Test-Taker's Checklist for the College Board Achievement Test Mathematics Level I

1. Review Chapter 2, entitled "Thirty-Three Strategies for Answering Multiple-Choice Mathematics Questions."

2. Review "What You Should Know" at the end of each chapter, making sure that you have memorized the facts and laws you need to recall. Be especially sure to remember:

   a. The Pythagorean Theorem
   b. The sum of the angles of a triangle
   c. The definitions of sine, cosine and tangent
   d. The values of trigonometric functions of special angles
   e. The basic trigonometric identities
   f. The Isosceles Triangle Theorem
   g. The formulas for areas of triangles and rectangles
   h. The formula for finding the distance between two points in a coordinate plane
   i. The formula for finding the midpoint of a segment when the coordinates of the endpoints are given
   j. The formula for the slope of a line
   k. The formulas for the standard forms of the equations of a line, a circle centered at the origin and a parabola with vertex at the origin
   l. The laws of exponents
   m. The laws of logarithms
   n. The formulas for volume and surface area of simple solids

3. Review the sample test results, paying special attention to questions you missed when you first took the tests.

4. Make dependable arrangements to get to the test center with time to spare.

5. Check to see that you have all the materials you will need, including several No. 2 pencils, a good eraser, a watch, a hand-held pencil sharpener and, perhaps, a snack.

6. As you take the test, remember to do the following:

   a. Budget your time. Calculate the time you can spend on each question so that you aren't caught short at the end. Be sure not to linger on a question you can't answer.
   b. Read the directions carefully to be sure you don't start out with a false assumption.
   c. Examine the answer choices given before answering the question. This will help ensure that you are on the right track.
   d. Mark your answers carefully. Use a No. 2 lead pencil, and blacken the choice completely. Your pencil mark must be kept within the oval. If you erase any marks, make sure they are completely erased. Don't make any stray marks on the test sheet.

HOW TO PREPARE FOR COLLEGE BOARD ACHIEVEMENT TESTS

MATHEMATICS
LEVEL I

UPDATE

This new feature of Barron's test preparation books represents our attempt to present the most comprehensive, up-to-date information on the examination as it is presently being given. Should there be any change in the types of questions asked, the subject matter covered, or the time allowed for completing the examination, we will publish a special UPDATE indicating these changes. This exclusive service, offered only by Barron's Educational Series, Inc., is available to you entirely free of charge.

If you are planning to take the Achievement Test in Mathematics Level I in the near future, the following schedule will tell you when the examination will be given:

Achievement Test Dates and Registration Deadlines

TEST DATES	
National and New York State	REGISTRATION DEADLINES
November 1, 1986	September 26, 1986
December 6, 1986	October 31, 1986
January 24, 1987	December 19, 1986
May 2, 1987	March 27, 1987
June 6, 1987	May 1, 1987

TEST
UPDATE
SERVICE

Register now to receive test UPDATES as they are published, at no additional cost.

Simply fill in and mail the coupon. If, within six months of our receipt of your coupon, we find that the examination has changed and we publish an UPDATE, you will automatically receive a copy.

-- -------------------------

TEST UPDATE SERVICE   **No. 2344-7**
Barron's Educational Series, Inc.
113 Crossways Park Drive, Woodbury, New York 11797

I would like to register for your free *Test Update Service*. I will be taking the College Board Achievement Test/Mathematics Level I on

_____

Name _____

Address _____

City _____ State _____ Zip _____

How to Prepare for
College Board Achievement Tests
MATHEMATICS LEVEL 1
Fourth Edition

JAMES J. RIZZUTO

DIRECTOR OF STAFF DEVELOPMENT
HAWAII PREPARATORY ACADEMY
KAMUELA, HAWAII

EDITOR

HOWARD P. DODGE
CHOATE ROSEMARY HALL
WALLINGFORD, CONNECTICUT

BARRON'S EDUCATIONAL SERIES, INC.

Woodbury, New York • London • Toronto • Sydney

All inquiries should be addressed to:
Barron's Educational Series, Inc.
113 Crossways Park Drive
Woodbury, New York 11797

Library of Congress Catalog Card No. 86-8079

International Standard Book No. 0-8120-3721-9

Library of Congress Cataloging in Publication Data

Rizzuto, James J.
  How to prepare for college board achievement test.
mathematics, level I.

  Includes index.
    1. Mathematics—Examinations, questions, etc.
  2. Mathematics—Outlines, syllabi, etc. I. Dodge,
  Howard P. II. Title. III. Title: Mathematics, level I.
- QA43.R59 1986 510©O38.76   86-8079
  ISBN 0-8120-3721-9   AACDR2

PRINTED IN THE UNITED STATES OF AMERICA
6789 410 12

To Shirley,

Rahna, Ticia and Tony

Contents

Editor's Preface

This book has been revised and enlarged three times to reflect changes over the last several years in the College Board's Mathematics Level I Achievement Test.

The first chapter of this Fourth Edition, "All about the CBAT/Math Level I Examination," answers the most frequently asked questions about the Mathematics Level I Test. The second chapter, "Thirty-Three Strategies for Answering Mutiple-Choice Mathematics Questions," reveals problem-solving techniques that will help you attack multiple-choice mathematics questions effectively. A diagnostic test, with explained answers, enables you to identify weak areas on which you need to focus your review.

The material is arranged so that the book can be used either in a classroom situation or as an aid for individual study. Chapters 5–31 provide an organized pathway through the topics of elementary mathematics which generally apear on the Level I Achievement Test, as well as some more advanced topics.

If you are a student who plans to use this book as an individual aid, you should begin at Chapter 1, which opens with a question typical of the ones appearing on the examination. If you can answer it correctly, you should proceed to the second question. If you cannot answer it successfully, you should read the section immediately following the question for an explanation of that particular topic. You should continue through the book in this fashion. When you have finished your review, you will find six sample tests at the end of the book that will give you some insight into the general nature of the examination and will help you pinpoint the areas in which you need still more work.

Students who have a strong background in mathematics will find this book useful as a review. If you are such a student, you should complete one or more of the sample tests at the end of the book. Since the questions are keyed to particular sections, you will be able to determine the areas that you need to review and the sections that will provide assistance.

Although this book is primarily a resource for students preparing to take the Level I examination, it is also an excellent starting point for students planning to take the Level II examination. All the Level I topics are presumed for Level II mastery, and students will find that as much as 70% of all material covered on the Level II examination is discussed here.

One final word to the student: there is no quick, shortcut method of preparing for achievement tests. To do your best, you should make long-range preparations. Several weeks before the test date, set aside a regular time each day to work on your review. In this way you will gain the most understanding of the material at hand.

HOWARD P. DODGE

Choate Rosemary Hall

Introduction

How MUCH intermediate math do you know? Or, what is more to the point, how much intermediate math *don't* you know? By this latter question we mean how much have you forgotten, never *really* learned, or never covered in your high school program in the first place?

The bulk of this book constitutes a review of intermediate math based on the recommendations of the College Board. The format presents an efficient method for discovering what you don't know and filling in these knowledge gaps.

While preparing this book we set out to accomplish five things:

1. to review the facts of intermediate math,
2. to review the methods, skills and techniques of intermediate math,
3. to further develop your ability to think mathematically,
4. to familiarize you with multiple-choice questions, and
5. to accomplish aims 1 through 4 with as little wasted effort as possible.

We've separated the topics usually found in elementary algebra, geometry, intermediate algebra and trigonometry into a little over 300 review sections spread over Chapters 5–31. Each section begins with a mutiple-choice question; the majority of the questions would be acceptable as test questions, but a few were chosen primarily to make a particular point.

Following each question is a discussion of the facts, skills and techniques necessary to answer it. The discussions average 200 words, and in all sections we've worked out the answer.

The development in most discussions is designed to help you learn to think mathematically and to expose the nature of proof, but we have by no means made ourselves slaves to rigor.

Most sections terminate in a short drill exercise with an average of three or four questions designed to help you remember what you've just reviewed.

The diagnostic test in Chapter 3 and the six sample test in Chapters 32–37 follow the guidelines of the Mathematics Level I Achievement Tests.

For further information on how this book can help you, read the section entitled "How Should I Use This Book?" in Chapter 1.

I am grateful for the encouragement given me by Dr. W. Eugene Ferguson, Head of the Mathematics Department, Newton High School, Newtonville, Massachusetts, and to my former colleagues in the Mathematics Department at The Gunnery: Rod Beebe, Anthony Golembeske and James Haddick. I would like to thank Ogden D. Miller, Headmaster of The Gunnery, for his support and to express my especial thanks to Chester E. Floyd, formerly Head of the Mathematics Department of the Danbury State College, and Howard P. Dodge of Choate Rosemary Hall; their advice and carefully detailed suggestions have contributed greatly to the accuracy and effectiveness of the text.

I am also grateful to Ruth Flohn, whose careful editing of this Fourth Edition has contributed to its clarity and readability.

1. All about the CBAT/Math Level I Examination

WHAT IS IT?
The CBAT/Math Level I Exam, like each of the other 13 achievement tests sponsored by the College Board, tests your knowledge of a particular subject—in this case, mathematics—and your ability to apply that knowledge. Unlike an aptitude test, an achievement test is curriculum-based and is intended to measure how much you have learned rather than how much learning ability you have.

The achievement tests are described, with sample questions, in a booklet entitled *Taking the Achievement Tests*, which is prepared by the Educational Testing Service. Copies are supplied to secondary schools for free distribution to interested students.

Registration forms for the tests are contained in the *Registration Bulletin for the SAT and Achievement Tests*, copies of which are also supplied to high schools. If your guidance or counseling office does not have a copy, write to:

College Board ATP
CN 6200
Princeton, New Jersey 08541-6200
or call whichever of the following is closer to you:
Princeton, NJ (609) 771-7600
Berkeley, CA (415) 849-0950

Achievement tests are usually given on five Saturday mornings during the academic year, in November, December, January, May and June, at hundreds of test centers around the country. Dates vary from year to year; those for the near future are given in the UPDATE in the front of this book. For other information on dates and test sites, write to the College Board Admission Testing Program at the address given above.

WHAT IS THE TEST FORMAT?
Each achievement test is 1 hour long, and your fee entitles you to take from one to three tests at one sitting.

The Math Level I Test contains 50 multiple-choice questions, each having five possible answers. All questions count equally. The penalty factor to discourage random guessing is a score calculation of the total right minus one fourth of the total wrong (answers left blank are neither right nor wrong and receive no points added or subtracted).

Mathematical symbols are kept simple and are intended to be clear from the context of the problem. For example, the symbol *AB* may be used to denote "line *AB*," "segment *AB*," "ray *AB*" or "length *AB*."

HOW IS THE TEST USED?
Colleges use achievement tests to predict an admission candidate's future success on the level of work typical at that college. Applicants to colleges use the tests to demonstrate their acquired knowledge in subject areas important to their future goals.

Some colleges, especially the most selective schools, have found achievement test results to be better predictors of success in related college courses than SAT scores and, frequently, the high school record. Because grading systems, standards and course offerings differ among secondary schools, a student's achievement test score may provide the college with more and better information about what the student knows than his or her high school transcript does.

Colleges also use achievement test results to place students in appropriate courses after they have been admitted.

High schools use achievement tests to examine the success of the school's curriculum and to indicate strengths and weaknesses.

WHAT IS THE DIFFERENCE BETWEEN LEVEL I AND LEVEL II?
The *Level I test* is a broad survey exam covering topics typical of 3 years of college-preparatory mathematics. It contains questions designed to determine knowledge (facts, skills and processes), comprehension (understanding and applying concepts) and higher mental processes (solution of nonroutine problems, logical reasoning and generalization of concepts).

Of the 50 questions on the test, the approximate number of questions pertaining to each topic of high school math is as follows:

Topic	Percent	Number of Questions
Algebra	30	15
Plane geometry	20	10
Solid geometry	6	3
Coordinate geometry	12	6
Trigonometry	8	4
Functions	12	6
Miscellaneous	12	6

The topic "functions" includes functional notation, composites, inverses and the value of a function. Solid geometry includes space perception of simple solids (spheres, rectangular solids, pyramids, etc.), including their surface areas and volumes. The trigonometry questions deal primarily with right triangle trigonometry and basic relationships among the trigonometric ratios.

The *Level II exam* is intended for students who have had 3½ or 4 years of college-preparatory math *or* an exceptionally strong 3-year math curriculum. The test involves more advanced work, with greater emphasis on trigonometry, elementary functions and material that is prerequisite to calculus.

An important difference from Level I is that plane Euclidean geometry is *not* directly tested on Level II, where the geometry questions deal with two- or three-dimensional coordinate geometry, transformations, solid Euclidean geometry and vectors. The trigonometry questions are concerned primarily with the properties and graphs of trigonometric functions, inverse trigonometric functions, identities and equations and inequalities in trigonometry.

The approximate allocation of questions is as follows:

Topic	Percent	Number of Questions
Algebra	18%	9
Solid geometry	8%	4
Coordinate geometry	12%	6
Analytical trigonometry	20%	10
Functions	24%	12
Miscellaneous	18%	9

As to *which test you should take*, it is generally to your advantage to select Level I if you have completed courses in elementary algebra and plane Euclidean geometry and are in the final stages of completing a third course in intermediate math that includes coordinate geometry and an introduction to functions and trigonometry. This is the normal situation in the spring term of your third year in a college-preparatory math program.

If, on the other hand, you have had sound preparation in analytical trigonometry, coordinate geometry of conic sections and elementary functions (including logarithmic and exponential functions) and have attained grades of B or better in your math courses, you should take the Level II test. This is true also if you are enrolled in an introductory calculus or advanced placement calculus course.

If you are adequately prepared for Level II, do not make the mistake of choosing Level I in the hope of receiving a higher score. Remember that the Level I test deals primarily with more elementary topics, which you probably studied some time ago. Also, because Level II is elected by a more talented and more highly prepared group of candidates, the test scores are placed higher on the reported scale, a distinct advantage for qualified candidates.

Finally, whichever level you select, keep in mind that you will not be expected to have studied every topic on the test, or required to answer every question.

HOW SHOULD I PREPARE FOR THE TEST?

There are four important long-range steps:

1. Enroll in secondary school courses in elementary algebra, plane Euclidean geometry and intermediate math (with trigonometry) in your first 3 years of high school.
2. Apply your best effort to these math courses to learn the material to best advantage.
3. Review thoroughly over a time period (several weeks or more) long enough to provide renewed mastery and understanding. Avoid "cramming," that is, a superficial, last-minute survey of a course undertaken in the shortest possible time.
4. Study sample testing material under exam conditions. In this way you will become familiar with what the actual test is like—the types of questions it contains, and how it is structured—and will thereby gain the confidence that comes from familiarity. You will learn how to use your time efficiently and will gain practice in problem-solving skills. You will diagnose your strong and weak areas and, through our explanations keyed to sections of the text, be directed to review sections designed to help you overcome weaknesses.

This book is designed to help you with the last two steps.

Here are some helpful last-minute tips:

1. Make dependable arrangements to get to the test center in plenty of time.
2. Have ready the things you will need: your ticket of admission, some positive form of identification, two or more No. 2 pencils (with erasers, or bring an eraser), a watch (though test centers *should* have clearly visible clocks) and a simple twist-type pencil sharpener (so that you need not waste time walking back and forth to a pencil sharpener if your point breaks). No books, calculators, rulers, scratch paper, slide rules, compasses, protractors or any other devices are allowed in the examination room.
3. The night before the test, spend a short time (no more than half an hour) reviewing important concepts or formulas. Then relax for the rest of the evening by doing something you enjoy—perhaps reading, watching television, jogging or chatting with friends.
4. Go to bed in time for a full night's rest.
5. On the day of the test, eat a moderate and balanced breakfast with adequate protein. Specifically avoid a sugary breakfast that may bring on feelings of anxiety when your blood sugar level drops rapidly an hour or two later.

WHAT DOES MY SCORE MEAN?

From your raw score, a scaled score is calculated. Scaled scores range from a low of 200 to a high of 800 with 550 the average of all Level I scores. Sixty-eight percent of all Level I scores fall between 450 and 640, and 84 percent are below 640. With your scaled score, you will receive a percentile ranking that shows what percentage of students scored below you and, by inference, above you.

For comparison purposes, the average for Level II is 670 and 68% of test-takers score between 570 and 760.

The College Board does not establish a passing grade. What constitutes "success" on the test depends on the college you wish to attend and your own personal aspirations. In general, you can be satisfied with any Level I test score that is 50 or more points higher than your math SAT score.

HOW SHOULD I USE THIS BOOK?

There is more here than the typical student will need. How much you need will depend on how much you already know. Proceed as follows:

1. Read the preceding sections of Chapter 1 (to familiarize yourself with the nature of the Mathematics Level I Test) and Chapter 2 (to learn successful methods that will help you answer multiple-choice mathematics questions).
2. Take and score the diagnostic test, and use the self-evaluation chart to pinpoint your weak areas.
3. Read over the concepts and formulas in Chapter 4, and check for periodic review the ones with which you are unfamiliar.
4. Now turn to Chapter 5 and note the title and the topic headings. On the diagnostic test did you get all the arithmetic questions correct? If so, skim the chapter. Skip over the questions that you know you can answer. If, however, you are doubtful about any question, work out the answer and check it against the one recorded in the answer section. If your answer is wrong, read the discussion following the question and work out the drill exercises.
5. When you have finished with Chapter 5, go on to Chapter 6. Again, if you answered all the real number questions correctly when you took the diagnostic test, skim the chapter and spend time only on problems about which you feel uncertain. If, however, you did poorly on questions dealing with real numbers, work through the chapter question by question, reading the discussion and doing the drill exercises for any problems you cannot solve correctly.
6. Review Chapters 5 through 24 and Chapter 31 in this manner.
7. If you have time, review also Chapters 25 through 30, which deal with material that may be helpful to you but is seldom tested.
8. When you have finished your review, turn to the six sample tests in Chapters 32 through 37. After reading the discussion that precedes them, work through the tests one by one, analyzing the results by means of self-evaluation charts and reviewing topics on which you are still weak.

2. Thirty-Three Strategies for Answering Multiple-Choice Mathematics Questions

Using actual multiple-choice test questions as examples, we'll explain problem-attack skills. Problem-solving skills are usually necessary to answer questions whose solutions have several steps. In several of our examples, we'll use more than one problem-solving technique to get the answer, but we'll focus on one method at a time in the discussion of each example.

1. Know what multiple-choice questions are like. A multiple-choice question involves given information, operations (sometimes stated but usually unstated) by which the correct answer is found and five answer choices. Only one choice is correct. (We'll call the incorrect choices "distractors.") Regard the answer choices as part of the given information since they help you focus your effort.

EXAMPLE 1

For what values of x is the equation

$$x^2 - \left(\frac{1}{b} + b\right)x + 1 = 0$$

true?

Ⓐ $2b, \dfrac{2}{b}$ Ⓑ $-b, -\dfrac{1}{b}$ Ⓒ $1, \dfrac{1}{b}$

Ⓓ $b, \dfrac{1}{b}$ Ⓔ $b^2, \dfrac{1}{b}$

The given information is the equation, the information that the desired result is the set of values of x that make the equation true, *and* the set of answer choices, which provide information about the type of answer desired.

Choice Ⓓ is the correct answer, and the remaining choices are the distractors. Note that the distractors generally represent possible incorrect results that stem from common errors. Choice Ⓑ, for example, results from an error in sign; Ⓐ, from a misuse of the quadratic formula (failure to divide by 2). This means that, if you make a predictable error in working out a test question, you are likely to find a matching distractor, which may give you unwarranted confidence in your answer.

Answering the question correctly requires both mathematical knowledge (specifically, that in a quadratic equation the second coefficient is the negative of the sum of the roots) and some ingenuity in applying this knowledge quickly and simply.

A student who knows the concept can find the answer by inspection. A student who doesn't know the concept but can solve the quadratic equation (by any of several methods) will find the correct answer, but only after expending considerable time and effort. A student who knows only that the product of the roots is the final coefficient, 1, can eliminate choices Ⓐ, Ⓒ and Ⓔ, but is forced to guess between Ⓑ and Ⓓ, a somewhat risky business, though in this case better than just leaving the answer blank. (There will be more about guessing later.)

2. Use the answers. Multiple-choice questions are particularly responsive to strategies because the answers are given. Therefore, it may be possible to answer a question correctly without knowing the mathematical procedure the test-maker used to derive the answer in the first place.

EXAMPLE 2

If $x^3 - x^2 - x - 2 = 0$, then $x =$

Ⓐ 0 Ⓑ 1 Ⓒ 2 Ⓓ -1 Ⓔ -2

To answer this question, you don't need to know how to solve a cubic equation. You would, though, if it weren't a multiple-choice question. And even if you did know how to solve a cubic equation, you would still be able to find the answer more quickly by checking the choices given. (The answer is Ⓒ.) Having your goal defined in advance allows you to work backward, a process we'll explain more thoroughly in further examples.

3. Do no more work than you have to. Unlike questions on classroom tests, College Board test items do not require complete solutions showing steps. You earn full credit by selecting the correct answer, not by showing work. Only the answer counts. Work carefully to avoid errors, but show only the steps *you* need to keep track of what you are doing. Painstakingly writing out elaborate procedures can waste time you need to answer other questions.

4. Recognize information implied by diagrams. For most problems, some information is implied, not stated. Figures, for example, provide information about the relationships between points and lines. They are drawn accurately unless the problem states that the figure is *not* drawn to scale. Size relationships in accurately drawn figures are helpful in suggesting ways to proceed and in estimating answers, *but should not be the only reason an answer is chosen*.

In addition, all figures are plane figures unless the problem states that the figure is three-dimensional.

5. Recognize information implied by terms. The values of a variable and the domain of a function are the set of all real numbers unless the question states otherwise. In some questions, however, special values *are* stated, especially the restriction of a domain to the set of *integers*. Therefore, it is extremely important to be familiar with the meanings of the terms "integer," "positive integer," "negative integer," "rational number," "real number" and "complex number." Furthermore, the meanings of all mathematical terms provide important implications you should use.

EXAMPLE 3

If a linear function has a graph with a positive slope and its *y*-intercept is also positive, then its *x*-intercept is

  Ⓐ Zero   Ⓑ Negative   Ⓒ Positive   Ⓓ Equal to the *y*-intercept   Ⓔ Greater than the *y*-intercept

To answer the question you need to know what is directly implied by the terms "linear function," "slope," "*y*-intercept" and "*x*-intercept."

You also need to know that a positive slope implies that the line (the "graph" of the "linear function") rises from left to right, which in turn implies that the *x*-intercept is negative in order to satisfy the given condition that the *y*-intercept is positive.

6. Know mathematical facts. Although most test questions require more skill than just the knowledge of mathematical facts, many elementary test questions require nothing more.

EXAMPLE 4

$(\sin 30°)(\cos 60°) =$

  Ⓐ $\dfrac{\sqrt{3}}{2}$ Ⓑ $\dfrac{\sqrt{3}}{4}$ Ⓒ $\dfrac{1}{4}$ Ⓓ $\dfrac{1}{2}$ Ⓔ $\dfrac{3}{4}$

The values of the sine and cosine of special angles are elementary facts of trigonometry. Answering this question requires no higher level of problem-solving skill than knowing these facts:

$$\sin 30° = \frac{1}{2}$$

$$\cos 60° = \frac{1}{2}$$

Therefore $(\sin 30°)(\cos 60°) = \left(\dfrac{1}{2}\right)\left(\dfrac{1}{2}\right) = \dfrac{1}{4}.$

EXAMPLE 5

Which of the following has a graph that is perpendicular to the *x*-axis and contains the points $(-2, 5)$?

  Ⓐ $x = 2$ Ⓑ $x = -2$ Ⓒ $y = -2$
  Ⓓ $x + y = 2$ Ⓔ $x - y = 2$

A line perpendicular to the *x*-axis is a vertical line. The graphs and equations of vertical and horizontal lines are basic facts in the study of linear equations. To answer this question, you need know only that $x = -2$ is the equation of the vertical line containing all points having -2 as their first coordinate.

7. Know mathematical methods. Some test questions require no more than the ability to apply routine algebraic processes to the given information.

EXAMPLE 6

If $\dfrac{2}{3}(x - 1) \le \dfrac{x + 4}{6}$, then

  Ⓐ $x \le \dfrac{5}{3}$ Ⓑ $x \le \dfrac{8}{3}$ Ⓒ $x \le \dfrac{5}{4}$ Ⓓ $x \ge \dfrac{5}{3}$
  Ⓔ $x \le 4$

The answer is found merely by applying routine steps of inequality solving. First, clear fractions by multiplying each side by 6:

$$6\left(\frac{2}{3}(x - 1)\right) \le 6\left(\frac{x + 4}{6}\right),$$

This gives

$$4(x - 1) \le x + 4,$$
$$4x - 4 \le x + 4,$$
$$3x \le 8,$$
$$x \le \frac{8}{3}.$$

EXAMPLE 7

At what points do the graphs of $2x + y = 6$ and $3x - 4y = 9$ intersect?

  Ⓐ $(0, 6)$ Ⓑ $(1, 4)$ Ⓒ $(6, 9)$ Ⓓ $(3, -4)$
  Ⓔ $(3, 0)$

Solving systems of linear equations in two variables is a routine procedure of elementary algebra. You either know how to do it, or you don't. If you do, that is all you need to answer the question. If you don't, no problem-solving strategy will produce the answer within a reasonable amount of time. (And, if you don't, be sure to review the pertinent section of this book!)

If $2x + y = 6$, then $y = 6 - 2x$. Substituting $6 - 2x$ for *y* in $3x - 4y = 9$ yields

$$3x - 4(6 - 2x) = 9,$$

which simplifies to

$$x = 3.$$

Because $x = 3$ and $y = 6 - 2x$, it follows that $y = 0$.

8. Draw inferences. When you have carefully studied the given information until you are sure of what it says and what it asks, you will sometimes see a solving process immediately. If not, examine the given information to see what inferences might be drawn. Each inference is a potential starting point. The most important question a problem solver can ask him- or herself is, "What can I conclude?" Search your memory for everything you can remember about concepts of the type given.

EXAMPLE 8

If quadrilateral *ABCD* is a parallelogram and the measures of angles *A* and *B* are $2x + 4$ and $3x - 4$, respectively, then $x =$

ⓐ 8
ⓑ 24
ⓒ 36
ⓓ 76
ⓔ 55

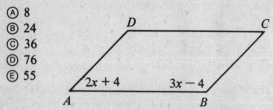

(Figure is not drawn to scale.)

There are dozens of implications that can be drawn from the fact that the figure is a parallelogram: (1) opposite sides are congruent, (2) opposite sides are parallel, (3) the diagonals bisect each other, (4) the opposite angles are congruent, (5) the adjacent angles are supplementary, etc.

Obviously, not all of these are useful in the solution of any one problem. In this problem it is clear that we need an inference about a pair of adjacent angles.

We've noted that adjacent angles are supplementary, so the measures of angles *A* and *B* must add up to 180:

$$(2x + 4) + (3x - 4) = 180,$$
$$x = 36.$$

Suppose that you could not remember any of the angle relationships. From the fact that the figure is a parallelogram, you can infer that opposite sides are parallel. From the fact that opposite sides are parallel, you can infer that the angles noted in the following diagram have the same measure:

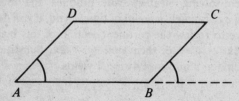

From the fact that the angles indicated have the same measure, you can infer that the adjacent angles are supplementary.

EXAMPLE 9

PQRS is a parallelogram and angle *T* is a right angle. $RT = 5$, $ST = 12$. $PQ =$

ⓐ 13 ⓑ 17
ⓒ 7   ⓓ 11
ⓔ 15

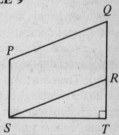

Because $\triangle RTS$ is a right triangle, you can conclude that $RS = 13$ from the Pythagorean Theorem:

$$RS^2 = RT^2 + ST^2$$
$$= 5^2 + 12^2$$
$$= 25 + 144$$
$$= 169,$$
$$RS = 13.$$

Because *PQRS* is a parallelogram, you can conclude that both pairs of opposite sides are congruent. Hence $PQ = RS = 13$.

Sometimes the place to look for inferences is not just the given facts but also the goals. In other words, always examine the suggested answers before attempting to draw conclusions.

EXAMPLE 10

If $a = xy$ and $b = xz$, then $a - b =$

ⓐ $x(y - z)$ ⓑ $xy(1 - xz)$ ⓒ $xz(1 - y)$
ⓓ $z(x - y)$ ⓔ $y(x - z)$

All of the answers are in factored form; therefore you can infer that, when you do find an expression for $a - b$, you must factor it before comparing it with the choices given:

$$a - b = xy - xz = x(y - z).$$

9. Seek alternative approaches when you reach a dead end. Is it possible to know too much relevant information? In the long run, probably not, but sometimes you may head off on the wrong track because you started with an unproductive inference.

EXAMPLE 11

If $Q(x)$ is any quadratic function and $f(x)$ is any linear function, then the number of possible solutions for $Q(x) = f(x)$ is

ⓐ 0 ⓑ 1 ⓒ 2 ⓓ None of these ⓔ All of these

Since $Q(x)$ is a quadratic function, you can infer that it can be written in the form

(1) $Q(x) = ax^2 + bx + c$.

Similarly, a linear function $f(x)$ can be written in the form

(2) $f(x) = px + q$.

If $Q(x) = f(x)$, then

(3) $ax^2 + bx + c = px + q$, and

(4) $ax^2 + (b - p)x + (c - q) = 0$.

Equation (4) is complicated enough to be a dead end for many test-takers, who would then abandon this line of reasoning and start over.

Starting over with a different set of inferences, we can note that the graph of a quadratic function is a parabola with a vertical axis and the graph of a linear function is a line. Since $Q(x)$ represents the whole family of parabolas with vertical axes and a line can intersect a parabola in zero, one, or two points, the correct answer is Ⓔ.

In most cases, however, mathematical paths that start with the same concept tend to reconnect later on. That complicated "dead-end" equation (4) would lead to the right conclusion for a student who recognized that it was still a quadratic equation and that a quadratic equation may have zero, one, or two solutions.

Your mind may travel a different logical path to a solution, but if your inferences are correct, your conclusion will be the same.

EXAMPLE 12

If $AB = AC$ and $BM = AM = AN = NC$, then $x =$

Ⓐ 20   Ⓑ 25   Ⓒ 30   Ⓓ 40   Ⓔ 60

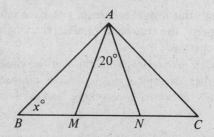

(Figure is not drawn to scale.)

Two different paths lead to the correct solution.

a. Because $AM = AN$, you may conclude that $\angle AMN$ and $\angle ANM$ have the same measure. Call this measure a; $a + a + 20 = 180$ since the sum of the measures of the angles of a triangle is 180.

$$2a = 160$$
$$a = 80$$

The measure of $\angle BAM$ is x because $AM = BM$. Also, $\angle AMN$ is an exterior angle of $\triangle BMA$. Since an exterior angle is the sum of the two nonadjacent interior angles,

$$80 = x + x,$$
$$80 = 2x,$$
$$40 = x.$$

b. A second approach is to note that $\angle BAM$ is x since $BM = AM$, $\angle C$ is x because $AB = AC$ and $\angle NAC$ is x because $AN = NC$.

Since the sum of the measures of the angles of $\triangle BAC$ is 180,

$$x + (x + 20 + x) + x = 180,$$
$$4x + 20 = 180,$$
$$4x = 160,$$
$$x = 40.$$

These two paths are not as different as they appear. One involves an inference that is a logical consequence of the other.

10. Correctly define your goal. The goal of a multiple-choice question is more precisely defined than that of any other type of mathematical problem because the goal is given as a choice; you are not asked to discover an unknown. Nevertheless, the goal can be misunderstood. Remember that many distractors are constructed on the basis of an imprecise understanding of the goal. Therefore, because your incorrect answer is one of the choices that are given, you may not realize you have made an error.

EXAMPLE 13

If m is the measure of an acute angle of a right triangle and $\tan m = \dfrac{b}{2}$, then $\sin m =$

Ⓐ $\dfrac{\sqrt{4 - b^2}}{b}$ Ⓑ $\dfrac{b}{\sqrt{4 - b^2}}$ Ⓒ $\dfrac{b}{\sqrt{4 + b^2}}$

Ⓓ $\dfrac{\sqrt{4 - b^2}}{2}$ Ⓔ $\dfrac{2}{\sqrt{4 + b^2}}$

In this problem, each of the distractors represents an error by confusing the meaning of "sine" or "tangent." The correct answer is Ⓒ. Answer Ⓔ is the cosine. Answers Ⓐ and Ⓑ result from confusing the meaning of "tangent" with that of "sine."

By giving, say, the cosine when the question asks for the sine, you are really answering the wrong question through your own misunderstanding of the meanings of the terms. The only remedy for this type of error is to learn the meanings of terms and to double-check your work to make sure you are using them correctly. This is only one of several ways in which you can make an error by answering the wrong question. We'll give other examples later.

11. Try to restate the goal in your own words. Such restatement helps clarify the meaning of the goal, although it can sometimes lead to errors if your restatement is not accurate.

EXAMPLE 14

If a polygon $ABCDEF$ is a regular hexagon with perimeter $36p^2$, then the length of side $AB =$

(A) $6p^2$ (B) $6p$ (C) 6 (D) p^2 (E) p

Since a regular hexagon has six equal sides, the perimeter is six times the length of a side. Dividing $36p^2$ by 6 gives $6p^2$.

Had you confused the meaning of "perimeter" with "area" (because $36p^2$ is a perfect square, which suggests area), you would be answering a far more complicated question.

If a precise restatement does not come easily to mind, the reason may be that no such restatement is possible.

EXAMPLE 15

If $x = \log_2 20$, then x is between what pair of consecutive integers?

(A) 0 and 1   (B) 1 and 2   (C) 2 and 3   (D) 4 and 5
(E) 16 and 32

The precise value of $\log_2 20$ is unnecessary in finding the answer. Since precise values of $\log_2 x$ are most readily determined when x is a power of 2, we can get all of the information we need by inspecting powers of 2 on either side of 20. Because $\log_2 16 = 4$ and $\log_2 32 = 5$, the correct answer is (D).

12. Answer the right question. Don't confuse the actual question with some other question suggested by the problem but not really asked.

EXAMPLE 16

The graphs of $x^2 + y^2 = 4$ and $x^2 = 4y$ intersect in how many points?

(A) 0   (B) 1   (C) 2   (D) 3   (E) 4

Look carefully and you will see that the question does not ask you to *find* the points of intersection but to tell *how many* there are. Perhaps you have had to find the points of intersection as part of your regular studies and on classroom tests. If so, you may rush into solving the system without realizing that it is unnecessary.

Because you can infer that the graph of the first equation is a circle with center at the origin and radius 2, and that of the second is a parabola with vertex at the origin, you can see by inspection that there are two points of intersection without ever working out what they are.

Answer (D), by the way, deserves special comment. Many students select it because they don't realize that the center of the circle is not a point of the circle.

13. Infer properties from the information in the question. Sometimes, to solve a problem you must infer new properties you may never have known before.

EXAMPLE 17

If the length of the side of an equilateral triangle is 10, then its area =

(A) 50   (B) 100   (C) 25   (D) $5\sqrt{3}$ (E) $25\sqrt{3}$

Chances are that you have not memorized the formula

$$A = \frac{\sqrt{3}}{4} s^2,$$

where A is the area of an equilateral triangle and s is the length of a side. Nor should you.

You can infer all of the information you need from the figure and the Pythagorean Theorem (or from the 30-60-90 triangle relationship). First draw a figure: an equilateral triangle ABC with altitude CD:

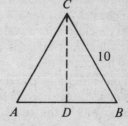

Altitude CD bisects AB, so $DB = 5$.

From the Pythagorean Theorem (or 30-60-90 triangle relationship), $CD = 5\sqrt{3}$.

From the formula for the area of a triangle,

$$\text{area of } \triangle ABC = \frac{1}{2}(AB)(CD)$$
$$= \frac{1}{2}(10)(5\sqrt{3})$$
$$= 25\sqrt{3}.$$

Through this logical sequence, you have inferred a new property, the area of an equilateral triangle, from other properties.

14. Infer properties from the answer choices. As noted earlier, multiple-choice questions are sometimes most easily answered by working backward from the choices.

EXAMPLE 18

The set R includes p, q, r and s. Multiplication in the set R is defined by a table, part of which is given below:

X	p	q	r	s
p	s			
q		0		
r			r	
s				q

Which of the following is 1?

Ⓐ p Ⓑ q Ⓒ r Ⓓ s Ⓔ None of these

The question becomes simple to answer once you realize that a property of 1 is $1 \times 1 = 1$. In the portion of the table given, each number is multiplied by itself, so we are looking for a number x such that $x \cdot x = x$. Since $r \cdot r = r$, the answer is Ⓒ. We discovered it by inferring properties about our goal, the number 1, and matching these properties with the given information.

15. Use trial and error effectively. Working backward takes many forms. One of these, trying and discarding answer choices, was introduced in Example 2 and is reviewed here.

EXAMPLE 19

If $\sqrt{5x - 4} + \sqrt{2x + 1} = 7$, then $x =$

Ⓐ -4 Ⓑ 4 Ⓒ 2 Ⓓ 1 Ⓔ 0

To answer the question by solving the equation involves a complicated and time-consuming procedure. Checking the answer choices in the equation takes only a few seconds, especially since the answer is Ⓑ.

16. Try specific cases. Often it is helpful to rephrase the given information in terms of specific cases.

EXAMPLE 20

If $f(x)$ is a function for which

$$f(a + b) = f(a) + f(b),$$

which of the following must also be true?

I. $f(a - b) = f(a) - f(b)$
II. $f(4a) = 4f(a)$
III. $f(ab) = f(a) \cdot f(b)$

Ⓐ I only   Ⓑ I and II only   Ⓒ II and III only
Ⓓ All   Ⓔ I and III only

Direct methods exist for answering this question, but let us suppose you are unable to think of one. You can still get a "feel" for the problem by trying a specific case. The problem deals with a function that has a simple property. The simplest of the functions are linear functions of the form $f(x) = mx$. A quick check shows that $f(x) = mx$ does have the desired property since

$$f(a + b) = m(a + b) = ma + mb$$
$$= f(a) + f(b).$$

Let us see what happens when we try I, II and III on $f(x) = mx$.

I. $f(a - b) = m(a - b) = ma - mb = f(a) - f(b)$

II. $f(4a) = m(4a) = 4(ma) = 4f(a)$
III. $f(ab) = m(ab) \neq (ma)(mb) = f(a) \cdot f(b)$

This special case shows that property III cannot be true and eliminates choices Ⓒ, Ⓓ and Ⓔ, narrowing down the possibilities to Ⓐ and Ⓑ.

Since $f(x) = mx$ is only one of many types of functions having the given property, we cannot assert that I and II must be true from working with this special case. But we can see that, for any function with the given property,

$$f(4a) = f(a + a + a + a)$$
$$= f(a) + f(a) + f(a) + f(a)$$
$$= 4f(a)$$

without looking at special cases.

Therefore the correct answer must be Ⓑ. We never really came to grips with property I; but then again, we never really had to in order to get the answer.

In some problems, there is nothing else you *can* do except try specific cases.

EXAMPLE 21

If x is an integer, then $\dfrac{x^2}{x - 4}$ is a positive integer when $x =$

Ⓐ 4 Ⓑ -4 Ⓒ 1 Ⓓ 3 Ⓔ 6

Unlike Examples 18 and 19, in which elementary algebraic processes do exist that will crank out an answer (despite the fact we chose not to use them), this example involves algebraic principles sufficiently unfamiliar to be a dead end for many students. You should, however, be able to check all of the answers within 10 to 15 seconds just by substituting them for x. That's less time than it may take even to begin searching for a different strategy.

17. Identify subgoals. A subgoal is a step partway between the given information and the final answer. Setting up subgoals is a process similar to drawing inferences.

EXAMPLE 22

If $\triangle ABC$ is a right triangle with right angle at C, what is the length of altitude CD?

Ⓐ 5 Ⓑ $3\frac{1}{2}$ Ⓒ 2

Ⓓ 3 Ⓔ $\dfrac{12}{5}$

(Figure is not drawn to scale.)

This question can be answered by determining two subgoals: (1) finding the length of AB and (2) finding the area of the triangle. Then, (3), we'll combine the information from (1) and (2) to get the answer.

Subgoal (1): From the Pythagorean Theorem,

$$AB^2 = BC^2 + AC^2.$$

Therefore $AB = 5$.

Subgoal (2): The area of a right triangle is one-half the product of the legs, or

$$\frac{1}{2}(3)(4) = 6.$$

Then

$$\text{area} = \frac{1}{2}(CD)(AB),$$

$$6 = \frac{1}{2}(CD)(5),$$

$$\frac{12}{5} = CD.$$

Subgoals are determined as part of the process of deciding what can be inferred. Clearly, both the area of the triangle and the missing hypotenuse can be inferred from the given lengths and the fact that the figure is a right triangle. By itself, each inference is a dead end. Together, the inferences combine to reach the goal.

This example, by the way, is an excellent case where understanding the mathematics used is not enough to answer the question. Proficiency in problem-solving strategy is essential.

18. Break out of circles. Your attempts to solve a problem may lead you around and around the same mental paths without reaching the desired conclusion. Either the inference you started with is not the basis of the answer, or the sequence of actions you are using won't lead to the answer. To break out of the circle, go back to the given information and look for other inferences. If you cannot see any other inferences, look for a different action sequence. Be aware, however, that you haven't really changed action sequences if your new one is merely a different way of doing the same thing your old one did.

EXAMPLE 23

The graph of the function $Q(x) = x^2 + bx + c$ intersects the x-axis in exactly one point. At that point, $x = r$. Therefore, $b =$

Ⓐ r Ⓑ $2r$ Ⓒ $\pm 2\sqrt{c}$ Ⓓ $\dfrac{bc}{r}$ Ⓔ $\dfrac{c}{r}$

At the point of intersection of the graph with the x-axis, $Q(x) = 0$. Your first approach might be to try to solve $x^2 + bx + c = 0$ to find an expression for the roots. Whether you do this by (1) factoring, (2) completing the square or (3) substituting the coefficients into the quadratic formula, you are on the same track,

despite the differences in the methods used. All three are equivalent action sequences. All spin you around the same circle.

If you discover that you cannot find the answer along that path, you should try to break out of the circle. Since you started by trying to infer results from the equation, you can change procedures by inferring results from the solutions.

The graph intersects in exactly one point, so the quadratic equation has a single solution; therefore the discriminant, $b^2 - 4ac$, is zero. Since $a = 1$,

$$b^2 - 4c = 0,$$
$$b^2 = 4c,$$
$$b = \pm 2\sqrt{c}.$$

Note that the root itself plays no role in answering the question.

19. Use destructive processes to narrow down to an answer. Simplifying expressions and solving equations are examples of what might be called "destructive" processes because they break down complex expressions and statements into increasingly simpler ones. In many test questions, the initial information is complex, the answer choices are simple and a destructive process leads directly to the correct conclusion.

EXAMPLE 24

If $f(x) = 7x - 4$, $g(x) = 2x + 8$, and $f(2a) = g(a)$, then $a =$

Ⓐ -1 Ⓑ 0 Ⓒ 1 Ⓓ -2 Ⓔ $\dfrac{1}{2}$

From the given information,

$$f(2a) = 7(2a) - 4$$

and

$$g(a) = 2a + 8.$$

Since $f(2a) = g(a)$, the following equation is true:

$$7(2a) - 4 = 2a + 8.$$

This can be solved by elementary processes to get

$$a = 1.$$

Sometimes a destructive process need not be carried all the way to the solution set of the variable.

EXAMPLE 25

If x is an acute angle for which $\tan x = \dfrac{1}{3}$ and $\cos x = \dfrac{1}{2}$, then $\sin x =$

Ⓐ 6 Ⓑ $\dfrac{1}{6}$ Ⓒ $\dfrac{2}{3}$ Ⓓ $\dfrac{3}{2}$ Ⓔ $\dfrac{5}{6}$

This question can be answered without carrying the solving process all the way to a value for x.

$$\tan x = \frac{1}{3}$$

$$\frac{\sin x}{\cos x} = \frac{1}{3}$$

$$\frac{\sin x}{\frac{1}{2}} = \frac{1}{3}$$

$$\sin x = \frac{1}{6}$$

EXAMPLE 26

If $5(1 + b) - a = 4a + 5$, then $a =$

Ⓐ 1   Ⓑ 5   Ⓒ 5b   Ⓓ b   Ⓔ $\frac{b}{5}$

Breaking the equation down through solving processes gets the desired result, even though it does not produce a value for a or for b. (As you will see, no unique value exists.)

$$5(1 + b) - a = 4a + 5$$
$$5 + 5b = 5a + 5$$
$$5b = 5a$$
$$b = a$$

20. Write an equation. Often, information is given about two quantities that are equal. In that case the question can usually be answered by setting up an equation and solving it.

EXAMPLE 27

Two rectangular boxes have equal volumes. Their dimensions are 8, 3, h and 4, 4, $(2h - 1)$, respectively. Then $h =$

Ⓐ $\frac{1}{16}$ Ⓑ -1 Ⓒ $\frac{4}{5}$ Ⓓ 4   Ⓔ 2

The volumes are found by multiplying the length times the width times the height, or:

Volume of the first box = 8(3)*(h)*
Volume of the second box = 4(4)(2h − 1).

Since the volumes are equal,

$$8(3)(h) = 4(4)(2h - 1),$$
$$24h = 32h - 16,$$
$$-8h = -16,$$
$$h = 2.$$

21. Use constructive processes to expand out to an answer. When the initial information is expressed in simpler form than the requested expression, the answer can usually be found by developing the latter from the former.

EXAMPLE 28

If $a - 3 = b$, which of the following is the value of $|a - b| + |b - a|$?

Ⓐ 0   Ⓑ -3 Ⓒ 3   Ⓓ -6 Ⓔ 6

The equation $a - 3 = b$ can be used to construct the expression $|a - b| + |b - a|$, thereby presenting the answer:

$$a - 3 = b,$$
$$a = b + 3,$$
$$a - b = 3 \quad \text{and} \quad b - a = -3,$$
$$|a - b| = 3 \quad \text{and} \quad |b - a| = 3.$$

Therefore $|a - b| + |b - a| = 3 + 3 = 6.$

22. Transform and combine. It is helpful to change an expression from a form you are unable to recognize into one that is easier to work with. At times this process will even enable you to answer a question for which you do not have adequate mathematical background. The following example was chosen because it involves a topic most Level I test-takers have not studied (and that is not part of the syllabus tested on Level I), yet all should be able to answer by using a transformation.

EXAMPLE 29

What is the graph of the following set of parametric equations in the xy-plane?

$$x = 6t - 2$$
$$y = 9t^2$$

Ⓐ A parabola   Ⓑ A line   Ⓒ A circle   Ⓓ An ellipse   Ⓔ A hyperbola

You may never have encountered "parametric" equations before, but this doesn't matter. Since you may be familiar just with the graphs of equations involving *only* x and y, transform the two equations by combining them into one that involves only x and y.

From the first equation, $x = 6t - 2$, we get

$$x + 2 = 6t,$$
$$\frac{x + 2}{2} = 3t.$$

Substituting for $3t$ in the second equation gives

$$\left(\frac{x + 2}{2}\right)^2 = 9t^2,$$

and we get

$$\left(\frac{x + 2}{2}\right)^2 = y.$$

Now you should see that the graph in the xy-plane is a parabola. This question was selected only to show you the power of the method. Questions involving parametric equations are *not* asked on the Level I test. Transformations solve simpler problems as well.

EXAMPLE 30

If $(\sin x + \cos x)^2 = \frac{5}{4}$, then $\sin x \cos x =$

Ⓐ $\frac{1}{2}$ Ⓑ $\frac{1}{8}$ Ⓒ $\frac{1}{5}$ Ⓓ $\frac{1}{4}$ Ⓔ $\frac{5}{4}$

Even though enough information is given to find values for x, you need only to find an expression involving x that can be found by transforming the left side of the equation.

$$(\sin x + \cos x)^2 = \frac{5}{4}$$

$$\sin^2 x + 2 \sin x \cos x + \cos^2 x = \frac{5}{4}$$

$$1 + 2 \sin x \cos x = \frac{5}{4}$$

$$2 \sin x \cos x = \frac{1}{4}$$

$$\sin x \cos x = \frac{1}{8}$$

EXAMPLE 31

If $x + y = 1$ and $x^2 - y^2 = 6$, then $x - y =$

Ⓐ 5   Ⓑ −6   Ⓒ 6   Ⓓ −3   Ⓔ 7

Transform $x^2 - y^2 = 6$ into

$$(x + y)(x - y) = 6.$$

Substitute 1 for $x + y$:

$$1(x - y) = 6.$$

Again, both x and y could have been determined from the given information by solving systems of simultaneous equations, but this was unnecessary since the desired result could be derived by transforming and combining.

EXAMPLE 32

If $\sin x = 3 \cos x$, then $\tan x =$

Ⓐ $\frac{\sqrt{3}}{2}$ Ⓑ $-\frac{1}{3}$ Ⓒ $\frac{1}{3}$ Ⓓ $\sqrt{3}$ Ⓔ 3

Since $\tan x = \frac{\sin x}{\cos x}$, transform the given equation into one involving $\tan x$ by dividing each side by $\cos x$:

$$\frac{\sin x}{\cos x} = 3 = \tan x.$$

23. Work both ends toward the middle. As already noted, some problems are easily resolved by starting with the initial information and working toward the goal, while others are best handled by working backward from the goal. Still a third group is best resolved by simultaneously working forward and backward to meet halfway.

EXAMPLE 33

If x and y are positive integers and 4 is a factor of xy, then which of the following must always be true?

Ⓐ 4 is a factor of x but not of y.   Ⓑ 4 is a factor of y but not of x.   Ⓒ 4 is a factor of both x and y.   Ⓓ 2 is a factor of both x and y.   Ⓔ 2 is a factor of at least one of x and y.

The complicating aspect here is the difference between what is "necessary" and what is "sufficient." The correct answer is Ⓔ. The number 2 must be a factor of at least one of x and y, though this is not sufficient to make 4 a factor of xy. In each of cases Ⓐ through Ⓓ, 4 can be a factor of xy without requiring the answer choice to be true. Yet, in each case, if the answer choice is true, 4 will be a factor of xy. To work this out, you must be constantly considering the initial information and the conclusion to join them in a train of thought at a point somewhere between the start and the finish.

In other words, without the answer choices, the problem is not defined, and from the answer choices alone, the goal is not defined.

This situation is very different from questions like 30 through 32, in which the answer can be found without knowing the choices offered.

24. Use general cases. Just as using special cases can point to a procedure, generalizing the problem is often helpful.

EXAMPLE 34

Which of the following points is on the line containing $(-1, 0)$ and $(1, 3)$?

Ⓐ $(0, -1)$ Ⓑ $(0, 3)$ Ⓒ $(0, \frac{3}{2})$ Ⓓ $(0, 5)$ Ⓔ $(0, -3)$

The equation of a line is a general condition satisfied by all points of the line. We can find the equation by first finding the slope of the line:

$$\frac{3 - 0}{1 - (-1)} = \frac{3}{2}.$$

Substituting the slope and one point into the point-slope form of the equation of the line gives us the general condition

$$y - 0 = \frac{3}{2}[x - (-1)]$$
$$= \frac{3}{2}(x + 1),$$
$$y = \frac{3}{2}x + \frac{3}{2}.$$

The points can now be checked quickly by letting $x = 0$.

EXAMPLE 35

The average of three numbers is $2a$. If two of the numbers are $-3a$ and $7a$, the third number is

Ⓐ $4a$ Ⓑ $-6a$ Ⓒ $10a$ Ⓓ a Ⓔ $2a$

In general, the average of three numbers, x, y and z, is given by the equation

$$\frac{x + y + z}{3} = \text{average.}$$

In this case, we are given x, y and the average, and we are asked to find z. Substituting into the general condition gives

$$\frac{-3a + 7a + z}{3} = 2a,$$
$$\frac{4a + z}{3} = 2a,$$
$$4a + z = 6a,$$
$$z = 2a.$$

25. Represent the answer symbolically. As we have already seen, representing the answer by a variable will help you set up equations, will suggest operations and will enable you to keep track of results.

EXAMPLE 36

The largest of four consecutive odd integers is one less than twice the smallest. Which of the following is the largest?

Ⓐ 7   Ⓑ 21   Ⓒ 11   Ⓓ 13   Ⓔ 5

Represent the consecutive odd integers by

$$x, x + 2, x + 4 \text{ and } x + 6.$$

If the largest, $x + 6$, is one less than twice the smallest, x, this fact can be represented symbolically by

$$x + 6 = 2x - 1,$$
$$6 = x - 1,$$
$$7 = x.$$

Hence the integers are 7, 9, 11 and 13.

26. Use diagrams. In most Level I tests, if a diagram is helpful, it is provided. There are exceptions, however, and for these you should draw your own diagrams.

EXAMPLE 37

Two vertices of an equilateral triangle are contained in the x-axis, and the third in the y-axis. The sum of the slopes of the three sides is

Ⓐ 0   Ⓑ 1   Ⓒ -1 Ⓓ 3   Ⓔ -3

First, draw a diagram showing the given information:

The diagram should suggest a number of possibilities. A plotting approach is to represent the coordinates of the vertices and, from these, the slopes of the sides. Let $A = (-a, 0)$ and $B = (a, 0)$. From the Pythagorean Theorem, or the $30 - 60 - 90$ triangle relation, OC can be found to be $\sqrt{3}$, making $C = (0, \sqrt{3}\,a)$. Therefore the slopes of BC and AC are, respectively,

$$\frac{a\sqrt{3}}{a} = \sqrt{3} \quad \text{and} \quad \frac{a\sqrt{3}}{-a} = -\sqrt{3}.$$

The slope of AB is 0, so the sum of all three slopes is 0.

An ingenious student noticing the y-axis symmetry of lines AC and BC would recognize that their slopes must be the negatives of each other and must add to 0, without doing any work.

Ah, well, there is no problem-solving tactic as valuable as ingenuity!

27. Substitution. Many test questions (including some we've already discussed) are answered quickly and directly by substitution.

EXAMPLE 38

The points at which the line $x = 4$ and the circle $x^2 + y^2 = 25$ intersect are

Ⓐ $(4, \pm 3)$ Ⓑ $(4, 0)$ and $(-4, 0)$ Ⓒ $(4, \pm 9)$
Ⓓ $(4, \pm 16)$ Ⓔ $(\pm 3, 4)$

Since $x = 4$, substitute 4 for x in

$$x^2 + y^2 = 25.$$

Then

$$4^2 + y^2 = 25,$$
$$y^2 = 9,$$
$$y = \pm 3.$$

Substitution usually plays an important role in questions involving functional notation.

EXAMPLE 39

If $f(x) = (4 - x)^x$, then $f(2) =$

(A) 2 (B) 1 (C) 0 (D) 16 (E) 4

The value of $f(2)$ is found by substituting 2 for x in $f(x) = (4 - x)^x$:

$$f(2) = (4 - 2)^2 = 2^2 = 4.$$

EXAMPLE 40

If $f(x) = ax$ and $f(f(x)) = 4x$, then $a =$

(A) ± 2 (B) ± 3 (C) 4 (D) $\frac{1}{2}$ (E) $\frac{1}{4}$

$$f(x) = ax$$
$$f(f(x)) = af(x) = a(ax) = a^2x$$

Since

$$f(f(x)) = 4x,$$

then

$$a^2x = 4x,$$
$$a^2 = 4,$$
$$a = \pm 2.$$

EXAMPLE 41

If $f(x) = 2x - 1$ and $g(x) = x + 4$, then $f(g(x)) =$

(A) $3x + 3$ (B) $x - 5$ (C) $2x + 7$ (D) $2x + 3$
(E) $-x + 5$

To find $f(g(x))$, substitute $g(x)$ for x in $f(x) = 2x - 1$:

$$f(g(x)) = 2(g(x)) - 1$$
$$= 2(x + 4) - 1$$
$$= 2x + 8 - 1$$
$$= 2x + 7.$$

28. Carry out operations. Many questions require merely the ability to carry out operations that are clearly stated in the given information.

EXAMPLE 42

$$\left(\frac{1}{x}\right)^4 + \left(\frac{2}{x^2}\right)^2 =$$

(A) $\frac{3}{x^4}$ (B) $\frac{5}{x^4}$ (C) $\frac{8}{x^2}$ (D) $5x^4$ (E) $3x^4$

The answer is found directly by raising each term to the indicated power and adding the results:

$$\frac{1}{x^4} + \frac{4}{x^4} = \frac{5}{x^4}.$$

EXAMPLE 43

If $\begin{vmatrix} a & b \\ c & d \end{vmatrix} = d(a - c) - c(b - d)$, then $\begin{vmatrix} 1 & 2 \\ 3 & 4 \end{vmatrix} =$

(A) 3 (B) 1 (C) 2 (D) -1 (E) -2

You need never have encountered the symbol $\begin{vmatrix} a & b \\ c & d \end{vmatrix}$ before to answer the question correctly. The symbol is well defined by the given information. Carry out the operations on $\begin{vmatrix} 1 & 2 \\ 3 & 4 \end{vmatrix}$ by substituting into the formula:

$$\begin{vmatrix} 1 & 2 \\ 3 & 4 \end{vmatrix} = 4(1 - 3) - 3(2 - 4)$$
$$= 4(-2) - 3(-2)$$
$$= -8 + 6$$
$$= -2.$$

29. Use ingenuity and insight. For many test questions, even ones that seem relatively simple, no problem-solving tactic can completely replace ingenuity and insight, even though all problem-solving tactics are designed to help inspire these mental qualities. Perceptive mental traits are best developed by (1) mastering fundamental facts and skills, (2) developing an understanding of mathematical concepts and (3) wrestling with problems that require ingenuity.

EXAMPLE 44

A pentagonal dodecahedron is a solid figure with 12 faces, each face having 5 sides. How many edges does this solid have?

(A) 60 (B) 30 (C) 45 (D) 17 (E) 48

Your first thought might be to multiply the number of faces, 12, by the number of sides of each face, 5, to get 60. But, if you visualize this solid in your mind, you'll realize that each edge of the solid is shared by 2 pentagons.

Therefore the answer you guessed first, 60, counts each side twice. The correct answer, then, must be half of 60, or 30.

EXAMPLE 45

If $M(x) = (x - a)^2 + (x - b)^2$, then the least value of $f(x)$ occurs when $x =$

(A) a (B) b (C) $a + b$ (D) $a - b$ (E) $\frac{a + b}{2}$

A bit of doodling with diagrams should help your insight. The functions defined by $(x - a)^2$ and $(x - b)^2$ have graphs that are parabolas opening upward with vertices on the x-axis and axes of symmetry at $x = a$ and $x = b$, respectively:

Their sum, $(x - a)^2 + (x - b)^2$, is also a quadratic function, so it must also be a parabola, which also opens upward. Without drawing $M(x)$ you should be able to see from the symmetry of the drawing that the parabola

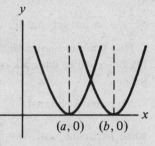

which is the sum of the parabolas must have its axis of symmetry halfway between a and b—in other words, at $\frac{a + b}{2}$ Since this is the "bottom" of the parabola, it must be the point that gives the minimum value.

Such questions test insight far more than they test any specific mathematical fact. It would not be assumed, for example, that a test-taker had ever encountered the function $M(x)$ as such before.

EXAMPLE 46

A belt is stretched tightly over two wheels having radii of 1 and 5 inches, respectively. If the centers of the wheels are 8 inches apart, what is the total length of the *straight* sections of the belt?

Ⓐ $4\sqrt{2}$ Ⓑ 6
Ⓒ 3 Ⓓ $8\sqrt{3}$
Ⓔ 7

(Figure is not drawn to scale.)

After experimenting by drawing radii to various points of the figure, you might have the insight to produce the following figure:

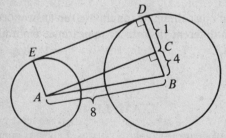

In the figure, $ACDE$ is a rectangle since BD is perpendicular to DE because a radius and a tangent are perpendicular at the point of tangency, and AC is drawn perpendicular to BD. Because AE is 1, CD must also be 1 and BC is 4. Using the Pythagorean Theorem on triangle ABC gives:

$$AB^2 = BC^2 + AC^2,$$
$$8^2 = 4^2 + AC^2,$$
$$64 = 16 + AC^2,$$
$$\sqrt{48} = AC = 4\sqrt{3} = DE.$$

Therefore each of the two straight sections of belt has length $4\sqrt{3}$ for a total of $2(4\sqrt{3}) = 8\sqrt{3}$.

Besides a knowledge of the Pythagorean Theorem and of the fact that radii are perpendicular to tangents at the point of tangency, the only (!) other requirement is ingenuity. Knowledge of the facts, however, provides a major boost to your insight.

30. Guess efficiently. Guessing is the ultimate problem-solving strategy—"ultimate" only because it is a last resort when all else has been tried unsuccessfully.

Trial-and-error methods sometimes result in the elimination of only one or two distractors, leaving you with three or four possible choices and no way to decide which is correct. When you cannot identify the correct choice but have eliminated one or more distractors, guessing may help your test score.

Efficient guessing procedures help you to save time and to keep track of which questions you have guessed on. Here is a procedure many students have found helpful.

If you decide to guess on a question, mark it as follows:

a. Place a question mark next to the question *in the test booklet* to remind yourself that you arrived at the answer by guessing.
b. In the test booklet (not on the answer sheet!) cross out the letters of the choices you feel are definitely incorrect (this avoids unnecessary pondering later).
c. In the test booklet (not on the answer sheet!) circle the response you wish to choose.
d. Postpone marking the answer sheet until the last few minutes of the test, or until you have completed all the questions you are sure of.
e. In the closing minutes of the test, scan the question-marked problems for new insights (more about that later).
f. Mark the answer sheet with the guessed choices.

Procedures that use time efficiently and reduce confusion are useful because two or three correct answers can have a significant effect on your final scaled score.

Let's go through the procedure with an example.

EXAMPLE 47

Which of the following is the probability of obtaining more tails than heads in five tosses of a fair coin?

Ⓐ $\frac{1}{2}$ Ⓑ $\frac{3}{5}$ Ⓒ $\frac{2}{5}$ Ⓓ $\frac{5}{8}$ Ⓔ $\frac{5}{32}$

Let's pretend the question is totally unfamiliar to you, which is most likely to be true if you, like many high school students, have studied no probability theory. That's why we chose this example for guessing.

Let's fumble our way through it as though we don't know much about probability but do have some experience with flipping coins. We'll suppose that all we know is that, when five coins are flipped, the possible outcomes are:

Tails	Heads
0	5
1	4
2	3
3	2
4	1
5	0

The bottom three lines show the situation described in the question, "more tails than heads," as the desired outcome, and the top three show "more heads than tails." Therefore the tossing of five coins seems to offer only two possibilities, more tails than heads and more heads than tails, with about the same results for each.

That's enough information to make us feel that answer choice ⒠ can be eliminated and that ⒜ is our best guess, even though it is not enough information to make us feel totally secure (it would if we were good students of probability).

We may want to think about this problem a little more before we commit choice ⒜ to the answer sheet, so we'll mark our test booklet as below and return to the question in the closing minutes of the test.

47. Which of the following is the probability of obtaining more tails than heads in five tosses of a fair coin?

   ⒜ $\frac{1}{2}$ ⒝ $\frac{3}{5}$ ⒞ $\frac{2}{5}$ ⒟ $\frac{5}{8}$ ⒠ $\frac{5}{32}$

You might be interested to know, by the way, that 68% of a group of high school students who tried to guess the answer to this question by intuition alone (they knew nothing of probability) chose answer ⒝, and the remainder chose ⒞. Our guess, based on just a bit more than intuition, is correct.

EXAMPLE 48

If $\frac{a}{b}$ is an integer, which of the following must also be an integer?

   ⒜ $a + b$ ⒝ $a - b$ ⒞ $\frac{b}{a}$ ⒟ $\frac{5a}{b}$ ⒠ ab

The quick and simple way to answer this question is to recognize that the set of integers is closed for multi-

plication—in other words, an integer times an integer is an integer. Since $\frac{a}{b}$ is an integer and 5 is an integer, $5(\frac{a}{b})$ is an integer and ⒟ is correct.

Had you not known this method, you would probably have had to fall back on trial and error and guessing.

You could eliminate ⒞ quickly by taking $\frac{a}{b}$ to be some particular case, say $\frac{6}{3}$. Then $\frac{b}{a} = \frac{1}{2}$.

You might then reason that ⒜ and ⒝ can both be eliminated since, if one is true, the other must also be true. If that wasn't enough for you, you could choose, say, $a = 1$ and $b = \frac{1}{2}$ and eliminate ⒜ and ⒝ in a different way. These same values would eliminate ⒠.

At this point, ⒟ is the only one left.

That's a different kind of guessing game from the one described in the answer to Example 47. Here our job was to guess values of a and b that would expose the right properties of the answers.

But suppose we had not thought to use fractional values of a and b. Then we would have had no other recourse but to eliminate only ⒞ and pick the best guess among the ones remaining.

Just how did we know to use fractional values for a and b? That's a result of our efforts to break out of a circle. Using integer values did not eliminate all distractors. Using other integer values kept us going around the same circle. To break it, we had to try a different set of numbers. Had we been especially adventurous, we might have tried irrationals such as $a = 2\sqrt{2}$ and $b = \sqrt{2}$.

Many different problem-solving strategies may prove useful in the same problem, as this example showed.

31. Don't eliminate distractors for the wrong reasons. Here are four wrong reasons for eliminating distractors.

a. Don't just eliminate (or choose!) an answer because it is different in form or appearance from all the rest.

EXAMPLE 49

Each of x cartons contains y boxes. Each box contains z marbles. How many marbles are there in all?

   ⒜ xyz ⒝ $\frac{yz}{x}$ ⒞ $x + y + z$ ⒟ $\frac{xy}{z}$ ⒠ $\frac{xz}{y}$

Choices ⒝, ⒟ and ⒠ are similar in form, a "clue" to some unsuspecting test-takers that this is the form of the correct answer (by a vote of 3 out of 5). They would then concentrate on these answers. But the correct answer is Ⓐ.

b. Don't assume that the correct answer must be somewhere in the middle of the choices with the incorrect answers at the extremes.

EXAMPLE 50

The points at which the graph of $2x - 3y = -4$ intersects the x-axis are

Ⓐ $(-2, 0)$ Ⓑ $(0, 0)$ Ⓒ $(4, 0)$ Ⓓ $(2, 0)$

Ⓔ $(0, -\frac{4}{3})$

The correct answer is Ⓐ, which in this case is at the extreme left of all the answer choices—both in the order listed *and* on the graph of the points.

c. Don't assume that there is any pattern to the answer choices. In other words, if you have marked answer choice Ⓐ more often than any other throughout the test, this does not mean that the next answer is less likely (or more likely!) to be Ⓐ. Because positions for correct answers are selected at random, there *should* be approximately 10 of each choice, but there does not *have* to be. Certainly, if you have marked 20 answers as Ⓐ, you have reason to be concerned and should suspect that some of these are wrong. But there is no pattern by which you can determine which ones are incorrect.

d. Don't assume that there is always enough information but that you just don't know how to use it. Occasionaly you will find a question for which one of the answer choices is "cannot be determined from the given information" and there really is not enough information given to get the answer.

Such questions can be especially trying and time consuming. You always think you've forgotten something and hope it will come to you if you just persevere!

EXAMPLE 51

Given the figure with the center of the circle at P. If $a = 50°$, then $b =$

Ⓐ 25°   Ⓑ 20°

Ⓒ $27\frac{1}{2}°$ Ⓓ $22\frac{1}{2}°$

Ⓔ Cannot be determined from the given information

Several inferences can be drawn about arc XY, but no information will relate a to b definitively. Your temptation is to approximate the value of b from the

figure and guess the measure that looks closest. In this case, guessing the choice that appears most obvious from the figure gives the wrong answer, even though it may actually *be* the correct measure!

Don't assume there is a way to "beat" the test— meaning to earn a satisfactory score without knowing a sufficient amount of mathematics. It is possible, unfortunately, to have a test score *lower* than it should be for a person of your mathematical skill because you have not been able to do your best work. But it is very unlikely that you can score higher than you should merely by using a system for eliminating distractors rather than your developed mathematical ability and knowledge.

32. Return later to difficult problems. Rarely is it a good idea to continue working on a problem past a reasonable deadline of a few minutes, and you should go on to other questions rather than bogging down.

But leaving a problem is not the same as giving up on it. In fact, leaving it temporarily may be all you need to do to eventually solve it!

When you return to a problem after working on others for a while, you will sometimes see a new approach. Some psychologists have suggested that your subconcious mind continues to work on the problem as your conscious mind solves others. Other psychologists feel that you merely bring a different mind-set with you the second time around, your original associations with the problem having been broken up by the intervening mental activity.

Returning with a "fresh mind" succeeds often enough to be part of your test-taking strategy, but only if you are familiar with the subject matter of the question. Don't waste time by returning to problems that have a mathematical basis you don't understand.

After taking a multiple-choice mathematics test, several students were asked to give examples of questions they were unable to answer the first time around but correctly solved on returning later. The following are three of the examples given.

EXAMPLE 52

For what values of x is $\frac{|x|}{x} = 1$?

Ⓐ $x = 0$ Ⓑ $x \geq 0$ Ⓒ $x \leq 0$ Ⓓ $x > 0$
Ⓔ $x < 0$

The student who selected this question said that her first attempt was to substitute values for x, which got her confused. This approach, by the way, would have worked had she been able to continue with it.

When she returned to the problem later, she immediately saw that the equation could be rewritten as $|x| = x$ (except for $x = 0$), which could be resolved quickly through the definition of absolute value. Within seconds, she had the correct answer, Ⓓ.

EXAMPLE 53

If $\dfrac{9a}{5} = 32$ and $\dfrac{9ab}{5} = 4$, then $b =$

Ⓐ 4   Ⓑ $\dfrac{1}{8}$ Ⓒ $\dfrac{1}{4}$ Ⓓ 16   Ⓔ Cannot be determined

The student who chose this question recognized that

$$\frac{9ab}{5} = \left(\frac{9a}{5}\right)(b)$$

and wrote the following for his scratch work:

$$\frac{9a}{5}(b) = 32(?) = 4.$$

He recognized that the missing number was the factor needed to produce 4 when multiplied by 32 but committed the simple mental lapse of thinking that 32 times 8 equals 4 rather than 8 times 4 equals 32.

Since 8 was not a choice, he left the problem temporarily. The second time around, this student made a new start and the error did not recur.

EXAMPLE 54

If $\log a = p$, then $\log 10a^2 =$

Ⓐ $\log 2a$ Ⓑ $2 \log a$ Ⓒ $1 + 2 \log a$
Ⓓ $10 \log a$ Ⓔ $20 \log a$

This student explained that the question came early on the test before he had really settled down, and his own lack of ease with logarithms caused him to panic. After building up his confidence on questions he found to be much easier, he returned to this question with a relaxed mind, reviewed the properties of logarithms that he remembered, and then transformed the equation to

$$\log 10 + \log a^2$$

and next to

$$\log 10 + 2 \log a.$$

He had forgotten that $\log 10 = 1$ in base 10 logs and did not remember this fact until he scanned the suggested choices looking for the answer. He then replaced $\log 10$ by 1 and got

$$1 + 2 \log a.$$

33. Remember your strategies. As an aid to recall, remember the acronym STEPS STIR SARGE. The letters in this sentence represent a 13-point summary of these problem-solving strategies in condensed form. In some cases, related strategies have been combined. The meaning of the acronym is shown below:

S   **Simplify** expressions that can be reduced, combined or altered by removing grouping symbols and by carrying out the operation of addition, subtraction, multiplication or division.

T   **Transform** expressions that can be written in a different form by factoring, using trigonometric or algebraic identities or replacing with equivalent expressions.

E   **Expand** expressions that are powers of monomials or binomials.

P   Look for **patterns** in the given information or in any expressions that result from your work on a question.

S   **Substitute** given values or other values that you have calculated for unknowns.

S   **Solve** equations that are given or that can be set up from the given information.

T   **Try** the suggested answer choices to see how they fit your work and the known information.

I   **Infer** properties and implications from the given information and the suggested answer choices.

R   **Represent** unknowns by variables as an aid to setting up and solving equations.

S   **Sketch** information that can be represented pictorially to aid the visual path of your mental processes.

A   Try **alternative** approaches to finding the answer if your original method reaches a dead end.

R   **Return** near the end of the test to questions you did not understand or could not answer the first time around.

GE   **Guess** only after **eliminating** at least one of the suggested answer choices.

Diagnose Your Weaknesses

3. Diagnostic Test

Before outlining a plan of study for the Math Level I examination, you should identify the areas in which you are weak and those in which you need little or no further preparation. In that way you can allot your time and focus your efforts to major advantage.

For this purpose the following diagnostic test has been provided. It is similar in number of questions, format and subject matter to the actual test, but is slightly more difficult.

Allow yourself 1 hour to take the test. Work steadily, without distractions. Answer as many questions as you can, but do not guess unless you can definitely eliminate at least one of the answer choices. If you need more time, make a note of where you were at the end of the hour and continue on until you have tried all questions. That way, you'll see how many questions you were able to answer during "regulation" time and you'll also get a chance to try all of the questions to identify all of your weak areas.

When you have finished, turn to the answer key and the answer explanations. Place a check mark next to each correct answer, and an X beside each incorrect answer. Then, for each question you got wrong, read the explanation carefully. Note that the italic numbers following an explanation refer you to the chapter and section of the book where you will find a fuller discussion of the mathematical skills or processes involved in solving the problem.

Fill out the self-evaluation chart that follows the answer explanations, noting the areas in which you did poorly, and calculate your score: (total number of correct answers $\times$ 4) $-$ (number of incorrect answers). Finally, record your score on page 299 by placing a dot opposite the nearest value on the vertical axis and above "Diagnostic" on the horizontal axis.

Note the following: All geometric figures are drawn as accurately as possible; unless otherwise specified, all figures lie in a plane.

You may assume that the domain of a function f is the set of all real numbers x for which $f(x)$ is a real number, unless the question indicates otherwise.

Now turn to the test.

ANSWER SHEET

Determine the correct answer for each question. Then, using a No. 2 pencil, blacken completely the oval containing the letter of your choice.

1. (A) (B) (C) (D) (E)   18. (A) (B) (C) (D) (E)   35. (A) (B) (C) (D) (E)
2. (A) (B) (C) (D) (E)   19. (A) (B) (C) (D) (E)   36. (A) (B) (C) (D) (E)
3. (A) (B) (C) (D) (E)   20. (A) (B) (C) (D) (E)   37. (A) (B) (C) (D) (E)
4. (A) (B) (C) (D) (E)   21. (A) (B) (C) (D) (E)   38. (A) (B) (C) (D) (E)
5. (A) (B) (C) (D) (E)   22. (A) (B) (C) (D) (E)   39. (A) (B) (C) (D) (E)
6. (A) (B) (C) (D) (E)   23. (A) (B) (C) (D) (E)   40. (A) (B) (C) (D) (E)
7. (A) (B) (C) (D) (E)   24. (A) (B) (C) (D) (E)   41. (A) (B) (C) (D) (E)
8. (A) (B) (C) (D) (E)   25. (A) (B) (C) (D) (E)   42. (A) (B) (C) (D) (E)
9. (A) (B) (C) (D) (E)   26. (A) (B) (C) (D) (E)   43. (A) (B) (C) (D) (E)
10. (A) (B) (C) (D) (E)   27. (A) (B) (C) (D) (E)   44. (A) (B) (C) (D) (E)
11. (A) (B) (C) (D) (E)   28. (A) (B) (C) (D) (E)   45. (A) (B) (C) (D) (E)
12. (A) (B) (C) (D) (E)   29. (A) (B) (C) (D) (E)   46. (A) (B) (C) (D) (E)
13. (A) (B) (C) (D) (E)   30. (A) (B) (C) (D) (E)   47. (A) (B) (C) (D) (E)
14. (A) (B) (C) (D) (E)   31. (A) (B) (C) (D) (E)   48. (A) (B) (C) (D) (E)
15. (A) (B) (C) (D) (E)   32. (A) (B) (C) (D) (E)   49. (A) (B) (C) (D) (E)
16. (A) (B) (C) (D) (E)   33. (A) (B) (C) (D) (E)   50. (A) (B) (C) (D) (E)
17. (A) (B) (C) (D) (E)   34. (A) (B) (C) (D) (E)

TEST

For each of the following, select the best choice—A, B, C, D or E—to answer the question or complete the statement. Then locate the number of the question on the answer sheet and indicate your choice by filling in completely the corresponding oval.

[1] Which property of the real numbers is illustrated by the equation $a(b + c) = (b + c)a$?

Ⓐ Commutative for addition   Ⓑ Commutative for multiplication   Ⓒ Distributive   Ⓓ Associative for addition   Ⓔ Associative for multiplication

[2] If the product of $2ab^2$ and $-3a^3b$ is divided by $-12ab$, the result is

Ⓐ $2a^3b^2$ Ⓑ $\dfrac{a^3b^3}{-2}$ Ⓒ $\dfrac{1}{2}a^3b^2$ Ⓓ $\dfrac{2}{a^3b^3}$
Ⓔ $-2a^3b^3$

[3] If $x < 0$, then

Ⓐ $|x| < 0$ Ⓑ $-x < 0$ Ⓒ $x < -x$
Ⓓ $-x < x$ Ⓔ $x = |x|$

[4] If a and b are any real numbers, then $a - b =$

Ⓐ $-(a + b)$ Ⓑ $-(b + a)$ Ⓒ $a - (-b)$
Ⓓ $b - (-a)$ Ⓔ $-b - (-a)$

[5] If $x < y$ and $c < -1$, which of the following is NOT true?

Ⓐ $x + c < y + c$ Ⓑ $x - c < y - c$
Ⓒ $cx < cy$ Ⓓ $\dfrac{x}{c} > \dfrac{y}{c}$ Ⓔ $x + c < y - c$

[6] The simplified form of

$$\frac{x^2 - 3x + 2}{x^2 - 2x - 3} \times \frac{x^2 - x - 6}{x^2 - 4}$$

is

Ⓐ 1 Ⓑ -1 Ⓒ $x^2 - 1$ Ⓓ $\dfrac{x - 1}{x + 1}$ Ⓔ x

[7] In $\triangle ABC$, $AB = BC$ and the measure of $\angle B$ is 70. What is the measure of $\angle A$?

Ⓐ 70   Ⓑ 110
Ⓒ 60   Ⓓ 35   Ⓔ 55

[8] A number such that one fourth of its square root is 3 is

Ⓐ $2\sqrt{3}$ Ⓑ $\dfrac{\sqrt{3}}{2}$ Ⓒ 12   Ⓓ 36   Ⓔ 144

[9] Which of the following has the graph shown?

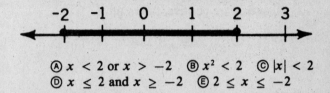

Ⓐ $x < 2$ or $x > -2$ Ⓑ $x^2 < 2$ Ⓒ $|x| < 2$
Ⓓ $x \le 2$ and $x \ge -2$ Ⓔ $2 \le x \le -2$

[10] In the circle with center at O, chord AB is 6″ long and 4″ from the center. In inches, the radius is

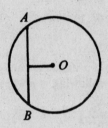

Ⓐ 3   Ⓑ 4   Ⓒ $4\dfrac{1}{2}$
Ⓓ 5   Ⓔ 6

[11] If $\dfrac{a}{b} = \dfrac{c}{d}$, then which of the following is NOT always true?

Ⓐ $\dfrac{a}{d} = \dfrac{c}{b}$ Ⓑ $ad = bc$ Ⓒ $ad = cb$
Ⓓ $\dfrac{a + b}{b} = \dfrac{c + d}{d}$ Ⓔ $\dfrac{a - b}{b} = \dfrac{c - d}{d}$

[12] If $x = 2$ which of the following has a value of 4?

Ⓐ $\dfrac{x - 4}{3x}$ Ⓑ $\dfrac{4x}{x - 2}$ Ⓒ $\dfrac{2x}{x - 1}$
Ⓓ $\dfrac{3(x - 2)}{2x}$ Ⓔ $\dfrac{2x^2}{3}$

[13] When two numbers, x and y, are added, the sum is a. The larger number is b more than twice the smaller. The smaller is

Ⓐ $\dfrac{a + b}{2}$ Ⓑ $\dfrac{a - b}{3}$ Ⓒ $a + b$ Ⓓ $a - b$
Ⓔ $\dfrac{a + b}{a - b}$

[14] If $(y + 1)(2y - 3) = 25$, then $y =$

Ⓐ -1 or 3   Ⓑ 4 or 8   Ⓒ 4 or $-\dfrac{7}{2}$
Ⓓ 6 or 2   Ⓔ 2 or $\dfrac{3}{2}$

[15] $\dfrac{3\sqrt{24} - 2\sqrt{18}}{-\sqrt{2}} =$

   Ⓐ $6\sqrt{2} + 6\sqrt{6}$ Ⓑ $6\sqrt{6} - 6\sqrt{2}$ Ⓒ $\sqrt{6}$
   Ⓓ $24 - 12\sqrt{3}$ Ⓔ $6 - 6\sqrt{3}$

[16] If $(a^3 b^{-2})^{-2}$ is simplified to a form in which all exponents are positive, the result is

   Ⓐ $\dfrac{b^4}{a^6}$ Ⓑ $\dfrac{1}{a^2 b}$ Ⓒ $\dfrac{a^6}{b^4}$ Ⓓ $a^2 b$ Ⓔ $\dfrac{a}{b^4}$

[17] What angle is determined by the hands of a clock at 2:00 o'clock?

   Ⓐ $10°$ Ⓑ $20°$ Ⓒ $30°$ Ⓓ $45°$ Ⓔ $60°$

[18] If a and x are any positive integers, which of the following is always an integer?

   Ⓐ $\dfrac{1}{x^{-a}}$ Ⓑ x^{-a} Ⓒ $\dfrac{1}{x^a}$ Ⓓ $\left(\dfrac{1}{x}\right)^a$ Ⓔ $(x^{-1})^a$

[19] If each of the answers below is a pair of numbers that indicate the length of the base and the altitude to that base of a different isosceles triangle, which triangle has a vertex angle of degree measure different from each of the others?

   Ⓐ Base = 4, altitude = 6 Ⓑ Base = 10, altitude = 15 Ⓒ Base = 9, altitude = 12 Ⓓ Base = 6, altitude = 9 Ⓔ Base = 2, altitude = 3

[20] Given that quadrilateral $ABCD$ is a parallelogram, which of the following statements would lead to the conclusion that $ABCD$ is a rectangle?

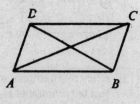

   Ⓐ AC and BD are the perpendicular bisectors of each other Ⓑ $AB = CD$ Ⓒ $AB = BC$
   Ⓓ $\angle DAB$ and $\angle CBA$ are supplementary
   Ⓔ $\angle DAB$ and $\angle CBA$ are equal in measure

[21] If the sum of the lengths of any three consecutive sides of a square is 9, the perimeter is

   Ⓐ 10 Ⓑ 12 Ⓒ 16 Ⓓ 18 Ⓔ Cannot be determined

[22] Rays BA and BC are tangent to a circle with center at O and with E the point of tangency of BA. If the measure of $\angle EOB$ is 30, what is the measure of $\angle DBC$?

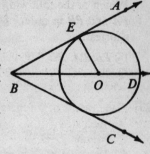

   Ⓐ 30 Ⓑ 45
   Ⓒ 20 Ⓓ 60 Ⓔ 55

[23] If D and F are the midpoints of the sides, then the ratio

$$\dfrac{\text{area of } \triangle ABE}{\text{area of } \square DEFC}$$

is

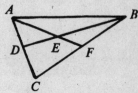

   Ⓐ $\dfrac{1}{2}$ Ⓑ $\dfrac{2}{3}$ Ⓒ $\dfrac{7}{8}$ Ⓓ 1 Ⓔ $\dfrac{3}{2}$

[24] If the radius, AB, of the circle is 6 and $\angle BAC$ has degree measure 40, what is the area of the shaded region?

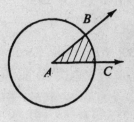

   Ⓐ 6π Ⓑ 4π
   Ⓒ 2π Ⓓ $(3\pi)^2$
   Ⓔ 3π

[25] If the sides of a triangle have lengths of 3, 4 and x, then

   Ⓐ $0 \leq x \leq 4$ Ⓑ $0 < x < 7$
   Ⓒ $1 < x < 7$ Ⓓ $3 < x < 4$
   Ⓔ $1 < x < 12$

[26] Segments AQ, BQ and CQ lie in plane E and have respective lengths of 4.4, 4.5 and 4.6. PQ is perpendicular to E.

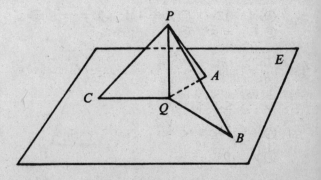

Which of the following is an arrangement of *PC*, *PA* and *PB* in order of length beginning with the shortest?

Ⓐ *PB, PA, PC*   Ⓑ *PB, PC, PA*   Ⓒ *PA, PB, PC*
Ⓓ *PA, PC, PB*   Ⓔ *PC, PA, PB*

[27] If the radius of a sphere is r, then the ratio of $\dfrac{\text{surface area}}{\text{volume}}$ is

Ⓐ $3\pi r$ Ⓑ π Ⓒ πr Ⓓ $3/r$ Ⓔ $9r$

[28] If $\dfrac{i+2}{1-3i} = a + bi$, then $(a, b) =$

Ⓐ $(-1, 7)$ Ⓑ $(\frac{1}{4}, \frac{1}{4})$ Ⓒ $(4, -\frac{1}{4})$

Ⓓ $(-\frac{1}{10}, 7)$ Ⓔ $(-\frac{1}{10}, \frac{7}{10})$

[29] If a ray is drawn from the origin through each of the following points, which ray makes the greatest angle with the nonnegative ray of the x-axis?

Ⓐ $(3, 1)$ Ⓑ $(2, 4)$ Ⓒ $(2, 7)$ Ⓓ $(3, 3)$
Ⓔ $(4, 2)$

[30] What is the slope of a line containing the points $(-1, 2)$ and $(3, 4)$?

Ⓐ 2 Ⓑ $\frac{1}{2}$ Ⓒ -2 Ⓓ $-(\frac{1}{2})$ Ⓔ 1

[31] If the graph of $x^2 + y^2 = c$ contains the point $(-3, 5)$, then $c =$

Ⓐ 4 Ⓑ 34 Ⓒ $-\sqrt{34}$ Ⓓ $\sqrt{-34}$ Ⓔ -4

[32] If an ellipse has foci $(0, 2)$ and $(0, -2)$ and $(0, -4)$ is a point of the ellipse, then an x-intercept is

Ⓐ 5 Ⓑ $2\sqrt{3}$ Ⓒ $2\sqrt{5}$ Ⓓ 3 Ⓔ $3\sqrt{2}$

[33] A parabola has a vertical axis of symmetry and contains points $(0, 0)$, $(1, 12)$, and $(-3, 108)$. Its equation is

Ⓐ $y = 12x^2$ Ⓑ $x = 12y^2$ Ⓒ $y = -12x^2$
Ⓓ $12y = x^2$ Ⓔ $12y = -x^2$

[34] If $y = |\sin x|$, then for all x the range of values of y is

Ⓐ $-1 \le y \le 1$ Ⓑ $0 \le y \le 1$
Ⓒ $-\dfrac{\sqrt{2}}{2} \le y \le \dfrac{\sqrt{2}}{2}$ Ⓓ $0 \le y \le \dfrac{\sqrt{2}}{2}$
Ⓔ $y \ge 0$

[35] If $x = \dfrac{\pi}{4}$, then $\sin x =$

Ⓐ $\csc x$ Ⓑ $\tan x$ Ⓒ $\cos x$ Ⓓ $\sec x$
Ⓔ $\cot x$

[36] If $1 - 2\cos^2 x = 2\sin^2 x - 1$, then $x =$

Ⓐ 0 only   Ⓑ Any real number from 0 to $\dfrac{\pi}{2}$
Ⓒ $\dfrac{\pi}{4}$ only   Ⓓ Any real number from 0 to π
Ⓔ Any real number

[37] If a central angle of a circle of radius 8 intercepts an arc of length $\dfrac{16\pi}{3}$, then its degree measure is

Ⓐ 30 Ⓑ 60 Ⓒ 90 Ⓓ 120 Ⓔ 150

[38] How many angles of a quadrilateral may have negative cosines?

Ⓐ 0 Ⓑ 1 Ⓒ 2 Ⓓ 3 Ⓔ 4

[39] If in a $\triangle ABC$ the sine of $\angle A = .504$, $BC = 7$ and $AC = 5$, then $\sin \angle B$ is

Ⓐ $.714$ Ⓑ $.360$ Ⓒ $.707$ Ⓓ $.504$ Ⓔ $.864$

[40] If $f(x) = -5x^2 - kx + 4$ and $f(-1) = 0$, then $k =$

Ⓐ -2 Ⓑ -1 Ⓒ 0 Ⓓ 1 Ⓔ 2

[41] If $f(x) = \dfrac{1}{|x| - 1}$, then the domain of f is

Ⓐ All real numbers   Ⓑ All real numbers except 0   Ⓒ All positive real numbers   Ⓓ All non-negative real numbers   Ⓔ All real numbers except 1 and -1

[42] If $f(x) = \sqrt{x - 1}$ and $g(x) = x^2 - 3$, then $f(g(2\sqrt{3})) =$

Ⓐ $2\sqrt{3}$ Ⓑ $3\sqrt{2}$ Ⓒ $2\sqrt{2}$ Ⓓ 3 Ⓔ 4

[43] If $\log_{10} x + \log_{10} 8 = \log_{10} 16$, then $x =$

Ⓐ 2 Ⓑ 4 Ⓒ 8 Ⓓ $\dfrac{1}{8}$ Ⓔ $\dfrac{1}{2}$

[44] Which of the following is NOT a function that is its own inverse?

Ⓐ $f(x) = x$ Ⓑ $f(x) = -x$ Ⓒ $f(x) = x + 1$ Ⓓ $f(x) = -x + 1$ Ⓔ $f(x) = -x - 1$

[45] If $\log_2 5 = M$, then $\log_2 10 =$

Ⓐ 1   Ⓑ $2M$ Ⓒ $\dfrac{1}{M}$ Ⓓ $1 + M$ Ⓔ $M - 1$

[46] If $3^{x+y} = \dfrac{1}{3}$ and $2^{x-y} = 1$, which of the following is (x, y)?

Ⓐ $(-1, -\dfrac{1}{2})$ Ⓑ $(-\dfrac{1}{2}, -\dfrac{1}{2})$ Ⓒ $(-1, 0)$

Ⓓ $(0, -1)$ Ⓔ $(\dfrac{1}{2}, \dfrac{1}{2})$

[47] Arcs AB and DC are semicircles with the same radius. Quadrilateral $ABCD$ is a square with sides of 4. The total surface area of the solid is

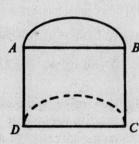

Ⓐ $12\pi + 16$
Ⓑ $16 + 20\pi$ Ⓒ 16
Ⓓ 12π Ⓔ 20π

[48] The seventh term in the expansion of $\left(1 - \dfrac{1}{m}\right)^{12}$ is

Ⓐ $-\dfrac{792}{m^6}$ Ⓑ $\dfrac{924}{m^7}$ Ⓒ $-\dfrac{792}{m^7}$ Ⓓ $\dfrac{924}{m^6}$ Ⓔ $\dfrac{495}{m^8}$

[49] If $\dfrac{1}{2}$, a, $\dfrac{3}{8}$ is a geometric sequence, then $a =$

Ⓐ $-\dfrac{\sqrt{3}}{4}$ Ⓑ $\dfrac{3}{4}$ Ⓒ $\dfrac{2}{5}$ Ⓓ $\dfrac{7}{16}$ Ⓔ $\dfrac{\sqrt{3}}{2}$

[50] If an auto license is to have four symbols, the first two of which are letters and the remainder digits, how many different license plates can be made? (I and O cannot be used as letters, but 0 can be used in either place as a digit.)

Ⓐ 642   Ⓑ 57,600   Ⓒ 49,680   Ⓓ 46,200
Ⓔ 6420

•

ANSWER KEY

1. B	11. A	21. B	31. B	41. E
2. C	12. C	22. D	32. C	42. C
3. C	13. B	23. D	33. A	43. A
4. E	14. C	24. B	34. B	44. C
5. C	15. E	25. C	35. C	45. D
6. D	16. A	26. C	36. E	46. B
7. E	17. E	27. D	37. D	47. A
8. E	18. A	28. E	38. C	48. D
9. D	19. C	29. C	39. B	49. A
10. D	20. E	30. B	40. D	50. B

ANSWER EXPLANATIONS

[1] Ⓑ The left member differs from the right member only in the order of the multiplication of the two factors a and $(b + c)$.   (6–3)

[2] Ⓒ $\dfrac{(2ab^2)(-3a^3b)}{-12ab} = \dfrac{-6a^4b^3}{-12ab} = \dfrac{a^3b^2}{2}$ (23–1)

[3] Ⓒ Since $x < 0$, it follows that $-x > 0$ so $x < -x$.   (6–7,8)

[4] Ⓔ $a - b = -b + a = -b - (-a)$.   (6–4)

[5] Ⓒ Multiplying both sides of an inequality by a negative number reverses the inequality.   (8–2)

[6] Ⓓ In factored form the product is:
$$\dfrac{(x - 2)(x - 1)}{(x - 3)(x + 1)} \times \dfrac{(x - 3)(x + 2)}{(x - 2)(x + 2)}$$
When common factors are removed we get:
$$\dfrac{(x - 1)}{(x + 1)}$$ (9–10)

[7] Ⓔ Since the sum of the measures of the angles of a triangle is 180:
$$(\angle A)° + (\angle C)° + 70 = 180$$
But $(\angle C)° = (\angle A)°$ by the Isosceles Triangle Theorem, so:
$$(\angle A)° + (\angle A)° + 70 = 180$$
$$2(\angle A)° = 110$$
$$(\angle A)° = 55$$ (12–4)

[8] Ⓔ Let $x =$ the number, then:
$$\dfrac{1}{4}\sqrt{x} = 3$$
$$\sqrt{x} = 12$$
$$x = 144$$ (6–12)

[9] Ⓓ The graph consists of all points that have coordinates greater than or equal to -2 *and* less than or equal to 2. This is the meaning of Ⓓ.

[10] Ⓓ The "distance" from a point to a line is the length of the perpendicular segment (in this case the ⊥ segment from 0 to AB; label the point of intersection X). Thus $OX = 4$ and $XA = 3$ (any perpendicular segment from the center to a chord will bisect the chord). By the Pythagorean Theorem:

$$(OA)^2 = 3^2 + 4^2$$
$$OA = 5 \qquad (16\text{--}1)$$

[11] Ⓐ If $\dfrac{a}{b} = \dfrac{c}{d}$ then $ad = bc$ by cross-multiplication.

Dividing both sides of this second equation by d^2, we get:

$$\frac{a}{d} = \frac{bc}{d^2}$$

which contradicts Ⓐ. $\qquad (15\text{--}2)$

[12] Ⓒ If $x = 2$, then $\dfrac{2x}{x-1} = \dfrac{2(2)}{2-1} = \dfrac{4}{1} = 4.$

$\qquad (9\text{--}1)$

[13] Ⓑ Let $x =$ the smaller, then:

$$x + y = a \quad \text{and} \quad y = 2x + b$$

Subtracting the second equation from the first, we get:

$$x = a - 2x - b$$
$$3x = a - b$$
$$x = \frac{a - b}{3} \qquad (22\text{--}3)$$

[14] Ⓒ $(y + 1)(2y - 3) = 25$
$$2y^2 - y - 3 = 25$$
$$2y^2 - y - 28 = 0$$
$$(2y + 7)(y - 4) = 0$$
$$2y + 7 = 0 \text{ or } y - 4 = 0$$
$$y = -\frac{7}{2} \text{ or } y = 4 \qquad (19\text{--}5)$$

[15] Ⓔ $\dfrac{3\sqrt{24} - 2\sqrt{18}}{-\sqrt{2}} = \dfrac{3\sqrt{24}}{-\sqrt{2}} - \dfrac{2\sqrt{18}}{-\sqrt{2}}$

$$= \frac{3\sqrt{4}\sqrt{3}\sqrt{2}}{-\sqrt{2}} + \frac{2\sqrt{9}\sqrt{2}}{\sqrt{2}}$$
$$= -6\sqrt{3} + 6 \qquad (6\text{--}14)$$

[16] Ⓐ $(a^3 b^{-2})^{-2} = (a^3)^{-2}(b^{-2})^{-2} = a^{-6}b^4 = \dfrac{b^4}{a^6}$

$\qquad (23\text{--}5)$

[17] Ⓔ The angle formed by the hands at 2:00 o'clock is $\dfrac{1}{6}$ of a rotation or $\dfrac{1}{6}(360°) = 60°.$ $\qquad (16\text{--}3)$

[18] Ⓐ $\dfrac{1}{x^{-a}} = x^a$, which will always be the product of a integers and hence an integer. $\qquad (23\text{--}1)$

[19] Ⓒ The ratio of altitude to base for all except Ⓒ is 3 to 2. For Ⓒ it is 4 to 3. All of the triangles are similar except Ⓒ. Similar triangles have corresponding angles of equal measure. If the vertex angle in Ⓒ *were* equal in measure to that of each of the others, the triangles would all be similar by *SAS*, and the altitude-base ratio would have to be the same for all. $\qquad (15\text{--}12)$

[20] Ⓔ Since $ABCD$ is a parallelogram, $AB \parallel CD$ and $\angle ADC$ is supplementary to $\angle BAD$. If they are also equal in measure as given in Ⓔ, they must be right angles. $\qquad (14\text{--}10)$

[21] Ⓑ Let x be the perimeter, then $\dfrac{3}{4}x = 9$ and $x = \dfrac{4}{3} \times 9 = 12.$

[22] Ⓓ $\angle OEB$ is a right angle since OE is a radius drawn to tangent EB. Thus $(\angle EBO)° = 60$, since the sum of the measures of the angles of a triangle is 180. But $(\angle OBE)° = (\angle OBC)°$ since BE and BC are tangents and ray BD contains the center of the circle. $\qquad (11\text{--}7)$

[23] Ⓓ Since $\triangle ABD$ and $\triangle CBD$ have equal bases (D is the midpoint) and equal altitudes (there is exactly *one* perpendicular to AC from B), then:

area $\triangle ABD =$ area $\triangle CBD = \dfrac{1}{2}$ area $\triangle ABC.$

By similar reasoning:

area $\triangle AFB =$ area $\triangle AFC = \dfrac{1}{2}$ area $\triangle ABC.$

Thus the union of the triangular regions determined by $\triangle ADB$ and $\triangle AFB$ is equal in area to the union of those determined by $\triangle AFC$ and $\triangle BDC$. If we subtract the sum of the areas of $\triangle ADE$ and $\triangle BEF$ from each of the unions mentioned in turn, we get the area of $\triangle AEB$ from the first subtraction and the area of quadrilateral $CDEF$ from the second. These areas are thus equal. $\qquad (17\text{--}3)$

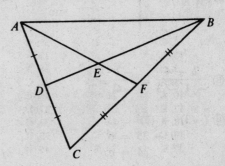

[24] Ⓑ With a radius of 6 the circle has an area of $\pi(6)^2 = 36\pi$. Since $(\angle BAC)° = 40$ and $\frac{40}{360} = \frac{1}{9}$, the area of the shaded region is $\frac{1}{9}(36\pi) = 4\pi$.

(17–22)

[25] Ⓒ The length of a side of a triangle must be less than the sum of the lengths of the other two sides, but greater than the absolute value of their differences.

(13–4)

[26] Ⓒ If we were to rotate segments QB and QA around point Q and into the plane of $\triangle PQC$ we would get:

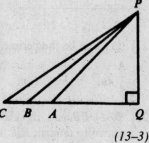

(13–3)

[27] Ⓓ Surface area $= 4\pi r^2$, volume $= \frac{4}{3}\pi r^3$

$$\frac{4\pi r^2}{4/3\pi r^3} = \frac{4\pi r^2}{4(1/3)\pi r^2 r} = \frac{1}{1/3r} = \frac{3}{r}$$

(30–6)

[28] Ⓔ $\dfrac{i+2}{1-3i} = \dfrac{2+i}{1-3i} \times \dfrac{1+3i}{1+3i} = \dfrac{-1+7i}{1+9}$

$$= -\frac{1}{10} + \frac{7}{10}i$$

(21–7)

[29] Ⓒ

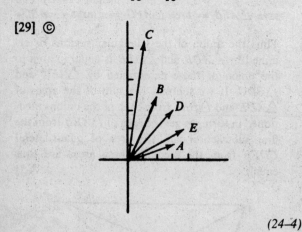

(24–4)

[30] Ⓑ $\dfrac{2-4}{-1-3} = \dfrac{-2}{-4} = \dfrac{1}{2}$

(18–6)

[31] Ⓑ $(-3)^2 + (5)^2 = c$
$9 + 25 = c$
$34 = c$

(18–11)

[32] Ⓑ Foci of $(0, 2)$ and $(0, -2)$ indicate that the ellipse is centered at the origin with major axis on the y-axis and is of the form

$$\frac{x^2}{b^2} + \frac{y^2}{a^2} = 1$$

where $(0, a)$ is the y-intercept and $(0, c)$ is a focus. Thus $c^2 = 4$, $a^2 = 16$ and $b^2 = a^2 - c^2$ (a relation which is true for all ellipses). So $b^2 = 16 - 4 = 12$ and the equation is thus:

$$\frac{x^2}{12} + \frac{y^2}{16} = 1$$

To find the x-intercepts, let $y = 0$ and solve for x.

$$\frac{x^2}{12} = 1$$
$$x^2 = 12$$
$$x = \pm\sqrt{12} = \pm 2\sqrt{3}$$

(18–30)

[33] Ⓐ If the axis is vertical then the parabola is of the form $y = ax^2$, which eliminates Ⓑ. The given point $(0, 0)$ satisfies each of the others, but $(1, 12)$ satisfies only Ⓐ.

(18–28)

[34] Ⓑ Sin x has a maximum value of 1 and a minimum value of -1. Thus the absolute value of sin x varies from 0 to 1.

(24–15)

[35] Ⓒ $x = \dfrac{\pi}{4}$ radians $= 45°$, and the trigonometric functions were calculated in section [12] of Chapter 24.

[36] Ⓔ $1 - 2\cos^2 x = 2\sin^2 x - 1$
$2 = 2\sin^2 x + 2\cos^2 x$
$1 = \sin^2 x + \cos^2 x$

The last equation is a fundamental trigonometric identity.

(24–14)

[37] Ⓓ Circumference $= \pi d = 16\pi$; thus $\dfrac{16\pi}{3}$, the length of the arc, represents $\dfrac{1}{3}$ of the circumference so its central angle is

$$\frac{1}{3}(360°) = 120°.$$

(24–13)

[38] Ⓓ For an angle of a quadrilateral to have a negative cosine the angle must be obtuse. Since the sum of the measures of the angles of a quadrilateral is 360, it may have as many as three obtuse angles but the final one must be acute (say 91°, 91°, 91°, 87°).

(24–9)

[39] Ⓑ In $\triangle ABC$, the Law of Sines states that:

$$\frac{\sin \angle A}{BC} = \frac{\sin \angle B}{AC}$$

Therefore:
$$\frac{.504}{7} = \frac{\sin \angle B}{5}$$
$$5(.072) = \sin \angle B$$
$$.360 = \sin \angle B \qquad (24\text{--}18)$$

[40] Ⓓ $f(-1) = -5(-1)^2 - k(-1) + 4 = -1 + k$
Since $f(-1)$ was given as equal to zero,

$$-1 + k = 0 \text{ and } k = 1 \qquad (20\text{--}7)$$

[41] Ⓔ When the domain of a function is not specified it is assumed to be all real numbers except those for which the function is meaningless. If $|x| - 1 = 0$ $(x = \pm 1)$, then f is undefined. $\qquad (20\text{--}6)$

[42] Ⓒ $g(2\sqrt{3}) = (2\sqrt{3})^2 - 3 = 12 - 3 = 9$
$f(g(2\sqrt{3})) = f(9) = \sqrt{9 - 1} = \sqrt{8} = 2\sqrt{2}$
$\qquad (20\text{--}9)$

[43] Ⓐ $\log_{10} x + \log_{10} 8 = \log_{10} 16$
$$\log_{10} 8x = \log_{10} 16$$
$$8x = 16$$
$$x = 2 \qquad (23\text{--}14)$$

[44] Ⓒ To find the inverse, $f^{-1}(x)$, replace $f(x)$ by x and x by $f^{-1}(x)$ and then solve for $f^{-1}(x)$. If $f(x) = x + 1$ as in Ⓒ, then:

$$x = f^{-1}(x) + 1$$
$$f^{-1}(x) = x - 1 \qquad (20\text{--}13)$$

[45] Ⓓ $\log_2 10 = \log_2 (2 \times 5) = \log_2 2 + \log_2 5 = 1 + \log_2 5 = 1 + M \qquad (23\text{--}14)$

[46] Ⓑ If $3^{x+y} = \frac{1}{3}$, then $3^{x+y} = 3^{-1}$ and

(1) $x + y = -1$
If $2^{x-y} = 1$, then $2^{x-y} = 2^0$ and
(2) $x - y = 0$.
Adding (1) and (2), we get:

$$2x = -1 \text{ and } x = -\frac{1}{2} \text{ and } y = -\frac{1}{2}$$

[47] Ⓐ Area of square $ABCD = (4)^2 = 16$ Length of arc $AB = \frac{1}{2}$ (circumference of circle of diameter $4) = \frac{1}{2}(4\pi) = 2\pi$, so area of curved surface $ABCD$ = height (4) times length of arc AB (2π) or 8π. Area of each semicircular base is $\pi r^2 = 4\pi$. Total $= 16 + 12\pi$. $\qquad (30\text{--}2)$

[48] Ⓓ $_{12}C_6(1)^6 \left(-\frac{1}{m}\right)^6 = \frac{12!}{6!6!} \left(\frac{1}{m^6}\right) = \frac{924}{m^6}$
$\qquad (29\text{--}2)$

[49] Ⓐ If $\frac{1}{2}, a, \frac{3}{8}$ is a geometric sequence, then

$$\frac{a}{1/2} = \frac{3/8}{a}$$
$$a^2 = \frac{3}{16}.$$
$$a = \pm\frac{\sqrt{3}}{4} \qquad (26\text{--}5)$$

[50] Ⓑ The first symbol is a letter and may be chosen in any of 24 ways (I and O cannot be used). The second symbol may also be chosen in 24 ways. The third, being a digit from 0 to 9, can be chosen in one of 10 ways as can the fourth:

$$24 \times 24 \times 10 \times 10 = 57,600 \quad (27\text{--}2)$$

SELF-EVALUATION CHART FOR DIAGNOSTIC TEST

SUBJECT AREA	QUESTIONS ANSWERED CORRECTLY	NUMBER OF CORRECT ANSWERS

Algebra
(15 questions)

1	2	3	4	5	6	8	11	12	13	14	15	16	18	49

_____

Plane geometry
(11 questions)

7	9	10	17	19	20	21	22	23	24	25

_____

Solid geometry
(3 questions)

26	27	47

_____

Coordinate geometry
(6 questions)

29	30	31	32	33	46

_____

Trigonometry
(5 questions)

34	35	36	37	39

_____

Functions
(6 questions)

40	41	42	43	44	45

_____

Miscellaneous
(5 questions)

24	28	38	48	50

_____

Total number of correct answers _____

Total score = total number of correct answers × 4   _____

minus number of incorrect answers − _____

_____

A Look Ahead

4. An Overview of Concepts and Formulas

ALGEBRA

25 IMPORTANT CONCEPTS

1. The term *set* designates a collection of objects named in such a way as to provide a test that will indicate whether or not some particular object belongs to (symbolized as "ε") the set.
2. Objects belonging to a set are called *elements* or *members* of the set.
3. A square root of a number x is a number y for which $y^2 = x$.
4. Two terms of a polynomial are like terms if they have the same variables and each variable has the same exponent.
5. The first step in factoring a polynomial is to look for a common factor and remove it by using the generalized Distributive Law:
   $$ab + ac + ad + \ldots = a(b + c + d + \ldots).$$
6. If a and b are any real numbers and if
   $$a < b \text{ and } b < c, \text{ then } a < c.$$
7. A rational expression is a fraction whose numerator and denominator are polynomials.
8. To solve an equation involving rational expressions, it is necessary to clear fractions by multiplying all terms by the lowest common denominator (LCD).
9. If $ax^2 + bx + c = 0$ and $ax^2 + bx + c$ can be factored into linear factors, then the solutions can be found by setting each factor equal to zero and solving for x.
10. A relation is a set of ordered pairs.
11. A function is a set of ordered pairs no two of which have the same first coordinate. Therefore a function is always a relation, but not all relations are functions.
12. The imaginary number i is defined by the equation $i^2 = -1$; in other words, $i = \sqrt{-1}$.
13. The standard form of a complex number is $a + bi$, where a and b are real.
14. In the complex number plane, the graph of $a + bi$ is the point whose coordinates are (a, b).
15. A system of equations can be solved in three ways: (1) by graphing, (2) by substitution, and (3) by addition, which involves eliminating a variable.
16. The terms *logarithm* and *exponent* are synonymous.
17. The common logarithm of a positive number can be expressed as the sum of an integer (called the *characteristic*) and the common log of a number (called the *mantissa*) between 1 and 0.
18. The values of a polynomial can be calculated quickly by synthetic division.
19. The number of linear factors of a polynomial of degree n is n.
20. An arithmetic sequence follows the pattern
    $$a, a + d, a + 2d, a + 3d, \ldots,$$
    $$a + (n - 1)d,$$
    where n is the number of the term.
21. A geometric sequence follows the pattern
    $$a, ar, ar^2, ar^3, ar^4, \ldots, ar^{n-1},$$
    where n is the number of the term and r is the ratio of any two consecutive terms.
22. If the first of two actions can be done in m ways and the second done in n ways, the number of ways the two actions can be done in order is $m \times n$.
23. The value of the expression $n!$, where n is any positive integer, is given by
    $$n! = n (n - 1)(n - 2) \ldots 3 \cdot 2 \cdot 1.$$
24. The total number of combinations of a set of n elements is the total number of those subsets that contain at least one element, and this number is
    $$2^n - 1.$$
25. If two events are mutually exclusive (i.e., they cannot both occur at the same time), and the first event can occur in m ways while the second can occur in n ways, then one or the other event can occur in $m + n$ ways.

25 FREQUENTLY USED ALGEBRA FORMULAS

1. $a^2 - b^2 = (a + b)(a - b).$
2. If $ax^2 + bx + c = 0$, then
   $$x = \frac{-b \pm \sqrt{b^2 - 4ac}}{2a}$$
3. $x^m \cdot x^n = x^{m+n}.$
4. $\dfrac{x^m}{x^n} = x^{m-n}.$
5. $(x^m)^n = x^{mn}.$
6. $(xy)^m = x^m y^m.$
7. $\left(\dfrac{x}{y}\right)^m = \dfrac{x^m}{y^m}.$
8. $x^{-m} = \dfrac{1}{x^m}.$

9. $x^{m/n} = \sqrt[n]{x^m}$ or $(\sqrt[n]{x})^m$.

10. $\log MN = \log M + \log N$.

11. $\log \dfrac{M}{N} = \log M - \log N$.

12. $\log M^n = n \log M$.

13. $\log \dfrac{1}{M} = -\log M$.

14. If $P(x_1, y_1)$ and $Q(x_2, y_2)$ are two points in a plane, then

(a) the slope of line $PQ = \dfrac{y_1 - y_2}{x_1 - x_2}$,

(b) the midpoint of segment $PQ =$
$(\dfrac{x_1 + x_2}{2}, \dfrac{y_1 + y_2}{2})$,

(c) the length of segment $PQ =$
$\sqrt{(x_1 - x_2)^2 + (y_1 - y_2)^2}$,

(d) an equation of line PQ is
$y - y_1 = \dfrac{y_1 - y_2}{x_1 - x_2}(x - x_1)$.

15. If m is the slope of a line and $(0,b)$ is the point at which it intersects the y-axis, then
$$y = mx + b$$
is the equation of the line.

16. If (h,k) is the center of a circle and r is its radius, then
$$(x - h)^2 + (y - k)^2 = r^2$$
is the equation of the circle. When the center is the origin, then $x^2 + y^2 = r^2$ is the equation.

17. If $f(x)$ is a second-degree function, then its graph is a parabola with equation
$$f(x) = ax^2 + bx + c$$
with vertex at the point $(\dfrac{-b}{2a}, \dfrac{4ac - b^2}{4a})$.

18. The equation of an ellipse with center at the origin is
$$\dfrac{x^2}{a^2} + \dfrac{y^2}{b^2} = 1$$
with axial intersections at the points $(\pm a, 0)$ and $(0, \pm b)$.

19. The equation of an hyperbola whose asymptotes intersect at the origin is
$$\dfrac{x^2}{a^2} - \dfrac{y^2}{b^2} = 1 \quad \text{(intercepts on the x-axis)},$$
or
$$\dfrac{x^2}{a^2} - \dfrac{y^2}{b^2} = 1 \quad \text{(intercepts on the y-axis)}.$$

The asymptotes are found by factoring the left side according to the difference of squares, then equating each factor with zero.

20. $a^2 - b^2 = (a + b)(a - b)$.

21. If a_n is any term of an arithmetic sequence, then
$$a_n = a_1 + (n - 1)d,$$
where a_1 is the first term, n is the number of terms, and d is the difference between any term and its successor.

22. If S_n is the sum of the first n terms of an arithmetic sequence, then
$$S_n = \dfrac{(a_1 + a_n)}{2}n.$$

23. If a_n is any term of a geometric sequence, then
$$a_n = a_1 r^{n-1},$$
where a_1 is the first term, n the number of terms and r the quotient found by dividing any term into its successor.

24. For a geometric series, the sum S_n is given by
$$S_n = \dfrac{a_1 - a_1 r^n}{1 - r}$$
where the variables have the same meaning as in 23.

25. For an infinite geometric series, the sum S_∞ is given by
$$S_\infty = \dfrac{a_1}{1 - r}$$
where the variables have the same meaning as in 23.

GEOMETRY

20 IMPORTANT CONCEPTS

1. A point has no width or thickness, only position.
2. A line is a set of points, has no thickness, is straight, and continues infinitely in two directions.
3. A plane is a set of points, is flat, has no depth (thickness), and continues infinitely in all directions.
4. The midpoint of a right triangle is equidistant from its vertices.
5. The sum of the measures of the angles of a triangle is 180.
6. The sum of the measures of the angles (interior) of any polygon is $180(n - 2)$, where n is the number of sides.
7. The sum of the measures of the exterior angles of a regular polygon is 360.

8. The measure of an angle inscribed in a circle is half the measure of the intercepted arc.

9. An angle inscribed in a semicircle is a right angle.

10. A triangle is a right triangle if and only if the square of the length of its longest side is equal to the sum of the squares of the lengths of the remaining two sides.

11. A right angle has degree measure 90.

12. An obtuse angle has a measure greater than 90.

13. An acute angle has a measure less than 90.

14. The measure of an exterior angle of a triangle is equal to the sum of the measures of its remote interior angles.

15. An altitude of a triangle is a segment containing the vertex of one angle of the triangle and is perpendicular to the opposite side.

16. In any 45-45-90 triangle, the sides are proportional to those shown at right.

17. In any 30-60-90 triangle, the sides are proportional to those shown at right.

18. Two lines are parallel if and only if they lie in the same plane and do not intersect.

19. Parallel lines are everywhere equidistant.

20. If R, S and T are three distinct points of a circle, then the measure of $\angle RTS$ is half the measure of arc RS.

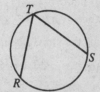

STANDARD ABBREVIATIONS FOR 10 GEOMETRIC LAWS

CP (or CPCT): Corresponding parts of congruent triangles are congruent. This is the definition of "congruent triangles."

ITT: Two sides of a triangle are congruent if and only if the angles opposite them are congruent. The Isosceles Triangle Theorem.

SAS: If two sides and the included angle of one triangle are each congruent to the corresponding parts of a second triangle, then the triangles are congruent. The Side-Angle-Side Postulate.

ASA: If two angles and the included side of one triangle are each congruent to the corresponding parts of a second triangle, then the triangles are congruent. The Angle-Side-Angle Postulate. (This is actually a theorem, but the proof is generally beyond the scope of elementary geometry students, so the law is just postulated.)

SSS: If the three sides of one triangle are each congruent to the corresponding sides of a second triangle, then the triangles are congruent. The Side-Side-Side Postulate. (Again, though the law is postulated for simplicity, it can be proved.)

AAS: If two angles and a side opposite one of the angles are each congruent to the corresponding parts of a second triangle, the triangles are congruent. The Side-Angle-Angle Theorem, also commonly abbreviated SAA.

HL: If the hypotenuse and one leg of a right triangle are congruent to the corresponding parts of a second right triangle, the two triangles are congruent. The Hypotenuse-Leg Theorem.

HA: If the hypotenuse and one acute angle of a right triangle are congruent to the corresponding parts of a second right triangle, the two triangles are congruent. The Hypotenuse-Angle Theorem.

SSS Similarity: A correspondence between two triangles is a similarity if all three pairs of corresponding sides are proportional.

AA Similarity: A correspondence between two triangles is a similarity if any two pairs of corresponding angles are congruent.

---

20 FREQUENTLY USED GEOMETRY FORMULAS

1. The area of a circle, A, is related to the radius by
$$A = \pi r^2.$$

2. The circumference of a circle, C, is related to the radius by
$$C = 2\pi r,$$
and to the diameter by
$$C = \pi d.$$

3. If A is the area of a square and s is the length of one side, then
$$A = s^2.$$
The perimeter, P, is $4s$.

4. If A is the area of a rectangle, l is its length and w its width, then
$$A = lw.$$
The perimeter, P, is
$$2l + 2w.$$

5. The area, A, of any triangle is related to the length, b, of any base and the altitude, a, to that base by

$$A = \frac{1}{2}ab.$$

6. If A and B are the midpoints of the sides of a triangle, then

$$AB = \frac{1}{2}CD$$
and
$$AB \parallel CD.$$

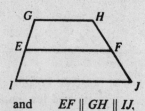

7. If $GH \parallel IJ$ and E and F are the midpoints of the sides of a parallelogram, then

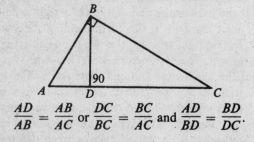

$$EF = \frac{1}{2}(GH + IJ) \quad \text{and} \quad EF \parallel GH \parallel IJ.$$

8. In right triangle ABC with $BD \perp AC$,

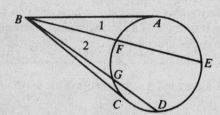

$$\frac{AD}{AB} = \frac{AB}{AC} \text{ or } \frac{DC}{BC} = \frac{BC}{AC} \text{ and } \frac{AD}{BD} = \frac{BD}{DC}.$$

9.

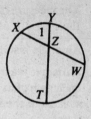

If AB and BC are tangents, then $AB = BC$, $(BE) \cdot (BF) = (BD) \cdot (BG) = (BA)^2 = (BC)^2$.
$\angle 1 = \frac{1}{2}(AE - AF)$. $\angle 2 = \frac{1}{2}(DE - FG)$.

10. If XW and YT are chords intersecting at point Z in the interior of a circle, then $(XZ)(ZW) = (YZ)(ZT)$ and

$$\angle 1 = \frac{1}{2}(XY + TW).$$

11. If V is the volume of a prism, h is the altitude (the perpendicular distance between the planes containing the bases), and B is the area of a base, then
$$V = hB.$$

12. If S_L is the lateral surface area of a prism, h is its altitude, and p is the perimeter of a base, then
$$S_L = hp.$$

13. If S_T is the total surface area of a prism, then
$$S_T = hp + 2B.$$

14. If A is the total surface area of a cube and e is the length of an edge, then
$$A = 6e^2.$$

15. If V is the volume of a cube and e is the length of an edge, then
$$V = e^3.$$

16. If V is the volume of a cylinder, h is its altitude, and B the area of its base, then
$$V + hB.$$

17. If S_c is the area of the curved surface of a cylinder, h is its altitude, and C is the circumference of the base, then
$$S_c + hC.$$
If S_T is the total surface area, then
$$S_T = hC = 2B.$$

18. If V is the volume of a pyramid, h its altitude, and B is the area of a base, then
$$V = \frac{1}{3}hB.$$

19. If V is the volume of a cone, h is its altitude, and B is the area of a base, then
$$V = \frac{1}{3}hB.$$

20. If V is the volume of a sphere, S is its surface, and r its radius, then
$$V = \frac{4}{3}\pi r^3 \quad \text{and} \quad S = 4\pi r^2.$$

TRIGONOMETRY

5 IMPORTANT CONCEPTS

1. In trigonometry, an angle is a rotation; therefore any real number (positive, negative or zero) may be the measure of an angle.

2. Since π radians = 180°:
   a. radians can be converted to degrees by multiplying each side of the equation
   $$1 \text{ radian} = \frac{180}{\pi} \text{ degrees}$$
   by the given number of radians and simplifying;
   b. degrees can be converted to radians by multiplying each side of the equation
   $$1 \text{ degree} = \frac{\pi}{180} \text{ radians}$$
   by the given number of degrees and simplifying.

3. To find values of trigonometric functions of angles with reference angles of 30 or 60, the 30-60-90 triangle is used:

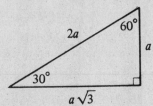

4. To find values of trigonometric functions of angles with reference angle 45, the isosceles right triangle is used:

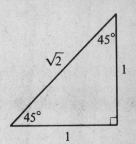

5. To find values of trigonometric functions of quadrantal angles (0, 90, 180, 270, 360, . . .), the diagram at right, with (x,y) the values given and $r = 1$ for each point, is used:

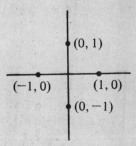

5 FREQUENTLY USED TRIGONOMETRY FORMULAS

1. If $\angle X$ is an acute angle of a right triangle, then
$$\sin \angle X = \frac{\text{opposite leg}}{\text{hypotenuse}},$$
$$\cos \angle X = \frac{\text{adjacent leg}}{\text{hypotenuse}},$$
$$\tan \angle X = \frac{\text{opposite leg}}{\text{adjacent leg}},$$
$$\cot \angle X = \frac{\text{adjacent leg}}{\text{opposite leg}},$$
$$\sec \angle X = \frac{\text{hypotenuse}}{\text{adjacent leg}},$$
$$\csc \angle X = \frac{\text{hypotenuse}}{\text{opposite leg}}.$$

2. If θ is an angle in standard position and (x, y) is a point on its terminal side at a distance r units from the origin, then
$$\sin \theta = \frac{y}{r}, \ \csc \theta = \frac{r}{y}, \ \cos \theta = \frac{x}{r},$$
$$\sec \theta = \frac{r}{x}, \ \tan \theta = \frac{y}{x}, \ \cot \theta = \frac{x}{y}.$$

3. For any $\angle X$, the following must be true:
$$(\sin \angle X)(\csc \angle X) = 1, \ \sin \angle X = \frac{1}{\csc \angle X}$$
$$\csc \angle X = \frac{1}{\sin \angle X};$$
$$(\cos \angle X)(\sec \angle X) = 1, \ \cos \angle X = \frac{1}{\sec \angle X}$$
$$\sec \angle X = \frac{1}{\cos \angle X};$$
$$(\tan \angle X)(\cot \angle X) = 1, \ \tan \angle X = \frac{1}{\cot \angle X}$$
$$\cot \angle X = \frac{1}{\tan \angle X}.$$

4. For any angle X,
$$\sin^2 \angle X + \cos^2 \angle X = 1, \ \tan^2 \angle X + 1 = \sec^2 \angle X;$$
$$\cot^2 \angle X + 1 = \csc^2 \angle X, \ \tan \angle X = \frac{\sin \angle X}{\cos \angle X}$$
$$\cot \angle X = \frac{\cos \angle X}{\sin \angle X}.$$

5. In any triangle with vertices X, Y, and Z,
$$\frac{YZ}{\sin \angle X} = \frac{XY}{\sin \angle Z} = \frac{XZ}{\sin \angle Y} \text{ (Law of Sines)},$$
$$XY^2 = YZ^2 + XZ^2 - 2(YZ)(XZ) \cos \angle Z$$
(Law of Cosines).

Strategies, Review, and Practice
Basic Topics

5.   Arithmetic

Key Terms

prime number   a number that is greater than 1 and has no other whole number factors except itself and 1. Examples: 5, 7.

least common multiple (LCM)   for two or more numbers, the smallest positive number in the set of common multiples. Example: For 4 and 5, the LCM = 20.

least common denominator (LCD)   for two or more fractions, the LCM of their denominators. Example: For $\frac{1}{3}$, $\frac{1}{4}$, and $\frac{1}{2}$, the LCD = 12.

reciprocal or **multiplicative inverse**   a number that, when used to multiply a given number, gives a product of 1. Example: $\frac{4}{5} \times \frac{5}{4} = 1$; $\frac{5}{4}$ is the reciprocal of $\frac{4}{5}$.

additive inverse   a number that, when added to a given number, gives a sum of zero. Example: $4 + (-4) = 0$; -4 is the additive inverse of 4.

---

[1] What is the value of
$$\frac{7 + 7 + 7 + 7 + 7}{5 + 5 + 5 + 5 + 5 + 5 + 5}?$$
Ⓐ 0   Ⓑ 1   Ⓒ 5   Ⓓ 7   Ⓔ 35

A student planning to take the Mathematics Level I Achievement Test should have a strong knowledge of the fundamentals of arithmetic. Just working with arithmetic skills as part of the study of algebra, geometry, trigonometry, and high school science, however, is adequate preparation in these elementary concepts for most students. Throughout this chapter the emphasis will be on some of the less routine aspects of arithmetic and the way they relate to basic skills. We will point out many of the common errors that plague even some of the best qualified students.

The question above illustrates not only some elementary arithmetic facts relating to addition and division, but also some of the devices test makers use to discover the student's level of mastery. Did you notice that the numerator is 5×7 (the sum of five 7's) and the denominator is 7×5 (the sum of seven 5's)? If you did, then you found the answer more quickly than the student who added all of the numbers and then divided.

TEST-TAKING TIP.

This familiarity with underlying mathematical principles is part of what testers are looking for. Rarely does a test question require much computation. Most can be answered quickly, often with no pencil-and-paper work at all.

¶ DRILL Can you discover a quick way to find the value of each expression?

(a) $(2 \times 13) + (18 \times 13) = ?$
(b) $(6 + 6 + 6) + (3 + 3 + 3 + 3 + 3) = ?$
(c) $(9.7 \times 157) + (.3 \times 157) = ?$
(d) $(25)(32.43)(4) = ?$

DOING OPERATIONS IN THE CORRECT ORDER

[2] Find the value of $4 + 7 \times 6 + 6 \div 2$.

Ⓐ 69   Ⓑ 49   Ⓒ 45   Ⓓ 36   Ⓔ 25

The order of operations in a mathematical expression is an agreement among mathematicians about which steps are to be done first. One way to remember this order is to think of the order of the first letters in the phrase "*My Dear Aunt Sally*." In other words, multiplication and division are carried out first, and addition and subtraction are done afterwards.

The expression above is really
$$4 + 42 + 3$$
since $7 \times 6 = 42$ and $6 \div 2 = 3$.

¶ DRILL Find the value of each of the following:

(a) $3 - 2 + 8 \times 7 - 4 \div 4$
(b) $100 - 2 \times 36 + 12 - 6$
(c) $10 \times 4 + 21 \div 7$
(d) $36 - 9 \div 3 + 6$
(e) $8 \div 2 \times 4 + 3 - 4 + 6$

[3] Find the value of $9 - 2(5 - 1) + (5 - 1)$.

Ⓐ 32   Ⓑ 5   Ⓒ 3   Ⓓ 12   Ⓔ 17

The order in which a series of operations is completed can be changed through the use of parentheses as grouping symbols. The operations enclosed in the parentheses are carried out first (using the MDAS order for operations inside the parentheses). Thus the expression above is really
$$9 - 2 \times 4 + 4 = 9 - 8 + 4 = 1 + 4.$$

Note the absence of a multiplication sign, $\times$, to designate the product of 2 and $(5 - 1)$. The multiplication sign is usually deleted when one or both multipliers are written in parentheses.

¶ DRILL Find the value of each of the following:

(a) $(3 + 2) 5$ (b) $(2 + 3) - (5 - 2)$
(c) $4 - 2 (3 - 1)$ (d) $(54 - 14 \div 7) \div 2$

FINDING THE LEAST COMMON MULTIPLE

[4] **What is the least common multiple of x and y if x and y are prime numbers?**

Ⓐ x Ⓑ y Ⓒ $x + y$ Ⓓ xy Ⓔ $\dfrac{x}{y}$

A number is *prime* if it is greater than 1 and has no whole number factors except itself and 1. Examples of primes are 2, 3, 5, 7, 11, 13, 17, and so forth.

A number p is a *multiple* of q if $p \div q$ is a whole number {0, 1, 2, 3, etc.}. Thus the multiples of 3 include {0, 3, 6, 9, 12, 15, . . .}, and the multiples of 5 include {0, 5, 10, 15, . . .}.

A *common multiple* of two numbers is a number that is a multiple of each.

Note that the common multiples of 3 and 5 include {0, 15, 30, . . .}. Thus 0 is a common multiple of every pair of numbers.

The *least common multiple* (LCM) of a set of two or more numbers is the smallest *positive* number in the set of common multiples. Therefore, the least common multiple of 5 and 3 is 15, and the least common multiple of 6 and 4 is 12.

One way to find the LCM is to write the first few members of the set of common multiples and choose the smallest positive number in this set. For example, the common multiples of 3 and 5 are {0, 15, 30, 45, . . .}, so the LCM is 15. A second method is sometimes quicker. To find the LCM of p and q, first write the prime factors of p and the prime factors of q. The LCM must contain each prime factor of p *and* each prime factor of q. The prime factors are each raised to a power equal to that of the greatest power of that prime factor in p or q, even if it appears in both.

For example, the prime factorizations of 12 and 45 are

$$12 = 2^2 \times 3,$$
$$45 = 3^2 \times 5.$$

The greatest powers of the primes are 2^2, 3^2 and 5 so the LCM is

$$2^2 \times 3^2 \times 5 = 180.$$

Note that 3 is a factor of both 12 and 45, but its greatest power in either is 3^2.

In the multiple-choice question above, x and y are both primes, so the LCM must be their product.

¶ DRILL Find the LCM of each:

(a) 2, 3 and 4   (b) 21, 30 and 54
(c) 15 and 35   (d) 18 and 21

FINDING THE GREATEST COMMON FACTOR

[5] **Which of the following is the greatest common factor of 36, 27, and 24?**

Ⓐ 2   Ⓑ 3   Ⓒ 6   Ⓓ 9   Ⓔ 12

When two or more numbers are multiplied together, each is called a *factor* of the result. The number 30, for example, can be written as 6 times 5, 2 times 15, 3 times 10, or 1 times 30, so its set of factors is

$$\{1, 2, 3, 5, 6, 10, 15, 30\}.$$

If a number is a factor of each of two or more given whole numbers, it is called a *common factor* of the given numbers. Note that the numbers given in the question above have the following sets of factors:

$36 \leftarrow\rightarrow \{1, 2, 3, 4, 6, 9, 12, 18, 36\},$
$27 \leftarrow\rightarrow \{1, 3, 9, 27\},$
$24 \leftarrow\rightarrow \{1, 2, 3, 4, 6, 8, 12, 24\}.$

Thus the factors common to *all three* of the given numbers are

$$\{1, 3\}.$$

The greater of these is, of course, 3.

This question was easily answered by listing the common factors, but a more efficient method exists. Write it as a product in which all factors are prime numbers —the *prime factorization*. The *greatest common factor* (GCF) will be the product of the prime factors found in both. Each is used only as many times as it occurs in *all* of the numbers. The latter part of that statement is easily misinterpreted. Study the following prime factorizations:

$$27 = 3 \times 3 \times 3,$$
$$36 = 3 \times 3 \times 2 \times 2,$$
$$24 = 3 \times 2 \times 2 \times 2.$$

The first number has three 3's. Do they *all* have three 3's? No, the numbers 36 and 24 do not. The number 36 has two 3's. Do they *all* have two 3's? No, just 36 and 27 have. The number 24 has one 3. Do they all have one

3? Yes. Since only one 3 is common, and no other factors are common, 3 is the GCF.

What is the GCF for 24 and 60?

$$24 = 3 \times 2 \times 2 \times 2$$
$$60 = 5 \times 3 \times 2 \times 2$$

Therefore the GCF is $3 \times 2 \times 2 = 12$ since the factors listed are the ones common to both—in other words, the ones both have.

¶ DRILL Find the GCF:

(a) 8 and 28   (b) 6, 8 and 10
(c) 8, 12 and 18   (d) 24, 36 and 108

REDUCING FRACTIONS TO LOWEST TERMS

[6] If the fraction $\frac{9}{45}$ were expressed in lowest terms, what factor common to numerator and denominator would have to be removed?

Ⓐ 3   Ⓑ 5   Ⓒ 9   Ⓓ 15   Ⓔ The fraction is already in lowest terms

A fraction is used to indicate that two numbers are to be divided; the number above the bar (the *numerator*) is to be divided by the number below the bar (the *denominator*). Two fractions that look very different may, in fact, indicate divisions having the same result. For example, $\frac{2}{5}$ and $\frac{4}{10}$ have the same result. This is so because

$$\frac{4}{10} = \frac{2 \times 2}{5 \times 2} = \frac{2}{5} \times \frac{2}{2} = \frac{2}{5} \times 1 = \frac{2}{5}.$$

The numbers 4 and 10 have the common factor 2, which has been removed by the process shown above.

The removal of common factors does not require the use of so many steps once the idea is understood. After the common factors have been identified, they may merely be crossed out:

$$\frac{9}{45} = \frac{1 \times 9}{5 \times 9} = \frac{1}{5}.$$

Thus $\frac{9}{45}$ and $\frac{1}{5}$ name the same number.

Fractions which name the same number are called *equivalent* fractions and the process of removing the common factors is called *reducing to lowest terms*.

Fractions may also be expressed as equivalent fractions in higher terms by reversing the process—in other words, by multiplying numerator and denominator by a common factor. Thus $\frac{2}{10}, \frac{3}{15}, \frac{4}{20}, \frac{5}{25}, \frac{6}{30}, \frac{7}{35}$, and so forth, are all expressions in higher terms for $\frac{1}{5}$.

TEST-TAKING TIP.

The ability to express fractions in higher or lower terms is required in many kinds of test questions and should be learned thoroughly.

¶ DRILL Reduce to lowest terms:

(a) $\frac{4}{12}$ (b) $\frac{25}{35}$ (c) $\frac{27}{36}$ (d) $\frac{100}{250}$

FINDING THE LEAST COMMON DENOMINATOR

[7] Find the least common denominator of the fractions $\frac{1}{60}$ and $\frac{5}{72}$.

Ⓐ $\frac{6}{360}$ Ⓑ $\frac{180}{360}$ Ⓒ 12   Ⓓ 360   Ⓔ 6

The *least common denominator* (LCD) of two or more fractions is the same number that is the LCM of their denominators and, therefore, is found by the method described in section [4] of this chapter.

$$60 = 5 \times 3 \times 2^2$$
$$72 = 3^2 \times 2^3$$
$$LCD = 3^2 \times 2^3 \times 5 = 360$$

To verify that 360 is a common denominator, you may check this result by dividing 360 by each of 72 and 60 as follows: $360 \div 60 = 6,$
$360 \div 72 = 5.$

TEST-TAKING TIP.

When taking tests, always check to make sure you are answering the question being asked and not a different one also suggested by the given information but not explicitly asked. A surprisingly large number of students misinterpret the directions "Find the least common denominator" to mean "Change the fractions to equivalent fractions with the least common denominator." You are merely being asked to discover what the LCD is and not to alter the fractions to have this LCD.

¶ DRILL For each of the following, first find the LCD and then change all fractions to equivalent fractions each with the LCD by multiplying the numerator and denominator of each by the necessary common factor:

(a) $\frac{1}{2}, \frac{1}{3}, \frac{1}{6}$ (b) $\frac{1}{3}, \frac{1}{9}, \frac{1}{27}$

(c) $\frac{3}{8}, \frac{5}{28}$ (d) $\frac{5}{48}, \frac{7}{54}$

[8] The value of $\frac{1}{2} - \frac{1}{3} + \frac{1}{4}$ is ?

(A) $\frac{1}{3}$ (B) 5 (C) $\frac{1}{4}$ (D) $\frac{1}{9}$ (E) $\frac{5}{12}$

Before a set of fractions can be added or subtracted, each fraction must be changed to an equivalent fraction with a denominator common to all. The LCD of $\frac{1}{2}$, $\frac{1}{3}$ and $\frac{1}{4}$ is 12.

$$\frac{1 \times 6}{2 \times 6} - \frac{1 \times 4}{3 \times 4} + \frac{1 \times 3}{4 \times 3}$$

Combining the fractions is completed by performing the indicated operations on the numerators and writing the result with the common denominator.

$$\frac{6 - 4 + 3}{12} = \frac{5}{12}$$

A common mistake made by many good students is to concentrate on combining the numerators and then to forget to write the denominator. Thus they would write the answer to the above as 5, rather than the correct fraction, $\frac{5}{12}$.

TEST-TAKING TIP.

In listing answer choices, testers use incorrect answers resulting from common mistakes as "distractors." Don't assume that the answer you have found must be correct solely on the basis that it appears as one of the answer choices.

¶ DRILL Combine:

(a) $\frac{1}{2} + \frac{9}{16}$　　(b) $\frac{3}{8} + \frac{1}{2} - \frac{27}{32}$

(c) $\frac{7}{8} - \frac{3}{4} + \frac{2}{3}$　　(d) $\frac{5}{8} + \frac{11}{12} - \frac{13}{16}$　　(e) $\frac{1}{3} + \frac{5}{12}$

MULTIPLYING FRACTIONS

[9] What is the value of $\frac{3}{8} \times \frac{4}{5} \times \frac{5}{6}$?

(A) $\frac{12}{19}$ (B) $\frac{1}{4}$ (C) $\frac{3}{8}$ (D) $\frac{3}{16}$ (E) 3

If a set of fractions is multiplied, the result is a fraction whose numerator is the product of the numerators and whose denominator is the product of the denominators. Thus one way of working out the answer to the question above is

$$\frac{3 \times 4 \times 5}{8 \times 5 \times 6} = \frac{60}{240} = \frac{1 \times 60}{4 \times 60} = \frac{1}{4}.$$

Note that the final step consisted of removing a factor common to numerator and denominator. A much more efficient procedure is to remove common factors before the multiplication is done. A common factor of any numerator and denominator may be removed, even if it is in different fractions. The numbers 3, 4 and 5 are common factors.

$$\frac{\cancel{3}}{\cancel{8}} \times \frac{\cancel{4}}{\cancel{5}} \times \frac{\cancel{5}}{\cancel{6}} = \frac{1 \times 1 \times 1}{2 \times 1 \times 2} = \frac{1}{4}$$

Students frequently confuse the procedure for multiplication of fractions with that for addition of fractions and start by changing to common denominators. Such a procedure just introduces many common factors that must be removed before the multiplication can begin.

TEST-TAKING TIP.

The result may be a number that does appear as an answer among the choices but is so different in form as to be unrecognizable at first glance. Therefore, when comparing your answer with the choices given, always consider the possibility that the correct answer is in a different form from the one you've calculated.

¶ DRILL Find the value:

(a) $\frac{2}{5} \times \frac{5}{16}$　　(b) $\frac{7}{12} \times \frac{4}{5}$

(c) $\frac{7}{12} \times 6$　　(d) $\frac{24}{35} \times \frac{21}{32} \times \frac{2}{3}$

USING MIXED NUMBERS AND IMPROPER FRACTIONS

[10] $4\frac{1}{3} - \frac{2}{3} = ?$

(A) $3\frac{1}{3}$ (B) 3 (C) $3\frac{2}{3}$ (D) 5 (E) $\frac{5}{3}$

The number $4\frac{1}{3}$ is an example of a mixed number. You should have no difficulty in dealing with such numbers if you understand that the operation relating the 4 and the $\frac{1}{3}$ is addition. Thus another way of writing it is

$$4\frac{1}{3} = 4 + \frac{1}{3} = \frac{4 \times 3}{1 \times 3} + \frac{1}{3} = \frac{12}{3} + \frac{1}{3} = \frac{13}{3}.$$

When a mixed number is written in fractional form, the numerator of the resulting fraction is always greater than the denominator, making it an *improper fraction*.

For changing mixed numbers to improper fractions, there is a shorter procedure than the one just described. Multiply the whole number by the denominator of the fraction and add the numerator of the fraction to this product. Then write this sum over the denominator of the fraction.

$$\frac{4 \times 3 + 1}{3} = \frac{13}{3}$$

¶ DRILL Change to improper fractions:

(a) $3\frac{2}{3}$ (b) $1\frac{1}{2}$ (c) $4\frac{3}{8}$ (d) $7\frac{1}{7}$

[11] If $2\frac{1}{3}$ is divided by $\frac{2}{3}$, the result is ?

ⓐ 2 ⓑ 3 ⓒ $3\frac{1}{2}$ ⓓ $\frac{1}{3}$ ⓔ 7

If the product of two numbers is 1, then each is called the *reciprocal,* or *multiplicative inverse,* of the other. For example, $\frac{2}{3}$ and $\frac{3}{2}$ are reciprocals since

$$\frac{2}{3} \times \frac{3}{2} = 1.$$

Dividing by a given number produces the same result as multiplying by its reciprocal, hence:

$$2\frac{1}{3} \div \frac{2}{3} = 2\frac{1}{3} \times \frac{3}{2}.$$

Before this division can be carried out, however, the number $2\frac{1}{3}$ must be changed from a mixed number to an improper fraction by following the procedure described in the preceding section.

$$2\frac{1}{3} = \frac{2 \times 3 + 1}{3} = \frac{7}{3}$$

$$\frac{7}{3} \times \frac{3}{2} = \frac{7}{2} = 3\frac{1}{2}$$

¶ DRILL Divide by multiplying by the reciprocal of the divisor:

(a) $\frac{1}{3} \div \frac{2}{3}$ (b) $2\frac{2}{3} \div \frac{8}{3}$

(c) $\frac{1}{5} \div 2\frac{2}{5}$ (d) $1\frac{1}{2} \div 2\frac{1}{4}$

CHANGING FRACTIONS TO DECIMALS

[12] If $\frac{3}{9}$ is written as a decimal, the result is ?

ⓐ $.\overline{3}$ ⓑ $.3$ ⓒ $.9$ ⓓ $.\overline{9}$ ⓔ $.39$

To change a fraction into decimal form, divide the denominator into the numerator *after reducing the fraction to lowest terms.*

EXAMPLE 1

To change $\frac{6}{8}$ to a decimal, first reduce it to $\frac{3}{4}$ and then divide:

$$\begin{array}{r} .75 \\ 4 \overline{)3.00} \end{array}$$

Therefore, $\frac{6}{8} = .75$.

Frequently the division cannot be completed because there is always a remainder. As the division is carried out, however, a pattern of repeating digits emerges.

EXAMPLE 2

To change $\frac{3}{11}$ to a decimal, divide 3 by 11.

$$\begin{array}{r} .2727 \\ 11 \overline{)3.0000} \\ \underline{2\ 2} \\ 80 \\ \underline{77} \\ 30 \\ \underline{22} \\ 80 \\ \underline{77} \\ 3 \end{array}$$

Note that this division cannot be completed since remainders of 8 and 3 will continue to alternate forever at each step. The result is called a "periodic" or "repeating" decimal and is generally written by placing a bar above the digits which repeat.

$$\frac{3}{11} = .\overline{27}$$

Whenever a given counting number is divided by another counting number, the result will be a decimal that terminates (meaning that the division is completed since a remainder of zero is reached) or repeats.

The fraction $\frac{3}{9}$ can first be reduced to $\frac{1}{3}$ and then changed to $.\overline{3}$ by division.

$$\begin{array}{r} .333 \\ 3 \overline{)1.000} \\ \underline{9} \\ 10 \\ \underline{9} \\ 10 \\ \underline{9} \\ 1 \end{array}$$

All repeating decimals can be changed to fractions having whole number terms; this procedure will be reviewed in the next chapter.

¶ DRILL Write as a decimal:

(a) $\frac{2}{4}$ (b) $\frac{1}{6}$ (c) $\frac{3}{7}$ (d) $\frac{9}{12}$

[13] If the number $7 \cdot 10^3 + 6 \cdot 10^1 + 5 \cdot 10^0 + 4 \cdot \frac{1}{10^2} + 3 \cdot \frac{1}{10^3}$ were written as a decimal, which of the following would be the result?

Ⓐ 76.543   Ⓑ 76.43   Ⓒ 706.543   Ⓓ 706.043
Ⓔ 7065.043

Numerical representation in the decimal system is based on place value. The number represented by each digit depends on how far to the left or the right of the decimal point it appears. Each digit represents the result of multiplying the value of the digit by the power of 10 determined by the position of the digit. The value of each place can be seen from the following table, where the arrow indicates the position of the decimal. The table is incomplete, of course, since the values continue to get larger to the left and smaller to the right, unendingly.

10^5	10^4	10^3	10^2	10^1	10^0	$\frac{1}{10^1}$	$\frac{1}{10^2}$	$\frac{1}{10^3}$

For example, the number 120.45 can be written as

$$1 \cdot 10^2 + 2 \cdot 10^1 + 0 \cdot 10^0 + 4 \cdot \frac{1}{10^1} + 5 \cdot \frac{1}{10^2}.$$

The latter form is called *expanded notation*. Negative exponents are sometimes used to simplify the writing of the terms on the right side of the decimal. The use of negative exponents will be reviewed later in this text.

¶ DRILL Write in expanded notation:

(a) 1.1   (b) 101.101   (c) .032   (d) 300.003

WORKING WITH DECIMAL NUMBERS

[14] What is the value of $2.2 + .38 - 1.4$?

Ⓐ 1.18   Ⓑ 5.6   Ⓒ 4.6   Ⓓ 5.28   Ⓔ 2.4

Addition and subtraction of decimal expressions are begun by first arranging the sum or difference vertically so that the decimal points are directly under each other in a vertical line. You may wish to annex zeros to the numerals being added so that each has the same number of decimal places.

$$\begin{array}{r} 2.20 \\ +\ \ .38 \\ \hline 2.58 \\ -\ 1.40 \\ \hline 1.18 \end{array}$$

¶ DRILL Add or subtract as indicated:

(a) $.023 + .4 - .05$
(b) $2.5 - .13 + .0048$
(c) $1.624 + 1.369 - 1.9$
(d) $.349 + 1.2 - .012$

[15] $.032 \times 1.85 = ?$

Ⓐ .0592   Ⓑ .5920   Ⓒ 5.92   Ⓓ 59.2   Ⓔ 592

When multiplying two decimal numerals, the number of decimal places in the result is the sum of the numbers of decimal places in the two multipliers. Count the total number of places in the multipliers. Point this total off in the product, counting from right to left. If you run out of places before you have all you need, prefix as many zeros to the left side of the number as you need to get enough decimal places. In the event that the product ends in one or more zeros, these zeros should be recorded and counted along with the others. For example:

$$.02 \times .05 = .0010.$$

The result of this example may, of course, be written as .001, but this zero should not be discarded until *after* the decimal point has been positioned.

¶ DRILL Carry out the multiplications:

(a) 2.07×5.9 (b) $.49 \times 62$
(c) $.380 \times .10$ (d) $.35 \times .02$

[16] The quotient $3.84 \div 18.2$ is the same as the quotient $38.4 \div 182$ because the removal of the decimal points is equivalent to multiplication by:

Ⓐ **100** Ⓑ **10** Ⓒ $\frac{10}{10}$ Ⓓ $\frac{100}{100}$ Ⓔ **1000**

To divide two decimal expressions, remove the decimal point from the divisor by shifting it as many places to the right as is necessary to make the divisor a whole number. Then move the decimal in the dividend (the number to be divided into) the same number of places to the right to compensate for the change you made in the divisor. The divisor and the dividend actually represent a fraction (dividend over divisor). The shift of the decimal point is the result of multiplying by a power of 10. The shift of the decimals in divisor and dividend is explained by the mathematical law that allows multiplication of the numerator and denominator of a fraction by a common factor. Thus:

$$3.84 \div 18.2 = \frac{3.84}{18.2} = \frac{3.84 \times 10}{18.2 \times 10}$$
$$= \frac{38.4}{182} = 38.4 \div 182.$$

Note that, to complete the division, the decimal point had to be moved only one place since the divisor contained only one decimal place.

$$18.2\overline{)3.84}$$

It is not necessary to remove the decimal points from *both* dividend and divisor.

¶ DRILL Divide:

(a) $3.024 \div .48$ (b) $4.653 \div .517$
(c) $.021 \div .00007$

CHANGING PERCENTS TO DECIMALS

[17] If $\frac{1}{2}\%$ is written as a decimal, what is the result?

Ⓐ **.5** Ⓑ **.05** Ⓒ **.005** Ⓓ **.0005** Ⓔ **5**

The term *percent* means "hundredths." A percent can be changed to a fraction by replacing the percent sign, %, with a denominator of 100. Thus:

5% is $\frac{5}{100}$, 87.3% is $\frac{87.3}{100}$ and $\frac{1}{2}\%$ is $\frac{\frac{1}{2}}{100}$.

Dividing a whole number or a decimal numeral by 100 is easily done by shifting the decimal point two places to the left. Hence:

$$\frac{5}{100} = .05 \quad \text{and} \quad \frac{87.3}{100} = .873.$$

When a fraction occurs in a percent, the new fraction that results when the percent sign is replaced by a denominator of 100 is a complex fraction. It can be simplified by first following the procedures of dividing fractions, and then by changing to a decimal through further division.

$$\frac{1}{2}\% = \frac{\frac{1}{2}}{100} = \frac{1}{2} \div 100 = \frac{1}{2} \times \frac{1}{100} = \frac{1}{200} = .005$$

A simpler procedure is to change the fraction to a decimal and then shift the decimal point two places to the left.

$$\frac{1}{2}\% = .5\% = .005$$

¶ DRILL Write as a decimal:

(a) 3% (b) $.6\%$ (c) $\frac{3}{8}\%$ (d) $12\frac{1}{4}\%$

CHANGING FRACTIONS TO PERCENTS

[18] When written as a percent, $3\frac{2}{5}$ is ?

Ⓐ **34%** Ⓑ **3.4%** Ⓒ **340%** Ⓓ **.034%**
Ⓔ **.34%**

Since percent means "hundredths," annexing a percent sign to a number is the same as dividing the number by 100. To compensate for this division, the number must, in some way, be multiplied by 100. This multiplication is usually accomplished by moving the decimal point two places to the right. For example:

$$3 = 300\%,$$
$$.5 = 50\%,$$
$$.01 = 1\%.$$

If a fraction is to be changed to a percent, it is usually best to change the fraction first to a decimal. For example:

$$\frac{1}{2} = .5 = 50\%,$$
$$\frac{3}{8} = .375 = 37.5\%,$$
$$3\frac{2}{5} = 3.4 = 340\%.$$

In each case, annexing a percent sign (in effect, dividing by 100) is compensated for by shifting the decimal point two places to the right (multiplying by 100).

¶ DRILL Write as percents:

(a) $\frac{2}{5}$ (b) $2\frac{1}{4}$ (c) $\frac{7}{20}$ (d) $\frac{15}{7}$

SOLVING PERCENTAGE PROBLEMS

[19] What percent of p is q?

Ⓐ **100%** Ⓑ $q\%$ Ⓒ $\frac{q}{p}\%$ Ⓓ $\frac{100q}{p}\%$
Ⓔ **Not enough information is given**

What percent of 5 is 3? Note that this question asks what fractional part of 5 the number 3 is, with the fraction being represented by use of the percent sign. The key idea to remember is that affixing a percent sign to a number is the same as dividing it by 100, so multiplication by 100 is necessary to counterbalance it.

$$\frac{3}{5} = \frac{3 \times 100}{5}\% = 60\%$$

The work on the example above was completed without resorting to decimals since the decimal representation could not be given in the multiple-choice question we are preparing to answer. The procedure for the sample question is, therefore, identical.

$$\frac{q}{p} = \frac{q \times 100}{p}\% = \frac{100q}{p}\%$$

TEST-TAKING TIP.

Note that, before attempting to answer the multiple-choice question, we rephrased it in terms of a simpler question involving the same basic idea. Many successful test-takers do this to help them think out the procedures for answering questions they do not, at first, understand.

¶ DRILL Answer the following:

(a) What percent of 12 is 4?

(b) What percent of 4 is 12?

(c) What percent of p is $\frac{1}{2}p$?

(d) What percent of $5p$ is $3p$?

[20] 4.2 is 20% of what number?

ⓐ 8.4   ⓑ .84   ⓒ .084   ⓓ 21   ⓔ 2.1

All percents can be written as common fractions, using the principle that "percent" means "hundredths."

$$6\% = \frac{6}{100} = \frac{3}{50}$$

$$120\% = \frac{120}{100} = \frac{6}{5}$$

$$20\% = \frac{20}{100} = \frac{1}{5}$$

Thus many types of percentage problems can be solved by setting up a proportion; in other words, by writing an equation between two fractions. In the question above, let x be the missing number. Then

$$\frac{4.2}{x} = \frac{20}{100}.$$

The procedure for solving a proportion is discussed in depth in Chapter 15, but we will describe it briefly here. In a proportion such as

$$\frac{a}{b} = \frac{c}{d},$$

the product ad equals the product bc regardless of what the numbers a, b, c and d are as long as the equation relating the fractions is true. This means that

$$(4.2)(100) = 20x,$$
$$420 = 20x,$$
$$21 = x.$$

¶ DRILL Answer the following:

(a) 5 is 20% of what number?

(b) 6 is 200% of what number?

(c) $\frac{1}{3}$ is 50% of what number?

(d) 4.4 is 4.4% of what number?

WORKING WITH SIGNED NUMBERS

[21] Which of the following is the additive inverse of $-\frac{1}{2}$?

ⓐ -2 ⓑ 2 ⓒ $\frac{1}{2}$ ⓓ $-\frac{1}{2}$ ⓔ 0

For each given real number there exists a number that when added to it results in a sum of zero. This number is called the *additive inverse* of the given number and is designated by prefixing a "$-$" to the given number.

The additive inverse of 3 is -3, because $-3 + 3 = 0$

The additive inverse of $\frac{2}{3}$ is $-\frac{2}{3}$, because $-\frac{2}{3} + \frac{2}{3} = 0$.

The additive inverse of -5 is $-(-5)$, because $-(-5) + (-5) = 0$. But $5 + (-5) = 0$, so $-(-5) = 5$.

Note that the additive inverse of a positive number is always negative and the additive inverse of a negative number is always positive. Zero is its own additive inverse.

¶ DRILL Write the additive inverse of each of the following:

(a) 2   (b) -8 (c) $\frac{2}{7}$ (d) $-3\frac{1}{4}$

[22] Find the sum of $5 + (-8) + (-2)$.

ⓐ -5 ⓑ -10 ⓒ 5 ⓓ 2 ⓔ -2

The rules of operations on signed numbers are expressed most simply in terms of the absolute value of the number. The *absolute value* of a positive number is the number itself. The absolute value of a negative number is its additive inverse. The absolute value of 0 is 0.

Absolute value is designated by a pair of vertical bars flanking the number.

$$|6| = 6$$
$$|32| = 32$$
$$|0| = 0$$
$$|-2| = 2$$
$$\left|-\frac{1}{2}\right| = \frac{1}{2}$$

Note that no absolute value can ever be negative.

To add signed numbers:

(a) if the numbers have like signs, add their absolute values and prefix the common sign;

(b) if the numbers have unlike signs, subtract the absolute values and prefix the sign of the addend with the greater absolute value.

EXAMPLES

To add $(-2) + (-4)$, add the absolute values, 2 and 4, then prefix the common "$-$" to get -6.

To add $(-5) + 3$, subtract the absolute values, 5 and 3, to get 2, then prefix the "$-$" sign because it is the sign of the number with the greater absolute value, -5. The result is -2.

To add 7 and (-4), subtract the absolute values, 7 and 4, to get 3, then prefix the "$+$" sign because it is the sign of the number with the greater absolute value, 7. The result is 3.

Remember that in a chain of calculations involving more than one operation, the operations are performed in order from left to right with the exceptions noted in sections [2] and [3] of this chapter. Hence

$$5 + (-8) + (-2) = -3 + (-2)$$
$$= -5.$$

TEST-TAKING TIP.

Testers assume a thorough knowledge of signed numbers and the ways to add, subtract, multiply and divide them. Distractors are frequently made from common errors in the use of signs.

¶ DRILL Find the value of each of the following:

(a) $-3 + (-7)$ (b) $4 + (-8)$
(c) $(-18) + 3$ (d) $(-5) + (-3)$

[23] Find the value of $3 - (-2) - 4$.

Ⓐ -5 Ⓑ -3 Ⓒ 3 Ⓓ 1 Ⓔ -1

To subtract a signed number, add its opposite. In other words, convert the problem from one of subtraction to one of addition and then follow the procedure outlined in the preceding section.

$$5 - (-3) = 5 + 3 = 8$$
$$-7 - 2 = (-7) + (-2) = -9$$
$$-4 - (-4) = -4 + 4 = 0$$
$$-5 - (-2) = -5 + 2 = -3$$

Again, in a chain of operations, work from left to right, completing the operations in order.

$$3 - (-2) - 4 = 3 + 2 + (-4)$$
$$= 5 + (-4)$$
$$= 1$$

¶ DRILL Find the value of each of the following:

(a) $-3 - 7$ (b) $4 - 8$
(c) $-18 - (-3)$ (d) $-5 - 3$

[24] Find the value of $(3 - 7)(1 - 4)\left(-\frac{1}{2}\right)$.

Ⓐ 3 Ⓑ -4 Ⓒ -6 Ⓓ 12 Ⓔ 6

To multiply signed numbers, multiply their absolute values and prefix a positive sign if the factors have like signs or a negative sign if the factors have unlike signs. In other words, the product of like signs is always positive; the product of unlike signs is always negative.

EXAMPLES

$$(-2)(-3) = 6$$
$$(-8)\left(\frac{1}{2}\right) = -4$$
$$(3)\left(-\frac{1}{3}\right) = -1$$

In the multiple-choice question, the operations inside the parentheses must be completed first, as explained in section [3] of this chapter; then the multiplication is carried out in order from left to right.

$$(3 - 7)(1 - 4)\left(-\frac{1}{2}\right) = (-4)(-3)\left(-\frac{1}{2}\right)$$
$$= (12)\left(-\frac{1}{2}\right)$$
$$= -6$$

¶ DRILL Find the value of:

(a) $(-2)(3 - 6)$
(b) $4(1 - 3) - 3(-3 + 2)$
(c) $(25)(-3) + (25)(-1)$
(d) $\left(-\frac{3}{4}\right)\left(-\frac{2}{3}\right)\left(\frac{2}{5}\right)$

[25] Find the value of $(-3) \div (-\frac{3}{2}) \div (-\frac{1}{8})$.

Ⓐ -36 Ⓑ -16 Ⓒ $\frac{9}{16}$ Ⓓ $-\frac{9}{16}$ Ⓔ 12

The rules of signs for division of signed numbers are the same as those for multiplication: like signs give a positive quotient, unlike signs give a negative quotient. The first step in the problem above is to divide -3 by $-\frac{3}{2}$. The like signs indicate that the solution is positive, so the procedure is merely to divide 3 by $\frac{3}{2}$; inverting the divisor and multiplying gives 2 as the result. To divide this result, 2, by $-\frac{1}{8}$, first determine the sign. Since the signs are unlike, the result must be negative; inverting and multiplying yields -16.

TEST-TAKING TIP.

The question illustrates one other important technique of taking multiple-choice tests. When tests are scored, a penalty factor for wrong answers is figured in to negate the effect of indiscriminate guessing. How this is done is explained in the introduction to the sample tests at the end of this book, but for our purpose at the moment it suffices to say that indiscriminate guessing will probably not help you and may hurt your score in the long run.

But what happens in a question where you may be able to eliminate one or more answer choices, though you are unable to determine the one correct answer? Take the above question as an example. Suppose you knew that the answer had to be negative because you knew your laws of signs, but you did not know how to work out the chain of operations. Thus you knew the correct answer had to be Ⓐ, Ⓑ, or Ⓓ, even though you could not choose which one. In such a case, your best procedure is to guess from among these choices, picking the one that seems to be the most reasonable to you. If you do this on every question for which you can eliminate at least one choice, the odds are that you will raise your score.

¶ DRILL Evaluate each of the following:

(a) $7 \div (-\frac{1}{7})$

(b) $-121 \div (-11) \div (-11)$

(c) $(-\frac{1}{3}) \div (-\frac{2}{3})$

(d) $(-.4) \div (-4) \div (.04)$

WHAT YOU SHOULD KNOW

KEY CONCEPTS

Handling Decimal Numbers

1. *To add (or subtract) decimal numerals*, line up the decimal points above each other when writing the numerals and add (or subtract) digits in the same column.

2. *To multiply decimal numerals*, ignore the decimal points and multiply as though the numerals represented whole numbers. Then count up the number of decimal places in the multipliers and point off this total in the answer, counting from right to left. Prefix as many zeros as needed to fill out the total before placing the decimal point.

3. *To divide decimal numerals*, reposition the decimal point by transferring it to the right of the divisor. Then transfer the decimal point the same number of places in the dividend. Position the decimal point in the quotient directly above the decimal point in the dividend.

Handling Fractions

1. *To reduce a fraction*, first factor the numerator and the denominator. Then strike out common factors.

2. *To raise a fraction to higher terms*, multiply the numerator and the denominator by the number needed to produce the desired denominator. This multiplier can be found by dividing the given denominator into the desired denominator.

3. *To add (or subtract) fractions*, change to a common denominator, then add (or subtract) numerators.

4. *To multiply fractions*, multiply numerators and multiply denominators. If a factor is common to any numerator and any denominator, it may be removed before multiplying.

5. *To divide fractions*, invert the divisor and multiply as in item 4.

Handling Conversions

1. *To change a fraction to a decimal*, divide the numerator by the denominator.

2. *To change a decimal to a percent*, shift the decimal point two places to the right and annex the percent sign.

3. *To change a percent to a decimal*, shift the decimal point two places to the left and remove the percent sign.

Handling Percentage Problems

1. *To calculate a percent of a given number*, change the percent to a decimal and multiply this decimal by the given number.
2. *To answer the question "What percent of* a *is* b*?"* set up the proportion

$$\frac{x}{100} = \frac{b}{a}$$

and solve it for *x*.
3. *To answer the question "*a *is* b% *of what number?"* set up the proportion

$$\frac{a}{x} = \frac{b}{100}$$

and solve it for *x*.

Handling Signed Numbers

1. *To add signed numbers with like signs*, add their absolute values and prefix the common sign.
2. *To add signed numbers with unlike signs*, subtract their absolute values and prefix the sign of the number with the greater absolute value.
3. *To subtract signed numbers*, change the sign of the number to be subtracted; then proceed as in addition.
4. *To multiply signed numbers with like signs*, multiply their absolute values.
5. *To multiply signed numbers with unlike signs*, multiply their absolute values and prefix a negative sign to the product.
6. *To divide signed numbers with like signs*, divide their absolute values.
7. *To divide signed numbers with unlike signs*, divide their absolute values and prefix a negative sign.

KEY FORMULAS

1. To find what percent (*x*) one number (*b*) is of another number (*a*):

$$\frac{x}{100} = \frac{b}{a}.$$

2. To find of what number (*x*) another number (*a*) is a given percentage (*b*%):

$$\frac{a}{x} = \frac{b}{100}.$$

TEST-TAKING STRATEGIES

• When dealing with an arithmetic question involving signed numbers, examine the answer choices carefully so that you can eliminate any in which signs are obviously used incorrectly.
• When dealing with decimal numbers, check to be sure the decimal is in the correct place in your answer. Often, distractors may be eliminated because the decimal point is improperly placed.
• Correct answers are always reduced fractions unless otherwise specified. An unreduced fraction is almost always an incorrect choice and can usually be eliminated unless the question specifically asks for an unreduced fraction. Keep this in mind.
• When numerical calculations appear to be very complicated and time-consuming, reread the question and check the answer choices to see if a simpler, more insightful, approach will get the desired answer.

ANSWERS

[1] Ⓑ
DRILL:
(a) $(2 + 18)(13) = 20 \times 13 = 260$
(b) $3 \times 6 + 6 \times 3 = 18 + 18 = 36$
(c) $(9.7 + .3)(157) = 10 \times 157 = 1570$
(d) $(4)(25)(32.43) = 100 \times 32.43 = 3243$

[2] Ⓑ
DRILL:
(a) $3 - 2 + 56 - 1 = 56$
(b) $100 - 72 + 12 - 6 = 34$
(c) $40 + 3 = 43$
(d) $36 - 3 + 6 = 39$
(e) $4 \times 4 + 3 - 4 + 6 = 16 + 3 - 4 + 6 = 21$

[3] Ⓑ
DRILL:
(a) $5 \times 5 = 25$
(b) $5 - 3 = 2$
(c) $4 - 2 \times 2 = 4 - 4 = 0$
(d) $(54 - 2) \div 2 = 52 \div 2 = 26$

[4] Ⓓ
DRILL:
(a) 12   (b) 1890
(c) 105   (d) 126

[5] Ⓑ
DRILL:
(a) $8 = 2^3$, $28 = 2^2 \times 7$, GCF $= 2^2$
(b) $6 = 2 \times 3$, $8 = 2^3$, $10 = 2 \times 5$, GCF $= 2$
(c) $8 = 2^3$, $12 = 2^2 \times 3$, $18 = 2 \times 3^2$, GCF $= 2$
(d) $24 = 2^3 \times 3$, $36 = 2^2 \times 3^2$,
$108 = 3^3 \times 2^2$, GCF $= 2^2 \times 3$

[6] Ⓒ
DRILL:
(a) $\frac{1}{3}$ (b) $\frac{5}{7}$ (c) $\frac{3}{4}$ (d) $\frac{2}{5}$

[7] Ⓓ
DRILL:

(a) $6; \dfrac{3}{6}, \dfrac{2}{6}, \dfrac{1}{6}$ (b) $27; \dfrac{9}{27}, \dfrac{3}{27}, \dfrac{1}{27}$

(c) $56; \dfrac{21}{56}, \dfrac{10}{56}$ (d) $432; \dfrac{45}{432}, \dfrac{56}{432}$

[8] Ⓔ
DRILL:

(a) $\dfrac{17}{16}$ or $1\dfrac{1}{16}$

(b) $\dfrac{12}{32} + \dfrac{16}{32} - \dfrac{27}{32} = \dfrac{1}{32}$

(c) $\dfrac{21}{24} - \dfrac{18}{24} + \dfrac{16}{24} = \dfrac{19}{24}$

(d) $\dfrac{30}{48} + \dfrac{44}{48} - \dfrac{39}{48} = \dfrac{35}{48}$

(e) $\dfrac{4}{12} + \dfrac{5}{12} = \dfrac{9}{12} = \dfrac{3}{4}$

[9] Ⓑ
DRILL:

(a) $\dfrac{1}{8}$ (b) $\dfrac{7}{15}$

(c) $\dfrac{7}{2}$ or $3\dfrac{1}{2}$ (d) $\dfrac{3}{10}$

[10] Ⓒ
DRILL:

(a) $\dfrac{11}{3}$ (b) $\dfrac{3}{2}$

(c) $\dfrac{35}{8}$ (d) $\dfrac{50}{7}$

[11] Ⓒ
DRILL:

(a) $\dfrac{1}{2}$ (b) 1

(c) $\dfrac{1}{12}$ (d) $\dfrac{2}{3}$

[12] Ⓐ
DRILL:

(a) $.\overline{5}$ (b) $.1\overline{6}$

(c) $.\overline{428571}$ (d) $.75$

[13] Ⓔ
DRILL:

(a) $1 \times 10^0 + 1 \times \dfrac{1}{10}$

(b) $1 \times 10^2 + 0 \times 10^1 + 1 \times 10^0 + 1 \times \dfrac{1}{10}$

$+ 0 \times \dfrac{1}{10^2} + 1 \times \dfrac{1}{10^3}$

(c) $0 \times \dfrac{1}{10} + 3 \times \dfrac{1}{10^2} + 2 \times \dfrac{1}{10^3}$

(d) $3 \times 10^2 + 3 \times \dfrac{1}{10^3}$

[14] Ⓐ
DRILL:

(a) .373 (b) 2.3748
(c) 1.093 (d) 1.537

[15] Ⓐ
DRILL:

(a) 12.213 (b) 30.38
(c) .038 (d) .007

[16] Ⓒ
DRILL:

(a) 6.3 (b) 9 (c) 300

[17] Ⓒ
DRILL:

(a) .03 (b) .006
(c) .00375 (d) .1225

[18] Ⓒ
DRILL:

(a) 40% (b) 225%
(c) 35% (d) $214.2857\overline{142857}\%$

[19] Ⓓ
DRILL:

(a) $33\dfrac{1}{3}\%$ (b) 300%

(c) 50% (d) 60%

[20] Ⓓ
DRILL:

(a) 25 (b) 3

(c) $\dfrac{2}{3}$ (d) 100

[21] Ⓒ
DRILL:

(a) -2 (b) 8

(c) $-\dfrac{2}{7}$ (d) $3\dfrac{1}{4}$

[22] Ⓐ
DRILL:

(a) -10 (b) -4
(c) -15 (d) -8

[23] Ⓓ
DRILL:

(a) -10 (b) -4
(c) -15 (d) -8

[24] Ⓒ
DRILL:

(a) 6 (b) -5

(c) -100 (d) $\dfrac{1}{5}$

[25] Ⓑ
DRILL:

(a) -49 (b) -1

(c) $\dfrac{1}{2}$ (d) 2.5

6.   The Real Numbers

Key Terms

natural number   any number in the set $\{1, 2, 3, \ldots\}$.

whole number   any number in the set $\{0, 1, 2, 3, \ldots\}$.

integer   any number in the set $\{\ldots, -3, -2, -1, 0, 1, 2, 3, \ldots\}$.

rational number   any number in the set $\{$all numbers that can be written in the form $\frac{p}{q}$, where p and q are integers and q is not zero$\}$. Examples: $\frac{1}{3} = 0.333\ldots$, $\frac{1}{4} = 0.25$.

irrational number   any number in the set $\{$all numbers that do not have repeating or terminal decimal representations$\}$. Examples: $\sqrt{2}$, $\sqrt{1}$, π, $-1010010001\ldots$

real number   any number in the set $\{$all rationals and irrationals$\}$.

NAMES FOR NUMBERS

[1] If N is the set of natural numbers, I the set of integers, Q the set of rational numbers, M the set of irrational numbers and R the set of real numbers, which of the following is NOT true?

Ⓐ I contains N.   Ⓑ Q contains N and I.   Ⓒ M contains N.   Ⓓ R contains Q.   Ⓔ R contains M.

Natural numbers $= \{1, 2, 3, \ldots\}$

Whole numbers $= \{0, 1, 2, 3, \ldots\}$.

Integers $= \{\ldots, -3, -2, -1, 0, 1, 2, 3, \ldots\}$.

Rational numbers $= \{$all numbers that can be written in the form $\frac{p}{q}$, where p and q are integers and q is not zero.$\}$

In decimal form the rational numbers are readily recognized since they either repeat digits infinitely (as in $\frac{2}{3} = 0.666\ldots$ and $\frac{1}{7} = 0.142857142857\ldots$) or terminate ($\frac{1}{2} = 0.5$, $\frac{2}{5} = 0.4$). Note that each of the sets just listed contains each of the sets which precede it.

Irrational numbers $= \{$all numbers that do not have repeating or terminating decimal representations$\}$. Therefore the set of irrational numbers (labeled M in the question above) contains no natural numbers, whole numbers, integers or rational numbers.

Examples of irrationals are $\pi = 3.14159\ldots$ and $\sqrt{2} = 1.4142\ldots$

Real numbers $= \{$all rationals and irrationals$\}$.

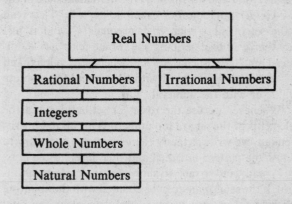

```
          Real Numbers
          /            \
 Rational Numbers    Irrational Numbers
      |
   Integers
      |
 Whole Numbers
      |
 Natural Numbers
```

¶ **DRILL** Give an example of:

(a) a whole number that is not a natural number
(b) an integer that is not a natural number
(c) a rational number that is not an integer
(d) an integer that is irrational
(e) an irrational number that is real

WORKING WITH SET THEORY

[2] If $P = \{x: x = 1\}$, Q is the set of all numbers which are equal to their squares, $R = \{0, 1\}$, $S = \emptyset$ and $T = \{0\}$, then which of the following is true?

Ⓐ $P = Q$ Ⓑ $Q = R$ Ⓒ $R = S$ Ⓓ $S = T$ Ⓔ $P = R$

To discuss much of intermediate math in contemporary terms we must first establish some of the fundamentals of set theory. We will review a few facts about sets in this section and others as needed in later chapters.

The term *set* is used to designate a collection of objects named in such a way as to provide a test that will indicate whether or not some object belongs to the set. Objects belonging to a set are called *elements* or *members* of the set. The symbol "$\in$" means "belongs to," as in $0 \in R$ of the multiple-choice question above.

Two common ways of naming sets are the "roster" and "description" methods. A roster consists of a pair of braces, { }, with the elements of the set listed inside and separated from each other by commas. The description method uses a verbal statement precise enough to determine membership. For example the roster {Tuesday, Thursday} and the description "the set of all days of the week which have "*T*" as their first letter" both refer to the same set. Two sets, such as these, that have exactly the same elements are called *equal* sets.

A third procedure for naming a set is a combination of the roster and description types and makes use of the *set-builder* notation. For example, $\{x: x = 1\}$ is read "the set of all x such that x equals 1" and is just another way of describing {1}. Some texts use "|" instead of ":" for "such that," but when written longhand "|" is too easily confused with the symbol for absolute value or with the numeral "1."

Whenever we use the roster or set-builder and the elements of the set are too numerous for all to be written out, we write as many elements as are necessary to show the pattern intended and then insert three dots, . . . , read "and so on," to show that the pattern continues. If the set is *finite* (can be counted with the counting coming to an end) we are careful to place the final element to the right of the three dots as in $A = \{1, 2, 3, 4, \ldots, 100\}$. If no element appears to the right of the dots, it indicates that the set is *infinite* and, therefore, continues on in the same pattern, as in $B = \{1, 2, 3, 4, \ldots\}$.

Note that sets A and B above are not equal (symbolized by $A \neq B$).

If a set contains no elements, we call it the *empty set* and use the symbol $\emptyset$ or { } Note that $\{0\} \neq \emptyset$ since $\{0\}$ contains the element 0 and $\emptyset$ contains no elements.

If every element of a set A is also an element of a set B, then we say that A is a *subset* of B. Further, we agree to consider $\emptyset$ to be a subset of every set. For example, the subsets of $A = \{a, b, c\}$ are $\emptyset$, $\{a\}$, $\{b\}$, $\{c\}$, $\{a, b\}$, $\{a, c\}$, $\{b, c\}$, $\{a, b, c\}$. Note that the last of these is A itself.

To answer the multiple-choice question above, use the given information to write a roster for each set: $P = \{1\}$, $Q = \{0, 1\}$, $R = \{0, 1\}$, $S = \{ \}$, $T = \{0\}$; then the correct answer becomes obvious.

TEST-TAKING TIP.

To answer comparison questions, it is usually helpful to put all items to be compared into the same form.

¶ DRILL Specify each of the following sets by roster, description and set-builder notations and indicate which are subsets of the others:

(a) A is the set of all positive whole numbers

(b) $B = \{1, 2, 4\}$

(c) $C = \{x: x$ is a perfect square$\}$

(d) D is the set of all negative numbers that have square roots

APPLYING THE FIVE LAWS OF ADDITION

[3] The following is a proof of the theorem "If a, b, and c are real numbers, then $(a + b) + c = (c + a) + b$." How many of the steps have the Commutative Law of Addition as a reason?

(1) $(a + b) + c = a + (b + c)$
(2) $\qquad = a + (c + b)$
(3) $\qquad = (a + c) + b$
(4) $\qquad = (c + a) + b$

Ⓐ None   Ⓑ 1   Ⓒ 2   Ⓓ 3   Ⓔ All

The fundamental procedures of elementary algebra can be derived from a relatively few basic assumptions about the operations of addition and multiplication. In this and the next several sections we will review eleven elementary statements that we will accept as the basic laws of the real numbers.

I CLOSURE LAW OF ADDITION
If a and b are real numbers, then $a + b$ is a real number.

II COMMUTATIVE LAW OF ADDITION
If a and b are real numbers, then $a + b = b + a$.

III ASSOCIATIVE LAW OF ADDITION
If a and b are real numbers, then $(a + b) + c = a + (b + c)$.

Law I asserts that the sum of any two real numbers will always be a real number. Law II guarantees that the result of addition does not depend on the order in which the terms are added.

Law III indicates that regrouping of the sum of three numbers does not change the sum. By definition the sum of three numbers, $a + b + c$, is the sum of the first two added to the last. It is thereby written $(a + b) + c$ since parentheses indicate operations which are to be performed first. In effect Law II guarantees that the sum $a + b + c$ is $a + (b + c)$ as well as $(a + b) + c$.

In the first step of the proof above, Law III has been used to regroup. Then $b + c$ is rearranged by Law II to become $c + b$. A second application of Law III again regroups. In the final step $a + c$ is commuted to $c + a$.

Therefore the Commutative Law of Addition is used in steps 2 and 4, but not in steps 1 and 3. The Associative Law of Addition is the proper reason for steps 1 and 3.

¶ DRILL Indicate which of the above laws justifies each equality:

(a) $(2 + 3) + 4 = 2 + (3 + 4)$
(b) $(2 + 3) + 4 = 4 + (2 + 3)$
(c) $(2 + 3) + 4 = (3 + 2) + 4$
(d) $(2 + 3) + 4 = (4 + 3) + 2$

[4] Which of the following steps in the proof of "If a and b are real numbers, then $b + [a + (-b)] = a$" has an incorrect reason?

Ⓐ $b + [a + (-b)]$ Commutative Law
$= [a + (-b)] + b$ of Addition
Ⓑ $= a + [(-b) + b]$ Associative Law
of Addition
Ⓒ $= a + [b + (-b)]$ Commutative Law
of Addition
Ⓓ $= a + 0$ Associative Law
of Subtraction
Ⓔ $= a$ Additive Identity Law

IV ADDITIVE INVERSE LAW

For every real number b there exists a number $-b$ (called the additive inverse of b) such that $b + (-b) + 0$.

V ADDITIVE IDENTITY

For every real number a, $a + 0 = a$.

Note that Law IV is the correct reason for step Ⓓ above rather than the Associative Law of Subtraction. Indeed, we have not mentioned subtraction up to this point and the operation of subtraction is not used anywhere in this proof. The proof does give us the opportunity to introduce subtraction and provides most of the reasoning for an important relationship between subtraction and the addition of inverses.

We define the difference $a - b$ to be that number x such that $b + x = a$.

With subtraction defined in this way we can prove that

6-1   If a and b are real numbers, then
$$a - b = a + (-b).$$

To prove this we need only show that $a + (-b)$ satisfies the condition for x in the equation above; in other words, when $a + (-b)$ is added to b the result is a. But the steps in question [4] above with the correct reason substituted for Ⓓ do precisely that!

Stated in words, Law 6-1 says, "To subtract a number, add its opposite."

Law V, though certainly not startling, is necessary in many rigorous proofs such as this one. Similar lines of reasoning can be used to demonstrate:

6-2   If a and b are real numbers, then
$$a - (-b) = a + b.$$

6-3   If a and b are real numbers, then
$$(-a) + (-b) = -(a + b).$$

Law 6-2 is really a slightly different way of writing, "To subtract a number, add its opposite." In this form, the law makes subtraction of negative numbers easier to visualize.

In words, Law 6-3 says, "The sum of the opposites of two numbers is the opposite of their sum."

¶ DRILL The following is the proof of statement 6-3. It is based on the fact that $-(a + b)$ is the additive inverse of $a + b$. In order to do this we must show that $(-a) + (-b)$ is also the inverse of $a + b$; and to do this we will prove $[(-a) + (-b)] + (a + b) = 0$. Fill in the reasons.

(a) $[(-a) + (-b)] + (a + b)$
     $= \{[(-a) + (-b)] + a\} + b$
(b) $= \{a + [(-a) + (-b)]\} + b$
(c) $= \{[a + (-a)] + (-b)\} + b$
(d) $= \{0 + (-b)\} + b$
(e) $= (-b) + b$
(f) $= 0$

APPLYING THE FIVE LAWS OF MULTIPLICATION

[5] The following is part of a proof of the theorem "If a and b are real numbers, and $ab = 0$, then $a = 0$ or $b = 0$."

(1) If $a \neq 0$, then $\frac{1}{a}$ is a real number.

(2) If $ab = 0$, then $\frac{1}{a}(ab) = \frac{1}{a}(0)$.

(3) $\frac{1}{a}(ab) = 0$.

(4) $\left(\frac{1}{a} \cdot a\right) b = 0$.

(5) $1 \cdot b = 0$.

(6) $b = 0$.

Which of the following is not used as a reason in this proof?

Ⓐ **Multiplication Property of Zero** Ⓑ **Multiplicative Identity** Ⓒ **Multiplicative Inverse**
Ⓓ **Associative Property of Multiplication**
Ⓔ **Commutative Property of Multiplication**

The following five laws of multiplication are similar to the assumptions already made for addition in the preceding section.

VI CLOSURE LAW OF MULTIPLICATION
If a and b are real numbers, the product of a and b, written ab, is a real number.

VII COMMUTATIVE LAW OF MULTIPLICATION
If a and b are real numbers then $ab = ba$.

VIII ASSOCIATIVE LAW OF MULTIPLICATION
If a, b and c are real numbers, then $(ab)c = a(bc)$.

Note that the product of three numbers is defined as the product of the first two multiplied by the third. Law VIII guarantees that the result of multiplying the first by the product of the second and third is the same as the defined product.

IX MULTIPLICATIVE INVERSE
For every nonzero real number, a, there exists a number, $\frac{1}{a}$, called the multiplicative inverse of a, such that $a(\frac{1}{a}) = 1$.

X MULTIPLICATIVE IDENTITY
For every real a, $a \cdot 1 = a$.

Laws VIII, IX and X are used in the multiple-choice question, as well as two properties not yet mentioned. We will agree that addition, subtraction, multiplication and division of any number can be done to both sides of an equation, the result being another equation, and this "Multiplication Property of Equality" is the reason for step 2. Step 3, in which $(\frac{1}{a})0$ has been replaced by 0, is justified by a statement frequently called the "Multiplication Property of Zero," the proof of which is found in the drill material.

The property whose proof forms the basis of the question above will be denoted 6-4 and is important in the solution of equations by factoring.

6-4 If a and b are real numbers and $ab = 0$, then
$$a = 0 \quad \text{or} \quad b = 0.$$

This property will be used in sections that review how to solve quadratic equations.

¶ DRILL Fill in the reasons for the proof of:

6-5 If a is a real number, then $a(0) = 0$.

PROOF

(a) $\quad 0 + 0 = 0$
(b) $\quad a(0 + 0) = a(0)$
(c) $a(0) + a(0) = a(0)$
(d) $a(0) + a(0) = a(0) + 0$
(e) $\quad a(0) = 0$

APPLYING THE DISTRIBUTIVE LAW

[6] Which of the following is an application of the Distributive Law for the real numbers?

Ⓐ $a[b + (-b)] = a[(-b) + b]$
Ⓑ $a[b + (-b)] = (ab) + (-b)$
Ⓒ $a[b + (-b)] = 0$
Ⓓ $a[b + (-b)] = ab + a(-b)$
Ⓔ $a[b + (-b)] = [b + (-b)]a$

The Distributive Law completes the set of eleven assumptions from which the properties of the real numbers derive. This law involves both addition and multiplication and provides the justification for much of the multiplication and factoring of algebraic expressions.

XI DISTRIBUTIVE LAW
If a, b and c are real, then
$$(1) \quad a(b + c) = ab + ac.$$
Many texts include a second statement,
$$(2) \quad (b + c)a = ba + ca,$$
as part of XI. Statement (2), however, can be derived from statement (1) and we therefore choose not to consider it as an assumption. We will, however, use the term "Distributive Law" to include both (1) and (2).

The proof of (2) follows:

(3) $(b + c)a = a(b + c)$ Law II
(4) $\qquad = ab + ac$ Law XI
(5) $\qquad = ba + ca$ Law VII

Law XI can be generalized to apply to multipliers of more than two terms. For example, the proof of a distributive law for three terms is left as a drill.

¶ DRILL Fill in the reasons for the proof of
$a(b + c + d) = ab + ac + ad$.

(a) $a(b + c + d) = a[(b + c) + d]$
(b) $\qquad = a(b + c) + ad$
(c) $\qquad = ab + ac + ad$

DERIVING LAWS OF SIGNS

[7] If a is a positive number and b is negative, which of the following is also negative?

Ⓐ $-(ab)$ Ⓑ $(-a)b$ Ⓒ $a(-b)$ Ⓓ $a - b$
Ⓔ ab

The laws of signs for the multiplication of positive and negative real numbers can now be derived from some of the preceding discussions in this chapter. These laws should be familiar to students of even the most elementary algebra but are included here for reference. The proofs of the first two are partially written out in the drill section and you should attempt to supply the reasons as a review of the last five sections.

In the multiple-choice question, since a is positive and b is negative, the number ab (choice Ⓔ) is negative. Since ab is negative, the number $-(ab)$ (choice Ⓐ) must be positive. Since $-a$ is negative and b is negative, $(-a)b$ (choice Ⓑ) is positive. Since a is positive and $-b$ is positive, $a(-b)$ (choice Ⓒ) is positive. Choice Ⓓ gives the greater number, a, minus the lesser number, b, so $a - b$ must be positive.

¶ **Drill** Supply the reasons:

> **6-6**   If a is a real number, then $a(-1) = -a$.

(a) $[a(-1)] + a = [a(-1)] + a \cdot 1$
(b) $= a[(-1) + 1]$
(c) $= a \cdot 0$
(d) $= 0$
(e) $= (-a) + a$
(f) Therefore $a(-1) = -a$

> **6-7**   If a and b are real, then $a(-b) = -(ab)$.

(g) $b + (-b) = 0$
(h) $a[b + (-b)] = 0$
(i) $ab + a(-b) = 0$
(j) ab is a real number
(k) There exists an inverse $-(ab)$ of ab such that $ab + [-(ab)] = 0$.
(l) $ab + a(-b) = ab + [-(ab)]$
(m) $a(-b) = -(ab)$

DEALING WITH INVENTED OPERATIONS

[8] The symbol $\odot$ is defined as follows: $A \odot B = 2A + 2B$, when A and B are real numbers. Which of the following properties is false?

Ⓐ There is a commutative property of $\odot$.

Ⓑ There is no associative property of $\odot$.

Ⓒ The identity element of $\odot$ is 0.

Ⓓ The set of real numbers is closed with respect to $\odot$.

Ⓔ The inverse of A with respect to $\odot$ is undefined.

TEST-TAKING TIP.

The operation $\odot$ is one that you have not encountered before since it was defined specifically for this question in order to test your general understanding of the properties of operations in number systems. Questions like this are frequently used by test-makers.

Ⓐ Is $A \odot B = B \odot A$? According to the definition of $\odot$ as given, $A \odot B = 2A + 2B$ and $B \odot A = 2B + 2A$. Since $2B + 2A = 2A + 2B$ by the Commutative Property of Addition, it follows that $A \odot B = B \odot A$.

Ⓑ Is $(A \odot B) \odot C = A \odot (B \odot C)$?
$(A \odot B) \odot C = 2(2A + 2B) + 2C$
$\qquad\qquad = 4A + 4B + 2C$
$A \odot (B \odot C) = 2A + 2(2B + 2C)$
$\qquad\qquad = 2A + 4B + 4C$

Ⓒ Is $A \odot 0 = A$?
$A \odot 0 = 2A + 2 \cdot 0 = 2A$

Ⓓ $A \odot B$ is defined by a series of applications of addition and multiplication. Since these basic operations are closed in the real number system, so must $\odot$ be.

Ⓔ Two members of a set are inverses of each other with respect to an operation if the application of the operation gives the identity element. "A operation inverse A equals identity." What is the identity element for $\odot$? Call it x and solve.
$$A \odot x = A$$
$$2A + 2x = A$$
$$A = -2x$$
$$-\frac{A}{2} = x$$

Thus $-\frac{A}{2}$ must be the identity element. Since $-\frac{A}{2}$ varies in value, no identity element exists. Without an identity element, no number can have an inverse.

¶ DRILL

(a) Verify that the statement "*A* operation inverse *A* equals identity" is true for the fundamental operations of addition and multiplication in the real number system.

(b) Let $x \odot y$ be finding the average of x and y, then $x \odot y = \dfrac{x + y}{2}$. Is the operation commutative? Associative? Closed for the real numbers? Does each number have an inverse? Is there an identity element?

SOLVING EQUATIONS INVOLVING ABSOLUTE VALUES

[9] If *a* is a negative real number, then which of the following is NOT true?

Ⓐ $|a| = -a$ Ⓑ $|a| = a$ Ⓒ $-|a| = a$
Ⓓ $|a|^2 = a^2$ Ⓔ If $x^2 = a^2$, then $|x| = |a|$

For every real number, *a*, except 0, either *a* or $-a$ will be a positive number. Note that $-a$ is a positive number when *a* is negative.

The *absolute value* of any number *a*, symbolized by $|a|$, is always the nonnegative choice of *a* or $-a$. If *a* is positive or zero, then *a* is its own absolute value.

(1) $|a| = a$ when *a* is positive or zero. (This contradicts choice Ⓑ).

If *a* is a negative number, then $-a$ is positive and is thereby the absolute value of *a*.

(2) $|a| = -a$ when *a* is negative. (This verifies choice Ⓐ).

Statement (2) is difficult for many students to grasp because, at first glance, it appears to say that a certain absolute value is negative. Remember that when *a* is negative $-a$ is positive!

¶ DRILL In each of the following *a* is positive and *b* negative. Determine the sign of each expression:

(a) ab (b) $|a| \, |b|$ (c) $|ab|$ (d) $a|b|$ (e) $|a|b$
(f) $a + |b|$ (g) $|a| - b$

[10] Which of the following sets contains all of the real values of *x* for which $|2x + 1| = 3$ is true?

Ⓐ $\{1\}$ Ⓑ $\{1, -1\}$ Ⓒ $\{-1\}$ Ⓓ $\{1, -2\}$
Ⓔ $\{1, 2\}$

A simple result of the definition of absolute value is that, when *a* is nonnegative and $|x| = a$, then *x* has the two values *a* and $-a$.

6-8   If $|x| = a$, then $x = a$ or $x = -a$.

This consequence is useful in solving equations involving absolute values.

EXAMPLE

Find *y* if $|3y - 2| = 4$.

SOLUTION: Since $|3y - 2| = 4$, then

$$
\begin{array}{lll}
3y - 2 = 4 & \text{or} & 3y - 2 = -4, \\
3y = 6 & \text{or} & 3y = -2, \\
y = 2 & \text{or} & y = -\dfrac{2}{3}
\end{array}
$$

The set of values that make the equation true is $\{2, -\dfrac{2}{3}\}$

In the multiple-choice question, since $|2x + 1| = 3$, it follows that

$$
\begin{array}{lll}
2x + 1 = 3 & \text{or} & 2x + 1 = -3, \\
2x = 2 & \text{or} & 2x = -4, \\
x = 1 & \text{or} & x = -2, \\
\multicolumn{3}{c}{\{-2, 1\}.}
\end{array}
$$

We will discuss absolute value further in Chapter 8.

¶ DRILL Solve each of the following for *x*:

(a) $|x| = 3$ (b) $|2x| = 5$
(c) $|x - 3| = 6$ (d) $|4x - 1| = 7$

CONVERTING REPEATING DECIMALS TO FRACTIONS

[11] If $x = .\overline{51}$, where the bar indicates that the digits under it repeat without stopping, write *x* as a fraction.

Ⓐ $\dfrac{51}{100}$ Ⓑ $\dfrac{5}{9}$ Ⓒ $\dfrac{51}{99}$ Ⓓ $\dfrac{510}{100}$ Ⓔ No fraction is possible

In section [1] of this chapter we defined a rational number as any number that could be written as the ratio of two integers *p* and *q* where *q* is not zero. At the same time we mentioned that rational numbers can be written as decimals that terminate or in which a block of digits repeats interminably. When a rational number appears as a decimal, it is frequently useful to convert the decimal to its fractional form. Doing this in the case of a terminating decimal is easy since the position of the decimal indicates the denominator, as in:

$$.5 = \frac{5}{10} = \frac{1}{2}, \; .51 = \frac{51}{100}, \text{ and } 4.581 = \frac{4581}{1000}.$$

For repeating decimals the procedure is shown by the following examples:

EXAMPLE 1

Convert $.\overline{51}$ to a fraction.

SOLUTION: Let $x = .\overline{51}$; then $100x = 51.\overline{51}$ (we chose 100 as a multiplier because we wanted to shift the decimal point two places, two being the number of repeating digits).

(1) $\qquad 100x = 51.\overline{51}$
(2) $\qquad\quad\; x = \;\;.\overline{51}$
(3) therefore $99x = 51$ by subtraction
(4) $\qquad\qquad x = \frac{51}{99}$

EXAMPLE 2

Convert $3.2\overline{164}$ to a fraction.

SOLUTION: Let $x = 3.2\overline{164}$; then $1000x = 3216.4\overline{164}$ (we chose 1000 because we wanted to shift the decimal three places).

(5) $\qquad 1000x = 3216.4\overline{164}$
(6) $\qquad\quad\; x = \;\;\;3.2\overline{164}$
(7) $\qquad 999x = 3213.2$
(8) $\qquad\quad x = \frac{3213.2}{999} = \frac{32132}{9990} = \frac{16016}{4995}$

¶ DRILL Convert each of the following to fractional form:

(a) $.\overline{3}$ (b) $.0\overline{3}$ (c) $2.0\overline{35}$ (d) $3.6\overline{831}$

WORKING WITH SIMPLE RADICALS

[12] Which of the following is not an irrational number?

Ⓐ .1010010001 ...   Ⓑ $\sqrt{3}$ Ⓒ $\sqrt{8}$
Ⓓ $\sqrt{\sqrt{4}}$ Ⓔ $\sqrt{-4}$

Most irrational numbers encountered in elementary algebra involve the radical sign. This sign, $\sqrt{}$, is used to denote the nonnegative square root of a nonnegative real number. In other words, if x and y are positive, then $\sqrt{x} = y$ if $x = y^2$. Furthermore, $\sqrt{0} = 0$.

In other words, $\sqrt{}$ is always used to indicate a number that is positive or zero. Though it is true, for example, that -2 is a square root of 4, it is not the square root represented by the radical sign, and the statement $-2 = \sqrt{4}$ is not true.

We have previously defined rational numbers as ratios of integers and pointed out that they have repeating or terminating decimal equivalents. Decimals that do not either terminate or repeat represent irrational numbers. Answer Ⓐ above is an example of a decimal for which no block of digits will repeat as long as the pattern indicated continues. Such nonrepeating, nonterminating decimals cannot be represented as the ratio of two integers and hence are nonrational. Merely being nonrational does not automatically make a number irrational. Choice Ⓔ is not rational but, certainly, cannot be found among any numbers we have mentioned since, if a real number x were equal to $\sqrt{-4}$, then $x^2 = -4$. But the product x^2 always involves the multiplication of real numbers with like signs and can result only in a positive real number.

We state without proof that $\sqrt{x}$, where x is a positive integer, is irrational as long as the prime factors of x (other than 1) do not all occur in pairs. It follows that Ⓑ and Ⓒ are irrational since Ⓑ has only the prime factor 3 and the prime factorization of Ⓒ is $2 \cdot 2 \cdot 2$ with the 2's not all in pairs. Ⓓ is just another name for $\sqrt{2}$ (since $\sqrt{4}$ can be replaced by 2) and hence is irrational.

TEST-TAKING TIP.

Do not select or reject an answer choice merely because it is not in the same form as all of the others. Choice Ⓐ, for example, does not have a radical sign and the others do. Choice Ⓓ has two radical signs, one inside the other. Nevertheless, all of the choices Ⓐ through Ⓓ satisfy the conditions of the question (they are irrational), although Ⓔ is the correct response.

¶ DRILL True or False:

(a) $\sqrt{4} = 2$ (b) $\sqrt{16} = \pm 4$
(c) -3 is a square root of 9   (d) $-\sqrt{4} = -2$

[13] Which of the following is not equal to $2\sqrt{6}$?

Ⓐ $\sqrt{6} + \sqrt{6}$ Ⓑ $\sqrt{3} + \sqrt{3}$ Ⓒ $\sqrt{24}$
Ⓓ $\sqrt{3}\sqrt{8}$ Ⓔ $\frac{\sqrt{96}}{2}$

We have reviewed the laws of multiplication for the real numbers and therefore for the irrationals. Since the irrationals commonly occurring in elementary algebra frequently involve radicals, we devote the next few sections to the techniques of operation with simple radicals.

6-9   If a and b are positive real numbers, then

$$\sqrt{ab} = \sqrt{a}\sqrt{b}.$$

Using this law to simplify radical expressions, we attempt to write the number as the product of a perfect square and some other integer.

EXAMPLES

(1) $\sqrt{18} = \sqrt{9 \cdot 2} = \sqrt{9}\sqrt{2} = 3\sqrt{2}$
(2) $\sqrt{12} = \sqrt{4 \cdot 3} = \sqrt{4}\sqrt{3} = 2\sqrt{3}$
(3) $\sqrt{2}\sqrt{3} = \sqrt{2 \cdot 3} = \sqrt{6}$
(4) $\sqrt{2}\sqrt{8} = \sqrt{16} = 4$

A frequent error is to apply a similar law for addition and to conclude that "the sum of the roots is the root of the sum." To verify that this is *not* true, note that such a "law" would have us believe that $\sqrt{16} + \sqrt{9} = \sqrt{25} = 5$, which is certainly not true since $\sqrt{16} = 4$, $\sqrt{9} = 3$ and $4 + 3 = 7$ not 5!

Ⓐ $\sqrt{6} + \sqrt{6} = 2\sqrt{6}$
Ⓑ $\sqrt{3} + \sqrt{3} = 2\sqrt{3}$
Ⓒ $\sqrt{24} = \sqrt{4 \cdot 6} = \sqrt{4}\sqrt{6} = 2\sqrt{6}$
Ⓓ $\sqrt{3}\sqrt{8} = \sqrt{24} = 2\sqrt{6}$
Ⓔ $\dfrac{\sqrt{96}}{2} = \dfrac{\sqrt{16 \cdot 6}}{2} = \dfrac{\sqrt{16}\sqrt{6}}{2} = \dfrac{4\sqrt{6}}{2} = 2\sqrt{6}$

¶ DRILL Simplify:

(a) $\sqrt{27}$ (b) $\sqrt{20}$ (c) $\sqrt{99}$ (d) $\sqrt{8} + \sqrt{18}$

Multiply and then simplify where necessary:

(e) $\sqrt{27}\sqrt{3}$ (f) $(3\sqrt{7})^2$
(g) $(5\sqrt{6})(4\sqrt{3})$ (h) $\sqrt{2}(\sqrt{32} - 3\sqrt{2})$

[14] Which of the following is equal to $\dfrac{3}{\sqrt{3}}$?

   Ⓐ $\sqrt{3}$ Ⓑ $3\sqrt{3}$ Ⓒ 3 Ⓓ 9 Ⓔ $\dfrac{\sqrt{3}}{3}$

A result of 6-9 follows:

6-10   If a and b are positive real numbers, then

$$\sqrt{\dfrac{a}{b}} = \dfrac{\sqrt{a}}{\sqrt{b}}.$$

This property provides one method for answering the question above:

$$\dfrac{3}{\sqrt{3}} = \dfrac{\sqrt{9}}{\sqrt{3}} = \sqrt{\dfrac{9}{3}} = \sqrt{3}.$$

Other examples of its use in simplification follow:

EXAMPLES

(1) $\sqrt{\dfrac{4}{9}} = \dfrac{\sqrt{4}}{\sqrt{9}} = \dfrac{2}{3}$
(2) $\sqrt{\dfrac{32}{9}} = \dfrac{\sqrt{32}}{\sqrt{9}} = \dfrac{4\sqrt{2}}{3}$
(3) $\sqrt{\dfrac{5}{4}} = \dfrac{\sqrt{5}}{\sqrt{4}} = \dfrac{\sqrt{5}}{2}$
(4) $\dfrac{\sqrt{50}}{5} = \dfrac{\sqrt{50}}{\sqrt{25}} = \sqrt{\dfrac{50}{25}} = \sqrt{2}$

¶ DRILL Simplify each of the following as far as possible:

(a) $\sqrt{\dfrac{27}{4}}$ (b) $\dfrac{\sqrt{125}}{5}$ (c) $\sqrt{\dfrac{49}{50}}$

RATIONALIZING DENOMINATORS THAT CONTAIN RADICALS

[15] If $\dfrac{\sqrt{10} - \sqrt{5}}{\sqrt{10}}$ were transformed to an expression with a rational denominator, the result would be:

   Ⓐ $\dfrac{\sqrt{10} - \sqrt{5}}{\sqrt{10}}$ Ⓑ $\dfrac{2 - \sqrt{2}}{2}$ Ⓒ $\dfrac{1}{2}$
   Ⓓ $\dfrac{\sqrt{10} + \sqrt{5}}{10}$ Ⓔ $\dfrac{5}{10 + 5\sqrt{2}}$

Though we are postponing our review of fractional expressions until Chapter 8, we will introduce an elementary property here:

6-11   If a, b, c and d are real numbers, neither b nor d being zero, then

$$\dfrac{a}{b} \times \dfrac{c}{d} = \dfrac{ac}{bd}.$$

Property 6-11, along with the Multiplicative Identity and Multiplicative Inverse Laws, provides the means for transforming many expressions that have irrational denominators to expressions with rational denominators.

6-12   If a and b are positive real numbers, then

$$\dfrac{\sqrt{a}}{\sqrt{b}} = \dfrac{\sqrt{ab}}{b} = \dfrac{1}{b}\sqrt{ab}.$$

We include the proof of 6-12 as a review of some of the laws of the real numbers; cover up the reasons and see if you can figure them out without looking.

PROOF

(1) $\dfrac{\sqrt{a}}{\sqrt{b}} = \dfrac{\sqrt{a}}{\sqrt{b}} \times 1$ — Multiplicative Identity

(2) $\quad = \dfrac{\sqrt{a}}{\sqrt{b}}\left[(\sqrt{b})\left(\dfrac{1}{\sqrt{b}}\right)\right]$ — Multiplicative Inverse

(3) $\quad = \dfrac{\sqrt{a}\sqrt{b}}{b}$ — 6-11 and definition of $\sqrt{}$

(4) $\quad = \dfrac{\sqrt{ab}}{b}$ — 6-9

EXAMPLES

(1) $\sqrt{\dfrac{1}{2}} = \dfrac{\sqrt{1}}{\sqrt{2}} = \dfrac{1}{\sqrt{2}} = \dfrac{1}{\sqrt{2}} \cdot \dfrac{\sqrt{2}}{\sqrt{2}} = \dfrac{\sqrt{2}}{2}$

(2) $\dfrac{\sqrt{2}}{\sqrt{3}} = \dfrac{\sqrt{2}}{\sqrt{3}} \cdot \dfrac{\sqrt{3}}{\sqrt{3}} = \dfrac{\sqrt{6}}{3}$

(3) $\dfrac{5}{\sqrt{5}} = \dfrac{5}{\sqrt{5}} \cdot \dfrac{\sqrt{5}}{\sqrt{5}} = \dfrac{5\sqrt{5}}{5} = \sqrt{5}$

(4) $\dfrac{\sqrt{10} - \sqrt{5}}{\sqrt{10}} = \dfrac{(\sqrt{10} - \sqrt{5})\,\sqrt{10}}{\sqrt{10}\,\sqrt{10}}$

$\quad = \dfrac{\sqrt{10}\,\sqrt{10} - \sqrt{5}\,\sqrt{10}}{10}$

$\quad = \dfrac{10 - \sqrt{50}}{10} = \dfrac{10 - 5\sqrt{2}}{10}$

$\quad = \dfrac{5(2 - \sqrt{2})}{5(2)} = \dfrac{2 - \sqrt{2}}{2}$

¶ DRILL Write each of the following with a rational denominator:

(a) $\dfrac{2}{\sqrt{11}}$ (b) $\dfrac{6\sqrt{3}}{\sqrt{8}}$ (c) $\dfrac{xy}{\sqrt{y}}$, y is positive

[16] If $\dfrac{\sqrt{10}}{\sqrt{10} - \sqrt{5}}$ were transformed to an expression with a rational denominator, the result would be:

Ⓐ $\dfrac{2 + \sqrt{2}}{5}$ Ⓑ $2 + \sqrt{2}$ Ⓒ $\dfrac{\sqrt{10}}{5}$ Ⓓ $\sqrt{2}$

Ⓔ $\dfrac{\sqrt{10}}{15}$

The procedure needed to answer this question is based on the following rule:

6-13 If x and y are real numbers, then

$$(x - y)(x + y) = x^2 - y^2.$$

PROOF (Cover the reasons and figure them out for yourself.)

(1) $(x - y)(x + y) = (x - y)x + (x - y)y$ — Law XI

(2) $\quad = x(x - y) + y(x - y)$ — Law VII

(3) $\quad = x^2 - xy + xy - y^2$ — 6-1, 6-7 and Law XI

(4) $\quad = x^2 - y^2$ — Law IV and 6-1

An immediate result of 6-13 is:

6-14 If a and b are positive integers, then

$$(\sqrt{a} - \sqrt{b})(\sqrt{a} + \sqrt{b}) = a - b.$$

Property 6-14 provides a method for rationalizing denominators which are sums with radicals.

EXAMPLES

(1) $\dfrac{1}{\sqrt{2} + \sqrt{3}} = \dfrac{1}{\sqrt{2} + \sqrt{3}} \cdot \dfrac{\sqrt{2} - \sqrt{3}}{\sqrt{2} - \sqrt{3}}$

$\quad = \dfrac{\sqrt{2} - \sqrt{3}}{2 - 3}$

$\quad = \sqrt{3} - \sqrt{2}$

(2) $\dfrac{4 + \sqrt{7}}{4 - \sqrt{7}} = \dfrac{4 + \sqrt{7}}{4 - \sqrt{7}} \cdot \dfrac{4 + \sqrt{7}}{4 + \sqrt{7}}$

$\quad = \dfrac{16 + 8\sqrt{7} + 7}{16 - 7}$

$\quad = \dfrac{23 + 8\sqrt{7}}{9}$

To answer the multiple-choice question, note the following:

$\dfrac{\sqrt{10}}{\sqrt{10} - \sqrt{5}} = \dfrac{\sqrt{10}\,(\sqrt{10} + \sqrt{5})}{(\sqrt{10} - \sqrt{5})(\sqrt{10} + \sqrt{5})}$

$\quad = \dfrac{10 + \sqrt{50}}{10 - 5}$

$\quad = \dfrac{10 + 5\sqrt{2}}{5}$

$\quad = 2 + \sqrt{2}$

¶ DRILL Rationalize the denominators of the following fractions:

(a) $\dfrac{2}{1 - \sqrt{5}}$ (b) $\dfrac{2 - \sqrt{5}}{3 - \sqrt{5}}$

(c) $\dfrac{1 - \sqrt{7}}{\sqrt{7} - 1}$

WHAT YOU SHOULD KNOW

KEY CONCEPTS

Mastering the Basic Laws of Real Numbers

1. **Closure Law of Addition:** If a and b are real numbers, then $a + b$ is a real number.
2. **Closure Law of Multiplication:** If a and b are real numbers, then ab is a real number.
3. **Commutative Law of Addition:** If a and b are real numbers, then $a + b = b + a$.
4. **Commutative Law of Multiplication:** If a and b are real numbers, then $ab = ba$.
5. **Associative Law of Addition:** If a and b are real numbers, then $(a + b) + c = a + (b + c)$.
6. **Associative Law of Multiplication:** If a and b are real numbers, then $(ab)c = a(bc)$.
7. **Additive Inverse Law:** If a is any real number, then there exists a number $-a$ such that $a + (-a) = 0$.
8. **Multiplicative Inverse Law:** If a is any real number except 0, then there exists a number $\frac{1}{a}$ such that
$$a(\frac{1}{a}) = 1.$$
9. **Additive Identity Law:** If a is any real number, then $a + 0 = a$.
10. **Multiplicative Identity Law:** If a is any real number, then $a(1) = a$.
11. **Distributive Law:** If $a, b,$ and c are any real numbers, then $a(b + c) = ab + ac$.
12. **Multiplication Property of Zero:** If a is any real number, then $a(0) = 0$.
13. **Addition, Subtraction, Multiplication and Division Properties of Equality:** If $a, b,$ and c are any real numbers and $a = b$, then:
$$a + c = b + c,$$
$$a - c = b - c,$$
$$ac = bc,$$
$$\frac{a}{c} = \frac{b}{c} \text{ when } c \neq 0.$$
14. **Multiplication Property of -1:** If a is any real number, then $-a = (-1)a$.

Handling Real Numbers

1. *To subtract any real number*, add its opposite:
$$a - b = a + (-b) \quad \text{or} \quad a - (-b) = a + b.$$
2. *To obtain the opposite of a sum,* add the opposites:
$$-(a + b) = (-a) + (-b).$$

3. *To obtain the absolute value of a number* a, take the nonnegative choice of a or $-a$. In other words,
$$|a| = a \quad \text{when } a \text{ is zero or positive,}$$
and
$$|a| = -a \text{ when } a \text{ is negative.}$$

Handling Radicals

1. A square root of a number x is a number y for which $y^2 = x$.
2. The nonnegative square root of x is denoted by $\sqrt{x}$ and is called the "principal" square root.
3. For any positive number x,
$$a\sqrt{x} + b\sqrt{x} = (a + b)\sqrt{x}.$$
4. *To simplify a radical expression*, identify the largest perfect square factor, a, of the radicand, and then apply the rule
$$\sqrt{ab} = \sqrt{a}\,\sqrt{b}.$$
5. *To multiply radicals,* apply the rule
$$\sqrt{a}\,\sqrt{b} = \sqrt{ab}.$$

Handling Fractions Whose Denominators Contain Radicals

1. *To rationalize the denominator of a fraction of the form* $\frac{a}{\sqrt{b}}$, multiply by $\frac{\sqrt{b}}{\sqrt{b}}$ to get the result,
$$\frac{a\sqrt{b}}{b}.$$

2. *To rationalize the denominator of a fraction of the form* $\frac{a}{\sqrt{b} + \sqrt{c}}$, multiply by $\frac{\sqrt{b} - \sqrt{c}}{\sqrt{b} - \sqrt{c}}$ to get
$$\frac{a\sqrt{b} - a\sqrt{c}}{b - c}.$$

TEST-TAKING STRATEGIES

- When you encounter a problem involving a specially defined operation, deal with it, within the framework of the definition, according to the basic rules for operations in number systems.
- Convert radicals to the simplest radical form and use common radical factors that may occur.
- Different texts sometimes use different names for basic laws of algebra. For example, the Identity Law of Multiplication is also known as the Multiplicative Identity Property. Rarely, however, will the exact wording of the name be a factor in determining the correct answer. Do not be confused by differences in nomenclature.
- Remember that all positive numbers have *two* square roots—one positive and the other negative. The negative root may lead to a correct answer when the positive root doesn't.

Because College Board Tests are short-answer exams, you'll never need to do a proof. On the other hand, keep in mind that some questions are devised to find out whether you know how proofs are done.

To ensure that you are able to recognize answers that are the same, be sure to rationalize any expressions with denominators that involve radicals.

The most common errors made on simple algebraic questions result from incorrect calculations with signs. If you cannot find your answer among the choices, look for a sign error in your calculations.

The Multiplication Property of Zero is a basic tool in solving equations of second degree or higher. When confronted with such an equation, factor the polynomial and determine the numbers that make each factor zero.

ANSWERS

[1] ©
DRILL:
(a) 0
(b) 0, −1, −2, etc.
(c) $\frac{1}{2}, \frac{3}{4}, \frac{2}{3}$, etc.
(d) None exist.
(e) Every irrational is real.

[2] ®
DRILL:
(a) $A = \{1, 2, 3, \ldots\} = \{x: x$ is a positive whole number$\}$
(b) $B =$ the set of powers of 2 with exponent 0, 1 or 2. $= \{2^x: x$ is 0, 1 or 2$\}$
(c) $C = \{1, 4, 9, 16, 25, \ldots\} =$ the set of perfect squares.
(d) $D = \emptyset = \{\ \}$.
D, being the empty set, is a subset of all the others. B and C are subsets of A.

[3] ©
DRILL:
(a) Associative Law of Addition.
(b) Commutative Law of Addition.
(c) Commutative Law of Addition.
(d) Commutative and Associative Laws of Addition.

[4] ⓓ
DRILL:
(a) Associative Law of Addition.
(b) Commutative Law of Addition.
(c) Associative Law of Addition.
(d) Additive Inverse Law.
(e) Additive Identity.
(f) Additive Inverse.

[5] Ⓔ
DRILL:
(a) Additive Identity.
(b) Property of Equality (Multiplication).
(c) Distributive Law (reviewed in next section).
(d) Additive Identity.
(e) Property of Equality (subtraction of $a \cdot 0$ from both sides).

[6] ⓓ
DRILL:
(a) Associative Law of Multiplication.
(b) Distributive Law.
(c) Distributive Law.

[7] Ⓔ
DRILL:
(a) Multiplicative Identity.
(b) Distributive Law.
(c) Additive Inverse.
(d) 6−5
(e) Additive Inverse.
(f) Property of Equality (subtraction of a from both sides of step (e)).
(g) Additive Inverse.
(h) 6−5.
(i) 6−5.
(j) Closure Law of Multiplication.
(k) Additive Inverse Law.
(l) Steps (i) and (k).
(m) Property of Equality (subtraction of ab from both sides of step (1)).

[8] Ⓔ
DRILL:
(a) $A + (-A) = 0$
$A(\frac{1}{A}) = 1$
(b) Commutative
Associative
Closed
Identity is the number itself, so no unique identity exists; thus no inverse exists.

[9] ®
DRILL:
(a) −   (b) +
(c) +   (d) +
(e) −   (f) +
(g) +

[10] Ⓓ
DRILL:

(a) ± 3 (b) $\pm \dfrac{5}{2}$

(c) $9, -3$ (d) $2, -\dfrac{3}{2}$

[11] Ⓒ
DRILL:

(a) $\dfrac{1}{3}$ (b) $\dfrac{1}{30}$

(c) $\dfrac{2015}{990}$ (d) $\dfrac{36795}{9990}$

[12] Ⓔ
DRILL:

(a) True.   (b) False.
(c) True.   (d) True.

[13] Ⓑ
DRILL:

(a) $3\sqrt{3}$ (b) $2\sqrt{5}$
(c) $3\sqrt{11}$ (d) $5\sqrt{2}$
(e) 9 (f) 63
(g) $60\sqrt{2}$ (h) 2

[14] Ⓐ
DRILL:

(a) $\dfrac{3\sqrt{3}}{2}$ (b) $\sqrt{5}$

(c) $\dfrac{7}{5\sqrt{2}} = \dfrac{7\sqrt{2}}{10}$

[15] Ⓑ
DRILL:

(a) $\dfrac{2\sqrt{11}}{11}$ (b) $\dfrac{3\sqrt{6}}{2}$

(c) $x\sqrt{y}$

[16] Ⓑ
DRILL:

(a) $-\dfrac{1 + \sqrt{5}}{2}$ (b) $\dfrac{1 - \sqrt{5}}{4}$

(c) -1

7. Polynomials and Factoring

Key Terms

monomial   an algebraic expression that is either a numeral, a variable, or the product of numerals and variables. Examples: 5, y, xy.

polynomial   an algebraic expression that is the sum (or difference) of two or more monomials. Examples: $3xy - 5$, $4x^2 - 6x + 3$.

like terms   two terms of a polynomial that have the same variables, with each variable having the same exponents. Example: y^3 and $4y^3$.

IDENTIFYING POLYNOMIALS

[1] If $3x^3 + 6x$ is subtracted from the sum of $8x^2 + 1$ and $-5x^2 + 6x - 3$, the result is:

(A) $3x^3 - 3x^2 + 2$ (B) $-3x^2 + 3x - 2$
(C) $-3x^3 + 3x^2 - 2x$ (D) $-3x^3 + 3x^2 - 2$
(E) **No result is possible**

A *monomial* is an algebraic expression that is either a numeral, a variable or the product of numerals and variables. The following are examples of monomials:

$$x, \quad 3x^2, \quad -2xy^3z, \quad \tfrac{1}{5}xy, \quad 7.$$

A monomial may contain one or several variables, each having a whole number as exponent. In more formal terminology, a monomial is an expression of the form

$$ax^n,$$

where a is any real number (called the *coefficient* of the monomial), x is any variable (or product of variables) and n is any whole number (including zero).

An expression that is the sum (or difference) of two or more monomials is called a *polynomial*. Polynomials may have one, two, three or more "terms," each term being a monomial. Examples include:

$$7w, \quad 5xy + 6, \quad 3x^2 + 7x - 5, \quad 9v^{10} - 3v.$$

In more formal terminology, an algebraic expression of the form

$$a_0x^n + a_1x^{n-1} + a_2x^{n-2} + \ldots + a_{n-1}x + a_n,$$

where n is any whole number and $a_0, a_1, \ldots, a_n$ (called the "coefficients") are real numbers, is called a *polynomial* over the reals. If the coefficients are all integers, the expression is a *rational integral polynomial*.

Polynomials may be added, subtracted, multiplied and divided by means of the properties of the real numbers.

ADDING AND SUBTRACTING POLYNOMIALS

Addition and subtraction are accomplished through the process known as "combining like terms." "Like" terms are terms that have the same variables raised to the same power.

EXAMPLE 1

Add $x^2 + 5x + 3$ and $3x^2 - 4x + 5$.

SOLUTION:

(1) $(x^2 + 5x + 3) + (3x^2 - 4x + 5)$
     $= x^2 + 3x^2 + 5x - 4x + 3 + 5$
(2) $= (1 + 3)x^2 + (5 - 4)x + (3 + 5)$
(3) $= 4x^2 + x + 8$

EXAMPLE 2

Add $4x^3 + 5x^2 - 6$ and $2x^2 + x$.

SOLUTION:

(1) $(4x^3 + 5x^2 - 6) + (2x^2 + x)$
     $= 4x^3 + 5x^2 + 2x^2 + x - 6$
(2) $= 4x^3 + (5 + 2)x^2 + x - 6$
(3) $= 4x^3 + 7x^2 + x - 6$

Before discussing subtraction of polynomials we repeat theorem 6-3 as:

> **7-1** If a and b are real numbers, then
> $$-(a + b) = (-a) + (-b).$$

PROOF

(1) $-(a + b) = -1(a + b)$ I-6
(2) $= (-1)a + (-1)b$ Law XI
(3) $= (-a) + (-b)$ I-6

7-2   If a, b and c are real numbers, then

$$a - (b + c) = a + [-(b + c)]$$
$$= a + (-b) + (-c).$$

This theorem tells us how to remove parentheses when they are preceded by a negative sign: we apply the negative sign to each term in the parentheses when the parentheses are removed, thereby changing the sign of each term in the parentheses. Therefore a difference such as

$$(x^2 + 5x + 3) - (3x^2 - 4x + 5)$$

can be found by changing the signs of the terms of the second polynomial and adding the new terms to like terms in the first polynomial.

$$(x^2 + 5x + 3) - (3x^2 - 4x + 5)$$
$$= x^2 + 5x + 3 + (-3x^2) + 4x + (-5)$$
$$= -2x^2 + 9x - 2$$

The multiple-choice question can be restated and simplified as follows:

$$(8x^2 + 1) + (-5x^2 + 6x - 3) - (3x^3 + 6x)$$
$$= 8x^2 + 1 - 5x^2 + 6x - 3 - 3x^3 - 6x$$
$$= -3x^3 + 3x^2 - 2.$$

¶ DRILL Perform the following operations:

(a) $(x^2 + 2) + (9x^2 + 7x - 5)$
(b) $(x^2 - x + 2) - (x - 3)$
(c) $(14x^3 - 21x^2 + 49x) + (6x^4 - 8x^3 + 10x)$
(d) $(18x^2 + 10x - 5) - (2x^4 + 4x^3 - 8x^2 + 6x)$

MULTIPLYING POLYNOMIALS

[2] Which of the following is NOT a term in the polynomial which is the product of $(x + 1)$, $(3x^2 + 6x)$ and $(2x^2 + 6x - 1)$?

Ⓐ $6x^5$ Ⓑ $36x^4$ Ⓒ $63x^3$ Ⓓ $-6x$ Ⓔ -1

Multiplying polynomials can be accomplished through repeated use of the Distributive Law as shown below:

EXAMPLE

$(2x^2 + 6x - 1)(3x^2 + 6x)$
$= (2x^2 + 6x - 1)3x^2 + (2x^2 + 6x - 1)6x$
$= (2x^2)(3x^2) + (6x)(3x^2) - (1)(3x^2) + (2x^2)(6x)$
$\quad + (6x)(6x) - (1)(6x)$
$= 6x^4 + 18x^3 - 3x^2 + 12x^3 + 36x^2 - 6x$
$= 6x^4 + 30x^3 + 33x^2 - 6x$

But such a procedure is exceedingly lengthy and we seldom do it this way in practice. We note instead that the above multiplication is the sum of the products of each term of one polynomial with each term of the other polynomial. A method which accomplishes this with less trouble follows. Note that each term of the lower polynomial in the arrangement below is multiplied by each term of the upper polynomial, forming two partial product polynomials. These partial products are written so that vertical columns contain the same powers of x. This arrangement allows ready addition of partial products.

$$\begin{array}{r} 2x^2 + 6x - 1 \\ 3x^2 + 6x \\ \hline 12x^3 + 36x^2 - 6x \\ 6x^4 + 18x^3 - 3x^2 \\ \hline 6x^4 + 30x^3 + 33x^2 - 6x \end{array}$$

To answer the multiple-choice question, perform the following operations:

$$\begin{array}{r} 3x^2 + 6x \\ x + 1 \\ \hline 3x^2 + 6x \\ 3x^3 + 6x^2 \\ \hline 3x^3 + 9x^2 + 6x \end{array}$$

$$\begin{array}{r} 3x^3 + 9x^2 + 6x \\ 2x^2 + 6x - 1 \\ \hline - 3x^3 - 9x^2 - 6x \\ 18x^4 + 54x^3 + 36x^2 \\ 6x^5 + 18x^4 + 12x^3 \\ \hline 6x^5 + 36x^4 + 63x^3 + 27x^2 - 6x \end{array}$$

TEST-TAKING TIP.

Rarely would a College Board question involve so much calculation, and most questions can be answered with no calculation at all. There is usually an insightful way of arriving at an answer with little pencil-and-paper work. So it is with this question. Since x is a factor of $3x^3 + 6x$, it will be a factor of each term in the product of the three polynomials. Therefore, without doing *any* calculation, you should be able to see that Ⓔ cannot be a term of the product.

¶ DRILL Carry out each of the following multiplications:

(a) $(a^2 + 7a - 2)(3a^2 - 2a + 5)$
(b) $(2x + 3)(5x^3 + 6x^2 - 8)$
(c) $(x^2 - x + 2)(x^2 + x + 1)$

DIVIDING POLYNOMIALS

[3] If $2x^4 - 7x^2 - 1 - 3x^3$ is divided by $3x - 1 + x^2$ which of the following is the remainder?

Ⓐ $-9x^3 - 5x^2$ Ⓑ $-9x^3 - 5x^2 - 1$
Ⓒ $22x^2 - 9x - 1$ Ⓓ $-75x + 21$
Ⓔ $25x - 7$

If a polynomial P_1 is divided by a second polynomial P_2, then P_1 is called the dividend and P_2 the divisor. We carry out the division by a process similar to long division.

Step 1 Arrange both of P_1 and P_2 in decreasing order of the powers of some variable found in both P_1 and P_2. Replace any missing power with a term of that power having a coefficient of 0.

Step 2 Divide the highest degree term of P_1 by the highest degree term of P_2 to find the highest degree term of the quotient.

Step 3 Multiply P_2 by the first term of the quotient and write the product under P_1, keeping like powers in the same column. Then subtract this product from P_1 to get a remainder.

Step 4 If P_1 has more terms than P_2, bring down the next term and use the sum of this term and the previous remainder (from step 3) as your new dividend. Repeat these four steps until the highest degree of the remainder is less than the highest degree of the divisor.

Applying this procedure to the question above, we first rearrange terms in descending powers of x to get:

divisor: $x^2 + 3x - 1$,
dividend: $2x^4 - 3x^3 - 7x^2 + (0)x - 1$.

We can now set up the division.

$$
\begin{array}{r}
2x^2 - 9x + 22 \\
x^2 + 3x - 1 \overline{\smash{\big)}\ 2x^4 - 3x^3 - 7x^2 + (0)x - 1} \\
\underline{2x^4 + 6x^3 - 2x^2} \\
-9x^3 - 5x^2 + (0)x \\
\underline{-9x^3 - 27x^2 + 9x} \\
22x^2 - 9x - 1 \\
\underline{22x^2 + 66x - 22} \\
-75x + 21
\end{array}
$$

Consequently the quotient is $2x^2 - 9x + 22$ with a remainder of $-75x + 21$.

¶ DRILL Perform each of the following divisions:

(a) $(x^2 + 3x - 5) \div (x - 2)$
(b) $(15y^3 - 3y + 1) \div (3y^2 + y + 6)$
(c) $(x^3 - 6x^2 + 12x - 8) \div (4 - 4x + x^2)$

FACTORING POLYNOMIALS

[4] If a and b are integers, which of the following represents the factored form of $ax - bx + ay - by$ over the integers?

Ⓐ $ax - bx + ay - by$
Ⓑ $(a - b)x + (a - b)y$
Ⓒ $(a - b)(x + y)$
Ⓓ $(\sqrt{a} + \sqrt{b})(\sqrt{a} - \sqrt{b})(x + y)$
Ⓔ $\sqrt{a} + \sqrt{b})(\sqrt{a} - \sqrt{b})(\sqrt{x} - i\sqrt{y})$
   $(\sqrt{x} + i\sqrt{y})$

A polynomial is in "factored form" over a set of numbers, S, if it is expressed as the product of other polynomials whose coefficients are all members of S. Factoring involves repeated use of the generalized distributive property mentioned in section [6] of Chapter 6.

$$a(b + c + d + \ldots) = ab + ac + ad + \ldots$$

When read from right to left, this property provides a way of writing a sum of n terms:

$$\underbrace{ab + ac + ad + \ldots}_{n \text{ terms}}$$

as a product of a common factor, a, and a second factor of n terms:

$$a\underbrace{(b + c + d + \ldots)}_{n \text{ terms}},$$

The first step in the factoring of any polynomial is the factoring out of common multipliers if any exist. Other steps will be discussed in subsequent sections.

EXAMPLE 1

Factor $3ax^2 + 9a^2x$ over the integers if a is an integer.

SOLUTION: After noting that each term has a factor of $3ax$, we write the above expression as:

$$3ax(x + 3a).$$

We can always check for errors in factoring by multiplying the factors to see if their product is the original expression.

EXAMPLE 2

Factor $y^3 - y^2 - 3y + 3$ completely over the integers.

SOLUTION: There is no factor common to all terms, but grouping the terms in pairs gives

$$(y^3 - y^2) - (3y - 3),$$

with each group being factored to get

$$y^2(y - 1) - 3(y - 1).$$

Each of the two new terms, $y^2(y - 1)$ and $-3(y - 1)$, has $(y - 1)$ as a factor. Applying the Distributive Law again, we get

$$(y - 1)(y^2 - 3),$$

which can be verified by multiplying this indicated product.

You may have noticed that each answer choice of the multiple-choice question [4] is a step in the factoring of $ax - bx + ay - by$ over the "complex" numbers, a system to which we will later devote an entire chapter. In Ⓐ no factoring has been done. In Ⓑ the expression has been grouped in pairs, with common factors recognized in each group, but the expression is still an indicated sum. In Ⓒ the factoring over the *integers* has been completed. In Ⓓ the factors are over the reals and in Ⓔ over the complex numbers. Ⓓ and Ⓔ will be discussed further in later sections.

TEST-TAKING TIP.

Suppose that you did not understand how to answer this question, but you did recognize that $\sqrt{a}$ is not always an integer when a is an integer. You would then be able to eliminate Ⓓ and Ⓔ. Having ruled out two choices, you would have increased your chances of guessing correctly and might improve your test score by making your best choice of Ⓐ, Ⓑ and Ⓒ. Since Ⓒ is the only one of these choices that is "factored," (written as a product) it would be a likely guess—and it is, in fact, the correct answer. You can verify this "guess" by working backward; multiply the two binomials in Ⓒ and you will get the given expression.

¶ **Drill** Factor over the integers:

(a) $10abx + 15b^2x$

(b) $x + xy - x^2y$

(c) $12x^4y^3 - 18x^3y^3 + 36x^3y^4$

(d) $x^2 - 2x + 3x - 6$

[5] If $32x^4 - 2y^8$ were factored completely over the integers, which of the following would **NOT** be one of the factors?

Ⓐ 2   Ⓑ $2x - y^2$ Ⓒ $2x + y^2$ Ⓓ $4x^2 + y^4$
Ⓔ $4x^2 - y^4$

We have noted that factoring results from the application of the Distributive Law from *right to left* whereas its application from *left to right* involves multiplication. In this way factoring can be thought of as "undoing" multiplication, and, as a matter of fact, we have verified our factoring by re-multiplying the factors. Multiplication also provides the means for the discovery of other laws of factoring. For example, property 6-13,

$$(x - y)(x + y) = x^2 - y^2,$$

suggests the factors for expressions involving the difference of squares.

EXAMPLES

(1) $x^2 - 4 = (x - 2)(x + 2)$

(2) $x^2 - y^4 = (x - y^2)(x + y^2)$

(3) $16a^2 - 25b^2 = (4a - 5b)(4a + 5b)$

(4) $16 - x^4 = (4 - x^2)(4 + x^2)$
$$= (2 - x)(2 + x)(4 + x^2)$$

(5) $x^2y + x^2 - 4y - 4 = x^2(y + 1) - 4(y + 1)$
$$= (x^2 - 4)(y + 1)$$
$$= (x - 2)(x + 2)(y + 1)$$

TEST-TAKING TIP.

Remember that, in all factoring, common factors should be considered first.

To answer the multiple-choice question, note the following:

$$32x^4 - 2y^8 = 2(16x^4 - y^8)$$
$$= 2(4x^2 + y^4)(4x^2 - y^4)$$
$$= 2(4x^2 + y^4)(2x - y^2)(2x + y^2).$$

Note that Ⓔ, $4x^2 - y^4$, is a factor at the third step, but it can be factored further. The question states that the expression is completely factored.

TEST-TAKING TIP.

You might not have answered this question correctly if you had not read it carefully. The word "completely" changes the answer. Careful reading of test questions is imperative.

¶ **Drill** Factor:

(a) $1 - x^4$ (b) $9x^2 - 81$

(c) $x^2 - (y + 1)^2$ (d) $4x^4 - 64$

FACTORING TRINOMIALS

[6] If $a^2x^2 + bx + c^2$ is the square of a binomial, which of the following is the correct relationship among a, b and c?

Ⓐ $b = ac$ Ⓑ $b^2 = a^2c^2$ Ⓒ $b = 2ac$
Ⓓ $b = 4ac$ Ⓔ $4b^2 = a^2c^2$

If a binomial, a polynomial of two terms, is squared, the result is a polynomial of three terms, a trinomial. The clues to the recognition and factoring of perfect square trinomials are provided by squaring the binomial $ax + c$:

$$(ax + c)^2 = a^2x^2 + 2acx + c^2.$$

Therefore the second coefficient, b, equals $2ac$. The coefficient of the center term is, thus, twice the product of the roots of the coefficients of the first and last terms.

EXAMPLES

(1) $x^2 + 2x + 1 = (x + 1)^2$

(2) $16x^2 - 24x + 9 = (4x - 3)^2$

¶ DRILL Factor each of the following:

(a) $x^2 + 6x + 9$ (b) $25x^2 - 30x + 9$

(c) $9x^2 - 12xy + 4y^2$

[7] If $2x^2 + 7x + 6$ is factored over the integers, which of the following is a factor?

Ⓐ $x + 6$ Ⓑ $2x - 6$ Ⓒ $2x - 3$ Ⓓ $x + 1$
Ⓔ $x + 2$

Many trinomials that are not squares of binomials are factorable. Developing the ability to factor them is a necessary preparation for solving some types of quadratic equations and for simplifying rational expressions. The simplest of these trinomials is the kind for which the coefficient of the second-degree term is 1,

$$(x + m)(x + n) = x^2 + (m + n)x + mn.$$

To factor we need only find a pair of numbers whose product is the final term and whose sum is the coefficient of the first-degree term.

EXAMPLES

(1) $x^2 - 5x + 6 = (x - 3)(x - 2)$
(2) $x^2 + 8x + 15 = (x + 3)(x + 5)$
(3) $y^2 - 5y - 14 = (y - 7)(y + 2)$

Factoring trinomials with leading coefficients other than 1 is more difficult and involves trial and error. As we can see from:

$$(px + m)(qx + n) =$$
$$pqx^2 + (mq + pn)x + mn,$$

we must find four numbers, p, q, m and n, such that two are factors of the first coefficient while the other two are factors of the last term. The middle term must be the sum of certain products of these factors, and finding just what products are needed is accomplished by trial and error. We must first list the possible factors of the first and last terms and then try summing various products until we discover the ones that yield the middle term.

EXAMPLE

Factor $3x^2 + 11x - 4$ over the integers.

SOLUTION: The first term can only be factored into $3x$ and x (or their negatives, but these we will take into consideration by listing the negatives of the final term). The last term yields the three possibilities 2 and -2, 1 and -4 and -1 and 4. The possible factorings these yield are therefore:

(1) $(3x + 2)(x - 2)$,
(2) $(3x - 2)(x + 2)$,
(3) $(3x + 1)(x - 4)$,
(4) $(3x - 4)(x + 1)$,
(5) $(3x - 1)(x + 4)$,
(6) $(3x + 4)(x - 1)$.

If we multiply out each of these, we get six different trinomials but only number (5) is $3x^2 + 11x - 4$.

Since this procedure may require numerous multiplications, we need a rapid way of multiplying binomials mentally. The FOIL device provides such a procedure. The diagram below indicates names for pairs of terms in the product of two binomials.

To multiply binomials, multiply the terms indicated in the order First, Outer, Inner, Last. The sum of the O and I terms gives the middle term of the trinomial and is a quick check for which of the possible factorings works. You should develop the ability to factor trinomials mentally.

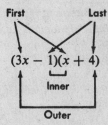

To answer the multiple-choice question,

$$2x^3 + 7x + 6 = (2x + 3)(x + 2).$$

¶ DRILL Factor:

(a) $x^2 - 10x - 75$ (b) $81x^2 + 144x + 64$
(c) $-x^2 - 4x + 77$ (d) $4x^2 + 28x + 48$
(e) $36x^2 + 12x - 35$ (f) $7x^2 - 30x + 8$

FACTORING THE SUM OR DIFFERENCE OF CUBES

[8] Which of the following is true?

Ⓐ $x^3 - 8 = (x - 2)^2$ Ⓑ $x^3 + 8 = (x + 2)^3$
Ⓒ $x^3 - 8 = (x^2 + 4)(x - 2)$
Ⓓ $x^3 + 8 = (x + 2)(x^2 - 2x + 4)$
Ⓔ $x^3 - 8 = (x - 2)(x^2 + 4x + 4)$

We sometimes find it useful to be able to factor the sum and difference of two cubes. The factors of each of $a^3 + b^3$ and $a^3 - b^3$ are not obvious but may be verified by carrying out the following multiplications:

$$(a + b)(a^2 - ab + b^2) = a^3 + b^3,$$
$$(a - b)(a^2 + ab + b^2) = a^3 - b^3.$$

EXAMPLES

(1) $x^3 + 8 = (x + 2)(x^2 - 2x + 4)$
(2) $x^3 - y^3 = (x - y)(x^2 + 2xy + y^2)$
(3) $8x^3 - 27y^3 = (2x - 3y)(4x^2 + 6xy + 9y^2)$
(4) $x + x^4 = x(1 + x^3) = x(1 + x)(1 - x + x^2)$

¶ DRILL Factor each of the following:

(a) $a^3 + 27b^3$ (b) $x^3 - 1$
(c) $16 + 2a^3$ (d) $64x^4 - 27x$

WHAT YOU SHOULD KNOW

KEY CONCEPTS

Adding, Subtracting, Multiplying and Dividing Polynomials

1. *To add polynomials*, add the coefficients of like terms.
2. *To subtract polynomials*, subtract the coefficients of like terms.
3. *To remove parentheses enclosing a polynomial when the parentheses are preceded by a positive sign*, merely remove the parentheses.
4. *To remove parentheses enclosing a polynomial when the parentheses are preceded by a negative sign*, remove the parentheses and change the signs of all terms within the parentheses.
5. *To multiply two polynomials*, multiply each term of one polynomial by every term of the other polynomial and combine like terms.
6. *To divide one polynomial by another*, first arrange both polynomials in descending order of the powers of a common variable and then proceed as in long division.

Factoring Polynomials

1. *To factor a polynomial*, first look for a common factor and remove it by using the generalized Distributive Law:
   $$ab + ac + ad + \ldots = a(b + c + d + \ldots).$$
2. A trinomial of the form $a^2x^2 + 2abx + b^2$ can be factored as
   $$(ax + b)(ax + b) = (ax + b)^2.$$
3. Trinomials of the form $ax^2 + bx + c$ may be factored into expressions of the form $(mx + n)(px + q)$, where
   $$mp = a, \qquad nq = c, \qquad mq + np = b.$$
   The values of m, n, p and q must be found by trial and error.

KEY FORMULAS

1. To factor the difference of two squares:
   $$a^2 - b^2 = (a + b)(a - b).$$

2. To factor the sum or difference of cubes:
   $$a^3 - b^3 = (a - b)(a^2 + ab + b^2),$$
   $$a^3 + b^3 = (a + b)(a^2 - ab + b^2).$$

TEST-TAKING STRATEGIES

- In factoring, consider common factors first.
- When working with polynomials, always put them in standard form to facilitate comparisons and operations.
- When subtracting polynomials, check your work to be sure all terms of the subtrahend polynomial are subtracted—not just the first term.
- When working with polynomials, if no insightful way of answering a question comes to you, try looking at the factors of the polynomial. For example, if two polynomials are to be divided, factoring may show common factors that can be removed first, simplifying the division process.
- When dividing polynomials, take the extra time to do each step carefully and fully. Polynomial division involves all polynomial operations, thereby creating numerous opportunities for small errors.
- Factoring of polynomials is a skill basic to most types of algebra questions. Before taking the CB Math Level I test, master fully the factoring of all types of second degree polynomials.
- On a CB Math Level I test, you will never be asked to give the meanings of terms like "trinomial" and "binomial," but be aware that these words may be used in questions in ways that will require your knowledge of their meanings.

ANSWERS

[1] Ⓓ
   DRILL:
   (a) $10x^2 + 7x - 3$
   (b) $x^2 - 2x + 5$
   (c) $6x^4 + 6x^3 - 21x^2 + 59x$
   (d) $-2x^4 - 4x^3 + 26x^2 + 4x - 5$

[2] Ⓔ
   DRILL:
   (a) $3a^4 + 19a^3 - 15a^2 + 39a - 10$
   (b) $10x^4 + 27x^3 + 18x^2 - 16x - 24$
   (c) $x^4 + 2x^2 + x + 2$

[3] Ⓓ
   DRILL:
   (a) $x + 5, R = 5$
   (b) $5y - \dfrac{5}{3}, R = 11 - \dfrac{94}{3}y$
   (c) $x - 2$

[4] ©
DRILL:
(a) $5bx(2a + 3b)$
(b) $x(1 + y - xy)$
(c) $6x^3y^3(2x - 3 + 6y)$
(d) $x(x - 2) + 3(x - 2) = (x + 3)(x - 2)$

[5] Ⓔ
DRILL:
(a) $(1 - x)(1 + x)(1 + x^2)$
(b) $9(x - 3)(x + 3)$
(c) $(x - y - 1)(x + y + 1)$
(d) $4(x - 2)(x + 2)(x^2 + 4)$

[6] ©
DRILL:
(a) $(x + 3)^2$
(b) $(5x - 3)^2$
(c) $(3x - 2y)^2$

[7] Ⓔ
DRILL:
(a) $(x - 15)(x + 5)$
(b) $(9x + 8)^2$
(c) $-1(x + 11)(x - 7)$
(d) $(2x + 9)(2x + 5)$
(e) $(6x - 5)(6x + 7)$
(f) $(7x - 2)(x - 4)$

[8] Ⓓ
DRILL:
(a) $(a + 3b)(a^2 - 3ab + 9b^2)$
(b) $(x - 1)(x^2 + x + 1)$
(c) $2(2 + a)(4 - 2a + a^2)$
(d) $x(4x - 3)(16x^2 + 12x + 9)$

8. Inequalities

Key Terms

degree of an inequality   the degree of an inequality is determined by the highest power of the variables involved. Thus a "second-degree inequality" has a second-degree term as its highest power.

equivalent inequalities   inequalities that have the same set of solutions.

THE MEANING OF INEQUALITY SIGNS

[1] If $a < b < c$ and $a < 0$, which of the following must be true?

    Ⓐ $b < 0$ Ⓑ $b > 0$ Ⓒ $c > 0$
    Ⓓ $c - b > 0$ Ⓔ $a - b > 0$

If a positive number, p, is added to any real number, a, the result is a different real number, b, that is greater than a. We formalize this intuitive idea in the following definition:

> If a and b are real numbers and $a < b$ (*read:* "a is less than b"), there exists a positive number p such that $a + p = b$. Furthermore, $a < b$ if and only if $b > a$ (*read:* "b is greater than a").

Because of this definition, when a lesser number is subtracted from a greater number, the result must be a positive number. For example, in Ⓓ of the multiple-choice question, $c - b$ must be positive since $b < c$. In choice Ⓔ, on the other hand, $b - a$ must be positive so $a - b$ must be negative.

We will also make the following assumption:

8-1 If a and b are any real numbers, then one and only one of the following is true,

$$a < b, \quad a = b \quad \text{or} \quad a > b.$$

APPLYING THE TRANSITIVE PROPERTY OF INEQUALITY

An immediate consequence of the definition is the "Transitive Property of Inequality."

8-2 If a and b are any real numbers and if

$a < b$ and $b < c$, then $a < c$.

We include the proof as an illustration of the value of the definition.

PROOF

(1) $a < b$ and $b < c$	Given
(2) There exist positive numbers p_1 and p_2 such that $a + p_1 = b$ and $b + p_2 = c$.	Definition of "$<$"
(3) $(a + p_1) + p_2 = c$	Substitution of $a + p_1$ for b
(4) $a < c$	By definition of "$<$" since $p_1 + p_2$ is positive

We sometimes write "$a < b$ and $b < c$" as $a < b < c$.

¶ **DRILL** Demonstrate your knowledge of the definition of "$<$" by finding the positive number p in each of the following:

    (a) $3 < 7$ (b) $-5 < 18$ (c) $-8 < -7$
    (d) $-\dfrac{3}{4} < -\dfrac{1}{2}$ (e) $a < b$ (f) $a < 0$

[2] If $3 - 2x < -5$, then which of the following is true of x?

    Ⓐ $x < -8$ Ⓑ $x < 4$ Ⓒ $x < -4$
    Ⓓ $x > 4$ Ⓔ $x < 8$

APPLYING THE MULTIPLICATION PROPERTY

Our definition of "$<$" and the rules of signs for the multiplication of real numbers allow us to deduce two properties that will aid us in the solution of inequalities.

8-3 If a, b and c are real numbers, then $a < b$ if and only if $a + c < b + c$.

PROOF We will deduce the "only if" part. (Cover the reasons and figure them out for yourself.)

(1) $a < b$ Given

(2) There exists some positive p
for which $a + p = b$.   Definition of "$<$"

(3) $(a + p) + c = b + c$ Property of Equality (addition)

(4) $(a + c) + p = b + c$ Laws II and III

(5) $a + c < b + c$ Definition of "$<$"

Therefore we may add the same number to both sides of an inequality and get an *equivalent* inequality (an inequality having the same set of solutions).

EXAMPLES

(1) $x + 5 < 6$
$$x < 1$$ (By adding -5 to both members)

(2) $-x - 6 < -4$
$$-2 < x$$ (By adding $x + 4$ to both members)

The Multiplication Property is a bit more complicated:

8-4 If a and b are real numbers and if $a < b$, then:

(1) $ac < bc$ when c is positive,

(2) $ac = bc$ when c is zero, and

(3) $bc < ac$ when c is negative.

Thus, if each side of the inequality $2 < 4$ is multiplied by 3, the resulting inequality, $3 \cdot 2 < 3 \cdot 4$, has the same sense, but if the inequality is multiplied by -3, the result, $-3 \cdot 2 > -3 \cdot 4$, has the opposite sense.

EXAMPLE 1

If $5 - x > 9$, then $-x > 4$ and $x < -4$.

EXAMPLE 2

$$-(x + 2) \leq 2x + 5$$
$$-x - 2 \leq 2x + 5$$
$$-x \leq 2x + 7$$
$$-3x \leq 7$$
$$x \geq -\frac{7}{3}$$

In the multiple-choice question,

$$3 - 2x < -5.$$

Adding -3 to each side gives

$$-2x < -8.$$

Dividing each side by -2 (and reversing the inequality sign) gives

$$x > 4.$$

¶ DRILL Solve each of the following inequalities:

(a) $7 - 4x > 15$

(b) $4x - 3 < 2x + 7$

(c) $3(x - 4) \geq 12$

(d) $8 - 2(1 + 2x) \leq 1 + x$

INEQUALITIES USING "AND" AND "OR"

[3] If $x - 1 \leq -3x + 2 \leq x + 6$, then which of the following is true of x?

Ⓐ $-1 \leq x \leq \frac{3}{4}$ Ⓑ $\frac{3}{4} \leq x \leq -1$

Ⓒ $-1 \leq x$ Ⓓ $x \leq 4$ Ⓔ No simpler equivalent statement is possible

The statement $a \leq b$ is equivalent to

$$a < b \quad \text{or} \quad a = b.$$

As with all statements connected by *or*, it is true whenever one of its composing statements is true.

The statement $a < b < c$ is equivalent to

$$a < b \quad \text{and} \quad b < c.$$

As with all statements connected by *and*, it is only true when *both* of its composing parts are true. Thus

$$5 < x \quad \text{and} \quad x < 6$$

is true when x is replaced by any number between 5 and 6 but is untrue for any other.

Inequalities of the form $a < b < c$ are often best handled by rewriting in the equivalent form and then applying properties 8-3 and 8-4.

EXAMPLE 1

Find the values of x for which

$$-3 < 2x - 1 < x + 4.$$

SOLUTION: Rewrite as:

$$-3 < 2x - 1 \quad \text{and} \quad 2x - 1 < x + 4.$$

Separate simplifications on both parts yield

$$-1 < x \quad \text{and} \quad x < 5,$$

which can be recombined to get

$$-1 < x < 5.$$

No special rearrangement is necessary to solve inequalities of the form $a \leq b$.

EXAMPLE 2

Solve for x: $3x - 5 \leq 4x$.

SOLUTION:

(1) $3x - 5 \leq 4x$

(2) $\quad - x \leq 5$ (By adding $5 - 4x$ to both sides)

(3) $\quad x \geq - 5$ (Remember to change the direction of the inequality sign when multiplying both sides by negatives)

In the multiple-choice question,

$$x - 1 \leq -3x + 2 \leq x + 6,$$

so

$$x - 1 \leq -3x + 2 \quad \text{and} \quad -3x + 2 \leq x + 6.$$

Adding $3x$ to each side of both inequalities gives

$$
\begin{aligned}
4x - 1 &\leq 2 & \text{and} && 2 &\leq 4x + 6, \\
4x &\leq 3 & \text{and} && -4 &\leq 4x, \\
x &\leq \frac{3}{4} & \text{and} && -1 &\leq x.
\end{aligned}
$$

Therefore $-1 \leq x \leq \frac{3}{4}$.

¶ DRILL Solve:

(a) $4 - (x - 1) > -(5 - 3x)$

(b) $-10 \geq 2 + 3x$

(c) $2 \leq 8x - 1 \leq -6$

(d) $4x \leq 6 - 2(1 - x) < 3x + 2$

FACTORING SECOND-DEGREE INEQUALITIES

[4] Which of the following is equivalent to $-2 < x < 3$?

   Ⓐ $x^2 - x - 6 < 0$ Ⓑ $3(x - 2) < 0$

   Ⓒ $x^2 < 9$ Ⓓ $x^2 - 5x + 6 < 0$ Ⓔ $x^2 < 6x$

All of the inequalities given as choices are of second degree (except Ⓑ, which can be readily eliminated using techniques already reviewed).

Second-degree inequalities can be factored and the laws of signs for products can then be applied to find solutions. As examples we will work out all of the above choices.

Ⓐ (1) $x^2 - x - 6 < 0$

    (2) $(x - 3)(x + 2) < 0$

The product of $x - 3$ and $x + 2$ will be negative whenever the factors are unlike in sign, so (2) is equivalent to:

(3) $[x - 3 > 0 \text{ and } x + 2 < 0]$ or $[x - 3 < 0 \text{ and } x + 2 > 0]$,

(4) $[x > 3 \text{ and } x < - 2]$ or $[x < 3 \text{ and } x > -2]$.

Since no number is both greater than 3 and less than 2, the statement on the left of the *or* has no values, but the statement on the right can be combined:

(5) $-2 < x < 3$.

Ⓑ does not involve a quadratic and is solvable by methods previously developed.

Ⓒ (1) $x^2 < 9$

    (2) $x^2 - 9 < 0$

    (3) $(x - 3)(x + 3) < 0$

    (4) $[x - 3 < 0 \text{ and } x + 3 > 0]$ or $[x - 3 > 0 \text{ and } x + 3 < 0]$

    (5) $[x < 3 \text{ and } x > -3]$ or $[x > 3 \text{ and } x < -3]$

The statement on the right has no solutions, while the one on the left gives $-3 < x < 3$.

Ⓓ simplifies to $2 < x < 3$.

Ⓔ (1) $x^2 < 6x$

    (2) $x^2 - 6x < 0$

    (3) $x(x - 6) < 0$

    (4) $[x < 0 \text{ and } x > 6]$ or $[x > 0 \text{ and } x < 6]$

    (5) $0 < x < 6$

¶ DRILL Solve:

(a) $x^2 - 5x - 6 < 0$

(b) $3x^2 - 7x - 6 \leq 0$

(c) $3x^2 < 9x$

SOLVING SECOND-DEGREE INEQUALITIES

[5] If $3x^2 - 7x - 6 > 0$, then which of the following is true for x?

   Ⓐ $x < -\frac{2}{3}$ and $x > 3$ Ⓑ $x < -\frac{2}{3}$ or $x > 3$

   Ⓒ $-\frac{2}{3} < x < 3$ Ⓓ $-\frac{2}{3} < x$ or $x < 3$

   Ⓔ $x > 3$ and $x > -\frac{2}{3}$

This inequality differs from the last one discussed since the quadratic expression is greater than zero rather than less than zero. Again, the technique for finding solutions involves factoring, but a different law of signs is applied.

To answer the multiple-choice question, perform the following steps:

(1) $3x^2 - 7x - 6 > 0$,

(2) $(3x + 2)(x - 3) > 0$.

The product of the factors $3x + 2$ and $x - 3$ can be positive when both factors are positive, and *also* when both factors are *negative*. Therefore the original statement is equivalent to:

(3) $[3x + 2 > 0$ and $x - 3 > 0]$ or
   $[3x + 2 < 0$ and $x - 3 < 0]$,

(4) $[x > -\frac{2}{3}$ and $x > 3]$ or $[x < -\frac{2}{3}$ and $x < 3]$.

But x is greater than *both* 3 and $-\frac{2}{3}$ when it is greater than 3. Similarly, x is less than both 3 and $-\frac{2}{3}$ only when it is less than $-\frac{2}{3}$. Therefore

(5) $x > 3$ or $x < -\frac{2}{3}$.

¶ DRILL Solve:

(a) $x^2 - 5x - 6 > 0$
(b) $3x^2 - 7x - 6 \geq 0$
(c) $3x^2 > 9x$

SOLVING INEQUALITIES INVOLVING ABSOLUTE VALUES

[6] **Which of the following statements is equivalent to $|2x - 1| < 5$ for all x?**

Ⓐ $x < 3$ Ⓑ $x > -2$ or $x < 3$ Ⓒ $x > -2$ and $x < 3$ Ⓓ $x > 3$ or $x < -2$ Ⓔ $x > 3$ and $x < -2$

The solution of inequalities involving absolute value is a topic of intermediate math, even though the major applications of such statements are in higher math. In this and the next section we will introduce, without proof, two properties which aid the solution process.

> **8-5** If $a > 0$ and x is any real number, then
> $$|x| < a \text{ if and only if } -a < x < a.$$

*Note that if $a \leq 0$ and $x \in R$, there is no value for which $|x| < a$ can be true.

To answer the multiple-choice question, note that, if $|2x - 1| < 5$, then
$$-5 < 2x - 1 < 5.$$
Adding 1 to each of the three members, we get
$$-4 < 2x < 6.$$
Dividing each member by 2 gives
$$-2 < x < 3.$$

> ### TEST-TAKING TIP.
> At first glance, this answer, $-2 < x < 3$, does not appear to be among the choices given, but that is only because it is in a slightly different form. You must be familiar with the many different forms an answer may have in order to be able to select correct responses.

EXAMPLE

If $|-3x - 4| \leq 3$, then:

(1) $-3 \leq -3x - 4 \leq 3$,
(2) $1 \leq -3x \leq 7$,
(3) $x \leq -\frac{1}{3}$ and $x \geq -\frac{7}{3}$,
(4) $-\frac{7}{3} \leq x \leq -\frac{1}{3}$.

¶ DRILL Solve:

(a) $|2x - 5| < 4$ (b) $|4x - 1| \leq 15$

[7] **If $|x| \geq x + 1$, then:**

Ⓐ x is no real number.   Ⓑ x is any real number.
Ⓒ x is zero only.   Ⓓ $x \geq 1$ or $x \leq \frac{1}{2}$.
Ⓔ $x \leq -\frac{1}{2}$.

> **8-6** If a is any real number and $|x| > a$, then
> $$x > a \text{ or } x < -a.$$

EXAMPLE 1

Solve $|x + 3| > 7$.

SOLUTION:

(1) $|x + 3| > 7$
(2) $x + 3 > 7$ or $x + 3 < -7$
(3) $x > 4$ or $x < -10$

EXAMPLE 2

Find all values of x if $|2x - 1| > x + 1$.

(1) $|2x - 1| > x + 1$.
(2) $2x - 1 > x + 1$ or $2x - 1 < -x - 1$
(3) $x > 2$ or $3x < 0$
(4) $x > 2$ or $x < 0$

EXAMPLE 3

Solve $|x| \geq x + 1$.

(1) $x \geq x + 1$ or $x \leq -(x + 1)$
(2) $0 \cdot x \geq 1$ or $x \leq -x - 1$
(3) $\emptyset$ or $2x \leq -1$
(4) $\emptyset$ or $x \leq -\frac{1}{2}$
(5) $x \leq -\frac{1}{2}$

¶ DRILL Find the sets of values that satisfy the conditions:

(a) $|7x + 2| \geq 12$
(b) $|x| > x$
(c) $|5 - 2x| > x - 1$

WHAT YOU SHOULD KNOW

KEY CONCEPTS

1. If $a < b$, then $a + p = b$ for some positive number p.
2. If $a < b$, then $b > a$.
3. If $a < b < c$, then $a < b$ and $b < c$.
4. If $ab > 0$, then $a > 0$ and $b > 0$ or $a < 0$ and $b < 0$.
5. If $ab < 0$, then $a > 0$ and $b < 0$ or $a < 0$ and $b > 0$.
6. If $a > 0$ and x is any real number for which $|x| < 0$, then $-a < x < a$.
7. If $a > 0$ and x is any real number for which $|x| > 0$, then $x > a$ or $x < -a$.

KEY PROPERTIES

1. If a and b are any real numbers and if $a < b$ and $b < c$, then $a < c$. (Transitive Property of Inequality)
2. If a, b and c are real numbers, then $a < b$ if and only if $a + c < b + c$.
3. If a and b are real numbers and if $a < b$, then:
   (1) $ac < bc$ when c is positive,
   (2) $ac = bc$ when c is zero, and
   (3) $bc < ac$ when c is negative. (Multiplication Property)

TEST-TAKING STRATEGIES

- If your solution to an inequality problem does not appear to be among the choices offered, try to recast your answer in a different form.
- Most of the rules for solving inequalities are identical to corresponding rules for solving equations. The major difference occurs when you must multiply or divide each side of an inequality by a negative number. When you do this, remember to change the direction of the inequality sign.
- Checking solutions to inequalities by trying numbers can be useful. However, be aware that the numbers you choose won't always tell you when your inequality is correct, though they may point out errors.
- If you cannot find a way to simplify an inequality, you may be able to eliminate many (or all) distractors by trying them out. Keep this possibility in mind.
- Remember that each positive number has a corresponding negative number with the same absolute value. Be sure to consider both when answering questions involving absolute value.

- Study the graphing of linear inequalities until it becomes second nature to you. Graphing helps you picture solutions, thereby providing a visual method of deciding which answer is correct.
- The product rules for inequalities parallel the laws of signs for multiplication, which may help you remember them. For example, the rule "If $ab > 0$, then $a > 0$ and $b > 0$ or $a < 0$ and $b < 0$" says that a product can be positive only if both factors are positive or if both factors are negative. Apply this relationship where appropriate.

ANSWERS

[1] ⓓ
DRILL:
(a) 4   (b) 23   (c) 1
(d) $\frac{1}{4}$ (e) $b - a$ (f) $-a$

[2] ⓓ
DRILL:
(a) $x < -2$ (b) $x < 5$
(c) $x \geq 8$ (d) $x \geq 1$

[3] ⓐ
DRILL:
(a) $\frac{5}{2} > x$
(b) $-4 \geq x$
(c) $\frac{3}{8} \leq x \leq -\frac{5}{8}$, hence no solution.
(d) $x \leq 2$ and $x > 2$, hence no solution.

[4] ⓐ
DRILL:
(a) $-1 < x < 6$ (b) $-\frac{2}{3} \leq x < 3$
(c) $0 < x < 3$

[5] ⓑ
DRILL:
(a) $x > 6$ or $x < -1$
(b) $x \geq 3$ or $x \leq -\frac{2}{3}$
(c) $x > 3$ or $x < 0$

[6] ⓒ
DRILL:
(a) $\frac{1}{2} < x < \frac{9}{2}$ (b) $-\frac{7}{2} \leq x \leq 4$

[7] ⓔ
DRILL:
(a) $x \geq \frac{10}{7}$ or $x \leq -2$ (b) $x < 0$
(c) $x < 2$ or $x > 4$

9. Rational Expressions

Key Terms

rational expression   a fraction whose numerator and denominator are polynomials.

Examples: $\dfrac{1}{4}$, $\dfrac{2}{y}$, $\dfrac{x^2 - 5}{x}$

reduce   to remove common factors from the numerator and denominator of a fraction.

EVALUATING RATIONAL EXPRESSIONS

[1] What is the value of $\dfrac{x - 2y}{\frac{1}{2} + xy}$ when $x = 1$ and $y = -\dfrac{1}{2}$?

Ⓐ 0   Ⓑ 1   Ⓒ -1   Ⓓ 2   Ⓔ No real number

Any expression that is the quotient of two polynomials is a *rational expression*. For example,

$$\frac{x^2 + 1}{x}, \quad \frac{xy + 3x^2}{2x + y}, \quad \frac{3}{x}.$$

The simplest of the polynomials are the integers, so the most elementary rational expressions are the rational numbers. For example,

$$\frac{1}{2}, \quad \frac{10}{3}, \quad \frac{-4}{5}.$$

To deal with division by zero, as in the multiple-choice question, we need to refer to the definition of division: If a and b are real numbers, then the quotient, $a \div b$, is the real number x for which $bx = a$. Since this definition expresses division in terms of multiplication, the properties of division are consequences of those already assembled for multiplication, and this fact helps us to understand division by zero. In the question above the substitution of 1 for x and $\frac{1}{2}$ for y yields $2 \div 0$. But if there exists some real number q that is the quotient $2 \div 0$, then by the definition of division,

$$q \times 0 = 2.$$

Since the product of 0 and every real number is 0, there can be no quotient $2 \div 0$.

Suppose the numerator had also been 0. By definition $0 \div 0 = x$ such that

$$0 \cdot x = 0,$$

and therefore x can be any real number.

> Our conclusion: division by zero does not fit the definition of division and is thus undefined.

¶ **DRILL** Fill in the blanks:

(a) $0 \div 2 = $ _____ since $2 \times $ _____ $= 0$
(b) $6 \div 0 = $ _____ since $0 \times $ _____ $= 6$
(c) $0 \div 0 = $ _____ since $0 \times $ _____ $= 0$
(d) $0 \div $ _____ $= 0$ since _____ $\times 0 = 0$

SIMPLIFYING RATIONAL EXPRESSIONS

[2] The simplest form of $\dfrac{-14a^3y^4}{-35a^3y^2}$ is:

Ⓐ $\dfrac{-2y^4}{-5y^2}$ Ⓑ $\dfrac{2y^4}{5y^2}$ Ⓒ $\dfrac{2y^2}{5}$ Ⓓ $\dfrac{5y^2}{2}$ Ⓔ $\dfrac{-2y^2}{-5}$

In Chapter 6 we introduced

> **6-11** If a, b, c and d are real numbers and neither b nor d is zero, then
>
> $$\frac{a}{b} \times \frac{c}{d} = \frac{ac}{bd}.$$

In future sections we will be using 6-11 to write products and quotients of rational expressions, but our immediate concern is in simplifying them. A rational expression is not in simplified form unless the numerator and denominator have no common factor other than 1. The principle by which we can remove common factors follows:

9-1   If a, b, and c are real numbers and neither b nor c is zero, then

$$\frac{ac}{bc} = \frac{a}{b}.$$

Note that c has been removed because it is a common (meaning that it appears in both numerator and denominator) factor (meaning it is *multiplied* by a and b).

PROOF   (The reasons will be left as drill and may be checked by looking in the answer section.)

(a) $\dfrac{ac}{bc} = \dfrac{a}{b} \times \dfrac{c}{c}$ (d) $= \dfrac{a}{b}\left(c \times \dfrac{1}{c}\right)$

(b) $= \dfrac{a}{b}\left(\dfrac{c \times 1}{1 \times c}\right)$ (e) $= \dfrac{a}{b} \times 1$

(c) $= \dfrac{a}{b}\left(\dfrac{c}{1} \times \dfrac{1}{c}\right)$ (f) $= \dfrac{a}{b}$

The proof above is fairly rigorous and contains more steps than necessary to convince you of the truth of 9-1. If, however, you cannot supply the reasons, you would do well to review your knowledge of the properties of multiplication.

The expression in the multiple-choice question,

$$\frac{-14a^3y^4}{-35a^3y^2},$$

can be written as

$$\frac{(-7a^3y^2)(2y^2)}{(-7a^3y^2)(5)}.$$

With the common factor $-7a^3y^2$ removed, the simplified form is $\dfrac{2y^2}{5}$.

¶ DRILL Find the value of x for which the fractions in each of the following pairs are equal:

(g) $\dfrac{1}{2}, \dfrac{2}{x}$ (h) $\dfrac{3}{4}, \dfrac{x}{16}$

(i) $\dfrac{3a^2}{2b^2}, \dfrac{3a^2x}{2b^2a^2}$ (j) $\dfrac{7p}{8q}, \dfrac{21pq^2}{8qx}$

MULTIPLYING AND DIVIDING RATIONAL EXPRESSIONS

[3] If $\dfrac{a}{x}$ is multiplied by $\dfrac{a}{x^2}$ and the product is divided by $-\dfrac{a^2}{x^3}$ the result is:

Ⓐ 1   Ⓑ -1 Ⓒ 0   Ⓓ a Ⓔ $-\dfrac{a}{x}$

We have agreed that the product of two rational expressions is a third rational expression whose numerator is the product of the original numerators and whose denominator is the product of the original denominators. With this property and the definition of division, we can prove the following property for the quotient of two rational expressions.

9-2   If a, b, c and d are real numbers such that none of b, c and d is zero, then

$$\frac{a}{b} \div \frac{c}{d} = \frac{a}{b} \times \frac{d}{c}.$$

This results in a familiar law: "When dividing fractions, invert the divisor and multiply."

PROOF   (As before the reasons are left as drill and are found in the answer section.)

(a) $\dfrac{a}{b} \div \dfrac{c}{d}$ is the number x such that $\left(\dfrac{c}{d}\right) x = \dfrac{a}{b}$

(b) $\dfrac{d}{c}\left[\dfrac{c}{d}(x)\right] = \dfrac{d}{c} \cdot \dfrac{a}{b}$

(c) $\left[\dfrac{d}{c} \cdot \dfrac{c}{d}\right] x = \dfrac{a}{b} \cdot \dfrac{d}{c}$

(d) $\left[\dfrac{d \cdot c}{c \cdot d}\right] x = \dfrac{a}{b} \cdot \dfrac{d}{c}$

(e) $1 \cdot x = \dfrac{a}{b} \cdot \dfrac{d}{c}$

(f) $x = \dfrac{a}{b} \cdot \dfrac{d}{c}$

EXAMPLE

$$\left(\frac{3xy^2}{5w^2v} \cdot \frac{4x^2y}{35wv}\right) \div \frac{24x^5y^6}{175w^3v^2} = ?$$

SOLUTION: We use property 9-2 to rewrite the above as above as

$$\frac{3xy^2}{5w^2v} \times \frac{4x^2y}{35wv} \times \frac{175w^3v^2}{24x^5y^6} = \frac{2100x^3y^3w^3v^2}{4200x^5y^6w^3v^2}.$$

After removing common factors we get

$$\frac{1}{2x^2y^3}.$$

To answer the multiple-choice question,

$$\frac{a}{x} \cdot \frac{a}{x^2} \div \left(-\frac{a^2}{x^3}\right) = \frac{a}{x} \cdot \frac{a}{x^2} \cdot \left(-\frac{x^3}{a^2}\right)$$

$$= -\frac{a^2x^3}{a^2x^3} = -1.$$

¶ DRILL Carry out the indicated operations:

(g) $\dfrac{4xy^3}{7x^2y} \times (7x^2y)$ (h) $\dfrac{44a^4b^4}{7x^2y^2} \div \dfrac{8a^4b^3}{21xy^2}$

(i) $\dfrac{7a}{x^2y^2} \times \dfrac{9xy}{a^3} \div \dfrac{3a}{xy}$

ADDING AND SUBTRACTING RATIONAL EXPRESSIONS

[4] If $\dfrac{-63a^3b^2}{-9a^2}$ is added to $\dfrac{81ab^3}{27a}$ and this sum is simplified, the result is:

Ⓐ $\dfrac{18a^4b^5}{18a^3}$ Ⓑ ab^5 Ⓒ $\dfrac{81ab^3 - 63a^3b^2}{-27a^2}$

Ⓓ $\dfrac{9b^3 + 7a^2b^2}{3a}$ Ⓔ $7ab^2 + 3b^3$

We begin by defining addition for rational expressions.

If a, b and c are real numbers and c is not zero, then

$$\frac{a}{c} + \frac{b}{c} = \frac{a + b}{c}.$$

Note that, though we have only defined the sum of two expressions which have the *same* denominator, we are not really hampered since property 9-1 enables us to change any expression to any denominator desired.

EXAMPLE 1

Add $\dfrac{x + 9}{3}$ to $\dfrac{x}{9} + 9$.

SOLUTION: Since we can rewrite $\dfrac{x + 9}{3}$ as

$\dfrac{x + 9}{3} \times \dfrac{3}{3}$ and 9 as $9 \times \dfrac{9}{9}$, we can write the above as

$$\frac{3(x + 9)}{9} + \frac{x}{9} + \frac{81}{9}.$$

Now that the denominators are all the same, the sum is

$$\frac{3(x + 9) + x + 81}{9} = \frac{4x + 108}{9}.$$

EXAMPLE 2

Simplify $1 + \dfrac{1}{a} + \dfrac{1}{a^2} + \dfrac{1}{a^3} + \dfrac{1}{a^4}$.

SOLUTION: Change the above so that all fractions have a^4 as denominator:

$$1 \cdot \frac{a^4}{a^4} + \frac{1}{a} \cdot \frac{a^3}{a^3} + \frac{1}{a^2} \cdot \frac{a^2}{a^2} + \frac{1}{a^3} \cdot \frac{a}{a} + \frac{1}{a^4},$$

and get

$$\frac{a^4}{a^4} + \frac{a^3}{a^4} + \frac{a^2}{a^4} + \frac{a}{a^4} + \frac{1}{a^4}.$$

Our sum is

$$\frac{a^4 + a^3 + a^2 + a + 1}{a^4}.$$

Property 9-3 below shows a similar principle for subtraction. Again as drill, fill in the reasons as a review of the properties of addition.

> **9-3** If a, b and c are real numbers, and c is not zero, then
>
> $$\frac{a}{c} - \frac{b}{c} = \frac{a - b}{c}.$$

PROOF

(a) $\dfrac{a}{c} - \dfrac{b}{c} = x$ such that $x + \dfrac{b}{c} = \dfrac{a}{c}$

If we can show that $\dfrac{a - b}{c}$ satisfies this requirement for x, we are finished.

(b) $\dfrac{a - b}{c} + \dfrac{b}{c} = \dfrac{(a - b) + b}{c}$

(c) $= \dfrac{[a + (-b)] + b}{c}$

(d) $= \dfrac{a + [(-b) + b]}{c}$

(e) $= \dfrac{a + 0}{c}$

(f) $= \dfrac{a}{c}$

Fractions can sometimes be reduced before adding, as in the multiple-choice question:

$$\frac{-63a^3b^2}{-9a^2} + \frac{81ab^3}{27a}.$$

Each fraction can be reduced:

$$\frac{(-9)\,(7)\,(a^2)\,(ab^2)}{-9a^2} + \frac{(27a)\,(3b^3)}{27a}$$
$$= 7ab^2 + 3b^3 \text{ (choice Ⓔ)}.$$

¶ DRILL Perform the following operations:

(g) $\dfrac{2}{a} + \dfrac{4}{b} + \dfrac{6}{c}$ (h) $\dfrac{3}{xy} - \dfrac{x}{zy}$

(i) $\dfrac{a}{4z} - \dfrac{5b}{12xy}$ (j) $\dfrac{19}{a - b} + \dfrac{7}{b - a}$

SOLVING SIMPLE EQUATIONS

[5] If $ax^2 = 3y$, then $\dfrac{a}{y} = ?$

Ⓐ 3   Ⓑ $3x^2$ Ⓒ $\dfrac{3}{x^2}$ Ⓓ $\dfrac{x^2}{3}$ Ⓔ x^2

An aid in solving simple equations involving rational expressions is the Cross-Multiplication Property.

9-4   The Cross-Multiplication Property

If a, b, c and d are real numbers and neither b nor d is zero, then

$$\frac{a}{b} = \frac{c}{d} \quad \text{if and only if} \quad ad = bc.$$

PROOF   (The reasons are left as drill.)

(a) $\dfrac{a}{b} = \dfrac{c}{d}$

(b) $bd \left(\dfrac{a}{b} \right) = bd \left(\dfrac{c}{d} \right)$

(c) $db \left(\dfrac{a}{b} \right) = bd \left(\dfrac{c}{d} \right)$

(d) $d \left(b\dfrac{a}{b} \right) = b \left(d\dfrac{c}{d} \right)$

(e) $da = bc$

(f) $ad = bc$

The above is actually a proof of just the "only if" part; turn the steps around (beginning with the last) and you will have a proof of the "if" part.

EXAMPLES

(1) If $\dfrac{x}{2} = \dfrac{3}{4}$, then $4x = 6$ and $x = \dfrac{3}{2}$.

(2) If $\dfrac{2}{5} = \dfrac{7}{x + 3}$, then $2(x + 3) = 35$ and $x = \dfrac{29}{2}$

(3) If $ax^2 = 3y$, then $\dfrac{a}{y} = ?$

In order for the cross-multiplication theorem to produce the result $ax^2 = 3y$, the original equation must be

$$\frac{a}{y} = \frac{3}{x^2}.$$

¶ DRILL Solve each of the following:

(g) $\dfrac{2}{3} = \dfrac{x}{6}$ (h) $\dfrac{x + 4}{3} = \dfrac{x}{2}$

(i) $\dfrac{3}{x} = \dfrac{x}{12}$ (j) $\dfrac{7x}{6x} = \dfrac{7}{6}$

[6] If the numbers $\dfrac{13}{23}, \dfrac{11}{15}$ and $\dfrac{13}{19}$ were written in order from least to greatest, which of the following arrangements would result?

(A) $\dfrac{13}{23}, \dfrac{11}{15}, \dfrac{13}{19}$ (B) $\dfrac{13}{19}, \dfrac{11}{15}, \dfrac{13}{23}$ (C) $\dfrac{11}{15}, \dfrac{13}{19}, \dfrac{13}{23}$

(D) $\dfrac{13}{23}, \dfrac{13}{19}, \dfrac{11}{15}$ (E) $\dfrac{13}{19}, \dfrac{13}{23}, \dfrac{11}{15}$

A property of inequality similar to 9-4 can be used to establish an ordering of the rational numbers.

9-5 If a, b, c and d are integers and both b and d are positive, then

$$\frac{a}{b} < \frac{c}{d} \quad \text{if and only if} \quad ad < bc.$$

---

*Note that the numerators, a and c, remain on their original sides of the inequality sign and the denominators are positive.

The proof of 9-5 is very similar to that of 9-4 and hence is omitted here.

By 9-5 we can determine that $\dfrac{13}{23}$ is less than $\dfrac{13}{19}$ since $13 \times 19 < 23 \times 13$ and $\dfrac{13}{19}$ is less than $\dfrac{11}{15}$ since $13 \times 15 < 11 \times 19$.

¶ DRILL Use 9-5 to demonstrate each of the following:

(a) $\dfrac{5}{7} < \dfrac{3}{4}$ (b) $\dfrac{7}{8} < \dfrac{14}{15}$ (c) $-\dfrac{14}{17} < -\dfrac{7}{9}$

[7] If $\dfrac{3}{a} + \dfrac{7}{2} = -\dfrac{15}{2a}$, then $a = ?$

(A) -3 (B) 3 (C) $-\dfrac{9}{7}$ (D) $\dfrac{9}{7}$ (E) $\dfrac{3}{7}$

Two closely related procedures may be used to solve equations involving rational expressions:

(1) carry out the additions and/or subtractions of both sides of the equation to get one rational expression on each side and then apply 9-4 (recommended method);

or

(2) multiply both sides of the equation by the lowest common denominator of all rational expressions appearing in the equation. The resulting equation will have no rational expressions.

If you recall the proof of 9-4 you will recognize method (2) as being the basis of its proof. As always you should check your solutions by substitution into the original equation; quite often the process of multiplying both sides of an equation by an expression involving a variable introduces solutions which do not satisfy the original equation.

EXAMPLE

Solve: $\dfrac{2}{3x} + 5 = \dfrac{1}{2x}$.

SOLUTION: We will use method (1) and rewrite the above as:

(1) $\dfrac{2 + 15x}{3x} = \dfrac{1}{2x}$,

(2) $30x^2 + 4x = 3x$,

(3) $30x^2 + x = 0$,

(4) $x(30x + 1) = 0$.

Since the product of two numbers can be 0 only when one or both of the numbers is 0, by 6-4, the solution becomes

(5) $x = 0$ or $30x + 1 = 0$.

Consequently,

(6) $x = 0$ or $x = -\dfrac{1}{30}$.

Only $-\dfrac{1}{30}$ is an acceptable result since substitution of 0 for x in the original equation leads to division by 0.

In the multiple-choice question,

$$\dfrac{3}{a} + \dfrac{7}{2} = -\dfrac{15}{2a}.$$

The least common denominator of the three fractions is $2a$. By method (2) we get:

$$2a\left(\dfrac{3}{a} + \dfrac{7}{2}\right) = 2a\left(-\dfrac{15}{2a}\right),$$
$$2a\left(\dfrac{3}{a}\right) + 2a\left(\dfrac{7}{2}\right) = 2a\left(-\dfrac{15}{2a}\right)$$
$$2(3) + a(7) = -15,$$
$$7a = -15 - 6 = -21,$$
$$a = -3.$$

¶ DRILL Solve for x:

(a) $\dfrac{1}{x} = 5$ (b) $3 - \dfrac{1}{x} = \dfrac{1}{2}$ (c) $\dfrac{1}{x} + \dfrac{1}{2x} = \dfrac{1}{3x}$

SOLVING INEQUALITIES

[8] If $\dfrac{3}{x} < 1$, then which of the following conditions describes the values of x?

Ⓐ $x > 3$ Ⓑ $x < -3$ Ⓒ x is any number
Ⓓ $x > 3$ or $x < 0$ Ⓔ $x < 0$

To solve an inequality involving rational expressions: (1) find the least common denominator of all of the expressions; (2) separate the solving process into two cases based on when this common denominator is positive and when negative (it can't be zero); and (3) for each case multiply both sides by the common denominator to clear the inequality of rational expressions. *Be sure to change the direction of the inequality in the case for which the common denominator is negative.*

EXAMPLE 1

If $\dfrac{3}{x} < 1$, then x satisfies what condition?

SOLUTION:

Case 1:   When $x > 0$, then $3 < x$.
Case 2:   When $x < 0$, then $3 > x$, but $3 > x$ for all $x < 0$, so all $x < 0$ is in the set of solutions.

Hence the condition on x is

$$\dot{x} > 3 \text{ or } x < 0.$$

EXAMPLE 2

Solve: $\dfrac{8}{x - 1} + 3 < x$.

SOLUTION: The least common denominator is $x - 1$.

Case 1: $x - 1 > 0$ (in other words, $x > 1$).
$$8 + 3(x - 1) < x(x - 1)$$
$$0 < x^2 - 4x - 5$$
$$0 < (x - 5)(x + 1)$$

The solutions are therefore $x < -1$ or $x > 5$ (see Chapter 8, section [5]). But only $x > 5$ is acceptable for this case since our initial restriction was $x > 1$.

Case 2: $x - 1 < 0$ (in other words, $x < 1$). Therefore
$$8 + 3(x - 1) > x(x - 1).$$

(Note that we changed the direction of the inequality since $x - 1$ is negative.)
$$0 > x^2 - 4x - 5$$

Consequently the solutions are $1 < x < 5$. But the domain of this case is $x < 1$ so it contains no solutions.

We conclude that the solutions contributed by both cases include all x such that $x > 5$.

¶ DRILL Solve for x:

(a) $\dfrac{1}{x} < 1$ (b) $\dfrac{1}{x} < -1$

(c) $\dfrac{1}{x} < x$ (d) $\dfrac{1}{x + 1} > x - 1$

REDUCING COMPLICATED EXPRESSIONS

[9] Which of the following reduces to $x + 4$?

Ⓐ $\dfrac{x^2 - 16}{x + 4}$ Ⓑ $\dfrac{x^2 + 8x + 16}{x - 4}$

Ⓒ $\dfrac{x^2 - 8x + 16}{4 - x}$ Ⓓ $\dfrac{x^2 + 8x + 16}{x^2 - 4}$

Ⓔ $\dfrac{-x^2 - 8x - 16}{-x - 4}$

In preceding sections we have already developed the techniques necessary to answer questions [9], [10], and [11]. The only new wrinkle here lies in the application of these techniques to numerators and denominators of many terms. Our experience is that students have more difficulty with this type of expression because they lose sight of the meaning of *reduce*. To *reduce* means to remove common *factors* from numerator and denominator. Many students indiscriminately "cancel" everything that looks the same in numerator and denominator regardless of whether these common entities are factors. We frequently see students who cancel the 2's in $\dfrac{2x + 1}{2x - 1}$ to get $\dfrac{x + 1}{x - 1}$, even though 2 is not a factor of either $2x + 1$ or of $2x - 1$. Agreed, 2 is a factor of $2x$, but $2x$ is just a term of the numerator and is not the entire numerator.

The first step in reducing complicated rational expressions is to rewrite the expression with numerator and denominator in completely factored form. Any factor that appears in both should then be struck from both numerator and denominator (the justification is 9-1). Remember that 1 is always a factor of any expression and, if all other factors are removed from either the numerator or the denominator, the factor 1 will remain. To illustrate we will work each of the answers above:

Ⓐ $\dfrac{x^2 - 16}{x + 4} = \dfrac{(x + 4)(x - 4)}{(x + 4) \cdot 1} = \dfrac{(x - 4)}{1} = x - 4.$

Ⓑ $\dfrac{x^2 + 8x + 16}{x - 4} = \dfrac{(x + 4)(x + 4)}{x - 4}$; no common factors.

Ⓒ $\dfrac{x^2 - 8x + 16}{4 - x} = \dfrac{(x - 4)(x - 4)}{-1(x - 4)}$

$\qquad = \dfrac{(x - 4)}{-1} = 4 - x.$

Ⓓ $\dfrac{x^2 + 8x + 16}{x^2 - 4} = \dfrac{(x + 4)(x + 4)}{(x - 4)(x + 4)} = \dfrac{x + 4}{x - 4}.$

Ⓔ $\dfrac{-x^2 - 8x - 16}{-x - 4} = \dfrac{-1(x + 4)(x + 4)}{-1(x + 4) \cdot 1}$

$\qquad = x + 4.$

¶ **DRILL** Reduce:

(a) $\dfrac{2a^2 - 5a + 3}{2a^2 - a - 3}$ (b) $\dfrac{2a^3 + a^2 - 15a}{8a^3 - 125}$

(c) $\dfrac{2a - 3b + 1}{4a^2 + 4a - 9b^2 + 1}$

[10] Which of the following equals $a - 8$?

Ⓐ $\dfrac{2a + 5}{4a^2 - 14a + 12} \times \dfrac{8a^3 - 27}{2a + 5}$

Ⓑ $\dfrac{2a^2 - 5a + 3}{9 - a^2} \times \dfrac{a^3 - 3a^2 - a + 3}{2a^2 - a - 3}$

Ⓒ $\dfrac{a^2 - 4}{a + 8} \div \dfrac{a^2 - 4}{a^2 - 64}$

Ⓓ $\dfrac{21ab - 28a}{14ab^2 - 14b^2} \div \dfrac{15ab - 20a - 21b + 28}{21 - a - 10a^2}$

Ⓔ $\dfrac{a^3 + 64}{a + 4} \times \dfrac{1}{a^2 - 4a + 16}$

TEST-TAKING TIP.

A question in which the answer choices are this complicated would rarely (if ever) appear on a College Board test. We have constructed this question to present a large number of mathematical problems to resolve.

Factor each numerator and denominator completely before carrying out any operation. Properties 6-11 and 9-2 tell how to write the product or quotient as a single rational expression. You may choose to write this single rational expression or remove common factors *before* doing so, always bearing in mind where these factors will occur in the product or quotient. Use the techniques of the preceding section to reduce the product or quotient and, finally, multiply together the remaining factors. To illustrate we will work out each of the answers above, beginning with their factored forms.

Ⓐ $\dfrac{(2a + 5)}{2(2a - 3)(a - 2)} \times \dfrac{(2a - 3)(4a^2 + 6a + 9)}{(2a + 5)}$

$\qquad = \dfrac{4a^2 + 6a + 9}{2a - 4}$

Ⓑ $\dfrac{(2a - 3)(a - 1)}{-1(a - 3)(3 + a)} \times \dfrac{(a - 1)(a + 1)(a - 3)}{(2a - 3)(a + 1)}$

$\qquad = \dfrac{(a - 1)^2}{-(3 + a)}$

Ⓒ $\dfrac{(a + 2)(a - 2)}{(a + 8)} \times \dfrac{(a + 8)(a - 8)}{(a + 2)(a - 2)} = a - 8$

Ⓓ $\dfrac{7a(3b - 4)}{14b^2(a - 1)} \times \dfrac{(7 - 5a)(3 + 2a)}{-1(7 - 5a)(3b - 4)}$

$\qquad = \dfrac{3a + 2a^2}{2b^2 - 2ab^2}$

Ⓔ $\dfrac{(a + 4)(a^2 - 4a + 16)}{(a + 4)(a - 4)} \times \dfrac{1}{a^2 - 4a + 16}$

$\qquad = \dfrac{1}{a - 4}$

¶ DRILL Simplify:

(a) $\dfrac{a^2 - 8a}{a - 5} \times \dfrac{a^2 - 25}{a^2 - 64}$

(b) $\dfrac{3a^2}{6b + 42} \div \dfrac{a}{b^2 - 49}$

(c) $\dfrac{a^2 - 16}{a^2 + 2a - 8} \div \dfrac{a^2 - 8a + 16}{a^2 + 3a - 10}$

(d) $\dfrac{2a^2 - 14a + 12}{a^3 - 4a^2} \div \dfrac{a^2 + a - 2}{a + 2}$

FINDING THE LEAST COMMON DENOMINATOR

[11] If $\dfrac{6x}{x^2 - 3x}$ is subtracted from the sum of

$\dfrac{3}{5x - 15}$ and $\dfrac{x + 3}{x - 3}$, the result is:

Ⓐ $-\dfrac{2}{3}$ Ⓑ $\dfrac{x + 2}{x - 3}$ Ⓒ $\dfrac{-5x}{x^2 - 3x}$

Ⓓ $\dfrac{5x - 12}{5x - 15}$ Ⓔ $\dfrac{x^2 + 2x}{x - 3}$

We will begin with a few comments about common denominators. The product of the denominators of two rational expressions will always be a common denominator, though not necessarily the least common denominator (LCD). To find the LCD, factor the given denominators completely. The LCD will contain every factor that occurs in either denominator, and the power of each factor is the same as its higher power in either given denominator. For example, the LCD for

$$\dfrac{1}{a^2(a - 2)(a - 3)^3} \quad \text{and} \quad \dfrac{1}{ab(a - 2)^3}$$

must be $a^2b(a - 2)^3(a - 3)^3$. Note that both b and $a - 3$ are factors of the LCD though they are factors of only one of the given denominators. Note also that the power of $a - 2$ in the LCD is 3 since its higher power in either denominator is 3.

Remember that when changing the denominator of a fraction you are actually multiplying the fraction by 1; to ensure this, you must multiply the numerator by the same expression by which you multiplied the denominator. For example, to change $\dfrac{1}{2}$ to fourths, multiply the $\dfrac{1}{2}$ by $\dfrac{2}{2}$; the value of the fraction is unchanged since multiplication by 1 cannot change it (Law X).

To write $\dfrac{x + 3}{x - 3}$ with denominator $5x(x - 3)$, multiply the fraction by $\dfrac{5x}{5x}$:

$$\dfrac{x + 3}{x - 3} \cdot \dfrac{5x}{5x} = \dfrac{5x(x + 3)}{5x(x - 3)}.$$

To answer the multiple-choice question, simplify

$$\dfrac{3}{5x - 15} + \dfrac{x + 3}{x - 3} - \dfrac{6x}{x^2 - 3x}$$

In factored form the denominators are

$$5(x - 3), \quad x - 3, \quad \text{and} \quad x(x - 3),$$

so the LCD is $5x(x - 3)$. Convert each fraction to the LCD as follows:

$$\dfrac{3}{5x - 15}$$
$$= \dfrac{3}{5(x - 3)} = \dfrac{3}{5(x - 3)} \cdot \dfrac{x}{x} = \dfrac{3x}{5x(x - 3)},$$

$$\dfrac{x + 3}{x - 3} = \dfrac{x + 3}{x - 3} \cdot \dfrac{5x}{5x} = \dfrac{5x(x + 3)}{5x(x - 3)},$$

$$\dfrac{6x}{x^2 - 3x}$$
$$= \dfrac{6x}{x(x - 3)} = \dfrac{6x}{x(x - 3)} \cdot \dfrac{5}{5} = \dfrac{30x}{5x(x - 3)}$$

Therefore:

$$\dfrac{3x}{5x(x + 3)} + \dfrac{5x(x + 3)}{5x(x - 3)} - \dfrac{30x}{5x(x - 3)}$$
$$= \dfrac{3x + 5x^2 + 15x - 30x}{5x(x - 3)},$$

$$\dfrac{5x^2 - 12x}{5x(x - 3)} = \dfrac{x(5x - 12)}{5x(x - 3)}$$
$$= \dfrac{5x - 12}{5x - 15}.$$

EXAMPLE

Simplify: $\dfrac{3a - 2}{4 - 4a + a^2} - \dfrac{a + 8}{4 - a^2} + \dfrac{9}{2 + a}$.

SOLUTION: The denominators in factored form are $(2 - a)^2$, $(2 - a)(2 + a)$, and $(2 + a)$ so the LCD is $(2 - a)^2(2 + a)$.

$$\dfrac{3a - 2}{(2 - a)^2} \times \dfrac{2 + a}{2 + a}$$

$$- \dfrac{a + 8}{(2 - a)(2 + a)} \times \dfrac{2 - a}{2 - a}$$

$$+ \dfrac{7}{2 + a} \times \dfrac{(2 - a)(2 + a)}{(2 - a)(2 + a)}$$

$$= \dfrac{(3a^2 + 4a - 4) - (16 - 6a - a^2) + (28 - 7a^2)}{(2 - a)^2(2 + a)}$$

$$= \dfrac{-3a^2 + 10a + 8}{a^3 - 2a^2 - 4a + 8}$$

¶ DRILL Simplify:

(a) $\dfrac{1}{a} + \dfrac{1}{b} + \dfrac{1}{c}$

(b) $\dfrac{2}{(a + b)c} - \dfrac{5}{(a + b)d}$

(c) $\dfrac{2a}{-a - b} + \dfrac{2b}{a - b} - \dfrac{2}{a^2 - b^2}$

[12] Simplify: $\dfrac{\dfrac{x^2 - 4}{x^2 - x - 6}}{\dfrac{x^2 + x - 6}{x^2 - 9}}$.

  Ⓐ **1** Ⓑ $x - 3$ Ⓒ $x + 2$ Ⓓ $x - 2$
  Ⓔ $x + 3$

A fraction whose numerator and denominator are rational expressions can be treated as an indicated division, using property 9-2. For example, we may rewrite the above as:

$$\dfrac{x^2 - 4}{x^2 - x - 6} \div \dfrac{x^2 + x - 6}{x^2 - 9}$$

$$= \dfrac{x^2 - 4}{x^2 - x - 6} \times \dfrac{x^2 - 9}{x^2 + x - 6}$$

$$= \dfrac{(x - 2)(x + 2)(x - 3)(x + 3)}{(x - 3)(x + 2)(x - 2)(x + 3)}$$

$$= 1$$

¶ DRILL Simplify:

(a) $\dfrac{\dfrac{x^3 y^4}{18}}{\dfrac{x^4 y^3}{36}}$ (b) $\dfrac{\dfrac{x^2 + 3x}{x^2 + 7x + 10}}{\dfrac{x^3 - 9x}{x + 2}}$

[13] Simplify: $\dfrac{1 + \dfrac{1}{x}}{1 - \dfrac{1}{x}}$.

  Ⓐ **1** Ⓑ -1 Ⓒ x Ⓓ $x + 1$ Ⓔ $\dfrac{x + 1}{x - 1}$

A mixed expression is the sum of a polynomial and a rational expression. To simplify a fraction in which either the numerator or denominator (or both) is a mixed expression, rewrite the mixed expressions as rational expressions and then apply the techniques of the preceding section.

EXAMPLE 1

$$\dfrac{x - \dfrac{4}{x}}{1 - \dfrac{2}{x}} = \dfrac{\dfrac{x^2 - 4}{x}}{\dfrac{x - 2}{x}} = \dfrac{x^2 - 4}{x} \times \dfrac{x}{x - 2} = x + 2$$

EXAMPLE 2

$$\dfrac{\dfrac{1}{a} - \dfrac{1}{b}}{\dfrac{a - b}{ab}} = \dfrac{\dfrac{b - a}{ab}}{\dfrac{a - b}{ab}} = \dfrac{b - a}{ab} \times \dfrac{ab}{a - b} = -1$$

To answer the multiple-choice question, multiply numerator and denominator by x and clear fractions:

$$\dfrac{x\left(1 + \dfrac{1}{x}\right)}{x\left(1 - \dfrac{1}{x}\right)} = \dfrac{x + 1}{x - 1}.$$

We picked x to multiply by because x is the LCD of the fractions that make up the terms of the complex fraction. This is an alternative method to the one explained above.

¶ DRILL Simplify:

(a) $\dfrac{\dfrac{1}{a} + 1}{a + 1}$ (b) $\dfrac{x - 2}{\dfrac{1}{x} - \dfrac{1}{2}}$ (c) $\dfrac{\dfrac{1}{a} + \dfrac{1}{b}}{\dfrac{1}{a} - \dfrac{1}{b}}$

(d) $\dfrac{\dfrac{z - y}{z} + \dfrac{z - y}{y}}{\dfrac{z - y}{y} - \dfrac{z - y}{z}}$

[14] If $\dfrac{1}{x - 1} = x - 1$, what does x equal?

  Ⓐ **1** Ⓑ **0** Ⓒ **1 or 0** Ⓓ **2** Ⓔ **0 or 2**

Applying the technique of section [7], we multiply both sides of the equation by the LCD, solve this simpler equation and then check all solutions—discarding any that may have been introduced by the multiplication step.

EXAMPLE 1

$$\dfrac{1}{x - 1} = x - 1$$
$$1 = x^2 - 2x + 1$$
$$0 = x^2 - 2x$$
$$0 = x(x - 2)$$

Therefore $x = 0$ or $x = 2$, both of which satisfy the original equation.

EXAMPLE 2

Find a if $\dfrac{1}{a} + \dfrac{2}{a + 1} = \dfrac{5}{6}$.

SOLUTION: The LCD is $6a(a + 1)$.

(1) $6a(a + 1)\left(\dfrac{1}{a} + \dfrac{2}{a + 1}\right) = 6a(a + 1)\left(\dfrac{5}{6}\right)$

(2) $\qquad\quad 6(a + 1) + 12a = 5a^2 + 5a$

$\qquad\qquad\qquad 18a + 6 = 5a^2 + 5a$

$\qquad\qquad\qquad\qquad 0 = 5a^2 - 13a - 6$

(3) $\qquad\qquad\qquad\quad 0 = (5a + 2)(a - 3)$

(4) Therefore $5a + 2 = 0$ or $a - 3 = 0$. The solutions are $-\dfrac{2}{5}$ and 3, both of which satisfy the original equation.

¶ DRILL Solve:

(a) $\dfrac{1}{x - 1} + \dfrac{2}{3} + \dfrac{2}{x - 1} = \dfrac{13}{6}$

(b) $\dfrac{15}{2x - 1} = x$

(c) $7 - \dfrac{7x}{x + 2} = \dfrac{3}{x + 5}$

THE OPPOSITE OF $x - y$

[15] Find the value of $\dfrac{a^2 - b^2}{b^2 - a^2}$.

Ⓐ -1 Ⓑ 1 Ⓒ 0 Ⓓ $a + b$ Ⓔ $a - b$

What is the additive inverse of $(x - y)$? Note that

$$-(x - y) = (-x) - (-y)$$
$$= -x + y$$
$$= y - x.$$

This important fact, $-(x - y) = y - x$, is frequently used in simplification of rational expressions, and it occurs in the question above. A useful way of dealing with it is to think of factoring out -1.

$$(x - y) = (-1)(y - x)$$

Therefore

$$\frac{a^2 - b^2}{b^2 - a^2} = \frac{a^2 - b^2}{(-1)(a^2 - b^2)} = \frac{1}{(-1)} = -1.$$

¶ DRILL Simplify each of the following:

(a) $\dfrac{5 - 2}{2 - 5}$

(b) $\dfrac{x - y^2}{-x + y^2}$

(c) $\dfrac{a^2 - b^2}{b^2 - 2ab + a^2}$

WHAT YOU SHOULD KNOW

KEY CONCEPTS

Handling Fractions

1. *To compare two fractions*, multiply the numerator of each by the denominator of the other and compare the products. The greater product contains the numerator of the greater fraction.
2. *To simplify a complex fraction*,
   a. express it as the division of the numerator by the denominator, then invert and multiply, *or*
   b. multiply the numerator and denominator of a complex fraction by the LCD of all the fractions that appear in either the numerator or the denominator.
3. To solve an equation in which both members are fractions, cross-multiply.

Handling Rational Expressions

1. *To simplify a rational expression*, first factor the numerator and the denominator, then remove common factors.
2. *To multiply rational expressions*, multiply the numerators and multiply the denominators.
3. *To divide rational expressions*, invert the divisor and multiply.
4. *To convert a rational expression to a different denominator*, multiply by $\dfrac{c}{c}$, where c is the factor needed to produce the desired denominator.
5. *To add (or subtract) rational expressions*,
   a. with the *same* denominator, add (or subtract) numerators and write the result with the common denominator.
   b. with *different* denominators, first change to the same denominator (see item 4 above) and then add (or subtract) (see 5a above).
6. *To solve an equation involving rational expressions*, clear fractions by multiplying all terms by the lowest common denominator (LCD).
7. *To gain additional opportunities to remove common factors*, replace the expression $a - b$ by the equivalent form $(-1)(b - a)$.

KEY PROPERTY

If a, b, c and d are real numbers and neither b nor d is zero, then

$$\frac{a}{b} = \frac{c}{d} \quad \text{if and only if} \quad ad = bc.$$

(Cross-Multiplication Property)

TEST-TAKING STRATEGIES

- Reducing a fraction means removing common factors from the numerator and denominator. This operation can best be carried out by thinking of the three words "remove common factors" as telling you what to do in reverse order. First *factor*. Then identify factors that are *common*. Then *remove* these common factors.
- Cross multiplication is an extremely useful way of comparing fractions and solving simple fractional equations. At first, it may look like a gimmick that has no reason for being true. Study the proof given in this text to assure yourself that cross multiplication is well supported by mathematical theory.
- Complex fractions look nastier than they really are. Simply multiply the numerator and denominator of a complex fraction by the LCD of all of the fractions of which it is composed. The result is always a simple fraction that is easy to work with.
- Don't overlook the simplification potential in knowing that $x - y$ and $y - x$ are opposites. In most applications, one can readily be converted into the other by a simple algebraic manipulation. By doing so, you can often markedly reduce the number of steps necessary to get an answer.
- Finding LCDs and reducing fractions requires the ability to factor quickly and accurately. Be sure to master your factoring skills before taking the CB Math Level I test.

ANSWERS

[1] Ⓔ

DRILL:
(a) 0, 0
(b) Undefined, no real number.
(c) Undefined, any real number.
(d) Any real number, any real number.

[2] Ⓒ

DRILL:
(a) 6–11. If $a, b, c, d \in R$ and neither b nor d is 0, then $\dfrac{a}{b} \times \dfrac{c}{d} = \dfrac{ac}{bd}$
(b) Multiplicative Identity.
(c) 6–11.
(d) Definition of division ($c \div 1 = x$ such that $1 \cdot x = c$), and Multiplicative Identity.
(e) Multiplicative Inverse.
(f) Multiplicative Identity.
(g) 4
(h) 12
(i) a^2
(j) $3q^2$

[3] Ⓑ

DRILL:
(a) Definition of division.
(b) Property of Equality (Multiplication).
(c) Associative Law of Multiplication.
(d) 6–11.
(e) Definition of division ($dc \div cd = q$ such that $q(cd) = dc$) and the Identity and Commutative Laws of Multiplication.
(f) Multiplicative Identity.
(g) $4xy^3$
(h) $\dfrac{33b}{2x}$
(i) $\dfrac{21}{a^3}$

[4] Ⓔ

DRILL:
(a) Definition of subtraction.
(b) Definition of addition for rational expressions.
(c) 6-2. If $a, b \in R$, then $a - b = a + (-b)$
(d) Associative Law of Addition.
(e) Additive Inverse Law.
(f) Additive Identity.
(g) $\dfrac{2bc + 4ac + 6ab}{abc}$
(h) $\dfrac{3z - x^2}{xyz}$
(i) $\dfrac{3axy - 5bz}{12xyz}$
(j) $\dfrac{12}{a - b}$ (Multiply $\dfrac{7}{b - a}$ by $\dfrac{-1}{-1}$ to get $\dfrac{-7}{a - b}$ and thus common denominators.)

[5] Ⓒ

DRILL:
(a) Given.
(b) Property of Equality (Multiplication).
(c) Commutative Law of Multiplication.
(d) Associative Law of Multiplication.
(e) Multiplicative Inverse and Identity Laws.
(f) Commutative Law of Multiplication.
(g) 4
(h) 8
(i) ± 6
(j) Any real number.

[6] Ⓓ

DRILL:
(a) $20 < 21$ (b) $7 \times 15 < 8 \times 14$
(c) $-14 \times 9 < -7 \times 17$

[7] Ⓐ

DRILL:

(a) $\dfrac{1}{5}$ (b) $\dfrac{2}{5}$

(c) No solutions.

[8] Ⓓ

DRILL:

(a) $x > 1$ or $x < 0$

(b) $-1 < x < 0$

(c) $x > 1$ or $-1 < x < 0$

(d) $-1 < x < \sqrt{2}$ or $x < -\sqrt{2}$

[9] Ⓔ

DRILL:

(a) $\dfrac{a-1}{a+1}$

(b) $\dfrac{a^2 + 3a}{4a^2 + 10a + 25}$ or $\dfrac{a(a+3)}{4a^2 + 10a + 25}$

(c) $\dfrac{1}{2a + 3b + 1}$

[10] Ⓒ

DRILL:

(a) $\dfrac{a^2 + 5a}{a + 8}$ or $\dfrac{a(a+5)}{a+8}$

(b) $\dfrac{ab - 7a}{2}$ or $\dfrac{a(b-7)}{2}$

(c) $\dfrac{a+5}{a-4}$

(d) $\dfrac{2a - 12}{a^3 - 4a^2}$ or $\dfrac{2(a-6)}{a^2(a-4)}$

[11] Ⓓ

DRILL:

(a) $\dfrac{bc + ac + ab}{abc}$

(b) $\dfrac{2d - 5c}{(a+b)cd}$

(c) $\dfrac{4ab - 2a^2 + 2b^2 - 2}{a^2 - b^2}$

[12] Ⓐ

DRILL:

(a) $\dfrac{2y}{x}$

(b) $\dfrac{1}{x^2 + 2x - 15}$ or $\dfrac{1}{(x+5)(x-3)}$

[13] Ⓔ

DRILL:

(a) $\dfrac{1}{a}$ (b) $-2x$

(c) $\dfrac{b+a}{b-a}$ (d) $\dfrac{y+z}{z-y}$

[14] Ⓔ

DRILL:

(a) 3 (b) $3,\ -\dfrac{5}{2}$

(c) $-\dfrac{64}{11}$

[15] Ⓐ

DRILL:

(a) -1 (b) -1

(c) $\dfrac{a+b}{a-b}$

10. Lines and Planes

Key Terms

A **point**   has no width or thickness, only position.

A **line**   is a set of points, has no thickness, is straight, and continues infinitely in two directions.

A **plane**   is a set of points, is flat, has no depth (thickness), and continues infinitely in all directions.

A **ray**   has no thickness, has one endpoint, and extends infinitely in one direction.

A **postulate**   is an agreement about the properties of algebraic or geometric elements.

IDENTIFYING INTERSECTIONS AND UNIONS

[1] **Which of the following sets of points could NOT be the intersection of a line and a plane?**

Ⓐ **The empty set**   Ⓑ **A single point**   Ⓒ **A line**
Ⓓ **A plane**   Ⓔ **The intersection of two lines**

Though geometry originated as the study of earth measurements and though many of its practical applications still lie in this area, contemporary school geometry is the study of sets of points. Some elementary aspects of sets have already been reviewed in Chapter 6, and others will be discussed in later chapters. In this section we will define the "union" (symbolized by ∪) and the "intersection" (symbolized by ∩) of two sets in order to simplify the statement of some of our geometric concepts.

The basic terms of geometry are *set, point, line,* and *plane.* Since these words initiate our study we cannot define them. We have no other words from which to formulate definitions. This lack of definitions will prove no obstacle because we will make some agreements about their use. These agreements, which we will call *postulates,* as well as our intuitive ideas of how we want points, lines and planes to behave, will guide us in formulating our geometry.

Texts vary in just what postulates they agree on at the outset, but the resulting theory derived from them is substantially the same. Since we do not want to confuse you by insisting on your memorization of precisely worded postulates that may only approximate those which you have already studied, we will state our agreements and derive their consequences informally. In general we will rely more on the motivation for each postulate than on its exact wording.

Our lines will be "straight" and will extend infinitely in two directions. Our points will have no thickness or depth. Our planes will be flat, with no thickness, and will extend infinitely in all directions.

Now back to sets. Two sets *intersect* when they have at least one point in common. The *intersection* of two sets is the set of points which belong to both. Consequently, if a point X belongs to the intersection of two sets, A and B, then X must belong to B and X must belong to A. If two sets do not intersect, we say their intersection is the empty set. Therefore, if a line L does not intersect a plane P, then $L \cap P = \emptyset$.

If a line pierces a plane but does not also lie in the plane, this intersection contains only a single point. If the line does lie in the plane, their intersection is the entire line, since every point of the line belongs to both.

Answer Ⓔ above is tricky. The intersection of a pair of lines can be either a single point, the empty set, or (in the case where the lines coincide) a line. All of these are also possible intersections of a line and a plane, so only choice Ⓓ will answer the question.

A point X belongs to the *union* of sets A and B if and only if it belongs to A *or* it belongs to B (or both). As long as it belongs to at least one of these sets it is in their union.

¶ DRILL

(a) The definition of the term *circle* will be reviewed in a later section. Using what you remember about circles, describe the possible intersections of a line and a circle.

(b) Draw three points, A, B and C, which do not all lie on the same line. Connect A, B and C with all possible segments of lines. What term can you apply to the union of these segments?

(c) The figure at the right shows a region of a plane containing three circular regions A, B and C Use vertical shading to indicate A ^{1} B. Use horizontal shading to indicate $A \cap C$.

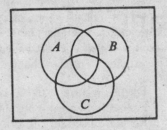

IDENTIFYING LINES, SEGMENTS AND RAYS

[2] M, N, P and Q are points of a line such that $MP + PQ = MQ$. N is the midpoint of PQ. In the following sentences each blank space represents one of the words "segment," "ray" or "line." What is the order in which these words are used to fill the blanks correctly?

_____ PN contains points M and Q.
_____ PN does not contain either M or Q.
_____ PN contains Q but not M.

  Ⓐ **Segment, Ray, Line**   Ⓑ **Ray, Line, Segment**
  Ⓒ **Line, Segment, Ray**   Ⓓ **Segment, Line, Ray**
  Ⓔ **Line, Ray, Segment**

We will have frequent use for the terms *collinear, coplanar, between, segment, midpoint* and *ray*. A set of points is *collinear* if there is one line that contains every point of the set. In the question above we were given that M, N, P and Q were collinear. Note that two points are always collinear, but three points need not be.

A set of points is *coplanar* if there is one plane which contains every point of the set. Three points are always coplanar. If the three points are not collinear, then there is exactly one plane that contains them. If they are collinear, infinitely many planes contain them.

When we wish to refer to the distance from point A to point B we use the symbol AB. This distance is a positive number and we choose to consider AB to be the same distance as BA. If A, B and C are distinct points on the same line and if $AB + BC = AC$, we say that B is *between* A and C. In the question above, we must conclude that P is between M and Q.

The union of points A, B, and the set of points between A and B, is called *segment AB*. A precise definition for *ray AB* is possible, though much more complex than is necessary to understand what a ray is. Suffice it to say that ray AB is that section of line AB that begins at A, passes through B and extends infinitely in the direction started.

It is customary in geometry courses to invent special symbols for segment, ray and line. We will not do so because such symbols are by no means standardized. When we want to distinguish among them we will write out the proper term.

A point B is the *midpoint* of segment AC if B is on line AC and if $AB = BC$. From the latter statement we may deduce that

$$AB = BC = \frac{1}{2}AC.$$

Now, with an understanding of the terms used, you should be able to see that the order of the points on the line in the multiple-choice question must be:

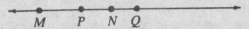

From the diagram, you can see that:

Line PN contains points M and Q.
Segment PN contains neither point M nor point Q.
Ray PN contains Q, but not M.

¶ DRILL In each of the following start with a pair of points labeled X and Y and draw the figure described:

(a) ray XY (b) segment XY (c) line XY
(d) ray YX (e) the ray of line XY opposite ray YX

UNDERSTANDING "STRAIGHTNESS" OF LINES

[3] If A and B are two different points which lie on a line CD and also on a line EF, which of the following is a correct conclusion?

  Ⓐ **Line CD and line EF are not coplanar.**
  Ⓑ **Lines CD and EF do not intersect.**   Ⓒ **Line CD intersects a plane containing line EF in exactly two points.**   Ⓓ **All the points A, B, C, D, E and F are collinear.**   Ⓔ **Ray CD and ray EF must be opposite rays.**

We stated in section [1] that we wanted our lines to be "straight" but said nothing about what this means. To rule out any possibility of a line that bends, we make the following agreement:

Postulate 1 If A and B are different points, there is one and only one line that will contain both.

To see that this actually does disallow a "non-straight" line, draw two points and then a line that contains both. Now try to draw a different line that also contains both. Unless you have allowed your second line to bend (or represented your original points by very fat dots) you cannot draw a second line.

We have called this Postulate 1 though we have actually made some informal agreements preceding it. Remember that we are attempting to review the major concepts of geometry and are not trying to recreate any of the many different rigorous systems available.

Can a pair of different lines intersect in more than one point? Suppose they did intersect in two (or more) points. Then these two points would be contained in both lines, which contradicts Postulate 1. We have just used an informal argument to deduce the following:

> **10-1** Two different lines will intersect in exactly one point (if they intersect at all).

Such deductions are called theorems, and this art of deduction has become perhaps the most important aspect of secondary school geometry.

To answer the multiple-choice question, note that, in order for both line *CD* and line *EF* to contain points *A* and *B*, line *CD* and line *EF* must be the same line.

¶ DRILL How many lines can be drawn containing each of the pairs of four different points if:

(a) all of the points are collinear
(b) three points are collinear but the fourth is not
(c) no more than two points are collinear

UNDERSTANDING "FLATNESS" OF PLANES

[4] If *A*, *B*, *C* and *D* are any four distinct points of a plane *P*, which of the following is true?

Ⓐ Line *AB* must intersect line *CD*. Ⓑ Line *AC* must intersect line *BD*. Ⓒ If lines *AD* and *BC* intersect in one point, this point will not lie in plane *P*. Ⓓ Line *AB* can contain a point not in plane *P*. Ⓔ Any point of intersection of any of the pairs of lines containing *A*, *B*, *C* and *D* must lie in plane *P*.

We have stated that we want our planes to be "flat" and to extend infinitely in all directions. We will make two agreements to guarantee this:

Postulate 2 Any plane that contains two distinct points of a line must contain every point of the line.

Postulate 2 provides the necessary restriction for "flatness."

Postulate 3 The intersection of two distinct intersecting planes is a line.

Among other things, Postulate 3 asserts that planes extend infinitely in all directions since lines extend infinitely in two directions.

A line, therefore, cannot intersect a plane in more than one point unless it lies in the plane, according to Postulate 2. We state this as a theorem:

> **10-2** The intersection of a line and a plane contains no more than one point (unless the line lies in the plane).

Answers Ⓒ, Ⓓ and Ⓔ all relate to these postulates. Answers Ⓐ and Ⓑ are, of course, incorrect since two lines may be contained in the same plane without intersecting—such lines are called "parallel" lines and will be studied in a later chapter.

¶ DRILL According to our postulates certain types of intersections are not possible. Make whatever distortions are necessary to draw these impossible situations:

(a) A line intersecting a plane in two points but not contained in it
(b) A pair of distinct lines intersecting in more than one point
(c) The vertices of a triangle lying in a plane that does not contain the triangle

Do you see how the postulates guarantee "flatness" and "straightness?"

IDENTIFYING PLANES

[5] A set of points is said to "determine" a plane if there is exactly one plane that contains all of the points. Which of the following does not determine a plane?

Ⓐ A triangle Ⓑ Any three points Ⓒ A line and a point not on the line Ⓓ A pair of intersecting rays Ⓔ A pair of intersecting lines

We will formalize an agreement already mentioned informally:

Postulate 4 There exists at least one plane that contains any three points. There is at most one plane that contains any three noncollinear points.

Thus three noncollinear points will determine a plane. A triangle also determines a plane since the three vertices of a triangle determine a plane, and this plane contains the sides by Postulate 2. Three collinear points do not determine a plane since infinitely many planes may contain all of them. Since a set containing two points of a line and a point not on the line is a set of three noncollinear points and since this line must lie in any plane which contains two of its points, we can conclude that Ⓒ determines a plane. Both Ⓓ and Ⓔ involve the same idea. Let *X* be the point of intersection of the two sets and let *Y* and *Z* each be another point of each of the sets. These noncollinear points determine a plane which then contains the rays or lines by Postulate 2.

¶ DRILL Which of the following sets of points determine a plane?

(a) Four points (b) A circle (c) Any three vertices of a cube (d) Any four vertices of a cube

[6] If a line is contained in a plane, the two sets of points of the plane that do not lie on the line may be called "sides" of the line. Which of the following statements is NOT true about S_1 and S_2 if they are the two sides of a line L in a plane M?

    Ⓐ If P and Q lie in S_1, then every point of segment PQ lies in S_1.   Ⓑ If P lies in S_1 and Q lies in S_2, then segment PQ must intersect line L.   Ⓒ The union of S_1 and S_2 is plane M.   Ⓓ The intersection of S_1 and S_2 is the empty set.   Ⓔ There exists at least one line completely contained in S_1.

In some texts the sides of a line are called "half-planes." We will occasionally use the notion of sides to help define more complicated regions of planes.

    Your intuition should tell you that Ⓐ is true. Sets of this kind (such that when P and Q are elements of the set, then segment PQ is completely contained in the set) are called *convex* sets. Experimentation should persuade you that Ⓑ is also true.

TEST-TAKING TIP.

Representing geometric information by diagrams is extremely helpful. Often the diagram alone is enough to suggest an answer or a problem-solving method.

    The following diagrams are useful in illustrating the information in several answer choices:

Ⓐ
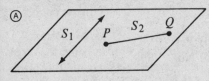

Ⓑ
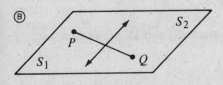

Ⓔ
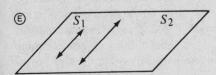

    Ⓒ cannot be true since line L by definition is not contained in either S_1 or S_2. Ⓓ is true since L makes a boundary between S_1 and S_2. Ⓔ is true—any line parallel to L will satisfy this condition.

¶ DRILL Using the definition of convex given above, indicate which of the regions marked I, II, III and IV are convex sets.

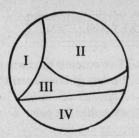

WHAT YOU SHOULD KNOW

KEY CONCEPTS

Handling Points and Lines

1. The *intersection* of sets A and B is the set of points that belong to both A and B.
2. The *union* of sets A and B is the set of all points belonging to either A or B.
3. A set of points is *collinear* if all are contained in the same line.
4. A set of points is *coplanar* if all are contained in the same plane.
5. A point B is *between* points A and C if and only if $AB + BC = AC$.
6. A point M is the *midpoint* of segment AC if and only if it is between A and C and $AM = CM = \frac{1}{2}AC$.
7. Two different points are contained in exactly one line.
8. If two different lines intersect, their intersection is a point.

Handling Planes

1. If two points of a line lie in a plane, the line lies in the plane.
2. If two planes intersect, their intersection is a line.
3. If a line intersects a plane and does not lie in the plane, the intersection is one point.
4. Any three points lie in a plane; any three noncollinear points lie in exactly one plane.
5. A set of points "determines" a plane if there is one and only one plane containing all points of the set.
6. A plane is determined by (a) three noncollinear points, (b) a line and a point not on the line, and (3) a pair of lines intersecting at exactly one point.
7. A line lying in a plane separates the plane into two sets (neither of which includes the points of the line) called *half-planes* or *sides* of the line. The half-planes are *convex*. If a point A is in one half-plane and a point B is in the other, segment AB must intersect the given line.

KEY THEOREMS

1. Two different lines will intersect in exactly one point (if they intersect at all).
2. The intersection of a line and a plane contains no more than one point (unless the line lies in the plane).

TEST-TAKING STRATEGIES

- If a question dealing with lines and planes does not provide a diagram to show relationships, draw your own diagram to represent the information given.
- Definitions and postulates of geometry vary a great deal from textbook to textbook. CB Math Level I exams are intended to test the ideas presented and not the wording used in any particular approach. For example, terms like "half-plane" and "convex" are not universally used in geometry texts, so it is unlikely you will see them on the CB Math Level I exam. We've used them here because they help you visualize the concepts they represent and make other definitions easier to understand. Do not be confused by varying terminology.
- CB Math Level I exams avoid using particular symbols to name rays, line segments and lines. Instead, be aware that they use the terms "ray," "line," and "line segment" to avoid any possibility of confusion.

ANSWERS

[1] ⓓ
 DRILL:
 (a) ∅, one point, two points
 (b) A triangle
 (c)

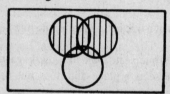

[2] ©
 DRILL:
 (a)
 (b)
 (c)
 (d)
 (e)

[3] ⓓ
 DRILL:
 (a) One.   (b) Four.
 (c) Six.

[4] ⓔ
 DRILL:
 (a)

 (b)

 (c)

[5] Ⓑ
 DRILL:
 (a) No.   (b) Yes.
 (c) Yes.   (d) No.

[6] ©
 DRILL:
 The regions marked I and IV are convex sets.

11. Angles

UNDERSTANDING SOME BASIC ASPECTS OF ANGLES

[1] Which of the following statements about angles is NOT true?

Ⓐ **An angle of a triangle may have a degree measure of 180.** Ⓑ **An angle of a triangle may not have a degree measure greater than 180.** Ⓒ **Two angles may be complementary without having a common side.** Ⓓ **The degree measure of an angle does not depend on the lengths of its sides.** Ⓔ **The interior of a triangle does not contain the interior of any of its angles.**

In this section we will review some elementary aspects of angles. By an *angle* we mean the union of two rays that (1) have a common endpoint and (2) do not lie on the same line:

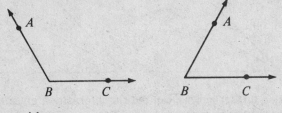

but neither

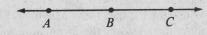

nor

Since an angle is the union of two rays, its sides cannot be segments. We will sometimes call the union of two segments an "angle" but what we will really mean is the angle whose sides contain the segments. When naming an angle we use the symbol ∠ followed by three capital letters. The first letter names a point on

one ray, the second names the vertex (the common endpoint of the rays) and the third names a different point on the remaining side. Thus the vertex of ∠ABC is *B*. When only one angle has a given point as its vertex, we frequently use the symbol ∠ with just the letter labelling that vertex.

For a point *P* to lie in the *interior of an angle*, ∠ABC, *P* must lie on the same side (see definition of "side" in Chapter 10) of line *AB* as point *C and* on the same side of line *BC* as point *A*. In the figure below, the vertical shading represents the set of all points on the side of line *BC* which contains *A* and the horizontal shading represents the set of all points on the side of line *AC* that contains *B*. The cross-hatching, therefore, designates the interior of ∠ACB. If a point is not on an angle and not in its interior, then it is in the *exterior* of the angle.

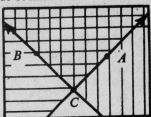

Two angles that (1) have a common vertex, (2) have a common side and (3) have interiors which don't overlap are called *adjacent* angles. For example, ∠ABD and ∠DBC are adjacent, but not ∠ABD and ∠ABC, in the figure below:

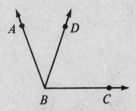

If the nonshared sides of a pair of adjacent angles are opposite rays, the angles formed are sometimes called a *linear pair*. For example, in the figure below, $\angle ABC$ and $\angle ABD$ are a linear pair:

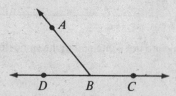

Your experience with measuring angles by protractor should prepare you to agree that every angle can be assigned a degree measure between 0 and 180 (but not either 0 or 180 since we have excluded "angles" with collinear sides). We formalize our agreements about angle measure in the following postulate.

Postulate 5 *The Angle Postulate* To each angle we assign a number between 0 and 180 to be called its "degree measure." Given a point A on a line AB and a number m such that $0 < m < 180$, there is one and only one angle that can be constructed with (1) ray AB as a side, (2) m as its degree measure, and (3) its interior contained in a given side of line AB.

When the sum of the measures of two angles is 180, we say these angles are *supplementary*. When their sum is 90, we call them *complementary* angles. Though we frequently encounter adjacent angles that are either supplementary or complementary, angles *do not* have to be adjacent to satisfy the definitions given.

If three points, A, B and C, are not collinear, then the union of segments AB, BC and AC is called a *triangle*.

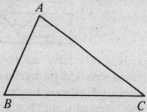

Note that the union of these three segments contains no points "inside" the triangle. The *interior* of a triangle is the intersection of the interiors of its three angles (the "angles" of a triangle are the angles which contain the sides of the triangle).

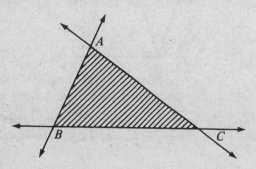

¶ DRILL Answer each of the following questions by referring to a definition or postulate that guarantees the answer is true.

(a) Can a point of a triangle lie in the interior of the triangle?

(b) Can a point lie on an angle of a triangle and not lie on the triangle?

(c) If the measures of the angles of a triangle are added, can the result ever be negative?

(d) What is the complement of an angle with degree measure of 110?

(e) Is there any angle with degree measure of $\sqrt{2}$?

WORKING WITH THE MEASURES OF ANGLES

[2] If (1) point P is in the interior of $\angle LMN$, (2) point W is in the interior of $\angle XYZ$, (3) the measures of $\angle LMN$ and $\angle XYZ$ are equal, and (4) the measures of $\angle PMN$ and $\angle WYZ$ are equal, which of the following is NOT true?

Ⓐ The measure of $\angle LMN$ equals the sum of the measures of $\angle LMP$ and $\angle PMN$.   Ⓑ The measure of $\angle XYW$ is the difference of the measures of $\angle XYZ$ and $\angle WYZ$.   Ⓒ The measure of $\angle ZYW$ must equal the measure of $\angle LMP$.   Ⓓ The measure of $\angle XYW$ equals the measure of $\angle LMP$.   Ⓔ $\angle LMP$ and $\angle PMN$ are adjacent angles.

When a geometric question is as complicated as this one, it helps to draw a figure:

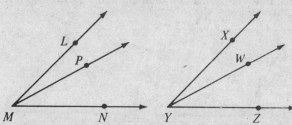

As a further aid, we can put the information given in more concise form. Abbreviations vary from text to text so writers of standardized tests avoid them and generally write out what they mean to avoid confusion. We will follow their lead in the formulation of questions but adopt a handy notation to simplify our discussions. When referring to the degree measure of $\angle ABC$ we will use

$$(\angle ABC)°.$$

Thus, we can summarize the given information as:

$$(\angle LMN)° = (\angle XYZ)°$$

and

$$(\angle PMN)° = (\angle WYZ)°.$$

You may well ask why we don't write $\angle LMN = \angle XYZ$. Remember that an angle is a set of points and equality of sets has already been defined to describe sets which have exactly the same elements. Our angles are equal in measure but do not contain the same points.

We will agree on the following:

Postulate 6 If a point P is in the interior of $\angle LMN$, then:

$$(\angle LMN)^\circ = (\angle LMP)^\circ + (\angle PMN)^\circ.$$

This agreement asserts the truth of answer Ⓐ. It also leads us to conclude that:

$$(\angle XYZ)^\circ = (\angle XYW)^\circ + (\angle WYZ)^\circ,$$

which is an affirmation of answer Ⓑ.

We can also conclude that:

$$(\angle LMN)^\circ - (\angle PMN)^\circ = (\angle LMP)^\circ,$$

and, therefore, by substitution we deduce:

$$(\angle XYW)^\circ = (\angle LMP)^\circ,$$

which supports answer Ⓓ.

Answer Ⓔ is an application of the definition of "adjacent." Answer Ⓒ *may* be true but *does not have to* be true. All of the others *must* be true.

We summarize these conclusions in the following theorem:

11-1 If D is in the interior of $\angle ABC$ and W is in the interior of $\angle XYZ$, then, when any two of

    (a) $(\angle ABC)^\circ = (\angle XYZ)^\circ$,
    (b) $(\angle ABD)^\circ = (\angle XYW)^\circ$, and
    (c) $(\angle DBC)^\circ = (\angle WYZ)^\circ$

are true, the third must also be true.

¶ DRILL Fill in the blanks if $(\angle AEC)^\circ = (\angle BED)^\circ$:

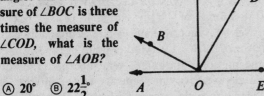

(a) $(\angle AEB)^\circ + (\angle BEC)^\circ$
    $= (\angle\ ?\ )^\circ$

(b) $(\angle BEC)^\circ + (\angle CED)^\circ$
    $= (\angle\ ?\ )^\circ$

(c) $(\angle\ ?\ )^\circ - (\angle BEC)^\circ$
    $= (\angle AEB)^\circ$

(d) $(\angle\ ?\ )^\circ - (\angle BEC)^\circ$
    $= (\angle CED)^\circ$

(e) $(\angle AEB)^\circ = (\angle\ ?\ )^\circ$

[3] If in the figure $\angle COE$ and $\angle BOD$ are right angles and if the measure of $\angle BOC$ is three times the measure of $\angle COD$, what is the measure of $\angle AOB$?

  Ⓐ 20° Ⓑ $22\frac{1}{2}°$
  Ⓒ 30° Ⓓ 45° Ⓔ 60°

We will call a pair of angles such as $\angle DOE$ and $\angle DOA$ a "linear pair" and agree that:

Postulate 7 The sum of the measures of the angles of a linear pair is 180.

When the angles of a linear pair have the same measure, x, then the sum of their measures, $x + x$, is 180 and x must be 90. An angle with measure 90 is called a *right* angle. If a pair of lines intersect to form a right angle, we say the lines are *perpendicular*.

Let $y = (\angle COD)^\circ$ in the figure above. Then $3y = (\angle COB)^\circ$ and $3y + y = 90$, since $\angle DOB$ is a right angle. Therefore $y = (\angle COD)^\circ = 22\frac{1}{2}$, and $3y = (\angle COB)^\circ = 67\frac{1}{2}$. Because $\angle COA$ is also a right angle,

$$(\angle BOA)^\circ = 22\frac{1}{2}.$$

¶ DRILL
(a) In the figure in section [3] name two linear pairs not already mentioned.
(b) Assume $(\angle DOE)^\circ = 2(\angle BOA)^\circ$, and find $(\angle COB)^\circ$.

[4] If $\angle AOB$ is a right angle, decide whether you can conclude that $\angle AOD$ and $\angle BOC$ have the same measure. Which of the following justifies your conclusion?

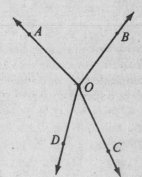

Ⓐ This conclusion cannot be justified from the information given.

Ⓑ Complements of angles having the same measure must also have the same measure. Ⓒ Supplements of angles with the same measure must also have the same measure. Ⓓ Vertical angles have the same measure. Ⓔ If two intersecting lines form one right angle, they must form four right angles.

Each of answers Ⓑ through Ⓔ is a provable geometric statement which we will verify while deciding on the correct choice.

Ⓑ and Ⓒ. If $\angle X$ and $\angle Y$ are any pair of angles such that $(\angle X)^\circ = (\angle Y)^\circ$, their complements and supplements must also be angle pairs of equal measure since $90 - (\angle X)^\circ$ must equal $90 - (\angle Y)^\circ$ and $180 - (\angle X)^\circ = 180 - (\angle Y)^\circ$. Our given information will not allow us to conclude that $\angle AOD$ and $\angle BOC$ are either complements or supplements of a pair of angles of equal measure.

Ⓓ Two angles are *vertical* angles if their sides form two pairs of opposite rays. In other words, they are formed only by two intersecting lines. No such situation occurs above. If the figure had been as shown at right, then ∠*AOD* and ∠*BOC* would be vertical angles. They must have the same measure since they are both supplements of ∠*AOB*.

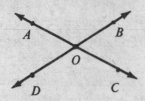

The statement in Ⓔ is a consequence of the vertical angle theorem just proved. If two lines intersect to form a right angle, then the two angles adjacent to the right angle must also have measures of 90 since they are supplements of the right angle. The nonadjacent angle forms a pair of vertical angles with the right angle. Again, the figure does not have a pair of intersecting lines so the correct answer is Ⓐ.

¶ DRILL In the figure at right ∠*DOB* and ∠*COA* are right angles. *BE* and *CF* are lines. Give a reason for each of the following:

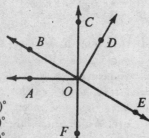

(a) (∠*COD*)° = (∠*BOA*)°
(b) (∠*BOC*)° = (∠*EOF*)°
(c) (∠*AOE*)° = (∠*DOF*)°

[5] In the figure ∠*AYB* and ∠*CXD* are right angles, *AY* = *CX*, and *BX* = *DX* = *CY*. Which of the following is NOT true?

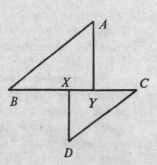

Ⓐ *BX* + *XY* = *BY*
Ⓑ *XY* + *CY* = *CX*
Ⓒ *XY* = *BY* − *BX*
   = *CX* − *CY*
Ⓓ *BX* = *CX*
Ⓔ *BY* = *CX*

(Figure is not drawn to scale.)

The only information given above that is necessary to the solution of the problem is *BX* = *DX* = *CY*. Ⓐ and Ⓑ are conclusions which follow from the definition of "between." If we solve each of Ⓐ and Ⓑ for *XY*, we get statement Ⓒ. We can use part of Ⓒ,

(1)   *BY* − *BX* = *CX* − *CY*,

along with part of the given information,

(2)   *BX* = *CY*,

to get statement Ⓔ,

(3)   *BY* = *CX*,

by the addition of (1) and (2). Since *BX* = *CY*, Choice Ⓓ, *BX* = *CX*, must be incorrect.

By similar arguments we may verify the following:

```
─────────────────────────────
A      B                    C
```

```
─────────────────────────────
X      Y                    Z
```

11-2 If *B* is between *A* and *C*, and *Y* is between *X* and *Z*, then, whenever any two of

(a) *AB* = *XY*,
(b) *BC* = *YZ*, and
(c) *AC* = *XZ*

are true, the third must also be true.

¶ DRILL In the figure at right *AC* = *BD*, *EF* = *GF*, *BF* = *CF*, *EH* = *DI* and *EA* = *DG*. Which of the following are true?

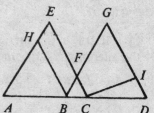

(a) *AB* = *DC*
(b) *EC* = *GB*
(c) *AH* = *GI*

[6] If ray *BD* is the bisector of ∠*ABC* in triangle *ABC*, which of the following is NOT true?

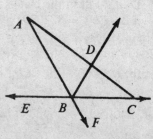

Ⓐ Every point of ray *BD* lies in the interior of ∠*ABC*.   Ⓑ If the measure of ∠*DBC* is 50, then ∠*ABC* is obtuse.   Ⓒ No matter how great the measure of ∠*ABC*, ∠*DBC* is always acute.   Ⓓ The bisector of ∠*ABE* is perpendicular to ray *BD*.   Ⓔ The ray opposite to *BD* bisects ∠*EBF*.

Ray *OX* is the *bisector* of ∠*MON* if and only if *X* is in the interior of ∠*MON* and (∠*MOX*)° = (∠*XON*)°. Answer Ⓐ is incorrect since point *B* does not lie in the interior of ∠*ABC*. Every other point of ray *BD* *does* lie in the interior of the angle—remember that the sides of an angle are rays, not segments, so the interior of an angle of a triangle extends far beyond the side opposite the angle. Ⓑ is true by definition since the measure of

$\angle ABC$ must be 100 if ray BD is the bisector. An *obtuse* angle is any angle with a measure between 90 and 180 An *acute* angle is an angle with measure between 0 and 90. Do you see that, since $\angle ABC$ could never have a measure even as great as 180, an angle with half this measure must always be less than 90? Thus Ⓒ is true.

If a and b are the measures of the angles of a linear pair, then $\frac{1}{2}a$ and $\frac{1}{2}b$ must be the measures of the angles formed when the angles of the linear pair are bisected. But $a + b = 180$ since the angles of a linear pair are supplementary, and this means

$$\frac{1}{2}(a + b) = \frac{1}{2}a + \frac{1}{2}b = 90.$$

Thus the measure of the angle formed by the bisectors of a linear pair must be 90 and Ⓓ must be true.

Answer Ⓔ is a consequence of the vertical angle theorem. Sketch in the ray opposite to BD and call it *BX*. By the vertical angle theorem,

(1) $(\angle FBX)° = (\angle ABD)°$

and

(2) $(\angle EBX)° = (\angle CBD)°.$

The definition of angle bisector assures us that

(3) $(\angle ABD)° = (\angle CBD)°,$

so we can conclude by substitution that:

(4) $(\angle FBX)° = (\angle EBX)°.$

Statement (4) indicates that ray BX satisfies the requirements for an angle bisector.

¶ DRILL If, in the figure at the upper right, ray OC bisects $\angle BOD$ and $(\angle AOB)° = (\angle DOE)°$, give a reason to support each of the following:

(a) $(\angle BOC)° = (\angle COD)°$
(b) $(\angle AOB)° + (\angle BOC)°$
$= (\angle AOC)°$
(c) $(\angle COD)° + (\angle DOE)°$
$= (\angle COE)°$
(d) $(\angle AOB)° + (\angle BOC)°$
$= (\angle COE)°$
(e) $(\angle AOC)° = (\angle COE)°$

WHAT YOU SHOULD KNOW

KEY CONCEPTS

1. Two angles are *adjacent* if they share a common side and their interiors do not intersect.
2. If two angles share a common side and their other sides form a line, then the angles are *supplementary* and the sum of their degree measures is 180.
3. Two angles are *supplementary* if and only if the sum of their degree measures is 180.
4. Perpendicular lines form right angles.
5. Two angles are *vertical* angles if their sides form two pairs of opposite rays.
6. Vertical angles are congruent.
7. Supplements of congruent angles are congruent.
8. Two angles are *complementary* if the sum of their degree measures is 90.
9. Complements of congruent angles are congruent.
10. Ray BD bisects $\angle ABC$ if and only if the degree measures of $\angle ABD$ and $\angle CBD$ are equal and each is half the measure of $\angle ABC$.

KEY THEOREMS

1. If D is in the interior of $\angle ABC$ and W is in the interior of $\angle XYZ$, then, when any two of

   (a) $(\angle ABC)° = (\angle XYZ)°,$
   (b) $(\angle ABD)° = (\angle XYW)°,$ and
   (c) $(\angle DBC)° = (\angle WYZ)°$

are true, the third must also be true.

2. If B is between A and C, and Y is between X and Z, then, whenever any two of

   (a) $AB = XY,$
   (b) $BC = YZ,$ and
   (c) $AC = XZ$

are true, the third must also be true.

TEST-TAKING STRATEGIES

- Whenever possible, use your knowledge of the symbols commonly used in geometry—$\angle ABC$, $\triangle ABC$, $(\angle ABC)°$, etc.—to express in more concise form the information about angles given in the question.
- Do not confuse "supplementary" with "complementary." If a question uses one of these terms, one of the distractors will almost always be the result of erroneously substituting the other term.

- Questions testing the ideas of angle measure reviewed in this chapter usually involve a figure with many different angles, some of whose measures are given. The question generally asks for one of the missing angles. Look for vertical angles first, then find supplementary or complementary angles. Having done so, you will almost always have found the measure of the missing angle.
- Though angles sharing a common side may be supplementary (or complementary), keep in mind that angles do not have to share a common side to be supplementary (or complementary).

ANSWERS

[1] Ⓐ
   DRILL:
   (a) No. Definition of triangle.
   (b) Yes. Definition of angle.
   (c) No. Definition of angle measure.
   (d) There is none. Definition of complement.
   (e) Yes. Definition of angle measure.

[2] Ⓒ
   DRILL:
   (a) *AEC*   (b) *BED*
   (c) *AEC*   (d) *BED*
   (e) *CED*

[3] Ⓑ
   DRILL:
   (a) ∠*COA* and ∠*COE,* ∠*BOA* and ∠*BOE.*
   (b) 60

[4] Ⓐ
   DRILL:
   (a) Both are complements of ∠*BOC.*
   (b) Both are supplements of ∠*COE,* or vertical angles are ≅.
   (c) They are supplements of ∠*AOB* and ∠*COD,* respectively, and $(\angle AOB)° = (\angle COD)°$.

[5] Ⓓ
   DRILL:
   All of (a), (b) and (c) are true.

[6] Ⓐ
   DRILL:
   (a) Definition of angle bisector.
   (b) Postulate 6.
   (c) Postulate 6.
   (d) Substitution of Given and step (a) in step (c).
   (e) Substitution of step (b) in step (d).

12.　Triangles

Key Terms

triangle　a three-sided, closed figure whose sides are line segments.

isosceles triangle　a triangle with two sides of equal length.

equilateral triangle　a triangle whose three sides are of equal length.

median of a triangle　a segment connecting a vertex of the triangle to the midpoint of the opposite side.

altitude of a triangle　a segment that contains the vertex of one angle of the triangle and is perpendicular to the opposite side

IDENTIFYING CONGRUENT TRIANGLES BY *CPCTC*, *SAS*, *ASA*, AND *SSS*

[1] If $\triangle ABC \cong \triangle PQR$ and $\triangle PQR \cong \triangle XYZ$, then which of the following is true?

Ⓐ **Every side of $\triangle ABC$ has the same length as every side of $\triangle XYZ$.** Ⓑ **There is at least one angle of $\triangle ABC$ for which no angle of $\triangle XYZ$ has the same measure.** Ⓒ **$\triangle ABC \cong \triangle XYZ$.** Ⓓ **All three triangles must lie in the same plane.** Ⓔ **Each of the three triangles must have a right angle.**

When we say two triangles are *congruent* we are expressing the intuitive idea that they have the same shape and size, or, in other words, that one of them can be fitted over the other in such a way that all of the sides and angles match exactly. To carry out this matching operation we must, of course, position the vertices so that *they* coincide and the sides will then coincide by Postulate 1. What we mean by a congruence between triangles, then, is a particular correspondence between the vertices of the triangles for which all of the matching ("corresponding") pairs of sides are equal in length and the corresponding pairs of angles have the same measure. As a shorthand notation to indicate which vertices we want to correspond to each other in a given congruence, we will write the letters for the vertices in corresponding order. Thus if $\triangle ABC \cong \triangle XYZ$, we will assume that A corresponds to X, B to Y, and C to Z. We summarize all this in the following definition of congruent triangles, which we will refer to with the letters *CP*.

Definition of congruent triangles (*CPCTC* or simply *CP*):

$\triangle ABC \cong \triangle XYZ$ if and only if $(\angle A)° = (\angle X)°$, $(\angle B)° = (\angle Y)°$, $(\angle C)° = (\angle Z)°$, $AB = XY$, $BC = YZ$ and $AC = XZ$.

Do you see that answer Ⓐ would mean that the lengths of all six sides of the two triangles would be the same number? To make this a true statement strike out the second "every," replace it with "the" and add "to which it corresponds" to the end of the sentence. Ⓑ directly contradicts *CP* while Ⓒ follows directly from *CP*.

The definition does not restrict congruences to triangles in the same plane so Ⓓ is false. Finally, though the given information would be true if each were a right triangle, it can also be true if none is.

¶ DRILL If $\triangle ABC \cong \triangle XYZ$ and $\triangle ABC$ has all of its sides of the same length (is "equilateral") and all of its angles of the same measure (is "equiangular"), how many correspondences between the vertices of $\triangle ABC$ and $\triangle XYZ$ are congruences?

[2] In which of the following can we NOT conclude that $\triangle ABC \cong \triangle XYZ$ from the information given?

Ⓐ **All pairs of corresponding sides have the same lengths and all pairs of corresponding angles have the same measures.** Ⓑ **$AB = XY$, $BC = YZ$ and $\angle B$ and $\angle Y$ have the same measure.** Ⓒ **$AB = XY$, $BC = YZ$ and $AC = XZ$.** Ⓓ **The measure of $\angle A$ equals that of $\angle X$ and of $\angle B$ equals that of $\angle Y$, $AB = XY$.** Ⓔ **All pairs of corresponding angles have the same measures.**

Start with a given angle, $\angle A$, and then mark off a pair of segments, AB and AC, on the sides of the angle as at right.

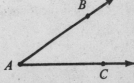

How many different segments can you draw that will complete a triangle which has the three parts mentioned? Do you see that only one such segment, BC, is

101

possible? Thus the given information uniquely determines the size and shape of a triangle. (When two sides of a triangle lie on the sides of an angle, as in this case, we say the sides "include" the angle.) The experiment above encourages us to make the following agreement:

Postulate 8 (*SAS*) If two sides and their included angle of one triangle are equal in length or measure to the corresponding parts of a second triangle, the two triangles are congruent.

Now start with a given segment *AB* and draw a pair of angles with vertices at *A* and *B*.

Do you see that the given information defines exactly one point, *C,* which can be the third vertex of a triangle having the given parts? (In such a case we say that ∠*A* and ∠*B* "include" segment *AB*.) We agree as follows:

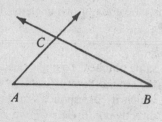

Postulate 9 (*ASA*) If two angles and their included side of one triangle are equal in measure or length to the corresponding parts of a second triangle, then the two triangles are congruent.

As a final experiment, take three sticks; tape them together at their ends, two sticks to a joint. The wooden triangle formed is "rigid" in a plane, meaning that it cannot be distorted into a different triangle in the same plane having the same dimensions. We agree then that the size and shape of a triangle are fixed when the lengths of the sides are fixed.

Postulate 10 (*SSS*) If all three sides of one triangle are equal in length to the corresponding sides of a second triangle, then the two triangles are congruent.

In the multiple-choice question:

Ⓐ is true by the definition of congruent triangles,
Ⓑ is true by *SAS,*
Ⓒ is true by *SSS,*
Ⓓ is true by *ASA,*
Ⓔ is false as shown by the diagram below, in which the corresponding angles are all congruent but the triangles are not.

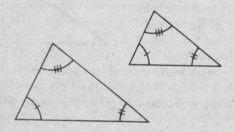

¶ DRILL In each of the following draw the figure based on the information given and indicate which of the postulates above (if any) allows you to conclude that the triangles asked for are congruent:

(a) Segments *AB* and *CD* intersect at *M,* their common midpoint. Is △*AMC* ≅ △*BMD*?

(b) *A, B, C,* and *D* are four coplanar points such that *B* and *D* lie on different sides of line *AC, BC = AD,* and *DC = BA.* Is △*ADC* ≅ △*CBA*? Will you arrive at the same answer if the points are not coplanar?

(c) Segment *AC* is perpendicular to segment *BD* with *C* being the point of intersection, (∠*CAD*)° = (∠*CAB*)°. Is △*ABC* ≅ △*ADC*?

(d) *C* and *D* lie on the same side of line *AB,* (∠*C*)° = (∠*D*)°, *CA = DB.* Is △*ACB* ≅ △*BDA*?

[3] *E* is the midpoint of both segments *AB* and *CD,* which are also perpendicular to each other. We can prove that *AD = BC.* If each of the following answers is a step in this proof, which of these could be left out with the remaining answers still constituting a proof?

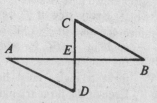

Ⓐ *AE = BE* and *CE = DE* by definition of midpoint.   Ⓑ ∠*CEB* and ∠*DEA* are right angles by definition of perpendicular.   Ⓒ ∠*CEB* and ∠*DEA* have the same measure since vertical angles are equal in measure.   Ⓓ △*AED* ≅ △*BEC* by Side-Angle-Side.   Ⓔ *AD = BC* by definition of congruent triangles.

In your geometry course you learned how to demonstrate the validity of various geometric statements in a formal way. The process is similar to one we have already reviewed in elementary algebra, though many students find geometric proofs easier to formulate since they can more readily visualize the necessary relationships from geometric diagrams.

In a formal proof we attempt to gather and organize logical evidence to support the statement we hope to justify. Each statement of evidence we set down must in turn be supported by some previously established theorem, definition or postulate. The hypothesis (or "if" part) of this theorem, definition or postulate must name a category into which some earlier step of the proof fits. For example, statement Ⓓ satisfies the hypothesis of the definition of congruent triangles used to support step Ⓔ. The conclusion (or "then" part) provides a category into which the statement of the same step must fit. For example, the conclusion of the reason in Ⓔ is that all pairs of corresponding parts of congruent triangles are equal in measure or length, while the statement in Ⓔ is that a pair of corresponding sides have the same length.

Merely assembling a collection of justified statements does not constitute proving a theorem. Each of these must in some way help to support the hypothesis of the final reason, even if only indirectly. For example, choice Ⓐ is used to help justify Ⓓ and, therefore, indirectly supports Ⓔ since Ⓓ supports Ⓔ. Accordingly, any step (except the final one) which does not justify a later step is unnecessary to the proof. Note that Ⓑ, though valid and correctly justified, does not contribute to any later step and can be omitted.

As a further example of how steps are interrelated, suppose we had inserted a step Ⓑ between Ⓑ and Ⓒ which stated "∠CEB and ∠DEA are equal in measure since all right angles have the same measure, 90." Do you see that we could then omit step Ⓒ?

¶ DRILL In the following proof, fill in the reasons for the statements and then omit unnecessary steps.

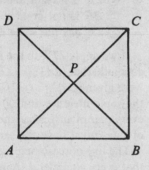

Given: *ABCD* is a square (meaning that all of its angles are right angles and all sides are the same length).

PROOF △*ADP* ≅ △*BCP*.

(a) (∠*DAB*)° = (∠*CBA*)° = (∠*ADC*)°
                 = (∠*BCD*)° = 90   ____
(b) *AD* ⊥ *DC*, *BC* ⊥ *CD*   ____
(c) △*ADC* is a right triangle   ____
(d) *AD* = *BC*   ____
(e) *AB* = *DC*   ____
(f) *AD* = *DC*   ____
(g) △*DAB* ≅ △*CBA*   ____
(h) (∠*CAB*)° = (∠*DBA*)°   ____
(i) (∠*CBD*)° = (∠*DAC*)°   ____
(j) (∠*DPA*)° = (∠*CPB*)°   ____
(k) (∠*ADC*)° = (∠*BCD*)°   ____
(l) *DC* = *DC*   ____
(m) △*ADC* ≅ △*BCD*   ____
(n) (∠*BDC*)° = (∠*ACD*)°   ____
(o) (∠*ADB*)° = (∠*BCA*)°   ____
(p) △*ADP* ≅ △*BCP*   ____

IDENTIFYING ISOSCELES TRIANGLES

[4] If, in the accompanying figure, *AD* ⊥ *DC*, *AD* ⊥ *BD* and *DC* = *BD*, which of the following statements is NOT necessarily true?
Ⓐ ∠*DBC* and ∠*DCB* are equal in measure.
Ⓑ △*ADB* ≅ △*ADC*. Ⓒ *AB* = *AC*. Ⓓ ∠*ABC* and ∠*ACB* are equal in measure. Ⓔ ∠*BAC* and ∠*BDC* have the same measure.

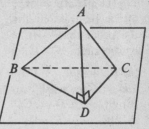

A triangle is *isosceles* if and only if it has a pair of sides of equal length.

12-1 (*ITT*) Two sides of a triangle have the same length if and only if the angles opposite these sides have the same measure.

We will refer to this as the Isosceles Triangle Theorem because it is a statement that is true of isosceles triangles, even though it never mentions the word *isosceles*.

To verify it, we use the figure at right, a triangle to which we have added a segment from one vertex, *A*, to the midpoint, *M*, of the opposite side. We know such a segment (called a *median* of the triangle) exists since the two points *A* and *M* determine a line by Postulate 1.

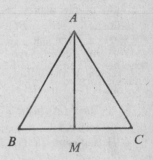

From the definition of midpoint we conclude that *BM* = *CM*. Of course, *AM* = *AM*. If we were given that *AB* = *AC*, do you see that △*ABM* ≅ △*ACM* by *SSS* and therefore (∠*B*)° = (∠*C*)° by *CP*? We did not really need segment *AM* to prove this part of the theorem. Instead, we could have noted that △*ABC* was congruent to its mirror-image, △*ACB*, by *SAS* (∠*BAC* is the included angle of both triangles) and therefore (∠*B*)° = (∠*C*)° by *CP*. Here we have used a correspondence between the vertices of a triangle and itself that was a congruence.

Suppose our given information had not been *AB* = *AC*, but (∠*B*)° = (∠*C*)°. Do you see that the mirror-image approach gives us △*ABC* ≅ △*ACB* by *ASA*? (*BC* is the included segment in both triangles.) Consequently *AB* = *AC* by *CP*.

In the multiple-choice question answer Ⓐ is true by *ITT*, Ⓑ is true by *SAS*, Ⓒ is true by *CP*, Ⓓ follows from *ITT*, and Ⓔ, though possible, is not necessarily true.

¶ DRILL Given that BC = ED and $AB = AE$, fill in the reasons for the proof that $\triangle ACD$ is isosceles:

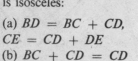

(a) $BD = BC + CD$, $CE = CD + DE$

(b) $BC + CD = CD + DE$

(c) $BD = CE$

(d) $(\angle B)° = (\angle E)°$

(e) $\triangle ABD \cong \triangle AEC$

(f) $(\angle ACD)° = (\angle ADC)°$

(g) $AC = AD$

(h) $\triangle ACD$ is isosceles

(i) Is it possible to justify $AD = AC$ by applying *ITT* to $(\angle B)° = (\angle E)°$?

IDENTIFYING ALTITUDES

[5] Given that C lies in plane E, D lies in plane F, the intersection of the planes is line AB, $AC = BC$, $AD = BD$ and ray DX bisects $\angle ADB$. Which of the following is (are) true?

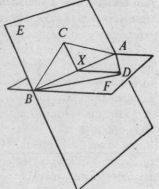

I Ray CX bisects $\angle ACB$.

II Segment CX is a median of $\triangle ACB$.

III Segment CX is an altitude of $\triangle ACB$.

Ⓐ All of I, II and III   Ⓑ I and II only   Ⓒ II and III only   Ⓓ I only   Ⓔ II only

We have already defined "median" and "angle bisector." In order to be an *altitude* segment CX must be perpendicular to side AB. In $\triangle ADB$ we conclude that $(\angle ADX)° = (\angle BDX)°$ by the definition of angle bisector so $\triangle ADX \cong \triangle BDX$ by *SAS* and $AX = BX$ by *CP*. It follows that $\triangle AXC$ is congruent to $\triangle BXC$ by *SSS*. This means $\angle ACX$ and $\angle BCX$ must have the same measure so ray CX is the bisector of $\angle ACB$. We have already shown $AX = BX$ so X is the midpoint of segment AB and thus segment CX is a median of $\triangle ACB$.

Because $\angle AXC$ and $\angle BXC$ are a linear pair the sum of their measures is 180. But $(\angle AXC)° = (\angle BXC)°$ since they are corresponding parts of the congruent triangles AXC and BXC. We conclude that each has a measure of 90 and consequently segment CX is an altitude.

Therefore CX is a median, an altitude and an angle bisector.

¶ DRILL

(a) If a segment is a median and an angle bisector of a triangle, must it also be an altitude?

(b) If it is an altitude and an angle bisector, must it also be a median?

(c) If it is an altitude and a median, must it be an angle bisector?

IDENTIFYING EQUILATERAL TRIANGLES

[6] If $\triangle ABC$ lies in plane E, $AC = BC$ and the measures of $\angle A$ and $\angle C$ are the same, which of the following is NOT true?

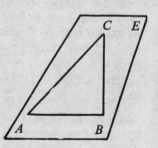

Ⓐ $\triangle ABC$ is equilateral.

Ⓑ $\triangle ABC$ is equiangular.

Ⓒ $\angle B$ is a right angle.

Ⓓ AC is not greater than AB.

Ⓔ $\angle A$ has the same measure as $\angle B$.

If we apply *ITT* to the statement $AC = BC$ we can conclude that $(\angle A)° = (\angle B)°$, so answer Ⓔ is true. We were given $(\angle A)° = (\angle C)°$; hence all of the angles have the same measure and Ⓑ is true. We now know that every pair of angles has the same measure so every pair of sides must have the same length by *ITT*.

The line of reasoning used above allows us to deduce that every equilateral triangle is equiangular and every equiangular triangle is equilateral.

The process of verification of Ⓐ and Ⓑ has also demonstrated the truth of Ⓓ and Ⓔ. As for Ⓒ, if $\angle B$ is a right angle, and, as we have just seen, it has the same measure as $\angle A$, then we have two perpendiculars from point C to line AB. How many should there be? Why? (We will review the number of perpendiculars from a point to a line in a later section of this chapter. From a point to a line, there is exactly one perpendicular.)

¶ DRILL

(a) If in the figure the measure of $\angle AVE$ is $2x$ and all three triangles are equilateral, find the measures of all other angles.

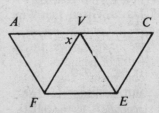

(b) Could we use an argument based on this figure and given information to prove that the sum of the measures of the angles of an equilateral triangle is 180? What assumption, not necessarily true, have we made which if absent would make the proof fallacious?

WORKING WITH TRIANGLES THAT ARE PARTS OF OTHER FIGURES

[7] Given that quadrilateral *MNOP* lies in plane *E*, *MN = PO*, *MP = NO* and *PX = NY*. Which of the following must be true?

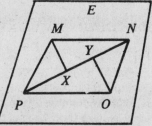

(A) *MX = OY*
(B) ∠*PMN* is a right angle (C) Ray *PN* bisects ∠*MPO* (D) Segment *MX* is perpendicular to segment *OY* (E) ∠*PMN* is obtuse

---

TEST-TAKING TIP.
We have already reviewed the useful technique of proving two segments to be of equal length, or two angles of equal measure, by demonstrating them to be corresponding parts of congruent triangles. Sometimes the triangles we need to use are parts of more complicated figures. When this happens we often must wander through a maze of seemingly unrelated relationships before we get to the one(s) we want.

For example, △*MPN* ≅ △*NOP* by *SSS* and this makes ∠*MPN* and ∠*ONP* corresponding parts of congruent triangles. But these angles are also corresponding parts of △*PMX* and △*NOY*. Thus △*PMX* ≅ △*NOY* by *SAS* and *MX = OY* by *CP*.

TEST-TAKING TIP.
If you chose any answer but (A), you were probably misled by some assumption you made from the way the figure looks. A figure may suggest certain promising relationships to explore further, but if these have not been given or cannot be established through the deductive process, you may not assume them to be true.

¶ DRILL Given that *BE = AD* and *BC = AC*, we can prove three pairs of triangles to be congruent. List them and indicate the congruence postulate which is their justification.

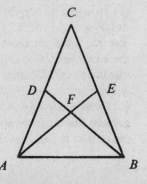

WORKING WITH PERPENDICULAR BISECTORS

[8] If L_1 and L_2 are the perpendicular bisectors of segments *XY* and *YZ*, which of the following must be true?

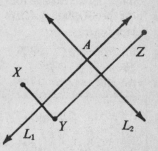

(A) *AX = AY = AZ*
(B) *AX > AZ* (C) *A*, *X* and *Z* are collinear
(D) L_1 and L_2 lie in the plane determined by *X*, *Y* and *Z* (E) L_1 contains a median of △*XYZ*

A line *L* is the *perpendicular bisector* of a segment *AB* if and only if line *L* is perpendicular to and contains the midpoint of segment *AB*. We can use congruent triangles to prove two important statements about perpendicular bisectors.

12-2 If *L* is the perpendicular bisector of segment *AB* and *X* is a point of *L*, then *X* is equidistant from *A* and *B*.

12-3 If *X* is equidistant from points *A* and *B*, then *X* lies on the perpendicular bisector of segment *AB*.

PROOF of 12-2 In the figure below, no matter what point *X* is of line *L*, the following must hold:

(1) *XM = XM*,
(2) ∠*XMA* and ∠*XMB* are right angles,
(3) *AM = BM*,
(4) △*XMA* ≅ △*XMB* (by *SAS*), and
(5) *XB = XA* (by *CP*).

PROOF of 12-3 If in the figure above we know only that *XA = XB* and *MA = MB*, we can conclude that △*XMA* ≅ △*XMB* by *SSS* (*XM = XM*, of course). Thus, no matter where *X* is in the plane, and as long as *XB = XA*, we know that ∠*XMA* and ∠*XMB* must be right angles since they are supplementary and equal in measure. Therefore the line that contains *X* and *M* is the perpendicular bisector of segment *AB*. Can there be more than one perpendicular bisector of *AB*? In other words, can there be more than one line passing through *M* and perpendicular to *L*? The answer is "no" if we limit the figure to a given plane; it is "yes" if we do not specify a plane figure. To visualize the latter case, ask yourself how many lines you can draw on the floor which will intersect the line formed by the joining of two walls. Thus L_1 and L_2 do not have to lie in plane XYZ and Ⓓ is false. We will review this further in the next section.

In the figure segments XY and YZ appear to be perpendicular but the information given does not require this.

TEST-TAKING TIP.

Remember that you cannot assume congruence, perpendicularity or parallelism from the way a figure is drawn. If, however, line segments *look* congruent, parallel or perpendicular, they may be so. Look for corroborating information that may suggest a way of solving the problem.

If XY and YZ were perpendicular, we would be able to prove that (C) is true.

We summarize 12-2 and 12-3 in the following statement: the perpendicular bisector of a segment is the set of all points of a plane that are equidistant from the endpoints of the segment.

Thus $AX = AY = AZ$.

¶ DRILL Given that L_1, L_2 and L_3 are three of the perpendicular bisectors of segment AB, $AZ = 4$, $AY = 3$ and $XB = 5$. Find BZ, BY and AX.

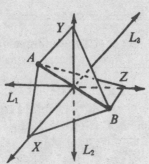

WORKING WITH PERPENDICULAR LINES

[9] If in the figure line L_2 intersects line L_1 at D, L_4 at C, and L_3 at B, and if all of L_1, L_3, and L_4 intersect at A, which of the following pairs of angles can BOTH be right angles?

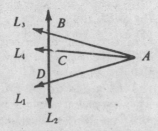

(Figure is not drawn to scale.)

Ⓐ $\angle BAD$ and $\angle CAD$ Ⓑ $\angle ACD$ and $\angle ABD$
Ⓒ $\angle CAD$ and $\angle CDA$ Ⓓ $\angle BAD$ and $\angle ABD$
Ⓔ $\angle BAD$ and $\angle ACD$

The figure above must be contained in the plane determined by L_2 and A since all of points B, C and D lie on L_2.

If (choice Ⓐ) $\angle CAD$ and $\angle BAD$ were both right angles, we would have two angles on the same side of line L_1 which have the same measure, 90, the same vertex, A, and a common side in L_1, ray AD. This contradicts Postulate 5. By a similar argument we can deduce the following:

12-4 Given point P on line L and in plane E, there is one and only one line in plane E which is perpendicular to L and contains P.

Suppose point P in 12-4 had not been a point of line L but was some other point of plane E. We argue as follows:

If two lines L_1 and L_2 contain P and are perpendicular to L, we may mark off a segment on line L_2 opposite to PN and of the same length to get $\triangle PNM \cong \triangle P'NM$ by *SAS*. The figure summarizes this. Then $(\angle PMN)° = (\angle P'MN)° = 90$ and this contradicts 12-4 by giving us lines $P'M$ and PM both perpendicular to L at M.

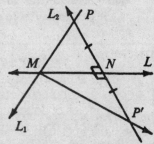

12-5 Given a point P not on line L, then there is one and only one line in the plane determined by P and L which contains P and is perpendicular to L.

If (choice Ⓑ) $\angle ACD$ and $\angle ABD$ were both right angles, then two lines, L_3 and L_4, would each be perpendicular to L_2.

If (choice Ⓒ) $\angle CAD$ and $\angle CDA$ were right angles, then L_4 and L_2 would be parallel since both are perpendicular to L_1.

Choice Ⓓ creates the same contradiction as Ⓒ. Choice Ⓔ can be true, though it does not look true since the figure is not drawn to scale.

¶ DRILL

(a) In $\triangle ABC$ at the beginning of this section may both $\angle B$ and $\angle C$ be right angles? Why?
(b) If any $\angle PMX$ and $\angle QMX$ are both right angles, what must be true of P and Q?
(c) How many lines are there in *space* that contain a point P and are perpendicular to a line L if P is not on L?

IDENTIFYING CONGRUENT TRIANGLES BY *AAS* AND *HL*

[10] If ∠*CDB* and ∠*ABD* have the same measure, and if ∠*DCB* and ∠*BAD* are right angles, then:

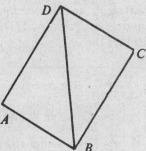

Ⓐ All points of the figure must lie in the same plane
Ⓑ The measure of ∠*DBC* is twice the measure of ∠*ADB*
Ⓒ *AD* = *DC*   Ⓓ ∠*ADB* and ∠*CDB* have the same measure   Ⓔ *AB* = *DC*

In this and the next section we will add to our list of congruence "postulates" for triangles. In your geometry course you undoubtedly learned them after other ideas such as inequalities in triangles or parallelism of lines had been developed and these "postulates" could be proved as theorems. We include them in this chapter because we are concentrating on triangle congruence. As a matter of fact, in an honors course you may have postulated only *SAS* and proved all four of the others (*ASA*, *SSS*, *AAS*, and *HL*). We omitted the proofs of *ASA* and *SSS* because of their difficulty.

Postulate 11 (*AAS*) In a given triangle if a pair of angles and one of their nonincluded sides have the same measures or length as the corresponding parts of a second triangle, the two triangles are congruent.

By *AAS* we can conclude △*DCB* ≅ △*BAD* and answer Ⓔ is correct. The figure may not at first appear to suggest this, but if you make a scale drawing and fold the paper along line *DB*, you should be able to visualize how perspective foreshortens △*DAB* to give the appearance shown. Imagine that the figure is a pyramid with points *A, B* and *C* in its base and point *D* above the base.

¶ **Drill** In a later chapter we will prove that the sum of the measures of the angles of a triangle is 180. How will this statement allow us to prove *AAS*?

[11] If in △*ADC* we know that ∠*ADC* is a right angle, with *AB* = *AC*, then:

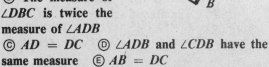

Ⓐ *AB* > *AC*
Ⓑ ∠*BAD* > ∠*DAC*
Ⓒ *BD* < *DC*
Ⓓ *AC* = *BD*
Ⓔ △*ABD* ≅ △*ACD*

Postulate 12 (*HL*) If the hypotenuse and one leg of a given right triangle have the same lengths as the corresponding parts of a second right triangle, then the two triangles are congruent.

In a right triangle the *hypotenuse* is the side opposite the right angle. The other two sides are called *legs*. From the figure, ∠*ADC* may not appear to be a right angle unless you realize that plane *E* is not the plane of the page.

Answer Ⓔ, △*ABD* ≅ △*ACD*, is correct by *HL* since the triangles are right triangles and they have congruent hypotenuses (*AB* = *AC*) and a pair of congruent legs (*AD* = *AD*).

¶ **Drill** In the figure (∠*ADC*)° = (∠*ACD*)°, (∠*ABD*)° = (∠*ABC*)° = 90. Fill in the reasons for each of the following:

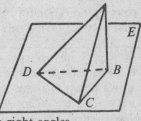

(a) *AD* = *AC*
(b) ∠*ABD* and ∠*ABC* are right angles
(c) △*ABD* and △*ABC* are right triangles
(d) *AB* = *AB*
(e) △*ABD* ≅ △*ABC*
(f) *DB* = *BC*
(g) (∠*BCD*)° = (∠*BDC*)°

WHAT YOU SHOULD KNOW

> KEY CONCEPTS

Handling Congruence

1. Two triangles are *congruent* if and only if all six pairs of corresponding sides and angles are congruent (abbreviated: *CPCTC*).

2. Two triangles are *congruent* if:
    a. two pairs of corresponding sides and their included angles are congruent (*SAS*),
    b. two pairs of corresponding angles and their included sides are congruent (*ASA*), *or*
    c. all pairs of corresponding sides are congruent (*SSS*).

3. Two triangles are *congruent* if:
    a. two pairs of angles and a pair of corresponding sides *not* included in the angles are congruent (*AAS*), *or*
    b. the triangles are right triangles and the hypotenuses and a pair of corresponding legs are congruent (*HL*).

4. If two sides of a triangle are congruent, the triangle is isosceles.
5. If two sides of a triangle are congruent, the angles opposite the sides are congruent (*ITT*).
6. If two angles of a triangle are congruent, the sides opposite the angles are congruent.

Handling Medians and Perpendicular Bisectors

1. The median to the base of an isosceles triangle bisects the vertex angle and is perpendicular to the base.
2. A line is the perpendicular bisector of a segment if it is perpendicular to the segment and contains its midpoint.
3. The perpendicular bisector of a segment is the set of all points equidistant from the endpoints of the segment. In a plane the perpendicular bisector is a line. In space the perpendicular bisector is a plane.
4. If two points of a line are each equidistant from the endpoints of a segment, the line is the perpendicular bisector of the segment.

Handling Perpendicular Lines

1. If point P is on line L in plane E, there is exactly one line in plane E that is perpendicular to L at P.
2. If a point P is *not* on line L and both are in plane E, there is exactly one line in plane E that is perpendicular to L and contains P.

```
KEY THEOREM
```

Two sides of a triangle have the same length if and only if the angles opposite these sides have the same measure. (Isosceles Triangle Theorem)

```
TEST-TAKING STRATEGIES
```

• If line segments appear to be congruent, parallel, or perpendicular in a given diagram, look for information that may corroborate this possibility and thereby suggest a solution to a triangle problem.
• When it is given that two sides or angles of a triangle are congruent, the Isosceles Triangle Theorem is almost always needed to answer the question. Master this theorem and its application.

ANSWERS

[1] Ⓒ
DRILL:
6

[2] Ⓔ
DRILL:
(a) *SAS.*
(b) *SSS,* yes.
(c) *ASA.*
(d) No, given information is *SSA.*

[3] Ⓑ
DRILL:
(a) Definition of right angle.
(b) Definition of perpendicular.
(c) Definition of right triangle.
(d)–(f) Definition of square.
(g) *SAS.*
(h) *CP.*
(i) Postulate 6.
(j) Vertical angles.
(k) All right angles are equal in measure.
(l) Identity.
(m) *SAS.*
(n) *CP.*
(o) Postulate 6.
(p) *ASA.*
Steps (b), (c), (f). (j), and (k) can be omitted.

[4] Ⓔ
DRILL:
(a) Definition of between.
(b) Addition of CD to both sides of given equation.
(c) Substitution.
(d) *ITT.*
(e) *SAS.*
(f) *CP.*
(g) Either *ITT* or *CP.*
(h) Definition of isosceles.
(i) No, these are parts of different triangles

[5] Ⓐ
DRILL:
(a) Yes (the proof is indirect).   (b) Yes.
(c) Yes.

[6] Ⓒ
DRILL:
(a) All triangles are congruent by *SSS* and all pairs of angles are congruent by *CP* so each acute angle has measure x. If A, V and C are *collinear,* then $3x = 180$ and $x = 60$. Thus the acute angles are 60° and the obtuse are 120°.
(b) Not without some assumption about parallels; the assumption made above is that A, V and C are collinear when the triangles are equilateral.

[7] Ⓐ
DRILL:
$\triangle DAB \cong \triangle EBA$ by *SAS,* $\triangle CEA \cong \triangle CDB$ by
SSS or *SAS,* $\triangle DFA \cong \triangle EFB$ by *ASA.*

[8] Ⓐ
DRILL:
$BZ = 4, BY = 3, AX = 5.$

[9] Ⓔ
DRILL:
(a) No, contradicts the uniqueness of perpendicu-
    lars from a point to a line. 12-5
(b) Lie on same line.
(c) One.

[10] Ⓔ
DRILL:
It will make the third pair of angles also equal in
measure and fulfill *ASA.*

[11] Ⓔ
DRILL:
(a) *ITT.*
(b) Definition of right angle.
(c) Definition of right triangle.
(d) Identity.
(e) *HL.*
(f) *CP.*
(g) *ITT.*

13.   Inequalities in Triangles

Key Term

exterior angle   an angle that forms a linear pair with any angle of the triangle.

IDENTIFYING EXTERIOR ANGLES

[1] **Each of the answers below is a true statement. Which of them is NOT a conclusion based on the following argument?**

D is the midpoint of segment *AC*. *E* is the point on ray *BE* for which *BD* = *DE*. ∠*ADB* has the same measure as ∠*CDE* since they are vertical angles. △*ADB* ≅ △*CDE*.

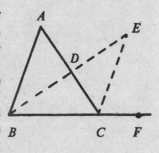

Ⓐ *AB* = *CE*   Ⓑ ∠*A* and ∠*DCE* have the same measure.   Ⓒ The measure of ∠*ACF* equals the sum of the measures of ∠*BAC* and ∠*ECF*.   Ⓓ ∠*ACF* > ∠*BAC*   Ⓔ The measure of ∠*ACF* equals the sum of the measures of ∠*A* and ∠*ABC*.

An angle is an *exterior* angle of a triangle if and only if it forms a linear pair with one of the angles of the triangle. In the figure above, ∠*ACF* is an exterior angle of △*ABC* since it forms a linear pair with ∠*ACB*. The two angles of the triangle which are not adjacent to a given exterior angle are called its *remote interior angles*. For example, ∠*BAC* and ∠*ABC* are remote interior angles of ∠*ACF*.

You may recall proving in your geometry course that the measure of any exterior angle of a triangle equals the sum of the measures of its remote interior angles. This is the statement of answer Ⓔ. But the verification of this theorem is not possible without an assumption about parallel lines which we will postpone until the next chapter. Answer Ⓔ, though true, does *not* follow from the given argument. The argument given, coupled with answers Ⓑ, Ⓒ and Ⓓ in sequential order, provides the basis for a different, but equally valuable, theorem on geometric inequalities.

> **13-1** An exterior angle of a triangle is greater than either of its remote interior angles.

When we say "∠*A* is greater than ∠*B*, or ∠*A* > ∠*B*," we mean (∠*A*)° > (∠*B*)°.

¶ DRILL

(a) Name three other exterior angles and their corresponding triangles.
(b) If one angle of a triangle is a right angle, what conclusion can you draw about the other two based on 13-1?
(c) If *BC* = *DB*, why is ∠*AEB* > ∠*BDC*?

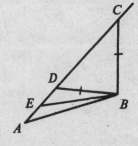

WORKING WITH SEGMENTS OF UNEQUAL LENGTH

[2] **If the angles have measures as indicated, which is the longest segment in the drawing?**

Ⓐ *BC*   Ⓑ *AB*
Ⓒ *AC*   Ⓓ Both *BC* and *AC* since *BC* = *AC*   Ⓔ Cannot be determined

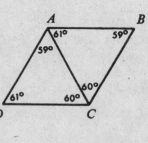

In a triangle, if two sides are not congruent, then the angles opposite them are not congruent and the greater angle is opposite the longer side. Furthermore, if two angles are not congruent, the longer side is opposite the greater angle.

110

13-2 In a $\triangle XYZ$, $XY > YZ$ if and only if $\angle Z > \angle X$.

In applying this theorem, be sure to realize it relates to parts of *one* triangle. In two different triangles, a shorter segment may be opposite a greater angle:

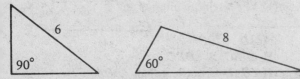

When two triangles share a common side, as in the multiple-choice question, comparing other parts with the common side may help you to determine the longest (or shortest) side in the figure.

If we apply 13-2 to the question we see that AC is the longest side of $\triangle ACD$. But AC is also a side of $\triangle ABC$ in which BC is opposite a greater angle. Conclusion: segment BC is the longest in the figure.

We include the proofs of both the "if" and "only if" parts of 13-2 because they will make you think.

PROOF

Only if: For this part our given information is $AB > BC$. On ray BC there is a point P such that $BP = BA$.

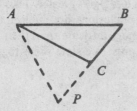

(1) By *ITT* $(\angle BPA)° = (\angle BAP)°$.
(2) But $\angle BAP > \angle BAC$. (Do you see that we must add some positive number to the measure of $\angle BAC$ to get the measure of $\angle BAP$ by Postulate 6?)
(3) $\angle BCA > \angle BPA$ by 13-1.

Combining (1), (2) and (3) we get:

$$\qquad\quad (3)\qquad (1)\qquad (2)$$
(4)$\qquad \angle BCA > \angle BPA = \angle BAP > \angle BAC$
(5)$\qquad\qquad \angle BCA > \angle BAC.$

If: Our given information is $\angle C > \angle A$ and we must derive $AB > BC$. We do this by eliminating the other two possibilities. If $AB = BC$, then $(\angle C)° = (\angle A)°$ by *ITT*. If $AB < BC$, then the proof of the "only if" part of this theorem shows that $\angle C$ must be less than $\angle A$. Thus AB must be greater than BC.

¶ **DRILL** If ray CX bisects $\angle ACB$, fill in the reasons for the proof of $BC > BX$.

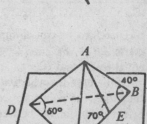

(a) $(\angle ACX)° = (\angle BCX)°$
(b) $(\angle CXB)° > (\angle ACX)°$
(c) $(\angle CXB)° > (\angle BCX)°$
(d) $BC > BX$

[3] Segment AC is perpendicular to plane E. The angles have the measures indicated while $\angle ADB$ and $\angle ABD$ have measures 70 and 50 respectively. If segments AD, AC, AE and AB are arranged in order from shortest to longest, which of the following is the result?

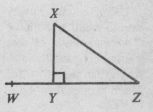

Ⓐ AE, AD, AB, AC Ⓑ AE, AB, AC, AD Ⓒ $AC,$ AB, AE, AD Ⓓ AC, AB, AD, AE Ⓔ $AC, AE,$ AD, AB

A line is perpendicular to a plane at a point B if and only if it is perpendicular to every line in the plane that passes through B. Thus we can assume $\angle ACD$ and $\angle ACB$ are right angles. Therefore AC must be less than any of the segments in the figure since it is always a side of a triangle that is opposite a lesser angle of the triangle. Certainly $AE < BE$ since the angle opposite BE in $\triangle AEB$ is 110° while the angle opposite AE is only 40°. But what of AB and AD? In $\triangle ABD$, AB is opposite the greater angle.

¶ **DRILL**

(a) We can prove that the hypoteneuse of a right triangle is always longer than the legs by proving that the angles opposite the legs are always acute. Use the figure given at right and show that $\angle X$ and $\angle Z$ are always acute when $\angle Y$ is a right angle.
(b) What is meant by the "distance" from a point to a line?

WORKING WITH THE TRIANGLE INEQUALITY LAW

[4] If A, B and C are any three points of a plane for which $AB = 5$ and $BC = 7$, which of the following can be the length of AC?

Ⓐ 0   Ⓑ 1   Ⓒ 2   Ⓓ 13   Ⓔ 15

The following theorem is frequently referred to as the "triangle inequality."

> **13-3** If A, B and C are three points of a plane, then $AB + BC \geq AC$.

Therefore we can eliminate answers Ⓓ and Ⓔ because $AB + BC = 12$, which is not greater than or equal to Ⓓ and Ⓔ.

In the case for which B is between A and C (and, therefore, the points are collinear), $AB + BC = AC$ by the definition of "between." This means that $AB + BC \neq AC$ when B is not between A and C. We will prove $AB + BC > AC$, leaving the reasons to you as a review of many things already discussed.

If B is not a point of line AC, then the union of the segments connecting the three points is $\triangle ABC$. On the ray opposite to ray CB we select a point X such that $CX = CA$.

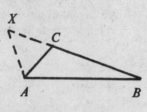

(a) C is in the interior of $\angle XAB$ so
$$(\angle XAC)° + (\angle CAB)° = (\angle XAB)°$$
(b) $(\angle CXA)° = (\angle XAC)°$
(c) $(\angle CXA)° + (\angle CAB)° = (\angle XAB)°$
(d) $\angle CXA < \angle XAB$
(e) $XB > AB$
(f) $XB = XC + CB$
(g) $XC + CB > AB$
(h) $AC + CB > AB$

There is one further case to mention. Suppose C were a point of AB that was not between A and B. As you can see, $AC + BC$ is still greater than AB.

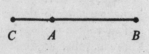

To answer the multiple-choice question draw a segment BC of 7 units and then a circle with center at B and radius 5. Do you see that the points of the circle are the only possible points that will do for A?

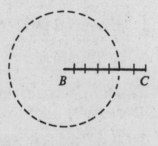

The intersection of the circle and the segment gives a location for A for which $AC = 2$, $AB = 5$ and $BC = 7$.

¶ **DRILL** In the text above, give reasons for (a) through (h).

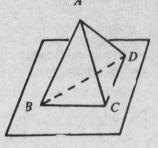

[5] If $AB = BD$, then two of the following four statements about the figure are contradictory. Which two are they?

I $AD = BC$
II $\angle ABC > \angle DBC$
III $\angle BAD$ is not less than $\angle BDA$
IV $AC = DC$

Ⓐ I and II　Ⓑ II and III　Ⓒ III and IV
Ⓓ I and III　Ⓔ II and IV

In the figure (right) all points are coplanar and $AP_1 = AP_2 = AP_3$. What appears to be the relationship between P_1B, P_2B and P_3B? Certainly as the angle, $\angle BAP_n$ gets greater the side opposite it becomes longer and, conversely, as BP_n gets longer $\angle BAP_n$ gets greater. These conclusions are subject to proof, but the proofs are more intricate than their importance in a review warrants. We state them together as a postulate.

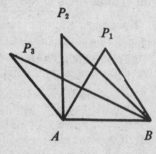

Postulate 13 When two sides of a triangle have the same lengths as the corresponding sides of a second triangle, then the included angle of the first pair is greater than the included angle of the second pair if and only if the remaining side of the first triangle is greater than the remaining side of the second triangle.

Do you see that this means statement II must contradict statement IV?

In the multiple-choice question, $\triangle ABC$ and $\triangle DBC$ have two pairs of congruent sides, $AB = BD$ and $BC = BC$. Since $\angle ABC > \angle DBC$ in statement II, then $AC > DC$, which contradicts IV.

¶ Drill

(a) If in the figure on p 112 P_1, P_2 and P_3 were not coplanar, would the three angles, $\angle P_nAB$, have to be of different measures? (Visualize a folded paper airplane).

(b) In the figure below would we contradict Postulate 13 if we said $\angle C > \angle D$ even though both are opposite segment AB?

(c) If $\triangle ABC$ is isosceles with $AB = BC$ and M is the midpoint of segment AC, use Postulate 13 to show that ray BM is the bisector of $\angle ABC$.

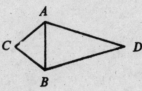

WHAT YOU SHOULD KNOW

1. The measure of an exterior angle of a triangle is greater than the measure of either of its remote interior angles.
2. If two sides of a triangle are not congruent, the angles opposite them are not congruent and the greater angle is opposite the longer side.
3. If two angles of a triangle are not congruent, the sides opposite them are not congruent and the longer side is opposite the greater angle.
4. The hypotenuse of a right triangle is the longest side.
5. The shortest segment from a point to a line is the perpendicular segment.
6. The sum of the lengths of two sides of a triangle is greater than the length of the third side.
7. If two pairs of corresponding sides of two triangles are congruent and their included angles are *not* congruent, the longer side is opposite the greater angle.

KEY THEOREMS

1. In a $\triangle XYZ$, $XY > YZ$ if and only if $\angle Z > \angle X$.
2. If A, B and C are three points of a plane, then $AB + BC \geq AC$. (Triangle Inequality Theorem)

TEST-TAKING STRATEGIES

• If two triangles in a given figure share a common side, try comparing other parts with this common side as an aid in determining the longest (or shortest) side of the figure.

• Questions involving triangle inequalities often require the ability to distinguish between a plane figure and a two-dimensional representation of a three-dimensional figure. Whenever a drawing is given, you may assume the points all lie in the same plane unless the directions say otherwise. Furthermore, familiarize yourself with the way three-dimensional objects are shown in two dimensions; this will help you visualize drawings that carry the qualifier "All points are not necessarily in the same plane."

ANSWERS

[1] Ⓔ
DRILL:
(a) $\angle FCE$ to $\triangle BEC$, $\angle BDC$ to $\triangle DCE$, $\angle BDC$ to $\triangle ABD$; there are others.
(b) Acute.
(c) $\angle AEB > \angle BCD$ by 13-1 and $(\angle BCD)° = (\angle BDC)°$ by ITT.

[2] Ⓐ
DRILL:
(a) Definition of angle bisector.
(b) 13-1.
(c) Substitution.
(d) 13-2.

[3] Ⓔ
DRILL:
(a) $90 = (\angle XYW)° > (\angle YXZ)°$ and $(\angle YZX)°$ by 13-1.
(b) The length of the perpendicular segment from the point to the line.

[4] Ⓒ
DRILL:
(a) Postulate 6.
(b) ITT.
(c) Substitution.
(d) Definition of ">".
(e) 13-2.
(f) Definition of "between."
(g) Substitution of step (f) in step (e).
(h) Substitution.

[5] Ⓔ
DRILL:
(a) No.
(b) No, because in different triangles.
(c) If $\angle ABM > \angle CBM$, then $AM > CM$ by Postulate 13. If $\angle ABM < \angle CBM$, then $AM < CM$ by Postulate 13.

14. Perpendiculars and Parallels

Key Terms

quadrilateral   a plane figure with four sides.

trapezoid   a quadrilateral with one and only one pair of parallel sides.

parallelogram   a quadrilateral for which one of the following is true:
   a. both pairs of opposite sides are parallel,
   b. both pairs of opposite sides are congruent,
   c. a pair of opposite sides is parallel and congruent,
   d. all pairs of consecutive angles are supplementary,
   e. both pairs of opposite angles are congruent, *or*
   f. the diagonals bisect each other.

rectangle   a parallelogram with four right angles.

square   a rectangle with all sides congruent.

rhombus   a parallelogram with all sides congruent.

WORKING WITH PERPENDICULARS

[1] Points *A*, *B*, *C* and *D* lie in plane *F*. Segment *CD* is the perpendicular bisector of segment *AB*. Segment *ED* is perpendicular to plane *F*. Which of the following gives a segment and the plane to which it is perpendicular?

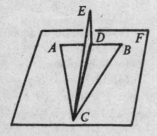

Ⓐ *EC*, plane *F*   Ⓑ *CD*, plane determined by *A*, *D* and *B*   Ⓒ *CD*, plane determined by *E*, *D* and *B*   Ⓓ *AD*, plane determined by *E*, *C* and *B*   Ⓔ *ED*, plane determined by *A*, *E* and *C*

By definition, a *line is perpendicular to a plane* at a point *B* if and only if it is perpendicular to every line lying in the plane and containing *B*. This definition is very useful when we are given a line perpendicular to a plane and are asked to draw conclusions; it is of less value when we wish to prove a line perpendicular to a plane because such would involve proving a line perpendicular to an infinite set of other lines. Through an involved proof which we will omit we could demonstrate the following:

> **14-1**   A line is perpendicular to a plane at a point *B* if it is perpendicular to any two lines lying in the plane and containing *B*.

In the figure above ∠*EDB*, ∠*EDC* and ∠*EDA* are all right angles by definition of "a line perpendicular to a plane." ∠*CDB* and ∠*CDA* are right angles by definition

of "perpendicular bisector." Thus *CD* is perpendicular to both line *ED* and line *DB*, so *CD* is perpendicular to the plane determined by *E*, *D* and *B* by 14-1.

TEST-TAKING TIP.

From the way the figure is drawn, you may think that *ED* is perpendicular to plane *F*, but there is not enough evidence to support this. You would need to know that *ED* is perpendicular to both *AB* and *CD* to conclude that it is perpendicular to the plane that contains them.

¶ **DRILL** In the figure at right *B*, *C* and *D* are points of plane *F*. ∠*ADB*, ∠*CDB* and ∠*ADC* are right angles, and *X* is any point of arc *BC*.

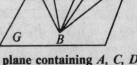

(a) What is the relationship between segment *AD* and plane *F*?
(b) What is the relationship between segment *AD* and segment *DX*? Why?
(c) Does your answer to part (b) depend on the fact that ∠*CDB* is a right angle?

[2] If in the figure at right all of the triangles shown are equilateral, then:

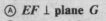

Ⓐ *EF* ⊥ plane *G*
Ⓑ ∠*E* is a right angle
Ⓒ *DF* > *EF*   Ⓓ *BF* ⊥ plane containing *A*, *C*, *D* and *E*   Ⓔ ∠*DFA* is a right angle

A plane is the *perpendicular bisecting plane of a segment* if and only if (1) it contains the midpoint of the segment and (2) it is perpendicular to the segment. We will prove the following:

14-2 Plane E is the perpendicular bisector of segment AB if and only if every point, X, of E is equidistant from A and B. In other words, $AX = BX$ for all X in E.

We will prove just the "only if" part, leaving the reasons as drill. Let plane E be the perpendicular bisector of AB at M and let X be any point of E.

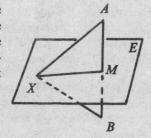

(a) $AM = BM$
(b) $AM \perp XM$
(c) $\angle AMX$ and $\angle BMX$ are right angles and thus have the same measure.
(d) $\triangle AMX \cong \triangle BMX$
(e) $AX = BX$

Statement 14-2 is more easily remembered as: "The set of all points equidistant from the end points of a segment is the perpendicular bisecting plane of the segment."

In the multiple-choice question above, because the triangles are equilateral, all of points A, D, E and C are equidistant from B and F so the plane containing A, D, E and C is the perpendicular bisecting plane of BF.

¶ DRILL

(a) In the question above, if you had been given just $AB = AF$, $BD = FD$, $EF = EB$ and $CF = CB$, rather than that the triangles were equilateral, would your conclusion be altered?
(b) What is the relationship between segments AC and BF? If their point of intersection is P, would this be the midpoint of both?

[3] Given a point P, a line L containing a point Q and a plane E containing a point M. If P, L and E do not intersect, then which of the following is false?

Ⓐ There is exactly one plane perpendicular to L at Q. Ⓑ There is exactly one line perpendicular to L at Q. Ⓒ There is exactly one line containing P and perpendicular to E. Ⓓ If segment PM is perpendicular to plane E, then $PM < PX$, where X is any other point of E. Ⓔ Any two lines that are perpendicular to E are coplanar.

Geometry presents few surprises; in general, points, lines and planes behave the way our intuition wants them to behave. It would not be efficient in a review of this sort to prove the obvious unless the proof itself contributed significantly to our understanding of a particular mathematical concept. Throughout the remainder of this chapter we will be selective about what we deduce and what we develop intuitively.

To represent the given information in a diagram, note that L must be parallel to E if they do not intersect. Remember that it is usually extremely helpful to represent information by a drawing whenever possible.

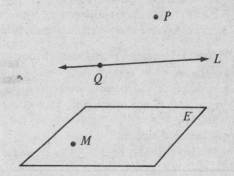

Ⓐ is true. Your intuition should persuade you that there is at *least* one plane which satisfies this. If there were two, their intersection could only be a single line (two different planes can intersect in at most one line) and yet each plane is the set of *all* lines perpendicular to L at Q. Ⓑ is false. There is a plane that is perpendicular to L at Q and this plane contains an infinite set of lines perpendicular to L at Q. Ⓒ is true. You can visualize it by letting your line be a piece of string with a weight at one end. If you tie the other end to the ceiling, gravity will pull the string into a single position perpendicular to the floor. Ⓓ is true. No matter where X is in plane E, $\triangle PMX$ will be a right triangle and PX will be the hypoteneuse. Ⓔ can be verified by an involved proof. Instead you can visualize this by noting that for any pair of exactly vertical objects (such as telephone poles or fence posts) you can move into a position where the nearer one lines up with the farther. The plane here is the one determined by the two poles.

¶ DRILL

(a) How would you define the distance from a point to a plane?
(b) Doesn't our response to (B) contradict a theorem already proved?
(c) Will the two lines in (E) ever intersect? If so, what strange triangle would be formed in the plane of the two lines?

WORKING WITH PARALLELS

[4] If lines L_1, L_2 and L_3 lie in plane P, which of the following is NOT sufficient to guarantee that L_2 and L_3 are parallel?

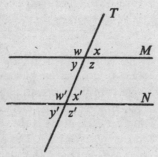

Ⓐ L_2 does not intersect L_3. Ⓑ L_2 and L_3 are both perpendicular to L_1. Ⓒ $\angle BAC$ has the same measure as $\angle EBD$. Ⓓ $\angle BAC$ has the same measure as $\angle ABF$. Ⓔ $\angle BAC$ has the same measure as $\angle DBA$.

Two lines are *parallel* if and only if they are contained in the same plane and do not intersect. Two lines in the same plane and perpendicular to a given line must be parallel; if they intersected, they would determine a triangle having two right angles.

If two lines, M and N, are intersected by a third line, T, as in the figure, then T is called a *transversal* and the angle pairs, $x \to x'$, $y \to y'$, $z \to z'$, and $w \to w'$ are called *corresponding angles*, while the pairs $y \to x'$, $z \to w'$ are called *alternate interior angles*.

If any pair of corresponding angles, say x and x', have the same measure, then lines M and N cannot intersect. If they were to intersect at some point A on the right of the transversal, then $\angle x$ would be an exterior angle of the triangle and would have to be greater than $\angle x'$. If they were to intersect at a point B on the left, then $\angle x'$ would be an exterior angle greater than its remote interior angle, $\angle y$. But $\angle y$ and $\angle x$ are vertical angles and must have the same measure. A similar line of reasoning supports the following:

> **14-3** If a pair of lines is intersected by a transversal and a pair of corresponding angles have the same measure, then the pair of lines is parallel.

An argument like the one above using exterior angles will also support the following:

> **14-4** If a pair of lines is intersected by a transversal and a pair of alternate interior angles have the same measure, then the pair of lines is parallel.

The foregoing arguments support all of answers Ⓐ through Ⓓ. You can see that Ⓔ must be false since there is no contradiction in allowing L_2 to intersect L_3 while $(\angle BAC)° = (\angle DBA)°$

¶ DRILL

(a) If a pair of corresponding angles have the same measure, will each of the other pairs of corresponding angles also be equal in measure?

(b) Would Ⓔ have been true if we had been given $\angle BAC$ and $\angle DBA$ as supplementary?

(c) In space, if two lines are each perpendicular to a third, must the first two be parallel?

(d) If a pair of corresponding angles are equal in measure, must a pair of alternate interior angles also be equal in measure?

[5] Given a plane containing the lines L_1, L_2 and L_3. L_1 intersects L_2 at a point P and L_3 intersects neither L_1 nor L_2. Which of the following must be true?

Ⓐ $L_1 \perp L_2$ Ⓑ L_1 and L_2 are two distinct lines that are both parallel to L_3 Ⓒ L_1 and L_2 are the same line Ⓓ L_3 is contained entirely in the interior of an angle with vertex at P Ⓔ $L_1 \parallel L_2$

This question would not be a fair test question, but we chose to include it since it clearly illustrates the point we are trying to get across in this section. If you, like almost every other high school student, have studied only geometries based on Euclid, you will probably see no ambiguity and conclude that answer Ⓒ is correct. No matter what geometry you've studied, you will automatically exclude Ⓔ because we were given that L_1 and L_2 intersect and Ⓐ because no restrictions, direct or indirect, were placed on angle measure. But what of Ⓑ? You may recall a statement which restricted the number of lines passing through a point and parallel to a given line. Euclid (and many geometers following him) tried to prove that only one such parallel existed because his intuition told him that only one should exist. No one who tried to prove this succeeded. But Euclid wanted his points, lines and planes to behave the way he felt they should so he postulated the existence of only one parallel. Some geometers tried to prove this statement by assuming that it was false and then attempting to find a contradiction. Their failure to do so set others thinking about the consequences of systems of postulates which did not have the same "parallel postulate" as Euclid's. One such non-Euclidean geometry postulates a statement much like the one in Ⓑ. For this particular type of geometry we can actually prove that Ⓓ is true!

You should be aware that other geometries besides the one you have studied are possible, and you should realize that these are formed by making up different postulates about the behavior of figures. Since our purpose is to review intermediate math, we have reminded you of the existence of non-Euclidean geometries; but we will continue to base our geometry on Euclid.

TEST-TAKING TIP.

The plane geometry tested on the College Board Mathematics Level I Test is Euclidean only. This test does not cover concepts of non-Euclidean geometries.

Postulate 14 If point P does not lie on line L, then there is exactly one line in the plane of L and P that passes through P and is parallel to L.

¶ DRILL A student attempted to "prove" the postulate above by reasoning as follows on the figure below: Assume L_1 and L_2 are both parallel to L_3, and L_4 is perpendicular to L_3. Then both L_1 and L_2 are perpendicular to L_4 (why?) which contradicts the fact that only one line through a point can be perpendicular to a given line. Thus the assumption that L_1 and L_2 are both parallel to L_3 must be a contradiction. What is wrong with the student's argument?

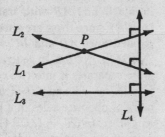

[6] If $L_1 \parallel L_2$ and L_3 intersects both L_1 and L_2 while the measure of $\angle 2 = 89°$, then:

Ⓐ $\angle 8$ is 89°. Ⓑ $\angle 7$ is 91°. Ⓒ $\angle 5$ is 89°. Ⓓ $\angle 6$ is 91°. Ⓔ $\angle 8$ and $\angle 2$ are supplementary.

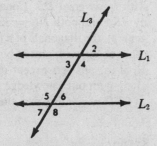

In this section we will review the converses of the statements of section [4]. In that section we started with some statements about lines and angles and proved certain pairs of lines to be parallel. In this section we start with the information that the lines are parallel and see what conclusions we can reach about pairs of angles.

14-5 If a pair of parallel lines is intersected by a transversal, then each pair of alternate interior angles is equal in measure.

The reasoning in this proof is novel and worth exploring. If $L_1 \parallel L_2$ and L_3 intersects both, as in:

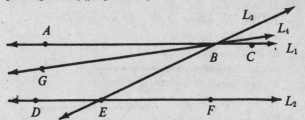

what would happen if $(\angle ABE)° \neq (\angle BEF)°$? Do you see that there would have to be some line L_4 passing through B with a point G such that $(\angle GBE)° = (\angle BEF)°$? And by 14-4 it follows that $L_4 \parallel L_1$ so we get a pair of lines passing through B and parallel to L_2, which contradicts Postulate 14. Once we have 14-5, the next few theorems follow immediately. We will leave their verification as drill.

14-6 If a pair of parallel lines is intersected by a transversal, then each pair of corresponding angles is equal in measure.

14-7 If three lines lie in a plane and two of them are parallel to the third, then all are parallel to each other.

14-8 If L_1, L_2 and L_3 lie in a plane and $L_1 \parallel L_3$ while $L_2 \perp L_1$, then $L_2 \perp L_3$.

In the multiple-choice question, $\angle 2$ and $\angle 4$ are supplementary because they are a linear pair. Also, $\angle 4$ and $\angle 8$ are congruent, because they are corresponding angles. Therefore $\angle 8$ and $\angle 2$ are supplementary (choice Ⓔ). Note that $\angle 5$, $\angle 7$ and $\angle 8$ are 91° and $\angle 6$ is 89°.

¶ DRILL Using the figure below:

If the measure of $\angle 1$ is 50°, find the measures of $\angle 2$, $\angle 3$, $\angle 4$, $\angle 5$ and $\angle 6$.

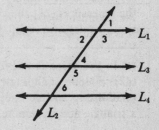

[7] If lines AD and BC are parallel and ∠EAC is 40° while ∠B is 60°, what is the measure of ∠EAB?

Ⓐ 60   Ⓑ 120   Ⓒ 40   Ⓓ 100   Ⓔ 140

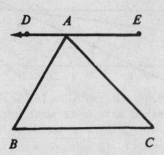

In the figure above (∠DAB)° = 60 by 14-5. But the sum of the measures of ∠DAB, ∠BAC and ∠EAC must be 180 since ∠DAC and ∠EAC are a linear pair. Therefore (∠BAC)° = 80, and (∠BAE)° = 120.

We can enlarge the scope of the problem a bit and prove the following important theorem:

14-9 The sum of the measures of the angles of a triangle is 180°.

PROOF Using the figure above and just the information that DA ∥ BC, we conclude:

(1) (∠DAB)° + (∠BAC)° + (∠CAE)° = 180 since ∠DAC and ∠CAE form a linear pair.

(2) (∠DAB)° = (∠CBA)° and (∠EAC)° = (∠BCA)° by 10-5.

(3) (∠CBA)° + (∠BAC)° + (∠BCA)° = 180 by substitution of (2) in (1).

¶ DRILL

(a) If two angles of a triangle have the same measures as the corresponding angles of a second triangle, what must be true of the remaining pair of angles?

(b) What is the sum of the measures of the acute angles of a right triangle?

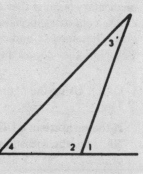

(c) In the figure above, (∠2)° = 180 − (∠1)°. Why? (∠2)° = 180 − (∠3 + ∠4)°. Why? What is the exact relationship, therefore, between an exterior angle of a triangle and its remote interior angles?

[8] In the figure, AB ∥ CD, AD ∥ BC and DC ≠ BC. Which of the following is NOT a correct conclusion?

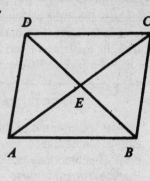

Ⓐ △ADC ≅ △CBA
Ⓑ ∠DCA has the same measure as ∠BCA
Ⓒ ∠ADC has the same measure as ∠CBA
Ⓓ AD = BC
Ⓔ DE = BE

Given four coplanar points A, B, C and D, no three of which are collinear, the union of segments AB, BC, CD and DA is a *quadrilateral*. The points A, B, C and D are called *vertices*. Any two sides which do not contain the same vertex are called *opposite* sides. A quadrilateral is a *parallelogram* if and only if both pairs of opposite sides are parallel. The figure above is thus a parallelogram. Furthermore, (∠DCA)° = (∠BAC)° since these are alternate interior angles of the parallel lines DC and AB with transversal AC. (∠DAC)° = (∠BCA)° since these are alternate interior angles of the parallel lines AD and BC with transversal AC. Thus △ADC ≅ △CBA. In general, a diagonal of a parallelogram separates it into two congruent triangles. Therefore DC = AB and AD = BC by CP. In general, both pairs of opposite sides of a parallelogram are equal in length. (∠ADC)° = (∠CBA)° by CP. In general, both pairs of opposite angles of a parallelogram are equal in measure. (∠BDC)° = (∠DBA)° because these are alternate interior angles of the parallel lines DC and AB with transversal DB. Consequently △DEC ≅ △BEA by ASA and both DE = EB and AE = EC by CP. In general, the diagonals of a parallelogram intersect each other at the midpoint of both. We have now supported all of the answers except Ⓑ. If Ⓑ were true, this fact, along with our knowledge that DE = EB, must make △CED ≅ △CEB and thereby, DC = BC.

¶ DRILL

(a) In the figure of the multiple-choice question, what is the relationship between ∠DCB and ∠CBA?

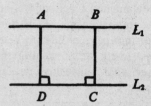

(b) How would you define the "distance" between any two parallel lines?

(c) If, in the figure above, $L_1 \parallel L_2$, AD ⊥ L_2 and BC ⊥ L_2, can you prove that L_1 and L_2 are everywhere equidistant?

[9] If the statement "ABCD is a parallelogram" means $AB \parallel CD$ and $BC \parallel AD$, then which of the following statements will NOT lead to the conclusion that ABCD is a parallelogram?

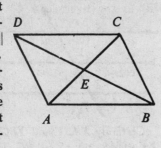

Ⓐ $AB = CD$ and $AD = BC$ Ⓑ $ED = EB$ and $AE = CE$ Ⓒ $AB = CD$ and $AB \parallel CD$ Ⓓ $DC = AB$ and $AD \parallel BC$ Ⓔ $AD = BC$ and $AD \parallel BC$

At first glance this question may appear to duplicate number [8]. But in [8] we were given a parallelogram and asked to draw conclusions about its parts, whereas here we are given information about the parts of a quadrilateral and asked whether this information will lead to the conclusion that the quadrilateral is a parallelogram.

If $AB = CD$ and $AD = BC$, then $\triangle ADC \cong \triangle CBA$ by SSS since $AC = AC$. Consequently, $(\angle DCA)° = (\angle BAC)°$ and $(\angle BCA)° = (\angle CAD)°$ by CP. Therefore both $DC \parallel AB$ and $AD \parallel BC$ because their pairs of alternate interior angles are equal in measure. In general, if both pairs of opposite sides of a quadrilateral are equal in length, the quadrilateral is a parallelogram.

If $DE = EB$ and $AE = EC$, then $\triangle DEC \cong \triangle BEA$ by SAS since $\angle CED$ and $\angle AEB$ are vertical angles. Accordingly, $(\angle EDC)° = (\angle EBA)°$ by CP so $DC \parallel AB$. Similar reasoning on $\triangle DEA$ and $\triangle BEC$ will yield $AD \parallel BC$. In general, if the diagonals of a quadrilateral bisect each other, the quadrilateral is a parallelogram.

If $AB = CD$ and $AB \parallel CD$, then $(\angle DCA)° = (\angle BAC)°$ and $(\angle CDB)° = (\angle DBA)°$ since they are alternate interior angles of parallel lines. Consequently, $\triangle EDC \cong \triangle EBA$ by ASA and $DE = BE$, $AE = CE$ by CP. Thus ABCD is a parallelogram since its diagonals bisect each other. In general, if a pair of sides of a quadrilateral are parallel and equal in length, then the quadrilateral is a parallelogram.

We have supported all of the answers except Ⓓ. Does the figure at right satisfy the information in Ⓓ?

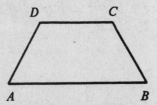

Figures like the one above are called trapezoids. A quadrilateral is a *trapezoid* if it has one and only one pair of parallel sides. It is an *isosceles trapezoid* if the non-parallel sides are equal in length.

¶ DRILL If in the figure at right both ADEF and BCEF are parallelograms, we can prove that ABCD is a parallelogram. Fill in the reasons:

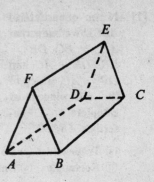

(a) $AD = EF$
(b) $AD \parallel EF$
(c) $BC = EF$
(d) $BC \parallel EF$
(e) $AD = BC$
(f) $AD \parallel BC$
(g) ABCD is a parallelogram

[10] Which of the following is (are) true?

   I A square is a parallelogram.
   II A square is a rectangle.
   III A square is a rhombus.

Ⓐ I only   Ⓑ II and III only   Ⓒ All of I, II and III   Ⓓ I and II only   Ⓔ II only

If a parallelogram ABCD has one right angle, say $\angle A$, then it must have four, since $(\angle A)° = (\angle C)°$ because they are opposite angles and both $(\angle A)° + (\angle B)° = 180$ and $(\angle A)° + (\angle D)° = 180$ since these are pairs of consecutive angles. A parallelogram is a *rectangle* if and only if it has a right angle. We have just shown that having one right angle means that all four angles will be right angles.

A parallelogram is a *rhombus* if and only if a pair of sides which contain the same vertex have the same length. Will all of the sides of a rhombus be equal in length? See part (a) of the drill below.

A parallelogram is a *square* if and only if all of its sides are equal in length and all of its angles are right angles.

Therefore a square is a parallelogram by definition, it is a rectangle because it has four right angles, and it is a rhombus because all sides are congruent.

¶ DRILL

(a) Is a rhombus equilateral?
(b) Is a rectangle a rhombus? a square? a parallelogram?
(c) Is a square a rhombus? a rectangle? a parallelogram?
(d) Is a rhombus a square? a rectangle? a parallelogram?

[11] If in quadrilateral *ABCD* we know that *AE* = *EC*, *DE* = *EB*, *DE* ⊥ *AC* and *DB* = *AC*, which of the following most completely describes *ABCD*?

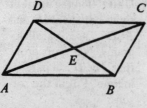

(Figure is not drawn to scale.)

Ⓐ **Trapezoid** Ⓑ **Parallelogram** Ⓒ **Rhombus**
Ⓓ **Rectangle** Ⓔ **Square**

The information that *AE* = *EC* and *DE* = *EB* (in other words, that the diagonals bisect each other) tells us that *ABCD* is a parallelogram as we have seen in section [9]. If, in addition, *DB* ⊥ *AC*, then △*AED* ≅ △*CED* and *AD* = *DC* by CP. In general, if the diagonals of a parallelogram are perpendicular, the parallelogram is a rhombus.

If *AC* = *BD* along with the other information, then △*DAB* ≅ △*CBA* and (∠*DAB*)° = (∠*CBA*)° by CP. But these two angles are supplementary so they are right angles. In general, if the diagonals of a quadrilateral bisect each other, are perpendicular and are equal in length, the quadrilateral is a square.

¶ **DRILL**

(a) If the diagonals of a quadrilateral have the same length, must it be a parallelogram?

(b) Suppose they are also perpendicular?

(c) Suppose one diagonal also bisects the other?

[12] In the figure *AB* ∥ *XY*, *DC* ∥ *XY*, *XD* = 3(*XA*) and *CY* = 6. Find *BC*.

Ⓐ 9 Ⓑ 8 Ⓒ 7
Ⓓ 6 Ⓔ 3

Suppose a set of three parallel lines L_1, L_2, and L_3, is intersected by a transversal, T_1, and cuts off segments of equal length, *XY* = *YZ*, in the figure at the upper right. If T_2 is a transversal parallel to T_1, then what is the relationship of *AB* to *BC*?

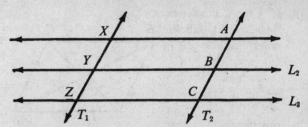

Certainly *XABY* and *YBCZ* are parallelograms, so *XY* = *AB* and *YZ* = *BC*. Thus *AB* = *BC*, since *XY* = *YZ*. In general, if a set of parallel lines cuts off segments of equal length on one transversal, it will cut off segments of equal length on any parallel transversal.

Suppose T_2 is not parallel to T_1. Then through *X* and *Y* we can construct lines parallel to T_2 as in the figure below.

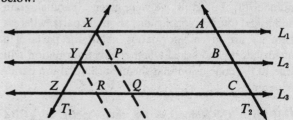

We know that *XY* = *YZ* and can demonstrate that (∠*XYP*)° = (∠*YZR*)° as well as (∠*XPY*)° = (∠*YRZ*)°. (Why? Answer this as part (a) of the drill below.) Consequently △*XYP* ≅ △*YZR* by SAA and *YR* = *XP* by CP. But *AB* = *XP* and *BC* = *YR* because these are opposite sides of a parallelogram. We conclude that *AB* = *BC* and state that, in general, if a set of parallel lines cuts off segments of equal length on one transversal, then it will cut off segments of equal length on *any* transversal.

To answer the multiple-choice question above, draw in two more lines that are parallel to *AB* and intersect segment *XD* between *X* and *D* to cut off segments of equal length (*DP* = *PQ* = *QX*). Since *XD* = *DP* + *PQ* + *QX* = 3(*XA*), then *CY* = *CP'* + *P'Q'* + *Q'Y* = 3(*YB*). Hence *YB* = 2 and *CB* = 8.

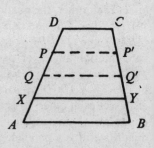

¶ **DRILL**

(a) In the text above.

(b) If a line bisects side *BC* of a triangle *ABC* and is parallel to side *AB*, must it also bisect *AC*? Why?

WHAT YOU SHOULD KNOW

KEY CONCEPTS

Handling Perpendiculars

1. A line is perpendicular to a plane E at a point B if it is perpendicular to any two lines in plane E at point B.
2. A plane is the perpendicular bisecting plane of a segment if it is perpendicular to the segment and contains its midpoint.
3. The perpendicular bisecting plane of a segment is the set of all points in space equidistant from the endpoints of the segment.
4. The distance between a point and a line is the length of the perpendicular segment.
5. The diagonals of a rhombus are perpendicular.

Handling Parallels

1. Two lines are parallel if and only if they lie in the same plane and do not intersect.
2. Parallel lines are everywhere equidistant.
3. If two parallel lines are intersected by a third line (a "transversal"), then:
   a. all pairs of corresponding angles are congruent,
   b. both pairs of alternate interior angles are congruent, *and*
   c. interior angles on the same side of the transversal are supplementary.
4. If two lines are intersected by a transversal, the following conditions will guarantee that the lines are parallel:
   a. a pair of corresponding angles is congruent,
   b. a pair of alternate interior angles is congruent,
   c. interior angles on the same side of the transversal are supplementary, *and*
   d. the lines are each perpendicular to the transversal.
5. Two lines that are parallel to a third line are parallel to each other.
6. If a quadrilateral is a parallelogram, then:
   a. both pairs of opposite sides are parallel,
   b. both pairs of opposite sides are congruent,
   c. both pairs of opposite angles are congruent,
   d. all pairs of consecutive angles are supplementary, *and*
   e. the diagonals bisect each other.
7. If a set of three or more parallel lines intercepts congruent segments on one transversal, it will intercept congruent segments on any transversal.

KEY THEOREMS

1. The sum of the measures of the angles of a triangle is 180.
2. The measure of an exterior angle of a triangle is equal to the sum of the measures of its remote interior angles. (Exterior Angle Equality Theorem)

TEST-TAKING STRATEGIES

- When a question involves possible perpendiculars, try to visualize the relationships involved in terms of familiar vertical objects, such as trees, that are perpendicular to the ground.
- Though seemingly facetious, a handy way of remembering all of the angle relationships for parallel lines cut by a transversal is to remember that when parallel lines are cut by a transversal, all of the angles that look congruent are congruent. Keep this in mind.
- In working with rectangles, rhombuses and squares, remember that all are parallelograms so all of the parallelogram relationships apply to them. For example, opposite angles are congruent, adjacent angles are supplementary, and the diagonals bisect each other.

ANSWERS

[1] ©
DRILL:
(a) Perpendicular by 14-1.
(b) Perpendicular by definition of "line perpendicular to plane."
(c) No.

[2] Ⓓ
DRILL:
(a), (b) Definition of perpendicular bisector.
(c) Definition of perpendicular.
(d) *SAS.*
(e) *CP.*
DRILL:
(a) No.
(b) Perpendicular bisectors, yes.

[3] Ⓑ
DRILL:
(a) Length of perpendicular segment from point to plane.
(b) No, a triangle with two right angles.

[4] Ⓔ
DRILL:
(a) Yes.   (b) Yes.
(c) No.   (d) Yes.

[5] Read the section.

DRILL:

Why are L_1 and L_2 perpendicular to L_4? This student cited the "alternate interior angle theorem," whose proof is based on the assumption that only one line through a given point is parallel to a given line. This will be explained in subsequent sections.

[6] Ⓔ

DRILL:

$\angle 1 = 50$	$\angle 2 = 50$
$\angle 3 = 130$	$\angle 4 = 50$
$\angle 5 = 130$	$\angle 6 = 50$

[7] Ⓑ

DRILL:

(a) Equal in measure.

(b) 90

(c) Linear pairs are supplementary; 14-8; its measure is equal to the sum of their measures.

[8] Ⓑ

DRILL:

(a) Supplementary.

(b) The length of the perpendicular segment from any point of one line to the other line.

(c) Yes, opposite sides of a rectangle are always equal in length.

[9] Ⓓ

DRILL:

(a)–(d) Opposite sides of a parallelogram.

(e)–(f) Substitution.

(g) It is a quadrilateral with a pair of opposite sides parallel and equal in length.

[10] Ⓒ

DRILL:

(a) Yes.

(b) No, no, yes.

(c) Yes, yes, yes.

(d) No, no, yes.

[11] Ⓔ

DRILL:

(a) No, it could be an isosceles trapezoid.

(b) (c) No, it could be a kite.

[12] Ⓑ

DRILL:

(a) Parallel lines cut by a transversal have all pairs of corresponding angles equal in measure.

(b) Yes.

15. Ratio, Proportion and Similarity

Key Terms

proportion   an equation in which both sides are ratios.

sequence   a set of numbers arranged in a prescribed order.

geometric mean   the nth root of the product of n numbers. Examples: the geometric mean of 9 and 4 is 6; the geometric mean of the numbers a and b is the number $\sqrt{ab}$.

WORKING WITH RATIOS

[1] If the ratio of the lengths of two segments measured in yards is $\dfrac{m}{n}$, then which of the following is the ratio of the lengths measured in inches?

(A) $3\left(\dfrac{m}{n}\right)$ (B) $12\left(\dfrac{m}{n}\right)$ (C) $36\left(\dfrac{m}{n}\right)$ (D) $\dfrac{m}{n}$

(E) $\dfrac{1}{36}\left(\dfrac{m}{n}\right)$

The *ratio* of p to q is the quotient $\dfrac{p}{q}$, where p and q are real numbers and $q \neq 0$. Representing ratios as fractions enables us to apply some of the ideas already reviewed in Chapter 9. Specifically, we will use 9-1 to answer this question.

9-1 If a, b and c are real numbers and neither b nor c is zero, then

$$\frac{ac}{bc} = \frac{a}{b}$$

Let us assume that the ratio $\dfrac{m}{n}$ in the question is in unsimplified form; in other words, that the length of one segment is m yards and of the other is n yards. Of course, this does not have to be the case since if $m = 2$ and $n = 6$, the ratio is $\dfrac{1}{3}$, but we will consider this possibility later.

If the lengths are m and n yards, then they are $36m$ and $36n$ inches. Thus the ratio in inches is

$$\frac{36m}{36n} = \frac{m}{n} \text{ by 5-1.}$$

Suppose $\dfrac{m}{n}$ *was* the simplified form. Then some common factor k has been removed from the numerator

and denominator such that the original lengths were km and kn yards. This gives $36km$ and $36kn$ inches which yields the ratio $\dfrac{36km}{36kn}$—the latter also reduces to $\dfrac{m}{n}$.

¶ **DRILL**

(a) What is the ratio of boys to girls in a school of 500 boys and 625 girls?

(b) Find two numbers that have the ratio $\dfrac{9}{4}$ if their sum is 39.

(c) What must be true of x and y if their ratio is $\dfrac{2}{3}$?

WORKING WITH PROPORTIONS

[2] If $\dfrac{9}{10} = \dfrac{x}{15}$ is to be a true proportion, then $x = ?$

(A) 14   (B) $13\dfrac{1}{2}$ (C) 13   (D) $12\dfrac{1}{2}$ (E) 12

An equation in which both sides are ratios is called a *proportion*. From 9-1 we conclude that when two fractions are equal it must be possible to find some number k which, when multiplied by the numerator and denominator of one fraction, yields, respectively, the numerator and denominator of the other. For example, in the question above we see that $15 = 10\left(\dfrac{3}{2}\right)$ so x must equal $9\left(\dfrac{3}{2}\right)$. A second process for finding an answer here is to use 9-4, the Cross-Multiplication Property.

9-4 If $a, b, c,$ and d are real numbers and neither b nor d is zero, then:

$$\frac{a}{b} = \frac{c}{d} \quad \text{if and only if} \quad ad = bc.$$

Using 9-4, we can rewrite $\frac{9}{10} = \frac{x}{15}$ as $9 \cdot 15 = 10x$. Thus $135 = 10x$ and $x = 13.5$.

¶ DRILL Find x in each of the following proportions:

(a) $\dfrac{3}{4} = \dfrac{9}{x}$ (b) $\dfrac{2x}{9} = \dfrac{3x}{4}$

(c) $\dfrac{x+1}{8} = \dfrac{1}{9}$ (d) $\dfrac{3(x-1)}{x} = \dfrac{2}{x-2}$

[3] If the sequence 5, x, y is proportional to the sequence x, 20, 32, which of the following is y?

Ⓐ 10   Ⓑ 12   Ⓒ 14   Ⓓ 16   Ⓔ 18

A *sequence* is a set of numbers arranged in a prescribed order. Two sequences,

(1) $a, b, c, \ldots$ and
(2) $a', b', c', \ldots,$

are *proportional* if and only if there is some real number k such that:

(3) $a = ka', \ b = kb', \ c = kc', \ldots.$

Equations (3) can be rewritten as

(4) $\dfrac{a}{a'} = k, \ \dfrac{b}{b'} = k, \ \dfrac{c}{c'} = k, \ldots.$

Since equations (4) indicate that each of the ratios given is equal to the same number, k (called the "proportionality constant"), we conclude:

(5) $\dfrac{a}{a'} = \dfrac{b}{b'} = \dfrac{c}{c'} = \ldots.$

Note that equation (5) (called a "proportionality") is equivalent to the separate equations:

(6) $\dfrac{a}{a'} = \dfrac{b}{b'}$ and $\dfrac{b}{b'} = \dfrac{c}{c'}$ and $\dfrac{a}{a'} = \dfrac{c}{c'},$ etc.

EXAMPLE

If the sequence $x, y, 3$ is proportional to 4, 5, 2, then what are x and y?

SOLUTION: We conclude:

$$\frac{x}{4} = \frac{y}{5} = \frac{3}{2},$$

which means

$$\frac{x}{4} = \frac{3}{2} \text{ and } \frac{y}{5} = \frac{3}{2},$$

so

$$2x = 12 \text{ and } 2y = 15 \text{ by 5-4.}$$

Thus $x = 6$ and $y = 7\frac{1}{2}.$

In the multiple-choice question,

$$\frac{5}{x} = \frac{x}{20} = \frac{y}{32}.$$

Because $\dfrac{5}{x} = \dfrac{x}{20}$, by cross-multiplying we get

$$x^2 = 100,$$
$$x = \pm 10.$$

Because $\dfrac{5}{10} = \dfrac{y}{32}$, by cross-multiplying we get

$$10y = 160,$$
$$y = 16$$

¶ DRILL Find the values of the variables if the sequences given are to be proportional. Also find k, the constant of proportionality.

(a) 3, 4, 13 is proportional to x, 2, y.
(b) 9, 21, 36 is proportional to x, y, 3.
(c) In a "proportion" is the sequence of numerators "proportional" to the sequence of denominators? Is a "proportion" always a "proportionality?"

[4] If $\dfrac{a}{2} = \dfrac{b}{3}$, then $\dfrac{b+3}{3} = ?$

Ⓐ $\dfrac{a+3}{3}$ Ⓑ $\dfrac{a+2}{2}$ Ⓒ $\dfrac{a+3}{2}$ Ⓓ $\dfrac{a+3}{6}$

Ⓔ $\dfrac{a+2}{6}$

A proportion is an equation and thereby is subject to the addition and subtraction properties of equality. Consequently, if

(1) $\dfrac{x}{y} = \dfrac{z}{w}$, then

(2) $\dfrac{x}{y} + 1 = \dfrac{z}{w} + 1$ and $\dfrac{x}{y} - 1 = \dfrac{z}{w} - 1.$

Hence

(3) $\dfrac{x}{y} + \dfrac{y}{y} = \dfrac{z}{w} + \dfrac{w}{w}$ and $\dfrac{x}{y} - \dfrac{y}{y} = \dfrac{z}{w} - \dfrac{w}{w},$

(4) $\dfrac{x+y}{y} = \dfrac{z+w}{w}$ and $\dfrac{x-y}{y} = \dfrac{z-w}{w}.$

We state these results formally in the following:

15-1 If x, y, z and w are real numbers such that $y \neq 0$ and $w \neq 0$, and if $\frac{x}{y} = \frac{z}{w}$, then

$$\frac{x + y}{y} = \frac{z + w}{w} \quad \text{and} \quad \frac{x - y}{y} = \frac{z - w}{w}.$$

You may recall that theorem 15-1 has applications to similar triangles which we will review in a later section.

Therefore, if $\frac{a}{2} = \frac{b}{3}$, then $\frac{a + 2}{2} = \frac{b + 3}{3}$.

¶ DRILL

(a) If $\frac{x}{3} = 2$, then $\frac{x + 3}{3} = ?$

(b) If $\frac{x}{y} = \frac{4}{3}$, then $\frac{x - y}{y} = ?$

(c) If $\frac{x}{y} = \frac{4}{3}$, then $\frac{x - 3}{y} = ?$

[5] If $\frac{a}{b} = \frac{c}{d}$, then $\frac{a}{c} = ?$

Ⓐ $\frac{a}{d}$ Ⓑ $\frac{c}{d}$ Ⓒ $\frac{b}{d}$ Ⓓ $\frac{d}{b}$ Ⓔ bd

15-2 If $\frac{a}{b} = \frac{c}{d}$, where $b \neq 0$ and $d \neq 0$, then

$$\frac{a}{c} = \frac{b}{d} \quad \text{and} \quad \frac{d}{b} = \frac{c}{a}.$$

PROOF

(1) $\frac{a}{b} = \frac{c}{d}$

(2) $ad = bc$

(3) $\frac{1}{cd}(ad) = \frac{1}{cd}(bc)$ and $\frac{1}{ab}(ad) = \frac{1}{ab}(bc)$

(4) $\frac{a}{c} = \frac{b}{d}$ and $\frac{d}{b} = \frac{c}{a}$

Thus, in a proportion, we may interchange either numerator with the denominator of the other term, and the resulting equation will still be a proportion.

¶ DRILL Verify 15-2 for each of the following:

(a) $\frac{1}{3} = \frac{6}{18}$ (b) $\frac{2}{5} = \frac{18}{45}$

[6] If $\frac{1}{2} = \frac{x}{4} = \frac{3}{6} = \frac{x + 4}{y}$, find y.

Ⓐ 9   Ⓑ 10   Ⓒ 11   Ⓓ 12   Ⓔ 13

15-3 For all a, b, c, ... and a', b', c', ..., such that none of the latter is zero,

$$\frac{a}{a'} = \frac{b}{b'} = \frac{c}{c'} = \ldots = \frac{a + b + c + \ldots}{a' + b' + c' + \ldots}.$$

PROOF

(1) $\frac{a}{a'} = \frac{b}{b'} = \frac{c}{c'} = \ldots$ means there is some k such that $a = a'k$, $b = b'k$, $c = c'k$, etc.

(2) Adding the equations of (1), we get:
$a + b + c + \ldots = a'k + b'k + c'k + \ldots$.

(3) Therefore
$a + b + c + \ldots = (a' + b' + c' + \ldots)k$.

(4) $k = \dfrac{a + b + c + \ldots}{a' + b' + c' + \ldots}$

But k was the proportionality constant in equations (1) so 15-3 is proved.

Note that the numerator of the final term in the proportionality of the multiple-choice question is the sum of the numerators of the other terms, so the denominator must be the sum of the denominators.

Therefore

$$2 + 4 + 6 = y.$$

¶ DRILL Find the numbers indicated by the question marks.

(a) $\frac{x}{y} = \frac{z}{w} = \frac{2}{3}$; therefore $\frac{x + z}{y + w} = \frac{2}{?}$

(b) $\frac{2}{x} = \frac{5}{?} = \frac{7}{x + 4}$

FINDING THE GEOMETRIC MEAN

[7] If $x = \sqrt{ab}$, then $\frac{x}{a} = ?$

Ⓐ $\frac{b}{x}$ Ⓑ $\frac{x}{b}$ Ⓒ bx Ⓓ ab Ⓔ $x\sqrt{b}$

15-4 If $\frac{x}{a} = \frac{b}{x}$ when $x > 0$, then

$$x^2 = ab \quad \text{and} \quad x = \sqrt{ab}.$$

When x satisfies the requirements of 15-4, it is called the *geometric mean* between a and b. Note that, if

$$\frac{x}{a} = \frac{b}{x},$$

then

$$\frac{b}{x} = \frac{x}{a}.$$

¶ DRILL Find the geometric mean between each of the pairs of numbers given.

(a) 3 and 12   (b) 2 and 8   (c) 4 and 5

(d) Find a pair of numbers, a and b, such that their geometric mean is equal to their arithmetic mean (the arithmetic mean is the average).

WORKING WITH SIMILARITY

[8] If $\triangle ABC \cong \triangle XYZ$, then which of the following is NOT necessarily true?

  Ⓐ The corresponding sides are proportional.
  Ⓑ The corresponding angles are proportional.
  Ⓒ The triangles are similar.   Ⓓ The triangles have the same area.   Ⓔ The triangles lie in the same plane.

If we take a photograph of a painting, the photograph and the painting will show figures that are exactly the same shape but different in size. We refer to this relationship as a "similarity." The formal definition follows:

A correspondence between the vertices of two triangles is a *similarity* if and only if all pairs of corresponding sides are proportional and all pairs of corresponding angles are equal in measure.

Thus, when we write $\triangle ABC \sim \triangle XYZ$, we mean:

(1) $\dfrac{AB}{XY} = \dfrac{BC}{YZ} = \dfrac{AC}{XZ}$, and

(2)
$(\angle A)^\circ = (\angle X)^\circ, (\angle B)^\circ = (\angle Y)^\circ, (\angle C)^\circ = (\angle Z)^\circ.$

If a correspondence is a congruence, is it also a similarity? Certainly all pairs of corresponding angles are equal in measure and the sides are proportional (with 1 as proportionality constant). Only answer Ⓑ is tricky: If $(\angle A)^\circ = (\angle X)^\circ$ and $(\angle B)^\circ = (\angle Y)^\circ$, then

(3) $\dfrac{(\angle A)^\circ}{(\angle X)^\circ} = 1,$

(4) $\dfrac{(\angle B)^\circ}{(\angle Y)^\circ} = 1.$

Therefore

(5) $\dfrac{(\angle A)^\circ}{(\angle X)^\circ} = \dfrac{(\angle B)^\circ}{(\angle Y)^\circ}$

Hence all pairs of corresponding angles and sides *are* proportional (with proportionality constant 1) because they are congruent. Congruent triangles, therefore, are also similar triangles and have the same area, but they need not lie in the same plane.

¶ DRILL
(a) Are any two quadrilaterals similar if their corresponding sides are proportional and their corresponding angles equal in measure?
(b) If the sides are proportional but the angles are not equal in measure?
(c) If the angles are equal in measure but the sides are not proportional?

[9] If $AY = BX$, $AX = 3$, $YC = 12$, and $XY \parallel BC$, find AC.

  Ⓐ 15   Ⓑ 18   Ⓒ 16
  Ⓓ 21   Ⓔ 20

The letters in the following postulate refer to the figure above, but the postulate will, of course, be considered true for all triangles that have two sides intersected by a line parallel to the third side.

Postulate 15 For any triangle ABC line XY intersects sides AB and AC and $XY \parallel BC$ if and only if

(1) $\dfrac{AB}{AX} = \dfrac{AC}{AY} = \dfrac{BC}{XY}.$

In other words, the segments that are cut off are proportional to the sides that contain them. Are the segments cut off also proportional to each other? By 15-1, if (1) above is true, then:

(2) $\dfrac{AB - AX}{AX} = \dfrac{AC - AY}{AY}.$

Since $AB - AX = XB$ and $AC - AY = YC$, we conclude:

(3) $\dfrac{XB}{AX} = \dfrac{YC}{AY}$

EXAMPLE 1

If $AX = 2$, $AB = 9$, $AY = 3$ in the figure above, find YC if XY is to be parallel to BC.

SOLUTION: By Postulate 15, $\dfrac{AB}{AX} = \dfrac{AC}{AY}$, so $\dfrac{9}{2} = \dfrac{AC}{3}$ and $AC = 13\frac{1}{2}$. Therefore $YC = AC - AY = 13\frac{1}{2} - 3 = 10\frac{1}{2}.$

EXAMPLE 2

Find m if $AX = 3m - 19$, $XB = m - 3$, $YC = 2m - 8$ and $AY = 8$, in the figure of the multiple-choice question.

SOLUTION:

$$\frac{3m - 19}{m - 3} = \frac{8}{2m - 8}$$
$$8m - 24 = 6m^2 - 62m + 152$$
$$0 = 6m^2 - 70m + 176$$
$$0 = 2(3m - 11)(m - 8)$$

Therefore $m = \frac{11}{3}$ or 8.

In the multiple-choice question,

$$\frac{AX}{BX} = \frac{AY}{CY}$$

Let $BX = AY = m$. Then

$$\frac{3}{m} = \frac{m}{12},$$
$$m^2 = 36,$$
$$m = 6 = AY.$$

Since $AC = AY + YC$,

$$AC = 6 + 12$$
$$= 18.$$

¶ DRILL

(a) Will the segment that connects the midpoints of two sides of a triangle always be parallel to the third? What will the ratio of these two segments be?

(b) In the figure of the multiple-choice question, write all of the ratios which are equal to $\dfrac{YC}{YA}$.

(c) Write all of the ratios that are equal to $\dfrac{BC}{XY}$.

(d) Is the following a correct proportion?

$$\frac{AX}{XB} = \frac{XY}{BC}$$

[10] If $AB \parallel WX \parallel YZ \parallel CD$, $AW = 2$, $WY = 3$, $YC = 1$ and $BD = 12$, find BX.

Ⓐ 2   Ⓑ 3   Ⓒ 4
Ⓓ 6   Ⓔ 8

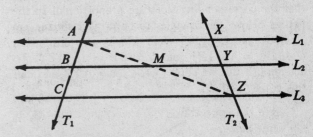

Postulate 15 enables us to prove the statement which follows. Try to think of a proof on your own before you review the one which accompanies it (hint: draw segment AZ).

15-5 Lines L_1, L_2 and L_3 are parallel if and only if they intersect transversals T_1 and T_2 in points A, B, C and X, Y, Z, respectively, such that

$$\frac{AB}{BC} = \frac{XY}{YZ}.$$

PROOF   *Only if:*

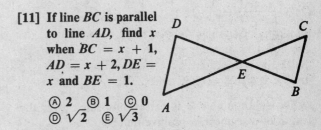

(1) $\dfrac{AB}{BC} = \dfrac{AM}{MZ}$ by Postulate 15

(2) $\dfrac{AM}{MZ} = \dfrac{XY}{YZ}$ by Postulate 15

(3) $\dfrac{AB}{BC} = \dfrac{XY}{YZ}$ by substitution in (1) and (2)

A similar law can be proved for sets containing four or more parallel lines. In the question which begins this section, let $ZD = a$. Then $XZ = 3a$ and $BX = 2a$, so $a + 3a + 2a = 12$ and $a = 2$.

¶ DRILL Describe how you can use 15-5 to separate a given segment, AB, into two parts in the ratio $\dfrac{3}{5}$ with only a straight-edge, compass and pencil.

[11] If line BC is parallel to line AD, find x when $BC = x + 1$, $AD = x + 2$, $DE = x$ and $BE = 1$.

Ⓐ 2   Ⓑ 1   Ⓒ 0
Ⓓ $\sqrt{2}$ Ⓔ $\sqrt{3}$

In a correspondence between two triangles for which two pairs of corresponding angles are equal in measure, will the third pair also be equal in measure? For any $\triangle ABC$ and $\triangle XYZ$, if $(\angle A)^\circ = (\angle X)^\circ$ and $(\angle B)^\circ = (\angle Y)^\circ$, then $(\angle A)^\circ + (\angle B)^\circ = (\angle X)^\circ + (\angle Y)^\circ$ and $180 - [(\angle A)^\circ + (\angle B)^\circ] = 180 - [(\angle X)^\circ + (\angle Y)^\circ]$. But $(\angle C)^\circ = 180 - [(\angle A)^\circ + (\angle B)^\circ]$ and $(\angle Z)^\circ = 180 - [(\angle X)^\circ + (\angle Y)^\circ]$ since the sum of the measures of the angles of a triangle is 180. Thus the third pair of angles, $\angle C$ and $\angle Z$, are equal in measure.

We can now prove:

15-6 (*AA*) A correspondence between two triangles is a similarity if two pairs of corresponding angles are equal in measure.

PROOF We have already shown that the third pair of angles must be equal in measure and need only show that the corresponding sides are proportional. In the figures below, the triangles to be proved similar are $\triangle ABC$ and $\triangle XYZ$, for which we are given $(\angle ABC)° = (\angle XYZ)°$ and $(\angle BAC)° = (\angle YXZ)°$. To accomplish this we copy $\triangle ABC$ on $\triangle XYZ$ and call this copy $\triangle A'B'C'$.

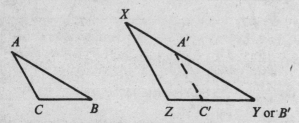

Line $A'C'$ must be parallel to line XZ since $(\angle X)° = (\angle A')°$. By Postulate 15 we conclude:

(1) $\dfrac{A'C'}{XZ} = \dfrac{B'C'}{YZ} = \dfrac{B'A'}{YX}.$

Since $\triangle A'B'C'$ is a copy of $\triangle ABC$, we can replace $A'C'$ by AC, $B'A'$ by BA and $B'C'$ by BC in (1) to get the required proportionality.

In the figure at the beginning of this section, the parallel lines give us two pairs of alternate interior angles of equal measure and thus the triangles are similar by *AA*. We need only solve the proportion:

(2) $\dfrac{x+1}{x+2} = \dfrac{1}{x}.$

(3) $x(x+1) = 1(x+2),$
$\qquad x^2 + x = x + 2,$
$\qquad\quad x^2 = 2,$
$\qquad\quad x = \pm\sqrt{2}.$

The solution $-\sqrt{2}$ is extraneous since x is the length of a segment, a positive number.

TEST-TAKING TIP.

Often, as in this example, the solution of an equation will not fit the given information because the equation represents a more general situation than the original information allows. Always check your answers to see whether they make sense in terms of the given information as well as making the deriving equation true.

¶ DRILL In each of the following indicate which triangles are similar by *AA*:

(a) Given that *ABCD* is a parallelogram.

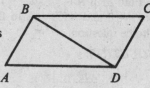

(b) Given $(\angle AXY)° = (\angle C)°.$

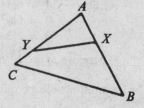

(c) Given $AB \perp BC$ and $BX \perp AC.$

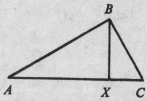

[12] In the figure $AD = 16$, $AB = 12$ and $AC = 9$. Both $\angle DAB$ and $\angle BAC$ have measures of 50. $\dfrac{DB}{BC} = ?$

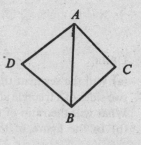

Ⓐ $\dfrac{4}{3}$ Ⓑ $\dfrac{16}{9}$ Ⓒ $\dfrac{3}{4}$

Ⓓ $\dfrac{9}{16}$ Ⓔ Cannot be determined

If, in $\triangle PMQ$ and $\triangle XYZ$ below,

(1) $\dfrac{PM}{MQ} = \dfrac{XY}{YZ}$

and $(\angle M)° = (\angle Y)°$, we can prove the two triangles are similar. To do this we have copied $\triangle XYZ$ on $\triangle PMQ$ to get $\triangle X'Y'Z'$ and have added line L parallel to segment PQ.

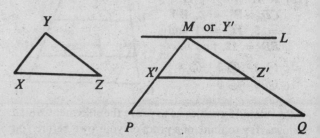

Since $X'Y' = XY$ and $Y'Z' = YZ$, we conclude:

(2) $\dfrac{PM}{MQ} = \dfrac{X'Y'}{Y'Z'}$ by substitution in (1) above, and

(3) $\dfrac{PM}{X'Y'} = \dfrac{MQ}{Y'Z'}$ by 15-2.

Therefore

(4) $\dfrac{PM - X'Y'}{X'Y'} = \dfrac{MQ - Y'Z'}{Y'Z'}$ by 15-1.

But $PM - X'Y' = PX'$ and $MQ - Y'Z' = QZ'$, so

(5) $\dfrac{PX'}{X'Y'} = \dfrac{QZ'}{Y'Z'}$.

The set of lines L, $X'Z'$ and PQ, therefore, cut off proportional segments on transversals PM and QM: this makes them parallel by 11-5. This means $(\angle Y'X'Z')° = (\angle P)°$ and, therefore, $(\angle YXZ)° = (\angle P)°$ so $\triangle XYZ \sim \triangle PMQ$ by AA. We have now proved the following:

15-7 (*SAS Similarity*) A correspondence between two triangles is a similarity if two pairs of corresponding sides are proportional and the included pair of corresponding angles are equal in measure.

In the multiple-choice question,

$$\frac{AD}{AB} = \frac{AB}{AC} \quad \text{since} \quad \frac{16}{12} = \frac{12}{9}.$$

Because we are given that $(\angle DAB)° = (\angle BAC)° = 50$, it follows that $\triangle ADB$ is similar to $\triangle ABC$ by SAS. Therefore the ratio of DB to BC must equal the ratio of the given pairs of corresponding sides (16 to 12, which reduces to 4 to 3):

$$\frac{AD}{AB} = \frac{4}{3} = \frac{DB}{BC}.$$

¶ DRILL

(a) Are any two isosceles triangles similar? How many pairs of angles must be proved equal in measure? Will any pair of corresponding angles do?

(b) Are any two equilateral triangles similar?

(c) If AC bisects $\angle BAD$ (see the figure at right), is $\triangle BAC$ ever similar to $\triangle CAD$? Suppose $AL = 1$, $AC = 3$ and $AD = 9$; Can the triangles be similar?

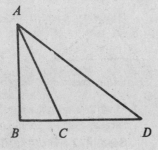

[13] What must the values of x and y be if we are to conclude that $\triangle ABC \sim \triangle EDF$?

  Ⓐ $x = 1, y = 2$ Ⓑ $x = 2, y = 3$ Ⓒ $x = 3, y = 4$ Ⓓ $x = 4, y = 5$ Ⓔ $x = 5, y = 6$

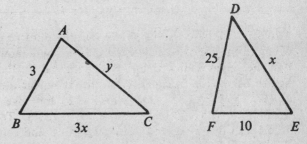

(Figures are not drawn to scale.)

15-8 (*SSS Similarity*) A correspondence between two triangles is a similarity if all three pairs of corresponding sides are proportional.

Many geometry courses omit theorem 15-8 entirely; we will omit only its proof. If our omission disturbs you, you may consider it a postulate.

In the question above we are given no information about the angles of the triangles and must apply 15-8 in order to conclude that they are similar. Thus we must find values of x and y such that

$$\frac{3}{x} = \frac{3x}{25} = \frac{y}{10}.$$

Using two fractions at a time, we get

$$\frac{3}{x} = \frac{3x}{25},$$
$$3x^2 = 75,$$
$$x^2 = 25,$$
$$x = \pm 5.$$

The solution -5 is extraneous since x is the length of a segment and must be a positive number. Using 5 for x in the above gives

$$\frac{3}{5} = \frac{y}{10},$$
$$\frac{3}{5}(10) = y,$$
$$6 = y.$$

¶ DRILL

(a) Name a similarity theorem or postulate that has no analogous congruence postulate.

(b) Name a congruence postulate that has no analogous similarity theorem or postulate.

[14] If the longest side of a right triangle is 13 while the shortest is 5, find the length of the altitude to the hypotenuse.

Ⓐ 5   Ⓑ $4\frac{8}{13}$ Ⓒ 6   Ⓓ $6\frac{5}{12}$ Ⓔ $6\frac{5}{13}$

To answer this question we'll develop two formulas based on the similar triangles found in a right triangle. If a $\triangle ABC$ has a right angle at B and if $BD \perp AC$ while $(\angle A)° = A$ 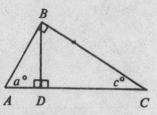 a and $(\angle C)° = c$, what are $(\angle ABD)°$ and $(\angle CBD)°$? Since $(\angle BDA)° = (\angle ABC)°$ and $(\angle BAD)° = (\angle BAC)°$, we conclude that the remaining pair of angles in $\triangle ABD$ and $\triangle ACB$ are also equal in measure so $(\angle ACB)° = (\angle ABD)° = c$. By a like argument we conclude that $(\angle CBD)° = a$.

Put these measures, c and a, in the appropriate angles of the sketch above so you can keep track of the corresponding angles. You should now see that:

(1) $\triangle ABC \sim \triangle ADB \sim \triangle BDC$

with the corresponding vertices given by the order of the letters in (1).

The corresponding sides of $\triangle ABD$ and $\triangle BCD$ must be proportional so:

(2) $\dfrac{BD}{DC} = \dfrac{AD}{BD}$,

(3) $(BD)^2 = (AD)(DC)$, and

(4) $BD = \sqrt{(AD)(DC)}$.

15-9   The altitude BD to the hypotenuse AC in a right triangle $\triangle ACB$ is the geometric mean of the lengths of the segments AD and DC into which it separates the hypotenuse:

$$BD = \sqrt{(AD)(DC)}.$$

The corresponding sides of $\triangle ABC$ and $\triangle ADB$ are proportional so:

(5) $\dfrac{AB}{AD} = \dfrac{AC}{AB}$,

(6) $(AB)^2 = (AD)(AC)$,

(7) $AB = \sqrt{(AD)(AC)}$.

Had we used $\triangle DBC \sim \triangle BAC$ we would have gotten:

(8) $BC = \sqrt{(DC)(AC)}$.

15-10   A leg BC of a right triangle is the geometric mean of the hypotenuse AC and that segment of the hypotenuse DC cut off by the altitude and adjacent to the leg:

$$BC = \sqrt{(DC)(AC)}.$$

We will use both 15-10 and 15-9 to answer the question at the beginning of the section. If $AC = 13$, let $DC = x$ and $BC = 5$. By 15-10,

(9) $5 = \sqrt{13x}$,

(10) $\dfrac{25}{13} = x$.

Thus the other segment of the hypotenuse is $13 - \dfrac{25}{13}$ or $\dfrac{144}{13}$. By 15-9 the altitude, BD, to the hypotenuse, AC, is the geometric mean of the two segments AD and DC, $\dfrac{25}{13}$ and $\dfrac{144}{13}$, respectively:

(11) $BD = \sqrt{\dfrac{25}{13} \times \dfrac{144}{13}} = \dfrac{60}{13}$.

¶ **DRILL** Answer the following questions. Refer to the figure of question [14].

(a) $AD = 3$, $DC = 27$; find BD and BC.
(b) $BC = 4\sqrt{3}$, $DC = 4$; find AC and BD.
(c) $AD = \sqrt{5}$, $BD = \sqrt{5}$; find DC and BA.

WHAT YOU SHOULD KNOW

KEY CONCEPTS

Handling Ratios and Proportions

1. If a, b and c are real numbers and $c \neq 0$, then $\dfrac{ac}{bc} = \dfrac{a}{b}$.

2. If $\dfrac{a}{b} = k$, then k is called the "constant of proportionality," and $a = kb$.

3. If two fractions are equal, their reciprocals are equal.

Handling Similar Triangles

1. Two triangles are similar if all pairs of corresponding angles are congruent and all pairs of corresponding sides are proportional.

2. If a line intersects two sides of a triangle and is parallel to the third, it cuts off segments proportional to the sides and forms a triangle similar to the original triangle.

3. Two triangles are similar if two pairs of corresponding angles are congruent (AA).

4. Two triangles are similar if two pairs of corresponding sides are proportional and their included angles are congruent (SAS).

5. Two triangles are similar if all pairs of corresponding sides are proportional (SSS).

Other

1. The segment connecting the midpoints of two sides of a triangle is parallel to the third and equal to half its length.

2. The altitude to the hypotenuse is the geometric mean between the segments into which it separates the hypotenuse.

KEY THEOREM

If a, b, c and d are real numbers and

$$\frac{a}{b} = \frac{c}{d},$$

then $ad = bc$. The terms a and d are called the "extremes," and b and c are the "means." The above law is sometimes stated, using these terms, as "The product of the means equals the product of the extremes." (Cross-Multiplication Theorem)

TEST-TAKING STRATEGIES

• When you solve an equation in a similarity problem, check your answer to see that it not only satisfies the deriving equation but also fits the given information.

• Roughly speaking, similar triangles have the same shape, though they are not necessarily of the same size. (Triangles of the same size and same shape are not only similar, but they are also congruent.) If triangles appear to have the same shape, look for ways of determining if they are similar so you can set up proportions to find the missing sides. This generally means finding a way to show that two pairs of angles are congruent.

ANSWERS

[1] Ⓓ

DRILL:

(a) $\frac{4}{5}$ (b) $\frac{27}{12}$ (c) $2y = 3x$.

---

[2] Ⓑ

DRILL:

(a) 12   (b) 0

(c) $-\frac{1}{9}$ (d) 3 or $\frac{2}{3}$

[3] Ⓓ

DRILL:

(a) $x = 1.5$, $y = 6.5$, $k = 2$

(b) $x = \frac{3}{4}$, $y = \frac{7}{4}$, $k = 12$

(c) Yes, yes.

[4] Ⓑ

DRILL:

(a) 3   (b) $\frac{1}{3}$

(c) $\frac{4y - 9}{3y}$

[5] Ⓒ

DRILL:

(a) $18 = 18$

(b) Not true since $90 \neq 45$.

[6] Ⓓ

DRILL:

(a) 3   (b) 4

[7] Ⓐ

DRILL:

(a) 6   (b) 4

(c) $2\sqrt{5}$ (d) Only 1 and 1.

[8] Ⓔ

DRILL:

(a) Yes.   (b) No.

(c) No.

[9] Ⓑ

DRILL:

(a) Yes, $\frac{1}{2}$ (b) $\frac{XB}{XA}$

(c) $\frac{AB}{AX}$, $\frac{AC}{AY}$ (d) No.

[10] Ⓒ

DRILL:

Draw any ray AX and, using any compass setting, find 8 points of AX equidistant from each other starting from A. Connect the last of these (call it P) to B and construct lines through the other points and parallel to line PB. These will separate AB into eight segments of equal length. The union of the first three of these and the union of the last five will be the desired parts.

[11] Ⓓ
DRILL:
(a) $\triangle ABD \sim \triangle CDB$; this is also a congruence.
(b) $\triangle AXY \sim \triangle ACB$.
(c) $\triangle ABC \sim \triangle BXC \sim \triangle AXB$.

[12] Ⓐ
DRILL:
(a) No, one pair of *corresponding* angles; yes.
(b) Yes.
(c) Only if $\triangle BAD$ is isosceles; then B, C and D cannot be collinear.

[13] Ⓔ
DRILL:
(a) AA.
(b) ASA, HL, SAA.

[14] Ⓑ
DRILL:
(a) 9, $9\sqrt{10}$.
(b) 12, $4\sqrt{2}$.
(c) $\sqrt{5}$, $\sqrt{10}$.

16. Circles

Key Terms

circle   the set of all points in a plane that are the same distance (called the *radius)* from a fixed point (called the *center)* in the plane.

radius   a line segment joining the center and any point on the circle.

chord   a line segment joining any two points on the circle.

diameter   a chord that passes through the center of the circle.

arc   a part of a circle that consists of two points and the set of points on the circle between them.

secant   a line that intersects a circle in more than one point.

tangent   a line that intersects a circle in exactly one point.

WORKING WITH TANGENTS AND CHORDS

[1] If line *MN* is tangent to the smaller circle at *X*, line *PQ* is tangent to the larger circle at *Z*, and *XZ* ⊥ *MN*, then which of the following is NOT necessarily true?

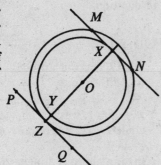

(A) *MX = XN*
(B) *PZ = QZ*
(C) *XZ ⊥ PQ*
(D) *MN ∥ PQ*
(E) *OX < OZ*

Given a point *O* and a positive number *r,* the set of all points that are *r* units from *O* is called a *circle.* The point *O* is called its *center* and *r* its *radius.* The term radius is also used to denote a segment with one endpoint at *O* and the other on the circle. Since point *O* is not *r* units from the center it is not a point of the circle. Two circles that have the same center are called *concentric* circles. The set of all points less than *r* units from *O* is called the *interior* of the circle and all those greater than *r* units from *O* comprise the *exterior* of the circle.

A line that intersects a circle in more than one point (such as line *MN* with the larger circle) is called a *secant.* Any segment whose endpoints lie on the circle (such as segments *MN* and *XY*) is a *chord.* Any chord of a circle which contains the center of that circle is a *diameter.*

A line is *tangent* to a circle if and only if it intersects the circle in exactly one point, *Z,* and is coplanar with the circle. *P* is called the point of "contact" or "tangency."

We can answer the multiple-choice question if we know the relationship of a tangent and the radius drawn to the point of contact.

16-1 A line, *L,* is perpendicular to a radius, segment *OX,* at a point *X* if and only if *L* is a tangent at point *X* to the circle with center *O.*

PROOF *Only if:* Suppose *OX* ⊥ *L* at *X* but *L* is not a tangent. Then *L* would have to intersect the circle at some other point *Y* as well (remember the definition of tangent?). *OX = OY* so $(\angle OXY)° = (\angle OYX)°$ by

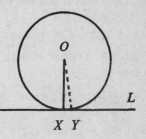

ITT and △*OXY* will have two right angles, which is impossible.

We could now use the "only if" part of 16-1, just verified, to support the "if" part. We will omit this proof.

In the multiple-choice question above, *XZ* is therefore perpendicular to both of lines *MN* and *PQ*. *OM = ON* because both are radii of the larger circle so △*OXM* ≅ △*OXN* by HL and *MX = NX.* In general:

16-2 A segment from the center of a circle which is perpendicular to a chord of the circle must bisect the chord.

In (B), though *PZ* looks equal to *ZQ, P* and *Q* can be any points of this line without contradicting the information that it is tangent.

¶ DRILL

(a) Suppose we were given $XM = XN$ instead of MN tangent at X. Could we *prove* $OX \perp MN$ and, thereby, MN tangent at X?

(b) Can a line intersect a circle in more than two points?

(c) If a line L intersects a chord PQ of a circle at its midpoint M, must L contain the center, O, of the circle?

[2] $\triangle ABC$ is equilateral with radius $OM \perp$ side AB, $OY \perp BC$, $OM = 6$, and $XM = 3$. Find the perimeter of quadrilateral $OYBX$.

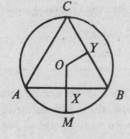

Ⓐ $6\sqrt{3}$ Ⓑ 6
Ⓒ 12 Ⓓ $6 + 6\sqrt{3}$
Ⓔ 15

The *distance* from a point to a line is defined to be the length of the perpendicular segment from the point to the line.

16-3 Two chords of a circle are equal in length if and only if they are equidistant from the center of the circle.

PROOF   *Only if:* If, in the figure at right, $CD = EF$, then:

(1) $\frac{1}{2}CD = \frac{1}{2}EF$.

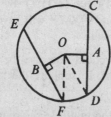

But $OB \perp EF$ and $OA \perp CD$ so OB must bisect chord EF and OA must bisect chord CD, both by 16-2. This means that

(2) $BF = \frac{1}{2}EF$ and

(3) $AD = \frac{1}{2}CD$.

Substitution of (2) and (3) in (1) yields $BF = AD$. Of course, $OF = OD$ since both are radii of the same circle. Therefore $\triangle OBF \cong \triangle OAD$ by HL and $OB = OA$.

In the multiple-choice question above, $AB = BC$ so $OX = OY = 3$. If we were to draw in radius OB we would get right triangle $\triangle OXB$ with hypotenuse of 6 ($OB = OM$ since both are radii) and leg OX of 3. To find XB, we need a relationship between the sides of a right triangle. We will informally introduce such a relationship here but postpone a more intense discussion until the next chapter.

If the sides of a right triangle have the lengths indicated in the figure at right, then $c^2 = a^2 + b^2$. You will find the skeleton of a proof of this equation in the drill exercises—this proof is based on similar triangles whereas the proof in the next chapter will be based on area.

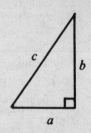

Thus

$$(OB)^2 = (OX)^2 + (XB)^2,$$
$$36 = 9 + (XB)^2,$$
$$\sqrt{27} = XB,$$
$$3\sqrt{3} = XB.$$

Since $CB = AB$ and X and Y are the respective midpoints of the sides, we know that $YB = XB$ and we now have all the lengths of the sides of the quadrilateral in question.

¶ DRILL

(a) If CD is the altitude to AB then: $a = ?$, $b = ?$, $y = ?$, $x = ?$ Since $x + y = c$, we can conclude $c = ?$ Therefore $c^2 = ?$

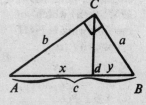

(b) If a chord is 3 inches from the center of a circle of radius of 5 inches, how long is the chord?

(c) If a chord is 6 inches long and is 1 inch from the center of the circle, what is the radius?

(d) If a chord is 8 inches long and the radius of the circle is 4, how far is the chord from the center of the circle?

FINDING THE DEGREE MEASURES OF ARCS AND ANGLES

[3] Which arc in the figure has the greatest degree measure?

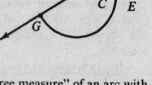

Ⓐ AB Ⓑ BC
Ⓒ AC Ⓓ DE
Ⓔ GF

Do not confuse the "degree measure" of an arc with the "length" of the arc. To define degree measure we will first define "minor arc," "major arc," and "central angle."

An angle is a *central angle* of a circle if and only if its vertex is the center of the circle. For example, $\angle AOB$ is a central angle of the circle with center at O (right).

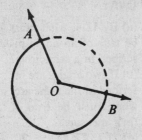

A *minor arc* of a circle is the set of all points of the circle which lie in the interior or on the sides of a given central angle. The dotted curve above indicates minor arc AB. Note that A and B are considered to be points of the arc.

A *major arc* of a circle is the set of points of the circle that lie in the exterior of, or on the sides of, a given central angle. The solid curve above, along with the points A and B, depicts major arc AB. Thus any given central angle determines two arcs, one minor and one major. When we write "arc AB" we will mean the minor arc.

The two arcs cut off by a diameter are called *semicircles* and include the endpoints of the diameter.

The *degree measure* of a minor arc is the degree measure of the central angle which determines it. The degree measure of a major arc is defined to be $360 - x$, where x is the degree measure of the determining central angle. The degree measure of a minor arc is always less than 180. The degree measure of a semicircle is 180. From the definitions above we can see that the total degree measure of a circle is 360.

In the multiple-choice question, arcs AB and GF are cut off by vertical angles and must each have the same degree measure. Arcs BC and DE also have the same measure because they are cut off by the same angle. Arc AC is a semicircle, and its degree measure must be greater than that of any minor arc.

¶ DRILL

(a) If $\angle AOB$ is a central angle of two different circles, what can you conclude about the circles?

(b) If A and B are points of one circle that has center O, while C and D are points of $\angle AOB$ on the second circle, what can you conclude about the measures of arc CD and arc AB? About the measures of major arc CD and major arc AB? About the measures of major arc CD and minor arc AB?

(c) Find the measures of each arc in the figure.

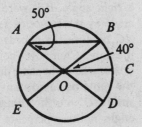

[4] If both circles have centers at O and the degree measure of minor arc CB is 40, what is the degree measure of major arc DE?

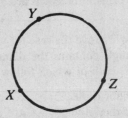

Ⓐ 220   Ⓑ 215
Ⓒ 210   Ⓓ 205   Ⓔ 200

Since the degree measure of a minor arc is defined to be the degree measure of its central angle, two minor arcs determined by the same central angle must have the same measure no matter what circle contains them. Thus, in the above figure:

$$(\text{arc } CB)° = (\text{arc } FE)°.$$

Before proceeding we will postulate the following:

Postulate 16 If Y is a point of an arc XZ (either major or minor), then:

$$(\text{minor arc } XY)° + (\text{minor arc } YZ)°$$
$$= (\text{arc } XYZ)°.$$

The use of the three letters in arc XYZ indicates the arc with endpoints X and Z that contains Y.

Postulate 16 could actually have been proved as a theorem, but the proof is tedious with several cases and the statement itself is straightforward.

Applying Postulate 16 to the above, we conclude

$$(\text{arc } FE)° + (\text{arc } FG)° + (\text{arc } GD)°$$
$$= (\text{major arc } ED)°.$$

The measures of arc FE and arc DG are 40. Arc GE is a semicircle with measure 180 so arc GF contains 140°. The answer requested is 220°.

¶ DRILL

(a) If two minor arcs are determined by central angles equal in measure, must the measures of the arcs be the same?

(b) If A and B are two points of a circle, what is the intersection of major arc AB with minor arc AB? What is their union? What is the sum of their measures?

(c) If all points of a semicircle AB are removed from a circle, is the set of points that remain also a semicircle?

[5] If the measure of ∠ABD is 50, what is the measure of ∠ACD?

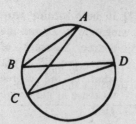

Ⓐ 25 Ⓑ 40 Ⓒ 50
Ⓓ 100 Ⓔ Cannot be determined

If X, Y and Z are any three distinct points of a circle, then ∠XYZ is called an *inscribed* angle. The arc determined by XZ and containing points of the interior of ∠XYZ is called the *intercepted arc* of ∠XYZ. The arc determined by XZ and containing points of the exterior of ∠XYZ is called the *inscribing* arc of ∠XYZ. ∠XYZ is said to *intercept* the former arc and to be *inscribed in* the latter arc.

> **16-4** The measure of an inscribed angle is half the measure of its intercepted arc.

PROOF We will prove the case for which one ray of the inscribed angle contains the diameter. There are two other cases, both of which follow from the first.

Case 1: If segment YZ is the diameter of the circle with center at O, then △XOY is isosceles. Let the measure of ∠Y be y; the measure of ∠X will also be y by ITT. If (arc XZ)° = p, then (∠XOZ)° = p

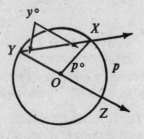

since ∠XOZ is a central angle that intercepts the arc. But y + y = p since ∠XOZ is an exterior angle of △OYX so y = ½ p, which was to be proved.

Case 2: To prove the case in which the diameter from the vertex of ∠XYZ passes through the interior of ∠XYZ, draw the diameter and apply Case I twice.

Case 3: The remaining case—the diameter from Y lies in the exterior of the angle—is similar to Case 2.

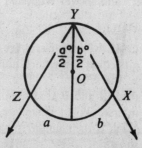

In the multiple-choice question, ∠ABD and ∠ACD are both inscribed angles intercepting the minor arc AD. Therefore they have the same measure, 50.

¶ **DRILL**

(a) By 12-4, what must be true of an angle inscribed in a semicircle?
(b) If two angles are inscribed in the same arc, what must be true of their measures?
(c) If (∠XZY)° = 70, (∠WXZ)° = 15, and (arc WX)° = 160, find the measures of each arc and angle in the figure.

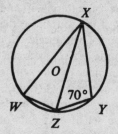

[6] If minor arc AC has the same degree measure as minor arc AB, which of the following CANNOT be true?

Ⓐ AC = AB Ⓑ AC = BC Ⓒ Segments AC and AB are equidistant from the center Ⓓ ∠ACB is a right angle Ⓔ ∠CAB is a right angle

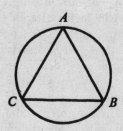

(Figure is not drawn to scale.)

As we have seen, a chord of a circle determines a major and a minor arc.

> **16-5** Two chords of a circle are equal in length if and only if their corresponding minor arcs are equal in measure.

PROOF Only if: In the circle at right, let XY = AB; then △OXY ≅ △OAB by SSS and (∠XOY)° = (∠AOB)° by CP. Since the measure of an arc equals the measure of the central angle which

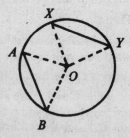

intercepts it, we conclude that (arc XY)° = (arc AB)°.

In the multiple-choice question, ∠ACB could not be a right angle. If it were, ∠ABC would also be a right angle by the Isosceles Triangle Theorem, since AB = AC because the chords have minor arcs of the same measure. Chord AC could equal BC since the three arcs can have the same degree measure. Chords AC and AB must be equidistant from the center of the circle since AC = AB. Though ∠CAB need not be a right angle, nothing prevents it from being a right angle.

¶ DRILL

(a) Suppose $AB = XY$ and AB and XY are chords of two different circles. Would the minor arcs be equal in measure if the radii were the same for both circles? If the radii were different?
(b) Suppose the major arcs of two chords are equal in measure. Would the chords have the same length?

[7] If lines AC and CD are tangent to the circle with center at O, and if the measure of $\angle DBC$ is 70, what is the measure of $\angle DAC$?

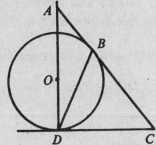

ⓐ 70   ⓑ 65   © 60
ⓓ 55   ⓔ 50

In the figure at right, rays XA and XB are tangent to the circle with center at O. $\angle XAO$ and $\angle XBO$ are right angles by 16-1. $AO = BO$ and $XO = XO$ so $\triangle XAO \cong \triangle XBO$ by HL.
We can now conclude each of the following:

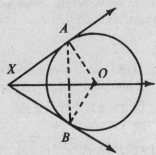

16-6 The ray from an external point X through the center of a circle bisects the angle formed by the tangent rays from X to the circle.

16-7 The tangent segments from a given external point to a circle are equal in length.

And, by *ITT*:

16-8 The angles formed by the two tangents from an external point with the secant connecting the points of tangency are equal in measure.

Theorem 16-8 could also be proved by use of the following:

16-9 The measure of a secant-tangent angle is one-half the measure of its intercepted arc.

PROOF In the figure at right, if YZ is tangent to circle O at Y and the measure of arc XY is m, then the measure of central $\angle XOY$ is also m. $\triangle OXY$ is isosceles so $(\angle OXY)° = (\angle OYX)°$. Let the measure of these two angles be n. Since the sum of the measures of the angles of $\triangle OXY$ must be 180, we conclude:

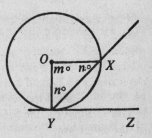

$$2n + m = 180,$$
$$2n = 180 - m,$$
$$n = \frac{180 - m}{2},$$
$$n = 90 - \frac{m}{2},$$
$$n + \frac{m}{2} = 90.$$

But $(\angle OXY)° + (\angle XYZ)° = 90$ since $\angle OYZ$ is a right angle by 16-1. Thus $(\angle XYZ)° = \frac{m}{2}$.

In the multiple-choice question, since $(\angle DBC)° = 70$, it follows that $(\angle BDC)° = 70$ and $(\angle C)° = 40$. Since $\angle ADC$ is a right angle, $\angle A$ must be the complement of $\angle C$ and $(\angle A)° = 50$.

¶ DRILL Given that segments DB, DE and EC are tangent to the circle, with $BD = 5$, $DE = 7$, $OB = 3$ and (arc GB)° = 96:

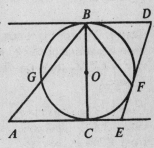

(a) Find the perimeter of quadrilateral $BCED$.
(b) Find $(\angle BAC)°$.

[8] Minor arc AB has degree measure 60 and $\angle CXD$ has degree measure 60. What is the degree measure of minor arc CD?

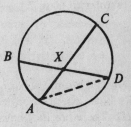

ⓐ 30   ⓑ 60   © 90
ⓓ 120   ⓔ 180

16-10 If two secants intersect in the interior of a circle, then the measure of any angle formed is one-half the sum of the measures of the arcs intercepted by the angle and its vertical angle.

16-11 If two secants intersect in the exterior of a circle, then the measure of the angle formed is one-half the difference of the measures of the two arcs intercepted by the angle.

PROOF Using the figure of the multiple-choice question, we want to prove that

$$(\angle AXB)^\circ = \frac{1}{2}[(\text{arc } AB)^\circ + (\text{arc } CD)^\circ].$$

By the theorem which states that the measure of an exterior angle of a triangle is the sum of the measures of its remote interior angles (the Exterior Angle Equality Theorem proved in Chapter 14 as a drill exercise), we conclude:

(1) $(\angle AXB)^\circ = (\angle CAD)^\circ + (\angle BDA)^\circ$.

But

(2) $(\angle BDA)^\circ = \frac{1}{2}(\text{arc } AB)^\circ$, and

(3) $(\angle CAD)^\circ = \frac{1}{2}(\text{arc } CD)^\circ$.

Substituting (2) and (3) in (1) gives the desired relationship.

To answer the multiple-choice question, substitute 60 for $(\angle CXD)^\circ$ and $(\text{arc } AB)^\circ$ in the equation:

$$(\angle CXD)^\circ = \frac{1}{2}[(\text{arc } AB)^\circ + (\text{arc } CD)^\circ],$$

$$60 = \frac{1}{2}[60 + (\text{arc } CD)^\circ],$$

$$120 = 60 + (\text{arc } CD)^\circ,$$

$$60 = (\text{arc } CD)^\circ.$$

¶ DRILL Each of the following refers to the figure in the question above.

(a) If $(\text{arc } AB)^\circ = 40$ and $(\text{arc } CD)^\circ = 50$, find $(\angle CXD)^\circ$.

(b) If $(\angle BXA)^\circ = 70$ and $(\text{arc } CD)^\circ = 60$, find $(\text{arc } BA)^\circ$.

[9] Find the measure of $\angle CXD$ if the degree measures of minor arcs CA, AB, and BD are, respectively, 120, 40, and 80.

Ⓐ 30   Ⓑ 35   Ⓒ 40
Ⓓ 45   Ⓔ 50

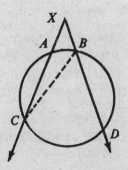

In the figure of the multiple-choice question:

(1) $(\angle CBD)^\circ = (\angle XCB)^\circ + (\angle CXD)^\circ$ by the Exterior Angle Equality Theorem,

(2) $(\angle XCB)^\circ = \frac{1}{2}(\text{arc } AB)^\circ$, and

(3) $(\angle CBD)^\circ = \frac{1}{2}(\text{arc } CD)^\circ$—both by the Inscribed Angle Theorem.

By substitution of (2) in (1) we get:

(4) $\frac{1}{2}(\text{arc } CD)^\circ = \frac{1}{2}(\text{arc } AB)^\circ + (\angle CXD)^\circ$, and

(5) $\frac{1}{2}[(\text{arc } CD)^\circ - (\text{arc } AB)^\circ] = (\angle CXD)^\circ$.

Substituting $(\text{arc } CD)^\circ = 120$ and $(\text{arc } AB)^\circ = 40$, we obtain

$$\frac{1}{2}(120 - 40) = \frac{1}{2}(80) = 40.$$

¶ DRILL Each of the following refers to the figure in the multiple-choice question.

(a) Find $(\angle CXD)^\circ$ if $(\text{arc } AB)^\circ = 30$ and $(\text{arc } CD)^\circ = 120$.

(b) Find $(\text{arc } BA)^\circ$ if $(\angle CXD)^\circ = 30$ and $(\text{arc } CD)^\circ = 110$.

(c) Find $(\text{arc } CD)^\circ$ if $(\angle CXD)^\circ = 40$ and $(\text{arc } AB)^\circ = 10$.

[10] If the measures of minor arcs AD, AB, and BC are, respectively, 30, 40 and 50, find the measure of $\angle Y$.

Ⓐ 170   Ⓑ 160
Ⓒ 150   Ⓓ 145
Ⓔ 140

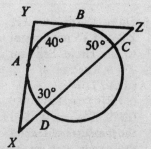

(Figure is not drawn to scale.)

16-12 If two tangents intersect, the measure of the angle formed is half the difference of the measures of the intercepted arcs.

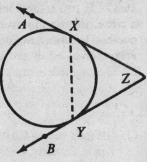

HANDLING CHORD RATIOS

[11] If $CE = 6, CD = 24$ and $AE = 4(EB)$, what is the length of AB?

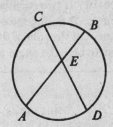

Ⓐ 8   Ⓑ 12   Ⓒ 10
Ⓓ $15\sqrt{3}$ Ⓔ 9

PROOF

(1) $(\angle YXZ)° + (\angle XZY)° = (\angle BYX)°$

(2) $(\angle XZY)° = (\angle BYX)° - (\angle YXZ)°$

(3) $(\angle BYX)° = \frac{1}{2}(\text{major arc } XY)°$

$(\angle YXZ)° = \frac{1}{2}(\text{minor arc } XY)°$

(4) $(\angle XZY)° = \frac{1}{2}[(\text{major arc } XY)°$

$- (\text{minor arc } XY)°]$

In the multiple-choice question,

$(\text{major arc } AB)° = 360 - (\text{minor arc } AB)°$
$= 320,$

$(\angle Y)° = \frac{1}{2}(320 - 40) = \frac{1}{2}(280) = 140.$

The proofs of 16-10, 16-11 and 16-12 have been quite similar. Once you become familiar with these proofs, you need not memorize the theorems—drawing the auxiliary segments should suggest the proper relationships. Test yourself by proving the following:

16-13 If a tangent and a secant intersect at a point in the exterior of a circle, then the measure of the angle formed is half the difference of the measures of the intercepted arcs.

¶ DRILL Segments XZ, ZV and XS are tangent to the circle. Segment TV is a secant. If $(\angle YXT)° = 80$, $(\angle YZW)° = 100$ and $(\angle WVU)° = 70$, find the measures of each of the minor arcs in the figure.

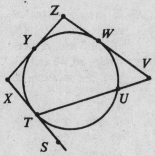

Let WX and YZ be two chords intersecting in a circle at a point E. Then $(\angle ZWX)° = (\angle XYZ)°$ since both are inscribed angles which intercept arc XZ. $(\angle WEZ)° = (\angle YEX)°$ since these are vertical angles. We conclude $\triangle WEZ \sim \triangle YEX$ by AA. Therefore:

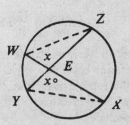

(1) $\dfrac{WE}{YE} = \dfrac{ZE}{XE}$

(2) $(WE)(XE) = (ZE)(YE)$

16-14 If WX and YZ are two chords of a circle intersecting at a point E, then

$$(WE)(XE) = (ZE)(YE).$$

In the multiple-choice question,

$(CE) \, (ED) = (AE)(BE),$
$(6) \, (18) = (4BE) \, (BE),$
$108 = 4(BE)^2,$
$27 = (BE)^2,$
$3\sqrt{3} = BE,$
$12\sqrt{3} = AE,$
$AB = AE + BE = 3\sqrt{3} + 12\sqrt{3}$
$= 15\sqrt{3}.$

¶ DRILL

(a) 16-14 tells us that to every point in the interior of a circle there can be assigned a positive number that is the product of the lengths of the segments of any chord containing the point. Find this number for the multiple-choice question above.

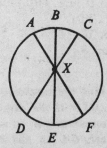

(b) If $AX = 2$, $XE = 4$ and $CX = 6$ find XD, XB and XF when the number described in (a) assigned to X is 12.

WHAT YOU SHOULD KNOW

KEY CONCEPTS

Handling Radii, Chords, Rays, and Tangents

1. A radius is perpendicular to a tangent at the point of tangency.
2. If a radius is perpendicular to a chord, then it bisects the chord.
3. Two congruent chords must be equidistant from the center of the circle.
4. Two chords have the same length if the degree measures of their minor arcs are equal.
5. If WX and YZ are two chords of a circle that intersect at a point E, then

$$(WE)(XE) = (ZE)(YE).$$

6. A ray from an external point X through the center of a circle bisects the angle formed by the tangent rays to the circle from X.
7. Tangent segments from an external point are congruent.

Handling Angles and Their Measures

1. A central angle of a circle is an angle whose vertex is the center of the circle.
2. The degree measure of a central angle is equal to the degree measure of its minor arc.
3. An inscribed angle is an angle with vertex on the circle and sides containing two other points of the circle.
4. The degree measure of an inscribed angle is half the degree measure of its intercepted arc.
5. The degree measure of a secant-tangent angle is half the measure of its intercepted arc.
6. If two secants intersect in the interior of a circle, the measure of each angle formed is half the sum of the measures of the arcs intercepted by the angle and its vertical angle.
7. If two secants intersect in the exterior of a circle, the measure of the angle formed is half the difference of the two arcs intercepted by the angle.
8. If two tangents intersect, the measure of the angle formed is half the difference of the measures of the intercepted arcs.
9. If a tangent and secant intersect at a point in the exterior of a circle, the measure of the angle formed is half the difference of the measures of the intercepted arcs.

KEY MEASURES

1. The degree measure of a *minor arc* is the degree measure of the central angle which determines it and is always less than 180.
2. The degree measure of a *major arc* is defined to be $360 - x$, where x is the degree measure of the determining central angle.
3. The degree measure of a *semicircle* is 180.
4. The total degree measure of a *circle* is 360.

TEST-TAKING STRATEGIES

- Take care not to confuse the "degree measure" and the "length" of an arc.
- Be sure to use the relationship between the measure of an angle and its intercepted arc when determining missing measures in a figure based on a circle.
- Always estimate the size of an angle to compare this number with the result you get by calculation. If an angle looks as if it measures 30 degrees and your calculation says it is 75 degrees, look for an error in your calculation.
- When given numerical information about parts of a figure, be sure to note this information in the appropriate place on your diagram. Often, this will immediately suggest the measures of missing parts.

ANSWERS

[1] Ⓑ
DRILL:
(a) Yes.
(b) No.
(c) Only if it is also perpendicular to PQ.

[2] Ⓓ
DRILL:
(a) $\sqrt{yc}, \sqrt{xc}, \dfrac{a^2}{c}, \dfrac{b^2}{c}, \dfrac{a^2}{c} + \dfrac{b^2}{c}, a^2 + b^2$
(b) 8
(c) $\sqrt{10}$
(d) Chord contains the center.

[3] Ⓒ
DRILL:
(a) They have the same center, 0.
(b) Equal; equal; their sum is 360.
(c) $BC = 40, BD = 100, CD = 60, AE = 100,$
$AB = 80 = ED.$

[4] Ⓐ
DRILL:
(a) Yes.
(b) Point A and B; the circle; 360.
(c) No, it has no endpoints.

[5] Ⓒ
DRILL:
(a) Right angle.
(b) Equal.
(c) (arc $WZY)° = 60$, $(\angle ZXY)° = 15$, $(\angle XWZ)° = 85$, $(\angle WZX)° = 80$, (arc $XY)° = 140$, and $(\angle WXY)° = 30$, $(\angle XYZ)° = 95$, (arc $YZ)° = 30$.

[6] Ⓓ
DRILL:
(a) Yes, no.
(b) Yes, if they are chords of the same or of congruent circles, otherwise, no.

[7] Ⓔ
DRILL:
(a) 20   (b) 48

[8] Ⓑ
DRILL:
(a) 45   (b) 80

[9] Ⓒ
DRILL:
(a) 45   (b) 50   (c) 90

[10] Ⓔ
DRILL:
$TY = 100$, $YW = 80$, $WU = 40$, $TU = 140$.

[11] Ⓓ
DRILL:
(a) 108
(b) $XF = 6$, $XB = 3$, $DX = 2$.

17. Area

WORKING WITH SQUARES AND TRIANGLES

[1] A square and a triangle have equal areas. If one side of the square and the base of the triangle have length b, what is the relationship between b and the altitude, h, of the triangle?

Ⓐ $\frac{1}{2}b = h$ Ⓑ $2b = h$ Ⓒ $b = h$ Ⓓ $b = 2h$

Ⓔ **Cannot be determined**

When we refer to the area of a "square," "triangle," "rectangle," or other polygon we really mean the area of the region *determined* by the polygon. This region is the union of the polygon and its interior. Strictly speaking, the polygon itself has no area since it is only the union of a finite number of segments.

We will make three assumptions as the basis of our theory of areas.

Area Postulate 1 Two triangles that are congruent have the same area.

Area Postulate 2 The area of a polygonal region is unique and is the sum of the areas of the polygonal regions that compose it.

When we use AP-2 we must be careful to separate the original region into regions that do not overlap, but that use all of the points of the original region. "Unique" reminds us that each triangle has one and only one area regardless of how this area is correctly computed.

The next assumption is not obvious, but we select it from all of the possible "unit" postulates because it greatly simplifies our later work. The purpose of any "unit" assumption is to give meaning to the term "area" by providing the area of some simple figure as a basis for the computation of the areas of all other figures. The area of a square is the customary choice,

but whereas few polygonal regions can be resolved into squares, all can be separated into triangles.

Area Postulate 3 The area of a triangle is one-half the product of the length of any side and the altitude to that side.

AP-3 yields the formula

$$A = \frac{1}{2}bh,$$

where A is the area of the triangle, b is the length of one side and h is the length of the altitude to that side. "Altitude" actually has two meanings: the altitude to a side is the segment from the opposite vertex drawn perpendicular to the line which contains the side and is also the length of this perpendicular segment.

For a right triangle the altitude to either one of the legs is the other leg (or the length of the other leg). Thus the area of a right triangle is one-half the product of the legs.

We will put the three assumptions together to derive the area of a square of side s.

Diagonal AC separates the square into two right triangles, the area of each of which is $\frac{1}{2}s^2$ by AP-3.

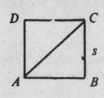

Since the area of a polygonal region is the sum of the areas of the composing regions (AP-2), the area of the square is

$$\frac{1}{2}s^2 + \frac{1}{2}s^2 = s^2.$$

The formula above can be used to solve the multiple-choice question. The area of the square is b^2, the area

of the triangle is $\frac{1}{2}bh$ and the areas were given as equal.
Therefore

$$b^2 = \frac{1}{2}bh,$$

$$b = \frac{1}{2}h \text{ or } h = 2b.$$

¶ DRILL If the area of a triangle, A_t, is $\frac{1}{2}bh$ and the area of a square, A_s, is s^2, find the missing elements of $\{A_s, A_t, s, b, h\}$ for each of the following.

(a) $A_s = A_t$, $s = 5$, $h = 4$
(b) $s = b$, $h = 2$, $A_s = 16$

WORKING WITH RECTANGLES

[2] If the area of a rectangle is doubled, but the length, b, of one side remains the same, what is the change in the length, a, of an adjacent side?

Ⓐ **Remains the same** Ⓑ **Quadruples** Ⓒ **Doubles** Ⓓ **Triples** Ⓔ **Cannot be determined**

Using our area assumptions, we can compute the formula for the area of a rectangle in exactly the same way we computed it for the square.

In a rectangle $WXYZ$, diagonal WZ separates the polygonal region into two right triangular regions with sides of length a and b.

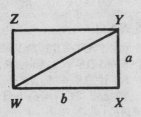

The area of each of these is $\frac{1}{2}ab$ so the area of the rectangle must be $\frac{1}{2}ab + \frac{1}{2}ab = ab$. Thus, if A is the area of a rectangle and a and b are the lengths of a pair of intersecting sides, then

$$A = ab.$$

To answer the multiple-choice question, solve for a to see how a relates to A and b:

$$a = \frac{A}{b}.$$

If A is doubled, the result is $2A$. Since

$$\frac{2A}{b} = 2\left(\frac{A}{b}\right) \quad \text{and} \quad \frac{A}{b} = a,$$

the new length of a is twice the original length.

¶ DRILL Find the missing element of $\{A, a, b\}$ if:
(a) $a = 12$, $b = 17$ (b) $A = 64$, $b = 8$
(c) $A = 10$, $a = \sqrt{10}$

WORKING WITH PARALLELOGRAMS

[3] Given parallelogram $ABCD$ with area X and $\triangle CDE$ with area Y, what is the relationship between X and Y?

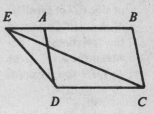

Ⓐ $X = Y$

Ⓑ $X = \frac{1}{2}Y$

Ⓒ $X = 4Y$

Ⓓ $Y = \frac{1}{2}X$

Ⓔ **Cannot be determined**

Diagonal PQ of parallelogram $PMQR$ separates it into two congruent triangles, $\triangle PMQ$ and $\triangle PRQ$. Since the distance, h, between two parallel lines is constant, both triangles have the

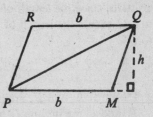

same altitude, h. The area of the parallelogram is the sum of the areas of the triangles. Both triangles have areas of $\frac{1}{2}hb$. Therefore the area, A, of the parallelogram is given by:

$$A = \frac{1}{2}hb + \frac{1}{2}hb$$
$$= hb,$$

where h is the distance between two parallel sides and b is the length of one of these parallel sides.

In the multiple-choice question, parallelogram $ABCD$ and $\triangle CDE$ have the same altitude (the distance between lines AB and CD) and the same base, CD. Since x, the area of the parallelogram, is the product of the altitude and the base, and y, the area of the triangle, is half the product of the altitude and the base,

$$y = \frac{1}{2}x.$$

¶ DRILL If A is the area of a parallelogram, b is the length of one side and h is the length of the altitude to that side, find the missing element of $\{A, h, b\}$ for each of the following:

(a) $A = 6$, $h = 4$ (b) $h = 2$, $b = 5$
(c) $A = \sqrt{2}$, $b = \sqrt{2}$

[4] If *M* is the midpoint of side *CD* of parallelogram *ABCD*, what is the relationship between the area, *X*, of △*AMD* and the area, *Y*, of △*BCM*?

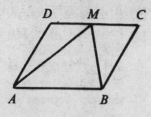

(A) $X = Y$ (B) $X = \frac{1}{2}Y$ (C) $X = 2Y$

(D) $X = \frac{1}{3}Y$ (E) $X = 3Y$

Since the area of a triangle is one-half the product of its altitude and base, two triangles that have equal altitudes and equal bases must have the same area. △*AMD* and △*BCM* have equal bases since *DM* = *MC*, because M is the midpoint of *DC*. They also have equal altitudes since the length of the perpendicular from *A* to *DC* equals the length of the perpendicular from *B* to *DC*.

¶ DRILL If L_1 and L_2 are parallel lines and points *A*, *B*, and *C* are on line L_1 while points *M* and *N* are on L_2, what is the relation between the areas of △*AMN*, △*NBM*, and △*CMN*?

[5] In △*ABC*, *BR* ⊥ *AC*, *CP* ⊥ *AB*, *CP* = 18, *AB* = 16 and *BR* = 12. What is the length of *AC*?

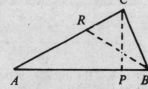

(A) Cannot be determined   (B) 20
(C) 15   (D) 10   (E) 24

(Figure is not drawn to scale.)

In AP-3 we construe "side" to mean *any* side. No matter which side of the triangle is selected as the base, the area is constant. For the multiple-choice question this means that

$$\frac{1}{2}(BR)(AC) = \frac{1}{2}(CP)(AB).$$

Substituting the given values into the equation produces

$$\frac{1}{2}(12)(AC) = \frac{1}{2}(18)(16),$$
$$6(AC) = 144,$$
$$AC = 24.$$

¶ DRILL
(a) If *AE* = 5, *BC* = 6 and *CD* = 3, find *AB*.
(b) If *CD* = 2, *AB* = 8 and *AE* = 4, find *BC*.
(c) If *BC* = 9, *CD* = 3 and *AB* = 9, find *AE*.

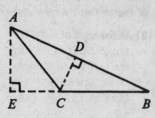

[6] Given parallelogram *ABCD* with segment *AF* perpendicular to the line that contains segment *DC*, *DE* ⊥ *BC*, *AF* = 7, *CD* = 9 and *DE* = 3. Find *BC*.

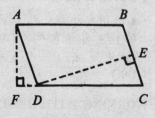

(A) 20   (B) 22   (C) 19   (D) 23   (E) 21

The area of a parallelogram is independent of the side chosen as base. The product of the length of any side and the altitude to that side must be the same as the product of the length of a different side and its respective altitude. In the question above, this means that

$$(DE)(BC) = (AF)(DC),$$
$$3(BC) = (7)(9) = 63,$$
$$BC = 21.$$

¶ DRILL
(a) If *AF* = 12, *BC* = 5 and *DE* = 3, find *AB*.
(b) If *DE* = 5, *AB* = 10 and *BC* = 6, find *AF*.

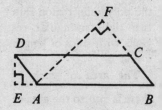

[7] If the area of parallelogram *ABCD* is 64 and the length of diagonal *AC* is 8, what is *DE* if *DE* ⊥ *AC*?

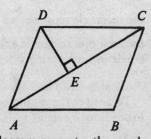

(A) 16   (B) 5   (C) 2
(D) 12   (E) 8

The diagonal of a parallelogram separates the parallelogram into two congruent triangular regions (*SSS*) which, therefore, have the same area. We can find the length of segment *DE* above by equating the area of △*ACD* as represented by $\frac{1}{2}(DE)(AC)$ with the area of △*ACD* as represented by one-half the area of the parallelogram:

$$\frac{1}{2}(DE)(8) = 32,$$
$$DE = 8.$$

WORKING WITH TRAPEZOIDS

[8] If the area of right triangle BCD is 12 and
the lengths of the seg-
ments are as shown in
the figure, what is the
area of trapezoid
$ABCE$ with $AB \parallel EC$?

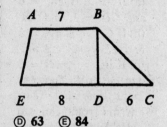

(A) 30   (B) 21   (C) 42   (D) 63   (E) 84

We have established a pattern for finding area formulas for polygonal regions: using diagonals we separate the polygonal regions into nonoverlapping triangular regions; then we add the areas of these triangular
regions. We will use this process to find the area formula for a trapezoid.

Trapezoid $ABCD$ has
parallel sides DC and AB
(called bases) with respective lengths b_1 and b_2.
The distance between DC
and AB is the length, h, of
any segment perpendicu-
lar to both and is called
the *altitude* of the trape-
zoid. Diagonal AC forms two triangles, $\triangle ACD$ with
base b_1 and $\triangle ABC$ with base b_2 as shown below.

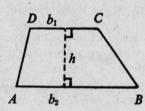

Since parallel lines are
everywhere equidistant, h
is the altitude of both triangles. The area of the
trapezoid is the sum of
the areas of $\triangle ADC$ and
$\triangle ABC$.

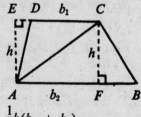

$$\frac{1}{2}hb_1 + \frac{1}{2}hb_2 = \frac{1}{2}h(b_1 + b_2)$$

In the multiple-choice question the lengths of the
bases are given but the altitude, BD, is missing. We can
find this altitude since it is a leg of a right triangle
whose area and other leg are given.

$$\frac{1}{2}(BD)(6) = 12$$
$$3BD = 12$$
$$BD = 4$$
$$\text{Area of } ABCE = \frac{1}{2}(4)(7 + 14)$$
$$= 2(21)$$
$$= 42$$

¶ DRILL Find the areas of each of the trapezoids whose
parts are given below:

(a) $h = 2, b_1 = 3, b_2 = 3$
(b) $h = 1, b_1 = 4, b_2 = 2$
(c) $h = 3, b_1 = \sqrt{2}, b_2 = \sqrt{18}$

[9] If the area of trape-
zoid $ABCD$ is 40 and
$ABED$ is a parallelo-
gram, find the area of
$\triangle BCE$.

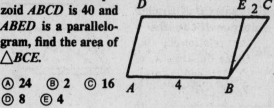

(A) 24   (B) 2   (C) 16
(D) 8   (E) 4

The area of a trapezoid is $\frac{1}{2}h(b_1 + b_2)$ and the opposite sides of a parallelogram have the same length. The
latter fact tells us that the length of DC is 6, and this,
with the trapezoid area formula, yields $h = 8$.

$$40 = \frac{1}{2}(h)(4 + 6) = \frac{1}{2}(10h)$$
$$= 5h$$
$$8 = h$$

Note that h is also an altitude of the parallelogram
and the triangle. The area we seek is $\frac{1}{2}(2)h$.

$$A = \frac{1}{2}(2h)$$
$$= h$$
$$= 8$$

¶ DRILL If the distance between parallel lines L_1 and
L_2 is 3 and $AB = 5$, where B is the midpoint of AC,
and if ED is also 5, find the areas of all triangles,
parallelograms and trapezoids in the following figure
that have all vertices on line L_1 or L_2.

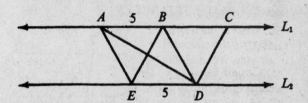

WORKING WITH RHOMBUSES

[10] If the area of a rhombus is 15 and the length of
one diagonal is 7, what is the length of the other
diagonal?

(A) $\frac{30}{7}$ (B) 30×7 (C) 15×7 (D) $15 \div 7$
(E) None of these

A rhombus is an equilateral parallelogram. The diagonals of a rhombus are perpendicular and bisect each
other. We use these facts and our established pattern to
develop a formula for the area of a rhombus in terms
of its diagonals.

If *ABCD* is a rhombus with diagonals $AC = a$ and $BD = b$, then $DE = BE = \frac{1}{2}b$ and $AE = CE = \frac{1}{2}a$. The diagonals form

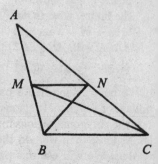

four right triangles with the sides, the area of each being

$$\frac{1}{2}(\frac{1}{2}a)(\frac{1}{2}b) = \frac{1}{8}ab.$$

The area of the rhombus is the sum of these four equal triangle areas:

$$4(\frac{1}{8})ab = \frac{ab}{2}.$$

The area is therefore half the product of the diagonals.

To answer the multiple-choice question, substitute 15 for *A* and 7 for *b* in the formula:

$$A = \frac{ab}{2},$$
$$15 = \frac{7b}{2},$$
$$30 = 7b,$$
$$\frac{30}{7} = b.$$

¶ DRILL Find the areas of the rhombuses that have the following as lengths of diagonals:

(a) 4, 2   (b) $\sqrt{2}, \sqrt{2}$ (c) $\sqrt{3}, 4$ (d) $\sqrt{3}, \sqrt{2}$

WORKING WITH TRIANGLES

[11] If *M* is the midpoint of side *AC* and the area of $\triangle ABM$ is 5, what is the area of $\triangle BMC$?

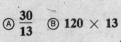

Ⓐ $\frac{5}{2}$ Ⓑ 5   Ⓒ 10

Ⓓ $\frac{7}{2}$ Ⓔ Cannot be determined

In $\triangle ABC$ there is only one segment which can be drawn from point *B* perpendicular to the line that contains *A* and *C*. This is segment *BD* as shown, and must, therefore, be an altitude of all three triangles, $\triangle ABC$, $\triangle ABM$ and $\triangle BMC$. Since *M* is the midpoint of segment *AC*,

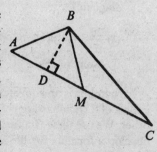

it follows that $AM = MC$ and $\triangle ABM$ has a base equal to a base of $\triangle BMC$. With equal bases and equal altitudes, triangles *ABM* and *BMC* must have the same area.

¶ DRILL In the figure at right, if *M* and *N* are the midpoints of the sides that contain them, name all of the triangles which have the same area as $\triangle AMN$. (Is $MN \parallel BC$?)

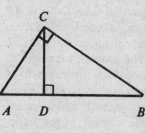

[12] If, in right triangle *ABC*, $BC = 12$ and $AC = 5$, what is the length of *CD*?

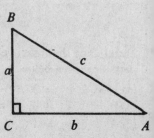

Ⓐ $\frac{30}{13}$ Ⓑ 120×13

Ⓒ $\frac{120}{13}$ Ⓓ $\frac{60}{13}$

Ⓔ 60×13

We will find *AB* and then use the fact that a triangle has exactly one number as its area:

$$\frac{1}{2}(AC)(BC) = \frac{1}{2}(CD)(AB),$$

from which we can compute *CD*. To find *AB* we will use a theorem already introduced and proved in Chapter 17. We will discuss this theorem and present a different proof as further drill in the use of area.

17-1 *The Pythagorean Theorem.* A triangle is a right triangle if and only if the square of the length of its longest side is equal to the sum of the squares of the lengths of the remaining two sides.

PROOF
Only if: Let $\triangle ABC$ be a right triangle with sides of length *a*, *b*, and *c* as shown.

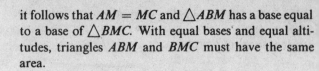

By constructing segments of lengths a and b along various perpendicular lines we build the following figure (our original triangle is the dotted one).

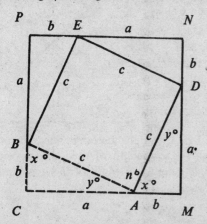

In this figure we can find: (1) four congruent right triangles with legs of a and b (congruent by *SAS*), (2) a square with sides of length $a + b$ (square *CMNP*), and (3) a square with sides of length c (square *ABED*).

Why is *ABED* a square? All of its sides have length c by *CP*. All of the angles are right angles by the following reasoning which we will trace out for $\angle BAD$.

(1) $x + y = 90$ (The acute angles of a right triangle are complementary)

(2) $n + x + y = 180$ (Ray *AC* and ray *AM* lie on the same line)

(3) $n = 90$ (Subtraction of (1) from (2))

The area $(a + b)^2$ of square *CMNP* is equal to the sum of the area of square *ADEB*, c^2, plus the areas of the four right triangles, each of which is $\frac{1}{2} ab$:

$$(a + b)^2 = c^2 + 4(\tfrac{1}{2} ab),$$
$$a^2 + 2ab + b^2 = c^2 + 2ab,$$
$$a^2 + b^2 = c^2.$$

Returning to the multiple-choice question, we see that $(AB)^2 = (BC)^2 + (AC)^2$ so AB is 13 since $BC = 12$ and $AC = 5$.

TEST-TAKING TIP.

Questions involving the use of the Pythagorean Theorem appear in one form or another on *every* College Board Mathematics Achievement Test.

An alternative method is described in section [14] of Chapter 15.

¶ DRILL If a and b are the lengths of the legs of a right triangle and c is the length of the hypotenuse, find the missing element of $\{a, b, c\}$:

(a) $a = 3, b = 4$ (b) $a = 5, c = 13$
(c) $a = \sqrt{2}, b = \sqrt{3}$ (d) $c = \sqrt{2}, a = 1$

[13] If *ABCD* is a trapezoid and the lengths of the segments are as shown, then the area of $\triangle FCB$ is?

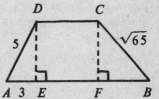

Ⓐ 7   Ⓑ Cannot be determined   Ⓒ 4
Ⓓ 14   Ⓔ 28

The given lengths of AD and AE will yield 4 as the length of DE by 17-1. CF also equals 4. By 17-1 we conclude $FB = 7$. With CF, FB and the area formula for right triangles we find the area of $\triangle CFB$ to be 14.

¶ DRILL In each of the following the given information is the length of the hypotenuse and one leg. Find the areas of the triangles by first using 17-1 to find the length of the missing leg.

(a) 6, 3   (b) 2, $2\sqrt{2}$ (c) 13, 5   (d) 2, $\sqrt{3}$

[14] What is the area of right triangle *ABC* if $\angle A$ and $\angle B$ both have measures of 45 while $AB = 5$?

Ⓐ Cannot be determined   Ⓑ 25
Ⓒ $\dfrac{25}{4}$ Ⓓ 100
Ⓔ 10

We can use 17-1 to develop an important relationship between the sides of an isosceles right triangle. If two sides of $\triangle ABC$, with right angle at C, have the same length, x, then the length of the hypotenuse, AB, is given by:

$$(AB)^2 = x^2 + x^2$$
$$= 2x^2,$$
$$AB = \sqrt{2x^2} = x\sqrt{2}.$$

This relationship is of enough importance in the remaining work of intermediate math—especially trigonometry—that you should memorize the figure at right. We will use it to compute the other two sides when one side is given; the following examples show the procedure.

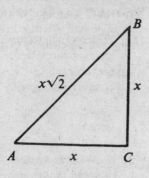

EXAMPLE 1

If a leg of an isosceles right triangle has length 4, what is the length of the hypotenuse?

SOLUTION: From the memorized figure, since $x = 4$ and the hypotenuse is $x\sqrt{2}$, the hypotenuse is $4\sqrt{2}$.

EXAMPLE 2

If the hypotenuse of an isosceles right triangle has length 5, what are the lengths of the legs?

SOLUTION: From the memorized figure the hypotenuse is $x\sqrt{2}$, so

$$x\sqrt{2} = 5 \quad \text{and} \quad x = \frac{5}{\sqrt{2}} \text{ or } \frac{5}{2}\sqrt{2}.$$

The results of Example 2 help us to answer the multiple-choice question by providing the lengths of the legs of the given right triangle. Since the area of a right triangle is half the product of the legs,

$$A = \frac{1}{2}(\frac{5}{2}\sqrt{2})(\frac{5}{2}\sqrt{2})$$
$$= \frac{1}{2} \cdot \frac{25}{4} \cdot 2$$
$$= \frac{25}{4}.$$

¶ DRILL If d is the length of the diagonal of a square and s is the length of each side, find the missing element of $\{d,s\}$ (hint: draw the diagonal and look for isosceles right triangles).

(a) $s = 5$ (b) $s = \sqrt{3}$
(c) $d = 2\sqrt{2}$ (d) $d = 3\sqrt{3}$

[15] If $\triangle ABC$ is equilateral with $BC = 6$, find the length of altitude CD.

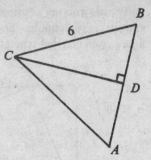

Ⓐ $3\sqrt{3}$ Ⓑ 3
Ⓒ $\frac{3}{\sqrt{3}}$ Ⓓ $\frac{\sqrt{3}}{3}$
Ⓔ $2\sqrt{3}$

17-2 In a triangle whose angle measures are 30, 60 and 90, the length of the side opposite the 30° angle is half the length of the hypotenuse.

PROOF If $\triangle CDB$ is a right triangle with angle measures as shown in the figure at right and if $DB = a$, construct a second 30° angle with vertex C and side CD. Then the line connecting segment DB will intersect ray CK at some point E. The measures of $\angle ECB$ and $\angle CBD$ are both 60, so the measure of $\angle CED$ must also be 60. But $\triangle BCD \cong \triangle ECD$ (ASA), so $DE = a$ and $BE = 2a$. Since $\triangle BCE$ is equiangular it is also equilateral, making $BC = 2a$.

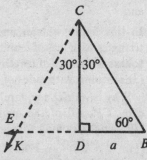

17-1 gives the length of the third side, CD, to be $a\sqrt{3}$. The figure at right puts together the relationships between sides and angles as proved. Memorize the figure for its use in later work.

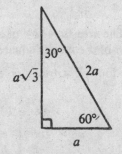

EXAMPLES

In each of the following, h is the length of the hypotenuse, t is the length of the side opposite the 30° angle and s is the length of the side opposite the 60° angle. Find the missing elements of $\{h, t, s\}$ for each of the following:

(1) Given $t = 5$:
Since t is opposite the 30° angle it is half of the hypotenuse, h, so $h = 10$. The side opposite the 60° angle, s, is $t\sqrt{3}$ so $s = 5\sqrt{3}$.

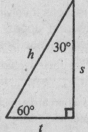

(2) Given $h = 8$:

Since t is opposite the 30° angle it is half of h, so $t = 4$. Again, $s = t\sqrt{3}$, so $s = 4\sqrt{3}$.

(3) Given $s = 6$: Since $s = t\sqrt{3}$ we conclude $6 = t\sqrt{3}$ so $t = \dfrac{6}{\sqrt{3}}$ or $2\sqrt{3}$. Because $h = 2t$, we get $h = 4\sqrt{3}$.

To answer the multiple-choice question, note that $\triangle BCD$ is a 30-60-90 triangle with BC the hypotenuse and CD the leg opposite the 60° angle. Using the 30-60-90 triangle relationship, we find that, if

$$BC = 2a = 6,$$

then

$$BD = a = 3$$

and

$$CD = a\sqrt{3} = 3\sqrt{3}.$$

¶ DRILL Use the directions for the above examples in each of the following:

(a) $t = 7$ (b) $h = 16$ (c) $s = 6\sqrt{3}$ (d) $s = 4$

[16] Find the area of $\triangle ABC$ if $BC = 4$, $\angle C$ has a measure of 30 and $\angle A$ has a measure of 45.

Ⓐ $\dfrac{2 + \sqrt{3}}{2}$

Ⓑ $2 + 2\sqrt{2}$

Ⓒ 8

Ⓓ $2 + 2\sqrt{3}$

Ⓔ 4

In the figure above construct altitude BD. By the 30-60-90 triangle relationship, $BD = 2$ and $CD = 2\sqrt{3}$. $\triangle ABD$ must be an isosceles right triangle, so $AD = 2$ also.

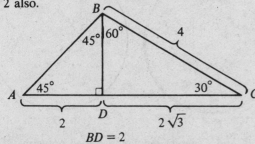

$$BD = 2$$

This yields $AC = 2 + 2\sqrt{3}$, and the area is

$$\frac{1}{2}(2)(2 + 2\sqrt{3}).$$

¶ DRILL In each of the following, find the area of the triangle if a and b are the lengths of two sides and $\angle C$ is their included angle:

(a) $a = 6$, $b = 5$ $(\angle C)° = 30$

(b) $a = 6$, $b = 5$, $(\angle C)° = 45$

(c) $a = 6$, $b = 5$, $(\angle C)° = 60$

FINDING AREAS OF COMPOSITE FIGURES

[17] Which of the follow-ing is a formula for the area of the ac-companying figure?

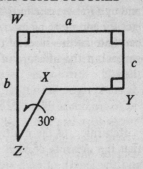

Ⓐ $ac + \dfrac{(b - c)^2}{2\sqrt{3}}$

Ⓑ ab

Ⓒ $ac + (b - c)$

Ⓓ $ac(b - c)$

Ⓔ $\dfrac{ac(b - c)^2}{\sqrt{3}}$

The figure is composed of a rectangular region (with sides of a and c) and a right triangular region (with an angle of 30° and a side of length $b - c$). Draw in a dotted segment that extends XY to meet WZ. The length of the dotted segment must be $\dfrac{b - c}{\sqrt{3}}$ by the 30-60-90 triangle relations. The area of the figure is the sum of the area of the rectangle (ac) and the area of the triangle $\left[\dfrac{1}{2} \times \dfrac{b - c}{\sqrt{3}} \times (b - c)\right]$.

WORKING WITH INSCRIBED POLYGONS

[18] If the perimeter of a regular inscribed po-lygon of six sides (a hexagon) is 48, what is its area?

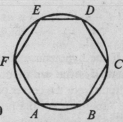

Ⓐ $96\sqrt{3}$ Ⓑ 384

Ⓒ 288 Ⓓ 96 Ⓔ 200

A polygon is *inscribed* in a circle if and only if the vertices of all of its angles lie on the circle. An inscribed polygon is *regular* if and only if all of its sides are equal in length and all of its angles are equal in measure.

To find the area of a regular inscribed polygon separate the figure into triangles by constructing all possible radii of the circle that intersect the vertices of the polygon as we have done for the in-scribed square at right.

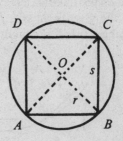

Each of the triangles formed is isosceles since two of the sides are radii of the circle no matter how many sides the polygon contains. The triangles are all congruent, then, by *SSS*. Each triangle contains a cen-tral angle—each of which has the same measure as each of the others by *CP*. This measure is $\dfrac{360}{n}$, where n is the number of sides (and hence the number of central angles). With this measure, along with the fact that the sum of the measures of the angles of a triangle is 180 and by *ITT,* we can find the measures of $\angle OAB$, $\angle OBA$, etc. By adding the measures of the adjacent angles we can find the measures of the angles of the polygon. In general, if the measure of an angle of a polygon is x, then

$$x = 180 - \frac{360}{n}.$$

Returning to the multiple-choice question, we find that the measure of each angle of the hexagon is 120 and the length of each side is 8.

Each of the altitudes of the triangle drawn from O will equal each of the others. Call this length a. The area of the polygon then is

(1) $\frac{1}{2}\,as + \frac{1}{2}\,as + \ldots + \frac{1}{2}\,as.$

n terms
(one for each of the n triangles)

Equation (1) simplifies to

(2) $\frac{1}{2}a(s + s + \ldots + s)$

n terms

But $s + s + \ldots + s$ is ns, which is the perimeter. Thus

(3) $A = \frac{1}{2}ap,$

where p is the perimeter of the polygon and a is the altitude from the center of the circle; a is referred to as the "apothem" of the polygon.

For the hexagon above we can find the length of the apothem by using the 30-60-90 triangle relationship.

If O is the center of the circle, consider $\triangle AOB$ below:

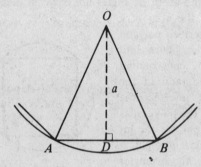

Since $AB = 8$, $BD = 4$ and $OD = 4\sqrt{3}$. Therefore the area is $\frac{1}{2}(4\sqrt{3})(48) = 96\sqrt{3}$.

¶ DRILL If each of the following gives data for a regular inscribed polygon where n is the number of sides, s is the length of a side and a is the length of the apothem, (1) draw the figure and separate it into triangles as indicated above, (2) find the measure of

each of the angles in the figure, and (3) find the area and perimeter.

(a) $n = 4$, $s = 2$, $a = 1$
(b) $n = 8$, $s = 1$, $a = 2$
(c) $n = 5$, $s = 3$, $a = 3$

FORMALLY DEFINING CIRCUMFERENCE

[19] **If an endless succession of regular polygons is inscribed in a circle, each polygon in turn having one more side than the one inscribed immediately preceding it, which of the following observations is (are) NOT true?**

   I The length of a side decreases and gets closer and closer to zero.

  II The polygons more and more closely approximate the circle, itself.

 III The length of the apothem increases but does NOT get closer and closer to any number.

Ⓐ **Only I is not true.**   Ⓑ **Only II is not true.**
Ⓒ **Only III is not true.**   Ⓓ **All are true.**   Ⓔ **All are not true.**

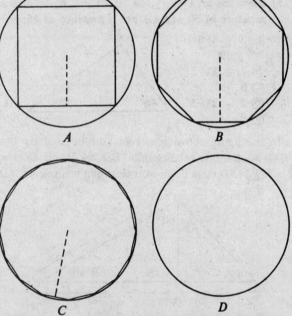

A

B

C

D

A, *B*, and *C* depict regular inscribed polygons of 4, 8, and 16 sides, respectively. The dotted segment is the apothem in each case. Note that as the number of sides increases from 4 to 16, several important things happen:

1. The vertices get closer and closer together and the sides shorter and shorter. Though the sides can never shrink to a length of zero (and still constitute a polygon) the lengths of the sides approach zero. We describe this situation by saying that the length of the sides approaches zero as a "limit."

2. The drawing of the polygon, though distinctly different from the drawing of the circle in diagram *A*, becomes less distinguishable from the sketch of the circle in *C*. Indeed, if we were to state that *D* was a picture of a million-sided polygon, anyone would be hard-pressed to prove us wrong. We are not suggesting for a moment that a circle is just a polygon with a large number of sides. But we are suggesting that a polygon more and more closely approximates a circle as the number of sides increases endlessly.

3. The apothems of the polygons more and more closely approximate the radius of the circle. We say that the apothem approaches the radius as a "limit" or more frequently that the radius is the "limit" of the apothem.

Using the ideas presented in these three observations, we can define "circumference of a circle." Since the polygons more and more closely approximate the circle as their number of sides increases, their perimeters more and more closely approximate "the distance around" the circle. Thus we will define *circumference* to mean the limit of the perimeters of the regular inscribed polygons as the number of sides of the polygons increases endlessly.

¶ DRILL If a regular polygon has a perimeter of 10, what is the length of each side if the number of sides is:

(a) 100   (b) 1000   (c) 100,000   (d) 1,000,000

(Do you see that by increasing the number of sides we can make the length of each side as short as we please?)

WORKING WITH CIRCLES

[20] The accompanying figure shows a pair of circles that have the same center. The radius of the inner circle is *r*; the radius of the outer circle is 5. If the other segments have the lengths indicated then *r* = ?

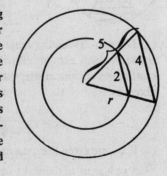

Ⓐ 1   Ⓑ 5   Ⓒ 4   Ⓓ 2   Ⓔ $\frac{5}{2}$

The multiple-choice question can be answered by comparing the sides of similar triangles. The numbers 2 and 4 are lengths of corresponding sides, as are *r* and 5:

$$\frac{r}{5} = \frac{2}{4} = \frac{1}{2},$$
$$r = \frac{5}{2}.$$

Though we have already answered the question, we will review a related concept leading to several important relationships between arcs, radii and chords of a circle.

Suppose the question had asked for the circumference of the smaller circle. We'll develop the formula that relates the circumference to the radius.

In the two circles below, *s* and *s'* denote the lengths of segments which are sides of polygons P_1 and *P* (not shown) of the same number of sides. The two central angles *θ* and *θ'* have the same measure ($\frac{360}{n}$). The two sides of the triangles that include these angles are in the same ratio, so the triangles are similar by *SAS*. This means that:

(1) $\frac{r}{r'} = \frac{s}{s'}$.

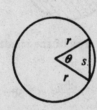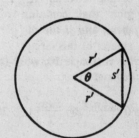

Multiplying the numerator and denominator of $\frac{r}{r'}$ by 2 and the numerator and denominator of $\frac{s}{s'}$ by *n*, we get:

(2) $\frac{2r}{2r'} = \frac{ns}{ns'}$.

But *ns* and *ns'* are the perimeters of the given polygons. Substituting perimeter *p* for *ns* and *p'* for *ns'* we get:

(3) $\frac{2r}{2r'} = \frac{p}{p'}$,

(4) $\frac{p'}{2r'} = \frac{p}{2r}$.

If we endlessly increase the number of sides then *p'* and *p* approach *C'* and *C*, the circumferences of the two circles:

(5) $\frac{C'}{2r'} = \frac{C}{2r}$.

The purpose of the foregoing discussion was to establish that the ratio of the circumference to the diameter is the same for all circles. Historically we have reserved the Greek letter π to indicate this constant ratio. The equation for the circumference of a circle is then

(6) $\dfrac{C}{2r} = \pi$ or $C = 2\pi r$.

Here π is an irrational number and cannot be evaluated exactly; any finite decimal representation such as 3.14 or 3.141592 is an approximation. Unless a specific approximation is requested, we generally express circumferences in terms of π.

¶ DRILL Find the missing elements of $\{C, r, d\}$, where C is the circumference, r is the radius and d is the diameter. Express your answers as multiples of π, and not as approximations.

(a) $C = 12\pi$ (b) $C = 12$ (c) $r = 2$ (d) $d = 3$

[21] If the point of tangency of circles A and B is the center of the circular region that contains them, and if the diameter of this circular region is 10, what is the area of the shaded region?

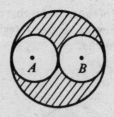

Ⓐ $\dfrac{25\pi}{2}$ Ⓑ $\dfrac{50\pi}{2}$ Ⓒ 25π Ⓓ $\dfrac{25\pi}{4}$ Ⓔ 50π

We have demonstrated the area of a polygon to be $\frac{1}{2}ap$, where a is the length of the apothem and p is the perimeter of the polygon. The limit of the apothem is the radius, and the limit of the perimeter is the circumference of the inscribing circle. If we let the number of sides of the polygonal regions increase endlessly, the area of the polygon will approach the *area of the circle* as a limit, and

$$A_c = \frac{1}{2}rC,$$

where A_c is the area of the circle, r is its radius and C its circumference. Substituting $2\pi r$ for C, we get:

$$A_c = \frac{1}{2}r(2\pi r) = \pi r^2.$$

This formula will give us the area of any circle when the radius is known.

In the multiple-choice question, since the diameter of the greater circle is 10, its radius is 5 and the radius of

each of the smaller circles is $\dfrac{5}{2}$. Therefore:

Area of greater circle $= 5^2(\pi) = 25\pi,$

Area of each smaller circle $= (\dfrac{5}{2})^2\pi = \dfrac{25}{4}\pi,$

Area of shaded region $= 25\pi - 2(\dfrac{25\pi}{4}),$

$$25\pi - \frac{25\pi}{2} = \frac{25\pi}{2}$$

¶ DRILL Find the missing element of $\{A_c, r\}$:

(a) $r = 2$ (b) $A_c = 9\pi$ (c) $r = \sqrt{2}$ (d) $A_c = 9$

[22] If the area of the circle is 9π and the area of the shaded region is 6π, what is the measure of $\angle AOC$?

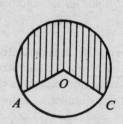

Ⓐ 130   Ⓑ 110
Ⓒ 90   Ⓓ 120
Ⓔ 60

A "sector" of a circle is a region shaped like a pie slice or a combination of pie slices. More formally it is defined as the region of a circle bounded by two radii and that arc of the circle whose end points lie on the radii. In the sketches below, both the shaded and unshaded regions are sectors of the circles. The area of a sector is a fractional part of the area of the circle. Once we have found what fractional part it constitutes, we may use this fraction to compute the area. Depending on the given information, we can compute this fraction in one of two different ways:

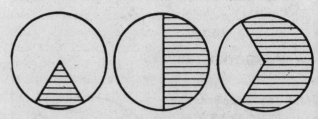

(1) If we are given the length of the arc which bounds the sector and enough information to compute the circumference of the circle, then the fractional part, f, is given by

$$f = \frac{\text{arc length}}{\text{circumference}}.$$

(2) If we are given the measure of the arc, then f is given by

$$f = \frac{\text{arc measure}}{360}$$

The area of the sector, A_s, is equal to f times the area of the circle, A_c.

In the multiple-choice question the sector constitutes $\frac{6\pi}{9\pi}$ or $\frac{2}{3}$ of the circle. The measure of $\angle AOC$ must then be $\frac{1}{3}$ of 360.

¶ DRILL Find (1) the fractional part of the circle, and (2) the area of the sector, for each of the following:

(a) $C = 4\pi$, arc length of sector $= \pi$
(b) $r = 2$, arc measure of sector $= 30$
(c) $r = 2$, arc length of sector $= 2$.

WHAT YOU SHOULD KNOW

KEY CONCEPTS

1. Congruent figures have equal areas.
2. Each region has one and only one area.
3. Two triangles with equal bases and equal altitudes have the same area.
4. The diagonal of a parallelogram forms two triangles of equal area with the sides.
5. A polygon is regular if it is convex, all of its sides are congruent and all of its angles are congruent.

KEY THEOREM and RELATIONSHIP

1. A triangle is a right triangle if and only if the square of the length of its longest side is equal to the sum of the squares of the lengths of the remaining two sides. (Pythagorean Theorem)
2. In a triangle whose angle measures are 30, 60 and 90, the length of the side opposite the 30° angle is half the length of the hypotenuse and the length of the side opposite the 60° angle is $\sqrt{3}$ times the length of the side opposite the 30° angle. (30-60-90 Relationship)

KEY FORMULAS

1. To find the area A of a triangle, where b is the length of any side and h is the altitude to that side:
$$A = \frac{1}{2} bh.$$

2. To find the area A of a square, where s is the length of any side:
$$A = s^2.$$

3. To find the area A of a rectangle, where a is the length of any side and b is the length of an adjacent side:
$$A = ab.$$

4. To find the area A of a parallelogram, where b is the length of any side and h is the altitude to that side:
$$A = bh.$$

5. To find the area A of a right triangle, where a is the length of one leg and b is the length of the other:
$$A = \frac{1}{2}ab.$$

6. To find the area A of a trapezoid, where a is the length of one base, b is the length of the other base, and h is the altitude to the bases:
$$A = \frac{1}{2}h\,(a + b).$$

7. To find the area A of a rhombus, where a is the length of one diagonal and b is the length of the other:
$$A = \frac{ab}{2}.$$

8. To find the measure of any angle, A, of a regular polygon of n sides:
$$(\angle A)° = 180 - \frac{360}{n}.$$

9. To find the perimeter P of a regular polygon of n sides, each with length s:
$$P = ns.$$

10. To find the area A of a regular polygon with perimeter P and apothem a:
$$A = \frac{1}{2}ap.$$

11. To find the circumference C of a circle of radius r:
$$C = 2\pi r.$$

12. To find the area A of a circle of radius r:
$$A = \pi r^2.$$

TEST-TAKING STRATEGIES

- Look for questions to which the Pythagorean Theorem applies.

- This theorem figures in more test questions than any other numerical law of geometry.

- Basic area formulas are not given on the test. Be prepared to supply them from your memory.

- When faced with a figure for which you have no area formula, try separating the figure up into composing triangles and (or) rectangles. Then calculate the areas of the composing pieces.

- Remember that an altitude can extend outside a figure. Don't limit yourself to the boundaries of the figure when drawing an altitude.

ANSWERS

[1] Ⓑ
DRILL:
(a) $A_s = 25 = A_t$, $b = 12.5$
(b) $s = 4 = b = A_t$

[2] Ⓒ
DRILL:
(a) 204   (b) 8   (c) $\sqrt{10}$

[3] Ⓓ
DRILL:
(a) $\dfrac{3}{4}$ (b) 10   (c) 1

[4] Ⓐ
DRILL:
$A_1 = A_2 = A_3$

[5] Ⓔ
DRILL:
(a) 10   (b) 4   (c) 3

[6] Ⓔ
DRILL:
(a) 20   (b) $\dfrac{25}{3}$

[7] Ⓔ

[8] Ⓒ
DRILL:
(a) 6   (b) 3   (c) $6\sqrt{2}$

[9] Ⓓ
DRILL:
$ABDE = 15, ADE = EBD = ADA = ABE = BDC = 7.5, AEDC = 22.5, EDCB = 15 = ADC.$

[10] Ⓐ
DRILL:
(a) 4   (b) 1
(c) $2\sqrt{3}$ (d) $\dfrac{\sqrt{6}}{2}$

[11] Ⓑ
DRILL:
$\triangle AMN, \triangle MNB, \triangle MNC.$

[12] Ⓓ
DRILL:
(a) 5   (b) 12   (c) $\sqrt{5}$ (d) 1

[13] Ⓓ
DRILL:
(a) $b = 3\sqrt{3}, A = \dfrac{9\sqrt{3}}{2}$
(b) $b = 2, A = 2$
(c) $b = 12, A = 30$
(d) $b = 1, A = \dfrac{\sqrt{3}}{2}$

[14] Ⓒ
(a) $d = 5\sqrt{2}$
(b) $a = \sqrt{6}$
(c) $s = 2$
(d) $s = \dfrac{3\sqrt{3}}{\sqrt{2}} = \dfrac{3\sqrt{6}}{2}$

[15] Ⓐ
DRILL:
(a) $s = 7\sqrt{3}, h = 14$
(b) $t = 8, s = 8\sqrt{3}$
(c) $t = 6, h = 12$
(d) $t = \dfrac{4\sqrt{3}}{3}, h = \dfrac{8\sqrt{3}}{3}$

[16] Ⓓ
DRILL:
(a) $h = 2.5, A = 7.5$
(b) $h = \dfrac{5\sqrt{2}}{2}, A = \dfrac{15\sqrt{2}}{2}$
(c) $h = \dfrac{5\sqrt{3}}{2}, A = \dfrac{15\sqrt{3}}{2}$

[17] Ⓐ

[18] Ⓐ
DRILL:
(a) $90, A = 4, p = 8$
(b) $67.5, A = 8, p = 8$
(c) Given information is self-contradictory.

[19] Ⓒ
DRILL:
(a) .1   (b) .01
(c) .0001   (d) .00001

[20] Ⓔ
DRILL:
(a) $r = 6, d = 12$ (b) $r = \dfrac{6}{\pi}, d = \dfrac{12}{\pi}$
(c) $d = 4, C = 4\pi$ (d) $r = 1.5, C = 3\pi$

[21] Ⓐ
DRILL:
(a) 4π (b) 3
(c) 2π (d) $\dfrac{3}{\sqrt{\pi}}$

[22] Ⓓ
DRILL:
(a) $f = \dfrac{1}{4}$, circle is 4π, sector is π.
(b) $f = \dfrac{1}{12}$, circle is 4π, sector is $\dfrac{\pi}{3}$
(c) $C = 4\pi, f = \dfrac{1}{2\pi}$, circle is 4π, sector is 2.

18. Coordinate Geometry

> *In this chapter, several topics are more typical of those tested on the Mathematics Level II exam than of those on the Level I exam. We have denoted these with an asterisk (*). Review of such topics may assist you in answering Level I questions, however, because they increase your general knowledge of mathematical ideas, methods and skills.*

Key Terms

coordinate any of an ordered set of numbers used to specify the location of a point on a line, on a surface, or in space.

parabola the set of all points that are equidistant from a given line and a given point that is not on that line.

ellipse the set of all points such that the sum of the distances from each of these points to two given points never varies.

hyperbola a set of points such that the difference of the distances from each point to each of two fixed points never varies.

DEFINING COORDINATES

[1] If p is the coordinate of point P and q is the coordinate of point Q, both on number line L, and $p < q$, then the distance from P to Q is:

Ⓐ p Ⓑ $p + q$ Ⓒ $p - q$ Ⓓ $|p - q|$ Ⓔ $|q|$

Our purpose in this chapter is to develop the fundamentals of a coordinate system in the plane. We shall start by reviewing a few basic ideas about coordinate systems on a line.

Coordinate Postulate 1 By first assigning 0 to a given point and 1 to a second point, both on a line L, a correspondence can be set up between the set of real numbers and the points on line L such that to every point on the line there corresponds a real number and to every real number there corresponds a point on L.

In this assumption the number assigned is called the *coordinate* of the point and the point is called the *graph* of the number. The point with coordinate 0 is termed the *origin,* and the point with coordinate 1 is the *unit point.* The positive integers are marked off on that ray of the line that contains the unit point, and the negative integers on the ray opposite to this. We assign integers in such a way that the distance between any two points associated with consecutive integers is the same as the distance between the origin and unit points. This, in fact, is where the "unit" point gets its name since the distance between it and the origin becomes the unit of measure for laying off the other points.

The points associated with the rational numbers (the numbers of the form $\frac{p}{q}$, where p and q are integers and $q \neq 0$) are assigned by dividing the unit segment into q congruent parts and then assigning to $\frac{p}{q}$ the point at the end of the pth one of these parts (counting away from the origin).

The irrational numbers that are roots of prime numbers may be marked off via the *Pythagorean Theorem:*

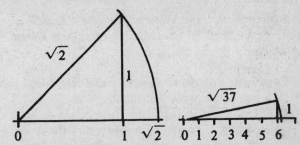

We will assume that all other irrational numbers have unique points of the line associated with them and that these can be approximated to any desired degree of accuracy by the use of rational approximations to the irrational number.

This correspondence is referred to as a *coordinate system on a line* or, more commonly, a *number line.*

The term *distance* between two points on a number line has no meaning until we define it. There are more obvious ways of accomplishing this than the one we are about to pursue, but it does have the virtue of brevity.

Coordinate Postulate 2 The distance between two points on a number line is the absolute value of the difference of their coordinates.

Note that, since the absolute value of $b - a$ is the same as the absolute value of $a - b$ (since $a - b$ is the negative of $b - a$ and each number has the same absolute value as its negative), the order of subtraction makes no difference. From this definition, the answer to the multiple-choice question is $|p - q|$. Answer Ⓒ looks similar, but note that $p - q$ must be negative since $p < q$. If $q - p$ had been a choice, it would have been correct since $q - p$ is positive.

¶ DRILL If the following pairs of numbers are coordinates of points on a number line, find the distance between them.

(a) 1 and 5   (b) −4 and 4
(c) −3 and 8   (d) −7 and −3
(e) −p and q (f) p and −q
(g) −p and −q

ESTABLISHING A COORDINATE SYSTEM IN A PLANE

[2] If $P = (3, 0)$, what is the second coordinate of the projection of P into the vertical axis?

Ⓐ 3   Ⓑ 0   Ⓒ −3   Ⓓ 4   Ⓔ −4

Now that we have given meaning to "coordinate system on a line," let us establish a coordinate system in a plane.

Coordinate Postulate 3 Given a plane determined by a pair of perpendicular number lines, L_1 and L_2, every point in the plane corresponds to an ordered pair of real numbers such that the first element of the ordered pair is the coordinate of the projection of the point into line L_1 and the second element of the ordered pair is the coordinate of the projection of the point into L_2.

Though any pair of number lines intersecting at any point will do the job, we assist the application of this assumption a bit with a series of conventions. We will agree that:

1. The number lines intersect at the point that is the origin for both.
2. Line L_1, called the x-axis, is horizontal with its positive ray extending to the right.

3. Line L_2, called the y-axis, must then be vertical with its positive direction upward.
4. The unit for each number line is the same.

The *projection* of a point into a line L is the point of intersection of line L with the line containing P and perpendicular to L. In each of the following sketches the point X is the projection of P into the x-axis and Y is the projection of P into the y-axis:

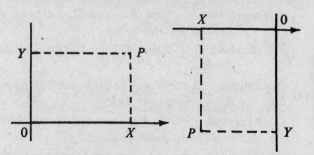

Note that, when P lies on one of the axes, the projection of P into the axis is P, itself, whereas the projection of P into the other axis is the origin.

In the multiple-choice question, $P(3, 0)$ is a point on the horizontal axis. Its projection into the vertical axis is the origin.

¶ DRILL Draw a coordinate system in a plane and locate each of the following:

(a) $A(3, 5)$ (b) $B(\frac{1}{2}, \frac{1}{2})$
(c) $C(-2, 1)$ (d) $D(-3, -2)$
(e) $E(8, -3)$ (f) $F(0, 0)$

[3] If a point $A(-a, b)$ is in quadrant IV, then which of the following is correct?

Ⓐ $a > 0, b > 0$ Ⓑ $a > 0, b < 0$ Ⓒ $a < 0, b > 0$ Ⓓ $a < 0, b < 0$ Ⓔ $a = 0, b = 0$

In the same way that a line separates a plane into two regions called "sides" yet does not belong to either region, the axes separate the coordinate plane into four parts called quadrants to which the axes do not belong. We name the quadrants, shown, by using Roman numerals.

II	I
III	IV

If a point lies in a given quadrant, the signs of its coordinates depend on the signs of the coordinates of the projections of the point into the axes. When (x, y)

is in quadrant I, $x > 0$, $y > 0$; in quadrant II, $x < 0$, $y > 0$; quadrant III, $x < 0$, $y < 0$; and in quadrant IV, $x > 0$, $y < 0$.

In the multiple-choice question, since the point is in quadrant IV, the first coordinate, $-a$, is positive and the second coordinate, b, is negative.

If $-a > 0$ and $b < 0$, then $a < 0$ and $b < 0$.

¶ DRILL Assuming a and b are both *negative* numbers, indicate which quadrant contains each of the following:

(a) (a, b) (b) $(-a, -b)$
(c) $(-a, b)$ (d) $(a, -b)$

[4] If $P = (3, 5)$ and $Q = (-1, 8)$, what is the length of the projection of segment PQ on the x-axis?

   Ⓐ 3   Ⓑ 5   Ⓒ −1   Ⓓ 8   Ⓔ 4

The projection of a segment AB into a line L is that segment of L whose endpoints are the projections of points A and B into L.

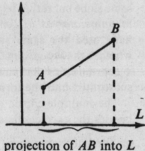

projection of AB into L

The length of the projection of a segment into a number line is the distance between the endpoints of the projection. By Coordinate Postulate 2, this distance is the absolute value of the difference of the coordinates on the number line.

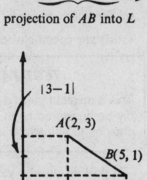

Note that the projection of a vertical segment into the horizontal axis is a point—thus the length of this projection is zero. The projection of a vertical segment into the vertical axis has the same length as the segment itself. Will the length of the projection of a segment ever be greater than the length of the segment itself? The projection will always be greater than or equal to 0 and less than or equal to the length of the segment itself.

The above definition of the projection of a segment into a line is still applicable when the segment and line intersect as at upper right. In each case segment PQ is the projection of segment AB.

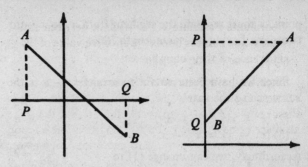

In the multiple-choice question, we note that the projections of P (3, 5) and Q (−1, 8) into the x-axis are, respectively, (3, 0) and (−1, 0). The distance between these points is 4.

¶ DRILL Find the lengths of the projections of the segments with the endpoints given into both axes:

(a) (2, 1), (0, 0)
(b) (3, 4), (8, 6)
(c) (−2, 3), (−4, −5)
(d) (−5, −6), (−1, −2)

[5] If $A = (a, b)$ and $B = (c, d)$, what is the second coordinate of the midpoint of segment AB?

   Ⓐ d Ⓑ b Ⓒ $\dfrac{b - d}{2}$ Ⓓ $\dfrac{b + d}{2}$

   Ⓔ $\dfrac{d - b}{2}$

If segment AB with $A = (x_1, y_1)$ and $B = (x_2, y_2)$ has its midpoint at M with coordinates (x, y), we can use the following figure to show how to represent the coordinates of M in terms of the coordinates of A and B.

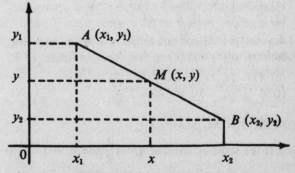

On the x-axis the point with coordinate x must be the midpoint of the segment with endpoints x_1 and x_2 since a set of parallel lines that cut off segments of equal length on one transversal (line AB) must cut off segments of equal length on any transversal (the x-axis in this case). The same will be true on the y-axis of the points with coordinates y, y_1 and y_2. Being the midpoint, x must separate the segment from x_1 to x_2 into two parts having the same length; thus

(1) $|x - x_1| = |x_2 - x|$.

Since we have been careful to arrange $x_2 > x > x_1$, we can state that

(2) $|x - x_1| = x - x_1$,
(3) $|x_2 - x| = x_2 - x$.

Accordingly, we can change (1) to

(4) $x - x_1 = x_2 - x$,
(5) $\qquad 2x = x_2 + x_1$,
(6) $\qquad x = \dfrac{x_2 + x_1}{2}$.

You may verify that (6) is also true when $x_2 < x < x_1$. A similar line of reasoning yields

(7) $y = \dfrac{y_2 + y_1}{2}$.

The coordinates of M, the midpoint of segment AB, are thus

(8) $\left(\dfrac{x_1 + x_2}{2}, \dfrac{y_1 + y_2}{2} \right)$.

Expression (8) is frequently called the "midpoint formula." Remember the formula as the "average of the coordinates," and you won't be confused over whether to add or subtract.

Applying this formula to the y-coordinate of points (a, b) and (c, d) of the multiple-choice question gives $\dfrac{b + d}{2}$.

¶ DRILL Find the coordinates of the midpoint of segment AB if:

(a) $A = (1, 6)$, $B = (5, 2)$
(b) $A = (-1, -4)$, $B = (-3, 0)$
(c) $A = (-8, -1)$, $B = (-2, -3)$
(d) $A = (5, -1)$, $B = (4, -2)$

If the midpoint M and one endpoint A are given below, substitute in (6) and (7) to find the coordinates of B.

(e) $A = (8, 1)$, $M = (-2, -3)$
(f) $A = (2, -5)$, $M = (-3, 4)$

DETERMINING SLOPES

[6] If the slope of segment AB is $\dfrac{1}{2}$ and $A = (-2, 5)$ which of the following could be the coordinates of B?

Ⓐ $(0, 6)$ Ⓑ $(2, 6)$ Ⓒ $(1, \dfrac{13}{4})$ Ⓓ $(6, 4)$ Ⓔ $(0, 0)$

For many reasons that will become apparent in later sections it is useful to be able to indicate the relative degree of slant or tilt of a line in the coordinate plane with respect to the axes.

To enable us to do this, we define a certain number m to be the "slope" of a nonvertical segment AB, where

$A = (x_1, y_1)$ and $B = (x_2, y_2)$. It is our purpose only to introduce this number m in this section while pursuing its applications in the next few sections. We define the slope, m, of line AB to be

(1) $m = \dfrac{y_2 - y_1}{x_2 - x_1}$.

A word of caution in determining slopes: note that we maintain a consistent order in the two subtractions involved in determining the slope of a segment. We are subtracting the coordinates of A from those of B. We will get the same slope if we reverse *both* subtractions since

$y_2 - y_1 = -(y_1 - y_2)$ and $x_2 - x_1 = -(x_1 - x_2)$;

substitution of these in (1) above yields:

(2) $m = \dfrac{y_2 - y_1}{x_2 - x_1} = \dfrac{-(y_1 - y_2)}{-(x_1 - x_2)} = \dfrac{y_1 - y_2}{x_1 - x_2}$.

If, however, we had reversed the order of *only one* of the subtractions, we would *not* have gotten the same slope but rather its negative. *Use the same order in numerator as in denominator.* Check that you have used the same subtraction order by noting whether the y-coordinate of each point is above the x-coordinate of that point when the coordinates are substituted into the formula.

The multiple-choice question has many answers besides the correct choice of those given. All points on the line containing $(-2, 5)$ with slope $\dfrac{1}{2}$ would satisfy the conditions for B.

TEST-TAKING TIP.

This is an example of a question that can probably be answered most quickly by checking the choices to see which is correct.

To do this quickly, you must be able to calculate slopes rapidly in your head. Since

$$\frac{6 - 5}{0 - (-2)} = \frac{1}{2},$$

the point $(0, 6)$ satisfies the conditions.

¶ DRILL If A and B are as given in each of the following, find the slope of segment AB:

(a) $A(1, 2)$, $B(3, 4)$ \qquad (b) $A(-1, -2)$, $B(-3, -4)$
(c) $A(-1, 2)$, $B(-3, 4)$ \qquad (d) $A(1, -2)$, $B(-3, 4)$

[7] If A, B, and C are points on the same line and the slope of segment AB is $\dfrac{2}{3}$, what is the slope of segment BC?

Ⓐ $\dfrac{3}{2}$ Ⓑ $\dfrac{4}{9}$ Ⓒ $\dfrac{2}{3}$ Ⓓ $-\dfrac{3}{2}$ Ⓔ $-\dfrac{2}{3}$

The first important fact about slopes that we will explore is that any two segments on the same nonvertical line will have the same slope.

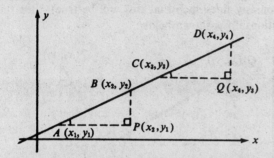

You may verify that the two triangles, *ABP* and *CDQ*, are similar by the Angle-Angle Similarity Theorem. Note that $DQ = y_4 - y_3$, $CQ = x_4 - x_3$, $BP = y_2 - y_1$ and $AP = x_2 - x_1$.

But similar triangles have corresponding sides in the same ratio, so

(1) $\dfrac{y_2 - y_1}{y_4 - y_3} = \dfrac{x_2 - x_1}{x_4 - x_3}.$

A little diligent application of algebra will transform (1) into

(2) $\dfrac{y_2 - y_1}{x_2 - x_1} = \dfrac{y_4 - y_3}{x_4 - x_3}.$

The two members of (2) are, respectively, the slopes of segments *AB* and *CD*. Though we have established this for only one of several possible cases, a similar argument will testify to the truth of the others. Thus it is meaningful to refer to *the* slope of a nonvertical line.

¶ DRILL If *A, B* and *C* are points on the same line, use the slope formula to verify that segments *AB* and *BC* have the same slope in each of the following:

(a) $A(0, 0)$, $B(1, 1)$, $C(5, 5)$
(b) $A(-2, 2)$, $B(-3, 3)$, $C(-15, 15)$
(c) $A(1, 3)$, $B(3, 6)$, $C(5, 9)$

[8] If $A = (5, 1)$, $B = (5, 3)$ and $C = (2, 3)$, what is the product of the slopes of line *AB* and line *BC?*

Ⓐ 0   Ⓑ 1   Ⓒ 5   Ⓓ 3   Ⓔ Undefined

So far we have avoided comment on the slopes of vertical and horizontal lines.

The characteristic feature of two points, *A* and *B*, which are on the same horizontal line is that their projections into the *y*-axis are the same point *P*.

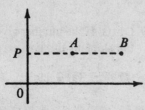

Thus any two points on the same horizontal line must have the same *y*-coordinate by definition of "*y*-coordinate." Let $A = (a, c)$ and $B = (b, c)$; the slope formula yields

(1) $\dfrac{c - c}{a - b} = \dfrac{0}{a - b} = 0$ $(a \neq b)$.

Consequently, the slope of any *horizontal* line is zero.

Similarly, the chief property of two points, *A* and *B*, on the same vertical line is that they have the same *x*-coordinate. Let $A = (c, a)$ and $B = (c, b)$. The slope formula yields

(2) $\dfrac{a - b}{c - c} = \dfrac{a - b}{0}$ $(a \neq b)$.

But the division of a real number by zero does not define any real number as its quotient so the slope of a vertical line is undefined. This does not handicap us too much since we can immediately recognize that any line with "undefined" slope is a vertical line.

In the multiple-choice question, line *AB* is vertical since points *A* (5, 1) and *B* (5, 3) have the same first coordinates. Therefore line *AB* has no slope. A product with a nonexistent factor is also undefined.

¶ DRILL Indicate whether each of the lines that contain *A* and *B* below is horizontal or vertical by attempting to determine its slope.

(a) $A(1, 5)$, $B(1, 9)$
(b) $A(-2, -\tfrac{1}{2})$, $B(-4, -\tfrac{1}{2})$
(c) $A(a, b)$, $B(c, b)$
(d) $A(2, 3)$, $B(3, 2)$

[9] If line *AB* is parallel to line *CD* and the slope of *AB* is -3, find the coordinates of *D* when $C = (2, 0)$.

Ⓐ No such point exists   Ⓑ *D* exists but is not unique   Ⓒ (5, 2)   Ⓓ $(-\tfrac{1}{2}, \tfrac{1}{2})$ Ⓔ (2, -3)

Another argument based on similar triangles provides us with a second major fact on slopes: two lines are parallel if and only if they have the same slope.

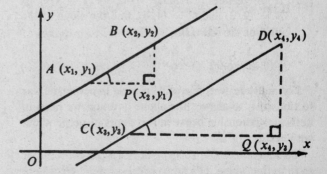

You may verify that triangles ABP and CDQ are similar by the Angle-Angle Similarity Theorem. Therefore, $AP = x_2 - x_1$, $BP = y_2 - y_1$, $CQ = x_4 - x_3$, and $DQ = y_4 - y_3$. Since similar triangles have proportional corresponding sides, then

(1) $\dfrac{y_2 - y_1}{y_4 - y_3} = \dfrac{x_2 - x_1}{x_4 - x_3}$.

Again, a little algebra will transform (1) into

(2) $\dfrac{y_2 - y_1}{x_2 - x_1} = \dfrac{y_4 - y_3}{x_4 - x_3}$.

There are other cases, but a like argument will support these; and, in general, we conclude that nonvertical parallel lines have the same slope.

Conversely, we will state without proof that two distinct lines which have the same slope are parallel.

In the multiple-choice question, lines AB and CD must have the same slope, -3, because they are parallel. Since C is the only point of CD that is given, D can be any other point of the line. Therefore D is not unique.

TEST-TAKING TIP.

One approach to this problem is to try the suggested answers. Choices Ⓒ, Ⓓ and Ⓔ can be eliminated by direct calculations. If, upon eliminating three choices of a question, you still cannot decide between the remaining two, be sure to pick the choice that seems more reasonable —don't just leave the answer blank because you aren't sure.

¶ DRILL Indicate whether lines AB and CD are parallel by finding their slopes:

(a) $A(-5, 4)$, $B(4, 9)$, $C(9, 0)$, $D(0, -5)$
(b) $A(0, 0)$, $B(1, 1)$, $C(-2, 2)$, $D(2, -2)$
(c) $A(4, 6)$, $B(-4, 8)$, $C(2, 8)$, $D(0, 0)$
(d) $A(-4, -2)$, $B(-2, 4)$, $C(2, -5)$, $D(8, -7)$

RELATING THE SLOPES OF PERPENDICULAR LINES

[10] If the vertices of triangle ABC are $A = (15, 1)$, $B = (9, 3)$ and $C = (4, 5)$, find the slope of the altitude to side AB.

Ⓐ $-\dfrac{2}{3}$ Ⓑ $\dfrac{2}{3}$ Ⓒ $\dfrac{4}{9}$ Ⓓ $-\dfrac{3}{2}$ Ⓔ 3

The altitude to a side of a triangle is perpendicular to that side; to answer the above question we need to know a relationship between the slopes of perpendicular lines.

If L_1 and L_2 are perpendicular lines intersecting at point $P(x, y)$ and if segments PQ and PQ' have the same length (note that we can always find points Q and Q' on any lines such that this will be true), then the relationship is shown below:

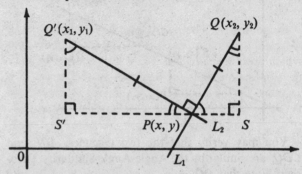

and triangles PQS and $PQ'S'$ are congruent by Angle-Side-Angle (verify that the angles are complements of congruent angles).

Thus $QS = PS'$ and $PS = Q'S'$, but $QS = y_2 - y$, $PS' = x - x_1$, $PS = x_2 - x$ and $Q'S' = y_1 - y$, so

(1) $QS = y_2 - y = PS' = x - x_1$,
(2) $PS = x_2 - x = Q'S' = y_1 - y$.

The slope of L_1 is $(y_2 - y)/(x_2 - x)$ and the slope of L_2 is $(y - y_1)/(x - x_1)$. Substituting equations (1) and (2) into the slope of L_2, we get:

(3) $\dfrac{y - y_1}{x - x_1} = \dfrac{-(y_1 - y)}{x - x_1} = \dfrac{-(x_2 - x)}{y_2 - y}$.

Now compare the right member of (3), our new expression for the slope of L_2, with

(4) $\dfrac{y_2 - y}{x_2 - x}$,

the slope of L_1.

You should see that (3) and (4) are the negative reciprocals of each other. Thus, if two lines with slopes m_1 and m_2 are perpendicular, then

(5) $m_1 = -\dfrac{1}{m_2}$,

and conversely.

In the multiple-choice question, the slope of A (15, 1) and B (9, 3) is

$$\frac{3 - 1}{9 - 15} = \frac{2}{-6} = -\frac{1}{3}.$$

The slope of the altitude must be the negative reciprocal, 3.

¶ DRILL If the number given is the slope of a line, find the slope of the line perpendicular to it:

(a) $-\dfrac{1}{2}$ (b) 2 (c) $\dfrac{1}{2}$ (d) $-\dfrac{3}{4}$

[11] Which of the following most completely describes the figure with vertices: $A(-5, 4)$, $B(4, 9)$, $C(9, 0)$, $D(0, -5)$.

   Ⓐ **Quadrilateral** Ⓑ **Trapezoid** Ⓒ **Parallelogram** Ⓓ **Rectangle** Ⓔ **Square**

By finding the slopes of the sides of a quadrilateral, we can tell which are parallel to each other, if any, and which are perpendicular, if any. But, as yet, we have developed no means for determining the length of a segment in the coordinate plane and, thereby, the lengths of the sides of a figure. We will pursue this now.

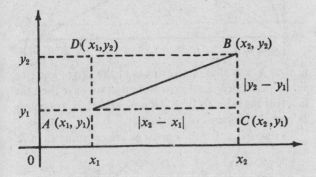

Verify that in the above figure, with lines BC and AD perpendicular to the x-axis and lines DB and AC perpendicular to the y-axis, triangle ABC is a right triangle. Verify, by noting their projections into the axes, that segment BC has length $|y_2 - y_1|$ and $AC = |x_2 - x_1|$. In the interest of a general proof we are *not* assuming $y_2 > y_1$ and $x_2 > x_1$, even though this is the way it appears in the figure.

The Pythagorean Theorem gives us

(1) $(AB)^2 = |x_2 - x_1|^2 + |y_2 - y_1|^2$.

Note that $|a| = a$ for $a \geq 0$ and $|a| = -a$ for $a < 0$, but both $(a)^2 = a^2$ and $(-a)^2 = a^2$ so $|a|^2 = a^2$ for all a. Using this fact we write equation (1) as

(2) $(AB)^2 = (x_2 - x_1)^2 + (y_2 - y_1)^2$,
(3) $AB = \sqrt{(x_2 - x_1)^2 + (y_2 - y_1)^2}$.

Equation (3) is referred to as the *distance formula* in a coordinate plane.

To answer the multiple-choice question, first plot the given points.

TEST-TAKING TIP.

Whenever it is possible to draw a diagram illustrating the given information, the diagram is usually useful in answering the question.

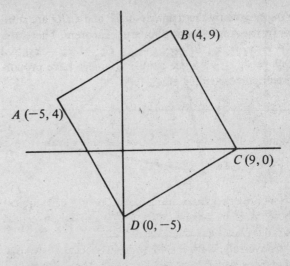

The above figure may suggest that all sides have the same length, but you may not be able to verify this solely from the sketch, since you will not have graph paper to use on the Level I exam.

The distance formula should erase any doubts:

$$AD = \sqrt{(-5 - 0)^2 + [4 - (-5)]^2}$$
$$= \sqrt{25 + 81}$$
$$= \sqrt{106},$$
$$CD = \sqrt{(9 - 0)^2 + [0 - (-5)]^2}$$
$$= \sqrt{81 + 25}$$
$$= \sqrt{106}.$$

From the diagram and the knowledge that adjacent sides are congruent, the figure can be judged to be a square.

¶ **DRILL** For each of the following, first let $A = (x_1, y_1)$ and $B = (x_2, y_2)$ and compute the distance from A to B. Then let $B = (x_1, y_1)$ and $A = (x_2, y_2)$ and compute the distance from B to A. Does the distance formula give the same result regardless of the order of the points?

(a) $A(4, -5)$, $B(-6, 2)$
(b) $A(-3, 5)$, $B(-3, -4)$
(c) $A(6, -3)$, $B(-4, 2)$
(d) $A(p, q)$, $B(0, 0)$

FINDING THE AREAS OF FIGURES DEFINED BY COORDINATES

[12] Find the area of triangle ABC if $A = (6, 6)$, $B = (14, -2)$ and $C = (4, -4)$.

   Ⓐ **24** Ⓑ **48** Ⓒ **48$\sqrt{2}$** Ⓓ **96** Ⓔ **None of these**

Graphing the points suggests that the triangle is isosceles and possibly equilateral.

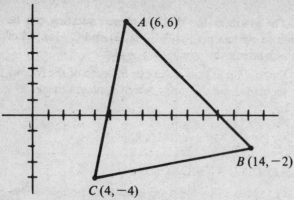

$AB = \sqrt{(14 - 6)^2 + (-2 - 6)^2}$

$\qquad = \sqrt{128} = 8\sqrt{2}$

$BC = \sqrt{(14 - 4)^2 + [-2 - (-4)]^2}$

$\qquad = \sqrt{104} = 2\sqrt{26}$

$AC = \sqrt{(6 - 4)^2 + [6 - (-4)]^2}$

$\qquad = \sqrt{104} = 2\sqrt{26}$

The distance formula applied to the sides of the above triangle proves it is isosceles. The altitude to the base (in this case, AB) of an isosceles triangle bisects the base. The midpoint formula will give the coordinates of the point of intersection of the altitude and the base, (10, 2). The distance formula gives the length of the altitude, using the coordinates of the midpoint of the base and of C, the vertex of the angle included by the sides of equal length:

$$\sqrt{(10 - 4)^2 + (2 + 4)^2} = \sqrt{72} = 6\sqrt{2}.$$

Therefore the area is $\frac{1}{2}$ (6 $\sqrt{2}$) (8 $\sqrt{2}$) = 48.

¶ DRILL Find the areas of the figures that have the following points as vertices. Where a quadrilateral is given, first find the slopes of the sides to see whether it is a parallelogram, rectangle or trapezoid.

(a) $A(8, 0)$, $B(-2, 3)$, $C(9, 3)$

(b) $A(-5, 18)$, $B(10, -2)$, $C(-5, -10)$

(c) A, B, C, and D are the respective midpoints of the sides of $P(0, 0)$, $M(5, 0)$, $N(0, -6)$ and $Q(5, -6)$

(d) $A(1, 1)$, $B(7, 1)$, $C(10, 3)$, $D(4, 3)$

USING COORDINATES TO COMPARE LENGTHS

[13] If in the accompanying figure, M and N are the midpoints of the diagonals of trapezoid $ABCD$, what is the relationship between MN and CD?

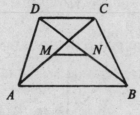

Ⓐ $MN = .3(AB - CD)$

Ⓑ $MN = .4(AB - CD)$ Ⓒ $MN = .5(AB - CD)$

Ⓓ $MN = .6(AB - CD)$ Ⓔ $MN = .7(AB - CD)$

(Hint: first use the midpoint formula to represent the coordinates of M and N.)

The methods of coordinate geometry frequently provide efficient means for verifying statements of geometry. The above question is a case in point. Let us first put the given figure on a set of coordinate axes

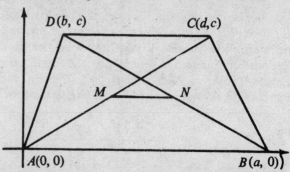

in such a way that one vertex is at the origin and one side is contained in an axis. Note that we have used the fact that the sides DC and AB are parallel to give points D and C the same y-coordinate.

The midpoint formula gives us the coordinates of M and N.

$$M = \left(\frac{d}{2}, \frac{c}{2}\right) \qquad N = \left(\frac{b + a}{2}, \frac{c}{2}\right)$$

(Do you see that this proves segment MN to be parallel to both segments AB and CD since all have slopes of zero?) Thus the length of MN is

$$\sqrt{\left(\frac{b + a}{2} - \frac{d}{2}\right)^2 + \left(\frac{c}{2} - \frac{c}{2}\right)^2},$$

which simplifies to

(1) $\dfrac{b + a - d}{2} = \dfrac{a - (d - b)}{2}.$

But the length of AB is a, and the length of DC is

(2) $\sqrt{(d - b)^2 + (c - c)^2} = d - b.$

The length of MN is, therefore, half of $(AB - DC)$.

¶ DRILL Using the following figure, verify that segment MN (M and N being the midpoints of the sides) is parallel to segment AB and has a length which is half the length of AB. (Hint: use the midpoint formula to represent the coordinates of M and N.)

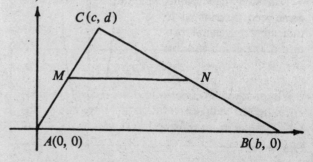

GRAPHING CURVES

[14] The figure on the right is part of the graph of which of the following conditions?

Ⓐ $y = x^3$
Ⓑ $y = 2x^3$
Ⓒ $y = x^2$
Ⓓ $x = y^3$
Ⓔ $x = 2y^3$

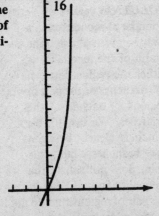

The graph of an ordered pair, (x, y), is the point in the coordinate plane whose x- and y-coordinates are given by the ordered pair. The graph of a condition in x and y is the set of all points (and only those points) with ordered pairs (x, y) that make the condition true.

In graphing a condition it is seldom useful (or even possible) to write out all of the ordered pairs in its solution set first, since most of the conditions discussed have infinite solution sets. When the condition is specified by an equation such as

$$y = 2x^2 + 1,$$

the most elementary approach to graphing it is to plot several points of the graph by finding several ordered pairs of its solution set. These points can be obtained most readily by selecting arbitrary values for x and solving the equation to find the companion values for y.

The table (right) shows a few pairs.

x	y
-2	9
-1	3
0	1
1	3
2	9

When enough points have been determined to indicate the general pattern of the graph and this number varies with the complexity of the graph, draw the simplest smooth curve which will contain all of the points, as shown at the right.

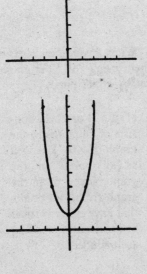

The graph in the multiple-choice question can be seen to contain points $(0, 0)$, $(1, 2)$ and $(2, 16)$, all of which satisfy the condition $y = 2x^3$.

¶ DRILL Plot at least six points for each of the following and draw the graph which contains them:

(a) $y = 3x + 1$ (b) $4x + 2y = -3$

(c) $y = \dfrac{1}{2} x^4 - 2$ (d) $y = |x|$

GRAPHING REGIONS

[15] Which of the following conditions best describes the graph to the right?

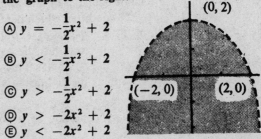

Ⓐ $y = -\dfrac{1}{2}x^2 + 2$

Ⓑ $y < -\dfrac{1}{2}x^2 + 2$

Ⓒ $y > -\dfrac{1}{2}x^2 + 2$

Ⓓ $y > -2x^2 + 2$

Ⓔ $y < -2x^2 + 2$

As we have seen, an equation in x and y has a graph that is a curve, a line, or a combination of curves or lines.

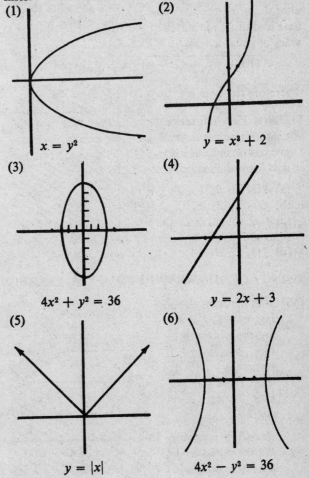

(1) $x = y^2$

(2) $y = x^3 + 2$

(3) $4x^2 + y^2 = 36$

(4) $y = 2x + 3$

(5) $y = |x|$

(6) $4x^2 - y^2 = 36$

These curves or lines separate the plane into regions that lie on either side of them. For example, (1) determines one region that lies between its extensions and another that lies outside the extensions, (2) determines a region above it and one below it, (3) cuts off a region as its interior and another as its exterior, (4) is a line and thus separates the plane into two half-planes, (5) is an angle and thus separates the plane into its interior and exterior, and (6) determines a region between its branches and a pair of regions outside the branches. We will state without proof that, when $A = B$ is an equation in x and y, then $A > B$ is the condition which describes one of the regions bounded by the graph of $A = B$, while $A < B$ is the condition which describes the other. (The graph of (6) is a special case; think of the region between as the "interior" and the pair of separated regions as the "exterior.") This fact provides us with a simple way of graphing inequalities in x and y.

1. First graph the boundary condition as a dotted figure.
2. Select any point that is clearly on one side of the boundary condition, and test it in the inequality. If it satisfies the inequality, shade in the region of the plane that contains the point. If it does not satisfy the inequality, shade in the other region.

EXAMPLE 1

Graph $x < 3y^2 + 6y + 4$.

SOLUTION: The boundary condition is $x = 3y^2 + 6y + 4$, which we graph as a dotted curve. We then test $(0, 0)$ in the original inequality:

$0 < 3(0)^2 + 6(0) + 4$.

Since it makes the inequality true, we shade in the region that contains $(0, 0)$.

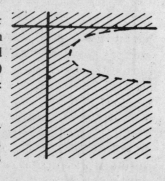

EXAMPLE 2

Graph $y < |x|$.

SOLUTION: The boundary condition is $y = |x|$. After graphing it as a pair of dotted rays, we test the point $(0, 6)$, which is clearly in the interior of the angle. Since $(0, 6)$ does *not* make the inequality true, we shade the region that does not contain it.

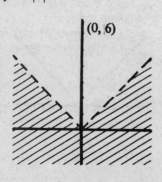

(0, 6)

EXAMPLE 3

Graph $4x^2 - y^2 > 36$.

SOLUTION: The boundary condition is $4x^2 - y^2 = 36$. The graph of the inequality is either the region between the branches or the pair of regions outside the branches. We test $(0, 0)$, which is clearly between the branches, but this point does not satisfy the inequality so we shade in the pair of regions that do not lie between the branches.

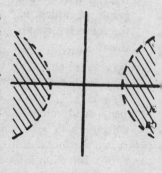

In the multiple-choice question, the labeled points $(-2, 0)$, $(0, 2)$ and $(2, 0)$ and the parabolic boundary show the dotted curve to be $y = -\frac{1}{2}x^2 + 2$. We can use $(0, 0)$ as a test point to decide between answers Ⓑ and Ⓒ.

¶ **DRILL** Draw the graph of each of the following:

(a) $y < x$ (b) $y > 2x + 5$
(c) $x^2 + y^2 < 9$ (d) $y > x^3$

[16] **Which of the following best describes the graph on the right?**

Ⓐ $x < 2$ or $x > -1$
Ⓑ $y < 2$ or $y > -1$
Ⓒ $y > 2$ and $y < -1$
Ⓓ $y < 2$ and $y > -1$
Ⓔ **None of these**

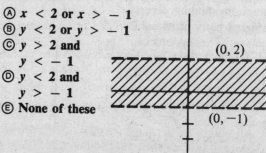

(0, 2)

(0, −1)

When a condition is expressed as a compound statement using "or," the graph consists of all points that satisfy either part.

(1) $y > 1$ or $x < 2$ consists of all points in the graph of $y > 1$ as well as all points in the graph of $x < 2$. In the graph (right) all points that have either vertical or horizontal shading are included.

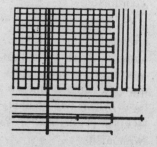

(2) $y \geq 3x$ means $y >$ $3x$ or $y = 3x$ and thus consists of all points of the graph of $y > 3x$ as well as all points of the graph of $y = 3x$. The graph contains all points of the line and all points above the line.

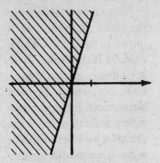

When a condition is expressed as a compound statement using "and," the graph consists of only those points that are found in the graphs of *both* composing conditions. If a point is found only in the graph of one of these conditions, it is *not* part of the graph of the compound condition.

(3) The condition $y > 1$ and $x < 2$ contains the points in the region of the graph of example (1) which has both horizontal and vertical shading.

In the multiple-choice question, the shaded region is bounded by the dotted lines with the equations $y = 2$ and $y = -1$. To lie in this region, a point must have a y-coordinate satisfying both the conditions $y < 2$ and $y > -1$.

¶ DRILL First draw the graph of the composing conditions and then graph each of the following:

(a) $\{(x, y): y > 2 \text{ or } y < 3\}$
(b) $\{(x, y): y > 2 \text{ and } y < 3\}$
(c) $\{(x, y): x > 4 \text{ and } x^2 + y^2 < 25\}$
(d) $\{(x, y): 3x + 2y \geq 5\}$

WRITING THE EQUATIONS OF LINES

[17] Which of the following is the point of intersection of the lines given by $y = 5$ and $x = -4$?

Ⓐ $(5, -4)$ Ⓑ $(4, -5)$ Ⓒ $(-4, 5)$
Ⓓ $(-4, -5)$ Ⓔ The lines don't intersect

All points on the same vertical line have the same x-coordinate since the projection of all of these points into the x-axis is the same point. Furthermore, no point that is *not* on the vertical line will have this x-coordinate. We can, therefore, give a complete description of any vertical line if we know what this common x-coordinate is.

If the x-coordinate is a, the condition

$$\{(x, y): x = a\},$$

which is read "the set of ordered pairs (x, y) for which the x-coordinate is a," will be true for all points of the line and false for any point not on the line. As we saw in the preceding section, we usually take the $\{(x, y): \quad \}$ notation for granted and write the condition without it.

This same situation exists for horizontal lines which, in general, can be described by equations of the form $y = b$, where b is the common y-coordinate.

In the multiple-choice question, the point of intersection must lie on the vertical line $x = -4$ and the horizontal line $y = 5$. Its coordinates must, therefore, be $(-4, 5)$.

¶ DRILL Write an equation for the line that contains the following points:

(a) $(3, 5)$, $(4, 5)$
(b) $(-\frac{1}{2}, 3)$, $(-\frac{1}{2}, \frac{1}{2})$
(c) $(8, -4)$, $(-8, -4)$
(d) $(\sqrt{2}, 3)$, $(\sqrt{2}, -\sqrt{2})$

[18] If $A = (1, 3)$ and $B = (-2, 4)$, which of the following is not an equation of the line that contains A and B?

Ⓐ $y - 3 = -\frac{1}{3}(x - 1)$

Ⓑ $y - 4 = -\frac{1}{3}(x + 2)$

Ⓒ $y - 1 = -\frac{1}{3}(x - 3)$

Ⓓ $y = -\frac{1}{3}x + 3\frac{1}{3}$

Ⓔ $3y + x - 10 = 0$

We have developed an important fact that will help us to describe any nonvertical line in the coordinate plane by an equation in x and y such as those in the above question. Recall that the slope of a given line is the same no matter what two points are used to compute it. Using this fact and given the points $A(a, b)$ and $B(m, n)$, we can write an equation in a and y such that the ordered pairs of numbers that make the sentence true are all of the ordered pairs (and only those ordered pairs) which represent points on the line which contains A and B. To accomplish this, we present the following argument.

Since x and y are variables that represent any real numbers, the symbol (x, y) is a variable that represents any ordered pair of real numbers, and, thereby, any point in the plane. Then

(1) $\dfrac{y - b}{x - a}$

represents the slope of any line in the plane that contains A, and

(2) $\dfrac{y - n}{x - m}$

represents the slope of any line in the plane that contains *B*. But we are interested only in the line that contains both *A* and *B*, and this will be the line for which (1) and (2) yield the same slope. Accordingly,

$$(3) \quad \frac{y - b}{x - a} = \frac{y - n}{x - m}$$

will be true only for those ordered pairs (x, y) that determine points on the line which contains *A* and *B*.

EXAMPLE

Determine an equation of the line that contains A $(1, 3)$ and B $(4, -2)$.

SOLUTION: $\dfrac{y - 3}{x - 1} = \dfrac{y - (-2)}{x - 4}$

We will develop other means for determining equations for lines and will not drill on this one.

In the multiple-choice question, the points A $(1, 3)$ and B $(-2, 4)$ can be used to determine the slope of line *AB*:

$$\frac{3 - 4}{1 - (-2)} = -\frac{1}{3}.$$

But each of the five choices is a line having $-\dfrac{1}{3}$ as a slope. Answer ©, however, has the coordinates reversed, because in the slope formula the *y*-coordinates are subtracted from each other and the *x*-coordinates are subtracted from each other.

TEST-TAKING TIP.

It would be easiest to solve this problem by inspection, as suggested above. A second method, though longer, involves the problem-solving technique of transformation. If each of the equations was simplified and changed to the same form, say that of choice ©, the maverick answer would readily stand out.

---

[19] If line *L*, with slope $\dfrac{1}{2}$, contains $(-1, 4)$ which of the following is an equation of line *L*?

Ⓐ $y + 1 = \dfrac{1}{2}(x - 4)$ Ⓑ $y - 4 = \dfrac{1}{2}(x + 1)$

© $x + 1 = \dfrac{1}{2}(y - 4)$ Ⓓ $x - 4 = \dfrac{1}{2}(y + 1)$

Ⓔ **None of these**

Given a point $A(a, b)$ in the plane, an infinite set of lines can be drawn which contain it. Some of these are shown in this figure. Each of these distinct lines must have a slope different from each of the others (two lines with the same slope would have to be parallel and, therefore, could not intersect at *A*). From this we can conclude that a given point, $A(a, b)$, and a given slope, *m*, determine one and only one line.

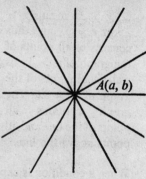

We can find the equation for this line in the following way:

Let (x, y) represent any point in the plane; then

$$(1) \quad \frac{y - b}{x - a}$$

represents the slope of any line that passes through *A*. But we are interested only in the one line that has a slope of *m*. If we set *m* equal to (1) we get

$$(2) \quad m = \frac{y - b}{x - a}$$

which is an equation that will be true only for those points such that their slope when computed with (a, b) is *m*. Thus the truth set of this equation is the set of all points of the given line *except* (a, b)—note that (a, b) leads to division by zero if we replace (x, y) by it. Hence we write (2) in the form:

$$(3) \quad y - b = m(x - a)$$

since the truth set of (3) is the same as (2) except that (3) *includes* (a, b).

EXAMPLE 1

Write the equation of the line that contains $(4, 5)$ and has a slope of -2.

SOLUTION: $y - 5 = -2(x - 4)$ (In equation (3) we have replaced (a, b) by $(4, 5)$ and *m* by -2.)

EXAMPLE 2

Write the equation of the line that contains A $(1, 3)$ and B $(-2, 4)$.

SOLUTION: First we use the slope formula to find the slope of line *AB*:

$$\frac{3 - 4}{1 + 2} = -\frac{1}{3}.$$

We then use equation (3) with *either A* or *B* to get *an* equation of the line:

$$y - 3 = -\frac{1}{3}(x - 1) \text{ or } y - 4 = -\frac{1}{3}(x + 2).$$

Verify that both equations can be transformed to:

$$x + 3y - 10 = 0.$$

The multiple-choice question can be answered directly by substituting $\frac{1}{2}$ for m and $(-1, 4)$ for (a, b) in equation (3), with Ⓑ as the result.

¶ DRILL Use equation (3) to write an equation of the line given by each of the following:

(a) Contains $(1, -2)$, slope 3

(b) Contains $(0, 4)$, slope $-\frac{1}{3}$

(c) Contains $(1, -2)$ and $(0, 4)$

[20] **Which of the following is NOT an equation for the same line as each of the others?**

Ⓐ $\dfrac{y - 4}{x + 1} = \dfrac{1}{2}$ Ⓑ $y - 4 = \dfrac{1}{2}(x + 1)$

Ⓒ $y = \dfrac{1}{2}x + \dfrac{9}{2}$ Ⓓ $x - 2y + 9 = 0$

Ⓔ $x + 2y - 9 = 0$

Every line can be expressed by an equation of the form

(1) $Ax + By + C = 0$,

where *not both* $A = 0$ and $B = 0$. Furthermore, every equation of this form is an equation of a line. For this reason equations that can be transformed to form (1) are called *linear equations.*

All equations of the same line, when transformed to form (1), are identical as long as any common factors of A, B and C are removed.

¶ DRILL Verify that each of the following pairs of equations determine the same line by writing them in form (1):

(a) $y - 4 = 2(x - 3)$ (b) $\dfrac{y + 3}{x - 2} = -\dfrac{7}{8}$

   $2x = y + 2$ $7x + 8y = -10$

(c) $4y = -3x + 24$ (d) $\dfrac{x}{3} + \dfrac{y}{5} = 1$

   $y = -\dfrac{3}{4}x + 6$ $y = -\dfrac{5}{3}x + 5$

FINDING INTERCEPTS

[21] **Which of the following choices lists *all* of the y-intercepts of $|x| + 12 = y$?**

Ⓐ There are none   Ⓑ $\{12, -12\}$ Ⓒ $\{12\}$
Ⓓ $\{-12\}$ Ⓔ $\{0\}$

The x-intercept of a graph is the x-coordinate of the point where the graph intersects the x-axis. It can be found most readily by substituting 0 for y in the graph of the condition and then solving for the values of x.

The y-intercept of a graph is the y-coordinate of the point where the graph intersects the y-axis. It can be found by substituting 0 for x in the condition and then solving for the values of y.

Intercepts are frequently the easiest points of a graph to find and, therefore, are ready aids to graphing.

The multiple-choice question is much simpler than it looks. Since you want the y-intercept, substitute 0 for x and solve the resulting equation for y:

$$|0| + 12 = y.$$

This provides the y-intercept, 12, directly.

¶ DRILL Find the x- and y-intercepts for each of the following:

(a) $\dfrac{x}{3} + \dfrac{y}{5} = 1$ (b) $6x + 3y = 2$ (c) $7 - 3y = 4x$

TESTING FOR SYMMETRY

*[22] **Which of the following completely describes the symmetry of the graph of $x^2 - 3y^2 = 3$?**

Ⓐ x-axis only   Ⓑ y-axis only   Ⓒ Both x- and y-axis   Ⓓ x-axis, y-axis and origin   Ⓔ Origin only

By definition, two points A and B are symmetric with respect to a point M if and only if M is the midpoint of segment AB. A graph is therefore symmetric with respect to the origin if for every point A of the graph there is some point B of the graph such that the origin is the midpoint of segment AB. If (a, b) is any point of the graph, then the midpoint formula shows us that $(-a, -b)$ must also be on the graph when the graph has origin symmetry. To test for origin symmetry, substitute $(-a, -b)$ into the equation and then substitute (a, b); if the resulting equations are the same, then the graph is symmetric with respect to the origin.

By definition, two points A and B are symmetric with respect to a line L if and only if line L is the perpendicular bisector of segment AB. If $A = (a, b)$ and the y-axis is the perpendicular bisector of segment AB, then $B = (-a, b)$. (Verify this by plotting.) If $A = (a, b)$ and the x-axis is the perpendicular bisector of AB', then $B' = (a, -b)$.

To check for y-axis symmetry substitute in your equation both (a, b) and $(-a, b)$ in turn. If the two resulting equations are the same, the graph has y-axis symmetry. To check for x-axis symmetry, apply the same test using (a, b) and $(a, -b)$.

In the multiple-choice question, the resulting equation is:

$$a^2 - 3b^2 = 3.$$

This is the same equation that results from substituting $(a, -b)$, $(-a, b)$ or $(-a, -b)$, so the graph has all three types of symmetry.

¶ DRILL Check each of the following for symmetry:

(a) $3x + 2y = 4$ (b) $x^2 + 3y = 1$
(c) $x^2 + y^2 = 4$ (d) $|x| = 2$

*[23] **Which of the following equations has a graph which is symmetric with respect to the line $y = 4$?**

Ⓐ $3x^2 + 2y = 4$ Ⓑ $4x + 9y = 8$
Ⓒ $4y^2 = x^2$ Ⓓ $x^2 + y^2 = 4$
Ⓔ $y^2 - 8y + 16 = x^2$

Recall that a graph is symmetric with respect to a line L if for every point A of the graph there is a point B of the graph such that line L is the perpendicular bisector of segment AB. In this section we will develop a test for symmetry with respect to *any* vertical line $x = k$ and *any* horizontal line $y = p$. We shall begin by proving the following statement:

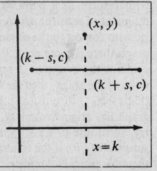

18-1 The line $x = k$ is the perpendicular bisector of the segment joining $(k - s, c)$ and $(k + s, c)$. The line $y = p$ is the perpendicular bisector of the segment joining $(d, p - s)$ and $(d, p + s)$.

PROOF   Let (x, y) represent any point in the plane. Then the distance from (x, y) to $(k - s, c)$ is

(1) $\sqrt{[x - (k - s)]^2 + (y - c)^2}$,

and the distance from (x, y) to $(k + s, c)$ is

(2) $\sqrt{[x - (k + s)]^2 + (y - c)^2}$.

Since the perpendicular bisector of a segment is the set of all points equidistant from its endpoints, the ordered pairs (x, y) for which (1) is equal to (2) must lie on the perpendicular bisector. Set (1) equal to (2), persevere through roughly ten steps of expansion and simplification, and you will get

$$x = k.$$

We recommend that you carry out this simplification process as practice in simple algebraic operations.

A similar line of reasoning will prove the second part of 18-1.

This theorem provides us with our test:

If $x = k + s$ produces the same value for y as does $x = k - s$ when both are substituted in turn in the equation to be tested, then the graph is symmetric with respect to $x = k$. If $y = p + s$ produces the same value for y as does $y = p - s$, then the graph is symmetric with respect to the line $y = p$.

EXAMPLE

Test the graph of $x^2 + 2x + y^2 - 6y = -5$ for symmetry with respect to the lines $x = -1$ and $y = 3$.

SOLUTION:

Case 1 Test for symmetry with respect to $x = -1$. Substitute $(-1 + s)$ for x and simplify.

$(-1 + s)^2 + 2(-1 + s) + y^2 - 6y = -5$
(3) $s^2 + y^2 - 6y = -4$

Substitute $(-1 - s)$ for x and simplify.

$(-1 - s)^2 + 2(-1 - s) + y^2 - 6y = -5$
(4) $s^2 + y^2 - 6y = -4$

Since equations (3) and (4) are the same and will therefore produce the same values for y when $x = -1 + s$ as when $x = -1 - s$, the graph is symmetric with respect to $x = -1$.

Case 2 Test for symmetry with respect to $y = 3$. Substitute $(3 - s)$ for y and simplify.

(5) $x^2 + 2x + s^2 = 4$

Substitute $(3 + s)$ for y and simplify.

(6) $x^2 + 2x + s^2 = 4$

Since (4) and (5) are the same equation, the graph is symmetric with respect to $y = 3$.

In the next section we will develop a simpler method of symmetry testing based on the method just described. For this reason we will postpone any drills until after the next section.

*[24] **Which of the following is a line of symmetry for: $x^2 + 4x + y^2 - 4y = 8$?**

Ⓐ $x = -2$ Ⓑ $x = 2$ Ⓒ $y = -2$
Ⓓ $x = 4$ Ⓔ $y = 4$

If all the like terms of an equation in x and y are collected and the only terms which involve x are of the form Ax^2 and Bx $(A \neq 0)$, then the variables that contain x can be written in the form $A(x - k)^2$ by completing the trinomial square as in the following:

(1) $y^2 = 3x^2 - 6x + 4,$
(2) $y^2 = 3(x^2 - 2x) + 4,$
(3) $y^2 = 3(x^2 - 2x + 1) + 4 - 3,$
(4) $y^2 = 3(x - 1)^2 + 1.$

Note that we subtracted 3 in step (3) since we added 3 by putting a 1 inside the parentheses. Do you see that every term inside the parentheses must be multiplied by the 3 outside the parentheses?

Similarly, if the only terms that involve y are Cy^2 and Dy ($C \neq 0$), then the variables that contain y can be written in the form $C(y - p)^2$. Note that in equation (1) above this means $y^2 = (y - 0)^2$. For those equations in which a Dy term ($D \neq 0$) also appears, we may again use the method of completing the square as used for x above.

Using our symmetry test on $A(x - k)^2$, we get

$$A(k + s - k)^2 = As^2$$

when $x = k + s$, and

$$A(k - s - k)^2 = As^2$$

when $x = k - s$. Thus the graph is symmetric with respect to the line $x = k$. A similar proof shows that when the terms involving y can be transformed to $C(y - p)^2$ the graph is symmetric with respect to $y = p$.

Thus for any equation of the form

$$Ax^2 + Bx + Cy^2 + Dy = E,$$

where not both $A = 0$ and $B = 0$ are true, we can find its horizontal and vertical lines of symmetry by completing the trinomial squares to put it in the form

$$A(x - k)^2 + C(y - p)^2 + F = 0.$$

The lines of symmetry will be $x = k$ and $y = p$. Equations in which no y^2 term appears will have no horizontal line of symmetry. Those in which no x^2 term appears will have no vertical lines of symmetry.

EXAMPLE

Find the lines of symmetry of

$$2y^2 + 6y = x.$$

SOLUTION: (1) $2(y^2 + 3y) = x$

(2) $2(y^2 + 3y + \frac{9}{4}) = x + \frac{9}{2}$

(3) $2(y + \frac{3}{2})^2 = x + \frac{9}{2}$

The only line of symmetry is $y = -\frac{3}{2}$.

The equation of the multiple-choice question can be transformed as follows:

$$x^2 + 4x + 4 + y^2 - 4y + 4 = 8 + 4 + 4$$
$$(x + 2)^2 + (y - 2)^2 = 16.$$

Therefore the vertical and horizontal lines of symmetry are

$$x + 2 = 0 \quad \text{and} \quad y - 2 = 0,$$
$$x = -2 \quad \text{and} \quad y = 2.$$

¶ DRILL Find all horizontal and vertical lines of symmetry for each of the following:

(a) $x^2 + 8x - 6y - 2 = 0$
(b) $x^2 + y^2 - 2x + 4y = 20$
(c) $3x^2 + 3y^2 + 10x - 6y - 12 = 0$

WRITING EQUATIONS OF CONIC SECTIONS, CIRCLES, PARABOLAS, ELLIPSES, AND HYPERBOLAS

*[25] Which of the following is NOT an equation of a conic section?

Ⓐ $x^2 + 2y = 1$ Ⓑ $x^2 + 2x + y^2 = 3$
Ⓒ $3x^2 - y^2 = 4$ Ⓓ $y = 4x^3$ Ⓔ $xy = 9$

The conic sections include the graphs of all equations of the form:

(1) $Ax^2 + By^2 + Cx + Dy + Exy + F = 0,$

where not all of A, B, C, D and E are zero. We will use the term "conic section" to mean the equation as well as the graph. With one exception (equations of the form $xy = k$) we will review only equations for which $E = 0$, in other words, equations with no xy term. Our work with symmetry prepares us to state that such conic sections will be lines (when $A = 0$, $B = 0$ and $E = 0$) or will have axes of symmetry parallel to the x- or y-axis (and frequently to both).

The term "conic section" stems from the fact that each graph can be represented by the intersection of a plane with a cone though we will not attempt to prove this, or even illustrate the intersections. You may choose to look these up in any text which covers simple analytic geometry.

There are other graphs which have equations of the form given by (1), the "degenerate" conics, but these are beyond the scope of this course. Indeed, a line is usually considered to be a "degenerate" conic.

We have already considered the line in detail and will devote the remainder of the chapter to the other conics with the development of two skills in mind: (1) writing the equation given the defining information, and (2) identifying the conic and its defining information, given the equation.

In the multiple-choice question, only Ⓓ cannot be put in the form of equation (1). It fails the test because the exponent of $4x^3$ is 3. The highest power in a conic equation is 2.

¶ DRILL (1) Indicate for each of the following whether it is a conic and, if so, (2) use the method of section [24] to find any axes of symmetry:

(a) $x^2 + y^2 - 6y - 8 = 0$
(b) $x^2 - 6x - 2y + 1 = 0$
(c) $x + 3y = 4$
(d) $x^2 + 8x + 3y^2 - 6y = 15$

*[26] **Which of the following is an equation of a circle with center at (3, −2) and radius 7?**

Ⓐ $x^2 + y^2 - 6x + 4y - 36 = 0$
Ⓑ $x^2 + y^2 = 62$
Ⓒ $x^2 - 6x + 9 + y^2 = 49$
Ⓓ $x^2 + y^2 + 4y + 4 = 49$
Ⓔ **None of these**

A *circle* is the set of all points that are at a given distance (the "radius") from a given point (the "center"). If we represent the center by $C(h, k)$ and the radius by r, and if $P(x, y)$ represents any point in the plane, then the distance from C to P is given by:

(1) $\sqrt{(x - h)^2 + (y - k)^2}$

according to the distance formula.

Setting (1) equal to r yields an equation that is true only when (1) equals r and, therefore, is true only for points $P(x, y)$ that are r units from $C(h, k)$:

(2) $\sqrt{(x - h)^2 + (y - k)^2} = r$.

Equation (2) must be an equation for the circle with center at C and radius r.

Squaring both sides gives the more useful form

(3) $(x - h)^2 + (y - k)^2 = r^2$.

We may readily write an equation for any circle, given the center and radius, by using (3).

EXAMPLE 1

Find an equation of a circle with center at $(-1, 4)$ and radius 11.

SOLUTION: Using (3), we obtain an equation:

$$[x - (-1)]^2 + (y - 4)^2 = (11)^2,$$
$$(x + 1)^2 + (y - 4)^2 = 121.$$

Given an equation of a circle, we can put it in the same form as (3) from which we can read off the center and radius.

EXAMPLE 2

Find the center and radius of:

$$x^2 + y^2 - 2x + 2y - 2 = 0.$$

SOLUTION: Completing the trinomial squares, we get.

(1) $x^2 - 2x + 1 + y^2 + 2y + 1 = 2 + 2$,
(2) $(x - 1)^2 + (y + 1)^2 = 4$,
(3) center, $(1, -1)$; radius, 4.

Equation (3) also provides the key to identifying an equation as a circle: the equation must contain both an x^2 and a y^2 term, and both of these terms must have the same coefficient.

The equation of the circle in the multiple-choice question (center at $(3, -2)$ and radius 7) is:

$$(x - 3)^2 + (y + 2)^2 = 7^2,$$
$$x^2 - 6x + 9 + y^2 + 4y + 4 = 49,$$
$$x^2 + y^2 - 6x + 4y - 36 = 0.$$

TEST-TAKING TIP.

The more experience you have with a concept or procedure, the quicker you can work through a problem and the more readily you can recognize a correct answer. If, for example, you've had lots of experience with the coordinate geometry of circles, the seemingly complicated question above can be answered in less than a minute without shortcuts. Beware of shortcuts that don't depend on sound mathematical principles. In this case, for example, you may be tempted to say that the constant must be 49, the square of the radius. As you can see from the process above, however, the number 49 is one of three constants in the equation, which, when combined, give the result −36.

Develop your skills and speed through practice, and avoid unsound shortcuts.

¶ DRILL Given the following, find the equation of the circle:

(a) Center $(-3, 4)$, radius 6
(b) Center $(-5, -2)$, radius 7

Given the following equations, find the center and radius:

(c) $x^2 + y^2 - 4x - 6y = 12$
(d) $x^2 + y^2 + 16x - 10y = -25$

[27] Which of the following is an equation of a parabola with focus $(-4, -\frac{3}{2})$ and vertex $(-4, -3)$?

Ⓐ $y^2 + 8y - 6x + 28 = 0$
Ⓑ $x^2 + 6x - 4y + 13 = 0$
Ⓒ $x^2 + 8x - 6y - 2 = 0$
Ⓓ $y^2 + 6y - 4x + 17 = 0$
Ⓔ $x^2 - 4x - 3y + 1 = 0$

A *parabola* is the set of all points that are equidistant from a given line (the "directrix") and a given point (the "focus") that is not on that line. We will deal only with parabolas that have either horizontal or vertical directrices. The line containing the focus and perpendicular to the directrix is the *axis* of symmetry, and its intersection with the parabola is called the *vertex*.

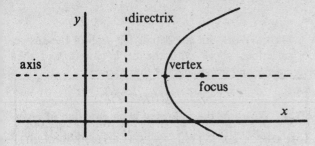

We will derive a general equation for any parabola with a vertical directrix. Let the vertex be $V(h, k)$ and the directed distance from the vertex to the focus be given by c ($c > 0$ if the focus is to the right of the vertex, $c < 0$ if to the left). Then the focus is $F(h + c, k)$ and the directrix is $x = h - c$. If $P(x, y)$ is any point in the plane, then the distance from F to P is

(1) $\sqrt{[x - (h + c)]^2 + (y - k)^2}$.

The distance from P to the line $x = h - c$ is not as straightforward but should be apparent from the figure at right and the following discussion.

The distance from a point to a line is defined to be the length of the perpendicular segment from the point to the line. Since the directrix is vertical, this perpendicular segment, DP, is always horizontal so the y-coordinates of P and D must always be the same. The x-coordinate of D must be $h - c$ since all points of the line $x = h - c$ have this x-coordinate. The distance formula then gives us

(2) $\sqrt{[x - (h - c)]^2 + (y - y)^2}$

as the distance from P to the directrix. If we set (1) equal to (2) and simplify, we get

(3) $(y - k)^2 = 4c(x - h)$.

A similar derivation for the case when the directrix is horizontal yields

(4) $(x - h)^2 = 4c(y - k)$.

Equations (3) and (4) are the standard forms of the parabolas with (a) vertical or horizontal directrices, (b) vertex at (h, k) and (c) directed distance, c, from vertex to focus. These equations provide the key for the recognition of parabolas: one and only one of x^2 or y^2 occurs, but the equation contains both variables.

The preceding discussion suggests two ways of writing the equation from the defining information: (1) by using the definition of parabola and (2) by using either equation (3) or (4).

EXAMPLE

Find the equation of the parabola with focus $(1, 3)$ and vertex $(1, -1)$.

SOLUTION: From the given information we can find the directrix to be $y = -5$ and the axis $x = 1$.

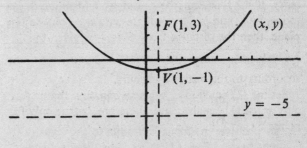

Method 1 (by definition). Let $P(x, y)$ be any point in the plane; then

$$PF = \sqrt{(x - 1)^2 + (y - 3)^2}.$$

Also, the distance from P to D (where D is any point of $y = -5$ on the same vertical line as $P(x, y)$) is

$$PD = \sqrt{(x - x)^2 + [y - (-5)]^2}.$$

Setting $PF = PD$ and simplifying, we get

$$(x - 1)^2 = 16(y + 1).$$

Method 2 (by equation (4)). The directed distance, c, from V to F is 4 and the vertex is $(1, -1)$ so the equation must be

$$(x - 1)^2 = 4(4)[y - (-1)].$$

¶ DRILL Write an equation for the parabola which satisfies each of the following:

(a) Directrix $y = 8$, focus $(0, -8)$
(b) Directrix $x = 6$, focus $(-6, 0)$
(c) Directrix $x = -4$, focus $(4, 0)$
(d) Directrix $x = -6$, focus $(2, 4)$

In the multiple-choice question, both the focus and the vertex have first coordinates -4, so the line $x = -4$ is the axis of symmetry. The equation must, therefore, be of the form:

$$[x - (-4)]^2 = 4c[y - (-3)],$$

where c is the directed distance from $(-4, -3)$ to $(-4, -\frac{3}{2})$, or $1\frac{1}{2}$.

$$(x + 4)^2 = 4(\tfrac{3}{2})(y + 3)$$
$$x^2 + 8x + 16 = 6(y + 3)$$
$$x^2 + 8x - 6y - 2 = 0$$

[28] Which of the following is a parabola with focus at $(-3, 5)$?

  Ⓐ $y^2 - 6y + 9 = 8x$
  Ⓑ $x^2 + 6x - 12y + 33 = 0$
  Ⓒ $y^2 - 2y + 12x - 11 = 0$
  Ⓓ $x^2 + 4x + 8y - 20 = 0$
  Ⓔ $x^2 + 8x - 12y + 52 = 0$

In the preceding section we developed the technique for doing this problem, and we are including this section to expand on what we have learned. Each of the above answers is a parabola, and we will go through the process for finding the focus, vertex, directrix and axis for each.

(A) $y^2 - 6y + 9 = 8x$
    $(y - 3)^2 = 8(x - 0)$

Therefore the vertex is $(0, 3)$, the axis is $y = 3$ and $c = 2$. Since the axis is horizontal and c is positive, the focus is 2 units to the right of the vertex, $F = (2, 3)$, and the directrix is a vertical line 2 units to the left of the vertex, $x = -2$.

(B) $x^2 + 6x - 12y + 33 = 0$
    $x^2 + 6x \qquad\qquad = 12y - 33$
    $x^2 + 6x + 9 \qquad = 12y - 33 + 9$
    $(x + 3)^2 = 12(y - 2)$

Therefore the vertex is $(-3, 2)$, the axis is $x = -3$ and $c = 3$. Since the axis is vertical and c is positive, the focus is 3 units above the vertex and is thus $(-3, 5)$. The directrix is the horizontal line 3 units below the vertex and is thus $y = -1$.

(C) $y^2 - 2y + 12x - 11 = 0$
    $y^2 - 2y \qquad\qquad = -12x + 11$
    $y^2 - 2y + 1 \qquad = -12x + 11 + 1$
    $(y - 1)^2 = -12(x - 1)$

Therefore the vertex is $(1, 1)$, the axis is $y = 1$ and $c = -3$. Since the axis is horizontal and c is negative, the focus is 3 units to the left of the

vertex and is $(-2, 1)$. The directrix is the vertical line 3 units to the right of the vertex and is $x = 4$.

(D) $x^2 + 4x + 8y - 20 = 0$
    $x^2 + 4x \qquad\qquad = -8y + 20$
    $x^2 + 4x + 4 \qquad = -8y + 20 + 4$
    $(x + 2)^2 = -8(y - 3)$

Therefore the vertex is $(-2, 3)$, the axis is $x = -2$, $c = -2$, the focus is $(-2, 1)$ and the directrix, $y = 5$.

(E) $x^2 + 8x - 12y + 52 = 0$
    $x^2 + 8x \qquad\qquad = 12y - 52$
    $x^2 + 8x + 16 \qquad = 12y - 52 + 16$
    $(x + 4)^2 = 12(y - 3)$

Vertex, $(-4, 3)$; axis, $x = -4$; $c = 3$; focus, $(-4, 6)$; directrix, $y = 0$.

¶ DRILL Work out the details for each of the answer selections above with the book closed, and then check your work against that shown.

*[29] Which of the following is an equation of an ellipse with foci of $(4, 0)$ and $(-4, 0)$, if $(5, 0)$ is a point on the ellipse?

  Ⓐ $25x^2 + 16y^2 = 1$ Ⓑ $25x^2 + 16y^2 = 400$
  Ⓒ $x^2 + y^2 = 400$ Ⓓ $\dfrac{x^2}{16} + \dfrac{y^2}{25} = 1$
  Ⓔ $\dfrac{x^2}{25} + \dfrac{y^2}{9} = 1$

An *ellipse* is the set of all points such that the sum of the distances from each of these points to two given points (the "foci") never varies. In intermediate math we are concerned only with ellipses which have horizontal and vertical axes of symmetry that intersect at the origin. We call the intersection of these axes the "center" of the ellipse and thus are studying only ellipses with center at the origin. The foci lie on one of these axes, termed the "major" axis, and the other is called the "minor" axis.

To derive the general equation with foci on the x-axis and center at the origin (as in the figure below),

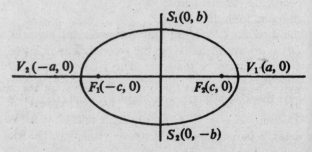

we will let the foci be $F_1(-c, 0)$ and $F_2(c, 0)$, and the intersections of the ellipse with the axes be as they are in the figure.

(1) $F_1V_1 = \sqrt{(a + c)^2 + (0 - 0)^2} = a + c$
(2) $F_2V_1 = \sqrt{(a - c)^2 + (0 - 0)^2} = a - c$

The sum of these distances is $2a$. Since this is the sum of the distances from a specific point of the ellipse to the two foci and the definition indicates that this sum never varies for a given ellipse, the equation of the ellipse is given by

(3) $\sqrt{(x - c)^2 + (y - 0)^2}$
$$+ \sqrt{(x + c)^2 + (y - 0)^2} = 2a.$$

We will omit the simplification process and merely state that (3) simplifies to

(4) $1 = \dfrac{x^2}{a^2} + \dfrac{y^2}{a^2 - c^2}$

Since S_1 is also a point on the ellipse, then $F_1S_1 + F_2S_1 = 2a$.

$$\sqrt{(-c - 0)^2 + (0 - b)^2}$$
$$+ \sqrt{(c - 0)^2 + (0 - b)^2} = 2a$$

This equation simplifies to

(5) $b^2 = a^2 - c^2$.

Equation (5) relates the coordinates of the foci and intercepts. Substituting b^2 for $a^2 - c^2$ in (4), we get

(6) $1 = \dfrac{x^2}{a^2} + \dfrac{y^2}{b^2}.$

Equation (6) is the general equation of the ellipse with foci on the x-axis. Equation (7) below follows from a similar derivation and is the equation of the ellipse with foci on the y-axis.

(7) $1 = \dfrac{x^2}{b^2} + \dfrac{y^2}{a^2}$

We can always differentiate a, the intercept on the major axis, from b, the intercept on the minor axis, because $a^2 > b^2$.

Deriving the equation of an ellipse from the definition is a needlessly lengthy process compared to the use of equations (5), (6) and (7) as exemplified below.

EXAMPLE 1

We will work the original question. The foci are $(4, 0)$ and $(-4, 0)$ so $c^2 = 16$, and the major axis is the x-axis. The given point $(5, 0)$ of the ellipse is on the x-axis so it must be one of the vertices. Therefore $a^2 = 25$. Since $b^2 = a^2 - c^2$, we conclude that $b^2 = 9$. We select equation (6) as the form we want since the foci

are on the x-axis. By substituting the values for a^2 and b^2 we get

$$1 = \frac{x^2}{25} + \frac{y^2}{9}.$$

EXAMPLE 2

Find the equation and foci of the ellipse with intercepts $(2, 0)$ and $(-2, 0)$ as well as $(0, 6)$ and $(0, -6)$.

SOLUTION: Since a and $-a$ are the intercepts on the major axis, we conclude that $a = 6$ and $b = 2$. We select (7) as the desired form since the major axis is the y-axis. Substituting 36 for a^2 and 4 for b^2, we get

$$1 = \frac{x^2}{4} + \frac{y^2}{36}.$$

We can find the foci from the fact that $b^2 = a^2 - c^2$.

$$4 = 36 - c^2$$
$$\pm\sqrt{32} = c$$
$$\pm 4\sqrt{2} = c$$

The foci are thus $(0, 4\sqrt{2})$ and $(0, -4\sqrt{2})$.

¶ DRILL Write an equation of each of the following ellipses:

(a) Foci $(4, 0)$, $(-4, 0)$, $a^2 = 36$
(b) Foci $(0, 2)$, $(0, -2)$, $b^2 = 5$
(c) Intercepts $(4, 0)$, $(-4, 0)$, $(0, \sqrt{7})$, $(0, -\sqrt{7})$

*[30] Which of the following ellipses has $(4\sqrt{2}, 0)$ as a focus?

ⓐ $16x^2 + 36y^2 = 576$ ⓑ $25x^2 + 16y^2 = 400$
ⓒ $25x^2 + 4y^2 = 100$ ⓓ $100x^2 + 25y^2 = 2500$ ⓔ $4x^2 + 36y^2 = 144$

In the preceding section we developed the techniques for answering this question and are including this section primarily to practice what has just been explained. All ellipses with centers at the origin and axes of symmetry parallel to the coordinate axes are of the forms designated by (6) and (7) in section [29]. These can be written as

(8) $a^2b^2 = b^2x^2 + a^2y^2$,
(9) $a^2b^2 = a^2x^2 + b^2y^2$,

by multiplying them by the lowest common denominators. In this form they provide the key for recognition of ellipses: each has only an x^2, y^2 and constant term, and the coefficients of the x^2 and y^2 terms are both of the same sign but are not equal. The first step in finding the foci and intercept of an ellipse in form (8) or (9) is to put it into either form (6) or (7).

To show the procedure, we'll find the intercepts and foci of Ⓐ, Ⓑ, and Ⓒ in the multiple-choice question.

Ⓐ $16x^2 + 36y^2 = 576$ can be written as

$$\frac{x^2}{36} + \frac{y^2}{16} = 1,$$

by dividing both sides by 576. Therefore $a^2 = 36$ and $b^2 = 16$. Since $b^2 = a^2 - c^2$, we find c^2 to be 20 and $c = \pm2\sqrt{5}$. Because a^2 is the denominator of the x^2 term, the major axis is the x-axis and the foci are $(2\sqrt{5}, 0)$ and $(-2\sqrt{5}, 0)$.

Ⓑ $25x^2 + 16y^2 = 400$ can be changed to

$$\frac{x^2}{16} + \frac{y^2}{25} = 1,$$

by dividing through by 400. Therefore $a^2 = 25$ and $b^2 = 16$. Since $b^2 = a^2 - c^2$, we conclude that $c^2 = 9$ and $c = \pm3$. Because a^2 is the denominator of the y^2 term, the major axis is the y-axis and the foci are $(0, 3)$ and $(0, -3)$.

Ⓒ $25x^2 + 4y^2 = 100$ can be changed to

$$\frac{x^2}{4} + \frac{y^2}{25} = 1.$$

Therefore $a^2 = 25$, $b^2 = 4$, $c^2 = 21$, $c = \pm\sqrt{21}$, the major axis is the y-axis and the foci are $(0, \pm\sqrt{21})$. We will leave the details of the remaining answers as a drill.

¶ DRILL Find the foci of each of the above answer selections with the book closed, and then check your work against the explanations given.

*[31] **Which of the following is an equation of a hyperbola?**

Ⓐ $x^2 + 3y^2 = 6$ Ⓑ $-\frac{x^2}{4} - \frac{y^2}{16} = 1$

Ⓒ $\frac{x^2}{4} + \frac{y^2}{16} = -1$ Ⓓ $\frac{x^2}{4} - \frac{y^2}{16} = -1$

Ⓔ **None of these**

A *hyperbola* is a set of points such that the difference of the distances from each point to each of two fixed points (the "foci") never varies. In intermediate math we are primarily concerned with hyperbolas which have horizontal and vertical axes of symmetry, and the intersection of these (called the "center") is at the origin. The foci lie on one of these axes, and this axis is called the "major" axis. The other axis is called the "transverse" axis.

To derive the general equation with foci on the x-axis and center at the origin (as in the following figure):

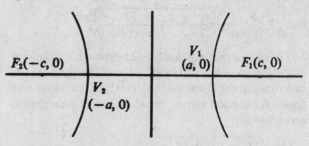

we let the foci and the intersections of the hyperbola with the major axis be as they are in the figure. Note that the hyperbola does not intersect the transverse axis.

$$F_1V_1 = c - a$$
$$F_1V_2 = c + a$$

Therefore

$$F_1V_2 - F_1V_1 = (c + a) - (c - a)$$
$$= 2a.$$

The definition of hyperbola indicates that $2a$ must be the difference for all points of the hyperbola so its equation must be given by

(1) $\sqrt{(x + c)^2 + (y - 0)^2}$
$$- \sqrt{(x - c)^2 + (y - 0)^2} = 2a.$$

Through some involved algebra we can simplify (1) to:

(2) $\dfrac{x^2}{a^2} - \dfrac{y^2}{c^2 - a^2} = 1.$

We let (3) $b^2 = c^2 - a^2$ (for the ellipse, b had a geometric meaning in terms of intercepts which we derived; for the hyperbola, b has no such meaning) and substitute to get

(4) $\dfrac{x^2}{a^2} - \dfrac{y^2}{b^2} = 1.$

Equation (4) is the general equation of the hyperbola with foci on the x-axis, and equation (3) relates the coordinates of the intercepts to the coordinates of the foci. Equation (5) below follows from a similar derivation and is the equation of the hyperbola with foci on the y-axis:

(5) $-\dfrac{x^2}{b^2} + \dfrac{y^2}{a^2} = 1.$

We can always determine which is a and which is b by noting that a provides meaningful intercepts and b doesn't.

Deriving the equation of an hyperbola from the definition is a needlessly lengthy process compared with the use of equations (3), (4) and (5) as exemplified on p. 175.

EXAMPLE 1

The foci of a hyperbola are $(3, 0)$ and $(-3, 0)$, and the curve intercepts the x-axis at $(1, 0)$. Find the equation of the hyperbola.

SOLUTION: Since the foci are as given, we conclude that $c^2 = 9$. Because $(1, 0)$ is an intercept, $a^2 = 1$. From equation (3) above, $b^2 = c^2 - a^2$ so $b^2 = 8$. The required equation can be found by substituting for a^2 and b^2 in (4).

$$\frac{x^2}{1} - \frac{y^2}{8} = 1$$

EXAMPLE 2

Find the equation and foci of the hyperbola with intercepts of $(0, 6)$ and $(0, -6)$ if one point on the graph is $(4, 6\sqrt{2})$.

SOLUTION: Since the foci are on the y-axis, the equation is of form (5) and $a^2 = 36$. If $(4, 6\sqrt{2})$ is a point of the hyperbola, it must satisfy the equation.

$$-\frac{x^2}{b^2} + \frac{y^2}{36} = 1$$

$$-\frac{4^2}{b^2} + \frac{(6\sqrt{2})^2}{36} = 1$$

$$-\frac{16}{b^2} + 2 = 1$$

$$b^2 = 16$$

Consequently, the required equation is

$$-\frac{x^2}{16} + \frac{y^2}{36} = 1.$$

Equations (4) and (5) provide the key to identifying the hyperbola with center at the origin and axes of symmetry the x- and y-axis. When the hyperbola is in the form $a^2x^2 - b^2y^2 = a^2b^2$ or $a^2y^2 - b^2x^2 = a^2b^2$, note that the operation connecting the y^2 and x^2 terms is always subtraction.

In the multiple-choice question:

Ⓐ is an ellipse, since both coefficients are positive.
Ⓑ is impossible since it can be transformed (by multiplying each side by -1) to

$$\frac{x^2}{4} + \frac{y^2}{16} = -1,$$

and the sum of two squares (which must each be positive or zero) cannot be negative.
Ⓒ is the same equation as B.
Ⓓ *looks* incorrect because the right-hand side is -1. If, however, each side is divided by -1, the characteristic form of the hyperbola can readily be seen.

¶ DRILL Write the equation for the hyperbola which satisfies each of the following:

(a) Foci $(2, 0)$ and $(-2, 0)$; intercepts $(\frac{1}{2}, 0)$ and $(-\frac{1}{2}, 0)$

(b) Foci $(0, 5)$ and $(0, -5)$; intercepts $(0, 1)$ and $(0, -1)$

*[32] Which of the following is an equation of a hyperbola which has $y = \frac{5}{2}x$ as an asymptote?

Ⓐ $\frac{x^2}{16} - \frac{y^2}{4} = 1$ Ⓑ $\frac{x^2}{36} - \frac{y^2}{16} = 1$

Ⓒ $\frac{y^2}{25} - \frac{x^2}{4} = 1$ Ⓓ $x^2 - 9y^2 = -36$

Ⓔ $\frac{x^2}{9} - \frac{y^2}{25} = 1$

In the equation of a hyperbola, as the value of x increases or decreases without bound the graph of the hyperbola approaches and remains close to two lines as shown.

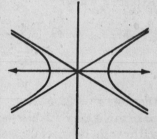

These lines are called the "asymptotes" of the hyperbola and are very useful in graphing the curve. They can be found by solving the equation of the hyperbola for y and then considering the expression that the right member approaches when x gets very large.

$$(1) \quad \frac{x^2}{a^2} - \frac{y^2}{b^2} = 1$$

$$-\frac{y^2}{b^2} = 1 - \frac{x^2}{a^2}$$

$$y^2 = \frac{b^2x^2}{a^2} - b^2$$

$$(2) \quad y = \pm\sqrt{\frac{b^2x^2}{a^2} - b^2}$$

As x becomes increasingly large in equation (2) the value of the right member closely approximates the value of

$$\pm\sqrt{\frac{b^2x^2}{a^2} - 0},$$

which simplifies to

$$\pm\frac{bx}{a}.$$

The asymptotes of a hyperbola with horizontal major axis are the lines $y = \pm\frac{bx}{a}$. You may verify that they are $y = \pm \dfrac{ax}{b}$ for a hyperbola with vertical major axis.

EXAMPLE

Find the foci and the equation of the asymptotes of

$$\frac{x^2}{16} - \frac{y^2}{4} = 1.$$

SOLUTION: The equation is of the form $\dfrac{x^2}{a^2} - \dfrac{y^2}{b^2} =$ 1 and has a horizontal major axis. Also, $a^2 = 16$ while $b^2 = 4$. Since $b^2 = c^2 - a^2$, we find $c^2 = 20$ and the foci are $(2\sqrt{5}, 0)$ and $(-2\sqrt{5}, 0)$. The asymptotes must be $y = \pm \dfrac{bx}{a}$ and therefore are $y = \pm \dfrac{x}{2}$.

To find the asymptotes without resorting to a memorized formula, replace the 1 by 0 and solve for y.

We'll use choice ⓒ as an example:

$$\frac{y^2}{25} - \frac{x^2}{4} = 1.$$

Replace 1 with 0:

$$\frac{y^2}{25} - \frac{x^2}{4} = 0,$$
$$\frac{y^2}{25} = \frac{x^2}{4},$$
$$y^2 = 25(\frac{x^2}{4}),$$
$$y = \pm \frac{5}{2}x.$$

¶ DRILL Find the foci and asymptotes of:

(a) $\dfrac{x^2}{36} - \dfrac{y^2}{16} = 1$ (b) $x^2 - 9y^2 = -36$

STUDYING INVERSE VARIATION

*[33] Which of the following is a vertex of the hyperbola $xy = -9$?

Ⓐ (3, 0)   Ⓑ (0, 3)   Ⓒ (3, 3)   Ⓓ (-3, 3)
Ⓔ None of these

An equation important to the study of inverse variation (and the only conic we will study that has an xy term) is the rectangular hyperbola, $xy = k$, where the constant k is any real number. A study of a sample graph (for $xy = 1$, right) provides the 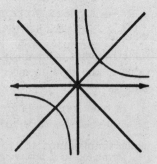 required information. The axes of symmetry are the lines $y = \pm x$, and the asymptotes are the x and y axes. Since the vertices are the points of intersection of the hyperbola with the major axis, $y = x$, they can be

found by substituting y for x in the equation and solving. We will not discuss the foci.

When k is negative, the asymptotes are still the coordinate axes, but the major axis is the line $y = -x$ and the vertices are found by substituting $-x$ for y in the equation and solving. The branches of these hyperbolas will lie in quadrants II and IV.

In the multiple-choice question,

$$xy = -9.$$

Replace y by $-x$ and solve for x:

$$-x^2 = -9,$$
$$x^2 = 9,$$
$$x = \pm 3.$$

Since $y = -x$, the vertices are $(3, -3)$ and $(-3, 3)$.

¶ DRILL For each of the following find the vertices and indicate which quadrants the branches of the graph will lie in:

(a) $xy = 16$ (b) $xy = -1$ (c) $xy = -12$

(d) $xy = \dfrac{1}{4}$

[34] The number of hours it takes to type a manuscript varies inversely with the number of typists assigned to the job. If it takes three typists 36 hours to complete a manuscript, how many hours will four typists take to do the job?

Ⓐ 27   Ⓑ 25   Ⓒ 20   Ⓓ 12   Ⓔ 18

Inverse variation is part of our chapter on coordinate geometry only because problems involving it may be solved by using the equation $xy = k$, where x and y represent the two quantities that vary inversely with respect to each other and k is the constant of variation.

In the given question let x represent the number of typists and y the number of hours; then

(1) $xy = k$

expresses the relationship between them. Once k is determined, equation (1) can be used to find the number of typists needed to do the job in a specified time or the number of hours the job will take for a given number of typists. The constant k can be found by using the given information of three typists and 36 hours:

$$(3)(36) = k = 108,$$

and equation (1) becomes

(2) $xy = 108.$

Let $x = 4$ and solve (2) to answer the question.

WHAT YOU SHOULD KNOW

KEY CONCEPTS

Handling Points and Lines

1. The distance between two points on a number line is the absolute value of the difference of their coordinates.
2. To every point in a plane there corresponds an ordered pair of numbers.
3. Every nonvertical line has exactly one slope.
4. If a line is vertical, it has no slope.
5. If a line is horizontal, its slope is zero.
6. If two lines are parallel, they have the same slope.
7. If two lines are perpendicular, the product of their slopes is -1.

Handling Equations of Lines, Circles, Parabolas, Ellipses, and Hyperbolas

1. If m is the slope of a line and (x_1, y_1) are the coordinates of a point on the line, an equation of the line is $(y - y_1) = m(x - x_1)$, where (x, y) is any point of the line.
2. If m is the slope of a line and b is its y-intercept, an equation of the line is $y = mx + b$, where (x, y) is any point of the line.
3. If (h, k) is the center of a circle and r its radius, then $(x - h)^2 + (y - k)^2 = r^2$ is an equation of the circle, where (x, y) is any point of the circle.
4. The equation of a parabola with vertex at the origin and focus $(0, c)$ is $x^2 = 4cy$.
5. The equation of a parabola with vertex at the origin and focus $(c, 0)$ is $y^2 = 4cx$.
6. An equation of an ellipse with foci on the x-axis is
$$\frac{x^2}{a^2} + \frac{y^2}{b^2} = 1,$$
where $a > b$.
7. An equation of an ellipse with foci on the y-axis is
$$\frac{x^2}{b^2} + \frac{y^2}{a^2} = 1,$$
where $a > b$.
8. An equation of a hyperbola with center at the origin and intercepts on the x-axis is
$$\frac{x^2}{a^2} - \frac{y^2}{b^2} = 1.$$
9. An equation of a hyperbola with center at the origin and intercepts on the y-axis is
$$\frac{y^2}{a^2} - \frac{x^2}{b^2} = 1.$$

10. To find the equation of the asymptotes of a hyperbola in either form (8) or (9), factor the left side of the equation and set each factor equal to zero:
$$\left(\frac{x}{a} - \frac{y}{b}\right) = 0 \quad \text{or} \quad \left(\frac{x}{a} + \frac{y}{b}\right) = 0.$$

Handling Graphs

1. To find the y-intercepts of the graph of an equation in x and y, replace x by zero and solve for y.
2. To find the x-intercepts of the graph of an equation in x and y, replace y by zero and solve for x.

Other

1. For an ellipse, if $2a$ is the length of the major axis, $2b$ the length of the minor axis and $2c$ the distance between foci, then $a^2 = b^2 + c^2$.
2. If $2a$ is the distance between the intercepts on the transverse axis of a hyperbola and $2c$ the distance between the foci, then $a^2 + b^2 = c^2$.

KEY FORMULAS

If the endpoints of a segment are (x_1, y_1) and (x_2, y_2), then:

a. The midpoint $M = \left(\dfrac{x_1 + x_2}{2}, \dfrac{y_1 + y_2}{2}\right)$.

b. The slope m of the line $= \dfrac{y_2 - y_1}{x_2 - x_1}$.

c. The distance between the points $=$
$$\sqrt{(x_1 - x_2)^2 + (y_1 - y_2)^2}.$$

TEST-TAKING STRATEGIES

- Look for coordinate geometry questions that can be answered most quickly by:
  a. checking each choice in turn to find the correct one,
  b. eliminating some choices by direct calculation, *or*
  c. using the technique of transformation, that is, putting all choices in the same form.
- Test questions involve both coordinate systems on a line and coordinate systems in a plane. Make sure you understand which is pertinent to the test question. You are likely to get confused when an equation in one variable is given. Such an equation can represent either a point on a line or a line (either vertical or horizontal) in a plane. Consult the given information to determine which is intended.
- Many beginning students are surprised to find that numbers in radical form represent finite lengths. Make sure you understand this so you don't discard a radical answer when the question asks for a length.

- Do not use decimal approximations for radicals unless the question specifically requests an approximation or the answer choices are in decimal form.
- When applying the slope formula, check yourself by asking four questions. Are both numbers in the numerator y-coordinates? Are both numbers in the denominator x-coordinates? Do the first numbers on top and bottom come from the same point? Do the second numbers on top and bottom come from the same point? The most common errors in applying the slope formula come from putting the numbers in the wrong places.
- To remember the midpoint formula, remember that the coordinates of the midpoint are the averages of the corresponding coordinates of the endpoints. The midpoint formula is the only formula in which the coordinates are added rather than subtracted.

ANSWERS

[1] Ⓓ

DRILL:

(a) 4   (b) 8
(c) 11   (d) 4
(e) $|q + p|$ (f) $|p + q|$
(g) $|q - p|$

[2] Ⓑ

DRILL:

(a) $A(3, 5)$
(b) $B(\frac{1}{2}, \frac{1}{2})$
(c) $C(-2, 1)$
(d) $D(-3, -2)$
(e) $E(8, -3)$
(f) $F(0, 0)$

[3] Ⓓ

DRILL:

(a) III   (b) I
(c) IV   (d) II

[4] Ⓔ

DRILL:

(a) x: 2, y: 1   (b) x: 5, y: 2
(c) x: 2, y: 8   (d) x: 4, y: 4

[5] Ⓓ

DRILL:

(a) (3, 4)   (b) (−2, −2)
(c) (−5, −2)   (d) (4.5, − 1.5)
(e) (−12, −7)   (f) (−8, 13)

[6] Ⓐ

DRILL:

(a) 1   (b) 1   (c) −1   (d) $-\frac{3}{2}$

[7] Ⓒ

DRILL:

(a) 1   (b) −1
(c) $\frac{3}{2}$

[8] Ⓔ

DRILL:

(a) Vertical.   (b) Horizontal.
(c) Horizontal.   (d) Neither.

[9] Ⓑ

DRILL:

(a) Parallel.   (b)–(d) Nonparallel.

[10] Ⓔ

DRILL:

(a) 2   (b) $-\frac{1}{2}$

(c) −2   (d) $\frac{4}{3}$

[11] Ⓔ

DRILL:

(a) $\sqrt{149}$ (b) 9
(c) $5\sqrt{5}$ (d) $\sqrt{p^2 + q^2}$

[12] Ⓑ

DRILL:

(a) 16.5   (b) 210
(c) 15   (d) 12

[13] Ⓒ

DRILL:

$$M = \left(\frac{c}{2}, \frac{d}{2}\right) \quad N = \left(\frac{b + c}{2}, \frac{d}{2}\right), \text{ slope of } MN$$

$$= 0, \quad MN = \frac{b}{2}$$

[14] Ⓑ

DRILL:

(a)   (b)

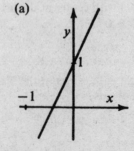
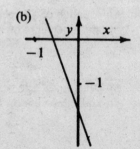

(c)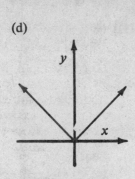

(d)

[15] Ⓑ
DRILL:

(a)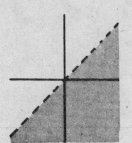

(b)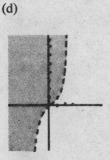

(c)

(d)

[16] Ⓓ
DRILL:
(a) The entire plane.
(b) The region between the lines $y = 2$ and $y = 3$.

(c)

(d)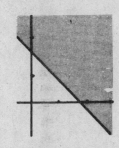

[17] Ⓒ
DRILL:

(a) $y = 5$ (b) $x = -\dfrac{1}{2}$

(c) $y = -4$ (d) $x = \sqrt{2}$

[18] Ⓒ

[19] Ⓑ
DRILL:

(a) $y + 2 = 3(x - 1)$ (b) $y - 4 = -\dfrac{x}{3}$

(c) $y - 4 = -6x$

[20] Ⓔ
DRILL:
(a) $2x - y - 2 = 0$
(b) $7x + 8y + 10 = 0$
(c) $3x + 4y - 24 = 0$
(d) $5x + 3y - 15 = 0$

[21] Ⓒ
DRILL:

(a) $x: 3,\ y: 5$ (b) $x: \dfrac{1}{3},\ y: \dfrac{2}{3}$

(c) $x: \dfrac{7}{4},\ y: \dfrac{7}{3}$

[22] Ⓓ
DRILL:
(a) None.   (b) y-axis only
(c) All.   (d) All.

[23] Ⓔ
DRILL:
All symmetries are correct.

[24] Ⓐ
DRILL:

(a) $x = -4$ (b) $x = 1,\ y = -2$

(c) $x = -\dfrac{5}{3},\ y = 1$

[25] Ⓓ
DRILL:
(a) Circle, $x = 0,\ y = 3$.
(b) Parabola, $x = 3$.
(c) Line, no axial symmetry.
(d) Ellipse, $y = 1,\ x = -4$.

[26] Ⓐ
DRILL:
(a) $x^2 + y^2 + 6x - 8y = 11$
(b) $x^2 + y^2 + 10x + 4y = 20$
(c) $C = (2, 3),\ r = 5$
(d) $C = (-8, 5),\ r = 8$

[27] Ⓒ
DRILL:
(a) $x^2 = -32y$
(b) $y^2 = -24x$
(c) $y^2 = 16x$
(d) $(x - 2)^2 = 20(y + 1)$

[28] Ⓑ

[29] Ⓔ
DRILL:
(a) $\dfrac{x^2}{36} + \dfrac{y^2}{20} = 1$ (b) $\dfrac{x^2}{5} + \dfrac{y^2}{29} = 1$
(c) $\dfrac{x^2}{16} + \dfrac{y^2}{7} = 1$

[30] Ⓔ

[31] Ⓓ
DRILL:
(a) $4x^2 - \dfrac{4y^2}{15} = 1$ (b) $y^2 - \dfrac{x^2}{24} = 1$

[32] Ⓒ
DRILL:
(a) $(\pm 2\sqrt{13}, 0)$, $y = \pm\dfrac{2}{3}x$
(b) $(0, \pm 2\sqrt{10})$, $y = \pm\dfrac{x}{3}$

[33] Ⓓ
DRILL:
(a) $(4, 4)$, $(-4, -4)$, I and III.
(b) $(1, -1)$, $(-1, 1)$, II and IV.
(c) $(2\sqrt{3}, -2\sqrt{3})$, $(-2\sqrt{3}, 2\sqrt{3})$, II and IV.
(d) $(\dfrac{1}{2}, \dfrac{1}{2})$, $(-\dfrac{1}{2}, -\dfrac{1}{2})$, I and III.

[34] Ⓐ

19. Quadratic Equations

Key Terms

quadratic equation   an equation of the form $ax^2 + bx + c = 0$, where $a \neq 0$.

trinomial square   the square of a linear binomial of the form $ax + b$.

FACTORING QUADRATICS

[1] For what value of k will the equation $x^2 - k = 0$ have the two solutions $\sqrt{2}$ and $-\sqrt{2}$?

Ⓐ ± 2 Ⓑ 2 Ⓒ $\pm\sqrt{2}$ Ⓓ $\sqrt{2}$ Ⓔ $\pm\sqrt{-2}$

19-1 If $x^2 - k = 0$, where k is positive, then $(x - \sqrt{k})(x + \sqrt{k}) = 0$ and $x = \pm\sqrt{k}$.

A *quadratic equation* is an equation of the form $ax^2 + bx + c = 0$, where $a \neq 0$. The equation above exemplifies the simplest type of quadratic:

$$x^2 + c = 0 \quad (a = 1, b = 0).$$

The first step in understanding the solution of any quadratic is to realize the circumstances for which any statement of the form $mn = 0$ is true. It should be clear that no product of two numbers can ever equal zero unless one (or both) of the factors is zero. We proved this in section [5] of Chapter 6.

Our procedure for finding solutions of quadratics, then, is to represent them as products of linear factors and then to discover which values of the variables cause these factors to equal zero.

The simple quadratic $x^2 + c = 0$ is factorable in the real number system only when c is negative.

EXAMPLE 1

Solve the equation $x^2 - 16 = 0$.

SOLUTION: The expression $x^2 - 16$ is the difference of squares and can be factored as follows (by 2–13):

$$(x - 4)(x + 4) = 0.$$

What values of x will make each of these factors equal zero? In other words, for which values of x is the statement

$$x - 4 = 0 \quad \text{or} \quad x + 4 = 0$$

true? The solutions must be 4 and -4. By similar reasoning we can state the following:

EXAMPLE 2

Find x if $9x^2 - 36 = 0$.

SOLUTION: If $9x^2 - 36 = 0$, then $x^2 - 4 = 0$. Thus $x^2 = 4$ and $x = \pm 2$.

EXAMPLE 3

Find x if $3x^2 - 2 = 0$.

SOLUTION: Divide both sides of the equation by 3 to get $x^2 - \dfrac{2}{3} = 0$. Then $x^2 = \dfrac{2}{3}$ and $x = \pm\sqrt{\dfrac{2}{3}} = \pm\dfrac{\sqrt{6}}{3}$.

¶ **DRILL** Solve each of the following:

(a) $x^2 = 9$ (b) $3x^2 - 12 = 0$ (c) $2x^2 - 2 = 0$

[2] What is the value of b if the roots of the equation $x^2 - 5bx + 4b^2 = 0$ are 2 and 8?

Ⓐ 1 Ⓑ 2 Ⓒ 3 Ⓓ 4 Ⓔ 5

Many trinomial quadratics (those for which $b \neq 0$) are also factorable into linear factors as we saw in section [7] of Chapter 7. To discover the circumstances under which this will occur, we will build a sample trinomial from the linear factors $x + m$ and $x + n$:

$$(x + m)(x + n) = x^2 + (m + n)x + mn.$$

The clue to factorization is thus to find a pair of numbers, m and n, such that their product is the constant term and their sum is the coefficient of the x term.

EXAMPLE 1

Find the solutions of $x^2 + 10x + 21 = 0$.

SOLUTION: We must find a pair of numbers whose product is 21 and whose sum is 10. Through trial and error (or insight developed with practice) we select 7 and 3. Thus

$$x^2 + 10x + 21 = 0,$$
$$(x + 7)(x + 3) = 0.$$

Since the product of two factors can be zero only when one of these factors is zero, we are interested in finding the values for which $(x + 7) = 0$ or $(x + 3) = 0$. Simple algebra indicates the solutions to be -7 and -3.

EXAMPLE 2

Solve the equation $2x^2 + 9x - 5 = 0$.

SOLUTION: Through practice in your Algebra I course you should have developed skills which will allow you to factor $2x^2 + 9x - 5$ in your head. If you do not have this facility, you can try dividing both sides of the equation by 2 to get

$$x^2 + \frac{9}{2}x - \frac{5}{2} = 0,$$

and attempt to discover two numbers with a product of $-\frac{5}{2}$ and a sum of $\frac{9}{2}$. Since the denominator of $\frac{9}{2}$ is 2, such a fraction must result from the addition of two fractions with denominators of 2 and such fractions will yield a product with denominator 4. With this in mind we change $-\frac{5}{2}$ to $-\frac{10}{4}$ and note from this the numbers $\frac{10}{2}$ and $-\frac{1}{2}$, which yield factors of

$$\left(x - \frac{1}{2}\right)\left(x + \frac{10}{2}\right) = 0$$

and roots of $\frac{1}{2}$ and $-\frac{10}{2} = -5$.

In the event that you are equally unable to master this method, this will prove little handicap in the solution of quadratics since we will develop two other, more mechanical methods in later sections.

In the multiple-choice question the equation $x^2 - 5bx + 4b^2 = 0$ can be factored into $(x - 4b)(x - b) = 0$, with roots represented by $4b$ and b. If the values of these roots are 2 and 8, then $b = 2$.

¶ DRILL Solve the equations:
  (a) $x^2 - x - 6 = 0$
  (b) $x^2 + 15x + 44 = 0$
  (c) $2x^2 - 10x - 28 = 0$
  (d) $2x^2 - 7x + 35 = -(5x - 3x^2)$

USING TRINOMIAL SQUARES

[3] **For what value of k is $x^2 - \frac{4}{5}x + k$ a trinomial square?**

  Ⓐ 5   Ⓑ $-\frac{4}{9}$ Ⓒ $\frac{4}{9}$ Ⓓ $\frac{4}{25}$ Ⓔ $-\frac{4}{25}$

The term *trinomial square* (Chapter 7, section [6]) applies to expressions that are the squares of linear binomials of the form $(ax + b)$. The simplest of these is the expansion of $(x + b)^2$:

$$(x + b)^2 = x^2 + 2bx + b^2.$$

In the equation above, the coefficient of the x term is $2b$ and the constant is b^2. In other words, the constant term is the square of half the coefficient of the x term, when the coefficient of the x^2 term is 1.

EXAMPLE 1

In each of the following replace the question mark with a constant making the trinomial a square:

  (a) $x^2 + 4x + ?$ (b) $x^2 + ?x + 16$
  (c) $x^2 + 5x + ?$ (d) $x^2 + ?x + 7$

SOLUTIONS:

  (a) The constant must be the square of half of 4 or $(2)^2$, giving $x^2 + 4x + 4$.
  (b) 16 is the square of half of the second coefficient, but 16 is the square of either 4 or -4. Hence the question mark is 8 or -8, giving $x^2 + 8x + 16$ or $x^2 - 8x + 16$.
  (c) Half of 5 is $\frac{5}{2}$, which when squared is $\frac{25}{4}$.
  (d) 7 is the square of either $\sqrt{7}$ or $-\sqrt{7}$ so the second coefficient can be either $2\sqrt{7}$ or $-2\sqrt{7}$.

EXAMPLE 2

Add a constant to both sides of $3x^2 + 4x + 5 = 0$ so that one side of the equation is a trinomial square.

SOLUTION: If $3x^2 + 4x + 5 = 0$, then $x^2 + \frac{4}{3}x + \frac{5}{3} = 0$. Thus:

$$x^2 + \frac{4}{3}x = -\frac{5}{3}.$$

We complete the trinomial square on the left side by adding $\dfrac{4}{9}$ to both sides:

$$x^2 + \frac{4}{3}x + \frac{4}{9} = \frac{4}{9} - \frac{5}{3},$$
$$\left(x + \frac{2}{3}\right)^2 = -\frac{11}{9}.$$

Would you now be able to find the roots of this equation? There will be more about this in the next section.

In the multiple-choice question, the trinomial is a square if

$$k = (\tfrac{1}{2}(\tfrac{4}{5}))^2$$
$$= (\tfrac{2}{5})^2$$
$$= \frac{4}{25}.$$

¶ DRILL Add a constant to both sides of each equation so that one side is a trinomial square.

(a) $x^2 + 2x = 8$

(b) $x^2 + 3x = 2$

(c) $3x^2 + 4x - 8 = 0$

(d) $2x^2 - 3x - 1 = 0$

[4] Which of the following are the roots of the equation $(x + 5)^2 - 3 = 0$?

Ⓐ $\sqrt{3}$ Ⓑ $\pm\sqrt{3}$ Ⓒ -5 Ⓓ ± 5

Ⓔ $-5 \pm \sqrt{3}$

Any quadratic equation, whether readily factorable or not, can be solved by completing the square and using the fact that when $x^2 = k$, then $x = \pm\sqrt{k}$.

EXAMPLE 1

Find the roots of $x^2 + 9x - 10 = 0$.

SOLUTION: Though this quadratic is readily factorable, $(x + 10)(x - 1) = 0$, we will use it to show the method of completing the square. First transform the equation so that the constant term is the right member:

$$x^2 + 9x = 10.$$

Then add to both sides the number that makes the left side a square trinomial:

$$x^2 + 9x + \frac{81}{4} = 10 + \frac{81}{4},$$
$$\left(x + \frac{9}{2}\right)^2 = \frac{121}{4},$$
$$x + \frac{9}{2} = \pm\frac{11}{2},$$
$$x = -\frac{9}{2} \pm \frac{11}{2}.$$

Therefore $x = 1$ or -10.

EXAMPLE 2

Solve $4x^2 + 6x - 9 = 0$.

SOLUTION: Divide both members by 4

$$x^2 + \frac{3}{2}x - \frac{9}{4} = 0,$$
$$x^2 + \frac{3}{2}x = \frac{9}{4}.$$

Complete the square:

$$x^2 + \frac{3}{2}x + \frac{9}{16} = \frac{9}{4} + \frac{9}{16},$$
$$\left(x + \frac{3}{4}\right)^2 = \frac{45}{16},$$
$$x = -\frac{3}{4} \pm \frac{\sqrt{45}}{4}.$$

In the multiple-choice question, the process of solution is similar to several steps in the process of solving by completing the square:

$$(x + 5)^2 - 3 = 0,$$
$$(x + 5)^2 = 3,$$
$$x + 5 = \pm\sqrt{3},$$
$$x = -5 \pm \sqrt{3}.$$

¶ DRILL Solve by completing the square:

(a) $x^2 + 3x - 2 = 0$ (b) $3x^2 + 4x - 4 = 0$

USING THE QUADRATIC FORMULA

[5] If $7x^2 - 12x + 3 = 0$, then $x = ?$

Ⓐ $\dfrac{6 + \sqrt{15}}{7}$ Ⓑ $\dfrac{6 + \sqrt{15}}{7}$ or $\dfrac{6 - \sqrt{15}}{7}$

Ⓒ $\dfrac{-6 + \sqrt{15}}{7}$ Ⓓ $\dfrac{-6 \pm \sqrt{15}}{7}$

Ⓔ No real number

In the preceding section we reviewed a method for solving any quadratic equation regardless of its factorability. The technique used provides the means for deriving a formula which will always yield the roots of a quadratic when the coefficients are known. We will state without proof:

19-2 If $ax^2 + bx + c = 0$ and $a \neq 0$, then

$$x = \frac{-b \pm \sqrt{b^2 - 4ac}}{2a}.$$

The above formula is called the "Quadratic Formula."

EXAMPLE

Find the roots of $x^2 - 8x + 6 = 0$.

SOLUTION: The coefficients are $a = 1$, $b = -8$ and $c = 6$. By formula:

$$x = \frac{-(-8) \pm \sqrt{64 - 24}}{2}$$
$$= 4 \pm \sqrt{10}.$$

In the multiple-choice question, since

$$7x^2 - 12x + 3 = 0,$$

$$x = \frac{-(-12) \pm \sqrt{(-12)^2 - 4(7)(3)}}{2(7)}$$
$$= \frac{12 \pm \sqrt{60}}{14}$$
$$= \frac{12 \pm 2\sqrt{15}}{14}$$
$$= \frac{6 \pm \sqrt{15}}{7}$$

¶ DRILL Use the Quadratic Formula to find the roots of:

(a) $2x^2 - x - 5 = 0$
(b) $3x^2 + 10x - 4 = 0$
(c) $x^2 - 5x + 6 = 0$

EXPRESSING INFORMATION AS A QUADRATIC EQUATION

[6] If the length of a rectangle exceeds its width by 1 foot, and if its area is 2 square feet, find the dimensions of the rectangle.

Ⓐ $1' \times 2'$ Ⓑ $2' \times 3'$ Ⓒ $\sqrt{2}' \times \sqrt{2}'$
Ⓓ $\frac{3}{2}' \times 3'$ Ⓔ No such rectangle is possible

Many common verbal problems can be resolved by first expressing the information given as a quadratic equation.

EXAMPLE 1

If the product of two numbers is 12 and the first exceeds the second by 1, find the numbers.

SOLUTION: Let x represent the smaller number; then $x + 1$ will represent the larger and $x(x + 1)$ will represent their product.

$$x(x + 1) = 12$$
$$x^2 + x - 12 = 0$$
$$(x + 4)(x - 3) = 0$$

Thus the smaller number can be either -4 or 3, and the larger -3 or 4.

EXAMPLE 2

An artist paints a picture which is 12 inches by 10 inches. He decides to put a uniform border around the picture which will have an area that is $\frac{4}{10}$ the area of the painting. What is the width of this border?

SOLUTION: Let x represent the width of the border. Then the total width of the painting and mounting will be $10 + 2x$ and the total length $12 + 2x$. The total area will be represented by $(10 + 2x)(12 + 2x)$. But the area of the painting is $12 \times 10 = 120$ and the area of the border is $\frac{4}{10}(120) = 48$. Therefore

$$(10 + 2x)(12 + 2x) = 120 + 48,$$

which simplifies to

$$(x + 12)(x - 1) = 0.$$

Since x is -12 or 1, the border must be 1 inch in width. The equation yields the root -12, but this answer is not applicable to the problem.

To answer the multiple-choice question, let x be the width. Then $x + 1$ represents the length and $x(x + 1)$ is the area. Therefore:

$$x(x + 1) = 2,$$
$$x^2 + x - 2 = 0,$$
$$(x + 2)(x - 1) = 0,$$
$$x = -2 \quad \text{or} \quad x = 1.$$

The solution -2 is extraneous since the width of a rectangle must be positive.

TEST-TAKING TIP.

Checking the answer choices may be an even quicker way of selecting the correct answer than solving the equation. Choices Ⓑ and Ⓓ give the wrong area, Ⓒ has the wrong relationship between length and width, Ⓐ has the right area and the right length-width relationship—both can be seen by inspection.

¶ DRILL

(a) If the sum of two numbers is 10 and the sum of their squares is 58, find the numbers.
(b) What are the dimensions of a rectangle whose area is 44 square inches and whose perimeter is 30 inches?

SOLVING NONQUADRATIC EQUATIONS

[7] Find the values of x if $(x^2 - 3x)^2 - 2(x^2 - 3x) = 8$.

Ⓐ $\{-1,1\}$ Ⓑ $\{2,1\}$ Ⓒ $\{4,-1\}$
Ⓓ $\{4,-1,2,1\}$ Ⓔ $\{-4,-1,-2,1\}$

Some equations, though not quadratic in themselves, can be solved by using the techniques developed for the solution of quadratic equations.

EXAMPLE 1

Find x if $x^4 - 3x^2 - 4 = 0$.

SOLUTION: Let $u = x^2$; then $x^4 - 3x^2 - 4 = 0$ can be rewritten as:

$$u^2 - 3u - 4 = 0,$$
$$(u - 4)(u + 1) = 0,$$
$$u = 4 \text{ or } u = -1.$$

But $u = x^2$, so $x^2 = 4$ or $x^2 = -1$,

$$x = \pm 2 \text{ or } x = \pm\sqrt{-1}.$$

The symbol $\sqrt{-1}$ should be familiar to students of intermediate math and would be an acceptable solution if the domain of the variable was the set of complex numbers. When, as in this case, no domain is specified, it is assumed to be the set of real numbers and thus excludes $\sqrt{-1}$. The required solution set is $\{2, -2\}$.

EXAMPLE 2

Solve $\left(\dfrac{1}{x} - 2\right)^2 - 6\left(\dfrac{1}{x} - 2\right) + 5 = 0$.

SOLUTION: Let $u = \dfrac{1}{x} - 2$; then:

$$u^2 - 6u + 5 = 0,$$
$$(u - 1)(u - 5) = 0,$$
$$u = 1 \text{ or } u = 5.$$

But $u = \dfrac{1}{x} - 2$, so:

$$\frac{1}{x} - 2 = 1 \text{ or } \frac{1}{x} - 2 = 5.$$

The solution set for x is thus $\{\dfrac{1}{3}, \dfrac{1}{7}\}$.

In the multiple-choice question above, let $u = x^2 - 3x$; then:

$$u^2 - 2u - 8 = 0,$$
$$(u - 4)(u + 2) = 0,$$
$$u = 4 \text{ or } u = -2.$$

But $u = x^2 - 3x$, so:

$$x^2 - 3x = 4 \text{ or } x^2 - 3x = -2.$$

The solution set for x is thus $\{4, -1, 2, 1\}$.

¶ DRILL Solve:

(a) $10 + \dfrac{1}{x} - \dfrac{3}{x^2} = 0 \left(\text{Let } u = \dfrac{1}{x}\right)$

(b) $\left(\dfrac{3}{2x} - 4\right)^2 + \left(\dfrac{3}{2x} - 4\right) = 2$

SOLVING EQUATIONS WITH RADICAL TERMS

[8] If $\sqrt{x} + \sqrt{x - 4} + 2 = 0$, then $x = ?$

Ⓐ 4   Ⓑ 4 or -4   Ⓒ 16   Ⓓ 8   Ⓔ No solution

When both sides of an equation are squared, the resulting equation does not necessarily have the same roots as the original equation. For example, the equation $x = 3$ has only 3 as a root, but the equation whose members are its squares, $x^2 = 9$, has the two roots 3 and -3. Whatever the roots of the original equation are, however, they will be among the roots of the new equation. One technique for solving equations that have radical terms consists of squaring the equation as many times as necessary to remove the radicals and then checking the roots of the new equation in the original equation.

EXAMPLE 1

Find the roots of $\sqrt{x + 1} = x - 1$.

SOLUTION: Squaring both sides, we get:

$$x + 1 = x^2 - 2x + 1,$$
$$0 = x^2 - 3x,$$
$$0 = x(x - 3),$$
$$x = 0 \text{ or } x = 3.$$

These are the roots of $x^2 - 3x = 0$, but only one is a root of the original equation because substitution of 0 for x yields $\sqrt{1} = -1$.

EXAMPLE 2

We will solve the multiple-choice question.

SOLUTION: You may have recognized immediately that this equation has no solutions since all three terms represent positive numbers and the sum of three positive numbers can never be zero.

TEST-TAKING TIP.

College Board test questions rarely involve many steps or much calculation. Always consider the possibility of a direct and quick solution.

To pursue a mechanical solution, first isolate one radical:

$$\sqrt{x - 4} = -\sqrt{x} - 2,$$

and then square both sides:

$$x - 4 = x + 4\sqrt{x} + 4.$$

(Note the square of the right side; remember that $(a + b)^2$ is $a^2 + 2ab + b^2$, not $a^2 + b^2$!) One radical remains, so we first simplify, isolate this radical, and then square both sides again:

$$-2 = \sqrt{x},$$
$$4 = x.$$

We are tempted to say that the solution of the original equation is 4, but substituting 4 for x we get:

$$\sqrt{4} + \sqrt{4 - 4} + 2 = 0,$$
$$4 = 0.$$

A word of caution: to remove a radical by squaring you must first isolate it on one side of the equation. Suppose you did not do this for an equation such as $\sqrt{x} + x = 6$. Your result by squaring would be $x + 2x\sqrt{x} + x^2 = 36$ and the radical would still be there! Had you isolated it first, $\sqrt{x} = 6 - x$, you would have gotten $x = 36 - 12x + x^2$ with no radicals.

¶ DRILL Solve each by the method of squaring:

(a) $\sqrt{x - 4} = 3$
(b) $2\sqrt{x - 5} + 4 = \sqrt{x - 5}$
(c) $x + \sqrt{x + 1} = 1$

DETERMINING THE NATURE OF ROOTS

[9] If $ax^2 + bx + c = 0$, $b > 1$, $b < 2\sqrt{ac}$, what is the nature of the roots of the quadratic equation?

Ⓐ One real, rational root   Ⓑ Two real, irrational roots   Ⓒ Two real, rational roots   Ⓓ One real, irrational root   Ⓔ No real roots

The Quadratic Formula can be used to determine the nature of the roots of a quadratic without actually calculating them. Recall that the expression $\sqrt{b^2 - 4ac}$ appears in the formula. The number $b^2 - 4ac$ is called the *discriminant*. When the discriminant is negative, there can be no real roots for the equation since no negative number has a square root in the real number system. When the discriminant is zero,

$$\sqrt{b^2 - 4ac} = 0,$$

and the formula gives

$$\frac{-b \pm \sqrt{0}}{2a} = \frac{-b}{2a}.$$

Thus the equation has only the real number $\frac{-b}{2a}$ as a root. If the discriminant is positive and a perfect square, then the equation has two real, rational roots since $\sqrt{b^2 - 4ac}$ will be rational. If the discriminant is positive, but not a perfect square, then the equation has two real irrational roots since $\sqrt{b^2 - 4ac}$ will be irrational.

EXAMPLES

(1) $x^2 - x + 1 = 0$; $b^2 - 4ac = -3$; no real roots
(2) $4x^2 - 12x + 9 = 0$; $b^2 - 4ac = 0$; one real root
(3) $x^2 - 5x + 6 = 0$; $b^2 - 4ac = 1$; two real rational roots
(4) $x^2 + 3x - 1 = 0$; $b^2 - 4ac = 13$; two real irrational roots

In the multiple-choice question $b > 1$ and $b < 2\sqrt{ac}$, meaning that $b^2 < 4ac$ and $b^2 - 4ac < 0$, so the equation has no real roots. The condition that $b > 1$ assures us that b is positive, and, hence, squaring both sides involves multiplying both sides of our inequality by positive numbers; the direction of the inequality was thus preserved.

¶ DRILL Without solving the equations below, indicate the nature of the roots:

(a) $2x^2 - 4x - 7 = 0$
(b) $21x^2 + 4x - 65 = 0$
(c) $4x^2 - 36x + 81 = 0$

[10] The roots of the equation $x^2 + 2bx + b^2 = 0$ are p and q. What can you conclude about b and q?

Ⓐ Both are positive   Ⓑ $b = q$ Ⓒ $b = -q$ Ⓓ $b > q$ Ⓔ $b < q$

We have seen that the roots of a quadratic equation $ax^2 + bx + c = 0$ are

$$r_1 = \frac{-b + \sqrt{b^2 - 4ac}}{2a}$$

and

$$r_2 = \frac{-b - \sqrt{b^2 - 4ac}}{2a}$$

If we add r_1 and r_2 we get

(1) $r_1 + r_2 = -\dfrac{b}{a}.$

Multiplying r_1 by r_2 gives

(2) $r_1 \cdot r_2 = \dfrac{c}{a}.$

The two numbers found in (1) and (2) are recognizable as the coefficients of the equation we get when we divide our original equation by a to get a first coefficient of 1.

(3) $x^2 + \dfrac{b}{a}x + \dfrac{c}{a} = 0$

Thus we state that, when the leading coefficient of a quadratic equation is 1, the second coefficient is the negative of the sum of the roots, and the constant term is the product of the roots.

The equation $x^2 + 2bx + b^2 = 0$ involves a perfect square trinomial so its roots are equal and their sum is $-2b$ (the sum of the roots is the negative of the coefficient of the x-term). If the roots are p and q, then $p = q$. Thus $q + q = -2b$ and q and b are negatives of each other. We can draw no conclusion about which of the two, q or b, is positive; certainly both cannot be. Since one is positive and the other negative, then one of $q > b$ or $b > q$ must be true, but we can draw no conclusion about which relationship it is.

¶ DRILL Without solving, indicate the sum and product of the roots of the equations given:

(a) $x^2 - 4x + 2 = 0$ (b) $x^2 = \dfrac{1}{3} - \dfrac{1}{2}x$

(c) $3x^2 = 5x + 7$

WHAT YOU SHOULD KNOW

KEY CONCEPTS

1. If $x^2 = k$ and $k > 0$, then $x = \pm\sqrt{k}$.
2. If $ax^2 + bx + c = 0$ and $ax^2 + bx + c$ can be factored into linear factors, then the solutions can be found by setting each factor equal to zero and solving for x.
3. To solve an equation of the form
$$\sqrt{ax + b} = c,$$
square each side to eliminate the radical and solve the resulting equation. Be sure to check all roots to see whether extraneous roots have been introduced by squaring.
4. To solve an equation involving more than one radical expression, first solve for one radical and square both sides to eliminate this radical. If any radicals remain, solve for another radical and square both sides. Continue the process until all radicals have been eliminated.
5. The equation $ax^2 + bx + c = 0$, has:
   a. no real roots if $b^2 - 4ac < 0$,
   b. one real root if $b^2 - 4ac = 0$, and
   c. two real roots if $b^2 - 4ac > 0$.

KEY FORMULA

If $ax^2 + bx + c = 0$ and $a \neq 0$, then
$$x = \frac{-b \pm \sqrt{b^2 - 4ac}}{2a}$$
(Quadratic Formula)

TEST-TAKING STRATEGIES

• If a verbal problem involves finding one or more factors of a product when the numerical value of the product is given, the solution generally requires a quadratic equation; for example, when the area is given and the length and width are unknown, but are

related to each other. Be thoroughly familiar with these equations and their application.
• The quadratic formula is a powerful tool for solving quadratic equations, but its use can be time-consuming. Before trying the formula, always check to see if the quadratic polynomial can be factored.
• Squaring both sides of an equation can introduce extraneous roots. (These are solutions of the squared equation that are not solutions of the original.) Always check your roots in the original equation.

ANSWERS

[1] Ⓑ
   DRILL:
   (a) $\{3, -3\}$ (b) $\{2, -2\}$ (c) $\{1, -1\}$

[2] Ⓑ
   DRILL:
   (a) $\{3, -2\}$ (b) $\{-4, -11\}$
   (c) $\{7, -2\}$ (d) $\{5, -7\}$

[3] Ⓓ
   DRILL:
   (a) 1 (b) $\dfrac{9}{4}$ (c) $\dfrac{4}{9}$ (d) $\dfrac{9}{16}$

[4] Ⓔ
   DRILL:
   (a) $\dfrac{-3 \pm \sqrt{17}}{2}$ (b) $\{\dfrac{2}{3}, -2\}$

[5] Ⓑ
   DRILL:
   (a) $\dfrac{1 \pm \sqrt{41}}{4}$ (b) $\dfrac{-5 \pm \sqrt{37}}{3}$
   (c) $\{3, 2\}$

[6] Ⓐ
   DRILL:
   (a) $\{7, 3\}$ (b) 4×11

[7] Ⓓ
   DRILL:
   (a) $\left\{-\dfrac{3}{5}, \dfrac{1}{2}\right\}$ (b) $\left\{\dfrac{3}{4}, \dfrac{3}{10}\right\}$

[8] Ⓔ
   DRILL:
   (a) $\{13\}$
   (b) No solution, 21 doesn't work.
   (c) $\{0\}$, 3 doesn't work.

[9] Ⓔ

DRILL:

(a) Discriminant: 72, two real irrational.

(b) Discriminant: 5476, which is 74^2, two real rational.

(c) Discriminant: 0, one real rational.

[10] Ⓒ

DRILL:

(a) $s = 4, p = 2$ (b) $s = -\frac{1}{2}, p = -\frac{1}{3}$

(c) $s = \frac{5}{3}, p = -\frac{7}{3}$

20. Relations and Functions

Key Terms

relation   a set of ordered pairs.

function   a set of ordered pairs no two of which have the same first coordinate.

domain of a relation (and, therefore, of a function)   the set of first coordinates. When not specified, it includes all real numbers.

range of a relation (and, therefore, of a function)   the set of all second coordinates.

IDENTIFYING FUNCTIONS AND RELATIONS

[1] Which of the following statements is (are) true?

    I A function is never a relation.
    II A function is always a relation.
    III All relations are functions.

    Ⓐ I only   Ⓑ II only   Ⓒ III only   Ⓓ I and II only   Ⓔ II and III only

It is frequently necessary in problem analysis to assign the elements of a set A to the elements of a second set B as directed by such rules as: (1) to every segment assign the positive real number that is its length, or (2) to every real number assign the number that is twice as great.

We are often concerned with pairings between sets of points and/or sets of numbers. Coordinate systems, for example, pair sets of points with sets of numbers or with sets of ordered pairs of numbers. Equations and inequalities in two variables pair a set of numbers with a second set of numbers. When we record the pairings of the elements of a set A with the elements of a set B, we generally use a fixed order that shows the sources of the entries of each pairing.

EXAMPLE

When we tabulate the ordered pairs of real numbers determined by an equation such as

$$y = 2x,$$

we always name the elements taken from the set of x values first. Some of these pairs are:

$$\{(2,4), (\tfrac{1}{2},1), (-3, -6), \ldots\}.$$

The second entry in each case is, of course, the y value.

Any set of ordered pairs is called a *relation*. Relations are not necessarily sets of ordered pairs of real

numbers, but we will deal primarily with those that are. The set of all first entries of the ordered pairs is called the *domain* of the relation. The set of all second entries is called the *range*. If a relation has the further characteristic that no two of its ordered pairs have the same first entry, then it is called a function. Thus a *function* is a set of ordered pairs for which no two ordered pairs have the same first entry. Therefore a function is always a relation, but not all relations are functions.

¶ DRILL The following are sets of ordered pairs of real numbers. Indicate which are relations, which are functions and which are both:

    (a) $\{(2, 3), (2, 4), (3, 4), (4, 3)\}$
    (b) $\{(2, 3), (4, 3), (8, 1), (1, 3)\}$
    (c) $\{(1, 2), (3, -4), (5, 6), (7, -8)\}$
    (d) $\{(1, 2), (1, 3), (1, 4), (1, 5)\}$

RECOGNIZING FUNCTIONS

[2] Which of the following statements does NOT describe a function?

    Ⓐ Assign to each triangle its area.   Ⓑ Assign to each day its date.   Ⓒ Assign to each book its number of pages.   Ⓓ Assign to each hour the temperature at that hour.   Ⓔ Assign to each positive number a number for which it is the absolute value.

Some of the possible answers above are examples of relations that do *not* assign numbers to numbers. Since all of them *do* establish ordered pairs by assigning the elements of one set to the elements of a second set, they are all relations. The set that is assigned is the range. The set that has the range elements assigned to it is the domain. In each of the relations except Ⓔ each element of the domain has only one element of the range assigned to it. Note that in Ⓔ every positive number has two numbers for which it is the absolute value. Since Ⓔ contains such ordered pairs as

$$\{(3, 3), (3, -3), (\tfrac{1}{2}, \tfrac{1}{2}), (\tfrac{1}{2}, -\tfrac{1}{2})\}$$

and more than one ordered pair has the same first element, Ⓔ cannot be a function.

¶ DRILL For each of the following, indicate whether it is a function:

(a) Assign to each person his weight at a given instant.
(b) Assign to each person his weight at 10 different instances, each a year apart.
(c) Assign to each integer between 100 and 200 the persons in your school who have these numbers as their weights to the nearest pound.
(d) Assign to each integer between 100 and 200 the persons in your family who have these numbers as their weights in pounds.

FINDING CARTESIAN PRODUCTS

[3] If $A = \{1,2,3\}$ and $B = \{4,5\}$, which ordered pair is NOT an element of $A \times B$?

Ⓐ (1,4)   Ⓑ (5,2)   Ⓒ (2,4)   Ⓓ (3,5)   Ⓔ (2,5)

The symbol "$A \times B$" designates the result of assigning the elements of a set B to the elements of a set A. It is called the *Cartesian product* (sometimes the cross-product or the Cartesian cross-product) and consists of the set of all possible ordered pairs which have a member of A as first entry and a member of B as second entry. If $C = \{a,b,c\}$ and $D = \{x,y,z\}$, then $C \times D =$

$$\{(a,x),(a,y),(a,z),(b,x),(b,y),(b,z),(c,x),(c,y),(c,z)\}.$$

Each element of D is thus paired with each element of C.

The most commonly used cross-product is $R \times R$, the set of all possible ordered pairs which have both first and second entries in the real number system. The graph of $R \times R$ is the real number plane discussed in Chapter 18.

Representing information by means of a table can be helpful in many types of problems, for example, in determining cross-products. In the multiple-choice question:

×	1	2	3
4	(1, 4)	(2, 4)	(3, 4)
5	(1, 5)	(2, 5)	(3, 5)

¶ DRILL Write out $A \times B$ where:

(a) $A = \{a,b\}$, $B = \{c,d\}$
(b) $A = \{a,b,c\}$, $B = \{d\}$
(c) $A = \{a\}$, $B = \{x,y,z\}$
(d) $A = \{a\}$, $B = \{z\}$

[4] Which of the following are graphs of functions?

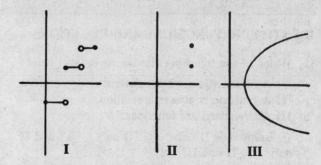

I   II   III

Ⓐ I only   Ⓑ II only   Ⓒ III only
Ⓓ I and III only   Ⓔ II and III only

We have defined a function as a set of ordered pairs for which no two have the same first entry. In Chapter 18 we learned to represent ordered pairs by points in the coordinate plane. A function can be graphed in the coordinate plane (as can a relation) by letting each first entry be the x-coordinate and each second entry be the y-coordinate. Since a function cannot have two ordered pairs with the same first coordinate, its graph cannot have two points on the same vertical line. A set of points, then, is the graph of a function if no vertical line intersects the graph in more than one point.

In the multiple-choice question, vertical lines strike more than one point of the graphs in both II and III; hence only I is a function.

¶ DRILL If each of the following geometric figures were graphed in the coordinate plane, the graph would designate a set of points. Which of the sets would define a function?

(a) A circle   (b) Any nonvertical line   (c) An acute angle that has a side parallel to the x-axis   (d) The interior of a triangle

[5] Which of the following sets of ordered pairs is a function?

Ⓐ $\{(x,y): y = x^3\}$ Ⓑ $\{(x,y): x = |y|\}$
Ⓒ $\{(x,y): y = \pm \sqrt{x}\}$ Ⓓ $\{(x,y): y < x\}$
Ⓔ All of these

The notation $\{(x,y): \quad \}$, with the blank space containing some mathematical sentence, means "the set of ordered pairs such that [the mathematical sentence] is true." The mathematical sentence is generally an equation, an inequality or a combination of equations and inequalities.

Intermediate math is primarily concerned with functions defined by equations. Other branches of math deal with other types of functions, but these are beyond the scope of our review.

No relation is completely specified unless its domain is established. We will agree that the domain of a relation when not explicitly stated is the set of all real numbers except those which make the relation meaningless. We will comment further on the latter statement in the next section, but return to the multiple-choice question now.

Ⓐ $y = x^3$ defines a function since no value of x yields more than one value for y. Since the domain is not explicitly stated, it is the set of all reals.

Ⓑ $x = |y|$ must have a domain restricted to nonnegative real numbers since negative real numbers cannot be absolute values. With the domain established we can determine that this is not a function since each value of x yields two values for y. (Note that, when $x = 3$, $y = 3$ or -3.)

Ⓒ $y = \pm \sqrt{x}$ has a domain also limited to nonnegative real numbers because no negative number has a square root in the real number system. Yet it is not a function because it, too, yields two values of y for each value of x.

Ⓓ $y < x$ yields infinitely many y values for each x value.

¶ DRILL Each of the following equations will define a relation, the set of ordered pairs that make the equation true. Which of these will also define a function?

(a) $y = x^2$ (b) $y^2 = x$
(c) $x^2 + y^2 = 4$ (d) $x = 3$

[6] **Which of the following statements describes the domain of the function defined as follows?**

$$y = \frac{\sqrt{x-3}}{(x-2)(x-\sqrt{3})}$$

Ⓐ **All real numbers except 2 and $\sqrt{3}$**   Ⓑ **All real numbers**   Ⓒ **All positive real numbers**
Ⓓ **All positive real numbers except 2 and $\sqrt{3}$**
Ⓔ **All real numbers except those less than 3**

When the domain of a function is not explicitly stated, we have agreed that it consists of all real numbers which are meaningful in the function. Among the common circumstances under which a real number will not be meaningful are (1) if it leads to division by zero, and (2) if it leads to the square root (fourth root, or any other even root) of a negative number. Both of these situations occur in the multiple-choice question. Note that 2 and $\sqrt{3}$ must be excluded from the domain

because they lead to division by zero. Similarly, all real numbers less than 3 must be excluded because they yield negative values for $x - 3$ and thus involve the square roots of negative numbers. Answer choice Ⓔ does not specifically mention 2 and $\sqrt{3}$ but excludes them both since they *are* less than 3.

¶ DRILL In each of the following indicate the values of x which must be excluded from the domain:

(a) $y = \dfrac{2x}{x^2 - 2}$ (b) $y = \dfrac{x^2 - 4}{x}$
(c) $y = \sqrt{x - 4}$ (d) $y = \sqrt{x^2 + 4}$

USING FUNCTION NOTATION

[7] **If $f(x) = x^3 - 2x$, then $f(3t) = ?$**

Ⓐ $t^3 - 2t$ Ⓑ $3t$ Ⓒ $3t^3 - 6t$ Ⓓ $27t^3 - 6t$
Ⓔ $2t^3 - 6$

A consequence of the definition of function is that three things are needed to specify a function: (1) a set called the domain, (2) a set called the range, and (3) a rule which assigns to each member of the domain exactly one member of the range.

It is customary to represent the rule by a letter of the alphabet such as "f." We use the symbol "$f(x)$" to mean "the member of the range that the rule, f, assigns to the member, x, of the domain."

EXAMPLES

(1) $f(x) = x^2$ means "the member of the range that f assigns to each member of its domain is the square of the domain member." In this function f will assign to 2 the number 4. This assignment is symbolized by $f(2) = 4$. If the member of the domain that has been selected is represented by some such expression as $2s$, then $f(2s)$ will be the square of $2s$, or $4s^2$.

(2) If $g(x) = 2x + 1$, then "the member of the range that g assigns to each member of the domain is one more than twice that member of the domain." Thus $g(1) = 3$, $g(-4) = -7$, $g(2s) = 4s + 1$, $g(t^2) = 2t^2 + 1$, $g(3t^2) = 6t^2 + 1$.

In the multiple-choice question, $f(3t) = (3t)^3 - 2(3t) = 27t^3 - 6t$.

¶ DRILL If $f(x) = |x - 1|$, $g(x) = 1 - x^2$ and $h(x) = 2x^2 - x + 3$, find each of the following:

(a) $f(-3) + g(-3)$
(b) $g(a^2) + h(a^2)$
(c) $g(0) \div h(0)$
(d) $3f(2) + 4g(-3) - 2h(1)$

IDENTIFYING ZERO, CONSTANT, AND IDENTITY FUNCTIONS

[8] Which of the following terms describe(s) $f(x) = 0$?

   I The zero function
   II The constant function
   III The identity function

   Ⓐ I and III only   Ⓑ II and III only   Ⓒ I and II only   Ⓓ All of I, II and III   Ⓔ I only

The *zero function* assigns 0 to every member of its domain. It consists of such ordered pairs as $\{(3, 0),$ $(-2, 0), (\frac{1}{2}, 0), \ldots\}$ and is usually symbolized by $y = 0$ or $f(x) = 0$. Its graph is the y-axis.

Any function that assigns the same constant, c, to every member of its domain is a *constant function*. It is usually symbolized by an equation such as $f(x) = c$ or $y = c$. The graph of any constant function is a horizontal line. Since 0 is a constant, the zero function is a constant function.

The *identity function* is the function that assigns every member to itself. It is usually symbolized by $y = x$ or $f(x) = x$. Its graph is the line that bisects the first and third quadrants.

¶ DRILL Classify each of the following in the categories defined above:

  (a) $y = 4$ (b) $y = \dfrac{3x - 3}{x - 1}, x \neq 1$

  (c) $f(x) = \dfrac{\sqrt{x^2}}{|x|}$ (d) $g(x) = 3x$

[9] If $f(x) = 2x$, $g(x) = \frac{1}{2}x$ and $f(g(x)) = 6$, what is x?

   Ⓐ 4 Ⓑ 12 Ⓒ 6 Ⓓ 3 Ⓔ 2

$f(g(x))$ is called "the composition of f with g." Using the functional notation described in the preceding section, we interpret $f(g(x))$ to mean "the value that f assigns to the value that g assigns to x."

In the multiple-choice question g assigns $\frac{1}{2}x$ to x and f assigns $2x$ to x. Thus $f(g(x))$ is $2(\frac{1}{2}x)$ or x since f must assign $2(\frac{1}{2}x)$ to $\frac{1}{2}x$. For this case we see that $f(g(x)) = x$ so $f(g(6)) = 6$ and x must be 6.

In general, to evaluate $f(g(x))$ substitute the expression which represents $g(x)$ for x in $f(x)$.

EXAMPLES

(1) If $f(x) = x^2$ and $g(x) = \dfrac{x}{3}$, then $f(g(x)) =$

$$[g(x)]^2 = \left(\frac{x}{3}\right)^2 = \frac{x^2}{9}.$$

(2) If $f(x) = x + 2$ and $g(x) = x^3$, then $f(g(x)) = g(x) + 2 = x^3 + 2$.

(3) If $f(x) = \dfrac{(8x + 1)}{4}$ and $g(x) = 3x$, then $f(g(x))$
$$= \frac{[8\,g(x) + 1]}{4} = \frac{(24x + 1)}{4}.$$

¶ DRILL If $f(x) = x^2$ and $g(x) = x - 3$ then:

  (a) $f(g(x)) = ?$ (b) $g(f(x)) = ?$
  (c) $f(f(-1)) = ?$ (d) $g(f(3a)) = ?$

FINDING THE INVERSE OF A FUNCTION

[10] If $f(x) = 3x + 2$, what is the inverse of f?

   Ⓐ $g(x) = -3x - 2$ Ⓑ $g(x) = 3x - 2$
   Ⓒ $g(x) = \dfrac{1}{3}x - \dfrac{2}{3}$ Ⓓ $g(x) = \dfrac{1}{3}x + \dfrac{2}{3}$
   Ⓔ $g(x) = -\dfrac{1}{3}x - \dfrac{2}{3}$

Two functions, f and g, are *inverses* if and only if for every (a, b) in f, (b, a) belongs to g and for every (b, a) in g, (a, b) belongs to f. It follows that the domain of f is the range of g and the range of f is the domain of g.

It also follows that $f(a) = b$ and $g(b) = a$. Substituting $g(b)$ for a in $f(a)$, we get

  (1) $f(g(b)) = b$.

If we substitute $f(a)$ for b in $g(b)$, we get

  (2) $g(f(a)) = a$.

Therefore for all x in the domain of both f and g,

  (3) $f(g(x)) = g(f(x)) = x$,

if and only if f and g are inverses. We can use (3) to derive the inverse (if it exists) of any given function.

EXAMPLE

Find the inverse of $f(x) = 4x - 7$.

SOLUTION: Find an expression for the value which f assigns to $g(x)$ by substituting $g(x)$ for x in the given function:

$$f(g(x)) = 4g(x) - 7.$$

But $f(g(x)) = x$ by equation (3) above, so:

$$x = 4g(x) - 7,$$
$$\frac{x + 7}{4} = g(x).$$

We can generalize the method to save a few steps. To find the inverse $g(x)$ of a function $f(x)$ replace every x with $g(x)$ and replace $f(x)$ with x; then solve for $g(x)$.

For example, in the multiple-choice question:

$$f(x) = 3x + 2,$$
$$x = 3(g(x)) + 2,$$
$$\frac{x - 2}{3} = g(x),$$
$$\frac{1}{3}x - \frac{2}{3} = g(x).$$

¶ DRILL In each case find $g(x)$ if g is to be the inverse of f:

(a) $f(x) = \dfrac{1}{2}x - 1$ (b) $f(x) = \sqrt{x}$

(c) $f(x) = x^3$ (d) $f(x) = \dfrac{1}{x}$

[11] If the figure at right is the graph of a function, which of the following is the graph of its inverse?

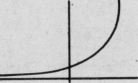

Ⓐ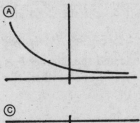

Ⓑ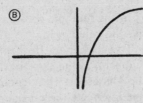

Ⓒ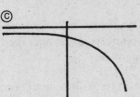

Ⓓ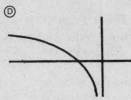

Ⓔ None of these

The definition of inverse functions provides the basis for discovering an important relationship between the graphs of a function, f, and its inverse, g. If the ordered pair $F(a, b)$ belongs to f, the ordered pair $G(b, a)$ must belong to g. The configuration of these points in the plane suggests that a search for a line of symmetry between them might be fruitful. The line of symmetry between two points is the perpendicular bisector of the segment for which the given points are endpoints. The perpendicular bisector of a segment is the set of all points equidistant from the endpoints of the segment. If $P(x, y)$ is any point in the plane, then the distance from P to F is given by:

(1) $\sqrt{(x - a)^2 + (y - b)^2}$,

and the distance from P to G by:

(2) $\sqrt{(x - b)^2 + (y - a)^2}$.

The line of symmetry is the set of points (x, y) for which $(1) = (2)$. If we set $(1) = (2)$ and simplify (we'll leave the details to the energetic reader) we get

(3) $x = y$.

We conclude that every function f is symmetric to its inverse g, with respect to the line $y = x$. The following graphs show examples of this symmetry:

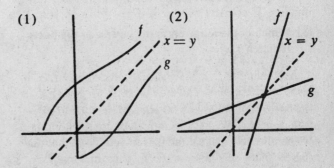

[12] Which of the following functions does NOT have an inverse?

Ⓐ $y = \sqrt{x}$ Ⓑ $y = 3x$ Ⓒ $y = x^3$
Ⓓ $y = -2x + 5$ Ⓔ $y = x^2$

We have defined the inverse of a function to be a *function*. But the set of ordered pairs, g, for which $f(g(x)) = g(f(x)) = x$ is *not* always a function:

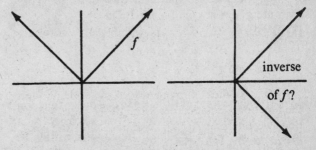

If g is *not a function*, then our definition of inverse excludes g from being the inverse of f and we say that f has no inverse.

How do you determine when a function has no inverse? When $F(a, b)$ is a point on the graph of a function, $G(b, a)$ is a point on the graph of its inverse. This means that the y-coordinates of f are the x-coordinates of g. By definition of function, g cannot be a function if two of its points have the same x-coordinate and this means no two points of f can have the same y-coordinate. Any two points of f that had the same y-coordinate would lie on the same horizontal line. Thus, if any horizontal line intersects the graph of a function in more than one point, the function can have no inverse.

Therefore, if a function has an inverse, for each x there is exactly one y and for each y there is exactly one x. Answer choice ⓔ is the only equation that gives multiple values of x for each value of y (when $y = 4$, for example, $x = \pm 2$), which prevents it from representing a function with an inverse.

¶ DRILL Sketch the graph of each of the following and then indicate whether or not it has an inverse:

(a) $y = 2$ (b) $y = 3x + 2$
(c) $y = 3x^2 + 2$ (d) $y = |x|$

[13] Which of the following is the inverse of the linear function $f(x) = -x - 1$?

ⓐ $g(x) = x + 1$ ⓑ $y = x + 1$ ⓒ $g(x) = -x - 1$ ⓓ $y = x - 1$ ⓔ $y = -x + 1$

A linear function is any function of the form $f(x) = ax + b$; $a \neq 0$. We have continued to use the notation $f(x)$ here to help make it familiar to you. Note that the ordered pairs of f are $(x, f(x))$, thus making $y = f(x)$. You may choose to think of the linear function as being defined by any equation of the form $y = ax + b$. Indeed, we will use the two interchangeably from now on.

The term "linear" refers to the facts that (1) the graph of every linear function is a line and (2) every nonvertical line has an equation which can be written in this form.

To find the inverse, g, of the linear function $f(x) = ax + b$, we will use the technique of section [10]: substitute $g(x)$ for x and x for $f(x)$:

$$x = a(g(x)) + b,$$
$$x - b = a(g(x)),$$
$$\frac{1}{a}x - \frac{b}{a} = g(x).$$

Memorizing the form of the inverse of a linear function is seldom useful since it can be derived so easily. As a matter of fact, when the linear function is written as $y = ax + b$, you need only interchange the x with the y and solve for the new y.

Therefore the inverse of the function

$$f(x) = -x - 1$$

is the inverse of $y = -x - 1$ and can be found by interchanging y and x, as follows:

$$x = -y - 1,$$
$$y = -x - 1.$$

¶ DRILL Write the equation of the inverse for each of the following:

(a) $y = x$ (b) $f(x) = 3x + 4$
(c) $y = \frac{1}{3}x - \frac{4}{3}$ (d) $f(x) = 2$

WORKING WITH SLOPES

[14] Find the value of a for which $y = ax + 4$ has a slope of -1.

ⓐ -1 ⓑ 4 ⓒ -4 ⓓ $\frac{1}{4}$ ⓔ $-\frac{1}{4}$

Since the equation $y = ax + b$ is true for $x = 0$, and $y = b$, one point on the line must be $P(0, b)$. Because the x-coordinate of P is 0, P will be the point of intersection of the line determined by $y = ax + b$ with the y-axis. For this reason, b is called the y-intercept of the function.

The equation $y = ax + b$ can be transformed as follows:

$$(1) \quad y = ax + b,$$
$$y - b = ax,$$
$$y - b = a(x - 0),$$
$$(2) \quad \frac{y - b}{x - 0} = a.$$

We know from Chapter 18 that $\dfrac{(y - b)}{(x - 0)}$ is called the *slope* of the line containing the points (x, y) and $(0, b)$. Thus a is the slope of the line determined by (1).

In the multiple-choice question, a is the slope and has the value -1.

To summarize: In the equation $y = ax + b$, the number a is the slope of the line and the number b is the y-intercept (the y-coordinate of the point where the line intersects the y-axis).

¶ DRILL Each of the following defines a linear function. Write each in slope-intercept form and then indicate the slope and y-intercept:

(a) $6x + 3y = 2$ (b) $\frac{x}{2} + \frac{y}{3} = 1$
(c) $2x + y = 0$ (d) $5 - 4x = 20y$

[15] If $f(z) = az + b$, what is the value of $\dfrac{f(b) - f(a)}{b - a}$?

ⓐ z ⓑ b ⓒ az ⓓ a ⓔ $az + b$

We have included this question as further practice in using $f(x)$ notation:

$$f(b) = ab + b,$$
$$f(a) = a^2 + b,$$
$$f(b) - f(a) = ab - a^2,$$
$$= a(b - a),$$
$$\frac{f(b) - f(a)}{b - a} = \frac{a(b - a)}{(b - a)} = a.$$

We could, of course, have predicted this outcome without any calculation since $(b, f(b))$ and $(a, f(a))$ are the coordinates of points on the graph of the given linear function. Hence the expression to simplify must be the slope of the line containing these points.

¶ DRILL If $f(z) = az + b$, evaluate:

(a) $f(2) + f(4)$ (b) $f(x + 1) - f(x - 1)$

(c) $f(3t) - f(-3t)$ (d) $[f(2x)][f(\frac{1}{2}x)]$

FINDING THE AXIS OF SYMMETRY

[16] The quadratic function $f(x) = 3x^2 - 12x + 16$ is symmetric with respect to which of the following lines?

   Ⓐ $x = 2$ Ⓑ $x = 12$ Ⓒ $x = 16$ Ⓓ $y = x$
   Ⓔ $x = 0$

If you could not answer this question we suggest that you review sections [27] and [28] of Chapter 18 before continuing.

A quadratic function is a function of the form $f(x) = ax^2 + bx + c$, where a, b and c are real numbers and $a \neq 0$. The graph of every quadratic function is a parabola whose line of symmetry is parallel to the y-axis. This line of symmetry can be readily determined by using the methods developed in the sections of Chapter 18 already mentioned to put the equation in the form

$$f(x) = a(x - k)^2 + p.$$

The axis of symmetry will be the line $x = k$. Then:

$$\begin{aligned}
f(x) &= 3x^2 - 12x + 16 \\
&= 3(x^2 - 4x) + 16 \\
&= 3(x^2 - 4x + 4) + 16 - 3(4) \\
&= 3(x - 2)^2 + 4.
\end{aligned}$$

Therefore the axis of the parabola given in the multiple-choice question is $x = 2$.

¶ DRILL Find the axis of symmetry:

(a) $y = x^2$
(b) $y = 3x^2 + 2$
(c) $y = -2x^2 + 4x + 1$
(d) $y = x^2 + 4x + 4$

FINDING MAXIMA OR MINIMA

[17] What is the minimum value which $f(x)$ can attain if $f(x) = 2x^2 + 8x - 1$?

   Ⓐ -1 Ⓑ -8 Ⓒ 9 Ⓓ -9 Ⓔ 7

The point of intersection of the axis of symmetry of a parabola with the parabola itself is called the *vertex*. For a parabola that opens upward ($a > 0$) the vertex is the lowest point of the graph. Similarly the vertex is the highest point on the graph of a parabola that opens downward ($a < 0$).

Recall that the axis of symmetry is $x = k$ for a parabola where $f(x) = a(x - k)^2 + p$. The x-coordi-

nate of the vertex must be k, which when substituted for x yields p as the y-coordinate. Thus the value of p is either the maximum or the minimum value of the function depending on whether the graph opens up or down. Obviously, a quadratic function cannot have both a maximum and a minimum value.

To find the minimum value of the function

$$f(x) = 2x^2 + 8x - 1,$$

transform it to

$$\begin{aligned}
f(x) &= 2(x^2 + 4x) - 1 \\
&= 2(x^2 + 4x + 4) - 1 - 2(4) \\
&= 2(x + 2)^2 - 9.
\end{aligned}$$

The minimum value occurs at the vertex of the parabola, which is the intersection of $f(x)$ with the axis, $x = -2$, of the parabola:

$$f(-2) = -9.$$

¶ DRILL Find any maximum or minimum values for each of the following:

(a) $y = -x^2 - 10x + 24$
(b) $y = x^2 + x + 4$
(c) $y = 2 + 10x - 10x^2$
(d) $y = 3x^2 + 6x - 8$

[18] A rectangular field is bordered on one side by a straight canal. If the total length of fencing used on the other three sides is 240 feet and the dimensions of the field are chosen so that the maximum area is enclosed, what are these dimensions?

   Ⓐ $60' \times 60'$ Ⓑ $60' \times 120'$ Ⓒ $90' \times 90'$
   Ⓓ $80' \times 80'$ Ⓔ $120' \times 2'$

A frequent problem in many diverse fields is that of finding the maximum or minimum results, given certain conditions. The solutions of most of these problems lie beyond the scope of intermediate math (usually requiring the calculus), but some can be found through the use of quadratic functions. The procedure is to express the desired value as a quadratic function and then find the vertex of the corresponding parabola.

EXAMPLE

Find the greatest rectangular region (in area) that can be enclosed by a string of length 48 inches.

SOLUTION: Let x be the length of the rectangle; then $24 - x$ will be the width and the following function represents the area:

$$\begin{aligned}
A(x) &= x(24 - x) \\
&= -1(x - 12)^2 + 144,
\end{aligned}$$

the second equation being the $a(x - k)^2 + p$ form of the first. The graph is a parabola that opens downward and has a vertex of (12, 144). Thus the maximum area that can be enclosed is 144, and this occurs when the length is 12.

To work the original problem, let w represent the width; then the length is $240 - 2w$ and the area function is:

$$A(w) = w(240 - 2w)$$
$$= -2(w - 60)^2 + 7200.$$

The vertex is (60, 7200), and the maximum area is 7200, which will occur when the width is 60.

¶ DRILL Express 12 as the sum of two numbers that have the maximum product possible.

WHAT YOU SHOULD KNOW

KEY CONCEPTS

1. The expression $f(x)$ represents the value of the function at x.
2. The expression $f(g(x))$ represents the value that f assigns to the value that g assigns to x.
3. The graph of a function is symmetric to the graph of its inverse with respect to the line $y = x$.
4. To find an equation of the inverse of a function, substitute x for y and y for x; then solve for y.
5. If a quadratic function is in the form
$$f(x) = a(x - p)^2 + k,$$
then $x = p$ is its axis and (p, k) is its vertex.

KEY EQUATIONS

1. For the zero function:
$y = 0$ or $f(x) = 0$.
2. For the constant function:
$f(x) = c$ or $y = c$.
3. For the identity function:
$y = x$ or $f(x) = x$.

TEST-TAKING STRATEGIES

• For appropriate problems, such as determining cross products, clarify information by representing it in the form of a table.

• Most questions about functions require the use of function notation—that is, $f(x) =$ an algebraic expression involving x. Be sure you understand the use of this notation in calculations and finding ranges.

ANSWERS

[1] Ⓑ
DRILL:
(a) R but not F.   (b) R and F.
(c) R and F.   (d) R but not F.

[2] Ⓔ
DRILL:
(a) Function.
(b) Not a function.
(c) Not a function.
(d) A function if no two persons have exactly the same weight.

[3] Ⓑ
DRILL:
(a) $\{(a, c), (a, d), (b, c), (b, d)\}$
(b) $\{(a, d), (b, d), (c, d)\}$
(c) $\{(a, x), (a, y), (a, z)\}$
(d) $\{(a, z)\}$.

[4] Ⓐ
DRILL:
(a) No.   (b) Yes.
(c) No.   (d) No.

[5] Ⓐ
DRILL:
(a) Yes.   (b) No.
(c) No.   (d) No.

[6] Ⓔ
DRILL:
(a) $\sqrt{2}, -\sqrt{2}$ (b) 0
(c) All $x < 4$.   (d) None.

[7] Ⓓ
DRILL:
(a) -4 (b) $a^4 - a^2 + 4$
(c) $\dfrac{1}{3}$ (d) -37

[8] Ⓒ
DRILL:
(a) Constant.   (b) Constant.
(c) Constant.   (d) None.

[9] ©

DRILL:

(a) $x^2 - 6x + 9$ (b) $x^2 - 3$

(c) 1   (d) $9a^2 - 3$

[10] ©

DRILL:

(a) $g(x) = 2x + 2$

(b) $g(x) = x^2$ with domain $x \geq 0$.

(c) $g(x) = x^{1/3}$

(d) $g(x) = \dfrac{1}{x}$

[11] ⑧

[12] Ⓔ

DRILL:

(a)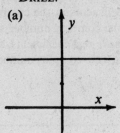

(b)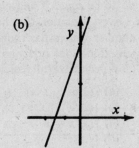

(c)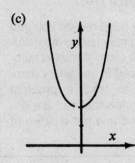

(d)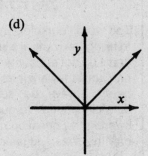

(a) No inverse.

(b) Has an inverse.

(c) No inverse.

(d) No inverse.

[13] ©

DRILL:

(a) $y = x$ (b) $g(x) = \dfrac{1}{3}x - \dfrac{4}{3}$

(c) $y = 3x + 4$ (d) No inverse.

[14] Ⓐ

DRILL:

(a) $y = -2x + \dfrac{2}{3}$, slope: -2, y-intercept: $\dfrac{2}{3}$

(b) $y = -\dfrac{3}{2}x + 3$, slope: $-\dfrac{3}{2}$, y-intercept: 3

(c) Slope: -2, y-intercept: 0

(d) Slope: $-\dfrac{1}{5}$, y-intercept: $\dfrac{1}{4}$

[15] Ⓓ

DRILL:

(a) $6a + 2b$ (b) $2a$

(c) $6ta$ (d) $a^2x^2 + \dfrac{5}{2}abx + b^2$

[16] Ⓐ

DRILL:

(a) $y = (x - 0)^2 + 0$, $x = 0$

(b) $y = 3(x - 0)^2 + 2$, $x = 0$

(c) $y = -2(x - 1)^2 + 3$, $x = 1$

(d) $y = (x + 2)^2 + 0$, $x = -2$

[17] Ⓓ

DRILL:

(a) Max: 49   (b) Min: $\dfrac{15}{4}$

(c) Max: $\dfrac{9}{2}$ (d) Min: -11

[18] ⑧

DRILL:

If x is one number, then $12 - x$ is the other, $P(x) = x(12 - x) = -1(x - 6)^2 + 36$ and the two numbers are 6 and 6 with a maximum product of 36.

21. Complex Numbers

DEFINING COMPLEX NUMBERS

[1] Which of the following equations has (have) solutions in the complex number system?

I $x^2 - 1 = 0$
II $x^2 - 2 = 0$
III $x^2 + 2 = 0$

Ⓐ I and II only   Ⓑ II and III only   Ⓒ I and III only   Ⓓ All of these   Ⓔ None of these

The extension of the number system from the integers to the rational numbers to the real numbers is motivated by the search for a number system that is "closed." A system is *closed* when every equation that has all of its coefficients in the system has all of its roots in the system.

The set of integers is not closed since it has no solution for $2x + 3 = 0$. The rational numbers fail to provide solutions for $x^2 - 3 = 0$. The extension of the number system to the real numbers incorporates additional elements (the irrationals), but these still don't provide solutions for $x^2 + 3 = 0$ since the square of no real number is negative. To produce a number system which is closed, we need introduce only one additional number and then define a system based on combinations of this new number with the real numbers.

The additional number, i, is termed the *imaginary unit* and is defined by the relation $i^2 = -1$. The extended system is called the *Complex Number System* (designated by C) and consists of the set of all numbers $a + bi$ in which a and b are real numbers and $i^2 = -1$. The $a + bi$ form is called the *standard* form of a complex number with a termed the *real part* and b the *imaginary part*. Note that the imaginary part is actually a real number.

The complex number system contains three categories of numbers: the reals, the imaginaries and the "pure" imaginaries. The *reals* are the numbers for which $b = 0$, such as $3 + 0i$, $-2 + 0i$, $\frac{1}{2} + 0i$, and $\pi + 0i$. These are, of course, the same real numbers we have studied throughout and differ only in form.

The *pure imaginaries* occur when $a = 0$ and $b \neq 0$: $0 + 3i$, $0 + (-2)i$, $0 + \frac{1}{2}i$, $0 + \pi i$, etc. The *imaginaries* are complex numbers for which $a \neq 0$ and $b \neq 0$, such as $3 + 2i$, $5 + (-2)i$, and $\frac{1}{2} + \pi i$.

We define two complex numbers, $a + bi$ and $c + di$, to be *equal* if and only if $a = c$ and $b = d$.

Every equation that has coefficients in the complex number system has roots in the complex number system. Equations I, II, and III have real coefficients, and (as noted above) all real numbers are complex numbers.

TEST-TAKING TIP.

The word "complex" may have misled you into thinking the roots are imaginary (since most students do not encounter the term "complex number" until they are introduced to imaginary numbers). Always be sure to read a problem carefully enough to guarantee that you are answering the question asked and not a different one that was suggested by it.

¶ DRILL Indicate which of the terms "real," "imaginary" and "pure imaginary" best describes each of the following:

(a) $5 + 0i$ (b) $3 + (-2)i$ (c) $4i$ (d) $\pi + 2i$

Put each of the following in standard form:

(e) i^2 (f) $-\frac{1}{4}$ (g) $6i - 2$ (h) $-4i$

[2] If $2x + 3yi = 1 + 4i^2$, then $y = ?$
Ⓐ $\frac{4i^2}{3}$ Ⓑ 0   Ⓒ $\frac{4}{3}$ Ⓓ 4   Ⓔ $\frac{1}{2}$

Since two complex numbers in standard form are equal if and only if their real parts are equal and their imaginary parts are equal, the best way to solve a first degree equation in two variables which involves the real and imaginary parts of complex numbers is to put both sides of the equation into standard form and set the real parts equal and the imaginary parts equal:

$$2x + 3yi = 1 + 4i^2$$
$$= 1 + 4(-1)$$
$$= -3$$
$$= -3 + (0)i.$$

Therefore $2x = -3$ and $3y = 0$, so $x = -\dfrac{3}{2}$ and $y = 0$.

¶ DRILL Solve each of the following for x and y:

(a) $x + yi = 4 + 5i$
(b) $2x + 2yi = 6 - 3i$
(c) $x - 4yi = 13i$

FINDING SOME POWERS OF i

[3] **Which of the following has the same value as i^{63}?**

Ⓐ i Ⓑ -1 Ⓒ $-i$ Ⓓ 1 Ⓔ **None of these**

We have defined i by the relation $i^2 = -1$. This leads to:

$i^0 = 1,$ $i^5 = i^4i = i,$
$i^1 = i,$ $i^6 = i^4i^2 = -1,$
$i^2 = -1,$ $i^7 = i^4i^3 = -i,$
$i^3 = i^2i = -i,$ $i^8 = i^4i^4 = 1.$
$i^4 = i^2i^2 = 1,$

You may verify for yourself that successive powers of i take on the values $i, -1, -i, 1$ which continue to repeat in the same order. Thus the higher powers of i can be found by breaking up the power of i into factors of i^4 times whatever power of i remains.

EXAMPLES

$$i^{11} = i^4i^4i^3 = 1 \times 1 \times i^3 = -i$$
$$i^{113} = \underbrace{i^4i^4 \ldots i^4i}_{28 \text{ factors}} = i$$

$$i^{63} = (i^4)^{15}(i^3)$$
$$= (1)^{15}(-1)$$
$$= -1$$

¶ DRILL Evaluate:

(a) i^7 (b) i^{19} (c) i^{99} (d) i^{4n+1}

ADDING COMPLEX NUMBERS

[4] **Express the sum of $\sqrt{-36} + \sqrt{-25} + \sqrt{-16}$ as a pure imaginary.**

Ⓐ 15 Ⓑ -15 Ⓒ $15i$ Ⓓ $-15i$ Ⓔ $5i$

When a is positive the symbol $\sqrt{a}$ stands for the positive number that when squared is a. When a is negative we define $\sqrt{a}$ to mean $i\sqrt{|a|}$. Thus $\sqrt{-36} = i\sqrt{36}$ or $6i$.

To answer the given question we must use some elementary facts about adding complex numbers. But remember that the real numbers are elements of C. Any laws we establish in C must in no way produce results for the real numbers in C which differ from the results we established for the reals before defining C. One way to help guarantee this uniformity is to accept as postulates for C the same laws we postulated in Chapter 6 for the reals, From here on we will assume that the properties postulated for the reals will hold true for C. Furthermore, we will make no definition which contradicts the established behavior of the reals.

Since, when $b = 0$ and $d = 0$, the numbers $a + bi$ and $c + di$ are real, we want the result of addition in C to accomplish

$$(a + 0i) + (c + 0i) = (a + c) + 0i.$$

We will, therefore, define addition in C to be

$$(a + bi) + (c + di) = (a + c) + (b + d)i.$$
$$\sqrt{-36} + \sqrt{-25} + \sqrt{-16}$$
$$= i\sqrt{36} + i\sqrt{25} + i\sqrt{16}$$
$$= 6i + 5i + 4i$$
$$= 15i.$$

¶ DRILL Add the following (put them in standard form and use the definition above):

(a) $\sqrt{-4} + \sqrt{-12}$ (b) $(2 + 3i) + (4 + 5i)$
(c) $4i + (3 - 9i)$ (d) $6 + (10i - 6)$

SUBTRACTING AND MULTIPLYING COMPLEX NUMBERS

[5] **If $z_1 = 3 + (-6)i$, $z_2 = 4 + 5i$ and $z_3 = 42 + (-9)i$, the operation which results in z_3 from z_1 and z_2 is:**

Ⓐ **Addition** Ⓑ **Subtraction** Ⓒ **Multiplication**
Ⓓ **Division** Ⓔ **None of these**

The following definitions for subtraction and multiplication are consistent with the same operations in the reals:

$$(a + bi) - (c + di) = (a - c) + (b - d)i,$$
$$(a + bi)(c + di) = (ac - bd) + (bc + ad)i.$$

The second definition may appear complicated but is motivated by the application of familiar procedures.

$$(a + bi)(c + di) = (a + bi)c + (a + bi)di$$
$$= ac + bci + adi + bdi^2$$

Since $i^2 = -1$ this becomes

$$= ac + bci + adi - bd$$
$$= (ac - bd) + (bc + ad)i.$$

Indeed you may find it easier to ignore the definition above and just repeat the procedure which motivates it. Note that the correct application of the definition necessitates that the numbers be in standard form.

We will postpone our review of division until the next section.

$$(z_1)(z_2) = (3 - 6i)(4 + 5i)$$
$$= 12 - 24i + 15i - 30i^2$$
$$= 12 - 9i + 30$$
$$= 42 - 9i$$

¶ DRILL Carry out the indicated multiplications and express the products in standard form:

(a) $(3 - i)(6 + i)$ (b) $i(1 + 2i)$
(c) $(-6 + 3i)(6 + 3i)$ (d) $(a - b)(a + bi)$

FINDING ADDITIVE INVERSES, RECIPROCALS, AND CONJUGATES

[6] If $z_1 = 6 + 2i$ and $z_2 = \dfrac{3}{20} + \dfrac{-1}{20} i$, then the term which best describes the relation between z_1 and z_2 is:

Ⓐ Additive inverses   Ⓑ Reciprocals   Ⓒ Conjugates   Ⓓ z_2 is the absolute value of z_1 Ⓔ No relation

As we saw in Chapter 5, the additive inverse of a number is defined to be the number that when added to the given number yields zero. We designate the additive inverse of z by $-z$. Since zero in standard form is $0 + 0i$, we can prove that $-(a + bi)$ is $-a + (-b)i$. You may verify this by showing that $-a + (-b)i$ when added to $a + bi$ gives zero.

The reciprocal, or multiplicative inverse, of z is the number that when multiplied by z yields 1. We designate the reciprocal of z by $\dfrac{1}{z}$. If the standard form of z is $a + bi$, the following discussion derives the standard form of $\dfrac{1}{(a + bi)}$.

Let $x + yi$ be the reciprocal of $a + bi$; then

$$(a + bi)(x + yi) = 1 + 0i,$$

by definition of reciprocal. Also,

$$(ax - by) + (ay + bx)i = 1 + 0i,$$

by definition of multiplication. And

$$(ax - by) = 1 \text{ and } (ay + bx) = 0,$$

by definition of "equal" for complex numbers. Solving the last two equations for x and y, simultaneously, produces

$$x = \frac{a}{a^2 + b^2} \text{ and } y = \frac{-b}{a^2 + b^2}$$

The *conjugate* of $a + bi$ is defined to be the number $a + (-b)i$ and could have been used to find the reciprocal. In fact the use of the conjugate of the divisor will simplify the division process in general. Note that the product of a complex number and its conjugate is real:

$$(a + bi)(a + (-b)i) = (a^2 + b^2) + (ab - ab)i$$
$$= a^2 + b^2.$$

We will use this fact to change the denominator of $\dfrac{1}{(a + bi)}$ into a real number and put it in standard form in relatively few steps.

$$\frac{1}{a + bi} \times \frac{a + (-b)i}{a + (-b)i} = \frac{a + (-b)i}{a^2 + b^2}$$
$$= \frac{a}{a^2 + b^2} + \frac{-b}{a^2 + b^2}i$$

In the multiple-choice question,

$$z_1 = 6 + 2i,$$
$$\frac{1}{z_1} = \frac{1}{6 + 2i} = \frac{1}{6 + 2i}\left(\frac{6 - 2i}{6 - 2i}\right)$$
$$= \frac{6 - 2i}{36 + 12i - 12i - 4i^2}$$
$$= \frac{6 - 2i}{40}$$
$$= \frac{3 - i}{20} = \frac{3}{20} - \frac{1}{20}i.$$

Therefore z_2 is the reciprocal of z_1.

We will postpone our review of "absolute value" until a later section.

¶ DRILL For each of the following find (1) its additive inverse, (2) its reciprocal and (3) its conjugate:

(a) $7 - i$ (b) $2i$ (c) $-i$ (d) $a - bi$

DIVIDING COMPLEX NUMBERS

[7] Evaluate $\dfrac{2 - i}{1 + i}$ and put it in standard form.

Ⓐ $\left(\dfrac{1}{2} - \dfrac{3}{2}\right) i$ Ⓑ $\dfrac{1}{2} + \left(-\dfrac{3}{2}\right) i$ Ⓒ $2 - \dfrac{1}{i}$
Ⓓ None of these   Ⓔ All of these

If z_1 and z_2 are complex numbers, then $\dfrac{z_1}{z_2}$ is that number z such that $z_2 \cdot z = z_1$. We could use this definition to divide complex numbers, but the process is a lengthy one and involves the solution of a pair of simultaneous equations in two variables. Instead we will multiply the numerator and denominator by the conjugate of the denominator. The resulting fraction will have a real denominator, and the complex number it represents can then be easily expressed in standard form.

EXAMPLE

Evaluate $\dfrac{5 + 2i}{6 + 4i}$.

SOLUTION: Multiply the numerator and denominator by the conjugate of the denominator:

$$\frac{5 + 2i}{6 + 4i} \times \frac{6 - 4i}{6 - 4i} = \frac{38 - 8i}{52}$$

$$= \frac{38}{52} + \frac{-8}{52}i$$

$$= \frac{19}{26} + \frac{-2}{13}i.$$

To evaluate the expression in the multiple-choice question,

$$\frac{2 - i}{1 + i} = \left(\frac{2 - i}{1 + i}\right)\left(\frac{1 - i}{1 - i}\right)$$

$$= \frac{2 - i - 2i + i^2}{1 + 1}$$

$$= \frac{1 - 3i}{2}$$

TEST-TAKING TIP.

Note that we did not carry out the final step to transform the expression into the exact form of the answer. You should do only as much work as is needed to decide which answer is correct. Additional work requires extra time, and time is a commodity you may not have enough of on test day.

¶ DRILL Perform the following divisions by the method of conjugates:

(a) $1 \div (3 + 2i)$
(b) $(2 + 3i) \div (5 + 4i)$
(c) $3i \div (8 + 3i)$
(d) $(3 + \sqrt{2i}) \div (3 - \sqrt{2i})$

USING THE QUADRATIC FORMULA

[8] If $r + si$ is a solution of $ax^3 + bx^2 + cx + d = 0$, where a, b, c and d are real, then another solution is:

Ⓐ $r - si$ Ⓑ $-r + si$ Ⓒ $-(r + si)$ Ⓓ All of these   Ⓔ None of these

Let us begin the discussion of the complex roots of a polynomial equation with a simpler situation than the one above and then extend our results.

As we learned in Chapter 19, when the domain of x for $ax^2 + bx + c = 0$ is the set of real numbers, we can derive the values of x by the Quadratic Formula. We state without proof that the same formula produces the solutions for $ax^2 + bx + c = 0$ when the domain of x is C and all of a, b, and c are real.

When the discriminant (see Chapter 19, section [9]), $b^2 - 4ac$, is negative, the solution set contains the two imaginary numbers.

$$\frac{-b \pm i\sqrt{|b^2 - 4ac|}}{2a}$$

You may verify that the two solutions above are conjugates of each other.

We will state without proof that, if the roots of a polynomial with *real* coefficients are imaginary, then these imaginary roots come in *conjugate* pairs.

In the multiple-choice question, $r + si$ is given as a root of an equation with real coefficients, so $r - si$ must also be a root.

¶ DRILL Use the Quadratic Formula to find the roots of:

(a) $3x^2 + x + 2 = 0$ (b) $x^2 + 2x + 1 = 0$
(c) $x^2 - 3x + 8 = 0$

If one of the roots of $ax^5 + bx^4 + cx^3 + dx^2 + ex + f = 0$, where a, b, c, d, e and f are real, is given in each of the following, find another root:

(d) $3 + i$ (e) $-5i$ (f) $i + 1$

[9] The solution set of $x^6 - 64 = 0$, with the set of complex numbers as its domain, contains:

Ⓐ $-1 + \sqrt{3}i$ Ⓑ 2 only   Ⓒ 2 and -2 only
Ⓓ No more than 4 distinct roots   Ⓔ No roots

We can use the Quadratic Formula to find the roots of equations of higher degree when these equations have members that can be factored into linear and quadratic factors. For example, the expression in the question above can be factored as follows:

$$x^6 - 64 = 0,$$
$$(x^3 - 8)(x^3 + 8) = 0,$$
$$(x - 2)(x^2 + 2x + 4)(x + 2)(x^2 - 2x + 4) = 0.$$

The linear factors yield the roots 2 and -2. The quadratic factors yield the roots $-1 \pm i\sqrt{3}$ and $1 \pm i\sqrt{3}$ from the Quadratic Formula.

¶ DRILL Find the solution sets of each of the following by expressing the polynomial as the product of linear and quadratic factors:

(a) $x^3 + 8 = 0$ (b) $x^3 + 3x^2 - 8x = 0$
(c) $x^4 - 4 = 0$

MULTIPLYING THE ROOTS OF NEGATIVE NUMBERS

[10] If a and b are real numbers, then under which of the following conditions is $\sqrt{a}\sqrt{b} = \sqrt{ab}$ NOT true?

Ⓐ $a > 0, b > 0$ Ⓑ $a < 0, b > 0$
Ⓒ $a < 0, b < 0$ Ⓓ $a > 0, b < 0$
Ⓔ $a = 0, b = 0$

When $x > 0$, we define $\sqrt{x}$ to be the nonnegative number that when squared is x. From this we may derive the statement $\sqrt{x}\sqrt{y} = \sqrt{xy}$ when x and y are positive by showing that $\sqrt{x}\sqrt{y}$ is the nonnegative number that when squared is xy. The rule can be extended if only one of x or y is negative, as in

$$\sqrt{-2}\sqrt{18} = \sqrt{-36} = 6i.$$

But it does lead to a contradiction when both $x < 0$ and $y < 0$. If the rule were applicable to the latter situation, then

$$\sqrt{-2}\sqrt{-2} = \sqrt{(-2)(-2)} = \sqrt{4} = 2.$$

The latter statement contradicts the meaning of $\sqrt{-2}$ since we want the square of $\sqrt{-2}$ to be -2.

Thus $\sqrt{a}\sqrt{b} = \sqrt{ab}$ is inconsistent with the definition of $\sqrt{}$ when both a and b are negative. This does not, however, leave us without a formula for the multiplication of the roots of negative numbers—our definition. Therefore

$$\sqrt{a} = i\sqrt{|a|} \quad \text{when} \quad a < 0$$

provides the clue:
If $a < 0$ and $b < 0$, then

$$\begin{aligned} \sqrt{a}\sqrt{b} &= i\sqrt{|a|}i\sqrt{|b|} \\ &= i^2\sqrt{|a|}\sqrt{|b|} \\ &= -\sqrt{|a|}\sqrt{|b|}. \end{aligned}$$

But $|a|$ and $|b|$ are positive real numbers, so

$$-\sqrt{|a|}\sqrt{|b|} = -\sqrt{|a||b|}.$$

¶ DRILL Carry out each of the following multiplications:

(a) $\sqrt{-3}\sqrt{-4}$ (b) $\sqrt{4}\sqrt{-3}$
(c) $\sqrt{-4}\sqrt{3}$ (d) $\sqrt{4}\sqrt{3}$

FINDING THE ABSOLUTE VALUE OF A COMPLEX NUMBER

[11] In the complex plane, which of the following does NOT determine a point on a circle of radius 1 with center at the origin?

Ⓐ 1   Ⓑ i Ⓒ $\frac{1}{2} - \frac{\sqrt{3}}{2}i$ Ⓓ $1 - i$
Ⓔ $-\frac{\sqrt{2}}{2} - \frac{\sqrt{2}}{2}i$

Recall that two complex numbers in standard form are equal if and only if the real parts are equal and the imaginary parts are equal. Thus, if $a \neq b$, then $a + bi \neq b + ai$. In other words each complex number determines a pair of real numbers for which the order makes a difference. The complex number $a + bi$ determines the ordered pair (a, b) and the number $b + ai$ determines (b, a). Our experience with ordered pairs suggests that we can form a coordinate plane with points determined by complex numbers, a complex number plane. We establish the horizontal axis as the *axis of reals* and agree that our x-coordinates shall be the real parts of the complex numbers. The vertical axis is the *axis of imaginaries,* and we shall let the y-coordinates be the imaginary parts of the complex numbers.

A reminder: the imaginary part of a complex number is a real number—the definition of "imaginary part" excludes the i.

To graph a point that corresponds to a given complex number, put the number in standard form, find the ordered pair it determines and then plot the ordered pair in the manner already established for the real number plane.

We define the *absolute value* of the complex number $a + bi$ to be its distance from the origin. Using the Pythagorean Theorem, we can demonstrate this distance to be $\sqrt{a^2 + b^2}$ and write the following:

$$|a + bi| = \sqrt{a^2 + b^2}.$$

Ⓐ $|1| = \sqrt{1^2 + 0^2} = \sqrt{1} = 1.$
Ⓑ $|i| = |0 + 1i| = \sqrt{0^2 + 1^2} = \sqrt{1} = 1.$
Ⓒ $|\frac{1}{2} - \frac{\sqrt{3}}{2}i| = \sqrt{(\frac{1}{2})^2 + (\frac{\sqrt{3}}{2})^2} = \sqrt{1} = 1.$
Ⓓ $|1 - i| = \sqrt{1^2 + 1^2} = \sqrt{2}.$
Ⓔ $|-\frac{\sqrt{2}}{2} - \frac{\sqrt{2}}{2}i| = \sqrt{\left(\frac{\sqrt{2}}{2}\right)^2 + \left(\frac{\sqrt{2}}{2}\right)^2} = 1.$

¶ DRILL Find the absolute value of each of the following:

(a) $2 + 4i$ (b) 0 (c) $5i - 2$ (d) $3 - i$

FACTORING OVER COMPLEX NUMBERS

[12] One of the factors of $4a^2 + 16y^2$ over the complex numbers is:

Ⓐ $2a + 4y$ Ⓑ $2a - 4y$ Ⓒ $4a + yi$
Ⓓ $a + 4yi$ Ⓔ $2a - 4yi$

Recall that $a^2 - b^2$ can be factored over the reals (not to mention the integers, rationals, etc.) since it is the difference of squares:

(1) $a^2 - b^2 = (a - b)(a + b).$

Recall also that $a^2 + b^2$ cannot be factored over the reals. But it can be factored over the complex numbers since it can be represented by

(2) $a^2 - (ib)^2$.

Expression (2) follows from $(ib)^2 = -b^2$. Thus

(3) $a^2 + b^2 = a^2 - (ib)^2 = (a + ib)(a - ib)$.

In the multiple-choice question we can represent the given expression by $(2a)^2 - (4yi)^2$. The factors are, therefore:

$$(2a - 4yi)(2a + 4yi).$$

¶ DRILL Factor each of the following over C:

(a) $x^2 + y^2$ (b) $x^2 - y^2$ (c) $2a^2 + 3b^2$

SOLVING OTHER COMPLEX NUMBER PROBLEMS

[13] Which of the following statements is (are) true?

    I The product of any two complex numbers that are conjugates of each other is a real number.
    II The sum of any two complex numbers that are conjugates of each other is imaginary.
    III The conjugate of i equals the reciprocal of i.

    Ⓐ I and II only   Ⓑ II and III only   Ⓒ I only
    Ⓓ III only   Ⓔ I and III only

  I. If $z = a + bi$, then the conjugate of z (designated by $\bar{z}$) has been defined to be $a - bi$ for every z in C. Thus:

$$z \cdot \bar{z} = (a + bi)(a - bi)$$
$$= a^2 + b^2 + (ab - ab)i$$
$$= a^2 + b^2 + (0)i.$$

Since a and b are both real, $a^2 + b^2$ is real and $z \cdot \bar{z}$ is real.
  II. Similarly,

$$z + \bar{z} = a + bi + a - bi$$
$$= 2a + (0)i.$$

Since a is real, $2a$ is real and $z + \bar{z}$ is real.
  III. Finally, the conjugate of i is $-i$. The reciprocal of i is $\dfrac{1}{i}$. But

$$\frac{1}{i} = \frac{1(i)}{i \cdot i} = \frac{i}{-1} = -i.$$

Thus $\bar{i} = \dfrac{1}{i}$.

[14] If z is a complex number and $\bar{z} = \dfrac{1}{z}$, then a possible value for z is:

    Ⓐ $1 + i$ Ⓑ 0 Ⓒ $2 + 2i$ Ⓓ $-1 + i$
    Ⓔ 1

When a single variable such as z is used to represent a complex number, it is sometimes preferable to express the number in standard form. In other words, let $z = x + yi$, where x and y are real numbers. This conversion allows you to use the familiar rules of the real numbers as well as those of the complex.
  To solve the multiple-choice question let $z = x + yi$; then

$$\bar{z} = \frac{1}{z},$$
$$x - yi = \frac{1}{x + yi},$$
$$x^2 + y^2 = 1.$$

In coordinate geometry the last equation defines a circle of radius 1 with center at the origin. Any complex number whose real part and imaginary part satisfy this equation will answer the question.
  For choice Ⓔ, $1 + 0i$, $x = 1$ and $y = 0$, so

$$x^2 + y^2 = 1.$$

TEST-TAKING TIP.

The method of testing each choice to see whether it satisfies the original conditions can be a lengthy and tedious process—a fact you will recognize immediately on trying it. The best method to use here was to transform the given condition into one that provided a simpler means of checking. Test-takers must be skilled in a great number of problem-solving strategies if they are to be consistently successful. No one method will always work best—or even work at all.

¶ DRILL True or False:

$$\left| \frac{z}{|z|} \right| = 1, \text{ when } z \neq 0.$$

WHAT YOU SHOULD KNOW

KEY CONCEPTS

1. The standard form of a complex number is $a + bi$, where a and b are real.
2. To find the value of i^n, where n is a positive integer, divide n by 4 to get the remainder, r. The value of i^n is i^r.
3. For $a < 0$, $\sqrt{a} = i \sqrt{|a|}$.

4. If a, b, c and d are real numbers, then:
   a. $(a + bi) + (c + di) = (a + c) + (b + d)i$,
   b. $(a + bi) - (c + di) = (a - c) + (b - d)i$,
   c. $(a + bi)(c + di) = (ac - bd) + (ad + bc)i$.

5. To find the value of $\dfrac{a + bi}{c + di}$, multiply by $\dfrac{c - di}{c - di}$ and simplify the result.

6. If $a + bi$ is a root of an equation with real coefficients, then $a - bi$ is also a root.

7. If $a < 0$ and $b < 0$, then
$$\sqrt{a}\sqrt{b} = -1\sqrt{|ab|}.$$

8. In the complex number plane, the graph of $a + bi$ is the point whose coordinates are (a, b).

KEY FORMULA

If $ax^2 + bx + c = 0$ and $a \neq 0$, then
$$x = \frac{-b \pm \sqrt{b^2 - 4ac}}{2a}.$$
(Quadratic Formula)

TEST-TAKING STRATEGIES

- If, in solving a complex number problem, you realize that the first method you try will be a lengthy process, abandon it in favor of another logical approach, and then if necessary try a third, since test questions rarely require long, tedious procedures.
- In dealing with high powers of i, look for cyclical patterns; for example, $i^2 = i^6 = i^{10} = i^{14} = \ldots = -1$.
- In operating with complex numbers, i can be treated as though it were a variable like x. When the result involves a power of i, calculate the power from the cyclical pattern of powers of i.

ANSWERS

[1] Ⓓ
DRILL:
(a) Real.   (b) Imaginary.
(c) Pure imaginary.   (d) Imaginary.
(e) $-1 + (0)i$ (f) $-\dfrac{1}{4} + 0(i)$
(g) $-2 + 6i$ (h) $0 + (-4)i$

[2] Ⓑ
DRILL:
(a) $x = 4, y = 5$ (b) $x = 3, y = -\dfrac{3}{2}$
(c) $x = 0, y = -\dfrac{13}{4}$

[3] Ⓒ
DRILL:
(a) $-i$ (b) $-i$
(c) $-i$ (d) i

[4] Ⓒ
DRILL:
(a) $0 + (2 + 2\sqrt{3})i$ (b) $6 + 8i$
(c) $3 + (-5)i$ (d) $0 + 10i$

[5] Ⓒ
DRILL:
(a) $19 + (-3)i$
(b) $-2 + i$
(c) $-45 + (0)i$
(d) $(a^2 - ab) + (ab - b^2)i$

[6] Ⓑ
DRILL:
(a) $-7 + i$; $\dfrac{7}{50} + \dfrac{1}{50}i$; $7 + i$
(b) $-2i$; $-\dfrac{1}{2}i$; $-2i$
(c) i; i; i
(d) $-a + bi$; $\dfrac{a}{a^2 + b^2} + \dfrac{b}{a^2 + b^2}i$; $a + bi$

[7] Ⓑ
DRILL:
(a) $\dfrac{3}{13} + \dfrac{-2}{13}i$ (b) $\dfrac{22}{41} + \dfrac{7}{41}i$
(c) $\dfrac{9}{73} + \dfrac{24}{73}i$ (d) $\dfrac{7}{11} + \dfrac{6\sqrt{2}}{11}i$

[8] Ⓐ
DRILL:
(a) $-\dfrac{1}{6} \pm \dfrac{\sqrt{23}}{6}i$ (b) -1
(c) $\dfrac{3}{2} \pm \dfrac{\sqrt{23}}{2}i$ (d) $3 - i$
(e) $5i$ (f) $1 - i$

[9] Ⓐ
DRILL:
(a) $\{-2, 1 \pm i\sqrt{3}\}$ (b) $\left\{0, \dfrac{-3 \pm \sqrt{41}}{2}\right\}$
(c) $\{\pm\sqrt{2}, \pm i\sqrt{2}\}$

[10] ©

DRILL:

(a) $-2\sqrt{3}$

(b) $2i\sqrt{3}$

(c) $2i\sqrt{3}$

(d) $2i\sqrt{3}$

[11] ©

DRILL:

(a) $2\sqrt{5}$

(b) 0

(c) $\sqrt{29}$

(d) $\sqrt{10}$

[12] ©

DRILL:

(a) $(x - yi)(x + yi)$

(b) $(x - y)(x + y)$

(c) $(a\sqrt{2} + bi\sqrt{3})(a\sqrt{2} - bi\sqrt{3})$

[13] ©

[14] ©

DRILL:

If you replace z by $x + yi$, then apply the definition of absolute value and simplify, you will discover that the statement is true.

22. Systems of Equations

Key Terms

linear equation   any equation of the form $ax + by + c = 0$, where a, b, and c are real numbers and not both of a and b are zero.

solution set of a linear equation   the set of ordered pairs, (x, y), that satisfy the equation.

system of linear equations   a set of two (or more) linear equations.

solution set of a system   the set of ordered pairs that satisfy the two equations of the system.

equivalent systems of equations   two systems that have the same solution set.

SOLVING A SYSTEM OF EQUATIONS BY GRAPHING

[1] Which of the following best describes the graph of the solution set of the system:

$$\begin{vmatrix} 2x + y = 4 \\ 2x - y = -8? \end{vmatrix}$$

Ⓐ A pair of intersecting lines Ⓑ A pair of parallel lines Ⓒ A point Ⓓ A single line Ⓔ The graph of the solution set contains no points

A *linear equation* is any equation of the form $ax + by + c = 0$, where a, b and c are real numbers and not both of a and b are zero. The *solution set of a linear equation* is the set of ordered pairs, (x, y), which satisfy the equation. The graph of this solution set is a line, hence the term "linear equation." A *system* of linear equations is a set of two (or more, though we will deal only with two) linear equations. We define the *solution set of a system* to be the set of ordered pairs that satisfy *both* equations, in other words, the intersection of the solution sets of the two equations of the system. When the graphs of the two linear equations are intersecting lines, the graph of the solution set of the system is a point; when the lines are parallel, the graph of the solution set of the system contains *no* points. If the two

linear equations are different equations for the same line, the solution set of the system is the set of all points on this line.

An elementary method of solving a system is to graph the composing lines and find the solution set by inspection.

EXAMPLE

Graph the system containing $2x + y = 4$ and $2x - y = -8$.

SOLUTION: The point of intersection has coordinates $(-1, 6)$. A common error is to consider the graph of the solution set to mean the same thing as the graph of the system. The graph of this system is the pair of intersecting lines, but the graph of its solution set is only the point $(-1, 6)$.

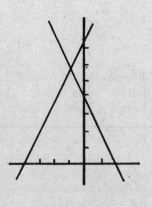

Solving a system by graphing has only limited practical value because coordinates that are not integers are hard to determine. In the next few sections we will review algebraic methods.

TEST-TAKING TIP.

Diagrams can be useful in suggesting relationships between algebraic quantities and parts of geometric figures. Diagrams can also suggest problem-solving approaches. Rarely, however, can precise information about lengths, measures and coordinates be judged accurately from a sketch. Don't rely solely on a sketch for precise information about lengths and measures.

¶ DRILL Solve the following systems graphically:

(a) $\begin{vmatrix} x - y = 5 \\ x + 2y = 2 \end{vmatrix}$ (b) $\begin{vmatrix} x + 2y = 2 \\ 3x - 4y = 6 \end{vmatrix}$

(c) $\begin{vmatrix} 5x + 2y = 13 \\ 4x + 3y = 9 \end{vmatrix}$

DETERMINING EQUIVALENT SYSTEMS

[2] Which of the following systems is equivalent to:

$$\begin{vmatrix} x + y = 6 \\ x - 2y = -6? \end{vmatrix}$$

Ⓐ $\begin{vmatrix} x = 2 \\ y = 4 \end{vmatrix}$ Ⓑ $\begin{vmatrix} y = 2 \\ x = 4 \end{vmatrix}$ Ⓒ $\begin{vmatrix} x = 6 \\ y = -6 \end{vmatrix}$

Ⓓ $\begin{vmatrix} x = 2 \\ y = 2 \end{vmatrix}$ Ⓔ $\begin{vmatrix} x = 4 \\ y = 4 \end{vmatrix}$

Two systems of equations are *equivalent* if and only if they have the same solution set. Algebraic methods of solving systems (sometimes called "simultaneous" equations) are procedures which transform a system into a simpler equivalent system. The simplest type of system is that which consists of a horizontal and vertical line, and its form is

$$\begin{vmatrix} x = h \\ y = k. \end{vmatrix}$$

Its solution set can be determined by inspection as follows: every point on the vertical line $x = h$ must have h as its x-coordinate and every point on $y = k$ must have k as its y-coordinate. In order for a point to lie on both, its coordinates must be (h, k).

To answer the multiple-choice question, find the solution of the system of simultaneous equations by any of the methods in the next two sections. Then represent the vertical and horizontal lines through the points.

¶ DRILL Graph each of the following systems, and determine from your graph an equivalent system consisting of a horizontal and a vertical line:

(a) $\begin{vmatrix} 3x - 2y = 19 \\ x + y = 23 \end{vmatrix}$ (b) $\begin{vmatrix} x + 2y = 3 \\ 3y + 4x = 2 \end{vmatrix}$

SOLVING A SYSTEM OF EQUATIONS BY SUBSTITUTION

[3] Which of the following systems are equivalent?

I $\begin{vmatrix} y = 5x - 4 \\ y = -3x + 2 \end{vmatrix}$

II $\begin{vmatrix} y = 5x - 4 \\ 5x - 4 = -3x + 2 \end{vmatrix}$

III $\begin{vmatrix} y = -3x + 2 \\ -3x + 2 = 5x - 4 \end{vmatrix}$

Ⓐ **All are equivalent**   Ⓑ **I and II only**   Ⓒ **II and III only**   Ⓓ **I and III only**   Ⓔ **No one is equivalent to any other**

The method of substitution provides a way of solving a system and is based on the fact that the following two systems are equivalent:

22-1

$$\begin{vmatrix} ax + by + c = 0 \\ y = mx + k \end{vmatrix} \leftrightarrow \begin{vmatrix} ax + b(mx + k) + c = 0 \\ y = mx + k \end{vmatrix}$$

We will use the symbol $\leftrightarrow$ to mean "is equivalent to." This equivalence may be verified by noting that the lower equations in the two systems are the same and that the only alteration in the upper equation is the substitution for y of the expression equal to y from the lower equation. The value of 22-1 to us lies in the fact that the new upper equation now contains only the variable x.

EXAMPLE 1

Solve the system:

$$\begin{vmatrix} 3x - y = 15 \\ 2x + y = 10. \end{vmatrix}$$

SOLUTION: We solve one equation (either one) for y, which transforms the system to:

$$\begin{vmatrix} 3x - y = 15 \\ y = -2x + 10. \end{vmatrix}$$

We then substitute $-2x + 10$ for y in the upper equation to get the equivalent system:

$$\begin{vmatrix} 3x - (-2x + 10) = 15 \\ y = -2x + 10. \end{vmatrix}$$

The latter system simplifies to:

$$\begin{vmatrix} x = 5 \\ y = -2x + 10. \end{vmatrix}$$

The solution set can now be determined by inspection since any ordered pair that satisfies it must have an x-coordinate of 5. The second equation gives us the companion y-value, $y = -2(5) + 10 = 0$.

EXAMPLE 2

Solve the system:

$$\begin{vmatrix} 6m - 2n = 1 \\ 3m + 10n = 6. \end{vmatrix}$$

SOLUTION: Applying the same procedure as in the preceding example, we first solve one equation for a variable, set up an equivalent system resulting from a substitution and then simplify.

$$\begin{vmatrix} 6m - 2n = 1 \\ \\ 3m + 10n = 6 \end{vmatrix} \leftrightarrow \begin{vmatrix} n = 3m - \dfrac{1}{2} \\ \\ 3m + 10(3m - \dfrac{1}{2}) = 6 \end{vmatrix}$$

$$\leftrightarrow \begin{vmatrix} n = 3m - \dfrac{1}{2} \\ \\ m = \dfrac{1}{3} \end{vmatrix}$$

Since $m = \dfrac{1}{3}$ and $n = 3m - \dfrac{1}{2}$, $n = 3(\dfrac{1}{3}) - \dfrac{1}{2} = \dfrac{1}{2}$ and the solution set contains only the ordered pair $(\dfrac{1}{3}, \dfrac{1}{2})$.

In the multiple-choice question, systems II and III are based on substitutions using the equations of system I. Each contains one equation from system I and a second equation that replaces y by its equivalent algebraic expression from the other equation in I.

¶ DRILL Solve each system in the Drill section of question [2] using the method of substitution.

SOLVING A SYSTEM OF EQUATIONS BY ELIMINATING A VARIABLE

[4] A system contains the equations $ax + by + c = 0$ and $dx + ey + f = 0$ whose graphs are a pair of intersecting lines. A second system contains the equations $ax + by + c = 0$ and $p(ax + by + c) + q(dx + ey + f) = 0$. For what values of p and q will the systems be equivalent?

Ⓐ $p = 0$ and $q = 0$ only   Ⓑ $q = 0$ only
Ⓒ All values of p and q Ⓓ No values of p and q
Ⓔ $p \neq 0$ or $q \neq 0$

If the original system,

$$(1) \begin{vmatrix} ax + by + c = 0 \\ dx + ey + f = 0, \end{vmatrix}$$

is a pair of intersecting lines, then their intersection is some point (m, n). Thus (m, n) satisfies both equations. In other words:

$$(2)\ am + bn + c = 0 \quad \text{and} \quad dm + en + f = 0.$$

The second system,

$$(3) \begin{vmatrix} ax + by + c = 0 \\ p(ax + by + c) + q(dx + ey + f) = 0, \end{vmatrix}$$

must also be satisfied by (m, n) from the following argument. We have already concluded that (m, n) satisfies the equations of the original system (see (2)). Thus

$$(4)\ p(am + bn + c) + q(dm + en + f)$$
$$= p(0) + q(0) = 0.$$

But if both p and q are zero, then

$$(5)\ p(ax + by + c) + q(dx + ey + f) = 0$$

is not a linear equation so the second system, (3), would consist of only one linear equation as well as the identity $0 = 0$. If only $q = 0$, we get a system containing two different equations for the same line:

$$(6) \begin{vmatrix} ax + by + c = 0 \\ p(ax + by + c) = 0. \end{vmatrix}$$

If only $p = 0$, then we get the original system, except that the second equation has been multiplied by a constant.

You may have noted that we are already well on the way to solving the system, but we will postpone our review of this until the next section. Be sure to do the following drill before going on.

¶ DRILL Write each of the following systems in the form of system (3) above, and then select values for p and q which will eliminate the y-terms from the lower equation:

(a) $\begin{vmatrix} 3x - 2y - 10 = 0 \\ 5x + 3y + 15 = 0 \end{vmatrix}$ (b) $\begin{vmatrix} 4x - y = 5 \\ x - 3y = 4 \end{vmatrix}$

(c) $\begin{vmatrix} 3x = 4y + 10 \\ 3y = -2x + 7 \end{vmatrix}$

SOLVING WORD PROBLEMS

[5] A boat takes two trips on a river. On the first trip it travels upstream for 5 hours and returns in 2 hours. On the second trip it goes downstream for 3 hours, turns around and heads back upstream. After spending 7 hours on the return trip it is still 2 miles from its starting point. Which of the following is the speed of the current in miles per hour?

Ⓐ 3   Ⓑ 4   Ⓒ 5   Ⓓ 6   Ⓔ 7

An important application of systems of equations is to the solution of word problems. We will review the method of solution through elimination by solving a few systems derived from word problems.

As with the majority of such problems, we let our variables represent the quantities asked for: b = rate of the boat exclusive of any effects of current (sometimes called its rate in still water) and s = rate of stream. Its speed going upstream is thus $b - s$ and going downstream is $b + s$. Since it takes 5 hours to cover the upstream leg of the first trip and $b - s$ miles is covered each hour, the distance upstream must be $5(b - s)$. By similar reasoning we find the distance back down to be $2(b + s)$. But these two distances must be the same. In other words,

$$5(b - s) = 2(b + s),$$

which becomes

(1) $3b - 7s = 0$.

For the second trip the first leg takes 3 hours downstream so the distance traveled is $3(b + s)$. When the boat comes back upstream for 7 hours, it covers a distance of $7(b - s)$ miles, but this is 2 miles short of the downstream distance. In other words,

$$3(b + s) - 2 = 7(b - s),$$

which becomes

(2) $2b - 5s + 1 = 0$.

From equations (1) and (2) we get the following system to solve:

(3) $\begin{vmatrix} 3b - 7s = 0 \\ 2b - 5s + 1 = 0. \end{vmatrix}$

System (3) is equivalent to

(4) $\begin{vmatrix} 3b - 7s = 0 \\ m(3b - 7s) + n(2b - 5s + 1) = 0. \end{vmatrix}$

We select values for m and n which will eliminate the b variable: $m = 2$, $n = -3$, and system (4) becomes

(5) $\begin{vmatrix} 3b - 7s = 0 \\ s = 3. \end{vmatrix}$

Since $s = 3$ and $3b = 7s$, then $b = 7$. The rate of the boat is thus 7 miles per hour and of the stream is 3 miles per hour.

EXAMPLE

We have two containers of sugar solution; the first is 4 percent and the second 8 percent. How much of each should we combine to get 40 gallons of a 5 percent solution?

SOLUTION: Let x represent the number of gallons of 4 percent solution and y the number of gallons of 8 percent solution in the *final* mixture. Then

(6) $x + y = 40$.

To get a second equation we note that the amount of sugar contributed by the 4 percent solution, 4 percent of x, when added to the amount of sugar contributed

by the 8 percent solution, 8 percent of y, must yield the amount of sugar in the final solution, 5 percent of 40. In other words,

(7) $.04x + .08y = .05(40)$.

From (6) and (7) we get the system:

$$\begin{vmatrix} x + y = 40 \\ .04x + .08y = 2. \end{vmatrix}$$

We multiply both sides of the lower equation by 100 to remove the decimals and then transform each equation until the right member is 0.

$$\begin{vmatrix} x + y - 40 = 0 \\ 4x + 8y - 200 = 0 \end{vmatrix}$$

This latter system is equivalent to

$$\begin{vmatrix} x + y - 40 = 0 \\ p(x + y - 40) + q(4x + 8y - 200) = 0. \end{vmatrix}$$

We choose $p = -4$ and $q = 1$ to get

$$\begin{vmatrix} x + y - 40 = 0 \\ y = 10. \end{vmatrix}$$

The proper solutions are 10 gallons of 8 percent solution and 30 gallons of 4 percent solution.

¶ DRILL Solve each of the systems by elimination:

(a) $\begin{vmatrix} 4x + 5y - 6 = 0 \\ 2x + 3y - 4 = 0 \end{vmatrix}$ (b) $\begin{vmatrix} 4x - 8y = 17 \\ 12x + 16y = -9 \end{vmatrix}$

(c) $\begin{vmatrix} 2x + 5y - 19 = 0 \\ 3x = -4y - 6 \end{vmatrix}$

[6] A father is 4 times as old as his son. Five years ago he was 9 times as old as his son was then. What is the son's present age in years?

   Ⓐ 6   Ⓑ 7   Ⓒ 8   Ⓓ 9   Ⓔ 10

In section [5] we began an exploration of the use of systems of equations to solve certain types of word problems. We will continue by analyzing the above question and several other examples.

Let f be the father's age now and s be the son's age. Since the father's age is 4 times the son's,

(1) $f = 4s$.

Five years ago, the father's age was $f - 5$ and the son's age was $s - 5$. Since the father was 9 times as old as the son, $f - 5 = 9(s - 5)$, and

(2) $f - 9s = -40$.

Which of the two methods, substitution or elimination, would you choose to solve the system containing (1) and (2)? Though both, of course, give the same answer, substitution is probably easier:

(3) $4s - 9s = -40$ (Substitution of $4s$ for f in (2)),

$- 5s = -40,$

$s = 8.$

EXAMPLE

A certain two-digit number has the following characteristics: (1) the tens digit when multiplied by 3 equals the sum of the digits, and (2) the number which is obtained by reversing the digits is 54 less than the product of 4 and the original number. Find the number.

SOLUTION: Let t equal the tens digit and u equal the units digit. A common error is to conclude from this that the number itself must then be $t + u$. Note, however, that a two-digit number, say 37, is equal to ten times the tens digit plus the units digit: $37 = 3 \times 10 + 7$. We conclude that the original number is $10t + u$ and the number obtained by reversing the digits is $10u + t$. We translate characteristic (1) to

(1) $3t = t + u,$

and characteristic (2) to

(2) $10u + t = 4(10t + u) - 54.$

Simplifying (1) and (2), we get

(3) $\begin{vmatrix} 2t - u = 0 \\ 6u - 39t + 54 = 0. \end{vmatrix}$

Since $2t - u = 0, u = 2t$. By the substitution method, $t = 2$ and $u = 4$, so the number is 24.

¶ DRILL

(a) The sum of two numbers is 10 and their difference is 4. Find the two numbers.

(b) If the perimeter of a certain square is increased by 100 inches, the area of the square becomes 325 more than three times its original area. Find the original dimensions.

GRAPHING LINEAR INEQUALITIES

[7] **Which geometric figure best describes the graph of the solution set of the system:**

$$\begin{vmatrix} x + y > 7 \\ 2x - y > 3? \end{vmatrix}$$

Ⓐ **An angle**   Ⓑ **The exterior of an angle**   Ⓒ **The interior of an angle**   Ⓓ **The exterior of a triangle**   Ⓔ **The interior of a triangle**

If a given line, L, has the equation $ax + by + c = 0$, then the inequalities $ax + by + c > 0$ and $ax + by + c < 0$ determine the regions on either side of L. L is called the boundary condition of the regions and provides a ready method for graphing them.

EXAMPLE 1

Draw the graph of $3x - 4y + 12 > 0$.

SOLUTION: The graph is one side of the line $3x - 4y + 12 = 0$. First graph the boundary condition, but indicate it as a dotted line since no point of the line satisfies the inequality. To discover which side of the line is the one in question, substitute the coordinates of some point which can be easily located on one side of the line. In this case we will choose the origin:

$$3(0) - 4(0) + 12 > 0.$$

Since this point clearly satisfies the inequality, the graph in question must be the region determined by the line and containing the origin.

Had the coordinates of our trial point not satisfied the inequality, we would have known just as assuredly that the graph was the other side of the line.

EXAMPLE 2

Represent graphically the solution set of the system:

$$\begin{vmatrix} x + 2y \leq 3 \\ 3y + x > 2. \end{vmatrix}$$

SOLUTION: Using the procedure of Example 1, we first graph $x + 2y = 3$ as a solid line and then check to see which side contains the origin. $(0, 0)$ satisfies $x + 2y \leq 3$ so the region is the one shown at right.

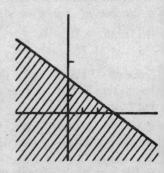

We then graph (dotted line) $3y + x = 2$. But $(0, 0)$ does not satisfy $3y + x > 2$ so we shade in the region above the line. The graph of the system is the cross-hatched region and includes the solid line.

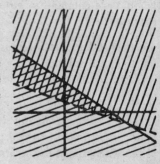

In the multiple-choice question, the cross-hatched region at right shows the graph of the solution set of the system of equations. Note that the region is the interior of an angle.

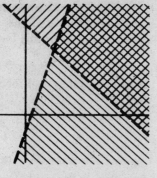

¶ DRILL Represent graphically the solution sets of the systems given:

(a) $\begin{vmatrix} x - y - 2 < 0 \\ x + 2y - 8 > 0 \end{vmatrix}$ (b) $\begin{vmatrix} x + 2y < 3 \\ 3y - 2x \le 6 \end{vmatrix}$

*[8] Which of the following systems is equivalent to

$$\begin{vmatrix} 2x + 4y - 3z + 9 = 0 \\ 3x + y - 2z - 4 = 0 \\ 5x + 2y + 4z - 28 = 0? \end{vmatrix}$$

Ⓐ $\begin{vmatrix} x = 3 \\ y = -2 \\ z = 4 \end{vmatrix}$ Ⓑ $\begin{vmatrix} x = 4 \\ y = 3 \\ z = -2 \end{vmatrix}$ Ⓒ $\begin{vmatrix} x = 3 \\ y = 4 \\ z = -2 \end{vmatrix}$

Ⓓ $\begin{vmatrix} x = -2 \\ y = 3 \\ z = 4 \end{vmatrix}$ Ⓔ $\begin{vmatrix} x = 4 \\ y = -2 \\ z = 3 \end{vmatrix}$

A common procedure for solving a system of three equations in three variables is to transform it to *triangular* form, using the method of elimination. A system is in triangular form if it resembles

$$\begin{vmatrix} T(1) & ax + by + cz + d = 0 \\ T(2) & ey + fz + g = 0 \\ T(3) & hz + m = 0. \end{vmatrix}$$

Note that T(1) contains all three variables, T(2) contains only two and T(3) contains only one. When the equation is in this form, the solution can be readily determined. We will show the procedure for the question above.

$$\begin{vmatrix} (1) & 2x + 4y - 3z + 9 = 0 \\ (2) & 3x + y - 2z - 4 = 0 \\ (3) & 5x + 2y + 4z - 28 = 0 \end{vmatrix}$$

We first write a combination of equations (1) and (2) which will eliminate the x-variable:

$$m(2x + 4y - 3z + 9) + n(3x + y - 2z - 4) = 0.$$

We accomplish this by letting $m = -3$ and $n = 2$ to get

(4) $-10y + 5z - 35 = 0.$

We then combine equations (2) and (3) to eliminate the same variable, x:

(5) $y + 22z - 64 = 0.$

Next, we combine (4) and (5) to eliminate y:

(6) $z - 3 = 0.$

The equivalent triangular form has any one of (1), (2) or (3) as its first equation; either one of (4) or (5) as its second equation; and (6) as its last equation. One satisfactory system is

$$\begin{vmatrix} (1) & 2x + 4y - 3z + 9 = 0 \\ (4) & -10y + 5z - 35 = 0 \\ (6) & z - 3 = 0. \end{vmatrix}$$

From the last equation we see that z must equal 3. If we substitute 3 for z in (4) we get $y = -2$, and if we substitute for both z and y in (1) we get $x = 4$.

¶ DRILL Solve each of the following systems:

(a) $\begin{vmatrix} 2x - y + 3z = 14 \\ 3x - 2y - z = 5 \\ 4x - 3y - 4z = -1 \end{vmatrix}$

(b) $\begin{vmatrix} x + 3y - 2z - 8 = 0 \\ 2x - 2y + 3z + 7 = 0 \\ 3x - y - 3z - 1 = 0 \end{vmatrix}$

*[9] How many points are there in the graph of the solution set of the system

$$\begin{vmatrix} 2x - y - 4 = 0 \\ y - x^2 + 4x - 5 = 0? \end{vmatrix}$$

Ⓐ 0   Ⓑ 1   Ⓒ 2   Ⓓ 3   Ⓔ 4

In Chapter 18 we reviewed the fact that the graph of every second-degree equation in two variables was a conic section: circle, ellipse, parabola or hyperbola. There are two exceptions, the so-called "degenerate" conics whose graphs are a pair of intersecting lines or a point, but these are not usually studied in intermediate math.

When a system contains one linear and one quadratic equation the number of possible points of intersection is 0, 1 or 2. Each of the following drawings shows a second-degree graph with three possible lines showing three different intersections:

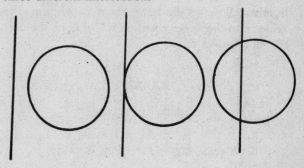

The usual procedure for solving such a system is the method of substitution: solve the linear equation for y and substitute in the second-degree equation.

EXAMPLE

Solve the system:

$$\begin{vmatrix} 3x + 2y - 6 = 0 \\ 9x^2 = 36 - 4y^2 \end{vmatrix}$$

SOLUTION: From the first equation we get $y = -\frac{3}{2}x + 3$. Substituting for y, we get:

$$9x^2 = 36 - 4(-\frac{3}{2}x + 3)^2.$$

If we simplify and solve we get $x = 0$ or $x = 2$. Substituting these values for x in the linear equation, we get $(0, 3)$ and $(2, 0)$.

¶ DRILL Solve each of the following systems:

(a) $\begin{vmatrix} y = -x + 7 \\ y^2 = 25 - x^2 \end{vmatrix}$ (b) $\begin{vmatrix} 4x^2 - 9y^2 - 28 = 0 \\ y = 2x - 6 \end{vmatrix}$

*[10] How many elements are contained in the solution set of the system:

$$\begin{vmatrix} xy = 8 \\ xy = 4x + 4y - 16? \end{vmatrix}$$

Ⓐ 0 Ⓑ 1 Ⓒ 2 Ⓓ 3 Ⓔ 4

Though the method of elimination sometimes works for quadratic-quadratic systems, the method of substitution is the more general procedure. For example, in the system above we could write a combination that would eliminate the xy term, but this combination would still have a term in x and a term in y. If, however, we solved the upper equation for y:

$$y = \frac{8}{x},$$

and substituted $\frac{8}{x}$ for y in the lower equation, we would get

$$x\left(\frac{8}{x}\right) = 4x + 4\left(\frac{8}{x}\right) - 16,$$

from which we get the values for x. Substituting these values into the upper equation will give us the corresponding values for y.

EXAMPLE

Solve the system:

$$\begin{vmatrix} x^2 + y^2 - 1 = 0 \\ x^2 - y - 1 = 0. \end{vmatrix}$$

SOLUTION: This system can be solved by elimination, but again we will use the more general method of substitution. From the lower equation we see that

$$x^2 = y + 1.$$

If we substitute $y + 1$ for x^2 in the upper equation, we find:

$$y + 1 + y^2 - 1 = 0,$$
$$y^2 + y = 0,$$
$$y = 0 \quad \text{or} \quad y = -1.$$

Substituting the two values for y gives the companion values of x.

¶ DRILL Solve:

(a) $\begin{vmatrix} 2x^2 = 30 - 3y^2 \\ x^2 = 13 - y^2 \end{vmatrix}$ (b) $\begin{vmatrix} 3y^2 = 4x^2 + 2 \\ 3x^2 + 4y^2 - 11 = 0 \end{vmatrix}$

WHAT YOU SHOULD KNOW

KEY CONCEPTS

1. *To solve a system of equations by graphing*, graph each equation and estimate the coordinates of the point of intersection.

2. *To solve a system of two equations by substitution*, solve one equation for a variable and substitute the resulting expression for that variable into the other equation. Then solve for the value of the second variable.

3. *To solve a system of two equations by addition*, eliminate a variable (we'll use x as an example) by the following steps:
   a. multiply the first equation by the coefficient of x in the second equation, then
   b. multiply the second equation by the negative of the coefficient of x in the first equation, then
   c. add the two equations, then
   d. solve for the value of y, then
   e. substitute the value of y for y in one of the original equations to find x.

KEY RELATIONSHIP

Equivalent Systems:

$\begin{vmatrix} ax + by + c = 0 \\ y = mx + k \end{vmatrix}$ $\leftrightarrow$ $\begin{vmatrix} ax + b(mx + k) + c = 0 \\ y = mx + k \end{vmatrix}$

• When you encounter a word problem with two un-knowns, set up a system of equations in which the variables represent the quantities the question asks for, then solve through elimination of a variable.

ANSWERS

[1] ©
DRILL:
(a) $(4, -1)$ (b) $(2, 0)$ (c) $(3, -1)$

[2] Ⓐ
DRILL:
(a) $x = 13$ and $y = 10$.
(b) $x = -1$ and $y = 2$.

[3] Ⓐ
DRILL:
See answers to [2] above.

[4] Ⓔ
DRILL:
(a) $p = 3, q = 2$ (b) $p = -3, q = 1$
(c) $p = 3, q = 4$

[5] Ⓐ
DRILL:
(a) $(-1, 2)$ (b) $\frac{5}{4} - \frac{3}{2}$ (c) $(2, -3)$

[6] ©
DRILL:
(a) 7 and 3.
(b) Let P = the original perimeter and A = original area; then

$$\left(\frac{P}{4}\right)^2 = A \quad \text{and} \quad \left(\frac{P + 100}{4}\right)^2 = 325 + 3A.$$

As with many simple problems susceptible to solution by systems of equations, this one is more easily done by solving a single equation in one unknown. The square has a side of 30 inches.

[7] ©
DRILL:
(a)   (b)
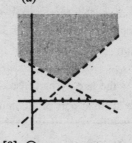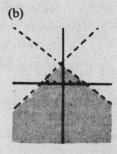

[8] Ⓔ
DRILL:
(a) $(2, -1, 3)$ (b) $(0, 2, -1)$

[9] Ⓑ
DRILL:
(a) $\{(3, 4), (4, 3)\}$ (b) $\{(4, 2), (4, -2)\}$

[10] ©
DRILL:
(a) $\{(3, 2), (3, -2), (-3, 2), (-3, -2)\}$
(b) $\{(\pm 1, \pm\sqrt{2})\}$

23. Exponents and Logarithms

> *In this chapter, several topics are more typical of those tested on the Mathematics Level II exam than of those on the Level I exam. We have denoted these with an asterisk (*). Review of such topics may assist you in answering Level I questions, however, because it increases your general knowledge of mathematical ideas, methods and skills.*
>
> *Be sure to read section [1] of this chapter even if you are able to answer the question.*

Key Terms

exponent   a number or letter written above and to the right of a mathematical expression (the *base*) to indicate that it is to be raised to a certain power. Example: x^5 means that x is to be used as a factor 5 times.

logarithm   an exponent that indicates to what power a base must be raised to produce a given number. Example: The logarithm of 25 to the base 5 is 2.

exponential function   a function of the form $\{(x, y) : y = a^x\}$, where a is any positive number except 1.

characteristic   the integer part of a common logarithm.

mantissa   the decimal part of a common logarithm.

APPLYING FIVE LAWS OF EXPONENTS

[1] Which of the following (where all exponents are integers) is NOT equal to xy?

(A) $(xy^2)y^{-1}$ (B) $\dfrac{12^0 x^{12}}{x^{11}y^{-1}}$ (C) $\dfrac{1}{x^{-1}y^{-1}}$

(D) $(x^n y)x^{1-n}$ (E) $(xy)^2(xy)^{-2}$

TEST-TAKING TIP.

The type of question used here—given five statements, select the incorrect one—will be used repeatedly throughout the chapter because it allows the presentation and resolution of many examples. It is not, however, a common format for Level I test questions.

In our review of exponents we will present five laws. You may consider them as assumptions since their proofs for all real numbers are largely beyond the scope of intermediate math. Indeed, our intention will be primarily the development of manipulative skills, since a rigorous course in exponents is not usually attempted in secondary schools.

To answer the given question we may use the following law:

EX-1 If a is a real number and m and n are integers, then

$$a^m a^n = a^{m+n}.$$

EX-1 has no meaning, however, until the followir definitions are understood.

Definition 1 If a is a real number and m is a *positive* integer, then

$$a^m = \underbrace{a \cdot a \cdot a \ldots a.}_{m \text{ factors}}$$

Definition 2 If a is a real number (except zero) and $m = 0$, then

$$a^m = 1.$$

(In other words, $a^0 = 1$.)

Definition 3 If a is a real number and $m = 1$, then

$$a^m = a.$$

(In other words, $a^1 = a$.)

Definition 4 If a is a real number and m is any integer ($a \neq 0$), then

$$a^m = \frac{1}{a^{-m}}.$$

EXAMPLES

$$a^{-1} = \frac{1}{a}, \ a^{-3} = \frac{1}{a^3}, \ \left(\frac{1}{2}\right)^{-2} = 4$$

Law EX-1 can be used to simplify each of the answer selections.

Ⓐ $(xy^2)y^{-1} = x(y^2 y^{-1})$ (Recognize the Associative Law of Multiplication?)

$\quad\quad = xy^{2 + (-1)}$ EX-1 with $a = y$, $m = 2$ and $n = -1$

$\quad\quad = xy^1$

$\quad\quad = xy$ Definition 3

Ⓑ $\dfrac{12^0 x^{12}}{x^{11} y^{-1}} = \dfrac{x^{12}}{x^{11} y^{-1}}$ Definition 3

$\quad\quad = \dfrac{x^{12}}{\dfrac{1}{x^{-11}} y^{-1}}$ Definition 4, $x^{11} = \dfrac{1}{x^{-11}}$

$\quad\quad = \dfrac{x^{12}}{\dfrac{1}{x^{-11}} \cdot \dfrac{1}{y}}$ Definition 4

$\quad\quad = \dfrac{x^{12}}{\dfrac{1}{x^{-11} y}}$

$\quad\quad = x^{12} x^{-11} y$

$\quad\quad = x^1 y$ By EX-1, with $a = x$, $m = 11$, $n = -11$

$\quad\quad = xy$

We used this somewhat complex process so as to avoid using EX-2, which will be reviewed in the next section:

Ⓒ $\dfrac{1}{x^{-1} y^{-1}} = \dfrac{1}{\dfrac{1}{x} \dfrac{1}{y}}$ Definition 4

$\quad\quad = \dfrac{1}{\dfrac{1}{xy}}$

$\quad\quad = xy$

Ⓓ $(x^n y)x^{1-n} = x^{1-n}(x^n y)$ (Recognize the Commutative Law of Multiplication?)

$\quad\quad = (x^{1-n} x^n)y$ (And the Associative Law?)

$\quad\quad = x^{1-n+n} y$ EX-1 with $a = x$, $m = 1 - n$, $n = n$

$\quad\quad = xy$

Ⓔ $(xy)^2 (xy)^{-2} = (xy)^{2+(-2)}$ EX-1 with $a = xy$, $m = 2$, $n = -2$

$\quad\quad = (xy)^0$

$\quad\quad = 1$ Definition 3

¶ DRILL Use EX-1 and the definitions to simplify each of the following where all exponents are integers:

(a) $y^2 y^4$ (b) $a^{2n} a$

(c) $x^a x^b$ (d) $a^x a^x$

(e) $y^{n-2} y^2 y^n$ (f) $(-x^{m+1})(-x^{m-1})$

[2] **Which of the following (where all exponents are integers) is NOT equal to w?**

Ⓐ $\dfrac{3w^2}{(3w)^2(3w)^{-1}}$ Ⓑ $\dfrac{w^2 x^6}{(wx^2)x^4}$ Ⓒ $\dfrac{w^{-2}}{w^{-3}}$

Ⓓ $\dfrac{w^{-3}}{w^{-2}}$ Ⓔ $\dfrac{w^{n-2}}{w^{n-3}}$

We could have used EX-1 to simplify each of these, but it is more expedient to introduce a second law to handle expressions that involve division.

EX-2   If a is a real number ($a \neq 0$) and m and n are *integers*, then

$$\frac{a^m}{a^n} = a^{m-n}.$$

As examples of the use of EX-2 we will simplify each of the answer selections.

Ⓐ $\dfrac{3w^2}{(3w)^2(3w)^{-1}} = \dfrac{3w^2}{3w}$ EX-1 with $a = 3w$, $m = 2$, $n = -1$

$\quad\quad = \dfrac{w^2}{w}$

$\quad\quad = \dfrac{w^2}{w^1}$ Definition 3

$\quad\quad = w^1$ EX-2 with $a = w$, $m = 2$, $n = 1$

Ⓑ $\dfrac{w^2 x^6}{(wx^2)x^4} = \dfrac{w^2 x^6}{w(x^2 x^4)}$

$\quad\quad = \dfrac{w^2 x^6}{wx^6}$

$\quad\quad = \dfrac{w^2}{w} \cdot \dfrac{x^6}{x^6}$

$\quad\quad = wx^0$ EX-2

$\quad\quad = w$

Ⓒ $\dfrac{w^{-2}}{w^{-3}} = w^{-2-(-3)}$ EX-2

$\quad\quad = w$

Ⓓ $\dfrac{w^{-3}}{w^{-2}} = w^{-3-(-2)}$ EX-2

$\quad\quad = w^{-1}$

$\quad\quad = \dfrac{1}{w}$ Definition 4

Ⓔ $\dfrac{w^{n-2}}{w^{n-3}} = w^{(n-2)-(n-3)}$ EX-2

$\quad\quad = w$

¶ DRILL Simplify:

(a) $x^{12} \div x^3$ (b) $y^{2n} \div y$ (c) $2^8 \div 2^4$

(d) $12m^3n^2 \div 2mn$ (e) $\frac{1}{2}x^6 \div \frac{1}{3}x^2$

(f) $(y - 4)^3 \div (y - 4)$

[3] **Which of the following (where all exponents are integers) is NOT true?**

Ⓐ $(2^2)^3 = 32$ Ⓑ $(x^3)^p = x^{3p}$
Ⓒ $(-b^{p+1})^2 = b^{2p+2}$
Ⓓ $(b^x)^{x+1} = b^{x^2+x}$ Ⓔ$(x^3)^0 = 1$

Again, we could have used EX-1 to simplify each of these, but we will introduce a third law to expedite the raising of a power to a power.

> **EX-3**   If a is a real number and m and n are integers, then
>
> $$(a^m)^n = a^{mn}.$$

Ⓐ $(2^2)^3 = 2^{2\times 3}$ EX-3
   $= 2^6$
   $= 64$ (By direct multiplication)

Ⓑ $(x^3)^p = x^{3p}$ EX-3

Ⓒ $(-b^{p+1})^2 = (b^{p+1})^2$ Since the square of every real number ˙equals the square of its negative.
   $= b^{(p+1)2}$ EX-3 with $a = b$, $m = p + 1$, $n = 2$
   $= b^{2p+2}$ (Recognize the Distributive Law?)

Ⓓ $(b^x)^{x+1} = b^{x(x+1)}$ EX-3 with $a = b$, $m = x$, $n = x + 1$
   $= b^{x^2+x}$ (The Distributive Law again)

Ⓔ $(x^3)^0 = x^{3\times 0}$ EX-3
   $= x^0$
   $= 1$ Definition 2

¶ DRILL Simplify:

(a) $(b^2)^5$ (b) $(b^{2p})^2$ (c) $(-c^3)^4$
(d) $(d^p)^q$ (e) $(-2^2)^3$ (f) $(r^8)^{8+1}$

[4] **Which of the following (where all exponents are integers) is NOT true?**

Ⓐ $(x^2y)^3 = x^6y^3$ Ⓑ $(2r^2s)^p = 2^p r^{2p}s^p$
Ⓒ $(3x)^2(2x^3) = 6x^5$ Ⓓ $(xy^2z^3)^4 = x^4y^8z^{12}$
Ⓔ $(x^3y^2)^3 \div x^3y = x^6y^5$

We introduce the next law to simplify the raising of a product to a power.

> **EX-4**   If a and b are real numbers and m is an integer, then:
>
> $$(ab)^m = a^m b^m.$$

The following argument shows EX-4 to be applicable to the product of three factors raised to a power.

$(xyz)^p = (xy)^p z^p$ EX-4 with $a = xy$, $b = z$, $m = p$
$= x^p y^p z^p$ EX-4

In general, the power of a product equals the product of the powers of its factors regardless of the number of factors.

Ⓐ $(x^2y)^3 = (x^2)^3 y^3$ EX-4
   $= x^{2\times 3}y^3$ EX-3
   $= x^6y^3$

Ⓑ $(2r^2s)^p = (2r^2)^p s^p$ EX-4
   $= 2^p(r^2)^p s^p$ EX-4
   $= 2^p r^{2p} s^p$ EX-3

Ⓒ $(3x)^2(2x^3) = 3^2 x^2 2x^3$ EX-4
   $= 9x^2 2x^3$
   $= 18x^2 x^3$
   $= 18x^5$ EX-1

Ⓓ $(xy^2z^3)^4 = x^4(y^2)^4(z^3)^4$ EX-4
   $= x^4y^8z^{12}$ EX-3

Ⓔ $(x^3y^2)^3 \div x^3y$
   $= (x^3)^3(y^2)^3 \div x^3y$ EX-4
   $= x^9y^6 \div x^3y$ EX-3
   $= x^6y^5$ EX-2

¶ DRILL Simplify:

(a) $(2x)^3(3x^2)$ (b) $(-3x^4)^2$

(c) $(2y)^3 \div (2y)^2$ (d) $(\frac{1}{2}x^{4p})^2$

(e) $(3x^{-1}y^{-2})^{-3}$ (f) $(x^{-1} + 2y)^{-1}$

[5] **Which of the following (where all exponents are integers) is NOT true?**

Ⓐ $\left(-\dfrac{2}{p}\right)^3 = -\dfrac{8}{p^3}$ Ⓑ $\left(\dfrac{3x^2}{y^4}\right)^3 = \dfrac{27x^6}{y^{12}}$

Ⓒ $\left(\dfrac{x^{-2}y^{-3}}{w^{-4}z^{-5}}\right)^{-1} = \dfrac{x^2y^3}{w^4z^5}$

Ⓓ $\dfrac{1}{(2/3)^{-1}} = \dfrac{3}{2}$ Ⓔ $\left(\dfrac{x^{-1}}{y^{-1}}\right)^{-1} = \dfrac{x}{y}$

EX-5 If a and b are real numbers ($b \neq 0$) and m is an integer, then

$$\left(\frac{a}{b}\right)^m = \frac{a^m}{b^m}.$$

Ⓐ $\left(-\frac{2}{p}\right)^3 = \left(\frac{-2}{p}\right)^3$

$\quad = \frac{(-2)^3}{p^3}$ EX-5

$\quad = \frac{-8}{p^3}$

$\quad = -\frac{8}{p^3}$

Ⓑ $\left(\frac{3x^2}{y^4}\right)^3 = \frac{(3x^2)^3}{(y^4)^3}$ EX-5

$\quad = \frac{3^3(x^2)^3}{y^{12}}$ EX-4

$\quad = \frac{27x^6}{y^{12}}$

Ⓒ $\left(\frac{x^{-2}y^{-3}}{w^{-4}z^{-5}}\right)^{-1}$

$\quad = \frac{(x^{-2}y^{-3})^{-1}}{(w^{-4}z^{-5})^{-1}}$ EX-5

$\quad = \frac{(x^{-2})^{-1}(y^{-3})^{-1}}{(w^{-4})^{-1}(z^{-5})^{-1}}$ EX-4

$\quad = \frac{x^2y^3}{w^4z^5}$ EX-3

Ⓓ $\frac{1}{(2/3)^{-1}} = \frac{2}{3}$ Definition 4 with $a = \frac{2}{3}$

Ⓔ $\left(\frac{x^{-1}}{y^{-1}}\right)^{-1} = \frac{(x^{-1})^{-1}}{(y^{-1})^{-1}}$ EX-5

$\quad = \frac{x^{(-1)(-1)}}{y^{(-1)(-1)}}$ EX-3

$\quad = \frac{x}{y}$

¶ **DRILL** Simplify:

(a) $\left(\frac{3x^2}{y}\right)^3$ (b) $\left(\frac{2}{3}\right)^3$

(c) $\left(\frac{x^{-1}}{y^{-2}}\right)^{-3}$ (d) $\left(\frac{x^2y}{z}\right)^{-2}$

AVOIDING IMPROPER APPLICATIONS

[6] Which of the following (where all exponents are integers) is NOT true? ($x \neq 0$)

Ⓐ $\frac{1}{x^m} \cdot \frac{1}{x^n} = x^{-m-n}$ Ⓑ $\frac{x^m}{x^{-n}} = x^{m+n}$

Ⓒ $x^m + x^n = x^{m+n}$

Ⓓ $(x^m + x^n)^{-1} = \frac{1}{x^m + x^n}$

Ⓔ $\left(\frac{x^{-1} + y^{-1}}{x^{-1}}\right)(x + y)^{-1} = \frac{1}{y}$

No new information is needed here; our purpose is to review errors frequently made by intermediate math students.

Ⓐ $\frac{1}{x^m} \cdot \frac{1}{x^n} = x^{-m}x^{-n}$ Definition 4

$\quad = x^{-m+(-n)}$ EX-1

$\quad = x^{-m-n}$

> Error to avoid: multiplying exponents in a product,
>
> $$x^{-m} \cdot x^{-n} \neq x^{(-m)(-n)}.$$

Ⓑ $\frac{x^m}{x^{-n}} = x^{m-(-n)}$ EX-2

$\quad = x^{m+n}$

> Error to avoid: adding exponents in a quotient,
>
> $$\frac{x^m}{x^{-n}} \neq x^{m+(-n)}$$

Ⓒ $x^{m+n} = x^m \cdot x^n$ EX-1

> Error to avoid: adding exponents in a sum,
>
> $$x^{m+n} \neq x^m + x^n.$$

Ⓒ $(x^m + x^n)^{-1}$

$\quad = \frac{1}{x^m + x^n}$ Definition 4

> Error to avoid: raising each term of a sum to a power when the sum is raised to the power,
>
> $$(x^m + x^n)^{-1} \neq x^{-m} + x^{-n}$$

Ⓔ $\left(\frac{x^{-1} + y^{-1}}{x^{-1}}\right)(x + y)^{-1}$

$\quad = \frac{\frac{1}{x} + \frac{1}{y}}{\frac{1}{x}} \cdot \frac{1}{x + y}$ Definition 4

$\quad = \frac{\frac{y + x}{xy}}{\frac{1}{x}} \cdot \frac{1}{x + y}$

$\quad = \frac{y + x}{xy} \cdot \frac{x}{1} \cdot \frac{1}{x + y} = \frac{1}{y}$

> Errors to avoid:
>
> $$x^{-1} + y^{-1} \neq \frac{1}{x + y}$$
>
> and
>
> $$(x + y)^{-1} \neq (x^{-1} + y^{-1}).$$

[7] Which of the following is NOT true?

  Ⓐ $X^{-1/3} = \dfrac{1}{\sqrt[3]{X}}$ Ⓑ $5^{2/3} = \sqrt[3]{5^2}$

  Ⓒ $(3X)^{-1/2} = \dfrac{1}{\sqrt{3X}}$ Ⓓ $64^{3/2} = 512$

  Ⓔ $\dfrac{1}{2X^{-1/3}} = \sqrt[3]{2X}$

We have reviewed, so far, only expressions in which the exponents were integers. Our purpose in this section will be to give meaning to rational exponents. We will be guided by a desire to define these exponents in such a way as to preserve the laws of exponents already assumed.

Definition 5 If a is a real number and q is any positive integer, then

$$a^{1/q} = \sqrt[q]{a} \quad (\textit{read: the principal } q\text{th root of } a).$$

In other words, $a^{1/q}$ is the number such that $(a^{1/q})^q = a$, with the following restrictions:

(1) If q is an even number and $a \geq 0$, then $a^{1/q}$ is the positive qth root.
(2) If q is an even number and $a \leq 0$, then $a^{1/q}$ defines no real number.
(3) If q is an odd number and $a \geq 0$, then
$$a^{1/q} \geq 0.$$
(4) If q is an odd number and $a < 0$, then
$$a^{1/q} < 0.$$

Definition 6 If a is a real number and p and q are integers ($q \neq 0$) then
$$a^{p/q} = (a^{1/q})^p = (a^p)^{1/q} = \sqrt[q]{a^p} = (\sqrt[q]{a})^p.$$

We will agree that all of the preceding definitions and laws of exponents will hold true when the domain of the exponents is all rationals.

  Ⓐ $X^{-1/3} = \dfrac{1}{X^{1/3}}$ Definition 4

          $= \dfrac{1}{\sqrt[3]{X}}$ Definition 5

  Ⓑ $5^{2/3}$ equals all of the following by Definition 6:
$$(5^{1/3})^2 = (5^2)^{1/3} = \sqrt[3]{5^2} = (\sqrt[3]{5})^2.$$

  Ⓒ $(3X)^{-1/2} = \dfrac{1}{(3X)^{1/2}}$ Definition 4

           $= \dfrac{1}{\sqrt[3]{3X}}$ Definition 6

  Ⓓ $64^{3/2} = (\sqrt[2]{64})^3$ Definition 6
         $= 8^3$
         $= 512$

  Ⓔ $\dfrac{1}{2X^{-1/3}} = \dfrac{1}{2(1/X^{1/3})}$ Definition 4

          $= \dfrac{1/2}{\sqrt[3]{X}}$ Definition 5

          $= \dfrac{\sqrt[3]{X}}{2}$

¶ **DRILL** Write each of the following in radical form and then simplify:

  (a) $3^{1/2} \times 4^{1/2} \times 3^{1/2}$ (b) $5^{1/3} \times 2^{5/2} \times 5^{2/3}$
  (c) $(-8)^{4/3} \times (-64)^{1/3}$ (d) $2^{-1} \times \left(\dfrac{4}{9}\right)^{1/2}$

CONVERTING RADICALS TO EXPONENTS

[8] Which of the following is not ALWAYS true?

  Ⓐ $\sqrt{x^2 y^6} = xy^3$ Ⓑ $(\sqrt[5]{\sqrt[6]{2}})^{30} = 2$
  Ⓒ $\sqrt[5]{128} = 2\sqrt[5]{4}$ Ⓓ $\sqrt[6]{x^4}\sqrt[6]{x^4} = x^{4/3}$
  Ⓔ $\sqrt{45} = 3\sqrt{5}$

We have agreed that EX-1 through EX-5, as well as their accompanying definitions, will apply as long as the domain of each exponent variable is the set of rational numbers.

  Ⓐ $\sqrt{x^2 y^6} = (x^2 y^6)^{1/2}$ Definition 5
           $= (x^2)^{1/2}(y^6)^{1/2}$ EX-4
           $= |x||y^3|$ Definition 5 and EX-3

(Note that we have introduced the absolute value bars because x and y represent any real numbers, positive or negative, but the exponent $\dfrac{1}{2}$ indicates the *principal* square root *only*, which is positive. Without these absolute value bars, the statement is false.)

  Ⓑ $(\sqrt[5]{\sqrt[6]{2}})^{30} = [(2^{1/6})^{1/5}]^{30}$ Definition 5
            $= (2^{1/30})^{30}$ EX-3
            $= 2$

  Ⓒ $\sqrt[5]{128} = (128)^{1/5}$ Definition 5
          $= (32 \times 4)^{1/5}$
          $= 32^{1/5} \times 4^{1/5}$ EX-4
          $= (2^5)^{1/5} \times (4)^{1/5}$
          $= 2(4)^{1/5}$ EX-3
          $= 2\sqrt[5]{4}$ Definition 5

  Ⓓ $\sqrt[6]{x^4}\sqrt[6]{x^4} = x^{4/6} \cdot x^{4/6}$ Definition 6
            $= x^{2/3} \cdot x^{2/3}$
            $= x^{4/3}$ EX-1

  Ⓔ $\sqrt{45} = (45)^{1/2}$ Definition 5
         $= (9 \times 5)^{1/2}$
         $= 9^{1/2} \times 5^{1/2}$ EX-4
         $= 3\sqrt{5}$ Definition 5

¶ DRILL Simplify:

(a) $(\sqrt[3]{7})^5$ (b) $(\sqrt[3]{2})(\sqrt[3]{4})$ (c) $(\sqrt[3]{9})^6$

(d) $(\sqrt{7})(\sqrt{3})$ (e) $\sqrt{a^3} \div \sqrt{a}$ (f) $\sqrt{75}$

SIMPLIFYING FRACTIONAL EXPONENTS

[9] Which of the following is NOT true?

Ⓐ $(xy)^{-2/5} = \left(\dfrac{1}{\sqrt[5]{xy}}\right)^2$

Ⓑ $y^{1/2}(y^{1/2} + y^{-1/2}) = y$

Ⓒ $y^{3/2} \cdot y^{1/2} \cdot y^{-3} = \dfrac{1}{y}$

Ⓓ $y^{1/2} \div y^{-1/2} = y$

Ⓔ $\sqrt[3]{\dfrac{y^6}{x^3}} = \dfrac{y^2}{x}$

We have included this problem as further review of topics already discussed.

Ⓐ $(xy)^{-2/5} = ((xy)^{-1/5})^2$ Definition 6

$\qquad = \left(\dfrac{1}{(xy)^{1/5}}\right)^2$ Definition 1

$\qquad = \left(\dfrac{1}{\sqrt[5]{xy}}\right)^2$ Definition 5

Ⓑ $y^{1/2}(y^{1/2} + y^{-1/2})$

$\qquad = y^{1/2} \cdot y^{1/2} + y^{1/2} \cdot y^{-1/2}$

$\qquad = y^1 + y^0$ EX-1

$\qquad = y + 1$ Definitions 2 and 3

Ⓒ $y^{3/2} \cdot y^{1/2} \cdot y^{-3}$

$\qquad = y^{3/2+1/2-3}$ EX-1

$\qquad = y^{-1}$

$\qquad = \dfrac{1}{y}$

Ⓓ $y^{1/2} \div y^{-1/2}$

$\qquad = y^{1/2-(-1/2)}$ EX-2

$\qquad = y$

Ⓔ $\sqrt[3]{\dfrac{y^6}{x^3}} = \left(\dfrac{y^6}{x^3}\right)^{1/3}$ Definition 5

$\qquad = \dfrac{y^2}{x}$ EX-5 and EX-3

¶ DRILL Simplify:

(a) $\left(\dfrac{125a^6}{27b^{-3}}\right)^{-1/3}$

(b) $\dfrac{a^{1/2}\sqrt[3]{b^{-3/2}}}{b^{-1/2}\sqrt{a^{-1}}}$

(c) $5^0 \cdot 16^{-3/4} \cdot 4^{-1/2}$

(d) $(x^{-1/2} + y^{-1/2})(x^{-1/2} - y^{-1/2})$

GRAPHING EXPONENTIAL FUNCTIONS

*[10] Which of the following could be the equation for the graph at right?

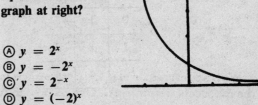

Ⓐ $y = 2^x$

Ⓑ $y = -2^x$

Ⓒ $y = 2^{-x}$

Ⓓ $y = (-2)^x$

Ⓔ $y = (-2)^{-x}$

An *exponential function* is a function of the form $\{(x, y): y = a^x\}$, *where a is any positive number except 1.* Its domain is the set of real numbers, and its range is the set of positive real numbers.

Two of the above answer selections define exponential functions, and we will discuss their graphs.

Ⓐ $y = 2^x$ is an exponential function for which $a = 2$. The domain of this function is defined to be the set of all real numbers, but we have not yet reviewed the meaning of irrational exponent.

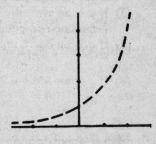

The graph at right shows the curve we might expect when the values of x are limited to the rationals and $y = 2^x$. The curve actually is not solid but, rather, full of holes. The holes are the points that have irrational first coordinates. The holes suggest a meaning for irrational exponents. We define the ordered pairs $(x, 2^x)$, where x is irrational, to be the coordinates of the points on the graph necessary to complete the curve. We rely heavily on your intuition, as we usually do in intermediate math, because a more rigorous approach necessitates the development of aspects of limit theory which are beyond the scope of this review.

Ⓑ By our definition, $y = -2^x$ is not an exponential function, but its graph is based on the graph in Ⓐ. The table on p. 182 shows the corresponding values of $y = -2^x$ and $y = 2^x$ and gives the information necessary to produce the graph shown.

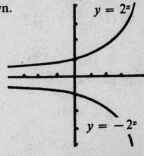

x	2^x	-2^x
-2	$\frac{1}{4}$	$-\frac{1}{4}$
-1	$\frac{1}{2}$	$-\frac{1}{2}$
0	1	-1
1	2	-2
2	4	-4

© $y = 2^{-x}$ does not, at first, appear to fit the definition of "exponential function," but recall that $2^{-x} = (2^{-1})^x$ by EX-3 (we have here made the assumption that the laws EX-1 through EX-5 hold for *all* reals). Thus we are dealing with $y = (\frac{1}{2})^x$, whose graph is the one given in the multiple-choice question.

Neither ⓓ nor ⓔ is an exponential function so we will not discuss them. Verify that neither could fit the given graph by taking some value such as $x = 1$ and showing that this does not yield a point on the curve. Try plotting these graphs by taking such sample values of x as 1, 2, 3, 4, $\frac{1}{2}$, and $\frac{1}{4}$ and note the complications that arise.

¶ DRILL Draw a graph of each of the following functions $(-2 \leq x \leq 2)$:

(a) $y = 3^x$ (b) $y = (\frac{1}{3})^x$

Use a full sheet of graph paper, and then find a rational approximation to $3^{\sqrt{2}}$ by intersecting the line $x = \sqrt{2}$ with the graph in (a).

*[11] Which of the following is NOT true?

ⓐ $(3^{\sqrt{3}})^{\sqrt{3}} = 27$ ⓑ $(10^{\sqrt{2}})(10^{\sqrt{2}}) = 100^{\sqrt{2}}$
© $(3^{1/\sqrt{2}})^{\sqrt{2}} = 3$ ⓓ $(9^{1/\sqrt{2}}) = 3^{\sqrt{2}}$ ⓔ $(\pi)^{\pi}$
$= 1$

We will agree that EX-1 through EX-5 as well as their accompanying definitions will be true for all real exponents.

ⓐ $(3^{\sqrt{3}})^{\sqrt{3}} = 3^3 = 27$ ⠀⠀ EX-3 and definition of $\sqrt{3}$

ⓑ $(10^{\sqrt{2}})(10^{\sqrt{2}})$
⠀⠀$= 10^{(\sqrt{2} + \sqrt{2})}$ ⠀⠀ EX-1
⠀⠀$= 10^{2\sqrt{2}}$
⠀⠀$= (10^2)^{\sqrt{2}}$ ⠀⠀ EX-3
⠀⠀$= 100^{\sqrt{2}}$

© $(3^{1/\sqrt{2}})^{\sqrt{2}}$
⠀⠀$= 3^{(1/\sqrt{2})\sqrt{2}}$ ⠀⠀ EX-3
⠀⠀$= 3$

ⓓ $9^{1/\sqrt{2}} = 9^{1/\sqrt{2} \cdot \sqrt{2}/\sqrt{2}}$
⠀⠀$= 9^{\sqrt{2}/2}$
⠀⠀$= (9^{1/2})^{\sqrt{2}}$ ⠀⠀ EX-3
⠀⠀$= 3^{\sqrt{2}}$

ⓔ We know that $\pi^0 = 1$ by Definition 2. π^{π} would equal 1 only if the exponent, π, equaled the exponent, 0. But $\pi = 3.14159\ldots \neq 0$.

¶ DRILL Simplify:

(a) $(4^{\sqrt{6}})^{-\sqrt{3}}$ (b) $(3^2)^{-3\sqrt{2}}$ (c) $\dfrac{10^{(2-2\sqrt{3})}}{100^{-\sqrt{3}}}$

RECOGNIZING THAT "LOGARITHM" AND "EXPONENT" ARE SYNONYMOUS

*[12] Which of the following is the inverse of $y = 2^x$?

ⓐ $y = (\frac{1}{2})^{-x}$ ⓑ $y = (\frac{1}{2})^x$ © $x = \log_2 y$
ⓓ $y = \log_2 x$ ⓔ $x = 2^{-y}$

We have defined an exponential function to be of the form

(1) $y = a^x; a > 0, a \neq 1$.

In Chapter 20 we discussed a simple procedure for finding the inverse of a function: interchange the range and domain variables. The inverse of $y = x^2$ is, therefore,

(2) $x = a^y; a > 0, a \neq 1$.

In defining functions we find it most expedient to express y in terms of x. No amount of algebraic manipulation, however, will allow us to do this with equation (2). To enable us to solve the inverse of an exponential function for y, we introduce the symbol *log* and make the following agreement:

(3) $\log_b N = m$ means $b^m = N$.

Applying (3) to equation (2), we get

(4) $y = \log_a x$.

Thus equations (1) and (4) define functions that are the inverses of each other.

The statement "$\log_b N = m$" is read "the logarithm to the base b of N is m." If you read this carefully, you will see that we are saying that m is a "logarithm." But m is also the exponent. Our agreement, then, is that the terms "logarithm" and "exponent" have the same meaning.

In summary: the table below is arranged so that the two statements in the same column are equivalent, whereas any two statements connected by line segments are inverses.

$$y = a^x \qquad\qquad x = a^y$$
$$x = \log_a y \qquad\qquad y = \log_a x$$

¶ DRILL For each of the following write (1) an equation that is equivalent, and (2) two different equations that define inverses:

(a) $y = 2^x$ (b) $y = (\frac{1}{2})^x$

(c) $y = \log_3 x$ (d) $y = \log_{1/3} x$

[13] Which of the following equations has 9 as a solution?

Ⓐ $\log_{10} (1 + y) = 2$ Ⓑ $\log_2 (3y - 5) = 3$
Ⓒ $\log_3 (1 + y)^2 = 2$ Ⓓ $x = 10^{\log_{10} 9}$
Ⓔ $x = \log_2 \sqrt{2}$

We have included this question to review the conversion from equations in exponential form to equations in logarithmic form. Do not fail to memorize the following statement (introduced in the preceding section):

$$\log_b N = m \text{ means } b^m = N.$$

Ⓐ $\log_{10} (1 + y) = 2$ means $10^2 = 1 + y$,
$$100 = 1 + y,$$
$$99 = y.$$

Ⓑ $\log_2 (3y - 5) = 3$ means $2^3 = 3y - 5$,
$$8 = 3y - 5,$$
$$13 = 3y,$$
$$\frac{13}{3} = y.$$

Ⓒ $\log_3 (1 + y)^2 = 2$ means $3^2 = (1 + y)^2$,
$$9 = y^2 + 2y + 1,$$
$$0 = y^2 + 2y - 8,$$
$$0 = (y + 4)(y - 2),$$
$$y = -4 \text{ or } y = 2.$$

Ⓓ $x = 10^{\log_{10} 9}$ means $\log_{10} x = \log_{10} 9$,
$$x = 9.$$

Ⓔ $x = \log_2 \sqrt{2}$ means $2^x = \sqrt{2}$,
$$2^x = 2^{1/2},$$
$$x = \frac{1}{2}.$$

¶ DRILL Solve:

(a) $\log_a 8 = 3$ (b) $\log_3 a = -2$

(c) $\log_3 \frac{1}{9} = a$ (d) $\log_a \frac{1}{4} = -\frac{1}{2}$

APPLYING EIGHT LAWS OF LOGARITHMS

[14] Which of the following is NOT true?

Ⓐ $\log 6 = \log 3 + \log 2$
Ⓑ $\log 12 - \log 2 = \log 6$
Ⓒ $\log 6 = (\log 3)(\log 2)$
Ⓓ $\log 6 = \log \frac{12}{2}$
Ⓔ $\log 6 = \frac{1}{2} \log 36$

As we have already reviewed, the terms "logarithm" and "exponent" are synonymous. It should be no surprise to discover that the laws of logarithms are the same as the laws of exponents. We will review two of them in this section and include their proofs as further practice in transformations of "log" and "exponential" notations.

LG-1 If $M > 0, N > 0, a > 0, a \neq 1$, then
$$\log_a (MN) = \log_a M + \log_a N.$$

PROOF

(1) Let $x = \log_a M$ and
$y = \log_a N$; then
(2) $a^x = M$ and $a^y = N$ Definition of log
(3) $MN = a^x a^y$
(4) $MN = a^{x+y}$ EX-1
(5) Therefore,
$\log_a (MN) = x + y$ Definition of log
(6) $\log_a (MN)$
$= \log_a M + \log_a N$ Substitution, step (1) in step (6)

LG-2 If $M > 0, N > 0, a > 0, a \neq 1$, then
$$\log_a \frac{M}{N} = \log_a M - \log_a N.$$

PROOF

(1) Let $y = \log_a M$ and
$x = \log_a N$; then
(2) $a^y = M$ and $a^x = N$ Definition of log
(3) $\frac{M}{N} = \frac{a^y}{a^x}$
(4) $\frac{M}{N} = a^{y-x}$ EX-2

Therefore, applying these laws to the answer choices in question [14], we get:

(5) $\log_a \frac{M}{N} = y - x$ Definition of log
(6) $\log_a \frac{M}{N}$
$= \log_a M - \log_a N$ Substitution, step (1) in step (6)

Ⓐ $\log 6$
$= \log (3 \times 2)$
$= \log 3 + \log 2$ LG-1

Ⓑ $\log 6$
$= \log (12 \div 2)$
$= \log 12 - \log 2$ LG-2

Ⓒ This statement contradicts what we just demonstrated for answer Ⓐ.

Ⓓ This is true since $\dfrac{12}{2} = 6$.

Ⓔ   log 36

$= \log (6 \times 6)$

$= \log 6 + \log 6$ LG-1

$= 2 \log 6$

$\dfrac{1}{2} \log 36 = \log 6$

¶ DRILL Use LG-1 and LG-2 to express each of the following as the logarithm of a single number:

(a) $\log_a 4 + \log_a 8$ (b) $\log_6 16 - \log_6 4$

(c) $2 \log_2 8 - \log_2 7$ (d) $\log_2 8 - \log_2 8$

[15] Which of the following is NOT equal to 1?

Ⓐ $\log_3 3$ Ⓑ $\log_{10} 10$ Ⓒ $\log_2 1$ Ⓓ $2^{\log_2 1}$

Ⓔ $3^{\log_4 1}$

LG-3   If $a > 0$, $a \neq 1$, then

$$\log_a a = 1.$$

PROOF

(1) $a^1 = a$ Definition 3

(2) $\log_a a = 1$ Definition of log

By LG-3 we can conclude that Ⓐ and Ⓑ are true.

LG-4   If $a > 0$, $a \neq 1$, then

$$\log_a 1 = 0.$$

PROOF

(1) Let $\log_a 1 = x$; then

(2) $a^x = 1$ Definition of log

(3) But $a^0 = 1$ Definition 2

(4) Thus $x = 0$ and $\log_a 1 = 0$

By LG-4 the logarithm of 1 is always zero regardless of the base of the logarithm—a consequence of this law is that the graph of every function $y = \log_a x$ contains the point $(1, 0)$.

From LG-4 we conclude that the expression in Ⓒ as well as the exponents in Ⓓ and Ⓔ must equal zero. We could now make our conclusion that Ⓓ and Ⓔ both equal 1 by Definition 2. We will, however, prove another law which relates to expressions of the type shown in Ⓓ.

LG-5   If $p > 0$, $p \neq 1$, then:

$$p^{\log_p q} = q.$$

PROOF

(1) Let $p^{\log_p q} = y$; then

(2) $\log_p y = \log_p q$ Definition of log

(3) $y = q$

(4) $p^{\log_p q} = q$ Substitution, step (1) in step (4).

¶ DRILL Simplify:

(a) $\log_2 4$ (Hint: let $\log_2 4 = \log_2 (2 \times 2)$.)

(b) $\log_e 1$ (c) $e^{\log_e e}$ (d) $16^{\log_4 2}$

[16] Which of the following is NOT true?

Ⓐ $\log_2 8 = 3$ Ⓑ $\log_3 81 = 4$

Ⓒ $\log_2 \left(\dfrac{1}{2}\right) = -1$ Ⓓ $-\log_3 \left(\dfrac{1}{3}\right) = \log_3 3$

Ⓔ $\log_{10} 3^{-1} = \dfrac{1}{3}$

Each of the above answer selections can be tested by the preceding laws of logs, but we will review two additional laws which are directly applicable.

LG-6   If a is a positive real number, $n \geq 0$ and $b > 0$ but $b \neq 1$, then

$$\log_b a^n = n \log_b a.$$

PROOF.   We will prove this law true for exponents that are integers, but accept it as true for all real values of n.

(1) $a^n = \underbrace{a \cdot a \cdot a \cdot a \cdot a \ldots a}_{n \text{ factors}}$ Definition 1

(2) $\log_b a^n$

$= \log_b \underbrace{(a \cdot a \cdot a \ldots a)}_{n \text{ factors}}$

(3) $= \underbrace{\log_b a + \log_b a + \ldots + \log_b a}_{n \text{ terms}}$ LG-1

(4) $= n \log_b a$

LG-7   If $a \geq 0$, $b > 0$, $b \neq 1$, then

$$\log_b \left(\dfrac{1}{a}\right) = -\log_b a.$$

PROOF

$$\log_b \left(\frac{1}{a}\right) = \log_b a^{-1}$$
$$= (-1) \log_b a \qquad \text{LG-6}$$
$$= -\log_b a$$

(A) $\log_2 8 = \log_2 2^3$
$$= 3 \log_2 2 \qquad \text{LG-6}$$
$$= 3 \qquad \text{LG-3}$$

(B) $\log_3 81 = \log_3 3^4$
$$= 4 \log_3 3 \qquad \text{LG-6}$$
$$= 4 \qquad \text{LG-3}$$

(C) $\log_2 \left(\frac{1}{2}\right) = -\log_2 2 \qquad \text{LG-7}$
$$= -1 \qquad \text{LG-3}$$

(D) $-\log_3 \left(\frac{1}{3}\right) = -(-\log_3 3) \qquad \text{LG-7}$
$$= \log_3 3$$
$$= 1 \qquad \text{LG-3}$$

(E) $\log_{10} 3^{-1} = \log_{10} \left(\frac{1}{3}\right)$

But $\log_{10} \left(\frac{1}{3}\right) \neq \frac{1}{3}$, since $\frac{1}{3} = \log_{10} 10^{1/3}$ by LG-5.

¶ DRILL Evaluate:

(a) $\log_2 \sqrt{8}$ (b) $\log_6 \left(\dfrac{36}{\sqrt{6}}\right)$

(c) $\log_5 \left(\dfrac{\sqrt[3]{5}}{125}\right)$ (d) $\log_3 3\sqrt{27}$

*[17] If $\log_3 x = 5$ and $\log_3 y = 2$, which of the following is $\log_y x$?

(A) 3   (B) $2\frac{1}{2}$ (C) $\frac{2}{5}$ (D) 10   (E) 7

It is sometimes useful to be able to express logarithms of one base as logarithms of a different base.

LG-8 If $a > 0$, $a \neq 1$, $b > 0$, $b \neq 1$, $N \geq 0$, then

$$\log_a N = \frac{\log_b N}{\log_b a}.$$

PROOF

(1) Let $y = \log_a N$; then
(2) $a^y = N$ Definition of log
(3) $\log_b a^y = \log_b N$
(4) $y \log_b a = \log_b N$ LG-6
(5) $y = \dfrac{\log_b N}{\log_b a}$
(6) $\log_a N = \dfrac{\log_b N}{\log_b a}$ Substitution, step (1) in step (6)

EXAMPLE

Show that $\log_3 5 = \dfrac{1}{\log_5 3}$.

SOLUTION: $\log_3 5 = \dfrac{\log_b 5}{\log_b 3}$ LG-8

Since the statement above will be true no matter what base is selected for b, let $b = 5$.

$$\log_3 5 = \frac{\log_5 5}{\log_5 3}$$
$$= \frac{1}{\log_5 3} \qquad \text{LG-3}$$

In the multiple-choice question,

$$\log_y x = \frac{\log_3 x}{\log_3 y} = \frac{5}{2}.$$

¶ DRILL Given $\log_{10} 3 = .4771$, $\log_{10} 2 = .3010$ and $\log_{10} 5 = .6990$, find the logs requested:

(a) $\log_2 3$ (b) $\log_3 2$ (c) $\log_5 6$ (d) $\log_2 15$

FINDING THE CHARACTERISTICS OF LOGARITHMS

[18] Which of the following has a characteristic of -2?

(A) $\log_{10} 150$ (B) $\log_{10} 15$ (C) $\log_{10} 1.5$
(D) $\log_{10} .15$ (E) $\log_{10} .015$

Every positive number, N, can be written in *scientific notation*. In other words, for all real positive N,

$$N = m \times 10^n,$$

where $1 \leq m \leq 10$ and n is an integer.

EXAMPLES

$$150 = 1.5 \times 10^2$$
$$15 = 1.5 \times 10^1$$
$$1.5 = 1.5 \times 10^0$$
$$.15 = 1.5 \times 10^{-1}$$
$$.015 = 1.5 \times 10^{-2}$$

Thus $\log_{10} N = \log_{10} (m \times 10^n)$
$$= \log_{10} m + \log_{10} 10^n$$
$$= \log_{10} m + n \log_{10} 10$$
$$= (\log_{10} m) + n$$

We have just demonstrated that the common logarithm of every positive N, $\log_{10} N$, can be expressed as the sum of an integer, n, and the common log of some number m between 1 and 10. The integer is called the *characteristic*, and the log of the number, m, is called the *mantissa*. Tables which give the mantissas of numbers between 1 and 10 are found in most intermediate math texts.

Therefore the exponents in the examples above are, in order, the characteristics of their logarithms. Use them to answer the multiple-choice question.

Every number in a table of mantissas involves a decimal point—this point is usually left out because its position is obvious. Each mantissa is the log of a number between 1 and 10 so is, itself, a number between 0 and 1 ($\log_{10} 1 = 0$, $\log_{10} 10 = 1$). The decimal point in a mantissa is, therefore, at the extreme left of the mantissa. Each mantissa is the log of a number between 1 and 10 so the decimal in this number is immediately to the right of the first digit, counting from the left.

EXAMPLE 1

A log table gives the mantissa 7536 for the sequence of digits 567. This means $\log_{10} 5.67 = .7536$.

No other rule for finding the characteristic of the logarithm of a number, N, is needed beyond that already described: put the number N in scientific notation and the characteristic is the exponent of the power of 10.

EXAMPLE 2

The characteristic of $\log_{10} 672.1$ is 2 since $\log_{10} 672.1 = \log_{10} (6.721 \times 10^2) = (\log_{10} 6.721) + 2$. The characteristic of $\log_{10} .00032$ is -4 since $\log_{10} .00032 = \log_{10} (3.2 \times 10^{-4}) = (\log_{10} 3.2) + (-4)$.

¶ DRILL Find the characteristic of each of the following:

(a) $\log_{10} .000057$ (b) $\log_{10} 7.23$
(c) $\log_{10} .708$ (d) $\log_{10} 4,678,000.02$

FINDING LOGS BY INTERPOLATION

[19] If $\log_{10} 604 = 2 + .7810$ and $\log_{10} 6.03 = .7803$, then which of the following is $\log_{10} 60.32$?

ⓐ 1.7803   ⓑ 1.7804   ⓒ 1.7805   ⓓ 1.7809
ⓔ 1.7810

Since the graph between two close points of $y = \log_a x$ differs only slightly from the line segment connecting them, we can approximate the coordinates of any point between them by the method of linear interpolation. As a review of this procedure we will find the log requested in the question above.

SOLUTION:

$$\log_{10} 60.32 = \log_{10} 6.032 + \log_{10} 10$$
$$= (\log_{10} 6.032) + 1$$

Thus we need to find $\log_{10} 6.032$ to answer the question. The given information will allow us to find $\log_{10} 6.030$ and $\log_{10} 6.040$, as explained below, both of which will be of value since $\log_{10} 6.032$ lies between them.

The given information yields $\log_{10} 6.03$ directly. It yields $\log_{10} 6.04 = .7810$ indirectly by the following reasoning:

$$\log_{10} 604 = \log_{10} 6.04 + \log_{10} 10^2$$
$$= (\log_{10} 6.04) + 2.$$

But we were given $\log_{10} 604 = .7810 + 2$ so $\log_{10} 6.04 = .7810$. Now that we have the two logs necessary to the question we can begin the process of linear interpolation.

Let x represent the difference between $\log_{10} 6.03$ and $\log_{10} 6.032$ and we set up our information in tabular form as below:

$$.010 \begin{cases} .002 \begin{cases} \log 6.040 = .7810 \\ \log 6.032 = .7803 + x \\ \log 6.030 = .7803 \end{cases} x \end{cases} .0007$$

The brackets represent the differences of the numbers indicated. To find x we set up the proportion.

$$\frac{.002}{.010} = \frac{x}{.0007}$$
$$\frac{2}{10} = \frac{x}{.0007}$$
$$.2 = \frac{x}{.0007}$$
$$.00014 = x$$

Since we cannot produce results more accurate than our given information and the given mantissas were accurate to only four decimal places, we round off x to .0001. Thus $\log_{10} 6.032 = .7804$ and $\log_{10} 60.32 = \log_{10} (6.032 \times 10^1) = 1 + .7804$.

¶ DRILL Given the following information, where all logs are base 10, interpolate to find the requested log:

(a) $\log_{10} 2.86 = .4564$, $\log_{10} 2.87 = .4579$, find $\log_{10} 2.865$
(b) $\log_{10} 45.1 = 1.6542$, $\log_{10} 45.2 = 1.6551$, find $\log_{10} 45.19$

*[20] If $\text{antilog}_{10} 8.2304 - 10 = .01700$, and $\text{antilog}_{10} 8.2279 - 10 = .01690$, which of the following is x if $\text{antilog}_{10} 8.2301 - 10 = x$?

ⓐ .01699   ⓑ .01700   ⓒ .01690   ⓓ .01689
ⓔ .01691

By definition,

$$\text{antilog}_b m = N \text{ means } \log_b N = m.$$

The information given above could have been written as follows:

$$\log_{10} .01700 = 8.2304 - 10,$$
$$\log_{10} .01690 = 8.2279 - 10.$$

The requested answer can be found by linear interpolation, but before doing this we will explain the form used for the characteristic. Historically, a major value of logarithms has been in rapid calculation, a role which computers and pocket calculators have usurped. To facilitate calculation, especially where a greater log must be subtracted from a lesser log, we replace a negative characteristic to maintain mantissa-characteristic pattern by $8 - 10$ for -2, $9 - 10$ for -1, $3 - 10$ for -7, etc. Thus ·

$$\log_{10} .01700 = 8.2304 - 10$$

is just another way of writing

$$\log_{10} .01700 = -2 + .2304.$$

To interpolate we let d represent the difference between antilog$_{10}$ $8.2301 - 10$ and antilog$_{10}$ $8.2279 - 10$ and set up our information in tabular form as:

$$0.0025 \left[0.0022 \left[\begin{array}{l} \text{antilog}_{10}\ 8.2304 - 10 = 0.01700 \\ \text{antilog}_{10}\ 8.2301 - 10 = 0.01690 + d \\ \text{antilog}_{10}\ 8.2279 - 10 = 0.01690 \end{array} \right] d \right] .00010$$

Again, the brackets represent the differences between the numbers indicated.

To find d we form the proportion

$$\frac{.0022}{.0025} = \frac{d}{.00010}$$

and compute d to be 0.00009. Hence

$$\text{antilog}_{10}\ 8.2301 - 10 = .01690 + .00009.$$

¶ DRILL Given the following information, find the antilog requested:

(a) antilog$_{10}$ .9058 = 8.05, antilog$_{10}$ .9063 = 8.06; find antilog$_{10}$ .9060
(b) antilog$_{10}$ 1.7324 = 54.0, antilog$_{10}$ 1.7332 = 54.1; find antilog$_{10}$ 1.7327

WHAT YOU SHOULD KNOW

KEY CONCEPTS

Handling Exponents

If a, b, m and n are real numbers, then:

a. $a^m \cdot a^n = a^{m+n}$,

b. $\dfrac{a^m}{a^n} = a^{m-n}$,

c. $(a^m)^n = a^{mn}$,

d. $(ab)^m = a^m b^m$,

e. $a^{-m} = \dfrac{1}{a^m}$,

f. $\left(\dfrac{a}{b}\right)^m = \dfrac{a^m}{b^m}$,

g. $a^{1/n} = \sqrt[n]{a}$, and

h. $a^{m/n} = \sqrt[n]{a^m} = (\sqrt[n]{a})^m$, $a > 0$.

Handling Logarithms

If $M > 0$, $N > 0$, $b > 0$, $b \neq 1$, $a > 0$ and $a \neq 1$, then:

a. $\log_b (MN) = \log_b M + \log_b N$,

b. $\log_b \left(\dfrac{M}{N}\right) = \log_b M - \log_b N$,

c. $\log_b N^x = x \log_b N$,

d. $\log_b b = 1$,

e. $\log_b 1 = 0$,

f. $\log_b \left(\dfrac{1}{N}\right) = -\log_b N$, and

g. $\log_b N = \dfrac{\log_a N}{\log_a b}$.

KEY STATEMENT

To convert an equation in exponential form to an equation in logarithmic form: If $N = b^m$, then $\log_b N = m$.

TEST-TAKING STRATEGIES

- Keep in mind that the terms "logarithm" and "exponent" are synonymous, and that the laws of logarithms are the same as the laws of exponents.
- Knowing the laws of exponents is critical to working successfully and quickly with exponential expressions. However, when exponents are numerals, you can often check your work by going back to the two very simplest principles. These are a^m means a is used as a factor m times and $a^{-m} = 1/a^m$. These allow you to write out the expressions as a succession of factors, thereby working with elementary algebraic principles. The method can be laborious, but remember that it also suggests a result when no other idea occurs to you.

ANSWERS

[1] Ⓔ
DRILL:
(a) y^6 (b) a^{2n+1}
(c) x^{a+b} (d) a^{2x}
(e) y^{2n} (f) x^{2m}

[2] Ⓓ

DRILL:

(a) x^9 (b) y^{2n-1}

(c) 2^4 (d) $6m^2n$

(e) $\dfrac{3x^4}{2}$ (f) $(y-4)^2$

[3] Ⓐ

DRILL:

(a) b^{10} (b) b^{4p}

(c) c^{12} (d) d^{pq}

(e) $-2^6 = -64$ (f) r^{s^2+s}

[4] Ⓒ

DRILL:

(a) $24x^5$

(b) $9x^8$

(c) $2y$

(d) $\dfrac{x^{8p}}{4}$

(e) $\dfrac{x^3y^6}{27}$

(f) $\left(\dfrac{1}{x} + 2y\right)^{-1} = \left(\dfrac{1+2xy}{x}\right)^{-1}$
$$= \dfrac{x}{1+2xy}$$

[5] Ⓓ

DRILL:

(a) $\dfrac{27x^6}{y^3}$ (b) $\dfrac{8}{27}$

(c) $\dfrac{x^3}{y^6}$ (d) $\dfrac{z^2}{x^4y^2}$

[6] Ⓒ

[7] Ⓔ

DRILL:

(a) 6   (b) $20\sqrt{2}$

[8] Ⓐ

DRILL:

(a) $7(\sqrt[3]{7})^2$ (b) 2

(c) 81   (d) $\sqrt{21}$

(e) a (f) $5\sqrt{3}$

[9] Ⓑ

DRILL:

(a) $\dfrac{3}{5a^2b}$ (b) a

(c) $\dfrac{1}{16}$ (d) $\dfrac{y-x}{xy}$ or $\dfrac{1}{x} - \dfrac{1}{y}$

[10] Ⓒ

DRILL:

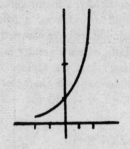 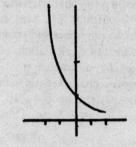

$y = 3^x; \; -2 \le x \le 2$ $y = \left(\dfrac{1}{3}\right)^x; \; -2 \le x \le 2$

Thus $3^{\sqrt{2}} = 4.7$

[11] Ⓔ

DRILL:

(a) $\dfrac{1}{4^{3\sqrt{2}}}$ or $\dfrac{1}{64^{\sqrt{2}}}$ (b) $\dfrac{1}{3^{6\sqrt{2}}}$ or $\dfrac{1}{729^{\sqrt{2}}}$

(c) 100

[12] Ⓓ

DRILL:

(a) $x = \log_2 y; \; y = \log_2 x, \; x = 2^y.$

(b) $x = \log_{1/2} y; \; y = \log_{1/2} x, \; \left(\dfrac{1}{2}\right)^y = x.$

(c) $3^y = x; \; y = 3^x, \; x = \log_3 y.$

(d) $x = \left(\dfrac{1}{3}\right)^y; \; y = \left(\dfrac{1}{3}\right)^x, \; x = \log_{1/3} y.$

[13] Ⓓ

DRILL:

(a) $a = 2$ (b) $a = \dfrac{1}{9}$

(c) $a = -2$ (d) $a = 16$

[14] Ⓒ

DRILL:

(a) $\log_a 32$ (b) $\log_6 4$

(c) $\log_2 \dfrac{64}{7}$ (d) $\log_2 1 = 0$

[15] Ⓒ

DRILL:

(a) 2   (b) 0

(c) e (d) 4

[16] Ⓔ

DRILL:

(a) $\dfrac{3}{2}$ (b) $\dfrac{5}{3}$

(c) $-\dfrac{8}{3}$ (d) $\dfrac{5}{2}$

[17] Ⓑ
DRILL:
(a) $\dfrac{.4771}{.3010}$ (b) $\dfrac{.3010}{.4771}$

(c) $\dfrac{.4771 + .3010}{.6990}$ (d) $\dfrac{.4771 + .6990}{.3010}$

[18] Ⓔ
DRILL:
(a) -5 (b) 0
(c) -1 (d) 6

[19] Ⓑ
DRILL:
(a) .4572   (b) 1.6550

[20] Ⓐ
DRILL:
(a) 8.054   (b) 54.04

24. Trigonometry

> In this chapter, some of the topics are more typical of those tested on the Mathematics Level II test than of those on the Level I test. We have denoted these with an asterisk (*). Review of such topics may assist you in answering Level I questions, however, because it increases your general knowledge of mathematical ideas, methods and skills.

Key Terms

angle   the union of two noncollinear rays (the *initial* and the *terminal* rays) that have a common endpoint with its degree measure defined as a number between 0 and 180.

degree measure   the number of degrees of rotation through which the initial ray would have to be turned to coincide with the terminal ray. The degree measure may be any real number.

straight angle   an angle with the degree measure of 180, formed when two rays lie on the same line but point in opposite directions.

angle in standard position   an angle that has its vertex at the origin and its initial side coincident with the positive ray of the *x*-axis.

reference angle   the smallest nonnegative angle between the terminal side of a given angle in standard position and the *x*-axis.

DEFINING TRIGONOMETRIC ANGLES AND THEIR MEASURES

[1] Which of the following statements is NOT true?

(A) The term "angle" is defined the same way in geometry as it is in trigonometry. (B) In trigonometry an angle has an initial ray and a terminal ray. (C) The measure of an angle in trigonometry is not unique. (D) The measure of an angle in trigonometry may be either positive or negative. (E) The measure of an angle in trigonometry can be zero.

In geometry we define an *angle* to be the union of two noncollinear rays which have a common endpoint (Chapter 11) with its degree measure defined as a number between 0 and 180. Such an interpretation simplifies the description of angles used in triangles and other plane figures. In trigonometry the definition is extended with the designation of one of the rays as the "initial" ray and the other as the "terminal" ray. The *degree measure* is then defined as the number of degrees of rotation through which the initial ray would have to be turned to coincide with the terminal ray. If this rotation is counterclockwise, the measure is positive. If the rotation is clockwise, the measure is negative. There are times when it is valuable to consider the two rays as coincident; in such cases the measure is defined as zero. If the two rays lie on the same line but point in opposite directions (forming "opposite rays"), the angle thus formed is termed a *straight angle* and has a degree measure of 180.

Considered in these terms, an angle has an infinite set of possible measures since the rotation of the terminal ray may be either positive or negative and is not even restricted to a single revolution. The figures below show three possible measures for the same angle:

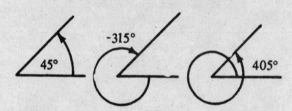

If these ambiguities were allowed in geometry, the subject would become considerably more complex through the necessity for quantifiers to indicate just what measure is intended. In this chapter "angle" will mean angle of trigonometry.

¶ DRILL Match up the following six angles into pairs which are coterminal (having the same terminal and initial rays):

(a) 74°   (b) −8°   (c) 352°
(d) 794°   (e) 434°   (f) −286°

FINDING THE RADIAN MEASURES OF ANGLES

[2] Which of the following is the radian measure of an angle whose degree measure is 135?

(A) $-\dfrac{\pi}{4}$ (B) $\dfrac{\pi}{4}$ (C) $\dfrac{3\pi}{4}$ (D) $\dfrac{3}{4}$ (E) $-\dfrac{3\pi}{4}$

Though the degree measure of an angle is useful, it is often more valuable to use a measure defined in terms of arc length. If an angle is a central angle of a circle of radius 1 unit (termed a "unit" circle), and the arc which it cuts off is also of length 1 unit, the measure of the angle is 1 *radian*. Since the circumference of this unit circle is 2π, such an arc (of length 1) can be laid off 2π times on the circle. In other words, a measure of 360° is equivalent to a measure of 2π radians, or

(1) π radians $= 180°$.

This yields the two equations most useful in converting from one unit to the other. Dividing both sides of (1) by π produces

(2) 1 radian $= \left(\dfrac{180}{\pi}\right)°.$

Dividing both sides of (1) by 180 produces

(3) $\dfrac{\pi}{180}$ radians $= 1°.$

To convert from radians to degrees, multiply the given number of radians times both sides of (2) and then simplify. To convert from degrees to radians, multiply the given number of degrees times both sides of (3) and then simplify.

Since $1° = \dfrac{\pi}{180}$ radians, it follows that

$$135(1°) = 135\left(\dfrac{\pi}{180}\right) \text{ radians,}$$

$$135° = 3(45)\left(\dfrac{\pi}{4(45)}\right) \text{ radians}$$

$$= \dfrac{3\,\pi}{4} \text{ radians.}$$

¶ DRILL Convert each of the following from radians to degrees or from degrees to radians:

(a) 5 radians (b) 60° (c) $\dfrac{\pi}{2}$ radians (d) $\left(\dfrac{\pi}{2}\right)°$

[3] If a central angle of a circle of radius 4 cuts off an arc of length 8, what is the radian measure of the angle?

Ⓐ 2π Ⓑ 2 Ⓒ 8 Ⓓ 4 Ⓔ 8π

As we have noted, the radian measure of an angle is determined by the length of the arc it cuts off on a unit circle. A theorem from geometry (Chapter 17, section [20]), however, states that arcs subtending central angles which have the same measure are in the same ratio as are their radii. Thus, if s and r are the respective lengths of arc and radius of one circle and s' and r' are the lengths of arc and radius of another circle, then

$$\frac{s}{r} = \frac{s'}{r'},$$

when the defining central angles have the same measure. In the unit circle where $r' = 1$ and $s' = \theta$ in radians, we get

$$\frac{s}{r} = \frac{\theta}{1}.$$

In short we can find the radian measure of an angle by dividing the subtended arc length by the radius. The latter formula may be used, of course, to find either the arc length or the radius of the circle when the other two of $\{s, r, \theta\}$ are known.

If $r = 4$ and $s = 8$, then

$$\theta = \frac{s}{r} = \frac{8}{4} = 2 \text{ radians.}$$

¶ DRILL Find the radian measure of the angle that subtends arc s on a circle of radius r:

(a) $s = 4, r = 5$ (b) $s = 2\pi, r = 2$
(c) $s = \pi, r = 1$

Now find the arc length of

(d) $\theta = \dfrac{\pi}{2}$ and $r = 2$

[4] If an angle is in standard position and the point $(-1, 0)$ is a point on the terminal side, in what quadrant does the terminal side lie?

Ⓐ I Ⓑ II Ⓒ III Ⓓ IV Ⓔ None of these

You will recall from geometry that a line separates the plane into two sets called "sides" or "half-planes" and the line does not belong to either of the sides. The coordinate axes are a pair of perpendicular lines that separate the plane into four regions called *quadrants*, and no point of either axis belongs to any quadrant.

An angle in *standard position* is one that has its vertex at the origin and its initial side coincident with the positive ray of the x-axis. The angle is said to *lie* in the quadrant through which the terminal ray passes, even though the interior of the angle may contain points of several quadrants. Two angles in standard position are referred to as *coterminal* when they have the same terminal side. Any angle which is coterminal with either ray of either axis does not lie in any quadrant and is called a *quadrantal angle*.

Since the point $(-1, 0)$ is on the negative ray of the x-axis, the angle defined is a quadrantal angle and does not lie in any quadrant.

¶ DRILL Given the following points to be on the terminal sides of angles in standard position, indicate in which quadrants the angles lie:

(a) $(-4, 3)$ (b) $(5, 1)$ (c) $(-2, -5)$ (d) $(0, 0)$

[5] If an angle has a radian measure of $\frac{5\pi}{4}$, what is the radian measure of its reference angle?

(A) $\frac{5\pi}{4}$ (B) $-\frac{5\pi}{4}$ (C) $\frac{3\pi}{4}$ (D) $\frac{\pi}{4}$ (E) $-\frac{\pi}{4}$

As we will see later, the concept of "reference angle" is useful in cutting down the size of trigonometric tables. Every angle in standard position has a *reference* angle (except for the quadrantal angles) which is defined to be the smallest nonnegative angle between the terminal side of the given angle and the x-axis. The ray of the x-axis you choose is the one which yields the smaller nonnegative angle.

The angle $\frac{5\pi}{4}$ terminates in the third quadrant, as you can see from the fact that $\frac{4\pi}{4}$ terminates on the negative ray of the x-axis. The angle formed by the negative ray of the x-axis and $\frac{5\pi}{4}$ is $\frac{\pi}{4}$.

¶ DRILL For each of the following, draw the angle in standard position and then find its reference angle:

(a) 45°   (b) 160°   (c) $-\frac{\pi}{3}$ radians   (d) $\frac{7\pi}{2}$ radians

FINDING THE COORDINATES OF A POINT ON THE TERMINAL SIDE

[6] If the x-coordinate of a point is −3 and its distance from the origin is 5, then its y-coordinate is?

(A) 4 or −4   (B) 4   (C) −4   (D) $\sqrt{34}$ (E) $\sqrt{34}$ or $-\sqrt{34}$

As noted in Chapter 18 on coordinate geometry, the absolute value of a coordinate of a point is the distance from that point to an axis. If a point $P(x, y)$ is r units from the origin, then the line segment from P to the x-axis completes a right triangle whose sides have length $|x|, |y|$ and r. Note that r, a distance, is always positive.

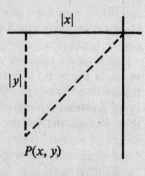

The Pythagorean Theorem yields

(1) $|x|^2 + |y|^2 = r^2$.

Since $|x| = x$ when $x \geq 0$ and $-x$ when $x < 0$ and since both of $(x)^2$ and $(-x)^2$ are equal to x^2, we rewrite (1) as

(2) $x^2 + y^2 = r^2$.

When two elements of $\{x, y, r\}$ are given, the other can be found by substituting for the known variables and solving for the third in (2). Whenever r is given with either x or y, the equation yields two values for the third unknown.

EXAMPLE

If $y = 2$ and $r = 3$, find x.

SOLUTION: $\quad x^2 + (2)^2 = (3)^2$
$$x^2 = 5$$
$$x = \pm\sqrt{5}$$

This would indicate that two different angles satisfy the given conditions as in the figure below for which $y = 2$, $r = 3$. When x and y are given, however, only one value is meaningful for r.

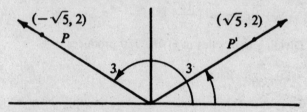

In the multiple-choice question, $x = -3$ and $r = 5$. Then:

$$x^2 + y^2 = r^2,$$
$$(-3)^2 + y^2 = 5^2,$$
$$9 + y^2 = 25,$$
$$y^2 = 16,$$
$$y = \pm 4.$$

¶ DRILL From the following given information about $\{x, y, r\}$ find the value of the missing coordinate or distance:

(a) $x = -2$, $y = 4$ (b) $y = 7$, $r = 13$
(c) $x = \sqrt{5}$, $r = \sqrt{7}$

WORKING WITH TRIGONOMETRIC FUNCTIONS

[7] If the terminal side of θ contains the point (3, 7) which of the following is NOT true?

(A) $\sin \theta = \frac{7}{\sqrt{58}}$ (B) $\cos \theta = \frac{3}{\sqrt{58}}$ (C) $\tan \theta = \frac{7}{3}$ (D) $\cot \theta = \frac{3}{7}$ (E) $\sec \theta = \frac{\sqrt{58}}{7}$

The trigonometric functions of an angle in standard position are defined as follows.

If $P(x, y)$ is a point on the terminal side of an angle θ and is r units from the origin $(r \neq 0)$ then:

$$\sin \theta = \frac{y}{r}, \quad \cos \theta = \frac{x}{r}, \quad \tan \theta = \frac{y}{x},$$
$$\csc \theta = \frac{r}{y}, \quad \sec \theta = \frac{r}{x}, \quad \cot \theta = \frac{x}{y}.$$

You may verify for yourself (using similar triangles) that the values of the functions do not depend on the point of the terminal side that is chosen. For a given angle, any point on the terminal side (other than the origin) will yield the same values for the trig functions of that angle as any other point on the terminal side.

The term "function" is used here properly since the sets of ordered pairs of the form $(\theta, \sin\theta)$, $(\theta, \cos\theta)$, etc., satisfy the definition of function. Note also that any two angles which are coterminal must have the same values for their trig functions, since their terminal sides contain exactly the same points. Thus $\sin 45° = \sin 405°$ and $\cos(-120°) = \cos 240°$.

To apply the definition of the trigonometric functions to the multiple-choice question, we must first find r. We are given $(x, y) = (3, 7)$. Then:

$$x^2 + y^2 = r^2,$$
$$9 + 49 = r^2,$$
$$58 = r^2,$$
$$\sqrt{58} = r.$$

Using $x = 3, y = 7, r = \sqrt{58}$ and the formulas for $\sin\theta$, $\cos\theta$, $\tan\theta$, $\cot\theta$ and $\sec\theta$, we see that

$$\sec\theta = \frac{\sqrt{58}}{3},$$

which disagrees with answer ⓔ, while all of the others agree with the corresponding choices.

¶ DRILL If each of the following is a point on the terminal side of an angle in standard position, find the value of the requested function:

(a) $(3, -2)$; $\sin\theta = ?$
(b) $(-\sqrt{2}, 4)$; $\csc\theta = ?$
(c) $(-4, -2)$; $\tan\theta = ?$

[8] $\triangle ABC$ is a right triangle with right angle at B. Find the cotangent of $\angle C$.

Ⓐ $\dfrac{1}{2}$ Ⓑ 2 Ⓒ $\sqrt{3}$

Ⓓ $\dfrac{2}{\sqrt{3}}$ Ⓔ $\dfrac{\sqrt{3}}{2}$

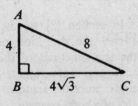

Two of the angles of a right triangle must be acute. If we position a right triangle in the coordinate plane so that one of the acute angles is in standard position, this angle will lie in the first quadrant. The lengths of the legs of the triangle tell us the coordinates of a point

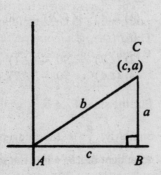

on the terminal side and the hypotenuse indicates the distance of this point from the origin. Using the trig function definitions from section [7], we can derive the following equations relating the trig functions of the acute angles of a right triangle to the lengths of the sides of the triangle:

If θ is an angle of a right triangle, then:

$$\sin\theta = \frac{\text{opposite leg}}{\text{hypotenuse}}, \quad \cos\theta = \frac{\text{adjacent leg}}{\text{hypotenuse}},$$
$$\tan\theta = \frac{\text{opposite leg}}{\text{adjacent leg}}, \quad \cot\theta = \frac{\text{adjacent leg}}{\text{opposite leg}},$$
$$\csc\theta = \frac{\text{hypotenuse}}{\text{opposite leg}}, \quad \sec\theta = \frac{\text{hypotenuse}}{\text{adjacent leg}}.$$

From the above equations we can find the values of the trig functions of the angles of a right triangle without using the coordinate plane definitions.

In the multiple-choice question, the adjacent leg for $\angle C$ is $BC = 4\sqrt{3}$, and the opposite leg is $AB = 4$. Therefore:

$$\cot\angle C = \frac{\text{adjacent leg}}{\text{opposite leg}}$$
$$= \frac{BC}{AB}$$
$$= \frac{4\sqrt{3}}{4}$$
$$= \sqrt{3}.$$

¶ DRILL In a right triangle, $\triangle ABC$ with right angle at C, if $AB = \sqrt{17}$, $AC = 4$ and $BC = 1$, find $\sin\angle B$, $\tan\angle A$ and $\cot\angle B$.

[9] If $\cos\theta = -\dfrac{1}{2}$ and $0 \le \theta < 360°$, then the set of possible values for θ is:

Ⓐ $\{60°, 300°\}$ Ⓑ $\{210°, 330°\}$ Ⓒ $\{240°, 300°\}$
Ⓓ $\{120°, 240°\}$ Ⓔ $\{135°, 225°\}$

It is possible to use the definitions of the trig functions to discover the sets of angles that have trig functions of a given value.

EXAMPLE 1

If $\sin\theta = \dfrac{\sqrt{3}}{2}$ and $0 \le \theta < 2\pi$, find θ.

SOLUTION: We conclude from the definition of sine that

$$(1)\; \frac{y}{r} = \frac{\sqrt{3}}{2}.$$

This, of course, does *not* mean that y must be $\sqrt{3}$ and r must be 2. As a matter of fact, *any* two numbers whose ratio is $\sqrt{3}{:}2$ will satisfy equation (1). Indeed, we may choose any value for r that we please since any point on the terminal side—whatever its distance, r, from the origin—will produce the same values for the trig functions as any other point. Once we have selected our arbitrary value for r, equation (1) tells us the value of y and $x^2 + y^2 = r^2$ yields the value of x.

For simplicity we let $r = 2$; then $y = \sqrt{3}$ and

(2) $x^2 + (\sqrt{3})^2 = 4$,

(3) $x^2 = 1$,

(4) $x = \pm 1$.

The points $P(1, \sqrt{3})$ and $P'(-1, \sqrt{3})$ lie on the terminal sides of angles which satisfy the given information, as shown below:

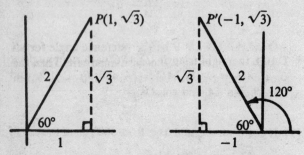

By dropping perpendiculars to the x-axis from points P and P', we form triangles with sides having the familiar ratios of the special 30–60–90 triangles (Chapter 17, section [15]):

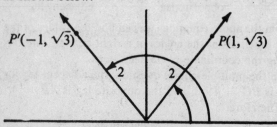

The angles between 0 and 2π, then, which satisfy the given information are 60° and 120°.

EXAMPLE 2

If $\tan \theta = -1$ and $\cos \theta > 0$, find θ.

SOLUTION: By definition of tan,

(5) $\dfrac{y}{x} = -1$.

Any pair of numbers in this ratio will yield a point on the terminal side so we can find such a point by an arbitrary selection for x, with the restriction that x be positive since we were given $\cos \theta > 0$. Let $x = 1$; then $y = -1$ and

(6) $x^2 + y^2 = r^2$, so

(7) $(1)^2 + (-1)^2 = r^2$, and

(8) $\sqrt{2} = r$.

From the figure and the special 45-45-90 triangle relationships (Chapter 17, section [14]) we see that θ is any angle coterminal with 315°

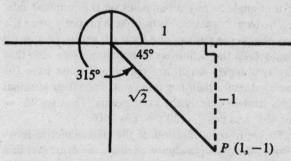

¶ DRILL Find all values of θ between 0 and 2π which satisfy:

(a) $\sec \theta = -2$ (b) $\sin \theta = \dfrac{\sqrt{2}}{2}$

(c) $\tan \theta = \dfrac{\sqrt{3}}{3}$

In the multiple-choice question, $\cos \theta$ is negative so θ represents angles terminating in quadrants II and III. From the 30–60–90 triangle, we see that $\theta = 60°$ gives a cosine of $\dfrac{1}{2}$. The angles in quadrants II and III with reference angle of 60 are

$180 - 60 = 120$ and $180 + 60 = 240$.

USING COFUNCTIONS

[10] If $\cot \theta = \tan 15°$, then $\theta = $?

Ⓐ 65° Ⓑ 75° Ⓒ 15° Ⓓ −15° Ⓔ None of these

In section [8] we discussed the definition of the trig functions of the acute angles of a right triangle. Since the acute angles of a right triangle are complementary, we can state for the triangle at right that

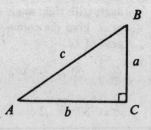

(1) $(\angle A)° + (\angle B)° = 90$.

Thus

(2) $(\angle B)° = 90 - (\angle A)°$ and

(3) $(\angle A)° = 90 - (\angle B)°$.

But the sine of $\angle A$ is $\dfrac{a}{c}$, which is also the cosine of $\angle B$.

Similarly, $\dfrac{a}{b}$ is the tangent of $\angle A$ as well as the cotangent of $\angle B$, while the secant of $\angle A$ is the cosecant of $\angle B$. Thus, if two angles, $\angle A$ and $\angle B$, are complementary, then

$$\sin \angle A = \cos \angle B,$$
$$\tan \angle A = \cot \angle B,$$
$$\sec \angle A = \csc \angle B.$$

Substituting the relations of (2) and (3) in each of the above produces

$$\sin \angle A = \cos (90 - \angle A),$$
$$\tan \angle A = \cot (90 - \angle A),$$
$$\sec \angle A = \csc (90 - \angle A).$$

We call the sine and cosine, tangent and cotangent, secant and cosecant, "cofunctions." Indeed, the prefix "co" serves to remind us of the complementary nature of the sine-cosine, etc., relationships.

In the multiple-choice question,

$$\cot \theta = \tan (90 - \theta) = \tan 15°.$$

Therefore:

$$90 - \theta = 15,$$
$$-\theta = -75,$$
$$\theta = 75.$$

¶ DRILL Express each of the following as a cofunction of a complementary angle:

(a) $\sin 45°$ (b) $\tan 13°$ (c) $\csc 53°$ (d) $\cot 42°$

USING REFERENCE ANGLES

[11] **Which of the following is (are) true?**

   I $\sin 45° = \sin 135°$

   II $\cos 83° = -\cos 263°$

   III $\tan 16° = -\tan 344°$

   Ⓐ I only   Ⓑ II only   Ⓒ I, II and III   Ⓓ I and II only   Ⓔ None

In section [5] we defined the term "reference" angle. We will now show how to express any trigonometric function of an angle as the same function of its reference angle. We will attack the task one quadrant at a time.

Quadrant I The reference angle of every first quadrant angle is the angle itself. Thus the functions of the angles are the same as the functions of the reference angles.

Quadrant II The reference angle of an angle, θ, in the second quadrant has measure $180 - \theta$. In the figure at upper right we constructed both θ and the angle in the first quadrant with measure $180 - \theta$. On the terminal sides we selected points P and P' to be r units from the origin and have dropped perpendiculars from these points to the x-axis. The two triangles thus formed are congruent by *SAA* and thus the pairs of corresponding legs must have the same length. Since we have chosen the

lengths of the corresponding legs to be a and b, the point P is $(-a, b)$ and P' is (a, b).

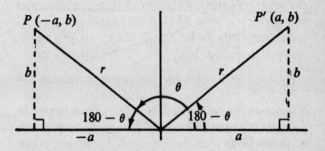

We draw the following conclusions from the figure:

(1) $\sin \theta = \dfrac{b}{r}$ and $\sin (180 - \theta) = \dfrac{b}{r}$,

   so $\sin \theta = \sin (180 - \theta)$;

(2) $\cos \theta = \dfrac{a}{r}$ and $\cos (180 - \theta) = \dfrac{-a}{r}$,

   so $\cos \theta = -\cos (180 - \theta)$;

(3) $\tan \theta = \dfrac{b}{a}$ and $\tan (180 - \theta) = \dfrac{-b}{a}$,

   so $\tan \theta = -\tan (180 - \theta)$.

Quadrant III Let θ be the reference angle for an angle terminating in the third quadrant. Then the angle itself can be designated as $180 + \theta$. From the figure below we see that

(4) $\sin \theta = -\sin (180 + \theta)$,

(5) $\cos \theta = -\cos (180 + \theta)$,

(6) $\tan \theta = \tan (180 + \theta)$.

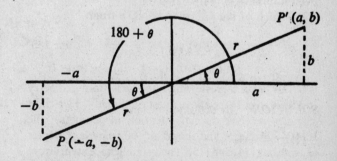

Quadrant IV Let θ be the reference angle for an angle terminating in the fourth quadrant. Then the angle itself can be designated as $360 - \theta$. From the figure on p. 194 we see that

(7) $\sin \theta = -\sin (360 - \theta)$,

(8) $\cos \theta = \cos (360 - \theta)$,

(9) $\tan \theta = -\tan (360 - \theta)$.

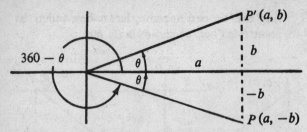

There is little value in memorizing equations (1) through (9). You should, instead, make a sketch of the given angle and its reference angle as positioned in quadrant I. Then compare the signs of the coordinates of the points at some fixed distance r from the origin on the terminal sides of both angles—the absolute values of these coordinates will not differ, of course. The relationship between the signs will be the desired relationship between the function of the angle and its reference angle.

¶ DRILL Express each of the following as the same function of its reference angle:

(a) sin 340°   (b) cos 192°
(c) csc 92°   (d) sec 270°

In the multiple-choice question,

I. The reference angle for 135 is 45, and 135 is in quadrant II, where sine is positive. Therefore sin 45 = sin 135.

II. The reference angle for 263 is 263 − 180 = 83, and 263 is in quadrant III, where cosine is negative. Therefore cos 83 = −cos 263.

III. The reference angle for 344 is 360 − 344 = 16, and 344 is in quadrant IV, where tangent is negative. Therefore tan 16 = − tan 344.

Hence all are true.

USING SPECIAL TRIANGLES

[12] Which of the following is NOT true?

Ⓐ $\sin \dfrac{\pi}{6} = \dfrac{1}{2}$ Ⓑ $\cos 45° = \dfrac{\sqrt{2}}{2}$ Ⓒ $\tan 135°$
$= -1$ Ⓓ $\sin 270° = -1$ Ⓔ $\cos 0° = 0$

Let us begin by reviewing some facts from geometry and then answer the above question directly. Two right triangles received special attention in geometry: the 30–60–90 triangle and the 45–45–90 triangle (Chapter 17, sections [14] and [15]. Their significance stems from the simple ratios of their sides. If you cannot remember the ratios, you will do well to review the sections of Chapter 17 just mentioned.

From the special triangles it is possible to determine the trig functions of angles of 30°, 45°, 60° and, through the application of the techniques of section [11], any other angles that have 30°, 45° or 60° as reference angles. We will use the answer selections above as examples.

Ⓐ Since $\dfrac{\pi}{6}$ radians = 30°,

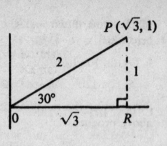

$\sin \dfrac{\pi}{6} = \sin 30°$. Since we are interested in a method which is as general as possible, we will construct a 30° angle in standard position and then select a point P on the terminal side such that $OP = 2$. (P may be any point on the terminal side so we have selected a point which will simplify our calculations.) If segment PR is perpendicular to the x-axis, then $PR = 1$, and $OR = \sqrt{3}$ by the 30–60–90 triangle ratios. Thus the coordinates of P are $(\sqrt{3}, 1)$ and $\sin \dfrac{\pi}{6} = \dfrac{1}{2}$.

Ⓑ Construct a 45° angle in standard position and choose a point P such that $OP = 1$ (another reminder that P may be any point on the terminal side and we have selected $OP = 1$ merely for simplicity). Then, if PR is perpendicular to the x-axis, $PR = \dfrac{\sqrt{2}}{2}$ and $OR = \dfrac{\sqrt{2}}{2}$ by the 45-45-90

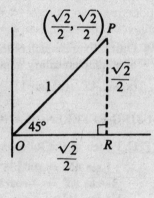

triangle ratios. Thus the coordinates of P are $\left(\dfrac{\sqrt{2}}{2}, \dfrac{\sqrt{2}}{2}\right)$ and $\cos 45° = \dfrac{\sqrt{2}}{2}$.

Ⓒ Construct an angle of 135° in standard position and choose a point P on the terminal side such that $OP = 1$. Then $PR = \dfrac{\sqrt{2}}{2}$ and $OR = \dfrac{\sqrt{2}}{2}$. But the x-coordinate of any point in Quadrant II is negative so $P = \left(-\dfrac{\sqrt{2}}{2}, \dfrac{\sqrt{2}}{2}\right)$ and

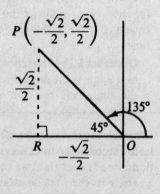

$$\tan 135° = \dfrac{\sqrt{2}/2}{-\sqrt{2}/2} = -1.$$

Ⓓ An angle of 270° is coterminal with the negative ray of the y-axis. Select $OP = 1$. Then $P = (0, -1)$ and $\sin 270° = -1$.

Ⓔ 0° is coterminal with the positive ray of the x-axis. Select $OP = 1$. Then $P = (1, 0)$ and cos 0° = 1.

¶ DRILL Find the following values:

(a) cos 120°   (b) sec 330°   (c) tan 180°

USING IDENTITIES

[13] Which of the following statements is NOT true for all values of the variable for which the function is defined?

Ⓐ $\cos^2 \theta + \sin^2 \theta = 1$
Ⓑ $\sec^2 \theta = 1 - \tan^2 \theta$
Ⓒ $\tan \theta = \dfrac{\sin \theta}{\cos \theta}$
Ⓓ $1 + \csc \theta = \dfrac{1 + \sin \theta}{\sin \theta}$
Ⓔ $(\cos^2 \theta)(\tan^2 \theta + 1) = 1$

Equations which are true for all values in the domain of the variable are referred to as *identities*. Such equations form an important part of trigonometry since they allow the transformation of an expression involving one or more functions into an expression involving other functions which may be more useful in a given problem.

Some of these are obvious, such as those suggested by the definitions of the functions themselves.

(1) $\sin \theta = \dfrac{y}{r} = \dfrac{1}{\frac{r}{y}} = \dfrac{1}{\csc \theta}$

(2) $\cos \theta = \dfrac{x}{r} = \dfrac{1}{\frac{r}{x}} = \dfrac{1}{\sec \theta}$

(3) $\tan \theta = \dfrac{y}{x} = \dfrac{1}{\frac{x}{y}} = \dfrac{1}{\cot \theta}$

Others follow from the definitions but are less obvious.

(4) $\tan \theta = \dfrac{y}{x} = \dfrac{y\left(\frac{1}{r}\right)}{x\left(\frac{1}{r}\right)} = \dfrac{\frac{y}{r}}{\frac{x}{r}} = \dfrac{\sin \theta}{\cos \theta}$ (answer Ⓒ)

(5) $x^2 + y^2 = r^2$, so $\dfrac{x^2}{r^2} + \dfrac{y^2}{r^2} = 1$. Therefore,

$$\cos^2 \theta + \sin^2 \theta = 1. \text{ (answer Ⓐ)}$$

Identities (1) through (5), which should be memorized, lead immediately to others through various substitutions.

$$\cos^2 \theta + \sin^2 \theta = 1$$
$$\frac{\cos^2 \theta}{\cos^2 \theta} + \frac{\sin^2 \theta}{\cos^2 \theta} = \frac{1}{\cos^2 \theta}$$
$$1 + \tan^2 \theta = \frac{1}{\cos^2 \theta} \qquad \text{Identity (4)}$$
$$(6) \qquad 1 + \tan^2 \theta = \sec^2 \theta \qquad \text{Identity (2)}$$

(Note: compare (6) with answer Ⓑ.)

They can also be used to prove the truth of others, as is demonstrated here for answers Ⓓ and Ⓔ.

Ⓓ $1 + \csc \theta = 1 + \dfrac{1}{\sin \theta}$ $\qquad$ Identity (1)

$$= \frac{\sin \theta}{\sin \theta} + \frac{1}{\sin \theta}$$
$$= \frac{(\sin \theta) + 1}{\sin \theta}$$

Ⓔ $(\cos^2 \theta)(\tan^2 \theta + 1)$

$$= (\cos^2 \theta)\left(\frac{\sin^2 \theta}{\cos^2 \theta} + 1\right) \qquad \text{Identity (4)}$$
$$= \sin^2 \theta + \cos^2 \theta$$
$$= 1 \qquad \text{Identity (5)}$$

¶ DRILL Use the identities in this section to transform the left sides of the following equations into the same expressions as are found on the right sides, thereby proving the two parts are always equal:

(a) $(\tan \theta)(\csc \theta) = \sec \theta$

(b) $\dfrac{(\cos \theta)}{(\sin \theta)(\cot^2 \theta)} = \tan \theta$

(c) $\sin \theta = \dfrac{\tan \theta}{\sec \theta}$

USING CONDITIONAL EQUATIONS

[14] The set $\{150°, 30°\}$ is the set of solutions for which of the following equations? (Assume the domain of the variable to be $0 \le \theta < 360$.)

Ⓐ $2 \sin \theta - 1 = 0$ Ⓑ $4 \tan \theta - 4 = 0$
Ⓒ $(\cos \theta)(\sin \theta) = 0$ Ⓓ $\sin^2 \theta + 2 \sin \theta = 3$
Ⓔ $2 \sin^2 \theta - 1 = 0$

In section [13] we reviewed trigonometric equations that were true for all defined values of the variable. In this section we will consider trigonometric equations that are true only for specific values of the variables—referred to as *conditional* equations.

Ⓐ $2 \sin \theta - 1 = 0$
$ 2 \sin \theta = 1$
$ \sin \theta = \dfrac{1}{2}$
$ \dfrac{y}{r} = \dfrac{1}{2}$

Using the method shown in section [9], we let $r = 2$, then $y = 1$. Since $x^2 + y^2 = r^2$, we conclude $x = \pm \sqrt{3}$. If we plot the points and use the 30-60-90 triangle relations as in the figure below, we get 30° and 150° for θ.

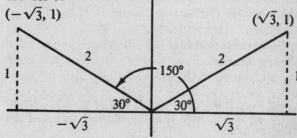

Ⓑ 4 tan θ − 4 = 0
    4 tan θ = 4
      tan θ = 1

$$\frac{y}{x} = 1$$

If we let $x = 1$, then $y = 1$ and $r = \sqrt{2}$. Plotting the point and applying the 45–45–90 triangle information, we get θ to be 45°. But we may also let $x = -1$, for which $y = -1$ and $r = \sqrt{2}$. From the latter information we find θ to be 225°.

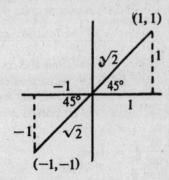

Ⓒ (cos θ)(sin θ) = 0

An important algebraic theorem (Chapter 6, section [5]) states that $ab = 0$ if and only if $a = 0$ or $b = 0$. If we apply this fact to the equation above, we get

    cos θ = 0 or sin θ = 0.

Since any angle that satisfies either part of this compound statement will satisfy the original equation, the solution set is {90°, 270°, 0°, 180°}. The first two elements are solutions of cos θ = 0; the second two are solutions of sin θ = 0.

Ⓓ $\sin^2 θ + 2 \sin θ = 3$
    $\sin^2 θ + 2 \sin θ - 3 = 0$
    $(\sin θ + 3)(\sin θ - 1) = 0$
    $\sin θ + 3 = 0$ or $\sin θ - 1 = 0$
    $\sin θ = -3$ or $\sin θ = 1$

Since no angle may have a sine less than −1, sin θ = −3 has no solutions, but sin θ = 1 is satisfied by 90°.

Ⓔ $2 \sin^2 θ - 1 = 0$
    $2 \sin^2 θ = 1$

$$\sin^2 θ = \frac{1}{2}$$

$$\sin θ = \pm\sqrt{\frac{1}{2}} = \pm\frac{\sqrt{2}}{2}$$

$$\frac{y}{r} = \pm\frac{\sqrt{2}}{2}$$

Let $r = 2$; then $y = \pm\sqrt{2}$ and $x = \pm\sqrt{2}$ (from $x^2 + y^2 = r^2$). Note that the absolute values of the

x- and y- coordinates are the same, so the triangles formed are isosceles right triangles (45–45–90) and the solutions are {45°, 135°, 225°, 315°}.

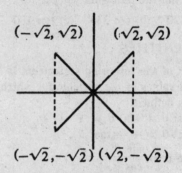

¶ DRILL Solve each of the following for $0 \le θ < 2\pi$: (Note that, since the domain is given in radians, all answers should be written in radians.)

(a) $2 \sin θ = \sqrt{2}$ (b) $\cos^2 θ - \sin^2 θ = \sin θ$

FINDING PERIODS AND AMPLITUDES

*[15] The graph below is part of $y = 2 \sin 2x$.

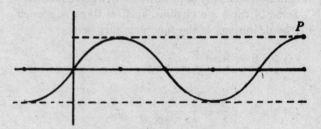

What are the coordinates of P?

Ⓐ $\left(\pi, \dfrac{1}{2}\right)$ Ⓑ $(\pi, 2)$ Ⓒ $(2\pi, 1)$

Ⓓ $\left(\dfrac{5\pi}{2}, 2\right)$ Ⓔ $\left(\dfrac{5\pi}{4}, 2\right)$

For a trig function, though no two ordered pairs have the same first coordinate, an infinite set of ordered pairs have each of the possible second coordinates. The complete graph of a trig function is an infinite series of identical sections, each beginning where the last left off. Such functions are termed "periodic." A function, $f(x)$, is *periodic* if and only if there is some number p such that:

$$f(x) = f(x + p) \quad \text{for all } x.$$

The smallest number p that indicates the distance between the points at the beginning and end of each cycle is called the *period* of the function. The table and the graphs on the next page show the functions defined by $y = \sin x$ (solid line) and $y = \cos x$ (dotted line) from 0° to 360°.

x	Sin x	Cos x
0	0	1
$\dfrac{\pi}{6}$	.5	$\dfrac{\sqrt{3}}{2}$ or .86
$\dfrac{\pi}{4}$	$\dfrac{\sqrt{2}}{2}$ or .71	$\dfrac{\sqrt{2}}{2}$ or .71
$\dfrac{\pi}{3}$	$\dfrac{\sqrt{3}}{2}$ or .86	.5
$\dfrac{\pi}{2}$	1	0
$\dfrac{2\pi}{3}$	.86	−.5
$\dfrac{3\pi}{4}$	.71	−.71
$\dfrac{5\pi}{6}$	.5	−.86
π	0	−1
$\dfrac{7\pi}{6}$	−.5	−.86
$\dfrac{5\pi}{4}$	−.71	−.71
$\dfrac{4\pi}{3}$	−.86	−.5
$\dfrac{3\pi}{2}$	−1	0
$\dfrac{5\pi}{3}$	−.86	.5
$\dfrac{7\pi}{4}$	−.71	.71
$\dfrac{11\pi}{6}$	−.5	.86
2π	0	1

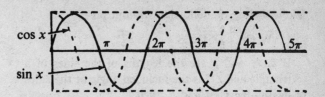

Note that, no matter how great θ becomes, neither $\sin \theta$ nor $\cos \theta$ takes values greater than 1 or less than −1.

The *amplitude* of the function is $\dfrac{1}{2}(p - q)$, where p is the maximum value of the function and q is the minimum value.

Many curves are based on the sine and cosine curves. Some of these are defined by equations of the form $y = A \sin Bx$ and $y = A \cos Bx$. We will state without proof that in such cases the amplitude is $|A|$ and the period is $\dfrac{2\pi}{B}$.

EXAMPLE

The function defined by $y = \dfrac{1}{4} \sin 3x$ varies between $-\dfrac{1}{4}$ and $\dfrac{1}{4}$, inclusive, while completing one full cycle from 0 to $\dfrac{2\pi}{3}$.

To answer the multiple-choice question, note that $y = 2 \sin 2x$ has a period of

$$\frac{2\pi}{2} = \pi$$

and an amplitude of 2. The period tells us that a cycle begins at 0 and ends at π. Point P is a quarter-cycle past π, so the first coordinate of P is

$$\pi + \frac{1}{4}\pi = \frac{5}{4}\pi.$$

Since the amplitude is 2, the second coordinate of P is 2.

¶ DRILL Find the period and amplitude of each of the following:

(a) $y = 3 \sin \dfrac{1}{2}x$ (b) $y = \dfrac{1}{2} \sin 2x$

USING THE LAW OF COSINES

*[16] If the lengths of two sides of a triangle are 5 and 6 while the measure of their included angle is 60, what is the length of the third side?

Ⓐ $\sqrt{31}$ Ⓑ $\sqrt{91}$ Ⓒ $\sqrt{61}$ Ⓓ $\sqrt{11}$
Ⓔ None of these

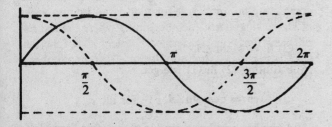

Since the terminal sides of θ, $\theta + 2\pi$, $\theta + 4\pi$, ..., $\theta + k \cdot 2\pi$ are coincident, the graph to the right of 2π is a series of repetitions of the section drawn above.

We will state the following without proof.

LAW OF COSINES

If a, b, and c are the lengths of the sides of a triangle and $\angle C$ is the included angle of the sides having length a and b, then

$$c^2 = a^2 + b^2 - 2ab \cos \angle C.$$

We can apply the Law of Cosines directly to the multiple-choice question allowing a to be 5, b to be 6. The cosine of $\angle C$ must be $\frac{1}{2}$ since $\angle C$ has a measure of 60. We'll leave the rest to you.

Since the given information for this question is side-angle-side, there is no ambiguity about the third side; you will recall that *SAS* is a congruence relation and thereby determines a triangle uniquely.

Third side ambiguity sometimes arises when the given information comprises two sides and an angle which is *not* included between them. In such cases, the third side may not be unique. You will recall the absence from geometry of a Side-Side-Angle congruence relation. (Indeed, the third side may not even exist, a situation we will review last.) The following figures show the two possible triangles based on the given information that $(\angle C)° = 60$ with $a = 5$ and $c = 6$.

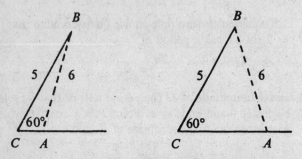

When applied to this situation, the Law of Cosines yields

$$36 = 25 + b^2 - 2 \cdot 5 \cdot b \cdot \frac{1}{2},$$
$$36 = 25 + b^2 - 5b,$$
$$0 = b^2 - 5b - 11.$$

Therefore, by formula,

$$b = \frac{5 \pm \sqrt{80}}{2}$$
$$= \frac{5 \pm 2\sqrt{5}}{2}.$$

The two solutions provide the lengths of the sides for both possible cases.

We can use the Law of Cosines to find the length of the missing side and the measures of the missing angles whenever the given information is two sides and an

angle. If all three sides are given, we can use the same law to find the three missing angles. This process of finding the missing parts is called *solving* the triangle.

In order to be solved, the triangle must, of course, exist. The figure at right shows a situation under which the triangle would not exist.

Given: $(\angle C)° = 30$, $a = 6$ and $c = 1$.

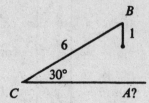

The side opposite angle C must be at least as long as the distance from point B to line AC in order for the triangle to exist.

¶ DRILL Given a triangle with sides of lengths 2, 5, and 6, use the Law of Cosines to find the cosine of each angle.

FINDING THE AREA OF A TRIANGLE

*[17] In $\triangle ABC$, if the area is $\frac{21}{2}$, $AC = 6$ and $BA = 7$, then which of the following can be the measure of $\angle A$?

Ⓐ 45° Ⓑ 60° Ⓒ 30° Ⓓ 40° Ⓔ $22\frac{1}{2}°$

As noted in Chapter 17, the area of a triangle is $\frac{1}{2}ab$, where b is the length of a side and a is the length of the altitude to that side. A formula for the area of a triangle can be derived based on the lengths of any two sides and the sine of their included angle.

Given acute $\triangle ABC$ with altitude h, $AB = c$ and $AC = b$. The area as indicated by the base-height formula is

(1) $\frac{1}{2}ch.$

But $\sin \angle A = \frac{h}{b}$, so

(2) $h = b \sin \angle A.$

Substituting (2) in (1), we get

(3) Area $= \frac{1}{2}cb \sin \angle A.$

A similar argument produces the same formula for the area of an obtuse triangle.

If we rearrange (3) to apply directly to the multiple-choice question we get

$$\sin \angle A = \frac{2 \times \text{Area}}{bc}$$

Applying this formula to the multiple-choice question gives

$$\sin \angle A = \frac{2(21/2)}{6(7)} = \frac{21}{42} = \frac{1}{2}.$$

If $\sin \angle A = \frac{1}{2}$, then $\angle A = 30°$.

¶ DRILL Find the area of $\triangle ABC$, given the following:

(a) $AB = 12$, $AC = 4$, $(\angle A)° = 45$

(b) $AC = 2$, $BC = 5$, $(\angle C)° = 150$

USING THE LAW OF SINES

*[18] If $\sin 48° = .7431$, $\sin 62° = .8829$ and the length of segment BC is 24.6, which of the following is the best approximation to the length of side AB?

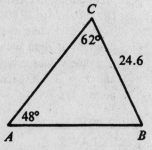

ⒶⒶ 18   Ⓑ 50   Ⓒ 45
Ⓓ 31   Ⓔ 29

In section [16] we presented a formula (Law of Cosines) for solving a triangle when two sides and an angle (or all three sides) were given. Here we will review a formula for solving a triangle when two sides and an angle opposite one of them or two angles and a side are given.

In section [17] we noted that the area of a triangle is one-half the product of the lengths of two sides and the sine of the included angle. If we apply this area formula to some triangle, $\triangle ABC$, we get the following three equations by exhausting the possible combinations of two sides and their included angle:

(1) $A = \frac{1}{2}ab \sin \angle C$,

(2) $A = \frac{1}{2}ac \sin \angle B$,

(3) $A = \frac{1}{2}bc \sin \angle A$.

But each of the formulas must give exactly the same area since the area of a triangle is unique, so

(4) $\frac{1}{2}ab \sin \angle C = \frac{1}{2}ac \sin \angle B = \frac{1}{2}bc \sin \angle A$.

If we multiply each member of equations (4) by $\frac{2}{abc}$, we get

(5) $\frac{\sin \angle A}{a} = \frac{\sin \angle B}{b} = \frac{\sin \angle C}{c}$

Equations (5) are referred to as the Law of Sines. In applying it we set up equations that contain only two members and solve them in the usual manner.

Applying the Law of Sines to the multiple-choice question gives

$$\frac{\sin 48}{24.6} = \frac{\sin 62}{AB}$$

Therefore

$$AB = \left(\frac{\sin 62}{\sin 48}\right)(24.6)$$
$$= \frac{.8829}{.7431}(24.6).$$

TEST-TAKING TIP.

Because we need to choose between answers that are given, rather than performing a careful calculation, we can settle for an approximation. The answer is about $\frac{88}{74}(25)$ or approximately $\frac{88}{3} \doteq 29$.

¶ DRILL In $\triangle ABC$ with $(\angle A)° = 135$, $(\angle B)° = 30$ and $AC = 5$, find BC.

WHAT YOU SHOULD KNOW

KEY CONCEPTS

Handling Angles

1. In trigonometry, an angle is a rotation; therefore any real number (positive, negative or zero) may be the measure of an angle.

2. An angle in standard position has the origin as its vertex and the positive ray of the x-axis as its initial ray. If the rotation to the terminal side is clockwise, the measure is negative. If it is counterclockwise, the measure is positive.

3. Since π radians $= 180°$,
   a. *to convert from radians to degrees,* multiply each side of the equation 1 radian $= \frac{180}{\pi}$ degrees by the given number of radians and simplify;
   b. *to convert from degrees to radians,* multiply each side of the equation 1 degree $= \frac{\pi}{180}$ radians by the given number of degrees and simplify.

4. If r is the radius of a circle, θ the measure of a central angle in radians and s the length of its intercepted arc, then

$$\theta = \frac{s}{r}.$$

5. If θ is an angle in standard position, its reference angle is the smallest positive angle between its terminal side and the nearer ray of the x-axis.

6. If (x, y) is a point r units from the origin, then

$$x^2 + y^2 = r^2.$$

Defining Trigonometric Functions

1. If (x, y) is a point on the terminal side of an angle θ in standard position and (x, y) is r units from the origin, then:

$$\sin \theta = \frac{y}{r}, \quad \csc \theta = \frac{r}{y},$$

$$\cos \theta = \frac{x}{r}, \quad \sec \theta = \frac{r}{x},$$

$$\tan \theta = \frac{y}{x}, \quad \cot \theta = \frac{x}{y}.$$

2. If θ is an acute angle of a right triangle, then:

$$\sin \theta = \frac{\text{opposite side}}{\text{hypotenuse}}, \quad \csc \theta = \frac{\text{hypotenuse}}{\text{opposite side}},$$

$$\cos \theta = \frac{\text{adjacent side}}{\text{hypotenuse}}, \quad \sec \theta = \frac{\text{hypotenuse}}{\text{adjacent side}},$$

$$\tan \theta = \frac{\text{opposite side}}{\text{adjacent side}}, \quad \cot \theta = \frac{\text{adjacent side}}{\text{opposite side}}.$$

3. If $\angle A$ and $\angle B$ are complementary, then:

$$\sin \angle A = \cos \angle B,$$
$$\sec \angle A = \csc \angle B,$$
$$\tan \angle A = \cot \angle B.$$

4. For all values of θ:

$$\sin^2 \theta + \cos^2 \theta = 1,$$

$$\tan \theta = \frac{\sin \theta}{\cos \theta},$$

$$\sin \theta = \frac{1}{\csc \theta},$$

$$\cos \theta = \frac{1}{\sec \theta},$$

$$\tan \theta = \frac{1}{\cot \theta}.$$

Finding Values of Trigonometric Functions of Angles

1. *To find values of trigonometric functions of angles with reference angles of 30 or 60, use the 30-60-90 triangle:*

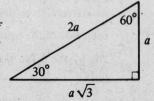

2. *To find values of trigonometric functions of angles with reference angle 45, use the isosceles right triangle:*

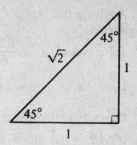

3. *To find values of trigonometric functions of quadrantal angles (0, 90, 180, 270, 360, . . .), use the diagram at right with (x, y) the values given and $r = 1$ for each point.*

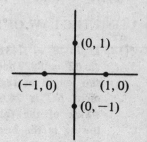

KEY LAWS

1. If a, b and c are *any* sides of *any* triangle and $\angle C$ is the angle opposite side c, then

$$c^2 = a^2 + b^2 - 2ab \cos \angle C.$$

(Law of Cosines)

2. If a, b and c are the sides of any triangle and $\angle A$, $\angle B$ and $\angle C$ are, respectively, the angles opposite these sides, then

$$\frac{\sin \angle A}{a} = \frac{\sin \angle B}{b} = \frac{\sin \angle C}{c}.$$

(Law of Sines)

TEST-TAKING STRATEGY

• Apply your knowledge of the ratios of the sides of 30-60-90 and 45-45-90 right triangles to find the trig functions of 30°, 45°, and 60° angles.

ANSWERS

[1] Ⓐ
(b) and (c); all of (a), (d), (e), (f).

[2] Ⓒ
DRILL:
(a) $\left(\dfrac{900}{\pi}\right)^{\circ}$ (b) $\dfrac{\pi}{3}$ radians.

(c) 90° (d) $\dfrac{\pi^2}{360}$ radians.

[3] Ⓑ
DRILL:

(a) $\dfrac{4}{5}$ radian   (b) π radians

(c) π radians   (d) π units

[4] Ⓔ
DRILL:

(a) II   (b) I

(c) III   (d) None (on the axis).

[5] Ⓓ
DRILL:

(a) 45°

(b) 20°

(c) $\dfrac{\pi}{3}$ radians

(d) This is a quadrantal angle coterminal with $\dfrac{\pi}{2}$.

[6] Ⓐ
DRILL:

(a) $2\sqrt{5}$ (b) $\pm 2\sqrt{30}$ (c) $\pm\sqrt{2}$

[7] Ⓔ
DRILL:

(a) $-\dfrac{2}{\sqrt{13}}$ (b) $\dfrac{\sqrt{18}}{4} = \dfrac{3\sqrt{2}}{4}$

(c) $\dfrac{1}{2}$

[8] Ⓒ
DRILL:

$\sin \angle B = \dfrac{4}{\sqrt{17}}$, $\tan \angle A = \dfrac{1}{4}$, $\cot \angle B = \dfrac{1}{4}$

[9] Ⓓ
DRILL:

(a) $\left|\dfrac{2\pi}{3}, \dfrac{4\pi}{3}\right|$ (b) $\left|\dfrac{\pi}{4}, \dfrac{3\pi}{4}\right|$

(c) $\left|\dfrac{\pi}{6}, \dfrac{7\pi}{6}\right|$

[10] Ⓑ
DRILL:

(a) $\cos 45°$ (b) $\cot 77°$

(c) $\sec 37°$ (d) $\tan 48°$

[11] Ⓒ
DRILL:

(a) $-\sin 20°$ (b) $-\cos 12°$

(c) $\csc 88°$ (d) On axis, none

[12] Ⓔ
DRILL:

(a) $-\dfrac{1}{2}$ (b) $\dfrac{2\sqrt{3}}{3}$

(c) 0

[13] Ⓑ
DRILL:

(a) $(\tan \theta)(\csc \theta) = \dfrac{\sin \theta}{\cos \theta} \times \dfrac{1}{\sin \theta}$
$$= \dfrac{1}{\cos \theta} = \sec \theta$$

(b) $\dfrac{\cos \theta}{(\sin \theta)(\cot^2 \theta)} = \dfrac{\cos \theta}{\dfrac{\cos^2 \theta}{\sin \theta}}$
$$= \dfrac{\cos \theta}{1} \times \dfrac{\sin \theta}{\cos^2 \theta} = \dfrac{\sin \theta}{\cos \theta}$$

(c) $\dfrac{\tan \theta}{\sec \theta} = \dfrac{\sin \theta}{\cos \theta}(\cos \theta) = \sin \theta$

We asked that this be transformed from left to right; merely reverse the steps.

[14] Ⓐ
DRILL:

(a) $\left|\dfrac{\pi}{4}, \dfrac{3\pi}{4}\right|$

(b) Convert the equation to $2 \sin^2 \theta + \sin \theta - 1 = 0$ and then factor; $\left|\dfrac{\pi}{6}, \dfrac{5\pi}{6}, \dfrac{3\pi}{2}\right|$.

[15] Ⓔ
DRILL:

(a) Amplitude: 3, period: 4π

(b) Amplitude: $\dfrac{1}{2}$, period: π

[16] Ⓐ
DRILL:

$\dfrac{19}{20}, \dfrac{5}{8}, -\dfrac{7}{20}$

[17] Ⓒ
DRILL:

(a) $12\sqrt{2}$ (b) $\dfrac{5}{2}$

[18] Ⓔ
DRILL:

$BC = 5\sqrt{2}$

Advanced Topics

25. Theory of Equations

> In this chapter, all topics are more typical of those tested on the Mathematics Level II exam than of those on the Level I exam. We have therefore denoted them with an asterisk (*). Review of such topics may assist you in answering Level I questions, however, because it increases your general knowledge of mathematical ideas, methods and skills.

Key Terms

polynomial in standard form   a polynomial in which the first term on the left contains the highest power of the variable and the remaining terms are arranged in descending order of the powers. Example: when $3 + x^2 + 5x$ is rewritten in standard form, the result is $x^2 + 5x + 3$.

degree of a polynomial   the degree of its term of highest power. Example: the degree of $x^{10} - x^4 + 2x^2 - 1$ is 10.

polynomial equation   an equation in which one member is a polynomial in standard form and the other member is zero. Example: $x^2 + 3x + 4 = 0$.

depressed equation   an equation found by dividing both sides of a polynomial equation by a factor of the polynomial.

root of an equation   a number that makes the equation true.

rational integral equation   an equation with integers for coefficients and rational numbers for roots.

---

*[1] If the polynomials

$$4x^3 + 8x - 5$$

and

$$(p - 1)x^3 + (q + 4)x^2 + \left(\frac{r}{2}\right)x + 10s$$

are equal, which of the following is (p, q, r, s)?

(A) $\left(5, -4, 16, -\frac{1}{2}\right)$ (B) $\left(5, 0, 16, -\frac{2}{1}\right)$

(C) $(5, -4, 16, -2)$ (D) $\left(5, -4, 4, -\frac{1}{2}\right)$

(E) $(5, 0, 16, -2)$

We have defined "polynomial" in Chapter 7. A polynomial in which the first term on the left contains the highest power of the variable while the remaining terms are arranged in descending order of the powers of the variable is said to be in *standard form*. When transforming a polynomial to standard form, fill in any missing terms with the appropriate power of x and assign a zero coefficient.

EXAMPLE

Arrange the polynomial $f(x) = 3x^2 + 2 + 5x^4$ in standard form.

SOLUTION: $f(x) = 5x^4 + 0 \cdot x^3 + 3x^2 + 0 \cdot x + 2$

Two polynomials in standard form are *equal* if and only if the coefficients of terms of like powers are equal. The *degree* of a polynomial is the degree of its term of highest power. Since $x^0 = 1$, the power of a polynomial such as $f(x) = 3$ is defined to be zero (3 may be written in standard form as $3x^0$).

Any equation of the form

$$a_0x^n + a_1x^{n-1} + a_2x^{n-2} + \ldots + a_{n-1}x + a_n = 0$$

is called a *polynomial equation*. In intermediate math we generally restrict our discussion to rational integral equations: equations with integral coefficients or coefficients that can be transformed into integers.

In the multiple-choice question,

$$p - 1 = 4, \quad q + 4 = 0, \quad \frac{r}{2} = 8 \quad \text{and}$$
$$10s = -5.$$

Therefore

$$p = 5, \quad q = -4, \quad r = 16 \quad \text{and} \quad s = -\frac{1}{2}.$$

¶ DRILL If $f(x) = 4x^4 - 3x^2 + 2$, find:

(a) $f(1)$ (b) $f(-1)$ (c) $f(2)$ (d) $f(a)$

(If you are unable to do these, review Chapter 20 on functions, especially functional notation.)

FACTORING POLYNOMIALS

*[2] If $x^{21} - 3x^7 + 2$ is divided by $x + 1$, which of the following is the remainder?

Ⓐ 0   Ⓑ 4   Ⓒ −4   Ⓓ 1   Ⓔ 2

If we divide a polynomial $f(x)$ by a linear expression, $(x - a)$, we get some polynomial quotient, $Q(x)$, and a remainder R such that

(1) $f(x) = (x - a)[Q(x)] + R$.

The value of f at a, or $f(a)$, can be found by replacing x by a wherever it occurs in (1).

(2) $f(a) = (a - a)[Q(a)] + R$
(3) $f(a) = 0 \times [Q(a)] + R$
(4) $f(a) = R$

Thus we see that, if a polynomial, $f(x)$, is divided by a linear binomial, $(x - a)$, until the remainder has no term involving x, then this final remainder is equal to the value of f at a, or $f(a)$.

In the multiple-choice question, finding the remainder is much more readily accomplished using equation (4) than by direct division. Since the linear binomial $(x - a)$ is $(x + 1)$, we conclude that $a = -1$ and

$f(a) = (-1)^{21} - 3(-1)^7 + 2 = -1 + 3 + 2 = 4$.

The remainder after division of $f(x)$ by $(x + 1)$ is 4.

¶ DRILL Without dividing, find the remainder in each of the following:

(a) $(x^{10} + x^4 + x^2 + x + 1) \div (x - 1)$
(b) $(x^4 + 3x^3 - x^2 + 11x - 4) \div (x + 4)$
(c) $(x^3 - 2x^2 + 3x - 4) \div (x - 2)$
(d) $(x^4 - 2x^3 + 3x^2 - x + 2) \div (x + 2)$

*[3] Given a polynomial $f(x)$ such that $f(4) = 4$ and $f(-2) = 0$, which of the following is a factor of $f(x)$?

Ⓐ $x + 4$ Ⓑ $x - 4$ Ⓒ $x + 2$ Ⓓ $x - 2$
Ⓔ Cannot be determined

In section [2] we reviewed a way to determine the remainder in the division of a polynomial by a linear binomial without actually dividing. If this remainder is 0, we can conclude that the binomial is a factor of the polynomial by the following argument:

Since $f(x) = (x - a)[Q(x)] + R$, then when $R = 0$, we get $f(x) = (x - a)[Q(x)]$ and $x - a$ must be a factor.

EXAMPLE

Determine whether $x - 1$ is a factor of $x^9 - 1$.

SOLUTION: If $f(x) = x^9 - 1$, then $f(1) = 0$, which means that the remainder after division of $f(x)$ by $x - 1$ must be 0. Therefore $x - 1$ is a factor of $x^9 - 1$.

In the multiple-choice question, since

$$f(-2) = 0,$$

it follows that $x + 2$ must be a factor.

¶ DRILL Determine whether the linear binomials given are factors of the accompanying polynomials:

(a) $x - 1$, $x^3 - 2x^2 + 3x - 2$
(b) $x - 2$, $x^3 - 3x^2 - 4x + 12$
(c) $x + 2$, $x^4 - 2x + 1$
(d) $x^n - a^n$, $x + a$, where n is an even integer greater than zero

*[4] If the polynomial $ax^4 + bx^2 + c$ has 5 as a zero (root), what is the remainder when the polynomial is divided by $(x - 5)$?

Ⓐ $5c$ Ⓑ c Ⓒ −5   Ⓓ 5   Ⓔ 0

A number, a, is a zero (or root) of the polynomial $f(x)$ if $f(a) = 0$. If $f(x)$ can be factored into some linear binomial, $(x - a)$, and some polynomial, $Q(x)$, then when $x = a$ the value of $(x - a)$ is zero. This means that the value of $(x - a)[Q(x)]$ is also zero, and we conclude that a is a zero of $f(x)$ if and only if it is a zero of a linear factor of $f(x)$.

EXAMPLE

Determine whether 3 is a zero of $2y^3 - 11y^2 + 12y + 9$.

SOLUTIONS: We can do this in two ways: (1) by applying the definition of "zero" directly or (2) by noting the relationship between zeros and linear factors.

(1) By definition a zero of $f(x)$ is a number such that the value of f is zero. The value of f at 3 by direct substitution is

$$2(3)^3 - 11(3)^2 + 12(3) + 9 = 0.$$

(2) Since the remainder on division of $f(x)$ by $x - 3$ is 0, $x - 3$ is a factor of $f(x)$. The factor $(x - 3)$ has the value 0 when $x = 3$, so $f(x)$ must be 0 when $x = 3$.

You may not see much difference between methods (1) and (2), but if you were to apply both to the multiple-choice question above, you would see that you cannot substitute 5 for x in $ax^4 + bx^2 + c$ and get a useful remainder. You must reason instead that, since 5 is a zero, $(x - 5)$ will be a factor and the remainder must be 0.

¶ DRILL Find the zeros of the factored polynomials given:

(a) $f(x) = (x - 3)(x + 4)(x - 1)$
(b) $f(x) = (x + 2)^3(x + 1)$
(c) $f(x) = x^2(x - 1)^2$

USING SYNTHETIC DIVISION

*[5] The polynomial $f(x) = 2x^4 - x^3 - 30x^2 - 8$ is to be divided by $(x + 4)$ by synthetic division which is set up below. The problem as set up contains an error. Which of the numbers is incorrectly calculated?

Ⓐ $-4\rfloor$ 2   Ⓑ -1 -30 Ⓔ 0 -8
             Ⓒ -8 36   264   1056
        2   -9 -66 264   1048
              Ⓓ

In Chapter 7, section [3], we reviewed a "long division" process for finding the quotient of two polynomials. If we were to analyze this process when the divisor is a linear binomial, discard repetitious steps, and then write the process in compact form, we would arrive at a simplified procedure called *synthetic division*. We will not give the details of the analysis but will go directly to a description of synthetic division through an example:

EXAMPLE

$$(2x^4 + 3x^2 + 4x - 36) \div (x + 2)$$

Directions	Results
(1) Write the polynomial in standard form filling in the missing terms.	$2x^4 + 0 \cdot x^3 + 3x^2 + 4x - 36$
(2) The coefficients form line 1.	2 0 3 4 -36 (line 1) (line 2) (line 3)
(3) Write the divisor in the form $(x - a)$.	$[x - (-2)]$
(4) The number a is the synthetic divisor.	$-2\rfloor$ 2 0 3 4 -36 (line 1) (line 2) (line 3)
(5) Bring the first coefficient down into line 3.	$-2\rfloor$ 2 0 3 4 -36 (line 1) (line 2) 2 (line 3)
(6) Multiply the first coefficient by the synthetic divisor and put this product in line 2 under the second coefficient.	$-2\rfloor$ 2 0 3 4 -36 (line 1) -4 (line 2) 2 (line 3)
(7) *Add* the second coefficient and the product just found.	$-2\rfloor$ 2 0 3 4 -36 (line 1) -4 (line 2) 2 -4 (line 3)
(8) Multiply this new result by the synthetic divisor and put the product under the third coefficient.	$-2\rfloor$ 2 0 3 4 -36 (line 1) -4 8 (line 2) 2 -4 (line 3)
(9) Carry out the pattern already described until the final coefficient has been added to a product.	$-2\rfloor$ 2 0 3 4 -36 (line 1) -4 8 -22 36 (line 2) 2 -4 11 -18 0 (line 3)

In line 3 the number farthest to the right is the remainder and the other numbers are the coefficients of the terms of the quotient arranged in standard form.

The correct synthetic division process for the multiple-choice question yields

$$
\begin{array}{r|rrrrr}
-4 & 2 & -1 & -30 & 0 & -8 \\
   &   & -8 & 36 & -24 & 96 \\
\hline
   & 2 & -9 & 6 & -24 & 88
\end{array}
$$

¶ DRILL Divide synthetically and write the quotient as a polynomial in standard form:

(a) $(x^4 - 4x^3 + 4x^2 - 2) \div (x - 3)$
(b) $(x^3 + x^2 - 3x - 2) \div (x + 2)$
(c) $(x^4 + 6x^2 + 2x - 3) \div (x + 1)$

FINDING THE ROOTS OF POLYNOMIALS

*[6] If the polynomial $f(x) = 5x^{15} - 15x^{12} + 30x + 25 = 0$ were completely factored over the complex numbers, how many linear factors would appear in the factored form?

Ⓐ 16 Ⓑ 4 Ⓒ 15 Ⓓ 14 Ⓔ 5

If a rational integral polynomial is of degree n, where $n \geq 1$, then it can be expressed as a product of n *linear* factors over the complex numbers. These factors need not all be different as in $x^2 + 4x + 4 = (x + 2)(x + 2)$. When a factor $(x - a)$ appears k times, it is called a *factor of multiplicity k* and the number a (which we showed to be a zero in section [4]) is called a *zero of multiplicity k*.

EXAMPLE

If $f(x) = 4x^5 + 2x^4 + 32x^2 - 36x + 12$ can be factored into $4(x - 1)(x - 1)(x - 1)(x - \sqrt{3})(x + \sqrt{3})$, then it has five linear factors (the number 4 is also a factor but is not linear since it is not of first degree). The factor $(x - 1)$ appears three times and, therefore, has multiplicity 3. The numbers 1, $\sqrt{3}$ and $-\sqrt{3}$ are the only distinct roots, and 1 is a root of multiplicity 3. (We sometimes say it is a "triple root.")

Therefore the 15th-degree polynomial of the multiple-choice question must have 15 linear factors, though not all factors need be different. In other words it could have 15 factors all of which are equal, 15 that are all different, 5 of one kind and 10 of another, or any other combination that totaled 15.

*[7] Given the polynomial $a_0 x^{n+2} + a_1 x^{n+1} + \ldots + a_{n+2} x + a_{n+3}$, where n is an integer and the set of numbers $\{a_0, a_1, \ldots, a_{n+3}\}$ contains only integers. If k represents the number of DISTINCT roots of the polynomial, which of the following is true?

Ⓐ $k = n + 2$ Ⓑ $k = n + 1$ Ⓒ $k = n$
Ⓓ $k \leq n + 2$ Ⓔ $1 \leq k \leq n + 2$

In section [6] we stated that every polynomial, $f(x)$, of nth degree can be expressed as the product of n linear factors:

$$f(x) = a(x - r_1)(x - r_2) \ldots (x - r_n).$$

These factors need not be distinct, and thus the numbers $r_1, r_2, \ldots, r_n$ need not be distinct. But each of $r_1, r_2, \ldots, r_n$ is a root (see section [4]). Since there are n of these, we are tempted to say that the number of roots is n, but we must consider the possibility that some or all of the factors are identical and yield the same root. To encompass this restriction we state:

The number of distinct roots of a polynomial of degree n is between 1 and n, and the sum of the multiplicities of the roots *is n*.

Since the degree of the polynomial given in the multiple-choice question is $n + 2$, the number of roots is $n + 2$ or less.

¶ DRILL Indicate (1) the maximum number of roots possible for each of the following, and (2) the sum of the multiplicities of the roots:

(a) $x^4 + 3x^2 + 6x - 5$ (b) $x^{19} + 17x^2 + 5$
(c) $x^{121} + x^{100} + x^{79} + x^{68} + x^2$

*[8] If the polynomial $ax^5 + bx^4 + cx^3 + dx^2 + ex + f$ (where a, b, c, d, e and f are all integers) has the numbers $2, 2 + 2i$, and $2 + \sqrt{2}$ in its solution set, which of the following is the complete solution set?

Ⓐ $\{2, 2 + 2i, 2 + \sqrt{2}\}$
Ⓑ $\{2, -2, 2 - 2i, 2 - \sqrt{2}\}$
Ⓒ $\{2, 2 + 2i, 2 - 2i, 2 + \sqrt{2}, 2 - \sqrt{2}\}$
Ⓓ $\{2, -2, 2 + 2i, 2 - 2i, 2 + \sqrt{2}\}$
Ⓔ **Cannot be determined**

For any polynomial equation $f(x) = 0$ with *real* coefficients, any imaginary roots must come in conjugate pairs. In other words, if $a + bi$ is a root of an equation with real coefficients, then $a - bi$ must also be a root. In the equation above the coefficients are integers and $2 + 2i$ is given as a root, so $2 - 2i$ must also be a root.

For any polynomial equation, $f(x) = 0$, with rational coefficients, whenever $a + \sqrt{b}$ (where a and b are rational, but b is not a perfect square) is a root, $a - \sqrt{b}$ must also be a root. In the equation above, since $2 + \sqrt{2}$ is given as a root, $2 - \sqrt{2}$ must be a root because the coefficients, being integers, are rational. The equation is of fifth degree and may not have more than the five roots we have now discovered.

EXAMPLE

The equation $x^4 - x^3 + x^2 + 2 = 0$ has coefficients that are integers and are thereby rational and real. If we are given that two of its roots are $1 + i$ and $-\frac{1}{2} + \frac{1}{2}i\sqrt{3}$, we can conclude that two other roots are $1 - i$ and $-\frac{1}{2} - \frac{1}{2}i\sqrt{3}$.

The polynomial of the multiple-choice question is of the fifth degree, so it must have at most five roots. Since all coefficients are integers, the rational roots and imaginary roots must be conjugate pairs. Since $2 + 2i$ is a root, $2 - 2i$ must be a root. Since $2 + \sqrt{2}$ is a root, $2 - \sqrt{2}$ is a root.

¶ DRILL If the numbers given are roots of a rational integral equation, list other numbers which must also be roots:

(a) $3 + 2i,\ 3 - \sqrt{2}$ (b) $5, \dfrac{1}{2} - i,\ 4 - \sqrt{3}$

USING DEPRESSED EQUATIONS TO FIND ROOTS

*[9] The polynomial $f(x) = x^5 - 3x^4 + 8x^2 - 9x + 3$ can be factored into $(x - 1)^3[Q(x)]$, where $Q(x)$ is a quadratic polynomial. There are only three distinct roots of $f(x)$. Find these three.

Ⓐ $\{-1, -1, -1\}$ Ⓑ $\{1, 1, 1\}$ Ⓒ $\{1, 3, -3\}$
Ⓓ $\{1, -1, 3\}$ Ⓔ $\{1, \sqrt{3}, -\sqrt{3}\}$

If $f(x) = (x - r_1)[Q(x)]$ one root of $f(x)$ is r_1 and the remaining roots of $f(x)$ are roots of $Q(x) = 0$. This latter equation is called a *depressed* equation. The following example shows how we may use depressed equations to find the roots of a polynomial equation when some are already known.

EXAMPLE

If two roots of $8x^4 - 14x^3 - 9x^2 + 11x - 2 = 0$ are 2 and -1, find the remaining roots.

SOLUTION: Since 2 is a root, $x - 2$ is a factor and we can find some $Q(x)$ such that

$$8x^4 - 14x^3 - 9x^2 + 11x - 2 = (x - 2)[Q(x)],$$

by synthetic division.

```
2 | 8  -14   -9    11   -2
   |     16    4  -10    2
   -------------------------
     8    2   -5     1 |  0
```

Thus $Q(x) = 8x^3 + 2x^2 - 5x + 1$, and any further roots of the original polynomial are roots of $Q(x)$. We can depress $Q(x)$ by using the given fact that -1 is a root.

```
-1 | 8    2   -5    1
   |     -8    6   -1
   ---------------------
     8   -6    1 |  0
```

This second depressed equation, $Q'(x)$, is

$$8x^2 - 6x + 1 = 0,$$

a quadratic which is solvable by factoring:

$$(-4x + 1)(-2x + 1) = 0,$$

$$x = \frac{1}{4} \text{ or } x = \frac{1}{2}.$$

Thus the factors of our original polynomial are

$$(x - 2)(x + 1)\left(x - \frac{1}{4}\right)\left(x - \frac{1}{2}\right).$$

If the polynomial of the multiple-choice question is divided by $(x - 1)^3$, the depressed equation is

$$x^2 - 3 = 0.$$

Its roots are $\pm\sqrt{3}$.

¶ DRILL If each of the equations below has the roots given, find the remaining roots:

(a) $2x^3 - 5x^2 + 1 = 0;\ \dfrac{1}{2}$

(b) $2x^4 + 5x^3 + 3x^2 + x - 2 = 0;\ -2, \dfrac{1}{2}$

(c) $2x^4 - 9x^3 + 13x^2 - 81x - 45 = 0;\ 3i$ (Hint: conjugate pairs?)

WRITING A RATIONAL INTEGRAL EQUATION TO FIT GIVEN ROOTS

*[10] Find the equation of lowest possible degree with integral coefficients and roots of a, ai, and 0 if a is an integer.

Ⓐ $x^3 + ax^2 + a^2x + a^3 = 0$
Ⓑ $x^4 - ax^3 + a^2x^2 + a^3x = 0$
Ⓒ $x^3 + ax^2 + aix = 0$
Ⓓ $ax^3 + a = 0$
Ⓔ $x^4 + ax^2 + ax = 0$

If $r_1, r_2, r_3, \ldots, r_n$ are the roots of a polynomial equation, then the equation can be written as

$$(x - r_1)(x - r_2)(x - r_3) \ldots (x - r_n) = 0.$$

Each of these factors may appear one or more times depending on the multiplicity of the root.

EXAMPLE

Given the roots 0, $5i$ and $\sqrt{2}$, find:
(a) a rational integral equation of lowest degree possible having these roots, and
(b) a rational integral seventh-degree equation having these roots.

SOLUTIONS:
(a) Since $5i$ and $\sqrt{2}$ are roots and the coefficients are real, $-5i$ and $-\sqrt{2}$ are also roots. The lowest degree possible is five.

$$(x - 0)(x - 5i)(x + 5i)(x - \sqrt{2})(x + \sqrt{2}) = 0$$
$$x(x^2 + 25)(x^2 - 2) = 0$$
$$x^5 + 23x^3 - 50x = 0$$

(b) A seventh-degree equation could be composed in several different ways, but each involves assigning a multiplicity of more than 1 to some of the factors. Let $(x - 0)$ have multiplicity 3.

$$(x - 0)(x - 0)(x - 0)(x - 5i)(x + 5i)$$
$$(x - \sqrt{2})(x + \sqrt{2}) = 0$$
$$x^7 + 23x^5 - 50x^3 = 0$$

We can assign a multiplicity of 2 to $(x - 5i)$, but this automatically gives a multiplicity of 2 to $(x + 5i)$ since the imaginary roots come in conjugate pairs. Similarly, we can give a multiplicity of 2 to $(x - \sqrt{2})$, which again gives $(x + \sqrt{2})$ a multiplicity of 2 since the equation is to have rational coefficients.

In the multiple-choice question, if ai is a root and the equation has integral coefficients, then $-ai$ must also be a root. The polynomial must, therefore, be composed of these factors:

$$(x - 0)(x - a)(x - ai)(x + ai) = 0,$$
$$x(x - a)(x^2 + a^2) = 0,$$
$$(x^2 - ax)(x^2 + a^2) = 0,$$
$$x^4 - ax^3 + a^2x^2 - a^3x = 0.$$

¶ DRILL For each of the following write a rational integral equation with the given roots and of the given degree:

(a) 1, -1, 2; third

(b) $1 + \sqrt{3}$, $-\dfrac{1}{2}$; lowest possible

(c) $2 + i$ is a root of multiplicity 2, and the degree is to be the lowest possible

(d) 5, $2 - 3i$; fifth

APPLYING DESCARTES'S RULE

*[11] If $f(x) = x^6 + x^2 + 2$, which of the following statements is true about the number and nature of the roots of $f(x)$?

   Ⓐ Six real roots   Ⓑ No positive real roots
   Ⓒ Three positive real roots   Ⓓ Three negative real roots   Ⓔ No roots are imaginary

One of the many significant contributions to mathematics by the French mathematician and philosopher René Descartes (1596–1650) is a method for determining the number and nature of the roots of a polynomial based on the number of variations of sign in the coefficients of the polynomial. A *variation* occurs when the signs of two successive coefficients differ (disregarding zero coefficients). Descartes' rule is as follows:

LAW OF SIGNS

The number of real positive roots of a rational integral polynomial, $f(x)$, is equal to the number of variations in sign occurring in $f(x)$, or is less than this number by an even integer. The number of negative roots of $f(x)$ is equal to the number of variations occurring in $f(-x)$, or is less than this number by an even integer.

EXAMPLE 1

Discuss the possible roots of

$$P(x) = x^3 - 4x^2 + 8x - 5.$$

SOLUTION: The signs of $P(x)$ are, in order,

$$+\smile\frown\smile\frown,$$

with the three variations noted. By Descartes' rule the number of positive roots is three or one.

$$P(-x) = -x^3 - 4x^2 - 8x - 5$$

The signs of $P(-x)$ are all alike so there are no negative roots for $P(x)$. The possible roots are:

(1) 3 positive, no negative, no imaginary, or

(2) 1 positive, no negative, 2 imaginary.

EXAMPLE 2

Discuss the roots of $P(x) = x^4 - 2x^3 - 3$.

SOLUTION: $P(x)$ has one variation in sign so it must have one positive root. $P(-x) = x^4 + 2x^3 - 3$ and has one variation in sign so $P(x)$ must have one negative root. The remaining two roots must be imaginary.

In the multiple-choice question, since

$$f(x) = x^6 + x^2 + 2$$

has no variations in sign, there are no positive roots. Also,

$$f(-x) = x^6 + x^2 + 2,$$

so there are no negative roots; all roots must be imaginary.

¶ DRILL Use Descartes' rule to discuss the possible roots of:

(a) $P(x) = x^5 + x^4 - x + 13$
(b) $P(x) = 2x^3 + 3x^2 - 4x - 1$
(c) $P(x) = 3x^5 - x^4 - x^2 - 2$

APPLYING THE RATIONAL ROOT LAW

*[12] Find all rational roots of the polynomial

$$P(x) = x^4 - 5x^2 - 6x - 5 = 0.$$

   Ⓐ $\{1, -1\}$ Ⓑ $\{5, -5\}$ Ⓒ $\{1, -1, 5, -5\}$
   Ⓓ $\{1\}$ Ⓔ The polynomial has no rational roots

The Quadratic Formula gives a direct relationship between the roots and coefficients of a quadratic polynomial. Complicated formulas exist for equations of higher degree, but we frequently rely on a simpler method that yields all rational roots of a polynomial regardless of degree.

If $\frac{p}{q}$ (where p and q are integers, $q \neq 0$) is a rational root of a polynomial equation with integral coefficients, then p is a factor of the constant term and q is a factor of the coefficient of the term with highest degree.

The application of this rational root law yields a set of rational numbers, not all of which are roots, but which contains all of the roots of the polynomial.

EXAMPLE

Find the rational roots of

$$2x^5 - 11x^4 + 14x^3 - 2x^2 + 12x + 9 = 0.$$

SOLUTION: If $\frac{p}{q}$ is a rational root, then p must belong to the set of factors of the constant term, 9:

$$p \in \{\pm 9, \pm 1, \pm 3\},$$

and q must belong to the set of factors of the coefficient of the term of highest degree, $2x^5$:

$$q \in \{\pm 2, \pm 1\}.$$

The possible values for $\frac{p}{q}$ are:

$$\frac{p}{q} \in \left\{ \pm \frac{9}{2}, \pm 9, \pm \frac{1}{2}, \pm 1, \pm \frac{3}{2}, \pm 3 \right\}.$$

Note: we have not said that these are all roots; rather, we have said that any rational roots must belong to this set. To discover which of these are actually roots we test them by synthetic division. We generally begin testing with positive integral roots (if Descartes' rule indicates that positive roots may exist) and start with the least of these.

```
1 | 2  -11   14   -2   12    9
  |      2   -9    5    3   15
    2   -9    5    3   15 |24
```

Since the remainder is 24, 1 is not a root and we continue with the next greater integer, 3.

```
3 | 2  -11   14   -2   12    9
  |      6  -15   -3  -15   -9
    2   -5   -1   -5   -3 | 0
```

The remainder is 0 so 3 is a root. It is always wise to test a root further to see if it has multiplicity greater than 1. We test 3 again in the depressed equation just formed.

```
3 | 2   -5   -1   -5   -3
  |      6    3    6    3
    2    1    2    1 | 0
```

We have discovered that 3 is a double root; we know that it cannot have a greater multiplicity since the new depressed equation may only have possible roots of ± 1 or $\pm \frac{1}{2}$ by the rational root law.

Further experiments show that $-\frac{1}{2}$ works.

```
-½ | 2    1    2    1
   |     -1    0   -1
     2    0    2 | 0
```

Our new depressed equation, $2x^2 + 2 = 0$, is quadratic. From the formula we get the further roots i and $-i$.

Applying the rational root theorem to the multiple-choice question, we see that

$$p \in \{\pm 5, \pm 1\},$$
$$q \in \{\pm 1\}.$$

Therefore

$$\frac{p}{q} \in \{\pm 1, \pm 5\}.$$

These must be tested to see which, if any, are roots. By synthetic division we can quickly see that *none* works, so the equation has *no* rational roots.

¶ DRILL Find the rational roots of:

(a) $x^4 + x^3 - 7x^2 - 5x + 10 = 0$
(b) $2x^3 - 3x^2 - 11x + 6 = 0$

WHAT YOU SHOULD KNOW

KEY CONCEPTS

1. If a polynomial $P(x)$ is divided by $x - a$, where a is any real number, then the remainder is $P(a)$.
2. If $x - a$ is a factor of $P(x)$, then $P(a) = 0$.
3. The values of a polynomial can be calculated quickly by synthetic division.
4. The number of linear factors of a polynomial of degree n is n.
5. The maximum number of roots of a polynomial of degree n is n.
6. If $a + bi$ is a root of a polynomial with real coefficients, then so is $a - bi$.
7. If $a + b\sqrt{c}$ is a root of a polynomial with rational coefficients, then so is $a - b\sqrt{c}$.

KEY LAWS

1. The number of real positive roots of a rational integral polynomial, $f(x)$, is equal to the number of variations in sign occurring in $f(x)$, or is less than this number by an even integer. The number of negative roots of $f(x)$ is equal to the number of variations occurring in $f(-x)$, or is less than this number by an even integer.
(Law of Signs: Descartes's Rule)

2. If $\frac{p}{q}$ (where p and q are integers, $q \neq 0$) is a rational root of a polynomial equation with integral coefficients, then p is a factor of the constant term and q is a factor of the coefficient of the term with highest degree.
(Rational Root Law)

TEST-TAKING STRATEGIES

- To facilitate finding the quotient of two polynomials, familiarize yourself with the procedure of synthetic division.
- Before attempting a laborious method of finding roots, use Descartes's rule of signs to determine the number and nature of the roots.

ANSWERS

[1] Ⓐ
DRILL:
(a) 3   (b) 3
(c) 54   (d) $4a^4 - 3a^2 + 2$

[2] Ⓑ
DRILL:
(a) 5   (b) 0
(c) 2   (d) 48

[3] Ⓒ
DRILL:
(a) Yes.   (b) Yes.
(c) No.   (d) Yes.

[4] Ⓔ
DRILL:
(a) $\{3, -4, 1\}$ (b) $\{-2, -1\}$
(c) $\{0, 1\}$

[5] Ⓓ
DRILL:
(a) $x^3 - x^2 + x + 3$ with remainder 7.
(b) $x^2 - x - 1$ with remainder 0.
(c) $x^3 - x^2 + 7x - 5$ with remainder 2.

[6] Ⓒ

[7] Ⓔ
DRILL:
(a) 4, 4   (b) 19, 19   (c) 121, 121

[8] Ⓒ
DRILL:
(a) $3 - 2i, 3 + \sqrt{2}$ (b) $\frac{1}{2} + i, 4 + \sqrt{3}$

[9] Ⓔ
DRILL:
(a) $1 \pm \sqrt{2}$ (b) $\frac{-1 \pm i\sqrt{3}}{2}$
(c) $\{-3i, 5, -\frac{1}{2}\}$

[10] Ⓑ
DRILL:
(a) $x^3 - 2x^2 - x + 2 = 0$
(b) $2x^3 - 3x^2 - 6x - 2 = 0$
(c) $x^4 - 8x^3 + 26x^2 - 40x + 25 = 0$
(d) $x^5 - 19x^4 + 148x^3 - 620x^2 + 1475x - 1625 = 0$ or $x^5 - 13x^4 + 82x^3 - 314x^2 + 689x - 845 = 0$

[11] Ⓔ
DRILL:
(a) 2 or 0 positive, 1 negative, 2 or 4 imaginary.
(b) 1 positive, 2 or 0 negative, 0 or 2 imaginary.
(c) 1 positive, no negative, 4 imaginary.

[12] Ⓔ
DRILL:
(a) $\{1, -2\}$ (b) $\{\frac{1}{2}, -2, 3\}$

26. Sequences and Series

> In this chapter, some topics are more typical of those tested on the Mathematics Level II exam than of those on the Level I exam. We have denoted these with an asterisk (*). Review of such topics may assist you in answering Level I questions, however, because it increases your general knowledge of mathematical ideas, methods and skills.

Key Terms

sequence   a set of numbers that have a prescribed order.

arithmetic sequence (arithmetic progression, A.P.)   a sequence that progresses by the addition to each term of some constant d. Example: 3, 6, 9, 12, where $d = 3$.

geometric sequence (geometric progression, G.P.)   a sequence in which each term is the product of some number r (called the *common ratio*) and the preceding term. Example: ¼, 1, 4, where $r = 4$.

arithmetic series   the indicated sum of the terms of an arithmetic sequence. Example: $3 + 6 + 9 + 12$.

geometric series   the indicated sum of the terms of a geometric sequence. Example: $¼ + 1 + 4 + 16$.

infinite geometric sequence   a geometric sequence that continues without end.

arithmetic means   in an arithmetic sequence, terms other than the first and last.

geometric means   in a geometric sequence, terms other than the first and last.

RECOGNIZING AN ARITHMETIC SEQUENCE

[1] From which of the following can we conclude that a, b, c is an arithmetic sequence?

(A) $a + b = b + c$ (B) $a + b = 2c$

(C) $b - a = c - b$ (D) $\dfrac{b}{a} = \dfrac{c}{b}$ (E) $\dfrac{a}{b} = c$

A *sequence* is a set of numbers that have a prescribed order. Every sequence is a function that associates with each positive integer n the number a_n. a_n is called a *term* and n is the *number of the term*. For example, in the sequence

$$2, 4, 6, 8, \ldots$$

the fifth term is 10, the sixth is 12, etc., and the function associates with each positive integer n the number $2n$. The majority of sequences dealt with in intermediate math have some such algebraic relationship between n and a_n.

The simplest is the *arithmetic sequence* which progresses by the addition to each term of some constant d resulting in the succeeding term.

The sequence

(1) 3, 7, 11, 15, . . .

is arithmetic since each term is four more than its predecessor. The relationship between each term in an arithmetic sequence, and the number of that term, is not obvious but can be found by a formula which we will develop in the next section. You may be able to guess by looking at sequence (1) that this relationship is $4n - 1$.

We can recognize an arithmetic sequence (sometimes called an "arithmetic progression" and hence symbolized by "A. P.") by noting that the difference between any two consecutive terms is always the same as the difference between the next two terms.

For the multiple-choice question, this means that

$$b - a = c - b.$$

¶ Drill Indicate whether each of the following is an A. P.

(a) 1, 2, 3, 4, 5, . . .   (b) 2, 4, 8, 16, . . .

(c) $\dfrac{1}{2}, \dfrac{1}{4}, 1, \dfrac{5}{4}, \ldots$ (d) $-3, 0, 3, 6, \ldots$

FINDING A TERM IN AN ARITHMETIC SEQUENCE

[2] Which of the following expressions is the general term of the sequence $-2, 1, 4, 7, \ldots$?

(A) $n + 3$ (B) $-2 + n$ (C) $-2 + 3$

(D) $-2 + 3n$ (E) $-2 + (n - 1)3$

The *general term* of a sequence is a formula for deriving each term from n, the number of the term. We may readily discover this formula for an A. P. by observing the following pattern, where a_1 is the first term, n is the number of the term and d is the difference between any two consecutive terms:

$$a_1 = a_1 + (0)d \qquad = a_1 + (1 - 1)d,$$
$$a_2 = a_1 + (1)d \qquad = a_1 + (2 - 1)d,$$
$$a_3 = (a_1 + d) + d \qquad = a_1 + (3 - 1)d,$$
$$a_4 = [(a_1 + d) + d] + d = a_1 + (4 - 1)d.$$

We conclude:

26-1 If $a_1, a_2, \ldots, a_n$ is an arithmetic sequence, then

$$a_n = a_1 + (n - 1)d.$$

We can use 26-1 to compute any term of an A. P. when several terms are given.

EXAMPLE 1

Find the 50th term of $\dfrac{1}{3}, \dfrac{2}{3}, 1, \ldots$.

SOLUTION: $a_1 = \dfrac{1}{3}, d = \dfrac{1}{3}, n = 50$; therefore:

$$a_n = \frac{1}{3} + (50 - 1)\frac{1}{3} = \frac{1}{3} + \frac{49}{3} = \frac{50}{3}$$

EXAMPLE 2

If the 10th term of an A. P. is 6 and the common difference between terms is -2, find the first term.

SOLUTION: $6 = a_1 + (10 - 1)(-2),$
$24 = a_1.$

EXAMPLE 3

If the third term of an A. P. is -9 and the 20th term is 59, find the first term.

SOLUTION: Since $a_3 = -9$,

(1) $-9 = a_1 + 2d.$

Since $a_{20} = 59$,

(2) $59 = a_1 + 19d.$

Solving (2) and (3) simultaneously, we get:

(3) $d = 4$ and $a_1 = -17$.

In the multiple-choice question, the first term is -2 and the common difference is 3 (found by subtracting any term from the next term).

Therefore:

$$a_n = -2 + (n - 1) \cdot 3.$$

¶ DRILL Find the missing one of $\{a_n, a_1, n, d\}$ for each of the following:

(a) $a_1 = 11, d = -2, n = 19$
(b) $a_1 = 4, n = 11, a_n = 64$
(c) $d = -2, n = 7, a_n = 3$
(d) $d = \dfrac{2}{3}, n = 8, a_n = 15$

FINDING THE SUM OF AN ARITHMETIC SERIES

*[3] Which of the following series has 35 as its sum?

Ⓐ $\displaystyle\sum_{k=3}^{k=7} (k + 2)$

Ⓑ $\displaystyle\sum_{k=1}^{k=4} \left(k^2 + \frac{1}{k} \right)$

Ⓒ $\displaystyle\sum_{k=2}^{k=8} \left(k + \frac{k}{2} \right)$

Ⓓ $\displaystyle\sum_{k=3}^{k=5} \left(\frac{k - 2}{3} \right)$

Ⓔ None of these

A *series* is the indicated sum of the terms of a sequence (caution: do not confuse the series with its sum). Given the sequence 5, 6, 7, 8, 9, its corresponding series is $5 + 6 + 7 + 8 + 9$ and its sum is 35.

We frequently use summation notation (Σ being the Greek letter corresponding to the first letter of "sum") as a shorthand for series. The following table (which expands the possible answers above) exemplifies this use. The numbers above and below the Σ are the initial and terminal values of k; k also takes each integral value in between them.

Σ notation (see above)	Series	Sum
Ⓐ	$5+6+7+8+9$	35
Ⓑ	$2+4\frac{1}{2}+9\frac{1}{3}+16\frac{1}{4}$	$32\frac{1}{2}$
Ⓒ	$3+4\frac{1}{2}+6+7\frac{1}{2}+9+10\frac{1}{2}+12$	$52\frac{1}{2}$
Ⓓ	$\frac{1}{3}+\frac{2}{3}+1$	2

In the Σ notation k does not necessarily represent the number of the term (as, indeed, it does not in any of the examples above).

When the series is infinite, we note this by placing the symbol ∞ above the Σ.

$$\sum_{k=1}^{\infty} \frac{1}{k^2} = 1 + \frac{1}{4} + \frac{1}{9} + \frac{1}{16} + \frac{1}{25} + \cdots$$

The three dots at the end of the indicated part of the series above tells us that it continues endlessly.

¶ DRILL Write all of the terms of each of the following series and find their sums:

(a) $\displaystyle\sum_{k=1}^{k=4} \frac{k^3}{10}$ (b) $\displaystyle\sum_{k=0}^{k=5} (k + 2)^2$

(c) $\displaystyle\sum_{k=1}^{\infty} \left(\frac{1}{2} \right)^k$

*[4] Which of the following is an arithmetic series of 21 terms with a sum of $10\frac{1}{2}$ and a common difference of -3?

Ⓐ $30.5 + 27.5 + 24.5 + \ldots + (-29.5)$
Ⓑ $(-29.5) + (-32.5) + (-35.5) + \ldots + 30.5$
Ⓒ $24.5 + 27.5 + 30.5 + \ldots + (-29.5)$
Ⓓ $24.5 + 21.5 + 18.5 + \ldots + (-30.5)$
Ⓔ None of these

The sum of a finite arithmetic series can be found by a simple formula which is intuitively appealing. It is the average of the first and last terms times the number of terms.

26-2 The sum of the first n terms of an arithmetic sequence, symbolized by S_n, is given by:

$$S_n = n\left(\frac{a_1 + a_n}{2}\right).$$

Though the verification of this equation is well within the scope of intermediate algebra, we will not include it here.

Applying this formula to the above question yields the sum 10.5 for both Ⓐ and Ⓑ, but Ⓑ could not be an arithmetic series if its last term is 30.5 while all other terms are negative.

By recalling that $a_n = a_1 + (n - 1)d$, we can transform 26-2 into

---

26-3 $S_n = n\left(\dfrac{a_1 + a_1 + (n-1)d}{2}\right)$

$\qquad = \dfrac{n}{2}[2a_1 + (n-1)d].$

Both 26-2 and 26-3 are useful; you should memorize the former and learn the substitution needed to get the latter.

EXAMPLE 1

Find the sum of the positive multiples of 3 that are less than 300.

SOLUTION: The series in question is:

$$3 + 6 + 9 + \ldots + 297.$$

Since 297 is 3(99), there are 99 terms in this arithmetic series. Applying 22-2, we get

$$S_{99} = 99\left[\frac{(3 + 297)}{2}\right] = 14{,}850.$$

EXAMPLE 2

How many terms are there in the series with a sum of 435 if the first term is -13 and the common difference is 6?

SOLUTION: Since the given information is S_n, a_1 and d, we will use 22-3:

$$435 = \frac{n}{2}[2(-13) + (n-1)6]$$
$$= -16n + 3n^2,$$
$$0 = 3n^2 - 16n - 435.$$

Therefore $n = 15$ ($n = \dfrac{-29}{3}$ is meaningless).

¶ DRILL. Find the sum of the arithmetic series with information as given:

(a) $a_1 = 7$, $a_n = 85$, $n = 14$
(b) $a_1 = 16$, $d = 11$, $n = 15$
(c) $a_1 = -11$, $d = 8$, $n = 7$
(d) $2 + 9 + 16 + \ldots$ to 15 terms

RECOGNIZING A GEOMETRIC SEQUENCE

[5] What is the value of a if $2a - 1$, $4a + 1$, $15a - 3$ is a geometric sequence?

Ⓐ 1 Ⓑ 2 Ⓒ 3 Ⓓ 4 Ⓔ -1

A sequence is *geometric* if each term is the product of some number r (called the *common ratio*) and the preceding term. For example, the sequence

$$\frac{1}{3}, 1, 3, \ldots$$

is geometric with $r = 3$. The common ratio can be found by dividing any term by the one preceding it. Since this number r must remain constant throughout the sequence, the answer to the above question is the solution of the equation

$$\frac{4a + 1}{2a - 1} = \frac{15a - 3}{4a + 1}.$$

We have

$$(4a + 1)(4a + 1) = (2a - 1)(15a - 3),$$
$$16a^2 + 8a + 1 = 30a^2 - 21a + 3,$$
$$0 = 14a^2 - 29a + 2$$
$$= (14a - 1)(a - 2),$$

$$14a - 1 = 0 \quad \text{or} \quad a - 2 = 0,$$
$$a = \frac{1}{14} \quad \text{or} \quad a = 2.$$

¶ DRILL Indicate which of the following are geometric sequences and find the common ratio:

(a) 2, 4, 6, 8, ... (b) $\dfrac{1}{2}, \dfrac{1}{4}, \dfrac{1}{8}, \ldots$

(c) $-4, 20, -100, \ldots$ (d) 1, $2x$, $4x^2$, ...

FINDING A TERM IN A GEOMETRIC SEQUENCE

[6] Which of the following is the eighth term of the sequence $1, \dfrac{\sqrt{3}}{2}, \dfrac{3}{4}, \ldots$?

Ⓐ $\dfrac{2 + 7\sqrt{3}}{2}$ Ⓑ $\dfrac{3\sqrt{3}}{8}$ Ⓒ $\dfrac{27}{64}$ Ⓓ $\dfrac{27\sqrt{3}}{128}$

Ⓔ $\dfrac{81}{256}$

The general term of a geometric sequence (or geometric progression and hence the abbreviation, G. P.) is a formula which relates each term to the number of that term. This formula for a G. P. can be derived by observing the way a G. P. develops as follows:

$$a_1 = a_1 r^0 = a_1 r^{1-1},$$
$$a_2 = a_1 r^1 = a_1 r^{2-1},$$
$$a_3 = a_1 r^2 = a_1 r^{3-1},$$
$$a_4 = a_1 r^3 = a_1 r^{4-1}.$$

We conclude:

26-4 If $a_1, a_2, \ldots, a_n$ is a geometric sequence, then

$$a_n = a_1 r^{n-1}.$$

EXAMPLE 1

Find the eighth term of $5, 10, 20, \ldots$.

SOLUTION: $a_1 = 5, r = 2, n = 8$
$$a_8 = 5(2^7) = 640$$

EXAMPLE 2

How many terms are there in the sequence

$$64, 32, 16, \ldots, \frac{1}{128}?$$

SOLUTION: $a_1 = 64$ and $r = \dfrac{1}{2}$

$$\frac{1}{128} = 64(\tfrac{1}{2})^{n-1}$$
$$\frac{1}{8192} = (\tfrac{1}{2})^{n-1}$$
$$(\tfrac{1}{2})^{13} = (\tfrac{1}{2})^{n-1}$$
$$13 = n - 1$$
$$14 = n$$

EXAMPLE 3

The fifth term of a G. P. is $32\sqrt{2}$, while the common ratio is $-\sqrt{2}$. What is the first term?

SOLUTION: $a_n = 32\sqrt{2}, r = -\sqrt{2}, n = 5$
$$32\sqrt{2} = a_1(-\sqrt{2})^4$$
$$= a_1(4)$$
$$8\sqrt{2} = a_1$$

In the multiple-choice question,

$$a_1 = 1,$$
$$r = \frac{\sqrt{3}}{2},$$
$$a_8 = a_1 r^7 = 1\left(\frac{\sqrt{3}}{2}\right)^7$$
$$= \frac{27\sqrt{3}}{128}.$$

¶ **DRILL** Find the requested term:

(a) The 8th term of $2, 4, 8, \ldots$

(b) The 7th term of $\dfrac{4}{5}, -\dfrac{8}{15}, \dfrac{16}{45}, \ldots$

(c) The 10th term of $0.3, 0.03, 0.003, \ldots$

FINDING THE SUM OF A GEOMETRIC SERIES

*[7] Each of the following represents a geometric series. Which one has $\dfrac{40}{81}$ as its sum?

Ⓐ $\displaystyle\sum_{k=1}^{k=10} (-1)^k$ Ⓑ $\displaystyle\sum_{k=1}^{k=10} (-2)^{k-1}$

Ⓒ $\displaystyle\sum_{k=0}^{k=9} \frac{1}{3^k}$ Ⓓ $\displaystyle\sum_{k=2}^{k=5} 3\left(\frac{1}{3}\right)^k$ Ⓔ **None of these**

We will introduce a formula and then answer this question directly.

26-5 For a geometric series, the sum S_n is given by

$$S_n = \frac{a_1 - a_1 r^n}{1 - r}.$$

Ⓐ In expanded form: $-1 + 1 + (-1) + \ldots + 1$. Therefore $a_1 = -1, r = -1$ and $n = 10$,

$$S_{10} = \frac{-1 - (-1)(-1)^{10}}{1 - (-1)} = 0.$$

Ⓑ In expanded form: $1 + (-2) + 4 + \ldots + (-512)$. Therefore $a_1 = 1, r = -2$ and $n = 10$,

$$S_{10} = \frac{1 - 1(-2)^{10}}{1 - (-2)} = \frac{1 - 1024}{3} = \frac{-1023}{3}.$$

Ⓒ Though the initial and terminal values of k are different from those in (1) and (2), you may verify that this series also has 10 terms. In expanded form: $1 + \dfrac{1}{3} + \dfrac{1}{9} + \ldots + \dfrac{1}{19,683}.$

Therefore $a_1 = 1$, $r = \dfrac{1}{3}$, $n = 10$,

$$S_{10} = \frac{1 - 1(1/3)^{10}}{1 - (1/3)} = \frac{1 - (1/59,049)}{2/3}$$

$$= \frac{59,048}{59,049} \times \frac{3}{2}$$

$$= \frac{29,524}{19,683}.$$

(D) In expanded form: $\dfrac{1}{3} + \dfrac{1}{9} + \dfrac{1}{27} + \dfrac{1}{81}$.

Therefore $a_1 = \dfrac{1}{3}$, $r = \dfrac{1}{3}$ and $n = 4$,

$$S_4 = \frac{1/3 - 1/3(1/3)^4}{1 - 1/3} = \frac{40}{81}.$$

¶ DRILL Find the sum of the given geometric series:

(a) $3 + 6 + 12 + \ldots$ to 6 terms

(b) $\dfrac{27}{4} + 9 + 12 + \ldots$ to 6 terms

(c) $2 + (-10) + 50 + \ldots$ to 5 terms

*[8] If a rubber ball is dropped from a height of 1 yard and continues to rebound to a height which is $\dfrac{9}{10}$ of its previous fall, find the total distance in yards that it travels on falls only.

(A) $\dfrac{81}{100}$ (B) 1   (C) 9   (D) 10   (E) Impossible to determine

As we add more terms to a finite series, the sum gets greater and greater. Accordingly it may at first seem impossible to find the sum of any infinite series, but we *can* attach a meaning to the term "sum" when the series is geometric and when the common ratio is between 1 and -1. Recall that the sum of the first n terms of any geometric series is given by:

26-6 $S_n = \dfrac{a_1 - a_1 r^n}{1 - r}$,

which can be written as:

$$S_n = \frac{a_1}{1 - r} - \frac{a_1 r^n}{1 - r}.$$

If we were to allow the number n to increase endlessly for a series such that $-1 < r < 1$, the value of r^n would approach zero and hence the value of $a_1 r^n/(1 - r)$ would also approach zero. With this in mind we define S_∞, the sum of an infinite geometric series with $|r| < 1$, to be:

26-7 $S_\infty = \dfrac{a_1}{1 - r}$.

EXAMPLE

Find the sum of the infinite series

$$1 + \frac{9}{10} + \frac{81}{100} + \ldots$$

SOLUTION: $S_\infty = \dfrac{1}{1 - 9/10} = 10$

(Note that this is the geometric series given by the falls of the ball in the above question.)

FINDING THE FRACTIONAL EQUIVALENT OF A REPEATING DECIMAL

[9] Which of the following is a fractional expression equal to $1.\overline{45}$ (the bar over the digits indicates that they repeat endlessly)?

(A) $1\dfrac{45}{100}$ (B) $\dfrac{5}{11}$ (C) $1\dfrac{5}{110}$ (D) $1\dfrac{9}{20}$ (E) $1\dfrac{5}{11}$

Recall that every rational number can be expressed as a repeating or terminating decimal. But a repeating decimal can be written as an infinite geometric series, and its fractional equivalent can be found by using formula 26-7.

EXAMPLE 1

Find the fractional equivalent of $.\overline{6}$ (remember that $.\overline{6} = .66666666 \ldots$ with the digit 6 repeating endlessly).

SOLUTION: $.\overline{6} = .6 + .06 + .006 + .0006 + \ldots$

Therefore $a_1 = .6$ and $r = .1$.

$$S_\infty = \frac{.6}{1 - .1} = \frac{.6}{.9} = \frac{2}{3}$$

EXAMPLE 2

(Example 2 is the multiple-choice question.)

What fraction represents $1.\overline{45}$?

SOLUTION:

$$1.\overline{45} = 1 + .45 + .0045 + .000045 + \ldots$$

Beginning with the second term, this is an infinite geometric series. We must first find the value of $.\overline{45}$ and then add it to 1.

$$S = \frac{.45}{1 - .01} = \frac{.45}{.99} = \frac{5}{11}$$

Therefore $1.\overline{45} = 1\dfrac{5}{11}$.

¶ DRILL Find the fractional equivalents of:

(a) $.\overline{4}$ (b) $.\overline{62}$ (c) $4.\overline{3}$ (d) $.23\overline{909}$

INSERTING ARITHMETIC MEANS

*[10] If nine arithmetic means are to be inserted between 6 and 20, one of them will be:

Ⓐ 10 Ⓑ 10.2 Ⓒ $7\frac{3}{11}$ Ⓓ 7 Ⓔ 11

In a finite arithmetic progression the first and last terms are called the extremes and the remaining terms, the *means*. To insert k arithmetic means between two numbers means to construct an A. P. with the given numbers as extremes and with k numbers in between. Such an A. P. will have $k + 2$ terms. To do this we use the formula for a_n, allowing a_1 and a_n to be the extremes and $n = k + 2$. In this way we find d, which we can then use to complete the A. P.

EXAMPLE

Insert 10 arithmetic means between -5 and 72.

SOLUTION: Let $a_1 = -5$, $n = 12$ (the 10 means plus the two extreme terms, -5 and 72), $a_n = 72$. Accordingly,

$$72 = -5 + (12 - 1)d,$$
$$7 = d.$$

The required sequence is

$$-5, 2, 9, 16, 23, 30, 37, 44, 51, 58, 65, 72.$$

In the multiple-choice question, the sequence will have 11 terms (the two given terms and nine means), the 11th term of which is 20. Therefore:

$$20 = 6 + (11 - 1)d,$$
$$14 = 10d,$$
$$1.4 = d.$$

Hence the sequence is

$$6, 7.4, 8.8, 10.2, 11.6, \ldots, 20.$$

¶ DRILL Insert the requested number of arithmetic means between the given numbers.

(a) Seven means between 4 and 20
(b) Five means between -11 and 25

INSERTING GEOMETRIC MEANS

*[11] If two geometric means were inserted between 128 and -2, their sum could be:

Ⓐ -24 Ⓑ 24 Ⓒ 12 Ⓓ -12 Ⓔ None of these

In a finite G. P. the intermediate terms between the first and last are called *geometric means*. To insert k geometric means between two numbers is to construct a G. P. of $k + 2$ terms for which the two given numbers

are a_1 and a_{k+2}. With this given information, we may use formula 26-4 to find the values of r. In general, we restrict such values of r to exclude imaginary numbers unless otherwise requested. Note that geometric means need not be numerically between the extremes. For 2, -4, 8, -16, 32, neither the -4 nor the -16 is numerically between the 2 and 32.

EXAMPLE

Insert four geometric means between 192 and 6.

SOLUTION: Let $a_n = 6$, $n = 6$ and $a_1 = 192$. Therefore

$$6 = 192(r)^5,$$
$$\frac{1}{32} = r^5,$$
$$r = \frac{1}{2},$$

and the requested progression is

$$192, 96, 48, 24, 12, 6.$$

In the multiple-choice question, the sequence must be of the form

$$128, 128r, 128r^2, 128r^3,$$

where

$$128r^3 = -2,$$
$$r^3 = -\frac{2}{128} = -\frac{1}{64},$$
$$r = -\frac{1}{4}.$$

Therefore the terms are

$$128, -32, 8, -2.$$

The sum of the inserted means is $-32 + 8 = -24$.

¶ DRILL

(a) Insert three geometric means between 81 and 256.
(b) Insert two geometric means between 108 and -500.

SOLVING WORD PROBLEMS

*[12] If \$900 is invested at 5 percent annual interest and this interest is compounded semiannually, find the total amount payable to the investor to the nearest dollar after $1\frac{1}{2}$ years.

Ⓐ \$945 Ⓑ \$968 Ⓒ \$969 Ⓓ \$990
Ⓔ \$970

If i is the interest rate for each unit period of time and P is the principal (or amount of money invested), the interest earned for the first unit of time is $P \times i$ and the amount due the investor at the end of this period is $P + Pi$ or $P(1 + i)$. When interest is compounded, the amount of money earned, $P \times i$, is added to the principal at the end of each time period to form the new principal for the next period. This process continues from period to period to form the G. P. which follows:

$$P, P(1 + i), P(1 + i)^2, P(1 + i)^3, \ldots,$$

for which the general term, P_n, is

$$P_n = P(1 + i)^n,$$

where n is the number of periods of time.

For the question above, $P = \$900$, $i = 2.5$ percent (since the interest is compounded each half-year and $\frac{1}{2}(5 \text{ percent}) = 2.5$ percent) and $n = 3$ (since there are 3 half-year periods in $1\frac{1}{2}$ years). Note that 2.5 percent is .025 when expressed as a decimal.

$$P_3 = 900(1 + .025)^3 = 900(1.077) = \$969.30$$

¶ DRILL A ranch had a herd of 8000 steers. The herd increased at the rate of 6 percent per year. How many steers were in the herd after 9 years?

WHAT YOU SHOULD KNOW

KEY CONCEPTS

1. An *arithmetic sequence* follows the pattern
$$a, a + d, a + 2d, a + 3d, \ldots,$$
$$a + (n - 1)d,$$
where n is the number of the term.
2. A *geometric sequence* follows the pattern
$$a, ar, ar^2, ar^3, ar^4, \ldots, ar^{n-1},$$
where n is the number of the term and r is the ratio of any two consecutive terms.

KEY FORMULAS

Handling Arithmetic Sequences

1. *To find a general term* in an arithmetic sequence where a_n is the nth term, a_1 is the first term, n is the number of the term, and d is the difference between two consecutive terms:
$$a_n = a_1 + (n - 1)d.$$
2. *To find the sum of the first n terms* of an arithmetic sequence, symbolized by S_n:
$$S_n = n\left(\frac{a_1 + a_n}{2}\right)$$

or

$$S_n = \frac{n}{2}(2a_1 + (n - 2)d).$$

Handling Geometric Sequences

1. *To find a general term* in a geometric sequence where a_1 is the first term, r is the ratio between two consecutive terms, n is the number of the term, and a_n is the nth term:
$$a_n = a_1 r^{n-1}.$$
2. *To find the sum of the first n terms* of a geometric series, symbolized by S_n:
$$S_n = \frac{a_1 - a_1 r^n}{1 - r}.$$
3. *To find the sum of an infinite geometric series* with $|r| < 1$, symbolized by S_∞ :
$$S_\infty = \frac{a}{1 - r}.$$

TEST-TAKING STRATEGY

- If a question requires you to find the next term in a sequence, first determine the relationship between the consecutive terms given in order to identify the progression as arithmetic or geometric.

ANSWERS

[1] Ⓒ
DRILL:
(a) Yes.   (b) No.
(c) No.   (d) Yes.

[2] Ⓔ
DRILL:
(a) $a_{19} = -25$ (b) $d = 6$
(c) $a_1 = 15$ (d) $a_1 = \frac{31}{3}$

[3] Ⓐ
DRILL:
(a) $\frac{1}{10} + \frac{8}{10} + \frac{27}{10} + \frac{64}{10} = 10$
(b) $4 + 9 + 16 + 25 + 36 + 49 = 139$
(c) This is an infinite series so all terms cannot be written; the first three are $\frac{1}{2} + \frac{1}{4} + \frac{1}{8}$.

The series does have a "sum" which will be discussed in section [8].

[4] Ⓐ
DRILL:

(a) 644   (b) 1395

(c) 91   (d) 765

[5] Ⓑ
DRILL:

(a) No.   (b) Yes, $\frac{\div}{2}$.

(c) Yes, -5.   (d) Yes, $2x$.

[6] Ⓓ
DRILL:

(a) $a_8 = 256$ (b) $a_7 = \dfrac{256}{3645}$

(c) .000 000 000 3

[7] Ⓓ
DRILL:

(a) 189   (b) $-3\left(\dfrac{27}{4} - \dfrac{1024}{27}\right)$

(c) 1042

[8] Ⓓ

[9] Ⓔ
DRILL:

(a) $\dfrac{4}{9}$ (b) $\dfrac{62}{99}$

(c) $\dfrac{13}{3}$ (d) $\dfrac{2654}{11100}$

[10] Ⓑ
DRILL:

(a) 6, 8, 10, 12, 14, 16, 18

(b) -5, 1, 7, 13, 19

[11] Ⓐ
DRILL:

(a) $r = \dfrac{4}{3}$, 108, 144, 192

(b) $r = -\dfrac{5}{3}$, -180, 300

[12] Ⓒ
13,516

27. Permutations and Combinations

> In this chapter, some topics are more typical of those tested on the Mathematics Level II exam than of those on the Level I exam. We have denoted these with an asterisk (*). Review of such topics may assist you in answering Level I questions, however, because it increases your general knowledge of mathematical ideas, methods and skills.

Key Terms

permutation any ordered arrangement of all the elements of a finite set. Example: b, a, c and b, c, a are two different permutations of the letters a, b, c.

combination a set of elements; a collection of elements in which the order makes no difference. Example: a committee consisting of the combination Alice, Bill, and Carol is the same as the committee consisting of Bill, Carol, and Alice.

factorial notation the use of the exclamation point to indicate the product of a sequence of descending integers. Example: $5! = 5 \cdot 4 \cdot 3 \cdot 2 \cdot 1$.

mutually exclusive events events that cannot occur simultaneously. Example: when a coin is flipped, "heads" and "tails" are mutually exclusive.

---

*[1] The expression $\dfrac{6!}{3!2!}$ is equal to which of the following?

Ⓐ 1! Ⓑ 1 Ⓒ 0! Ⓓ 60 Ⓔ 60!

In this chapter we will review some of the elementary techniques of counting and their applications. We will frequently use factorial notation to simplify long products and define it here.

For every positive integer n the notation $n!$ represents the product of the first n integers.

$$n! = n(n - 1)(n - 2)(n - 3) \ldots 3 \times 2 \times 1.$$

For example,

$$3! = 3 \times 2 \times 1 = 6,$$
$$6! = 6 \times 5 \times 4 \times 3 \times 2 \times 1 = 720.$$

Furthermore, we define

$$0! = 1$$

in order to be consistent with formulas we will develop later.

EXAMPLE 1

Find the value of $\dfrac{12!}{10!}$.

SOLUTION:
$$\frac{12!}{10!} = \frac{12 \times 11 \times 10 \times 9 \times 8 \times 7 \times 6 \times 5 \times 4 \times 3 \times 2 \times 1}{10 \times 9 \times 8 \times 7 \times 6 \times 5 \times 4 \times 3 \times 2 \times 1}$$
$$= 12 \times 11 = 132$$

EXAMPLE 2

$$\frac{(k + 1)!}{k!} = \frac{(k + 1)k!}{k!} = k + 1$$

EXAMPLE 3

Simplify $\dfrac{8!(k + 1)!k}{7!(k - 1)!}$.

SOLUTION: This expression in expanded form is:
$$\frac{(8 \times 7 \times 6 \times 5 \times 4 \times 3 \times 2 \times 1)(k + 1)(k)(k - 1)!(k)}{(7 \times 6 \times 5 \times 4 \times 3 \times 2 \times 1)(k - 1)!}$$
$$= 8k^2(k + 1) = 8k^3 + 8k^2.$$

In the multiple-choice question,
$$\frac{6!}{3!\,2!} = \frac{6 \times 5 \times 4 \times 3 \times 2 \times 1}{3 \times 2 \times 1 \times 2 \times 1}.$$

Removing common factors, we obtain
$$6 \times 5 \times 2 = 60.$$

TEST-TAKING TIP.

Note that answers Ⓐ, Ⓑ and Ⓒ are different in form only. The numbers 1!, 1 and 0! are all equal. Since only one choice can be correct, all three can be eliminated. Answer Ⓔ can be eliminated simply because it is far too great to be correct. Thus, even if you can readily simplify the given expression, you can more quickly determine the answer by scanning the choices first.

¶ DRILL Simplify:

(a) $\dfrac{6!}{2!}$

(b) $\dfrac{6!}{3!4!}$

(c) $[(x - y) - 1]!(x - y)$

(d) $\dfrac{(x - 4)!}{(x - 3)!}$

USING THE FUNDAMENTAL PRINCIPLE OF COUNTING

*[2] In how many ways can a three-digit number be formed from the set of digits $\{1, 2, 3, 4, 5, 6, 8\}$ if no digit may appear twice?

Ⓐ 8   Ⓑ 210   Ⓒ 336   Ⓓ 27   Ⓔ 343

Suppose 16 boys and 15 girls attend a dance, and the host, in order to assure that no one is left out, rotates the couples so that every boy dances with every girl. How many different couples can he make up? He can select the boy in 16 different ways, and for each boy he can choose 15 different girls. This means that each boy will be part of 15 different couples. Since there are 16 boys, the total number of couples is $16 \times 15 = 240$. (Some dance!)

The analysis of this example illustrates the *Fundamental Principle of Counting*:

27-1   If the first of two actions can be done in m ways and the second done in n ways, the number of ways the two actions can be done in order is $m \times n$.

In the multiple-choice question three actions are being performed: the actions of selecting digits. There are seven ways to select the first digit. The second digit can be selected in only six ways since no digit may appear more than once. The last digit may be selected in five ways so the total number of ways of forming the three-digit number is

$$7 \times 6 \times 5 = 210.$$

EXAMPLE 1

If a customer buys lunch at a restaurant which offers four kinds of soups, seven kinds of sandwiches and three kinds of pies, how many different soup-sandwich-pie lunches can she choose?

SOLUTION: The three possible actions are the selections of a soup, a sandwich and a pie.

$$4 \times 7 \times 3 = 84$$

EXAMPLE 2

If a bag contains eight marbles, each of different color, how many different pairs of marbles can be chosen from the bag?

SOLUTION: The action of selecting the first marble can be done in eight different ways. Once the first marble is selected, the second can be selected in seven ways.

$$8 \times 7 = 56.$$

¶ DRILL

(a) If a man has six different shirts, four different ties, three different suits and two different pairs of shoes, how many different business outfits can he make up?
(b) Three people get on a bus which has seven vacant seats. In how many ways can they be seated?

*[3] How many different three-digit even numbers can be formed from the set of integers from 1 to 9 inclusive if no repetitions are allowed?

Ⓐ 224   Ⓑ 504   Ⓒ 84   Ⓓ 104   Ⓔ 94

This is an example of a problem in which a restriction is placed on the way in which one or more actions can take place. It is usually easiest to analyze such a case by 27-1 and by performing the restricted action(s) first. In the above the restricted action is that of selecting the final digit; it may be only a 2, 4, 6 or 8, yielding four ways. Once this digit is selected, the next can be chosen from the remaining ones in eight ways and the first in seven ways.

$$4 \times 8 \times 7 = 224$$

EXAMPLE 1

Mr. Haddick selects a baseball squad from among nine men. Each player except the pitcher and catcher can play any position. How many different fielding arrangements can Mr. Haddick make?

SOLUTION: There are nine actions (the actions of selecting nine positions for nine men) which are to be performed. By selecting the pitcher and catcher first we get

$$1 \times 1 \times 7 \times 6 \times 5 \times 4 \times 3 \times 2 \times 1.$$

EXAMPLE 2

In how many ways may six boys be seated around a table if two specific boys are not allowed to sit next to each other?

SOLUTION: We seat the antagonists first. There are six ways in which the first boy may be seated, but only three ways in which the second boy may be seated so that he is not sitting next to the first boy. There are four remaining seats to be filled yielding four ways for the third boy, three ways for the fourth, two ways for the fifth and one way for the sixth.

$$6 \times 3 \times 4 \times 3 \times 2 \times 1 = 432$$

Had we construed the problem to make a difference only in the order of seating rather than in the actual selection of seats, then the first boy's choice is in effect only that of selecting a reference point for the remaining boys. Each of the six choices for a reference point is no different from the others so that he is, in effect, making one choice rather than six different choices. The answer under these circumstances is

$$1 \times 3 \times 4 \times 3 \times 2 \times 1 = 72.$$

This problem admits of at least one other method of solution. First find the total number of ways in which six boys could be arranged and then subtract from this the total number of ways that the two specific boys would be seated next to each other.

$$6 \times 5 \times 4 \times 3 \times 2 \times 1 - 6 \times 2 \times 4 \times 3 \times 2 \times 1$$
$$= 720 - 288 = 432$$

¶ DRILL

(a) In how many ways may five different girls be seated in a row if one particular girl must always be seated in one of the end seats?

(b) How many three-digit numbers can be made from the digits 1, 2, 3, 4, 5 if no number may be greater than 399?

WORKING WITH PERMUTATIONS

*[4] How many different seating arrangements can be made for eight students in a row of eight chairs?

Ⓐ 8   Ⓑ 64   Ⓒ 10,080   Ⓓ 40,320   Ⓔ 10,000

This problem could be solved using 27-1, but we will introduce a second counting principle which will simplify the process.

Any ordered arrangement of all the elements of a finite set is called a *permutation.* Since the process of selecting the n elements in each permutation of a set involves n actions, and since the first action can be done in n ways with the next done in $n - 1$ ways and the next in $n - 2$ ways, etc., until all elements have been used, we conclude the following:

> 27-2 The number of possible permutations or orderings of a finite set of n elements is always $n!$

EXAMPLE 1

How many different orderings are possible of the letters in the word "SOME"?

SOLUTION: There are four elements in the set of letters in the word "some" so the number of different permutations is $4! = 24$.

EXAMPLE 2

How many different football line-ups can Mr. Beebe choose from his 11 players if every man can play any position?

SOLUTION: We are after the number of permutations of 11 things taken all at a time.

$$11! = 11 \times 10 \times 9 \times 8 \times 7 \times 6 \times 5 \times 4 \times 3 \times 2 \times 1$$
$$= 39,916,800$$

In the multiple-choice question, the number of possible arrangements of 8 different objects in a row is 8!

*[5] How many different six-letter arrangements can be made using the letters of the name of a Hawaiian fish, POOPAA?

Ⓐ 6   Ⓑ 720   Ⓒ 120   Ⓓ 6   Ⓔ 90

The repetitions of letters which appear in the word above cause some permutations to be identical with others. For example, the geological term for a type of lava is "aa." Whereas the usual two-letter word has two permutations, both permutations of "aa" are identical and thus we say the word has only one permutation. If a letter appears p times, then the number of identical permutations is $p!$ In general:

> 27-3 The number of distinct permutations of n things, a of which are alike of one kind, b of which are alike of another kind, etc., is given by:
>
> $$\frac{n!}{a!b! \ldots}$$

EXAMPLE

How many distinct permutations are there of the letters of the word "STRUCTURE"?

SOLUTION: The nine-letter word "structure" has two "t's", two "r's" and two "u's."

$$\frac{9!}{2!2!2!} = \frac{9 \times 8 \times 7 \times 6 \times 5 \times 4 \times 3 \times 2 \times 1}{2 \times 2 \times 2}$$
$$= 45,360$$

Our Hawaiian fish name has six letters, but three pairs are identical.

$$\frac{6!}{2!2!2!} = \frac{6 \times 5 \times 4 \times 3 \times 2 \times 1}{2 \times 2 \times 2}$$
$$= 90$$

¶ DRILL In how many ways may seven books be arranged on a shelf if three are identical algebra books, two are identical geometry books, one is a chemistry book and the remaining one is a history book?

*[6] If you were to pick a three-letter name for a college fraternity from among the 24 letters of the Greek alphabet and no name could have the same letter appearing twice, how many possible names could you choose?

Ⓐ 2160   Ⓑ 216   Ⓒ 72   Ⓓ 8   Ⓔ 12,144

In this problem we are asked to find the number of possible permutations of a set of 24 elements taken three at a time. To do this we must analyze three actions, the first performed in 24 ways, the next in 23 and the last in 22. Thus the answer is

$$\underbrace{24 \times 23 \times 22}_{3 \text{ factors}}.$$

In general, when we are finding the number of permutations of an n-element set taken r at a time, we start the factorial representation of n but carry it down only to r factors:

$$\underbrace{n(n - 1)(n - 2) \ldots}_{r \text{ factors}} = n(n - 1)(n - 2) \ldots [n - (r - 1)].$$

A simpler notation for the right member of the above equation is

$$\frac{n!}{(n - r)!}$$

27-4 The number of possible permutations of a set of n elements taken r at a time is indicated by the symbol $_nP_r$ (other symbols sometimes used are $P\binom{n}{r}$ and $P(n, r)$) and is equal to

$$\frac{n!}{(n - r)!}$$

EXAMPLE 1

In how many different arrangements may four people seat themselves in six seats at the theatre?

SOLUTION: Our problem is to find the number of permutations of six chairs taken four at a time:

$$_6P_4 = \frac{6!}{(6 - 4)!} = 6 \times 5 \times 4 \times 3 = 360.$$

EXAMPLE 2

In how many ways can a five-digit number be written from the digits 1 to 8 inclusive if no repetitions of digits are allowed?

SOLUTION: Our problem is to find the number of permutations of eight digits taken five at a time:

$$_8P_5 = \frac{8!}{3!} = 8 \times 7 \times 6 \times 5 \times 4 = 6720.$$

EXAMPLE 3

If $_nP_4 = 6(_nP_3)$, find n.

SOLUTION: $_nP_4 = \frac{n!}{(n - 4)!}$ and $_nP_3 = \frac{n!}{(n - 3)!}$

Therefore the given information can be written as:

(1) $\dfrac{n!}{(n - 4)!} = 6\left(\dfrac{n!}{(n - 3)!}\right),$

(2) $(n - 3)!n! = 6n!(n - 4)!,$

(3) $(n - 3)! = 6(n - 4)!,$

(4) $(n - 3)(n - 4)! = 6(n - 4)!$ because $(n - 3)! = (n - 3)(n - 4)!,$

(5) $n - 3 = 6,$

(6) $n = 9.$

¶ DRILL

(a) Find n if $_nP_4 = 30(_nP_2)$.

(b) How many different five-letter "words" can be made up if a "word" is any collection of five letters for which no repetitions are allowed?

(c) In how many ways can you arrange any eight volumes of a 12-volume encyclopedia?

*[7] In how many different ways can six keys be arranged on a key ring?

Ⓐ 720   Ⓑ 120   Ⓒ 24   Ⓓ 60   Ⓔ 180

We briefly touched on an idea in section [3] to which we will return now. Most of our work so far has been with *linear* permutations, arrangements of objects lined up in a row. Arranging the same elements in a circle changes the number of permutations possible.

For example, if the letters of $\{A, B, C\}$ were arranged in a row, then the order ABC is different from the order BCA. But if these were arranged in a circle, the order ABC is identical to BCA.

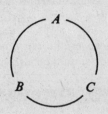

27-5 The number of circular permutations in a plane of n objects taken n at a time is

$$\frac{n!}{n} = (n - 1)!$$

EXAMPLE 1

In how many different arrangements can seven guests be seated at a circular dining table?

SOLUTION: This is an example of circular permutations in a plane, so the number of arrangements possible is $(7 - 1)! = 6! = 720$.

EXAMPLE 2

In how many ways may eight differently colored beads be arranged on a bracelet?

SOLUTION: In any situation where the circular arrangement may be meaningfully flipped over, a given clockwise permutation and its counterclockwise reflection are considered the same. Note that they were considered to be different for circular permutations in a plane. We must then modify our formula since we now have half the number of permutations The new formula is $\frac{(n - 1)!}{2}$. Such a situation is given in this problem and is referred to as a "cyclic permutation in space."

$$\frac{(8 - 1)!}{2} = \frac{7!}{2} = 2520$$

Since a key ring can be turned over, we use this concept to answer the multiple-choice question. The six keys can be arranged in

$$\frac{(6 - 1)!}{2} = \frac{5!}{2} = 60 \text{ ways.}$$

¶ DRILL

(a) Using the letters A, B, C, D and E, in how many different ways can the vertices of a pentagon drawn on a piece of paper be labeled?
(b) In how many different ways may the letters A, B, C, D and E be used to label the vertices of a pentagon constructed of wire and suspended from the ceiling?

WORKING WITH COMBINATIONS

[8] How many possible committees can be formed from a group of seven people if each committee can have any number of members from one to seven?

Ⓐ 7   Ⓑ 49   Ⓒ 5040   Ⓓ 127   Ⓔ 98

A *combination* of elements is a set of elements; in other words, it is a collection of elements in which the order makes no difference. For example, though the arrangements ABC and BAC are different permutations of these three elements, they are the same combination because they consist of the same three elements.

27-6 The total number of combinations of a set of n elements is the total number of its subsets which contain at least one element, and this number is:

$$2^n - 1.$$

The committees in the above problem would be combinations rather than permutations since the order of the people in the committees does not alter them. For example, a committee containing Rod, Jim, Tony and Chester is the same committee as the one composed of Jim, Chester, Tony and Rod. Remember: order is the determining factor in deciding whether you use a permutations or combinations formula for a particular counting problem.

The answer to the multiple-choice question would, therefore, be

$$2^7 - 1 = 128 - 1 = 127.$$

EXAMPLE

In how many ways may I make up a theater party from one, two or all three of my friends, if I go along, too?

SOLUTION: The question asks for the total number of one-, two-, or three-element subsets that can be made from the set of three friends. (Since taking Larry and Harry is the same as taking Harry and Larry, these are combinations.) Because $n = 3$,

$$2^n - 1 = 7.$$

¶ DRILL If I have one penny, one nickel, one dime, one quarter and one half-dollar, how many different sums of money can I make up?

[9] How many lines can be drawn such that each contains two points of a set of nine points, and no three of the points of this set are collinear?

Ⓐ 224   Ⓑ 7560   Ⓒ 27   Ⓓ 84   Ⓔ 36

Each combination of r elements has $r!$ permutations. Therefore

$$(_nC_r)(r!) = \,_nP_r,$$

where $_nC_r$ represents the number of combinations of n things taken r at a time. Hence:

27-7 $\quad _nC_r = \dfrac{_nP_r}{r!} = \dfrac{n!}{r!(n-r)!}.$

In the question above, we are interested in learning the number of two-point subsets there are in a set of nine points. This is a combinations problem since line AB is identical to line BA.

$$_9C_2 = \frac{9!}{7!2!} = \frac{9 \times 8}{2} = 36$$

EXAMPLE 1

Find the number of different five-card hands a poker player can draw from a deck of 52 cards.

SOLUTION: We are interested in the number of five-element subsets of a set of 52 cards.

$$_{52}C_5 = \frac{52!}{5!47!} = 2{,}598{,}960$$

EXAMPLE 2

From a group of eight men and 10 women in how many ways may a game of tennis "doubles" be set up involving two men and two women?

SOLUTION: There are $_8C_2 = 28$ ways of selecting the men and $_{10}C_2 = 45$ ways of selecting the women. By 23-1, there are 28×45 ways of making up the game.

¶ DRILL

(a) From a drama class of 16 students, how many different casts can be made up for a play containing five characters?

(b) In how many ways can a committee of three boys and three faculty members be made up in a school of 50 boys and 10 faculty?

[10] **In how many ways can we select a collection of three red or three white marbles from a bag of six white marbles and four red marbles?**

  Ⓐ **80**   Ⓑ **210**   Ⓒ **24**   Ⓓ **5040**   Ⓔ **5**

Two events are *mutually exclusive* if they do not occur simultaneously.

27-8 If two events are mutually exclusive and the first of these can occur in m ways while the second can occur in n ways, then one or the other event can occur in $m + n$ ways.

In the question above the number of ways we can select three red marbles from among four red marbles is $_4C_3 = 4$, and the number of ways of selecting three white marbles from six white marbles is $_6C_3 = 20$. Then the number of ways of accomplishing one selection *or* the other selection is 24. Note that this is a far different problem from one which asks the number of ways of accomplishing a first selection *and* a second selection. Had we been asked the number of ways of selecting three reds and three whites, six marbles altogether, we would have gotten 4×20 or 80 by 23-1; such actions would not be mutually exclusive.

EXAMPLE

A man has seven foxes and 12 chickens which he must take from their cages and ferry across a river. His boat can hold four animals (for obvious reasons, this means four chickens *or* four foxes). In how many different ways can he select the first load?

SOLUTION: He can select four foxes in $_7C_4 = 35$ ways, and four chickens in $_{12}C_4 = 495$ ways. This means that he can select four foxes *or* four chickens in $495 + 35 = 530$ ways.

¶ DRILL In how many ways can a committee of five be made up from a group of 12 men and nine women if the committee must be all men or all women?

WHAT YOU SHOULD KNOW

KEY CONCEPTS

Handling Permutations and Combinations

1.   The value of the expression $n!$, where n is any positive integer, is given by

$$n! = n(n-1)(n-2) \ldots 3 \cdot 2 \cdot 1.$$

2. The number of distinct permutations of n things, a of which are alike of one kind, b of which are alike of another kind, etc., is given by

$$\frac{n!}{a!b!c!\ldots}.$$

3. The number of possible permutations of a set of n elements, taken r at a time, is indicated by the symbol $_nP_r$ and is equal to

$$\frac{n!}{(n-r)!}.$$

4. The number of ways that r things can be chosen from a set containing n different things is

$$_nC_r = 2\frac{n!}{r!(n-r)!}.$$

Handling Mutually Exclusive Events

1. Two events are mutually exclusive if they cannot both occur at the same time.
2. If two events are mutually exclusive and the first of these can occur in m ways while the second can occur in n ways, then one or the other event can occur in $m + n$ ways.

KEY PRINCIPLES

1. If the first of two actions can be done in m ways and the second done in n ways, the number of ways the two actions can be done in order is mn. (Fundamental Principle of Counting)
2. The number of possible permutations or orderings of a finite set of n elements is always $n!$ (Principle of Permutation)
3. The total number of combinations of a set of n elements is the total number of its subsets which contain at least one element, and this number is $2^n - 1$. (Principle of Combination)

TEST-TAKING STRATEGY

• Use the criterion of order (Does it matter in which order the objects or people occur or are placed?) to decide whether to use a permutations or a combinations formula to solve a counting problem.

ANSWERS

[1] Ⓓ
DRILL:
(a) 360   (b) 5
(c) $(x - y)$ (d) $\dfrac{1}{x - 3}$

[2] Ⓑ
DRILL:
(a) 144   (b) $7 \times 6 \times 5 = 210$

[3] Ⓐ
DRILL:
(a) 48   (b) 75

[4] Ⓓ

[5] Ⓔ
DRILL:
(a) 420

[6] Ⓔ
DRILL:
(a) 8
(b) $26 \times 25 \times 24 \times 23 \times 22$
(c) $12 \times 11 \times 10 \times 9 \times 8 \times 7 \times 6 \times 5 = 19{,}958{,}400$

[7] Ⓓ
DRILL:
(a) 24   (b) 12

[8] Ⓓ
DRILL:
(a) 32 (counting 0 cent).

[9] Ⓔ
DRILL:
(a) 4368
(b) $19{,}600 \times 120 = 2{,}352{,}000$

[10] Ⓒ
DRILL:
$792 + 126$

28. Probability

In this chapter all topics are more typical of those tested on the Mathematics Level II exam than of those on the Level I exam. We have therefore denoted them with an asterisk (*). Review of such topics may assist you in answering Level I questions, however, because it increases your general knowledge of mathematical ideas, methods and skills.

Key Terms

probability   analysis of the chances an event will occur.

statistical probability   a method of analysis based on observed occurrences by actual count.

a priori probability   a method of analysis based on determining equally likely outcomes from the circumstances of an event.

sample space   the set of all possible outcomes of an experiment.

sample point   any of the possible outcomes that comprise the sample space.

event   any subset of a sample space.

---

*[1] A golfer concludes that the chances of a hole-in-one are one out of two and cites the laws of probability as her reason, since the outcome can happen in only one of two ways: the ball either goes into the cup or it doesn't. What is wrong with her argument?

Ⓐ There is a third outcome: the golf club could miss the ball entirely.   Ⓑ The golfer did not consider the length of the grass on the green. Ⓒ The argument does not reflect the skill of the golfer.   Ⓓ A hole-in-one is really impossible. Ⓔ The two events are not equally likely.

The sporting nature of this question is not limited to the subject discussed; you may rightly conclude that this is not a case of figures lying but of liars figuring. *Probability* is an analysis of the different ways an event may occur based on the assumption that all outcomes are equally likely.

This golfer could have come to a better understanding of her chances through *statistical probability:* from the accumulated evidence of her past record of driving balls from the tee she could figure her total past outcomes and the number of these which were holes-in-one. Statistical probability bases its analysis on observed occurrences by actual count and is used by insurance companies and others.

When the number of possible outcomes can be calculated in advance, we use *a priori probability*. For example, the number of ways in which a perfect cubical block of wood can come to rest on a different face is easily reckoned to be six. If five of these faces are painted green and one red, the chances that the block will land on a green face are five out of six.

¶ DRILL For each of the following decide whether the probability can be figured by *a priori* or whether it must be computed through statistical methods. If a priori, indicate the total possible outcomes.

(a) The chances of drawing a red marble from a bag containing eight marbles of different colors, one of which is red.

(b) The probability that a baseball player will get a hit at his next time at bat.

(c) The probability that a machine part put out by a specific worker will be defective.

(d) The probability that a hexagonal pencil when rolled on a flat table will come to rest with the manufacturer's name on the top face.

FINDING THE SAMPLE SPACE

*[2] Four cards in a pile are labeled *A*, *B*, *C* and *D*. Prior to figuring the probability that the first two drawn will be an *A* and a *C*, we must determine the sample space of the experiment. Which of the following is the sample space for the selection?

Ⓐ {(*A, B*), (*A, C*), (*A, D*), (*B, C*), (*B, D*), (*C, D*)}   Ⓑ {(*A, B*)}   Ⓒ {(*A, B*), (*B, A*)} Ⓓ {(*C, D*)}   Ⓔ {(*A, B*), (*B, A*), (*A, C*), (*C, A*), (*A, D*), (*D, A*), (*B, C*), (*C, B*), (*B, D*), (*D, B*), (*C, D*), (*D, C*)}

The *sample space* of an experiment is the set of all possible outcomes. We frequently designate a sample space by a set of ordered pairs, triples, etc., as in the above question. In this case the order of each pair represents the order in which the cards are drawn. Each outcome is represented by an element of the sample space and is called a *sample point*.

EXAMPLE

Find the sample space for an experiment in which three coins are tossed.

SOLUTION: Each of the three actions of flipping a coin can turn out in two ways. By 27-1 we can expect the sample space to have $2 \times 2 \times 2 = 8$ outcomes. The branching diagram below indicates how these outcomes can be ascertained:

First Coin   Second Coin   Third Coin   Sample Point

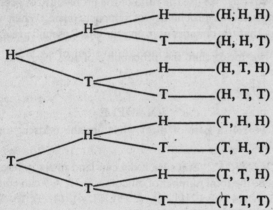

		H	(H, H, H)
	H		
		T	(H, H, T)
H		H	(H, T, H)
	T		
		T	(H, T, T)
		H	(T, H, H)
	H		
		T	(T, H, T)
T		H	(T, T, H)
	T		
		T	(T, T, T)

In the multiple-choice question, a sample space is the set of all ordered pairs for which the first entry is A, B, C or D and the second entry is different from the first. Choice Ⓔ fits this description.

¶ DRILL In an experiment in which a pair of dice are rolled, determine the sample space. (The six faces of a die are numbered from 1 to 6.)

*[3] Two boys choose blind dates at random from among a group of three girls. If the boys know nothing about the girls when they choose, how many elements are there in the "event" that is the set of all sample points for which a specific girl does not have a date?

Ⓐ 1   Ⓑ 2   Ⓒ 3   Ⓓ 4   Ⓔ 6

An *event* is any subset of a sample space. Label the boys A and B. Label the girls X, Y and Z with Z being the girl in question. We want to find that subset of the set of matchings that contains all the sample points for which Z is dateless. We set up the sample space by means of the following table (*dl* stands for "dateless"):

	X	Y	Z
(1)	A	B	dl
(2)	B	A	dl
(3)	A	dl	B
(4)	B	dl	A
(5)	dl	A	B
(6)	dl	B	A

Each sample point is a set of three elements, for example {AX, BY, dateless Z}, rather than an ordered triple. This is so because the ordered triples: (BY, AX, dateless Z), (AX, dateless Z, BY) and (AX, BY, dateless Z), etc., all result in the same dating couples.

The event in question is the set that contains the first two rows of the table above. (Those of you who are interested in set theory will note that this event is a set of sets and is in turn a subset of the set that is the sample space.)

Event: {{AX, BY, dateless Z}, {BX, AY, dateless Z}}.

EXAMPLE

A bag contains a red ball, a blue ball and a white ball. Each of the three balls is drawn in turn from the bag and not replaced. Set up the sample space for the experiment and the event for which the first ball drawn is white.

SOLUTION: The sample space will be a set of ordered triples since the order of the drawing is specified in the action of the experiment. In the table below the numbers represent the order of the draw:

Red	White	Blue	Sample Point
1	2	3	(R, W, B)
1	3	2	(R, B, W)
2	1	3	(W, R, B)
2	3	1	(B, R, W)
3	1	2	(W, B, R)
3	2	1	(B, W, R)

The sample space is the set of ordered triples in the column on the right, and the event is the subset {(W, R, B), (W, B, R)}.

¶ DRILL Two perfect coins are flipped. Set up the sample space and the event that the coins are not the same.

FINDING THE PROBABILITY OF AN EVENT

*[4] A chewing gum vending machine contains red, yellow and green gum-balls. The number of red is the same as the number of green but is half the number of yellow. If the balls were placed in the machine at random when it was loaded, what is the probability that a customer will get a red one on a given purchase?

(A) $\frac{1}{4}$ (B) $\frac{1}{2}$ (C) 1   (D) 2   (E) 4

PROBABILITY
May be defined as follows:

Suppose a sample space contains n sample points (outcomes), each equally likely (no outcome occurring more frequently than any other), and suppose that a certain event E, having e possible outcomes, is a subset of the sample space. Then the probability of the event E is $\frac{e}{n}$ and is designated by $P(E)$.

In the question above let n represent the total number of gum-balls (this will be the number of sample points) in the machine. Then $(\frac{1}{4})n$ is the number of red ones. By the definition of probability the answer is

$$\frac{(1/4)n}{n} = \frac{1}{4}.$$

EXAMPLE

If we take the spades from a pinochle deck, we get 12 cards, two each of 9, 10, J, K, Q and A. If after shuffling these cards and placing them face down on the table we draw a card, what is the probability that it will be an ace?

SOLUTION: The sample space contains 12 sample points (the 12 different cards which can be drawn). The event in question contains two sample points, the two aces.

$$P(E) = \frac{2}{12} = \frac{1}{6}$$

¶ DRILL

(a) In the multiple-choice question, figure out the probability of drawing a yellow.
(b) In the Example, figure the probability of drawing a face card (the face cards are J, K, Q, A).

*[5] Before the start of a horse race, and based on the past performances of the horses entered, the spectators are told that the chances are 4 to 1 that

"Old Rosebud" will lose. What is the probability that Old Rosebud will win?

(A) $\frac{1}{4}$ (B) 4   (C) 5   (D) $\frac{1}{5}$ (E) $\frac{4}{5}$

The probability of the occurrence of an event ranges from 0 (impossible) to 1 (certainty) because the number of sample points in the event can range from 0 to n, where n is the total number of possible outcomes. If the event of occurrence contains e elements, then the event of nonoccurrence contains $n - e$ elements. The probability of occurrence is defined to be $\frac{e}{n}$ and of nonoccurrence to be

$$\frac{n - e}{n} = 1 - \frac{e}{n}.$$

Thus, when the probability of an event is $\frac{2}{7}$, the probability of nonoccurrence is $\frac{5}{7}$.

When we express probability as "chances for" or as "odds on," we use the ratio of the probability of occurrence to the probability of nonoccurrence. When we say that the chances of losing for Old Rosebud are 4 to 1, we mean that the probability of loss is $\frac{4}{5}$ and of victory is $\frac{1}{5}$.

EXAMPLE
If we roll a pair of dice, what are the odds against rolling a 7?

SOLUTION: Since each die can land in six different ways, the total number of outcomes is 36. A 7 can come up in six ways: {(1, 6), (2, 5), (3, 4), (4, 3), (5, 2), (6, 1)}. The odds against a 7 are thus 5 to 1 (reduced from 30 to 6).

¶ DRILL If the letters of the word "PIPE" are written on separate pieces of paper, dropped into a hat and then drawn out one at a time, what are the odds that the two "P's" will emerge on successive draws?

FINDING THE PROBABILITY OF MUTUALLY EXCLUSIVE EVENTS

*[6] A bag contains 12 marbles; six are red, four are blue and two are white. If one marble is drawn from the bag, what is the probability that it is either white or blue?

(A) $\frac{1}{6}$ (B) $\frac{1}{18}$ (C) $\frac{1}{2}$ (D) 2   (E) 1

Two or more events are *mutually exclusive* if success in one event necessitates failure for the others. For example, if a die is rolled on a flat table, each outcome excludes all of the others (the die cannot turn up with both a 2 and a 4 at the same time). The outcome of selecting a marble of one color from the bag above excludes each of the other colors.

28-1 If two events are mutually exclusive and *a* is the probability of the first event while *b* is the probability of the second event, then the probability of either one or the other event is *a* + *b*.

The probability of selecting a white marble is $\frac{2}{12}$; of selecting a blue marble, $\frac{4}{12}$. The probability of selecting one *or* the other is

$$\frac{2}{12} + \frac{4}{12} = \frac{6}{12} = \frac{1}{2}.$$

EXAMPLE

If the letters of the word "STATISTICS" are written on separate cards, shuffled and dropped into a hat, and if a card is drawn at random, what is the probability it will be either an "S" or a "T"?

SOLUTION: The events are mutually exclusive since drawing a given letter indicates failure at drawing any other letter. The probability of an "S" is $\frac{3}{10}$ and of a "T" is $\frac{3}{10}$, so the probability of "S or T" is $\frac{6}{10} = \frac{3}{5}$.

¶ DRILL In the example above, find the probability that the letter drawn will be a vowel or a "T."

FINDING THE PROBABILITY OF INDEPENDENT EVENTS

*[7] **The six faces of a perfect cubical wooden block are painted so that four are red and two are green. If the block is rolled twice, what is the probability that it will come to rest on a green face both times?**

Ⓐ $\frac{2}{3}$ Ⓑ $\frac{1}{9}$ Ⓒ $\frac{1}{2}$ Ⓓ $\frac{1}{18}$ Ⓔ $\frac{1}{3}$

Two or more events are *independent* if success on one has no bearing on the success of any other. In the question above the first roll does not influence the second roll in any way.

28-2 When two events are independent and if the probability of the occurrence of the first is *a* while the probability of the second is *b*, then the probability that both will occur is *ab*.

EXAMPLE

A coin is tossed three times. What is the probability that all three will be "heads?" All three "tails?" All three the same?

SOLUTION: Each flip is independent of any other flip. The probability of "heads" for a given flip is $\frac{1}{2}$. The probability of "tails" on a given flip is also $\frac{1}{2}$, so the probability of all "tails" is $\frac{1}{8}$. The probability of all being the same means that all are "heads" or all are "tails." Since these two events are mutually exclusive, the probability of all coins the same is $\frac{1}{8} + \frac{1}{8} = \frac{1}{4}$.

In the multiple-choice question, the result of the second toss is independent of the result of the first toss. The probability of landing with a green face down on one toss is $\frac{1}{3}$, two faces out of six, and on both tosses is $(\frac{1}{3})(\frac{1}{3}) = \frac{1}{9}$.

¶ DRILL Two balls are drawn in order from a bag containing four reds and five whites. If the first ball is replaced before the second ball is drawn, what is the probability that both will be white?

*[8] **Two cards are drawn at random from a standard deck of 52 cards containing four different suits of 13 cards each. If the first card is not replaced before the second card is drawn, what is the probability that both cards will be of a given suit?**

Ⓐ $\frac{12}{51}$ Ⓑ $\frac{3}{51}$ Ⓒ $\frac{1}{16}$ Ⓓ $\frac{1}{2}$ Ⓔ $\frac{1}{4}$

In this problem, the outcome of the first draw changes the experiment and alters the probability of the second. In such a case the probability of *both* outcomes happening is, again, the product of the probabilities, but the probability of the second trial is based on the assumption that the first trial was successful. Do you see that if we assumed the first trial to be unsuccessful, the probability of *both* events occurring would be 0? The probability of the first card drawn is $\frac{13}{52}$ or $\frac{1}{4}$, and, if this trial was successful, then the second probability is $\frac{12}{51}$ and the compound probability is

$$(\frac{1}{4})(\frac{12}{51}) = \frac{3}{51}.$$

This problem could, of course, have been worked directly from the definition of probability. The number of outcomes in the event is the number of permutations of the 13 cards in a suit taken two at a time or 13 × 12. The number of outcomes in the sample space is the number of permutations of the whole deck taken two at a time or 52 × 51. The probability is therefore:

$$\frac{13 \times 12}{52 \times 51} = \frac{3}{51}.$$

Another way to approach this is to say that, since any card is a satisfactory first card, its probability is 1. In order to get a second card of the same suit, the probability is $\frac{12}{51}$.

$$1 \cdot \frac{12}{51} = \frac{12}{51}$$

Suppose the question had asked for the probability that the cards would be of the *same* suit rather than one given suit. This means both are hearts or both clubs, etc. Since these are mutually exclusive and the probability has just been figured at $\frac{3}{51}$, the total probability is

$$\frac{3}{51} + \frac{3}{51} + \frac{3}{51} + \frac{3}{51} = \frac{12}{51}.$$

¶ DRILL A box contains four red marbles and four white marbles. If two marbles are drawn at random and the first is *not* replaced before the second is drawn, what is the probability that both are white?

WHAT YOU SHOULD KNOW

KEY CONCEPTS

1. If an event E can occur in e possible, equally likely ways out of a sample space containing n equally likely outcomes and $0 \le e \le n$, then the probability of E is $\frac{e}{n}$.
2. Two or more events are *mutually exclusive* if success in one event must result in failure for the other(s).
3. Two or more events are *independent* if success in one event has no bearing on the success or failure of the other(s).

KEY PRINCIPLES

1. For *mutually exclusive* events:
   If two events are mutually exclusive and a is the probability of the first event while b is the probability of the second event, then the probability of either one or the other event is $a + b$.

2. For *independent* events:
   If two events are independent and the probability of the first is a while the probability of the second is b, then the probability that both will occur is ab.

TEST-TAKING STRATEGIES

- To find the sample space for a given experiment or other situation, set up a table showing the elements that comprise each sample point.
- Be clear on when probabilities are multiplied (independent events) and when they are added (mutually exclusive events).

ANSWERS

[1] The question is purposely facetious; read the section. The best answer is Ⓔ.
DRILL:
(a) A priori, 8. (b) Statistical.
(c) Statistical. (d) A priori, 6.

[2] Ⓔ
DRILL:
{(1, 1), (1, 2), (1, 3), (1, 4), (1, 5), (1, 6),
(2, 1), (2, 2), (2, 3), (2, 4), (2, 5), (2, 6),
(3, 1), (3, 2), (3, 3), (3, 4), (3, 5), (3, 6),
(4, 1), (4, 2), (4, 3), (4, 4), (4, 5), (4, 6),
(5, 1), (5, 2), (5, 3), (5, 4), (5, 5), (5, 6),
(6, 1), (6, 2), (6, 3), (6, 4), (6, 5), (6, 6)},

[3] Ⓑ
DRILL:
Sample space: {(H, H), (T, T), (H, T), (T, H)}.
Event: {(H, T), (T, H)}.

[4] Ⓐ
DRILL:
(a) $\frac{1}{2}$ (b) $\frac{2}{3}$

[5] Ⓓ
DRILL:
Probability: $\frac{6}{12} = \frac{1}{2}$; odds: 1 to 1.

[6] Ⓒ
DRILL:
$\frac{3}{5}$

[7] Ⓑ
DRILL:
$\frac{25}{81}$

[8] Ⓑ
DRILL:
$\frac{3}{14}$

29. The Binomial Theorem

> *In this chapter all topics are more typical of those tested on the Mathematics Level II exam than of those on the Level I exam. We have therefore denoted them with an asterisk (*). Review of such topics may assist you in answering Level I questions, however, because it increases your general knowledge of mathematical ideas, methods and skills.*

Key Term

binomial an expression of the form $a + b$.

LEARNING THE BINOMIAL FORMULA

*[1] How many terms are there in the expansion of $(x + 2)^{k-2}$?

Ⓐ $k + 1$ Ⓑ k Ⓒ $k - 1$ Ⓓ $k - 2$
Ⓔ $k - 3$

Any expression of the form $a + b$ is called a *binomial*. In this section we will make some observations about expressions that result from raising binomials to positive integral powers. By direct multiplication we arrive at the following:

$(a + b)^0 = 1,$
$(a + b)^1 = a + b,$
$(a + b)^2 = a^2 + 2ab + b^2,$
$(a + b)^3 = a^3 + 3a^2b + 3ab^2 + b^3,$
$(a + b)^4 = a^4 + 4a^3b + 6a^2b^2 + 4ab^3 + b^4,$
$(a + b)^5 = a^5 + 5a^4b + 10a^3b^2 + 10a^2b^3 + 5ab^4 + b^5.$

From this evidence we will make five general statements about the expansion of $(a + b)^n$ where n is a positive integer; these statements are suggested by the sample expansions above and can be proved by methods beyond the scope of this course.

(1) The expansion has $n + 1$ terms.

(2) Some power of b is a factor of every term except the first, and some power of a is a factor of every term but the last.

(3) The first term is always a^n and in each succeeding term the power of a decreases by 1.

(4) The sum of the exponents of a and b for each term is n.

(5) The coefficient of each term relates to that of the succeeding term as follows: when the binomial coefficient of a term is multiplied by the exponent of a and divided by the number of the term, the result is the binomial coefficient of the succeeding term.

These observations are summarized in the following expression, called the binomial formula:

$$(a + b)^n = a^n + na^{n-1}b + \frac{n(n - 1)}{2}a^{n-2}b^2$$
$$+ \frac{n(n - 1)(n - 2)}{2 \cdot 3}a^{n-3}b^3 + \ldots + b^n.$$

In the multiple-choice question, the exponent of the expansion is $k - 2$. Since the number of terms is one more than this exponent, the answer is

$$(k - 2) + 1 = k - 1.$$

¶ **DRILL** Use the above observations to write the terms of the expansion of each of the following:

(a) $(x + y)^3$ (b) $(a + 3)^5$
(c) $(x - y)^4$ (d) $\left(a + \dfrac{1}{a}\right)^5$

*[2] If the fifth term of the expansion of $\left(x^3 - \dfrac{1}{2}\right)^{10}$ is $\dfrac{105}{8}x^{18}$, which of the following is the sixth term?

Ⓐ $-\dfrac{189}{4}x^{21}$ Ⓑ $-\dfrac{189}{4}x^{18}$ Ⓒ $-\dfrac{189}{4}x^{15}$

Ⓓ $-\dfrac{63}{8}x^{15}$ Ⓔ $-\dfrac{63}{8}x^{18}$

In the preceding section we introduced the binomial formula, and we will continue our discussion here with an emphasis on finding coefficients. Each term in the expansion of $(a + b)^n$ consists of three factors: a binomial coefficient, a power of a and a power of b. For example, the first term has 1 as its binomial coefficient, the power of a is a^n and the power of b is b^0. For the second term the power of a is a^{n-1}, the power of b is b^1, and the binomial coefficient is n. But when a and b represent expressions that also involve coefficients (as in $(x + 2y)^4$, where $a = x$ and $b = 2y$, or in $(3v - \frac{1}{2}w)^6$, where $a = 3v$ and $b = -\frac{1}{2}w$) the final coefficient of each term is not just the binomial coefficient. To expand such a binomial apply the binomial formula, but do not simplify each term before continuing; remember that the binomial formula expresses the binomial coefficients in terms of other binomial coefficients and *not* in terms of the final coefficient.

EXAMPLE 1

Expand $(x + 2y)^4$.

SOLUTION: $a = x$, $b = 2y$ and $n = 4$.

$(x + 2y)^4 = x^4 + 4x^3(2y)^1 + \dfrac{4 \times 3}{2} x^2(2y)^2$

$+ \dfrac{4 \times 3 \times 2}{2 \times 3}x(2y)^3 + \dfrac{4 \times 3 \times 2 \times 1}{2 \times 3 \times 4}(2y)^4,$

$= x^4 + 8x^3y + 24x^2y^2 + 32xy^3 + 16y^4$

EXAMPLE 2

Write the first four terms of $(3v - \frac{1}{2}w)^6$.

SOLUTION: $a = 3v$, $b = -\frac{1}{2}w$ and $n = 6$

$(3v - \dfrac{1}{2}w)^6$

$= (3v)^6 + 6(3v)^5(-\dfrac{1}{2}w) + \dfrac{6 \times 5}{2}(3v)^4(-\dfrac{1}{2}w)^2$

$+ \dfrac{6 \times 5 \times 4}{2 \times 3}(3v)^3(-\dfrac{1}{2}w)^3 + \cdots$

$= 729v^6 - 729v^5w + \dfrac{1215}{4}v^4w^2$

$- \dfrac{135}{2}v^3w^3 + \cdots.$

In the multiple-choice question, the sixth term must be:

$\dfrac{10 \cdot 9 \cdot 8 \cdot 7 \cdot 6}{2 \cdot 3 \cdot 4 \cdot 5}(x^3)^5(-\dfrac{1}{2})^5 = -\dfrac{63}{8}x^{15}.$

> ## TEST-TAKING TIP.
>
> Suppose that you did not know how to find the coefficient but did know that the exponent of x must decrease from each term to the next. This information alone would be enough to eliminate (A), (B) and (E) since you are given that the exponent is 18 in the fifth term. In such situations, guessing among the remaining choices would probably help your score.

¶ DRILL Write the first three terms in the expansion of each of the following:

(a) $(2x - y)^8$ (b) $(y - 4)^4$ (c) $\left(\dfrac{w}{2} - \dfrac{v}{3}\right)^5$

FINDING THE GENERAL TERM OF A BINOMIAL SERIES

*[3] Which of the following is the sixth term of the expansion of $(1 + xy)^{10}$?

  (A) $210x^4y^6$ (B) $210x^5y^5$ (C) $252x^5y^5$
  (D) $252x^6y^6$ (E) $252x^4y^6$

In this section we will attempt to aid your memorization of the binomial theorem by introducing a formula for the general term of a binomial series. We will assume familiarity with factorial notation and with the formula which yields the number of combinations of n things taken r at a time. If you are unfamiliar with these, please review Chapter 27.

The general term of $(a + b)^n$, where n is a positive integer, is given by

$$_nC_{t-1}a^?b^{t-1},$$

where t is the number of the term. The question mark represents an exponent more easily found than its algebraic expression $(n - t + 1)$ suggests: recall that the sum of the exponents is always n, and you need not memorize the expression $(n - t + 1)$.

EXAMPLE 1

Find the fifth term of $(2x - y)^7$.

SOLUTION: Since $a = 2x$, $b = -y$, $n = 7$ and $t = 5$, the fifth term is

$$_7C_4(2x)^3(-y)^4 = \dfrac{7!}{4!3!}(8x^3y^4) = 280x^3y^4.$$

EXAMPLE 2

Find the middle term of $(x^2 - y)^6$.

SOLUTION: Since $n = 6$ there are seven terms and the middle term is the fourth. Therefore $a = x^2$, $b = -y$, $n = 6$ and $t = 4$. The fourth term is

$$_6C_3(x^2)^3(-y)^3 = \frac{6!}{3!3!} x^6(-y)^3 = -20x^6y^3.$$

In the multiple-choice question, the sixth term of the expansion is

$$_{10}C_5(1)^5(xy)^5 = \frac{10!}{5!5!} x^5y^5 = 252x^5y^5.$$

¶ **DRILL** Find the requested term:

(a) The sixth term of $(x + y)^{15}$

(b) The fourth term of $(2a - b)^9$

(c) The middle term of $(x^2 - \frac{1}{2})^{12}$

USING OTHER METHODS TO FIND TERMS

*[4] One of the terms of $\left(x - \dfrac{1}{\sqrt{x}}\right)^{12}$ contains no variable. Which of the following is the simplified form of that term?

Ⓐ 4620   Ⓑ −495   Ⓒ 495   Ⓓ −4620
Ⓔ 4965

We will answer this question directly. Since $a = x$ and $b = -(\frac{1}{\sqrt{x}})$, each term, exclusive of binomial coefficient, can be written as

(1) $x^p\left(-\dfrac{1}{\sqrt{x}}\right)^q$, where $p + q = 12$.

But $-\dfrac{1}{\sqrt{x}} = -x^{-1/2}$ and so expression (1) becomes

(2) $x^p(-x^{-1/2})^q = -x^{p-(1/2)q}$.

The term requested must have $p - (\frac{1}{2})q = 0$ if it has no variable, so p and q are solutions to the system

$$\begin{cases} p + q = 12 \\ p - (\frac{1}{2})q = 0. \end{cases}$$

Thus $p = 4$ and $q = 8$.

Since q is always one less than the number of the term, the requested term is the ninth:

$$_{12}C_8(x^4)\left(-\dfrac{1}{\sqrt{x}}\right)^8 = \frac{12!}{4!8!}(-1)^8 = 495.$$

¶ **DRILL** Find the term independent of x in $\left(x^2 - \dfrac{1}{x}\right)^9$.

*[5] Which of the following is the third term in the expansion of $(x^2 - 9)^{3/2}$?

Ⓐ $\dfrac{243}{8x}$ Ⓑ $-\dfrac{243}{8x}$ Ⓒ $-\dfrac{27x}{2}$ Ⓓ $\dfrac{27x}{2}$

Ⓔ $\dfrac{243x}{8}$

When n is not a positive integer and $|a| > |b|$, the expansion of $(a + b)^n$ yields an infinite series. The use of the combinatorial notation is not applicable, and the expansion must be done according to the binomial formula presented at the beginning of this chapter.

EXAMPLE 1

Expand $(1 + x)^{1/2}$ to four terms.

SOLUTION: $a = 1, b = x, n = \dfrac{1}{2}$

$$(1 + x)^{1/2} = 1^{1/2} + \frac{1}{2}(1)^{-1/2}(x)^1$$
$$+ \frac{1/2(1/2 - 1)}{2}(1)^{-3/2}x^2$$
$$+ \frac{1/2(1/2 - 1)(1/2 - 2)}{2 \times 3}(1)^{-5/2}x^3 + \cdots$$
$$= 1 + \frac{1}{2}x - \frac{1}{8}x^2 + \frac{1}{16}x^3 + \cdots$$

EXAMPLE 2

Write the first four terms of $(1 - x)^{-3}$.

SOLUTION: $a = 1, b = -x, n = -3$

$$(1 - x)^{-3} = 1^{-3} + (-3)(1)^{-4}(-x)^1$$
$$+ \frac{(-3)(-3 - 1)}{2}(1)^{-5}(-x)^2$$
$$+ \frac{(-3)(-3 - 1)(-3 - 2)}{2 \times 3}(1)^{-6}(-x)^3$$
$$= 1 + 3x + 6x^2 + 10x^3 + \cdots$$

In the multiple-choice question,

$$(x^2 - 9)^{3/2} = (x^2)^{3/2}$$
$$+ \frac{3}{2}(x^2)^{1/2}(-9)$$
$$+ \frac{3/2(3/2 - 1)}{2}(x^2)^{-1/2}(-9)^2 + \cdots$$
$$= x - \frac{27}{2}x + \frac{243}{8}\left(\frac{1}{x}\right) + \cdots.$$

¶ **DRILL** Write the first three terms of:

(a) $(4x + 3y)^{-1/2}$ (b) $(a^3 - x^3)^{-1/3}$

(c) $(1 + x)^{-2}$

WHAT YOU SHOULD KNOW

KEY CONCEPTS

1. If $(a + b)^n$ is written in expanded form, the following statements are true of the result:
   a. The expansion has $n + 1$ terms.
   b. A power of b is a factor of each term except the first, and a power of a is a factor of each term but the last.
   c. The first term is always a^n, and in each succeeding term the power of a decreases by 1.
   d. The sum of the exponents of a and b for each term is n.
   e. The coefficient of each term relates to that of the succeeding term as follows: when the binomial coefficient of a term is multiplied by the exponent of a in that term and divided by the number of the term, the result is the binomial coefficient of the succeeding term.
2. The general term of $(a + b)^n$ is

$$_nC_{t-1}a^{n-t+1}b^{t-1},$$

   where t is the number of the term. Note that the sum of the exponents is n. The second exponent is easier to remember, and the first can be calculated from it by subtracting it from n.

KEY FORMULA

$$(a + b)^n = a^n + na^{n-1}b + \frac{n(n-1)}{2}a^{n-2}b^2$$
$$+ \frac{n(n-1)(n-2)}{2 \cdot 3}a^{n-3}b^3 + \ldots + b^n.$$

(Binomial Formula)

TEST-TAKING STRATEGY

- Keep in mind that the binomial formula expresses the binomial coefficents in terms of other binomial coefficients, not in terms of the final coefficient; therefore do not simplify each term before continuing the expansion.

ANSWERS

[1] Ⓒ
DRILL:
(a) $x^3 + 3x^2y + 3xy^2 + y^3$
(b) $a^5 + 15a^4 + 90a^3 + 270\,a^2 + 405a + 243$
(c) $x^4 - 4x^3y + 6x^2y^2 - 4xy^3 + y^4$
(d) $a^5 + 5a^3 + 10a + 10a^{-1} + 5a^{-3} + a^{-5}$

[2] Ⓓ
DRILL:
(a) $256x^8 - 1024x^7y + 1792x^6y^2 + \ldots$
(b) $y^4 - 16y^3 + 96y^2 + 1 + \ldots$
(c) $\dfrac{w^5}{32} - \dfrac{5w^4v}{48} + \dfrac{5w^3v^2}{36} + \ldots$

[3] Ⓒ
DRILL:
(a) $3003x^{10}y^5$
(b) $-5376a^6b^3$
(c) $\dfrac{231x^{12}}{16}$

[4] Ⓒ
DRILL:
The seventh term is $84(x^2)^3 \left(-\dfrac{1}{x} \right)^6 = 84$.

[5] Ⓐ
DRILL:
(a) $\dfrac{1}{2}x^{-1/2} - \dfrac{3}{16}x^{-3/2}y + \dfrac{27}{256}x^{-5/2}y^2$
(b) $a^{-1} + \dfrac{1}{3}a^{-4}x^3 + \dfrac{2}{9}a^{-7}x^6$
(c) $1 - 2x + 3x^2$

Other Topics

30. Volume and Surface Area

> *In this chapter, some topics are more typical of those tested on the Mathematics Level II exam than of those on the Level I exam. We have denoted these with an asterisk (*). Review of such topics may assist you in answering Level I questions, however, because it increases your general knowledge of mathematical ideas, methods and skills.*

Key Terms

prism   a solid figure determined by a pair of congruent polygons lying in a pair of parallel planes. Example: a cube.

circular cylinder   a solid figure determined by a pair of congruent circles lying in a pair of parallel planes.

pyramid   given a plane containing a polygon, P, and given a point, X, not contained in the plane: a *pyramid* is the union of all segments such that (1) X is an endpoint, and (2) the other endpoint lies within P.

cone   given a plane containing a circle, C, and a point, X, not contained in the plane: a *cone* is the union of all segments such that (1) X is an endpoint, and (2) the other endpoint lies within C.

sphere   given a point, O, and a positive number, r: a *sphere* consists of the set of all points in space that are r units from O.

WORKING WITH PRISMS

[1] The number of units in the volume of a certain cube is equal to the number of units in its surface area. Find the length of an edge of the cube.

  Ⓐ 1 Ⓑ 2 Ⓒ 4 Ⓓ 6 Ⓔ 8

A cube is an example of a solid figure known as a prism. A *prism* is determined by a pair of congruent polygons, P and P', lying in a pair of parallel planes. If A and A' are corresponding vertices of polygons P and P', then the prism determined by P and P' is the union of all segments XX' such that (1) X lies in the region determined by P, (2) X' lies in the region determined by P', and (3) segment XX' is parallel to segment AA'.

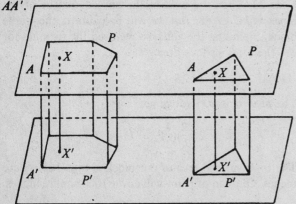

The polygonal regions P and P' are called the *bases*. The segments connecting corresponding vertices are called *lateral edges*, and the sides of the polygons are called the *basal edges*. The region determined by a pair of basal edges and their connecting lateral edges is called a *lateral face*. A lateral face is always a parallelogram (and, when a lateral edge is perpendicular to a base, also a rectangle). The union of all lateral faces is called the *lateral surface*. The union of the lateral surface and the bases is the *total surface*.

If a lateral edge is perpendicular to the plane containing a base, the prism is a *right prism*—frequently referred to as a *rectangular solid*.

The distance between the two parallel planes is called the *altitude* of the prism.

The volume of a prism is given by the formula

(1) $V = hB$,

where h is the altitude of the solid and B is the area of the base. In the multiple-choice question we deal with a cube, which could be called a "right" (meaning the lateral edges are perpendicular to the base) "square" (meaning the defining polygonal bases are squares) "prism." Let e represent the length of an edge. All of the edges, lateral and basal, are equal in length. Thus formula (1) gives us $V = e^3$ for the volume of a cube.

The lateral surface area, S_L, of a prism is given by

(2) $S_L = hp$,

where h is the altitude of the solid and p is the perimeter of a base. If e represents the edge of a square, then $4e$ is the perimeter of its base and $S_L = 4e^2$.

The total surface area, S_T, of a prism is the lateral surface area plus the sum of the areas of the bases:

(3) $S_T = hp + 2B$.

If e represents the edge of a square, then $S_L = 4e^2$ and $2B = 2e^2$ so $S_T = 6e^2$.

Therefore, in the multiple-choice question, we are looking for e such that $e^3 = 6e^2$. Dividing each side by e^2, we get $e = 6$.

¶ Drill Find (1) the volume, (2) the lateral surface area and (3) the total surface area of each of the following:

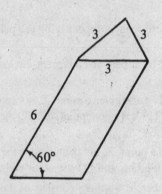

(a) A cube with edge of 2.

(b) A rectangular solid with dimensions $1 \times 2 \times 3$.

(c) The triangular prism shown at right.

WORKING WITH CIRCULAR CYLINDERS

[2] A certain toy block is a right circular cylinder 4 inches long with a volume of 154 cubic inches. A small can contains enough paint to cover an area of 1000 square inches. Approximately how many blocks can be painted completely with one can if you use $\frac{22}{7}$ for π?

(A) 1   (B) 2   (C) 4   (D) 6   (E) 8

A *circular cylinder* is determined by a pair of congruent circles, C and C', lying in a pair of parallel planes. The segment containing the centers, O and O', is called the *axis* of the cylinder. The cylinder determined by circles C and C' is the union of all segments XX' such that (1) X lies in the region determined by C, (2) X' lies in the region determined by C', and (3) segment XX' is parallel to the axis.

(Note the similarities between the definitions of "prism" and "cylinder.")

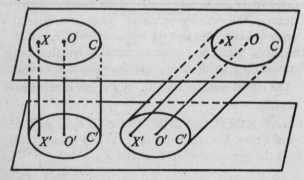

The circular regions are called the *bases*. The union of all segments connecting the circles (but not the circular regions) is called the *curved surface*. When the axis is perpendicular to the planes of the bases, the solid is a *right circular cylinder*. The distance between the parallel planes is called the *altitude* of the cylinder.

The formula for the volume of a cylinder is identical to that for a prism:

(1) $V = hB$,

where h is the altitude and B is the area of the base (B is, of course, figured differently for a cylinder and a prism).

In the multiple-choice question we can use the given length, 4, as h and compute the radius (approximately) by using the approximation $\frac{22}{7}$ for π:

$$154 = 4(\frac{22}{7})r^2,$$
$$\frac{7}{88} \times 154 = r^2,$$
$$\frac{49}{4} = r^2,$$
$$\frac{7}{2} = r.$$

The formula for the curved surface area, S_C, is

(2) $S_C = hC$,

where C is the circumference of the base. (The circumference of a circle is analogous to the perimeter of a polygon—note the similarity between equation (2) of this section and equation (2) of section [1].)

For the multiple-choice question we have computed r to be $\frac{7}{2}$ so we can find C to be 7π using $C = 2\pi r$. Approximating π as $\frac{22}{7}$ gives us an approximation for C of 22. Thus the area of the curved surface of the block is hC or 88. But we will be painting the whole block, including the ends, so we need the formula for S_T, the total surface area.

(3) $S_T = hC + 2B$

The area B is πr^2 so we get

$$2B = 2(\frac{22}{7})(\frac{7}{2})^2 = 11 \times 7 = 77.$$

The total surface area of our block is thus 165 square inches. Our can of paint will cover 1000 square inches.

$$\frac{1000}{165} = 6\frac{2}{33}$$

We can paint roughly six blocks.

¶ DRILL Find (1) the volume, (2) the curved surface area, and (3) the total surface area for each of the following:

(a) A right circular cylinder with radius of 5 and height of 1.

(b) A right circular cylinder whose volume equals its curved surface area.

WORKING WITH PYRAMIDS

*[3] A pyramid and a prism have equal altitudes and bases of equal area. What is the ratio of their volumes?

Ⓐ $\frac{1}{2}$　Ⓑ $\frac{1}{3}$　Ⓒ $\frac{1}{4}$　Ⓓ $\frac{1}{5}$　Ⓔ $\frac{1}{6}$

Given a plane containing a polygon, P, and given a point X not contained in the plane. A *pyramid* is the union of all segments such that (1) X is an endpoint, and (2) the other endpoint lies in the polygonal region determined by P. The polygonal region is the *base* of the pyramid, and the distance from X to the plane containing P is the *altitude*.

The formula for the volume, V, is

$$V = \frac{1}{3}hB,$$

where h is the altitude and B is the area of the base.

Compare the volume of a *pyramid*,

$$\frac{1}{3}hB,$$

with the volume of a prism of the same altitude and base,

$$hB.$$

The ratio of the volumes is $\frac{1}{3}$, which is answer Ⓑ of the multiple-choice question.

¶ DRILL Find the volume of the following *pyramids:*

(a) A square pyramid (meaning that the base is a square) with basal edge of 3 and height 4.

(b) A rectangular pyramid with basal edges of 3 and 4 and a height of 5.

(c) A pyramid all of whose faces are equilateral triangles with sides of length 6.

WORKING WITH CONES

*[4] If a solid brass cone with a height of 4 inches and a circular base of radius 4 inches is melted down and recast into two circular cones of height 2 inches and with circular bases of radius 4 inches, how many cubic inches of brass will be left over?

Ⓐ There is exactly enough brass to do the job
Ⓑ There is not enough brass　Ⓒ 1　Ⓓ π
Ⓔ 4

Given a plane containing a circle, C, and a point, X, not contained in the plane. A *cone* is the union of all segments such that (1) X is an endpoint, and (2) the other endpoint lies in the circular region determined by C. The circular region is called the *base* of the cone, and the distance from X to the plane of the base is the *altitude*.

The volume formula is

$$V = \frac{1}{3}hB,$$

where h is the altitude and B is the area of the base.

In the multiple-choice question the original cone has volume V_1,

$$V_1 = \frac{1}{3}(4)(16\pi) = \frac{64\pi}{3} \text{ cubic inches.}$$

Each of the smaller cones has volume V_2,

$$V_2 = \frac{1}{3}(2)(16\pi) = \frac{32\pi}{3} \text{ cubic inches.}$$

Thus there is exactly enough metal to accomplish the recasting.

¶ DRILL Find the volume of each of the following cones:

(a) A right circular cone with altitude 6 and base of radius 2.

(b) A right circular cone with radius 4 for which the distance from the *vertex* of the cone (the point X of the definition) to any point of the circle that defines the base is 5.

(c) A cone whose axis is not perpendicular to the base and for which the following are true: segment AB is a basal diameter of length 4, $XB \perp AB$ and $XA = 5$.

WORKING WITH SPHERES

*[5] An irregularly shaped chunk of metal is immersed in a pail which has been filled to the brim with water. The amount of water displaced by the immersion is 36π cubic inches. If the metal chunk were melted and recast in the shape of a spherical solid, what would the number of units be in the surface area of the new solid?

Ⓐ 1　Ⓑ 3　Ⓒ 6　Ⓓ 36　Ⓔ 36π

Given a point, O, and a positive number, r, the set of all points in space that are r units from O is called a *sphere*. O is the center and r is the radius. The set of all points X such that $OX \leq r$ is called a *spherical solid*.

The volume, V, of a spherical solid is given by the formula

$$V = \frac{4}{3}\pi r^3.$$

In the multiple-choice question we find the radius of the sphere to be

$$36\pi = \frac{4}{3}\pi r^3,$$
$$27 = r^3,$$
$$3 = r.$$

The surface area of a sphere is given by

$$S = 4\pi r^2.$$

For the multiple-choice question the surface area is

$$4\pi(3)^2 = 36\pi.$$

¶ DRILL Find (1) the volume and (2) the surface area of each of the following:

(a) A sphere of radius 5.
(b) A sphere for which the surface area equals the volume.

WHAT YOU SHOULD KNOW

KEY CONCEPTS

1. Volume is generally determined by using a memorized formula.
2. Surface area must by found by analyzing the shapes of the surfaces and choosing formulas that apply to these plane figures.
3. Prisms and cylinders are related forms and use similar formulas.
4. Pyramids and cones are related forms and use similar formulas.

KEY FORMULAS

A. Volume

1. *To find the volume of a prism:*
   If h is the altitude (the perpendicular distance between the planes containing the bases), and B is the area of a base, then
   $$V = hB.$$
2. *To find the volume of a cube:*
   If e is the length of an edge, then
   $$V = e^3.$$
3. *To find the volume of a cylinder:*
   If h is the altitude and B is the area of its base, then
   $$V = hB.$$

4. *To find the volume of a pyramid:*
   If h is the altitude and B is the area of a base, then
   $$V = \frac{1}{3}hB.$$
5. *To find the volume of a cone:*
   If h is the altitude and B is the area of a base, then
   $$V = \frac{1}{3}hB.$$
6. *To find the volume of a sphere:*
   If r is the radius, then
   $$V = \frac{4}{3}\pi r^3.$$

B. Surface Area

1. *To find the lateral surface area of a prism:*
   If h is the altitude and p is the perimeter of a base, then
   $$S_L = hp.$$
2. *To find the total surface area of a prism:*
   If h is the altitude, p is the perimeter of a base, and B is the area of a base, then
   $$S_T = hp + 2B.$$
3. *To find the total surface area of a cube:*
   If e is the length of an edge, then
   $$A = 6e^2.$$
4. *To find the area of the curved surface of a cylinder:*
   If h is the altitude, and C is the circumference of the base, then
   $$S_c = hC.$$
5. *To find the total surface area of a circular cylinder:*
   If h is the altitude, C is the circumference of the base, and B is the area of the base, then
   $$S_T = hC + 2B.$$
6. *To find the surface area of a sphere:*
   If r is the radius, then
   $$S = 4\pi r^2.$$

TEST-TAKING STRATEGY

- Before attempting to answer a volume or surface area question, note carefully what solid figure is involved, and, if a diagram is given, identify the base, lateral and basal edges, altitude, and other relevant parts.

ANSWERS

[1] ⓓ
   DRILL:
   (a) $V = 8$, $S_L = 16$, $S_T = 24$.
   (b) $V = 6$; any one of the six faces can be the base. We'll assume it is a 1×2 face; thus $S_L = 18$, $S_T = 22$.
   (c) $V = \dfrac{81}{4}$, $S_L = 27\sqrt{3}$, $S_T = \dfrac{63\sqrt{3}}{2}$.

[2] Ⓓ
DRILL:
(a) $V = 25\pi$, $S_C = 10\pi$, $S_T = 60\pi$
(b) The circular cylinder may be of any height as long as the radius of the base is 2 since $V = \pi r^2 h$ and $S_C = 2\pi rh$, yielding $\pi r^2 h = 2\pi rh$ and $r^2 = 2r$ so $r = 2$.

[3] Ⓑ
DRILL:
(a) 12
(b) 20
(c) Area of base $= 9\sqrt{3}$.
Altitude of the pyramid is $2\sqrt{6}$.
Volume is $18\sqrt{2}$.

[4] Ⓐ
DRILL:
(a) 8π
(b) Height must be 3, volume $= 16\pi$.
(c) Height must be 3, volume $= 4\pi$.

[5] Ⓔ
DRILL:
(a) $V = \dfrac{500\pi}{3}$ $S = 100\pi$
(b) $\dfrac{4\pi r^3}{3} = 4\pi r^2$, so $r = 3$, $V = 36\pi = S$.

31. Miscellaneous

HANDLING COMPUTERLIKE QUESTIONS

[1] If the instructions given below are carried out by a computer in the order shown, what would be printed by the time the computer stops?

1. LET $X = 1$
2. LET $Y = 2$
3. IF $X - Y < 0$, GO ON TO INSTRUCTION 6
4. IF $X - Y = 0$, GO ON TO INSTRUCTION 7
5. IF $X - Y > 0$, GO ON TO INSTRUCTION 8
6. PRINT A
7. PRINT B
8. PRINT C
9. LET X BE REPLACED BY $X + 1$ AND GO BACK TO INSTRUCTION 2

(A) A (B) A, B (C) A, B, C (D) A, B, C, C
(E) The computer does not stop

To show the procedure, we will work our way through this question, beginning with step 1.

The first two steps merely provide us with values to record and use later. After noting this information, we pass on to step 3.

Step 3 requires that a simple calculation be performed in order to follow the directions it gives. Since $X = 1$ and $Y = 2$, it follows that $X - Y = -1$, which is less than 0. Since the conditions of the "If" part of the instructions are satisfied, we must follow the command to go directly to step 6, skipping the intervening steps.

At step 6, we receive the information to print the letter A. After doing this we immediately proceed to step 7. *We do not return to step 4* because the directions at step 3 required us to pass over 4 and 5. Remember to follow the instructions in order from the step you have reached; in this case we must move to step 7 and print the letter B. Thus, at this stage we have printed

$$A, B.$$

Continuing to step 8, we print the letter C and now have

$$A, B, C.$$

Moving to step 9, we receive the command to change the initial value of X from 1 to $1 + 1 = 2$ and then return to step 2. Instead of being finished, we find ourselves almost at the start again, this time with new values!

When we repeat a section of the program, we are performing a "loop." Loop-type questions are the usual form selected for standardized achievement tests.

Since $X - Y$ is now 0, because X and Y are both 2, we must ignore step 3 and go to step 4, which directs us to step 7, at which point we receive the instruction to print the letter B again. We now have

$$A, B, C, B.$$

From 7 we go to 8 and print C again to get

$$A, B, C, B, C.$$

On to step 9. We now must replace the current value of X (which is 2) with the value $2 + 1 = 3$ as instructed in step 9. This step then directs us to return to step 2. This time we begin the loop with $X - Y = 1$, a positive number, so we ignore steps 3 and 4 and go to 5. The conditions are satisfied, and we follow the instructions to step 8, at which point we print C again.

We now have

$$A, B, C, B, C, C.$$

From step 8, we go to 9 and discover that X must be changed from 3 to 4, yielding an $X - Y$ that is positive and greater than before! Thus we learn that we are going to be looping forever as we jump from 5 to 8, print a C, then increase X again at 9. The computer continues on forever printing a chain of C's.

¶ DRILL In place of the drill normally found at the end of a review section, we are substituting two more computerlike questions.

[2] What is the final value of A if the following instructions are carried out?
 1. LET $A = 2$
 2. REPLACE THE VALUE OF A BY 2^A
 3. IF $A < 20$, GO BACK TO INSTRUCTION 2
 4. IF A IS NOT < 20, GO ON TO INSTRUCTION 5
 5. WRITE THE FINAL VALUE OF A

Ⓐ 2^5 Ⓑ 2^4 Ⓒ 20 Ⓓ 2^{16} Ⓔ 2

The infinite loop that developed in question [1] would be very upsetting to a computer, and the computer would probably even refuse to begin work on it once it scanned the program and discovered there was no way to stop. Wise computer programers build such discretionary powers into their processing software. By contrast, question [2] is an example of a loop that eventually attains a boundary value and quits. We shall see this as we work through the problem.

At step 1, the value of A is 2.

At step 2, the value of A is 4 because we must replace A by 2^4, which is 2^2. Then we go on to step 3. Since A is now 4 and, therefore, less than 20, we must follow the command to return to instruction 2.

On this return trip our value of A is 4, but the directions require us to replace this value with 2^4 or 16. Continuing on to step 3 again, we see that A is still less than 20 (it is 16, remember?) and we must again return to step 2. Now we replace A by 2^{16}. This is clearly greater than 20, so we can ignore step 3 and go on to step 4. The requirements of step 4 are satisfied (2^{16} is clearly not less than 20), and we pass on to step 5, thereby printing the final value of A, 2^{16}.

Since a computer receives its instructions typed along a line, it could not, of course, understand the symbol 2^4, but would really have to have it translated into a form such as $2\uparrow A$. As already noted in the first section of this chapter, CB tests do not favor any specific computer language, and all directions are made as easy to comprehend as possible.

[3] What value of X is written in instruction 7?
 1. LET $X = 1$
 2. LET $S = X^2 - 3X - 4$
 3. IF $S = 0$, GO TO INSTRUCTION 7
 4. IF S IS NOT 0, GO TO INSTRUCTION 5
 5. REPLACE THE VALUE OF X BY $X + 1$
 6. GO BACK TO INSTRUCTION 2
 7. WRITE THE PRESENT VALUE OF X

Ⓐ 1 Ⓑ -1 Ⓒ 2 Ⓓ 3 Ⓔ 4

Let's go through the loop and then see if there are any shortcuts.

Substituting 1 for X in step 2, we find that S is -6. Since S is not 0, we follow instruction 4 and go on to step 5. At step 5, we increase X from 1 to 2 and start over at step 2.

How many times must we go through the loop? Each time that we fail to get a root for S when our new value of X is given, we must increase X by 1 and start over. Obviously, we can shorten our work by figuring out the roots for S directly. Setting $S = 0$, we get

$$x^2 - 3x - 4 = 0,$$
$$(x - 4)(x + 1) = 0,$$
$$x = 4 \text{ or } x = -1.$$

We may disregard the -1 since X began at 1 and is always increasing. Thus we see that we will continue to loop until X becomes 4; only then will we satisfy instruction 3 and go on to instruction 7.

We could, of course, have found the answer by continuing to replace X by greater and greater values until we hit upon the correct result, but this takes more time. The procedure we used here, that of working with specific values until we become familiar with the problem, then deducing the answer, is a good basic approach to a large range of questions.

RESOLVING A FRACTION INTO A PAIR OF FRACTIONS

[4] Find the value of A if

$$\frac{2}{(x - 5)(x + 3)} = \frac{A}{x - 5} + \frac{B}{x + 3}$$

Ⓐ 1 Ⓑ 3 Ⓒ 5 Ⓓ -5 Ⓔ $\frac{1}{4}$

Procedures for combining rational expressions are a standard part of the study of intermediate math. A question like the one above, however, asks not how to *combine* fractions but how to *resolve* a fraction into a pair of fractions for which the given fraction is the sum.

This can be done by using the techniques already learned for combining fractions. What is the result of adding $\dfrac{A}{x-5}$ and $\dfrac{B}{x+3}$? The LCD is $(x-5)(x+3)$, so the result is

$$\dfrac{A(x+3)}{(x-5)(x+3)} + \dfrac{B(x-5)}{(x+3)(x-5)}$$
$$= \dfrac{Ax+3A+Bx-5B}{(x+3)(x-5)}$$
$$= \dfrac{(A+B)(x)+(3A-5B)}{(x+3)(x-5)}.$$

In order for the last rational expression to be equal to the given expression,

$$\dfrac{2}{(x-5)(x+3)},$$

the numerators must be equal. Therefore

(1) $\qquad 2 = (A+B)x + (3A-5B).$

Since the left side has no x term, the coefficient of any x term must be zero.

(2) $\qquad\qquad A+B = 0$

Since the constant term, 2, must equal the constant term, $(3A-5B)$, we get

(3) $\qquad\qquad 3A-5B = 2.$

Solving the system composed of equations (2) and (3) simultaneously will give us the desired information. We begin by solving (1) for B,

$$B = -A,$$

and replacing B with $-A$ in equation (3):

$$3A - 5(-A) = 2,$$
$$8A = 2,$$
$$A = \dfrac{1}{4}.$$

We could continue to find B, but the additional work is unnecessary since only A is requested.

If the left side of equation (1) had included a term involving x, we would have set $A+B$ equal to the coefficient of x in that expression and proceeded in the same way. For example, to resolve

$$\dfrac{3x-1}{x(x-1)} = \dfrac{A}{x} + \dfrac{B}{x-1}$$

we first write

$$\dfrac{A}{x} + \dfrac{B}{x-1} = \dfrac{A(x-1)}{x(x-1)} + \dfrac{Bx}{(x-1)x}$$
$$= \dfrac{(A+B)x - A}{x(x-1)}.$$

Therefore

$$3x - 1 = (A+B)x - A.$$

For this equation to be true, both of the following must hold:

$$A + B = 3,$$
$$-A = -1.$$

All that remains is to determine A and B; this is left as an exercise.

¶ DRILL Find A and B if:

(a) $\dfrac{2x+1}{x(x+1)} = \dfrac{A}{x} + \dfrac{B}{x+1}$

(b) $\dfrac{7}{6x^2+x-2} = \dfrac{A}{3x-2} + \dfrac{B}{x+1}$

WORKING WITH SINES AND COSINES

[5] If x is positive, but less than $\dfrac{\pi}{2}$, what is the least value of x for which $\cos\left(x+\dfrac{\pi}{6}\right) = 0$?

ⓐ $-\dfrac{\pi}{6}$ ⓑ $\dfrac{\pi}{6}$ ⓒ 0 ⓓ $\dfrac{\pi}{2}$ ⓔ $\dfrac{\pi}{3}$

To answer this question, you need to have a basic understanding of how the cosine function varies. Refer to the graph of the cosine found in section [15] of Chapter 24. Do you see that the smallest positive number that yields a cosine of 0 is $\dfrac{\pi}{2}$? Since $\cos\dfrac{\pi}{2} = 0$ and $\cos\left(x+\dfrac{\pi}{6}\right) = 0$, it follows that

$$\cos\left(x+\dfrac{\pi}{6}\right) = \cos\dfrac{\pi}{2}.$$

Therefore

$$x + \dfrac{\pi}{6} = \dfrac{\pi}{2},$$
$$x = \dfrac{\pi}{2} - \dfrac{\pi}{6}$$
$$= \dfrac{\pi}{3}.$$

¶ DRILL Find x if $0 < x < \dfrac{\pi}{2}$.

(a) $\sin\left(x+\dfrac{\pi}{6}\right) = 1$

(b) $\cos\left(x+\dfrac{\pi}{3}\right) = 0$

[6] What is the least positive number x for which

$$\cos\left(\dfrac{\pi}{6}-x\right) = \sin\left(\dfrac{\pi}{4}+2x\right)?$$

ⓐ $\dfrac{\pi}{6}$ ⓑ $\dfrac{\pi}{9}$ ⓒ $\dfrac{\pi}{3}$ ⓓ $\dfrac{\pi}{12}$ ⓔ $\dfrac{\pi}{15}$

As we have already reviewed in section [10] of Chapter 24, the sine and cosine functions are cofunctions, meaning that the cosine of an angle is the sine of its complement. Expressed in radians, this may be stated in either of two ways:

$$\sin x = \cos \left(\frac{\pi}{2} - x\right)$$

or

$$\cos x = \sin \left(\frac{\pi}{2} - x\right).$$

The same is true, of course, for secant and cosecant as well as for tangent and cotangent. In other words, when cofunctions are equal, the sum of the angle measures is $\frac{\pi}{2}$.

Applying this information to the question above, we get

(1) $\left(\frac{\pi}{6} - x\right) + \left(\frac{\pi}{4} + 2x\right) = \frac{\pi}{2}$,

(2) $\left(\frac{2\pi}{12} + \frac{3\pi}{12}\right) + x = \frac{6\pi}{12}$,

(3) $\frac{5\pi}{12} + x = \frac{6\pi}{12}$,

(4) $x = \frac{\pi}{12}$.

A common mistake made in approaching a question like this is to say that sine and cosine are equal for $\frac{\pi}{4}$ only on the domain specified so that both

(5) $\frac{\pi}{6} - x = \frac{\pi}{4}$ and $\frac{\pi}{4} + 2x = \frac{\pi}{4}$,

but the two equations given in (5) result in two different values for x! In fact, there is no basis to assume that the cosine and sine are operating on the same number.

¶ DRILL Find x:

(a) $\sin \left(x - \frac{\pi}{3}\right) = \cos \left(x + \frac{\pi}{2}\right)$

(b) $\cos (2x - \pi) = \sin \left(\frac{x}{2} + \pi\right)$

[7] Let $a = \cos \frac{p}{2}$, let $b = \cos p$ and let $c = \cos 2p$, where $0 < p < \frac{\pi}{4}$. Arrange a, b and c in order from least to greatest.

Ⓐ a, b, c Ⓑ a, c, b Ⓒ b, c, a Ⓓ b, a, c Ⓔ c, b, a

The cosine of x is a decreasing function as x increases from 0 to π. You can clearly see this from the graph of cosine in section [10] of Chapter 24. This means that the cosine gets smaller as x gets larger on this interval. In the question above, the number of which we are taking the cosine progresses from least at $\frac{p}{2}$ to greatest at $2p$. This means that the cosine is *decreasing* from $\frac{p}{2}$ through p to $2p$. Thus the corresponding values of cosine, $a, b,$ and c are decreasing. The order must be reversed to cause them to go from least to greatest.

¶ DRILL For what values of x from $0 \le x \le 2\pi$ will the following be (1) increasing and (2) decreasing?

(a) $\sin x$ (b) $\cos x$ (c) $\tan x$

[8] Suppose θ is a number between 0 and $\frac{\pi}{2}$ for which $\sin \theta = \frac{120}{169}$ and $\cos \theta = \frac{119}{169}$. Which of the following would be the closest approximation to the value of θ?

Ⓐ $\frac{\pi}{12}$ Ⓑ $\frac{\pi}{6}$ Ⓒ $\frac{\pi}{4}$ Ⓓ $\frac{\pi}{3}$ Ⓔ $\frac{\pi}{2}$

Students frequently pass up easy questions like this one because they look much more complex than they are. The most important information given above is that $\sin \theta$ and $\cos \theta$ are nearly equal, differing only by $\frac{1}{169}$. At what point do the graphs of $y = \cos \theta$ and $y = \sin \theta$ cross? Expressed in another way, under what circumstances will the ratio of the opposite side of an acute angle of a right triangle to the hypotenuse be equal to the ratio of the adjacent side to the hypotenuse? The latter question is answered by noting that this can occur when adjacent and opposite are equal, thus making the triangle an isosceles right triangle with angles of 45° (a measure of $\frac{\pi}{4}$ in radians). The former question (where do the graphs cross?) can be answered directly by referring to the graphs in section [10] of Chapter 24.

The given information that θ is between 0 and $\frac{\pi}{2}$ actually reduces the complexity of the problem by eliminating the alternatives.

¶ DRILL

(a) If the restriction of the domain in the question above had not been given, what would the answer have been?

(b) For what values between 0 and $\frac{\pi}{2}$ will $\sin \theta$ be equal to $\tan \theta$?

WORKING WITH REMAINDERS

[9] When p is divided by 7, the remainder is 1. When q is divided by 7, the remainder is 2. What will the remainder be if the product pq is divided by 7?

Ⓐ 1   Ⓑ 2   Ⓒ 3   Ⓓ 5   Ⓔ 7

TEST-TAKING TIP.

You probably have never seen a question like this one before, and, chances are, when you encounter questions relating to unfamiliar material on the Mathematics Level I Test, you will skip them. Skipping unfamiliar questions in order to devote time to the familiar ones can be a wise procedure, but do not reject a question you have not read carefully. Quite often a simple approach will get the answer quickly, as is true in this case.

Certainly a great deal of mathematical machinery can be cranked up to work on the problem of remainders after division by prime numbers. The development of theories about such things may be the life's work of a theoretical mathematician, but only a bit of common sense is needed on this one.

Choose a pair of numbers that satisfy the requirements for p and q; for example, 8 and 9. The remainders are, respectively, 1 and 2. Their product is 72. Dividing 72 by 7 gives a remainder of 2. The question has been answered.

Will the remainder always be 2? A more involved approach to the question proves that it will be. To satisfy the requirements, p must be of the form $7m + 1$ and q of the form $7n + 2$, where m and n are whole numbers. The product of these numbers is

$$(7m + 1)(7n + 2) = 49mn + 14m + 7n + 2$$
$$= 7(7mn + 2m + n) + 2.$$

The number in parentheses must be a whole number since it is composed of sums and products of wholes. Therefore the expression $7(7mn + 2m + n)$ must be divisible by 7 since it clearly has a factor of 7. Hence, the remainder must be 2 no matter what p and q are.

¶ DRILL Using the numbers 9 and 17 with a divisor of 5, answer the following questions about the remainders:

(a) Is the sum of the remainders the remainder of the sum?

(b) Is the product of the remainders the remainder of the product?

(c) Is the quotient of the remainders the remainder of the quotient?

(d) Is the difference of the remainders the remainder of the difference?

TEST-TAKING TIP.

Have you noticed how our discussion has moved in a very interesting direction, even though the question that started it has already been answered? Interesting questions *should* stimulate interesting points for you to ponder, but your first goal when taking an achievement test is to answer as many questions as quickly and accurately as possible. Some fine students have done poorly merely because they have devoted more time than necessary to mulling over the ramifications of questions they have already answered. By all means, explore the fascinating aspects of mathematical questions, but do it after the test is over.

DETERMINING INTEGRAL SOLUTIONS TO EQUATIONS IN TWO VARIABLES

[10] If $9x + 3y = 25$ and x and y are positive integers less than 25, how many ordered pairs (x, y) are solutions of the equation?

Ⓐ 0   Ⓑ 1   Ⓒ 2   Ⓓ 3   Ⓔ 4

A moment's study will show that there are no methods for "solving" this equation since it involves two unknowns and only one equation. Can you work it out just by trial and error? In other words, can you just pick positive integers that will satisfy the equation? Trying all possible pairs of integers from 1 to 25 would certainly be a lengthy process, and achievement test questions rarely require lengthy solutions.

Do you see that the left side, $9x + 3y$, has a factor of 3? Thus

$$3(3x + y) = 25,$$
$$3x + y = \frac{25}{3} = 8\frac{1}{3}.$$

But addition and multiplication involving integers must always result in an integer. Thus the left side can never result in $8\frac{1}{3}$. The equation can never be true for a pair of integers.

¶ DRILL Indicate which of the following can have integral solutions:

(a) $2x + 3y = 15$ (b) $5x - 10y = 3$
(c) $2x - 6y = 1$

WORKING WITH FUNCTIONS

[11] The function $f(x)$ has the value 0 if and only if x is a member of the set $\{-3, 0, 1\}$. For what values of x is $f(x - 3) = 0$?

Ⓐ $\{-3, 0, 1\}$ Ⓑ $\{0, 1\}$ Ⓒ $\{0, 3, 4\}$
Ⓓ $\{-6, 0, -2\}$ Ⓔ $\{3, 0, -2\}$

The symbol $f(a) = b$ represents the fact that f is a rule that results in b when it works on a. This has already been reviewed in section [7] of Chapter 20. In the given information about the function f, above, we discover that f can result in 0 only when it works on -3, 0, or 1. This means that when f works on $x - 3$, it is the $x - 3$ that must be -3, 0, or 1 in order to yield 0. Thus

$$x - 3 = -3 \rightarrow x = 0$$
$$= 1 \rightarrow x = 4$$
$$= 0 \rightarrow x = 3.$$

¶ **DRILL** Let $f(x)$ be the function $x^2 - 2x - 3$.

(a) For what values of x is $f(x) = 0$?
(b) Substitute $x + 1$ for x in $f(x)$ and simplify it.
(c) Find the values of x for which $f(x + 1)$ is zero by an analysis of the function you found in (b).
(d) Now find the values for which $f(x + 1) = 0$, using the method explained in the text above.

[12] If $f(x) = \dfrac{3x - 2}{4}$, where $x > 0$, for what values of x is $f(x) < 0$?

Ⓐ $0 < x < \dfrac{2}{3}$ Ⓑ $0 < x < 2$
Ⓒ $-2 < x < 4$ Ⓓ $0 < x < 3$
Ⓔ **No value of x**

Students often misinterpret $f(x) < 0$ to mean $x < 0$. Remember that a function is a set of ordered pairs whose members can be represented by the ordered pair

$$(x, f(x)),$$

where the rule, f, tells how $f(x)$ is derived from x. Thus x and $f(x)$ represent two different quantities.

Therefore, in the question above, $f(x) < 0$ means

$$\frac{3x - 2}{4} < 0.$$

To solve this inequality, first multiply each side by 4 (there is no change in the direction of the inequality because the multiplier is positive).

$$3x - 2 < 0$$
$$3x < 2$$
$$x < \frac{2}{3}$$

There was, however, an initial restriction that x was to be positive. Combining the restrictions, we get

$$0 < x < \frac{2}{3}.$$

¶ **DRILL**

(a) With $f(x)$ as defined above, when is $f(x) > 0$?
(b) If $g(x) = 4x + 1$, find the values of x for which $g(x) < 0$.
(c) For what values of x will $g(x^2)$ above be equal to 0?

[13] If $f(x) = \dfrac{1}{x} + x + \dfrac{1}{x} + x$, for all real numbers, which of the following will be true?

Ⓐ $f(0) = 0$ Ⓑ $f(x) = f(\dfrac{1}{x})$ Ⓒ $f(x) = f(-x)$

Ⓓ $f(x) = x$ Ⓔ $f(x) = \dfrac{1}{f(x)}$

This question illustrates several different aspects of functions, which we will review by discussing each of the choices given. First, however, note that $f(x)$ can be simplified:

$$f(x) = 2(\frac{1}{x}) + 2x$$
$$= 2(\frac{1}{x} + x).$$

Ⓐ Since no domain is specified, the values that may be used for x include all real numbers except those that produce meaningless operations. The number 0 is the only one that causes complications since it cannot be used as a divisor. Hence $f(0)$ is meaningless.

Ⓑ To find $f(\dfrac{1}{x})$, replace x by $\dfrac{1}{x}$ wherever x occurs. Therefore

$$f(\frac{1}{x}) = 2\left(\frac{1}{\frac{1}{x}} + \frac{1}{x} \right)$$
$$= 2(x + \frac{1}{x})$$
$$= 2(\frac{1}{x} + x).$$

The latter is, of course, $f(x)$.

Ⓒ To find $f(-x)$, replace x by $(-x)$:

$$f(-x) = 2(\frac{1}{-x} + (-x)) = -2(\frac{1}{x} + x).$$

The latter is not $f(x)$, but is $-f(x)$. Any function for which $f(-x)$ is $-f(x)$ is referred to as an "odd function." If $f(-x) = f(x)$, it is an "even function."

Ⓓ $f(x) \neq x$, since $2(\frac{1}{x} + x) \neq x$.

(E)

$$\frac{1}{f(x)} = \frac{1}{2(\frac{1}{x} + x)}$$

$$= \frac{1(x)}{2(\frac{1}{x} + x)(x)}$$

$$= \frac{x}{2(1 + x^2)}$$

$$\neq 2(\frac{1}{x} + x).$$

¶ DRILL For each of the following find $f(\frac{1}{x})$ and $f(-x)$:

(a) $f(x) = \frac{1}{x}$ (b) $f(x) = \frac{1}{x^2}$

(c) $f(x) = \frac{-1}{x - 1}$

WORKING WITH ABSOLUTE VALUES

[14] If $a + 5 = b$, then which of the following is
$$|b - a| + |a - b|?$$

Ⓐ 0   Ⓑ 10   Ⓒ 5   Ⓓ −5   Ⓔ Cannot be determined

Since $a + 5 = b$, it follows that
$$b - a = 5 \quad \text{and} \quad a - b = -5,$$
by subtracting the appropriate expressions from each side. Therefore both $|b - a|$ and $|a - b|$ are 5.

¶ DRILL

(a) Is $|b - a| = |a - b|$ always true?
(b) Is $|a - b|^2 = (a - b)^2$ always true?
(c) Is $-(a - b) = b - a$ always true?

WORKING IN THREE-DIMENSIONAL COORDINATE GEOMETRY

[15] If point O is the origin and point P is (3, 4, 12), what is the distance between P and M, where M is the midpoint of segment OP?

Ⓐ $6\frac{1}{2}$ Ⓑ 4   Ⓒ 9   Ⓓ 7   Ⓔ 3

Many of the formulas for plane coordinate geometry can be extended to space. In three-dimensional coordinate geometry, each point of space is represented by an ordered triple of numbers where each number is found

in terms of the projected distance along each of three perpendicular axes as shown.

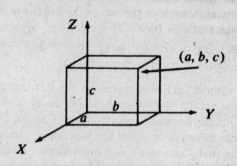

The distance between any two points (x_1, y_1, z_1) and (x_2, y_2, z_2) is given by
$$\sqrt{(x_1 - x_2)^2 + (y_1 - y_2)^2 + (z_1 - z_2)^2}.$$
The midpoint of the segment connecting them is
$$\left(\frac{x_1 + x_2}{2}, \frac{y_1 + y_2}{2}, \frac{z_1 + z_2}{2} \right).$$

If you compare these with the corresponding formulas in sections [11] and [5] of Chapter 18 you will see the great similarity.

The question above can be answered quite simply without using the midpoint formula, however. Just find the distance between the origin and point P, then divide it by 2.

$$\begin{aligned} OP &= \sqrt{(3 - 0)^2 + (4 - 0)^2 + (12 - 0)^2} \\ &= \sqrt{9 + 16 + 144} \\ &= \sqrt{169} \\ &= 13 \end{aligned}$$

Therefore

$$OM = \frac{1}{2}OP = 6\frac{1}{2}.$$

¶ DRILL Find the distances between the following pairs of points and the midpoints of the segments that contain them.

(a) (1, 1, 2), (2, −1, 1)
(b) (0, 1, 0), (0, 0, 1)
(c) (1, 2, 3), (1, 2, −3)
(d) (3, 4, 6), (2, −1, 6)

WORKING WITH EQUAL EXPONENTIAL EXPRESSIONS

[16] Find the value of x if $4^x = 8$.

Ⓐ 2   Ⓑ $\frac{1}{2}$ Ⓒ $\frac{3}{2}$ Ⓓ 3   Ⓔ Cannot be determined

If two exponential expressions are equal and have the same base, then the exponents must be equal. Thus the procedure for working out the question above is to express each side of the equation as an exponential form with the same base. Do you see that both 4 and 8 are powers of 2? Since $4 = 2^2$ and $8 = 2^3$, it follows that

$$4^x = 8$$

is the same as

$$(2^2)^x = 2^3.$$

Applying the laws of exponents gives

$$2^{2x} = 2^3.$$

Since the expressions are equal and the bases are equal, the exponents must be equal.

$$2x = 3$$
$$x = \frac{3}{2}$$

TEST-TAKING TIP.

One of the advantages to the student of a multiple-choice test is that the correct answer is given. Thus a student who did not know the procedure for finding x directly could probably get the answer just as quickly by trying each of the choices.

¶ DRILL Solve each of the following for x.

(a) $2^{x-1} = 16$ (b) $3^{-x} = \frac{1}{27}$ (c) $8^x = \frac{1}{2}$

DRAWING CONCLUSIONS ABOUT ODD AND EVEN NUMBERS

[17] If a and b are odd numbers, c is an even number and $x = a + bc$, which of the following must be true of x?

Ⓐ x is always odd. Ⓑ x is always even.
Ⓒ x is even when a, b, and c are positive and odd when they are negative. Ⓓ x is even when all of a, b, and c are negative and odd when they are all positive. Ⓔ Nothing can be determined about whether x is odd or even.

One way to represent odd and even numbers algebraically in forms that will allow conclusions to be drawn is to let $2p$ represent any even number and $2q + 1$ any odd number where p and q are always

integers. If two different odd numbers are to be expressed, then $2q + 1$ and $2r + 1$ will do the job.

. To answer the question above let $a = 2q + 1$, $b = 2r + 1$ and $c = 2p$, then

$$(1)\ a + bc = 2q + 1 + (2r + 1)(2p).$$

The form of equation (1) must be changed before any conclusions can be drawn. We seek to represent the result in a form recognizable as *even* (meaning having a factor of 2) or *odd* (meaning that it can be represented as 1 plus a number with a factor of 2).

$$(2)\ a + bc = 2q + 1 + 4pr + 2p$$
$$(3)\qquad\quad = 4pr + 2p + 2q + 1$$
$$(4)\qquad\quad = 2(2pr + p + q) + 1$$

Since $2pr + p + q$ must be an integer (it is the sum of integers) the expression in (4) is in the form $2m + 1$, so it must be odd.

¶ DRILL Use the representations given for odd and even numbers to indicate whether the results of the operations given are odd or even.

(a) The sum of two odd numbers.
(b) The product of two odd numbers.
(c) The sum of an odd and an even number.
(d) The product of two even numbers.

WHAT YOU SHOULD KNOW

KEY CONCEPTS

1. No computer background is needed to answer questions written in computer format. The only skill required is the ability to follow directions.
2. Computerlike questions are not written in any standard computer language.
3. The sine and cosine functions are cofunctions; that is, the cosine of an angle is the sine of its complement.
4. Addition or multiplication involving integers must always result in an integer.
5. The expression $f(a) = b$ means that f is a rule that results in b when it works on a.
6. If two exponential expressions are equal and have the same base, then the exponents must be equal.

KEY FORMULAS

1. The distance between any two points (x_1, y_1, z_1) and (x_2, y_2, z_2) is given by
$$\sqrt{(x_1 - x_2)^2 + (y_1 - y_2)^2 + (z_1 - z_2)^2}.$$

2. The midpoint of the segment connecting them is given by

$$\left(\frac{x_1 + x_2}{2} , \frac{y_1 + y_2}{2} , \frac{z_1 + z_2}{2} \right).$$

TEST-TAKING STRATEGIES

- To solve a computerlike problem, always carry out the instructions in the order given unless one of the steps tells you specifically to do otherwise.
- Know how to represent even and odd numbers algebraically. Use $2m$ for even numbers and $2n + 1$ for odd, where m and n are any integers.

ANSWERS

[1] Ⓔ

[2] Ⓓ

[3] Ⓔ

[4] Ⓔ
DRILL:
(a) $Ax + A + Bx = 2x + 1$; therefore $A = 1$, $B = 1$.
(b) $Ax + A + 3Bx - 2B = 7$, so $A = \frac{21}{5}$,
$B = -\frac{7}{5}$

[5] Ⓔ
DRILL:
(a) $\frac{\pi}{3}$ (b) $\frac{\pi}{6}$

[6] Ⓓ
DRILL:
(a) $\frac{\pi}{6}$ (b) $\frac{\pi}{5}$

[7] Ⓔ
DRILL:

(a) Increasing at $0 < x < \frac{\pi}{2}$ or $\frac{3\pi}{2} < x < 2\pi$,
decreasing at $\frac{\pi}{2} < x < \frac{3}{2}$.
(b) Increasing at $\pi < x < 2\pi$, decreasing at $0 < x < \pi$.
(c) Always increasing on any interval not including $\frac{\pi}{2}$ and $\frac{3\pi}{2}$.

[8] Ⓒ
DRILL:
(a) $2n\pi + \frac{\pi}{4}$, $2n\pi + \frac{5\pi}{4}$, where n is any integer.
(b) None, $\tan \theta$ is always greater than $\sin \theta$ on the interval.

[9] Ⓑ
DRILL:
(a) $4 + 2 \neq 1$; no.
(b) $4 \cdot 2 \neq 3$; no.
(c) $\frac{9}{17}$ is not a whole number so division by 5 does not produce a "remainder"; no.
(d) $4 - 2 \neq 3$; no.

[10] Ⓐ
DRILL:
(a) Yes, for example (3, 3)
(b) No, $x - 3y = \frac{3}{5}$
(c) No, $x - 3y = \frac{1}{2}$

[11] Ⓒ
DRILL:
(a) $(x - 3)(x + 1) = 0$; $x = 3$ or $x = -1$
(b) $x^2 - 4$
(c) $(x - 2)(x + 2) = 0$, $x = 2$, or $x = -2$
(d) $x + 1 = 3$ so $x = 2$; $x + 1 = -1$ so $x = -2$

[12] Ⓐ
DRILL:
(a) $x > \frac{2}{3}$
(b) $4x + 1 = 0$, so $x < -\frac{1}{4}$.
(c) $4x^2 + 1 = 0$, therefore no values of x.

[13] Ⓑ
DRILL:
(a) $f\left(\frac{1}{x}\right) = x$, $f(-x) = -\frac{1}{x}$
(b) $f\left(\frac{1}{x}\right) = x^2$, $f(-x) = \frac{1}{x^2}$
(c) $f\left(\frac{1}{x}\right) = \frac{-x}{1 - x} = \frac{x}{x - 1}$
$f(-x) = \frac{-x}{-x - 1} = \frac{x}{x + 1}$

[14] Ⓑ
DRILL:
(a) Yes.   (b) Yes.   (c) Yes.

[15] Ⓐ
DRILL:

(a) Distance $= \sqrt{6}$, $mp = \left(\dfrac{3}{2}, 0, \dfrac{3}{2} \right)$

(b) Distance $= \sqrt{2}$, $mp = \left(0, \dfrac{1}{2}, \dfrac{1}{2} \right)$

(c) Distance $= 6$, $mp = (1, 2, 0)$

(d) Distance $= \sqrt{26}$, $mp = \left(\dfrac{5}{2}, \dfrac{3}{2}, 0 \right)$

[16] Ⓒ
DRILL:
(a) 5
(b) $x = 3$
(c) $x = -\dfrac{1}{3}$

[17] Ⓐ
DRILL:
(a) Even.   (b) Odd.
(c) Odd.   (d) Even.

Test Yourself

SOME FACTS ABOUT THE SAMPLE TESTS

Directions for the Sample Tests

Each Mathematics Level I Achievement Test is composed of 50 multiple-choice questions with a time limit of 1 hour. Thus the candidate who completes the test (80% of the test-takers do, according to CB) averages 1 minute and 12 seconds per question. Though it is unrealistic for most students to expect to answer every question accurately, you should not let yourself get bogged down—obviously, the more questions you answer correctly, the better your final score. An announcement of elapsed time is made every 20 minutes, but you would do well to bring your own watch. A good guideline is to spend no more than 2 minutes on a given question.

In general the questions get progressively more difficult; this is tempered somewhat by your preparation. For example, if you have a thorough grounding in trigonometry but your experience with radicals is negligible, you might find question 44 of Test 1, which follows, to be easier than question 1.

The most important thing you can learn from taking practice achievement tests is how to pace yourself without getting bogged down. When taking these tests try to approximate testing conditions as closely as possible —arrange for an undistracted hour with no other materials than several sharpened pencils and the test itself. You may want to use scratch paper, but all scratchwork on the College Boards must be done in the test booklet. No scratchwork counts toward your score; only the answer recorded on the answer sheet is graded.

When you grade your sample test, give yourself 4 points for each correct answer and -1 for each incorrect answer. Note that there is a difference between an incorrect answer and an answer left blank. No points are added or subtracted for an answer left blank. The -1 point for each incorrect answer is computed as a penalty for indiscriminant guessing. If you were to guess at five questions which you knew nothing at all about, the probability is that you would guess one correctly and four incorrectly. Adding together the 4 points for the one correct answer and the $4(-1)$ points for the four incorrect answers gives you a net score of 0.

Thus the probability is that indiscriminate guessing will not help your score and may actually hurt it. If, however, you knew enough about each question to be able to eliminate at least one of the choices given, the probability would be in your favor, and you might aid your score by selecting for each question the one among the remaining answers that seemed most likely.

In general, you should not guess unless you can definitely eliminate at least one of the possible answers given for a particular question. By doing this, you are in no way attempting to "beat" the test, but are just trying to get credit for knowing something about the question.

Most CB Mathematics Level I Achievement Tests contain approximately 15 questions of an elementary nature, questions that seem quite easy to a person who is well prepared. Among such easy questions might be:

[1] If $2x = 5$, which of the following is $4x$?

    Ⓐ $\dfrac{5}{2}$ Ⓑ 10   Ⓒ 20   Ⓓ $\dfrac{5}{4}$ Ⓔ $\dfrac{4}{5}$

or

[2] $\sin^2 x + \cos^2 x = ?$

    Ⓐ -1 Ⓑ 0   Ⓒ 1   Ⓓ $\sin 2x$ Ⓔ **No answer is possible unless x is known.**

The answer to [1] can be readily found by doubling both sides, and the answer to [2] should be recognized easily as being the result of a basic fact of trigonometry. You should have quickly arrived at Ⓑ and Ⓒ in a matter of seconds.

In order to make the most efficient use of your review time, we have replaced the easy questions normally found on the Level I tests with others that are slightly more difficult. The result is that our sample tests, with one exception, will seem quite a bit harder than the actual Level I test that you will eventually take on examination day. The practice you get by taking more difficult sample tests should sharpen your ability to work quickly on the test that counts. Do not let the more difficult nature of our sample tests scare you away from taking the Level I test. It will be easier than any of the sample tests that follow. You will probably not finish any of our sample tests in the one-hour time limit, but the actual CB tests are designed to allow the majority of students (80%) to finish them, while all students complete at least 37 or 38 questions.

Sample test 6, however, is only slightly more difficult than actual Level I tests and should give you a good idea of the degree of difficulty of these tests.

All geometric figures are drawn as accurately as possible **except** when a specific problem states that its figure is not drawn to scale; unless otherwise specified, all figures lie in a plane.

You may assume that the domain of a function f is the set of all real numbers x for which $f(x)$ is a real number, unless the question indicates otherwise.

Diagnostic Key

The majority of the questions in the sample tests pertain directly to one or more sections of this text. Wherever possible, we have indicated, along with the explanation of the answer, the section of the book that most closely relates to the test question. Thus, when you see the number *23-3* following the explanation of the answer, it means that you will find a more comprehensive description of the mathematical skills used in section [3] of Chapter 23.

Self-Evaluation Charts

Each sample test is followed by a self-evaluation chart on which to monitor your progress. Each test question is assigned to an appropriate subject matter category on each chart.

To monitor your progress, place a check (✓) in the box below each question that you have answered correctly. Use an X to mark each question you have answered incorrectly. Leave the box blank below every question you have not answered.

The chart enables you to compute not only your total score for the test, but also a separate score for each

topic that will appear on the Level I test, such as algebra, coordinate geometry, or functions. In this way you can easily spot the areas in which you are weak and need further review before taking the next test.

The number of questions selected from each subject area varies slightly from test to test, just as it does on the actual CB Math Level I Achievement Test. Furthermore, a particular question might just as easily have been classified under a different subject heading because it involves several kinds of knowledge and skills. In such cases the question was assigned to the subject area in which you are most likely to have studied questions like it. For example, a question that involves both the knowledge that the sum of the measures of the angles of a triangle is 180 and the ability to set up and solve algebraic equations is assigned to the plane geometry section, not the algebra section.

After completing each test, calculate your score by multiplying the number of correct answers (marked by checks) by 4 and subtracting the number of incorrect answers (marked by X's). Then record your score on page 299 by placing a dot opposite the nearest value on the vertical axis and above the appropriate test number on the horizontal axis. As you progress from one test to the next, the graph of your progress should show a steady rise from Test 1 to Test 5 and a marked jump for Test 6, which, you will recall, is less difficult than the others.

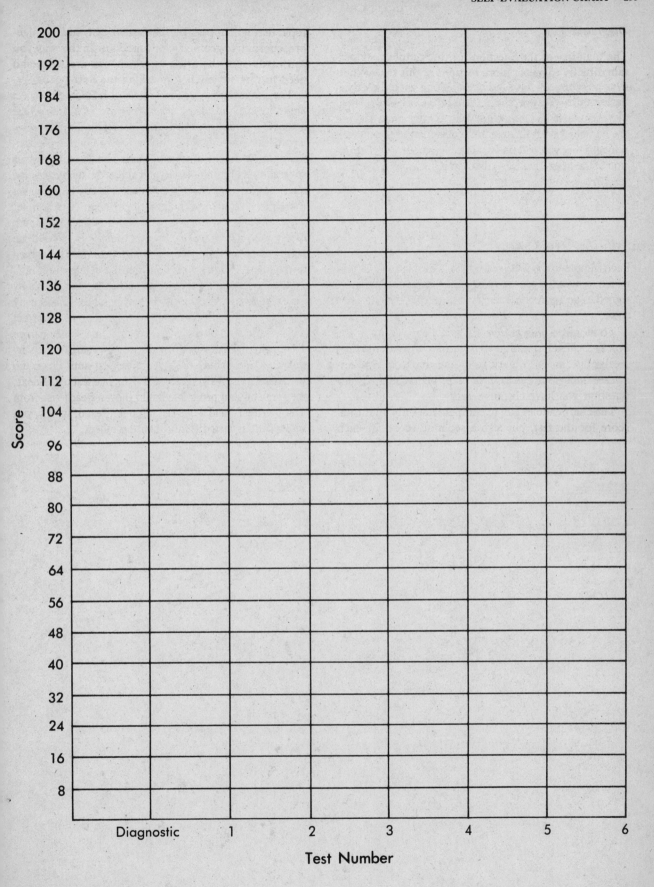

ANSWER SHEET FOR TEST 1

Determine the correct answer for each question. Then, using a No. 2 pencil, blacken completely the oval containing the letter of your choice.

1. Ⓐ Ⓑ Ⓒ Ⓓ Ⓔ
2. Ⓐ Ⓑ Ⓒ Ⓓ Ⓔ
3. Ⓐ Ⓑ Ⓒ Ⓓ Ⓔ
4. Ⓐ Ⓑ Ⓒ Ⓓ Ⓔ
5. Ⓐ Ⓑ Ⓒ Ⓓ Ⓔ
6. Ⓐ Ⓑ Ⓒ Ⓓ Ⓔ
7. Ⓐ Ⓑ Ⓒ Ⓓ Ⓔ
8. Ⓐ Ⓑ Ⓒ Ⓓ Ⓔ
9. Ⓐ Ⓑ Ⓒ Ⓓ Ⓔ
10. Ⓐ Ⓑ Ⓒ Ⓓ Ⓔ
11. Ⓐ Ⓑ Ⓒ Ⓓ Ⓔ
12. Ⓐ Ⓑ Ⓒ Ⓓ Ⓔ
13. Ⓐ Ⓑ Ⓒ Ⓓ Ⓔ
14. Ⓐ Ⓑ Ⓒ Ⓓ Ⓔ
15. Ⓐ Ⓑ Ⓒ Ⓓ Ⓔ
16. Ⓐ Ⓑ Ⓒ Ⓓ Ⓔ
17. Ⓐ Ⓑ Ⓒ Ⓓ Ⓔ

18. Ⓐ Ⓑ Ⓒ Ⓓ Ⓔ
19. Ⓐ Ⓑ Ⓒ Ⓓ Ⓔ
20. Ⓐ Ⓑ Ⓒ Ⓓ Ⓔ
21. Ⓐ Ⓑ Ⓒ Ⓓ Ⓔ
22. Ⓐ Ⓑ Ⓒ Ⓓ Ⓔ
23. Ⓐ Ⓑ Ⓒ Ⓓ Ⓔ
24. Ⓐ Ⓑ Ⓒ Ⓓ Ⓔ
25. Ⓐ Ⓑ Ⓒ Ⓓ Ⓔ
26. Ⓐ Ⓑ Ⓒ Ⓓ Ⓔ
27. Ⓐ Ⓑ Ⓒ Ⓓ Ⓔ
28. Ⓐ Ⓑ Ⓒ Ⓓ Ⓔ
29. Ⓐ Ⓑ Ⓒ Ⓓ Ⓔ
30. Ⓐ Ⓑ Ⓒ Ⓓ Ⓔ
31. Ⓐ Ⓑ Ⓒ Ⓓ Ⓔ
32. Ⓐ Ⓑ Ⓒ Ⓓ Ⓔ
33. Ⓐ Ⓑ Ⓒ Ⓓ Ⓔ
34. Ⓐ Ⓑ Ⓒ Ⓓ Ⓔ

35. Ⓐ Ⓑ Ⓒ Ⓓ Ⓔ
36. Ⓐ Ⓑ Ⓒ Ⓓ Ⓔ
37. Ⓐ Ⓑ Ⓒ Ⓓ Ⓔ
38. Ⓐ Ⓑ Ⓒ Ⓓ Ⓔ
39. Ⓐ Ⓑ Ⓒ Ⓓ Ⓔ
40. Ⓐ Ⓑ Ⓒ Ⓓ Ⓔ
41. Ⓐ Ⓑ Ⓒ Ⓓ Ⓔ
42. Ⓐ Ⓑ Ⓒ Ⓓ Ⓔ
43. Ⓐ Ⓑ Ⓒ Ⓓ Ⓔ
44. Ⓐ Ⓑ Ⓒ Ⓓ Ⓔ
45. Ⓐ Ⓑ Ⓒ Ⓓ Ⓔ
46. Ⓐ Ⓑ Ⓒ Ⓓ Ⓔ
47. Ⓐ Ⓑ Ⓒ Ⓓ Ⓔ
48. Ⓐ Ⓑ Ⓒ Ⓓ Ⓔ
49. Ⓐ Ⓑ Ⓒ Ⓓ Ⓔ
50. Ⓐ Ⓑ Ⓒ Ⓓ Ⓔ

32. Model Test 1

TEST

For each of the following, select the best choice—A, B, C, D or E—to answer the question or complete the statement. Then locate the number of the question on the answer sheet, and indicate your choice by filling in completely the corresponding oval.

[1] $\dfrac{\sqrt{10}\sqrt{2}}{\sqrt{15}} =$

Ⓐ $\dfrac{2}{5}$ Ⓑ $\dfrac{2\sqrt{5}}{5}$ Ⓒ $\dfrac{\sqrt{3}}{6}$ Ⓓ $\dfrac{2\sqrt{3}}{3}$ Ⓔ $\dfrac{\sqrt{6}}{3}$

[2] What is the relationship between the areas of $\triangle ABC$ and $\triangle DBC$ in the figure below?

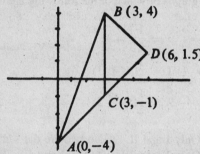

Ⓐ Equal Ⓑ Area of $\triangle ABC = \dfrac{1}{2}$ Area of $\triangle DBC$ Ⓒ Area of $\triangle ABC >$ Area of $\triangle BDC$
Ⓓ Area of $\triangle ABC + 1 =$ Area of $\triangle BDC$
Ⓔ Area of $\triangle ABC = \dfrac{1}{3}$ Area of $\triangle DBC$

[3] If $a \neq b$, then $\dfrac{a-b}{a+b} - 1 =$

Ⓐ 0 Ⓑ $\dfrac{a-b-1}{a+b}$ Ⓒ $\dfrac{-2b}{a+b}$ Ⓓ $\dfrac{2a}{a+b}$
Ⓔ $\dfrac{a^2+b^2}{a+b}$

[4] If the given angles have the measures indicated, what are the measures of x and y?

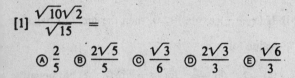

Ⓐ $x = 100, y = 90$ Ⓑ $x = 120, y = 85$
Ⓒ $x = 120, y = 90$ Ⓓ $x = 100, y = 85$
Ⓔ $x = 110, y = 90$

[5] If $3 + y = a$ and $3 - y = a$, then

Ⓐ $a = 5, y = 2$ Ⓑ $a = 1, y = -1$
Ⓒ $a = 2, y = -1$ Ⓓ $a = 3, y = 1$
Ⓔ $a = 3, y = 0$

[6] If the first three digits of $N = \dfrac{(8.42)^2(95.1)}{(.982)(69.4)}$ are 988, which of the following is the best approximation to N?

Ⓐ 988 Ⓑ 98.8 Ⓒ 9.88 Ⓓ 9880 Ⓔ 98,800

[7] If $\dfrac{x-1}{x+1} = \dfrac{2}{3}$, then $x =$

Ⓐ 3 Ⓑ 2 Ⓒ No value possible Ⓓ 4 Ⓔ 5

[8] If ray OA is perpendicular to line BD and $\angle AOE$ has degree measure of 15, then the measure of $\angle COD$ is

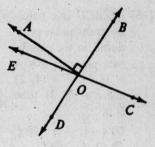

Ⓐ 75 Ⓑ 95
Ⓒ 100 Ⓓ 105
Ⓔ 110

[9] If $4^{x/2} = 16$, then $x =$

Ⓐ -2 Ⓑ 1 Ⓒ 2 Ⓓ 4 Ⓔ -4

[10] If $\dfrac{x^2-1}{3} = 5$ and $y\left(\dfrac{x^2-1}{3}\right) = 15$, then $y =$

Ⓐ 5 Ⓑ 3 Ⓒ $\sqrt{3}$ Ⓓ 15 Ⓔ Cannot be determined

[11] $\cos 30° - \sin 60° =$

Ⓐ 0 Ⓑ 1 Ⓒ -1 Ⓓ $\dfrac{\sqrt{3}}{2}$ Ⓔ $\dfrac{1}{2}$

[12] Arc CD is a semicircle. $AB \perp CD$, $BC = 3$, $BD = 4$. Then the length of $AB =$

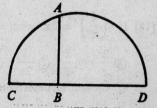

Ⓐ $2\sqrt{3}$ Ⓑ $3\sqrt{2}$
Ⓒ 3 Ⓓ 4 Ⓔ 5

[13] If $(b + c)(ab - ac) = b^2 - c^2$, then $a =$

  Ⓐ 0 Ⓑ 1 Ⓒ -1 Ⓓ b Ⓔ c

[14] If $x = 2$, $y = 3$ and $z = 4$, then $\dfrac{x^3 + yz^2}{-2(2 - 3y)} =$

  Ⓐ 5 Ⓑ -5.6 Ⓒ -5 Ⓓ 5.6 Ⓔ 4

[15] If the radii of the circles are 5 and 3, the centers are A and B and both $\angle FAG$ and $\angle DBC$ are right angles, what is the perimeter of $\triangle CEG$?

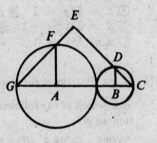

  Ⓐ 32 Ⓑ $16 + 16\sqrt{2}$ Ⓒ 30
  Ⓓ $16 + 10\sqrt{2}$
  Ⓔ Cannot be determined

[16] If $ABCD$ is a parallelogram and is positioned in the coordinate plane so that $A = (1,1)$, $B = (4, 2)$ and $E = (3, 3)$, then D is

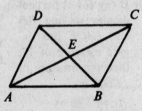

  Ⓐ $(-4, -2)$ Ⓑ $(-4, 2)$
  Ⓒ $(2, 4)$ Ⓓ $(2, -4)$ Ⓔ $(-2, -4)$

[17] If $AD = 2$ and $DB = 3$, then the ratio

$$\dfrac{\text{area } \triangle ADC}{\text{area } \triangle ABC}$$

is

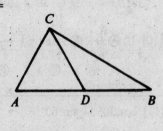

  Ⓐ $\dfrac{2}{3}$ Ⓑ $\dfrac{3}{2}$ Ⓒ $\dfrac{2}{5}$
  Ⓓ $\dfrac{3}{5}$ Ⓔ $\dfrac{5}{3}$

[18] If $f\left(\dfrac{1}{x}\right) = 2x$, what is $f(x)$?

  Ⓐ $\dfrac{2}{x}$ Ⓑ $\dfrac{x}{2}$ Ⓒ $\dfrac{1}{2x}$ Ⓓ 2
  Ⓔ Cannot be determined

[19] $\angle D$ and $\angle B$ are right angles. $AD = AB$, $BC = DC$, and $AB \neq BC$. How many circles can be drawn that contain A, B and C, but not D?

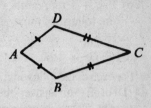

  Ⓐ None Ⓑ 1
  Ⓒ 2 Ⓓ 3 Ⓔ Infinitely many

[20] If $\left(x - \dfrac{1}{2}\right)\left(x - \dfrac{3}{2}\right) < 0$, then the greatest negative value for x is

  Ⓐ -1 Ⓑ $-\dfrac{1}{2}$ Ⓒ $-\dfrac{3}{2}$ Ⓓ 0 Ⓔ No negative value of x will make the inequality true

[21] The graphs of which of the following are the same?

  I $y = \dfrac{1}{2}x + \dfrac{1}{2}$

  II $y + 1 = \dfrac{1}{2}(x + 3)$

  III $y - 2 = \dfrac{1}{2}(x - 3)$

  Ⓐ Only I and II. Ⓑ No two are the same.
  Ⓒ Only II and III. Ⓓ Only I and III. Ⓔ All three.

[22] In 10 minutes, the number of degrees the hour hand of a clock rotates is

  Ⓐ 1 Ⓑ 6 Ⓒ $6\dfrac{2}{3}$ Ⓓ 5 Ⓔ 10

[23] If $\dfrac{1}{x} + \dfrac{1}{\sqrt{x}} = 0$, then $x =$

  Ⓐ 0 Ⓑ 1 Ⓒ -1 Ⓓ 111 Ⓔ No real value possible

[24] If $(\sin x)(\csc x) = 1$, then $x =$

  Ⓐ 0 Ⓑ $\dfrac{\pi}{4}$ Ⓒ 1 Ⓓ All real numbers except $n\pi$, where n is an integer Ⓔ No real numbers

[25] If $\dfrac{1}{x} < \dfrac{1}{2}$, then

  Ⓐ $x > 2$ Ⓑ $x > 2$ or $x < 2$ Ⓒ $x > 2$ and $x < 2$ Ⓓ $x > 2$ or $x < 0$ Ⓔ x is any real number except zero

[26] If $k + 1$ represents a given odd integer, which of the following must also be an odd integer?

     Ⓐ $2(k + 1)$ Ⓑ $k(k + 1)$ Ⓒ $(k + 1)(k + 2)$
     Ⓓ $(k + 1)(k - 1)$ Ⓔ $(k + 1)^2 - 1$

[27] If $(a^2 - 3a)(a + 3) = 0$ then $a =$

     Ⓐ $\{3\}$ Ⓑ $\{-3\}$ Ⓒ $\{3, -3\}$ Ⓓ $\{0, 3, -3\}$
     Ⓔ $\{0, -1, 3, -3\}$

[28] If the right angles and sides are as marked, the area of trapezoid $ABCD$ is 18, and $a = 2b$, then $c =$

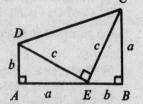

     Ⓐ $2\sqrt{5}$ Ⓑ $4\sqrt{5}$
     Ⓒ 4 Ⓓ 2 Ⓔ
Cannot be determined

[29] If $f(x) = -\dfrac{1}{x^3}$ and x takes on successive values from -10 to $-\dfrac{1}{10}$, then

     Ⓐ $f(x)$ increases throughout   Ⓑ $f(x)$ decreases throughout   Ⓒ $f(x)$ increases, then decreases   Ⓓ $f(x)$ decreases, then increases   Ⓔ $f(x)$ remains constant throughout

[30] If in a $\triangle ABC$, $\angle C$ is a right angle, $BC = 1$ and $\tan \angle B = p$, then $\cos \angle A =$

     Ⓐ $\dfrac{1}{\sqrt{p^2 + 1}}$ Ⓑ $\dfrac{p}{p + 1}$ Ⓒ $\dfrac{p}{\sqrt{p^2 + 1}}$
     Ⓓ $\dfrac{\sqrt{p^2 + 1}}{p}$ Ⓔ $p^2 + 1$

[31] A gold bar with dimensions $2' \times 3' \times 4'$ has all of its faces rectangular. If it is melted and recast into three cubes of equal volumes, what is the length of an edge of each cube?

     Ⓐ 1 Ⓑ 2 Ⓒ 3 Ⓓ 4 Ⓔ 5

[32] If $\dfrac{n!}{2} = (n - 2)!$ then $n =$

     Ⓐ 1 Ⓑ 2 Ⓒ 3 Ⓓ 4 Ⓔ 5

[33] If $\log x = \dfrac{1}{2} \log a - \log b$ and $a = 4b^2$, then $x =$

     Ⓐ 1 Ⓑ 2 Ⓒ 4 Ⓓ 8 Ⓔ 16

[34] If p, m and n are prime numbers, none of which is equal to the other two, what is the greatest common factor of $24pm^2n^2$, $9pmn^2$ and $36p(mn)^3$?

     Ⓐ $3pmn$ Ⓑ $3p^2m^2n^2$ Ⓒ $3pmn^2$ Ⓓ $3pm^2n^2$
     Ⓔ $3pm^3n^3$

[35] If the perpendicular bisector of the segment with endpoints A $(1, 2)$ and B $(2, 4)$ contains the point $(4, c)$, then the value of c is

     Ⓐ 7 Ⓑ $\dfrac{7}{4}$ Ⓒ -7 Ⓓ 4 Ⓔ -4

[36] If $f(x) = \dfrac{1}{x}$ and $f[f(x)] = f(x)$, then x is

     Ⓐ 1 only   Ⓑ -1 only   Ⓒ 1 or -1 Ⓓ no real number   Ⓔ any real number

[37] If in the figure line DE is parallel to line AB, and $CD = 3$ while $DA = 6$, which of the following is NOT a correct conclusion?

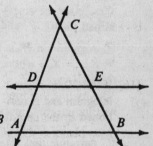

     Ⓐ $\triangle CDE \sim \triangle CAB$
     Ⓑ $\dfrac{CD}{DA} = \dfrac{CE}{EB}$
     Ⓒ Area of $\triangle CDE = \dfrac{1}{9}$ Area of $\triangle CAB$
     Ⓓ $\dfrac{\text{Area } \triangle CDE}{\text{Area } \triangle CAB} = \left(\dfrac{CD}{CA}\right)^2$
     Ⓔ If $AB = 4$, then $DE = 2$

[38] If $x = 3i$, $y = 2i$ and $z = 1 + i$, then $xy^2z =$

     Ⓐ 0 Ⓑ -1 Ⓒ $1 - i$ Ⓓ $12 - 12i$ Ⓔ $6 - 6i$

[39] If $a < b$, then which of the following is NOT true for all a and b?

     Ⓐ $-a < |b|$ Ⓑ $-a > -b$ Ⓒ $-b^2 < a^2$
     Ⓓ $-a^2 < b^2$ Ⓔ $0 < -(a - b)$

[40] A singer has memorized 12 different songs. If every time he performs he sings any three of these songs, how many different performances can he give?

     Ⓐ 4 Ⓑ 12 Ⓒ 110 Ⓓ 220 Ⓔ 440

[41] The measure of $\angle AOD$ and $\angle BOY$ is 90, and the measure of $\angle DOY$ is between 40 and 50. What is the range of possible values of the measure of $\angle AOC$?

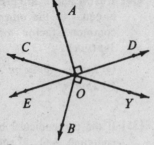

(A) 30 to 40 (B) 40 to 50 (C) 50 to 60 (D) 40 to 60 (E) Cannot be determined

[42] If a circle is tangent to both the x- and y-axis and has a radius of 1, then its equation is

(A) $(x - 1)^2 + (y + 1)^2 = 1$ (B) $x^2 + y^2 = 1$ (C) $x^2 + (y + 1)^2 = 1$ (D) $(x + 1)^2 + y^2 = 1$ (E) $(x - 1)^2 + y^2 = 1$

[43] If two planes, P_1 and P_2, are parallel, then

(A) Any line in P_1 is parallel to any line in P_2.
(B) $AB = CD$ whenever A and C are in P_1 and B and D are in P_2.
(C) Any line that intersects P_1 in exactly one point will intersect P_2 in exactly one point.
(D) Any line parallel to P_1 will intersect P_2.
(E) Any line that intersects P_1 in more than one point must intersect P_2 in more than one point.

[45] The number of points in the intersection of the graphs of $y = |x + 2|$ and $y = -|x| + 2$ is

(A) Infinitely many (B) A finite but indeterminable number (C) 3 (D) 2 (E) 0

[46] If $\sin x > 0$ and $\cos x = -\dfrac{4}{5}$, then $\tan x =$

(A) $\dfrac{3}{5}$ (B) $-\dfrac{3}{5}$ (C) $\dfrac{4}{3}$ (D) $-\dfrac{3}{4}$ (E) $-\dfrac{4}{3}$

[47] If $x = \sqrt{yz}$, $x > 0$, $y > 0$ and $z > 0$, then log $y =$

(A) $\dfrac{x^2}{z}$ (B) $\dfrac{\log x^2}{\log z}$ (C) $\dfrac{2 \log x}{\log z}$ (D) $2 \log x - \log z$ (E) $2(\log x - \log z)$

[48] A parallelogram has an area of 36 square feet and two sides of lengths 6 feet and 9 feet. Which of the following is the sine of an angle of the parallelogram?

(A) $\dfrac{2}{3}$ (B) $\dfrac{3}{2}$ (C) $\dfrac{4}{9}$ (D) $\dfrac{5}{9}$ (E) $-\dfrac{5}{6}$

[49] Three cards, Card One, Card Two, and Card Three, are drawn from a deck. One of these is a queen, one an ace and one a king. One and only one of the following statements is true.

I Card Two is NOT a queen.
II Card Three IS a queen.
III Card One is NOT an ace.

Based on this information, which of the following is true?

(A) Card One is a queen. (B) Card One is an ace. (C) Card Two is a king. (D) Card Three is an ace. (E) Card Three is a queen.

[50] If a cube has an edge of length 10, then the length of the segment connecting the center of a face of the cube to *any* vertex not contained in the plane of that face is

(A) $\sqrt{6}$ (B) $5\sqrt{6}$ (C) $6\sqrt{5}$ (D) $3\sqrt{5}$ (E) $10\sqrt{6}$

ANSWER KEY

1. D	11. A	21. E	31. B	41. B
2. A	12. A	22. D	32. B	42. A
3. C	13. B	23. E	33. B	43. C
4. B	14. E	24. D	34. C	44. B
5. E	15. B	25. D	35. B	45. A
6. B	16. C	26. D	36. C	46. D
7. E	17. C	27. D	37. E	47. D
8. D	18. A	28. A	38. D	48. A
9. D	19. B	29. A	39. A	49. B
10. B	20. E	30. C	40. D	50. B

ANSWER EXPLANATIONS

[1] (D) $\dfrac{\sqrt{10}\sqrt{2}}{\sqrt{15}} = \dfrac{\sqrt{5}\sqrt{2}\sqrt{2}}{\sqrt{5}\sqrt{3}} = \dfrac{2}{\sqrt{3}}$

$\qquad = \dfrac{2\sqrt{3}}{\sqrt{3}\sqrt{3}} = \dfrac{2\sqrt{3}}{3}$ (6–14)

[2] (A) Altitude from A to segment BC is 3 and $BC = 5$, so area of $\triangle ABC = \dfrac{1}{2} \times 5 \times 3 = \dfrac{15}{2}$.

Altitude from D to segment BC is 3 and $BC = 5$, so area of $\triangle BCD = \dfrac{1}{2} \times 5 \times 3 = \dfrac{15}{2}$.

(18–12)

[3] © $\dfrac{a-b}{a+b} - 1 = \dfrac{a-b}{a+b} - \dfrac{a+b}{a+b} =$

$\dfrac{(a-b)-(a+b)}{a+b} = \dfrac{-2b}{a+b}$ (9–11)

[4] Ⓑ Angle adjacent to 130° is 50° and $x = 70 + 50 = 120$ since the measure of an exterior angle ($\angle x$) of a triangle equals the sum of the measures of its remote interior angles. Also $50 + 45 + y = 180$ since the sum of the measures of the angles of a triangle is 180. Therefore $y = 180 - 95 = 85$.   (9–7)

[5] Ⓔ If $x = 3$, then $3 + y = a$ and $3 - y = a$ so $3 + y = 3 - y$ and $y = 0$. Thus $3 + 0 = a$, using the first equation given.   (22–4)

[6] Ⓑ Since the sequence of digits is given, we need only find the decimal point. Round off the numbers as follows: $(8.42)^2 = (8.4)^2 = 71$, $95.1 = 95$, $.982 = 1$ and $69.4 = 69$. Thus $\dfrac{71 \times 95}{69} = 98$.   (22–4)

[7] Ⓔ $\dfrac{x-1}{x+1} = \dfrac{2}{3}$ so $3(x-1) = 2(x+1)$, and $3x - 3 = 2x + 2$; $x = 5$.   (9–5)

[8] Ⓓ $(\angle COD)° = (\angle BOE)°$ since they are vertical angles.
$(\angle BOE)° = (\angle EOA)° + (\angle AOB)° = 15 + 90 = 105$ (11–4)

[9] Ⓓ $16 = 4^2$ so $4^{x/2} = 4^2$ and $\dfrac{1}{2}x = 2$. Thus $x = 4$.

[10] Ⓑ Since $\dfrac{x^2 - 1}{3} = 5$ then $y(5) = 15$ and $y = 3$.   (22–3)

[11] Ⓐ 30° and 60° are complementary so any trigonometric cofunctions are equal.   (24–12)

[12] Ⓐ There are at least three different ways of doing this question using areas, similar triangles or special relationships such as the following: The altitude to the hypotenuse is the geometric mean of the segments of the hypotenuse. Join C and A; A and D. $\triangle CAD$ is a right $\triangle$ because $\angle CAD$ is inscribed in a semicircle.
$AB = \sqrt{(CB)(BD)} = \sqrt{3 \times 4} = 2\sqrt{3}$

(15–14 and 16–5)

[13] Ⓑ The left member can be transformed as follows: $(b + c)(ab - ac) = (b + c)(b - c)a = (b^2 - c^2)a$.
It is thus a times the right member so $a = 1$.   (7–2)

[14] Ⓔ $\dfrac{(2)^3 + (3)(4)^2}{-2(2 - 3 \cdot 3)} = \dfrac{8 + 48}{14} = \dfrac{56}{14} = 4$ (9–1)

[15] Ⓑ $\triangle GEC$ is an isosceles right triangle since $(\angle G)° = (\angle C)° = 45$. GC is composed of two radii from each triangle so $GC = 16$. From the special triangle relations $GE = EC = \dfrac{16}{\sqrt{2}} = 8\sqrt{2}$, and the sum is $16 + 16\sqrt{2}$.   (17–14)

[16] © Diagonals of a parallelogram bisect each other so E is the midpoint. Using the midpoint formula to find $D(x,y)$:
$\dfrac{x+4}{2} = 3$ and $\dfrac{y+2}{2} = 3$ so $x = 2$ and $y = 4$.   (18–11)

[17] © Altitudes are equal so ratio of areas is ratio of bases. $AB = 2 + 3 = 5$.   (17–11)

[18] Ⓐ Replace x with $\dfrac{1}{x}$ so $f(x) = f\left(\dfrac{1}{1/x}\right) = 2\left(\dfrac{1}{x}\right)$.   (20–7)

[19] Ⓐ AC is the hypotenuse of both $\triangle ADC$ and $\triangle ABC$. The midpoint, M, of AC must be equidistant from the vertices of the right triangles. M must be the center of any circle containing A, B and C, and this circle must contain D since $MD = MA = MB = MC$.   (16–5)

[20] Ⓔ Any negative values of x will make *both* factors negative and thus give a positive product.   (8–5)

[21] Ⓔ Solve II and III for y and simplify; you will get equation I in both cases.   (18–20)

[22] Ⓓ In 1 hour the hour hand will rotate $\dfrac{1}{12}$ of a revolution or $\dfrac{1}{12}$ of 360° = 30°. In 10 minutes it will rotate $\dfrac{1}{6}$ of this distance or $\dfrac{1}{6}$ of 30° = 5°.   (16–3)

[23] Ⓔ If $\dfrac{1}{x} + \dfrac{1}{\sqrt{x}} = 0$, then $\dfrac{1}{x} = \dfrac{-1}{\sqrt{x}}$ and $\sqrt{x} = -x$. But $x > 0$ for $\sqrt{x}$ to exist ($x = 0$ leads to division by 0) and "$\sqrt{}$" is defined to be positive. $-x$ is negative. *(19–8)*

[24] Ⓓ $(\sin x)(\csc x) = (\sin x)\dfrac{1}{\sin x} = 1$ when $\sin x \neq 0$
But $\sin x = 0$ only when $x = n\pi$, where n is an integer. *(24–13)*

[25] Ⓓ There are two cases to consider: $x > 0$ and $x < 0$ ($x = 0$ leads to division by 0).

Case I, $x > 0$

If $\dfrac{1}{x} < \dfrac{1}{2}$ then $2 < x$.

Case II, $x < 0$

If $\dfrac{1}{x} < \dfrac{1}{2}$ then $2 > x$, but $2 > x$ for all x in this case, which includes only $x < 0$.
Thus $x > 2$ or $x < 0$. *(8–2)*

[26] Ⓓ If $k + 1$ is odd, then k is even, and k^2 is even. $(k + 1)(k - 1) = k^2 - 1$ and $k^2 - 1$ is odd.

[27] Ⓓ If $(a^2 - 3a)(a + 3) = 0$, then $a(a - 3)(a + 3) = 0$. But the latter equation is true for any number that makes a factor equal to zero. Thus $a = 0$ or $a - 3 = 0$ or $a + 3 = 0$. *(6–5)*

[28] Ⓐ Replace a by $2b$ wherever it occurs. Using the formula for the area of a trapezoid:

$$18 = \dfrac{1}{2}(3b)(b + 2b)$$

from which

$$b = 2 \text{ and } a = 4 \text{ (since } a = 2b).$$

But
$$c^2 = a^2 + b^2$$
$$c^2 = 20$$
$$c = 2\sqrt{5} \qquad (17\text{–}12)$$

[29] Ⓐ $f(-10) = -\dfrac{1}{(-10)^3} = \dfrac{1}{1{,}000}$

$f(-5) = -\dfrac{1}{(-5)^3} = \dfrac{1}{125}$

$f(-1) = -\dfrac{1}{(-1)^3} = 1$

$f\left(-\dfrac{1}{10}\right) = -\dfrac{1}{(-1/10)^3} = 1000$ *(20–6)*

The representative values of $f(x)$ shown above suggest that $f(x)$ increases throughout the interval.

[30] Ⓒ $\operatorname{Tan} \angle B = \dfrac{AC}{BC} =$

$\dfrac{AC}{1} = p$; therefore

$AC = p$

By the Pythagorean Theorem:

$$(AB)^2 = p^2 + 1^2$$
$$AB = \sqrt{p^2 + 1}$$

Thus $\cos \angle A = \dfrac{AC}{AB} = \dfrac{p}{\sqrt{p^2 + 1}}$ *(24–8)*

[31] Ⓑ Volume of bar $= 2 \times 3 \times 4 = 24$
Volume of cube $= e^3 = \dfrac{1}{3}(24) = 8$
Therefore $e = 2$ *(30–1)*

[32] Ⓑ $\dfrac{n!}{2} = \dfrac{n(n-1)(n-2)(n-3)\ldots 3 \times 2 \times 1}{2}$
$(n - 2)! = (n - 2)(n - 3)\ldots 3 \times 2 \times 1$
Thus, if we divide both sides of the given equation by $(n - 2)!$, we get:
$$\dfrac{n(n-1)}{2} = 1$$
$$n^2 - n - 2 = 0$$
$$(n - 2)(n + 1) = 0 \qquad (27\text{–}1)$$
$\{2, -1\}$ But $n!$ is not defined for -1.

[33] Ⓑ If $\log x = \dfrac{1}{2}\log a - \log b$, then
$$\log x = \log \dfrac{\sqrt{a}}{b} \text{ and } x = \dfrac{\sqrt{a}}{b}$$
But $a = 4b^2$ so $\sqrt{a} = 2b$ and $x = \dfrac{2b}{b} = 2$

[34] Ⓒ $24pm^2n^2 = (3pmn^2)(8m)$
$9pmn^2 = (3pmn^2)(3)$
$36p(mn)^3 = (3pmn^2)(12m^2n)$ *(23–14)*

[35] Ⓑ $(4, c)$ must be equidistant from A and B so:
$$\sqrt{(4 - 1)^2 + (c - 2)^2} = \sqrt{(4 - 2)^2 + (c - 4)^2}$$
$$\sqrt{9 + c^2 - 4c + 4} = \sqrt{4 + c^2 - 8c + 16}$$
$$c^2 - 4c + 13 = c^2 - 8c + 20$$
$$4c = 7$$
$$c = \dfrac{7}{4} \qquad (18\text{–}11)$$

[36] © $f[f(x)] = f\left(\dfrac{1}{x}\right) = x$ and $f(x) = \dfrac{1}{x}$, so $x = \dfrac{1}{x}$. Thus $x^2 = 1$ and $x = 1$ or $x = -1$.

(20–9)

[37] Ⓔ $CA = CD + DA = 3 + 6 = 9$
$\dfrac{CD}{CA} = \dfrac{DE}{AB}$ so $\dfrac{3}{9} = \dfrac{DE}{4}$ and $DE = \dfrac{12}{9} = \dfrac{4}{3}$

(15–9)

[38] Ⓓ $(3i)(2i)^2(1 + i) = (3i)(-4)(1 + i) = -12i$
$(1 + i) = -12i - 12i^2 = 12 - 12i$ *(21–5)*

[39] Ⓐ Let $a = -5$ and $b = -4$. Thus $-a = 5$ and $|b| = 4$ so $-a > |b|$ in contradiction to Ⓐ.

(6–7, 8)

[40] Ⓓ The question asks for the number of combinations of 12 songs taken three at a time, which is (by formula):

$$\dfrac{12!}{9!\,3!} = 220$$ *(27–9)*

[41] Ⓑ $(\angle AOC)^\circ + (\angle COE)^\circ = 90$ and $(\angle COE)^\circ = (\angle DOY)^\circ$. Thus $(\angle AOC)^\circ = 90 - (\angle DOY)^\circ$. When $(\angle DOY)^\circ = 40$, then $(\angle AOC)^\circ = 50$ and when $(\angle DOY)^\circ = 50$, then $(\angle AOC)^\circ = 40$.   *(11–4)*

[42] Ⓐ Since the radius to the point of tangency is always ⊥ to the tangent, and since this radius is 1, the center of any such circle is one of the points $\{(1, 1), (1, -1), (-1, 1), (-1, -1)\}$. The center of the circle in Ⓐ is $(1, -1)$.   *(18–26)*

[43] © The two planes are parallel so that a line which pierces P_1 cannot bypass P_2.   *(14–5)*

[44] Ⓑ Let $\dfrac{y}{2} = \theta$; then $\tan \theta = \sin \theta$ is given. But $\tan \theta = \dfrac{\sin \theta}{\cos \theta}$ for any θ whose cosine is defined, so $\cos \theta = 1$ and $\theta = 0$. Since $\dfrac{y}{2} = \theta$, we conclude that $\dfrac{y}{2} = 0$ so $y = 0$, and $\cos y \doteq 1$.

(24–14)

[45] Ⓐ From the graph below, the intersection is a segment (which contains infinitely many points).

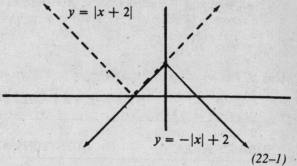

$y = |x + 2|$

$y = -|x| + 2$

(22–1)

[46] Ⓓ $\sin^2 x + \cos^2 x = 1$
$$\sin^2 x + \dfrac{16}{25} = 1$$
$$\sin^2 x = \dfrac{9}{25}$$
$$\sin x = \pm \dfrac{3}{5}$$

But $\sin x$ was given as positive so $\sin x = \dfrac{3}{5}$.

$$\tan x = \dfrac{\sin x}{\cos x} = \dfrac{3/5}{-4/5} = -\dfrac{3}{4}$$ *(24–13)*

[47] Ⓓ If $x = \sqrt{yz}$, then $x^2 = yz$ and $y = \dfrac{x^2}{z}$. Thus

$\log y = \log \dfrac{x^2}{z} = \log x^2 - \log z = 2 \log x - \log z$.

(23–16)

[48] Ⓐ Let h be the altitude to a 9-foot side; then $9h = 36$ and $h = 4$. The sine of $\angle A$ is $4/6 = 2/3$.

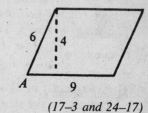

A 9 6 4

(17–3 and 24–17)

[49] Ⓓ By trial and error, let each statement be true and the others false. Each such trial will lead to a contradiction except III true and both I and II false.

[50] Ⓑ $AB = 10$
(given)
$AC = 10\sqrt{2}$
(Pyth. Th.)
$AM = 5\sqrt{2}$
(M is midpoint as given).
$(BM)^2 = (AB)^2 + (AM)^2$
(Pyth. Th.)
$BM = \sqrt{100 + 50}$
$= \sqrt{150} = 5\sqrt{6}$ *(20–1 and 18–12)*

SELF-EVALUATION CHART FOR TEST 1

SUBJECT AREA	QUESTIONS ANSWERED CORRECTLY	NUMBER OF CORRECT ANSWERS
Algebra (15 questions)	1 3 5 7 9 10 13 14 20 23 25 27 32 39 47	_____
Plane geometry (10 questions)	4 8 12 15 17 19 28 35 37 41	_____
Solid geometry (3 questions)	31 43 50	_____
Coordinate geometry (5 questions)	2 16 21 42 45	_____
Trigonometry (7 questions)	11 22 24 30 44 46 48	_____
Functions (5 questions)	14 18 29 33 36	_____
Miscellaneous (7 questions)	6 26 32 34 38 40 49	_____
Total number of correct answers		_____

Total score = total number of correct answers × 4   _____

minus number of incorrect answers − _____

_____

ANSWER SHEET FOR TEST 2

Determine the correct answer for each question. Then, using a No. 2 pencil, blacken completely the oval containing the letter of your choice.

1. Ⓐ Ⓑ Ⓒ Ⓓ Ⓔ	18. Ⓐ Ⓑ Ⓒ Ⓓ Ⓔ	35. Ⓐ Ⓑ Ⓒ Ⓓ Ⓔ
2. Ⓐ Ⓑ Ⓒ Ⓓ Ⓔ	19. Ⓐ Ⓑ Ⓒ Ⓓ Ⓔ	36. Ⓐ Ⓑ Ⓒ Ⓓ Ⓔ
3. Ⓐ Ⓑ Ⓒ Ⓓ Ⓔ	20. Ⓐ Ⓑ Ⓒ Ⓓ Ⓔ	37. Ⓐ Ⓑ Ⓒ Ⓓ Ⓔ
4. Ⓐ Ⓑ Ⓒ Ⓓ Ⓔ	21. Ⓐ Ⓑ Ⓒ Ⓓ Ⓔ	38. Ⓐ Ⓑ Ⓒ Ⓓ Ⓔ
5. Ⓐ Ⓑ Ⓒ Ⓓ Ⓔ	22. Ⓐ Ⓑ Ⓒ Ⓓ Ⓔ	39. Ⓐ Ⓑ Ⓒ Ⓓ Ⓔ
6. Ⓐ Ⓑ Ⓒ Ⓓ Ⓔ	23. Ⓐ Ⓑ Ⓒ Ⓓ Ⓔ	40. Ⓐ Ⓑ Ⓒ Ⓓ Ⓔ
7. Ⓐ Ⓑ Ⓒ Ⓓ Ⓔ	24. Ⓐ Ⓑ Ⓒ Ⓓ Ⓔ	41. Ⓐ Ⓑ Ⓒ Ⓓ Ⓔ
8. Ⓐ Ⓑ Ⓒ Ⓓ Ⓔ	25. Ⓐ Ⓑ Ⓒ Ⓓ Ⓔ	42. Ⓐ Ⓑ Ⓒ Ⓓ Ⓔ
9. Ⓐ Ⓑ Ⓒ Ⓓ Ⓔ	26. Ⓐ Ⓑ Ⓒ Ⓓ Ⓔ	43. Ⓐ Ⓑ Ⓒ Ⓓ Ⓔ
10. Ⓐ Ⓑ Ⓒ Ⓓ Ⓔ	27. Ⓐ Ⓑ Ⓒ Ⓓ Ⓔ	44. Ⓐ Ⓑ Ⓒ Ⓓ Ⓔ
11. Ⓐ Ⓑ Ⓒ Ⓓ Ⓔ	28. Ⓐ Ⓑ Ⓒ Ⓓ Ⓔ	45. Ⓐ Ⓑ Ⓒ Ⓓ Ⓔ
12. Ⓐ Ⓑ Ⓒ Ⓓ Ⓔ	29. Ⓐ Ⓑ Ⓒ Ⓓ Ⓔ	46. Ⓐ Ⓑ Ⓒ Ⓓ Ⓔ
13. Ⓐ Ⓑ Ⓒ Ⓓ Ⓔ	30. Ⓐ Ⓑ Ⓒ Ⓓ Ⓔ	47. Ⓐ Ⓑ Ⓒ Ⓓ Ⓔ
14. Ⓐ Ⓑ Ⓒ Ⓓ Ⓔ	31. Ⓐ Ⓑ Ⓒ Ⓓ Ⓔ	48. Ⓐ Ⓑ Ⓒ Ⓓ Ⓔ
15. Ⓐ Ⓑ Ⓒ Ⓓ Ⓔ	32. Ⓐ Ⓑ Ⓒ Ⓓ Ⓔ	49. Ⓐ Ⓑ Ⓒ Ⓓ Ⓔ
16. Ⓐ Ⓑ Ⓒ Ⓓ Ⓔ	33. Ⓐ Ⓑ Ⓒ Ⓓ Ⓔ	50. Ⓐ Ⓑ Ⓒ Ⓓ Ⓔ
17. Ⓐ Ⓑ Ⓒ Ⓓ Ⓔ	34. Ⓐ Ⓑ Ⓒ Ⓓ Ⓔ	

33. Model Test 2

TEST

For each of the following, select the best choice—A, B, C, D or E—to answer the question or complete the statement. Then locate the number of the question on the answer sheet, and indicate your choice by filling in completely the corresponding oval.

[1] If $a = 3b + 5$ and $c = 3a$, then $c =$

  Ⓐ $9b + 15$ Ⓑ $3b + 5$ Ⓒ $b + \frac{5}{3}$ Ⓓ $9b$

  Ⓔ $3b + \frac{5}{3}$

[2] The length of arc AC is twice the length of arc BC. Which of the following is NOT true?

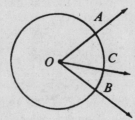

  Ⓐ The degree measure of $\angle AOC$ is twice the degree measure of $\angle BOC$.
  Ⓑ The degree measure of arc AC is twice the degree measure of arc BC. Ⓒ The radian measure of $\angle AOC$ is twice the radian measure of $\angle BOC$.
  Ⓓ The radius of arc AC is equal to the radius of arc BC. Ⓔ The length of line segment AC is twice the length of line segment BC.

[3] If $a = 3^2$, $b = \frac{1}{a}$ and $c = b^4$, then

  Ⓐ $a > b > c$ Ⓑ $a < b < c$
  Ⓒ $a < c < b$ Ⓓ $c < a < b$ Ⓔ $b < c < a$

[4] If $\frac{x - 2}{y} = 4$ and $y - 1 = 0$, what is the value of x?

  Ⓐ No value possible   Ⓑ 6   Ⓒ 5   Ⓓ 4   Ⓔ 3

[5] Lines L_1 and L_2 are NOT parallel and will intersect at some point to the right of the page. Which of the following is NOT true?

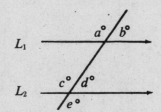

Ⓐ $c = e$ Ⓑ $b > d$
Ⓒ $d + e = 180$ Ⓓ $a = c$
Ⓔ $c > 180 - b$

[6] If $A = (-1, 2)$ and $B = (2, -1)$, where A and B are two points in the coordinate plane, then what is the length of segment AB?

  Ⓐ 1   Ⓑ 2   Ⓒ 3   Ⓓ $3\sqrt{2}$ Ⓔ $2\sqrt{3}$

[7] An operation, $\circ$, on the numbers a and b is defined by the formula $a \circ b = 2(a + 2b)$. For what values of x and y is $x \circ y = y \circ x$?

  Ⓐ All real values   Ⓑ Only when $x = y$
  Ⓒ Only when both x and y are 0   Ⓓ Only when $x = -y$ Ⓔ Only when x and y are both 1

[8] If the area of a square is 1.44 square feet, its perimeter is

  Ⓐ 1.2   Ⓑ 4.8   Ⓒ 14.4   Ⓓ 12   Ⓔ 14

[9] The arc measures are as shown, $L_1 \parallel L_2$ and L_1 is tangent to the circle whose center is O. Which answer is NOT true?

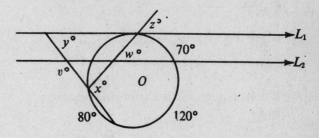

  Ⓐ $z = 45$ Ⓑ $x = 95$ Ⓒ $y = 50$ Ⓓ $w = 70$ Ⓔ $v = 130$

[10] If $\sqrt{x^2 - 6x + 9} = x - 3$, then $x =$

  Ⓐ No real number
  Ⓑ Any real number   Ⓒ 3 or -3 only
  Ⓓ 3 only   Ⓔ $x \geq 3$

[11] If $\frac{a}{b} = 5$, which of the following is NOT true?

  Ⓐ a cannot be zero.   Ⓑ b cannot be zero.
  Ⓒ a and b cannot both be integers.   Ⓓ a and b must both have the same sign.   Ⓔ a and b can have infinitely many values.

[12] What is the simplified form of

$$\frac{\dfrac{m + n}{m - 1} + n}{\dfrac{m + n}{m - 1} - 1}?$$

(A) $\dfrac{m + n}{m - 1}$ (B) 1   (C) m (D) -1 (E) $m^2 - n^2$

[13] If $\angle A$ is positioned on a set of coordinate axes so that its vertex is at the origin and one of its sides is the nonnegative ray of the x-axis, and if its other side passes through the point $(-8, 15)$, then sine $\angle A =$

(A) $-\dfrac{8}{15}$ (B) $\dfrac{15}{8}$ (C) $\dfrac{8}{15}$ (D) $\dfrac{15}{17}$ (E) $-\dfrac{8}{17}$

[14] If $a = -\dfrac{1}{2}$ and $b = -8$, then $\dfrac{a^2}{b} + b$

(A) -8 (B) $-\dfrac{257}{32}$ (C) -6 (D) $\dfrac{1}{32}$ (E) -10

[15] If, in $\triangle ABC$, $AB = 4$, $\sin \angle A = .695$ and $AC = 10$, what is the area of $\triangle ABC$?

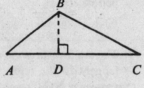

(A) 13.9   (B) 12.9   (C) 14.9   (D) 27.8   (E) 25.8

[16] If $f(x) = 2 - |x| + x^2$, then $f(-2) =$

(A) 0   (B) 4   (C) 2   (D) -2 (E) -4

[17] If $x - 1, x, x - 1$ is a geometric sequence, then $x =$

(A) $-\dfrac{1}{2}$ (B) $\dfrac{1}{2}$ (C) 2   (D) 1   (E) -1

[18] A circle with center $(-3, 4)$ is tangent to the x-axis. Which of the following is a point of intersection of the circle with the y-axis?

(A) $(0, -4 - \sqrt{7})$ (B) $(0, 9)$
(C) $(0, +4 - \sqrt{7})$ (D) $(0, 1)$ (E) $(0, -1)$

[19] Ray AD is the bisector of $\angle CAB$, and the measure of $\angle ACD$ is y. What must be the measure of $\angle ADC$ in order for line AB to be parallel to line CD?

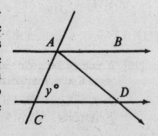

(A) $90 - y$
(B) $90 - \dfrac{y}{2}$ (C) $180 - \dfrac{y}{2}$ (D) $180 - y$
(E) $90 + y$

[20] $\sqrt{108} - \dfrac{2}{3 - \sqrt{27}} =$

(A) $\dfrac{19\sqrt{3} + 1}{3}$ (B) $3 + 3\sqrt{3}$ (C) -2 (D) $6 + 2\sqrt{27}$ (E) $4\sqrt{108}$

[21] If $|x|^2 - |x| - 6 = 0$, then $x =$

(A) $\{3, 2\}$ (B) $\{-3, 2\}$ (C) $\{3, -3\}$
(D) $\{\pm 3, \pm 2\}$ (E) $\{-3, -2\}$

[22] The radius of the circle is 4, and the measure of $\angle AOC$ is 120. What is the length of chord AC?

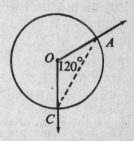

(A) 5   (B) $2\sqrt{2}$
(C) $4\sqrt{2}$ (D) 8
(E) $4\sqrt{3}$

[23] If $\tan 36° = .727$ and $\tan 37° = .754$, which of the following is the best approximation to $\tan 36.8°$?

(A) .734   (B) .745   (C) .736   (D) .737   (E) .749

[24] For what value of c will $2x^2 - 3x + c = 0$ have one and only one real root?

(A) 4   (B) 1   (C) -4 (D) $\dfrac{9}{8}$ (E) 0

[25] If $f(x) = x + 1$ and $g(x) = x^2 - 1$, for what value(s) of x does $g(f(x)) = 0$?

(A) 0 only   (B) 1 and -1 only   (C) 1 only
(D) -2 only   (E) 0 and -2

[26] If $(a^x)^{2/3} = \dfrac{1}{a^2}$, then $x =$

(A) -1 (B) -2 (C) -3 (D) 2   (E) 1

[27] A rectangular box is inscribed in a cylinder of height 5 and with a circular base of radius $2\dfrac{1}{2}$ and $AB = 4$. The volume of the box is

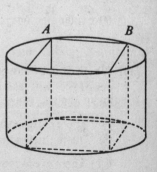

(A) 20   (B) 45
(C) 15   (D) 30   (E) 60

[28] If $x^2 - 2x - 3 > 0$, then

Ⓐ $x > 2$ Ⓑ $1 < x < 3$ Ⓒ $-1 < x < 3$
Ⓓ $x > 3$ or $x < 1$ Ⓔ $x > 3$ or $x < -1$

[29] If $f(x) = \dfrac{3x + 1}{x}$, and $f(2b) = 2f(b)$, then b is

Ⓐ Any real number   Ⓑ Any real number except
0 Ⓒ $-\dfrac{1}{2}$ only   Ⓓ No real number   Ⓔ 0 and

$-\dfrac{1}{2}$ only

[30] The points of intersection of the line $y = 3x$ and the hyperbola $y^2 - x^2 = 2$ are

Ⓐ $(\pm\dfrac{1}{4}, \pm\dfrac{3}{4})$ Ⓑ $(\pm\dfrac{1}{2}, \pm\dfrac{3}{2})$ Ⓒ $(\pm 1, \pm 3)$
Ⓓ $(\pm 2, \pm 6)$ Ⓔ $(0, 0)$

[31] If the cosine of each of $\angle A$, $\angle B$, $\angle C$ and $\angle D$ is $-\dfrac{1}{2}$, which of the following can be concluded?

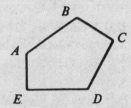

Ⓐ Points A, E, and D are collinear
Ⓑ $\cos \angle E = \dfrac{1}{2}$
Ⓒ $\angle AED$ is a right angle   Ⓓ $\angle AED$ and $\angle EDC$ are complementary   Ⓔ The given information is self-contradictory

[32] If $\log_{\sqrt{2}}(x - 1) = 4$, then $x =$
Ⓐ 1   Ⓑ 2   Ⓒ 3   Ⓓ 4   Ⓔ 5

[33] If, in $\triangle ABC$, $AB = 12$, $AC = 14$ and $BC = 16$, then $\cos \angle A =$

Ⓐ $\dfrac{6}{7}$ Ⓑ $\dfrac{11}{16}$ Ⓒ $\dfrac{7}{8}$ Ⓓ $\dfrac{1}{4}$ Ⓔ $\dfrac{3}{4}$

[34] Which of the following statements about the values of $f(x)$ will lead to the conclusion that f does NOT define a function?

Ⓐ There exists some a such that $f(a) = f(-a)$.
Ⓑ There exists some a such that $f(a) \neq f(-a)$.
Ⓒ There exists some a such that $f(a) = f\left(\dfrac{1}{a}\right)$.

Ⓓ There exist some a and b such that $f(a) \neq f(b)$ but $a = b$.
Ⓔ There exist some a and b such that $f(a) = f(b)$ and $a = b$.

[35] A rectangular aquarium is $\dfrac{2}{3}$ filled with water and then is tilted on its side until the water level coincides with one edge of the bottom. During the tilting process, 6 quarts of water are poured out. What is the volume of the tank in quarts?

Ⓐ 12   Ⓑ 24   Ⓒ 36   Ⓓ 48   Ⓔ 64

[36] If $\log_{10}(x + 4) + \log_{10}(x - 4) = 1$, then

Ⓐ $-\sqrt{6}$ Ⓑ $\sqrt{26}$ Ⓒ 5   Ⓓ $\sqrt{6}$ Ⓔ $\dfrac{5}{4}$

[37] An equation for the line containing the point $(-2, 1)$ and parallel to $4x - 2y = 3$ is
Ⓐ $y = 2x + 5$ Ⓑ $y = 2x - 1$ Ⓒ $y = x - 2$ Ⓓ $y = \dfrac{1}{2}x$ Ⓔ $y = 2x - 2$

[38] Point O is the center of the circle. The measure of arc XB is $\dfrac{1}{3}$ the measure of arc AB, and the measure of arc YC is $\dfrac{1}{2}$ the measure of arc DC. If the measure of $\angle AXB$ is 140, then the measure of $\angle DYC$ is

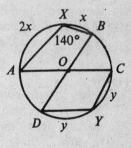

Ⓐ 120   Ⓑ 140   Ⓒ 135   Ⓓ 145   Ⓔ $137\dfrac{1}{2}$

[39] If $f(a) = 2^a$, then $\log_2 f(a) =$
Ⓐ 2   Ⓑ $f(a)$ Ⓒ a Ⓓ $\dfrac{1}{2^a}$ Ⓔ a^2

[40] Which of the following is the set of all points in space that are equidistant from two given points?
Ⓐ A sphere   Ⓑ An ellipse   Ⓒ A parabola
Ⓓ A plane   Ⓔ A line

[41] Which term in the expansion of $\left(\dfrac{1}{x} + x^2\right)^9$ contains no power of x?

Ⓐ No term   Ⓑ Sixth   Ⓒ Fifth   Ⓓ Third
Ⓔ Fourth

[42] Both $\angle XAB$ and $\angle XYZ$ are right angles, $XB = 6, BY = 2$ and $AB = 4$.

The ratio of $\dfrac{\text{area of } \triangle XAB}{\text{area of } \triangle XYZ}$ is

Ⓐ $\dfrac{3}{5}$ Ⓑ $\dfrac{5}{16}$ Ⓒ $\dfrac{9}{25}$
Ⓓ $\dfrac{4}{5}$ Ⓔ $\dfrac{3}{25}$

[43] The range of $f(x) = -\dfrac{1}{4}\sin 4x$ is

Ⓐ $-\dfrac{1}{4} \le y \le 0$ Ⓑ $-\dfrac{1}{4} \le y \le \dfrac{1}{4}$

Ⓒ $0 \le y \le \dfrac{1}{4}$ Ⓓ $-1 \le y \le 1$

Ⓔ $-4 \le y \le 4$

[44] Three planes, E, F and G, intersect so that each is perpendicular to the other two. A segment AB is positioned so that the length of its projection on the intersection of E and F is 1, on the intersection of F and G is 2, and on the intersection of E and G is 3. What is the length of AB?

Ⓐ $\sqrt{14}$ Ⓑ 4   Ⓒ 5   Ⓓ 6   Ⓔ $\sqrt{12}$

[45] A bag contains seven marbles, three red and four green. If three marbles are drawn from the bag at random, what is the probability that all three will be red?

Ⓐ $\dfrac{3}{35}$ Ⓑ $\dfrac{3}{7}$ Ⓒ $\dfrac{1}{35}$ Ⓓ $\dfrac{3}{4}$ Ⓔ $\dfrac{4}{7}$

[46] The values of m for which the following has no real value defined:
$$\dfrac{\dfrac{1}{m^2 - m - 2}}{m^2 - 4}$$
are

Ⓐ $\{-2, -1\}$ Ⓑ $\{-1, 2, -2\}$ Ⓒ $\{2, -2\}$
Ⓓ $\{-1, 2\}$ Ⓔ $\{1, -1, 2, -2\}$

[47] If $\log_{10}(x - 5) > 0$, then

Ⓐ $x > 5$ Ⓑ $x > 6$ Ⓒ $x > 1$ Ⓓ $x > 0$
Ⓔ $x < 5$

[48] If one solution for $x^3 + 2x^2 + x + 2$ is i, where $i = \sqrt{-1}$, which of the following sets contains all other solutions?

Ⓐ $\{-i\}$ Ⓑ $\{-i, 2\}$ Ⓒ $\{-i, -2\}$
Ⓓ $\{2, -2\}$ Ⓔ $\{2\}$

[49] If $f(x) = -\sqrt{x}$ and g is the inverse of f, which of the following describes the domain of g?

Ⓐ $y \ne 0$ Ⓑ All rational numbers   Ⓒ All real numbers   Ⓓ $y \ge 0$ Ⓔ $y \le 0$

[50] If $0 \le x \le 2\pi$ and $4\sin^2 x + 4\cos x - 1 = 0$, which of the following sets contains all values of x?

Ⓐ $\left[\dfrac{\pi}{3}, \dfrac{\pi}{6}\right]$ Ⓑ $\left[\dfrac{\pi}{3}, \dfrac{2\pi}{3}\right]$ Ⓒ $\left[\dfrac{2\pi}{3}, -\dfrac{2\pi}{3}\right]$

Ⓓ $\left[\dfrac{\pi}{3}, -\dfrac{\pi}{3}\right]$ Ⓔ $\left[\dfrac{2\pi}{3}, \dfrac{4\pi}{3}\right]$

ANSWER KEY

1. A	11. C	21. C	31. B	41. E
2. E	12. C	22. E	32. E	42. B
3. A	13. D	23. E	33. D	43. B
4. B	14. B	24. D	34. D	44. A
5. D	15. A	25. E	35. C	45. C
6. D	16. B	26. C	36. B	46. B
7. B	17. B	27. E	37. A	47. B
8. B	18. C	28. E	38. B	48. C
9. D	19. B	29. C	39. C	49. E
10. E	20. A	30. B	40. D	50. E

ANSWER EXPLANATIONS

[1] Ⓐ If $c = 3a$, then $a = \dfrac{c}{3}$ and $\dfrac{c}{3} = 3b + 5$

$c = 3(3b + 5) = 9b + 15$ ⠀⠀⠀⠀ (22-3)

[2] Ⓔ Arc length, arc measure and angle measure are all directly proportional. To see that Ⓔ is not true, note the figure (right) showing a similar situation for which OX bisects $\angle ZOY$. $(\angle ZOY)° = 2(\angle XOY)°$, but if $ZY = 2XY$, then $ZX + XY = ZY$ which is impossible.

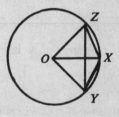

⠀⠀⠀⠀⠀⠀⠀⠀⠀⠀⠀⠀⠀⠀⠀⠀ (16-6)

[3] Ⓐ $a = 3^2 = 9 \quad b = \dfrac{1}{a} = \dfrac{1}{9} \quad c = b^4 = (\dfrac{1}{9})^4$

$= \dfrac{1}{6561}$

[4] Ⓑ If $y - 1 = 0$, then $y = 1$. Thus:

$$\dfrac{x - 2}{1} = 4$$
$$x - 2 = 4$$
$$x = 6 \qquad (22\text{-}3)$$

[5] Ⓓ If $a = c$ then the lines must be parallel since a pair of corresponding angles are equal in measure. $(14\text{-}4)$

[6] Ⓓ $AB = \sqrt{(-1 - 2)^2 + (2 + 1)^2}$

$= \sqrt{9 + 9} = \sqrt{9 \times 2} = 3\sqrt{2}$
$(18\text{-}11)$

[7] Ⓑ If $x \circ y = y \circ x$, then $2(x + 2y) = 2(y + 2x)$ and $x + 2y = y + 2x$ so $y = x$.

[8] Ⓑ Let $x = $ length of a side, then

$$x^2 = 1.44$$
$$= (1.2)^2$$
$$x = 1.2$$

Perimeter $= 4x = 4(1.2) = 4.8 \qquad (17\text{-}2)$

[9] Ⓓ $\angle x$ is an inscribed angle and is thus $\dfrac{1}{2}$ the measure of its intercepted arc:

$$x = \dfrac{1}{2}(70 + 120) = \dfrac{1}{2}(190) = 95.$$

The angle adjacent to $\angle z$ is a secant-tangent angle and is thus $\dfrac{1}{2}$ the measure of its intercepted arc:

$$\dfrac{1}{2}(70 + 120 + 80) = \dfrac{1}{2}(270) = 135, \text{ so}$$
$$z = 45.$$

$\angle w$ and $\angle z$ are corresponding angles so $w = 45$. The remaining arc in the figure is:

$$360 - (70 + 120 + 80) = 90.$$

$\angle y$ has a measure equal to $\dfrac{1}{2}$ the difference of the measures of its intercepted arcs:

$$\dfrac{1}{2}(190 - 90) = 50.$$

$\angle v$ and $\angle y$ are supplementary so $v = 130$.
$(16\text{-}5, 7)$

[10] Ⓔ $\sqrt{x^2 - 6x + 9} = \sqrt{(x - 3)^2} = x - 3$ only when $x - 3 \geq 0$ by definition of "$\sqrt{}$".
$(19\text{-}8)$

[11] Ⓒ Let $a = 10$ and $b = 2$. $(9\text{-}1)$

[12] Ⓒ $\dfrac{\dfrac{m + n}{m - 1} + n}{\dfrac{m + n}{m - 1} - 1} = \dfrac{\dfrac{m + n}{m - 1} + \dfrac{n(m - 1)}{m - 1}}{\dfrac{m + n}{m - 1} - \dfrac{m - 1}{m - 1}}$

$= \dfrac{\dfrac{m + n + mn - n}{m - 1}}{\dfrac{m + n - m + 1}{m - 1}}$

$\dfrac{m + n + mn - n}{m + n - m + 1} = \dfrac{m + mn}{n + 1} = \dfrac{m(1 + n)}{1 + n}$

$= m \qquad (9\text{-}13)$

[13] Ⓓ Sin $\angle A = \dfrac{y}{r}$, where r is the distance of the point (x, y) from the vertex and (x, y) is on the terminal side. The point $(-8, 15)$ is at a distance of $\sqrt{(8 - 0)^2 + (15 - 0)^2} = 17$ units from the origin so $\sin \angle A = \dfrac{15}{17}$ $(24\text{-}7)$

[14] Ⓑ $\dfrac{(-1/2)^2}{-8} + (-8) = \dfrac{1/4}{-8} - 8 = \dfrac{1}{4}\left(-\dfrac{1}{8}\right) - 8$

$= -\dfrac{1}{32} - 8 = -\dfrac{1}{32} - \dfrac{256}{32}$

$= -\dfrac{257}{32} \qquad (9\text{-}1)$

[15] Ⓐ $\sin \angle A = \dfrac{BD}{AB}$

$.695 = \dfrac{BD}{4}$

$2.78 = BD$

Area $= \dfrac{1}{2}(BD)(AC) = \dfrac{1}{2}(2.78)(10)$

or, Area $= \dfrac{1}{2}(AB)(AC)\sin(\angle A)$

$= \dfrac{1}{2} \cdot 4 \cdot 10 \cdot (.695)$

$= 13.9 \qquad (24\text{-}17)$

[16] Ⓑ $f(-2) = 2 - |-2| + (-2)^2 = 2 - 2 + 4$
$= 4 \qquad (20\text{-}7)$

[17] Ⓑ $\dfrac{x}{x - 1} = \dfrac{x - 1}{x}$

$$x^2 = (x - 1)^2$$
$$x^2 = x^2 - 2x + 1$$
$$0 = -2x + 1$$
$$\dfrac{1}{2} = x \qquad (26\text{-}5)$$

[18] Ⓒ From the figure the radius is 4 so the equation of the circle is:

$(x+3)^2 + (y-4)^2 = 4^2$

Let $x = 0$ to find the y-intercept.

$9 + y^2 - 8y + 16 = 16$

$y^2 - 8y + 9 = 0$

By quadratic formula:

$y = \dfrac{8 \pm \sqrt{28}}{2}$

$= \dfrac{8 \pm 2\sqrt{7}}{2}$

$= 4 \pm \sqrt{7}$ (18-26)

[19] Ⓑ For $AB \parallel CD$, $\angle ACD$ and $\angle CAB$ must be supplementary so $(\angle CAB)^\circ = 180 - y$. Thus:

$$(\angle BAD)^\circ = \frac{1}{2}(180 - y) = 90 - \frac{y}{2}$$

by definition of angle bisector and $(\angle ADC)^\circ = (\angle BAD)^\circ$ since parallel lines must have pairs of alternate interior angles equal in measure.

(14-6)

[20] Ⓐ $\sqrt{108} - \dfrac{2}{3 - \sqrt{27}} = 6\sqrt{3} - \dfrac{2}{3 - 3\sqrt{3}}$

$= 6\sqrt{3} - \dfrac{2(3 + 3\sqrt{3})}{(3 - 3\sqrt{3})(3 + 3\sqrt{3})}$

$6\sqrt{3} - \dfrac{6 + 6\sqrt{3}}{9 - 27} = 6\sqrt{3} - \dfrac{6(1 + \sqrt{3})}{-18}$

$= 6\sqrt{3} + \dfrac{1 + \sqrt{3}}{3}$

$\dfrac{18\sqrt{3} + 1 + \sqrt{3}}{3} = \dfrac{19\sqrt{3} + 1}{3}$ (6-15)

[21] Ⓒ Let $u = |x|$; then $u^2 - u - 6 = 0$

$(u + 3)(u + 2) = 0$

$u = 3$ or $u = -2$

Replace u with $|x|$:

$|x| = 3$ or $|x| = -2$

$x = \pm 3$ but $|x| = -2$ has no solutions.

(19-7)

[22] Ⓔ The figure shows the given triangle with a segment from O and $\perp$ to AC. M must be the midpoint of AC, so $OM = 2$, $AM = 2\sqrt{3}$, by the 30–60–90 triangle relations.

$\therefore AC = 4\sqrt{3}$

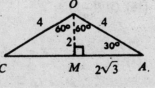

(17-15)

[23] Ⓔ The necessary interpolation is shown below:

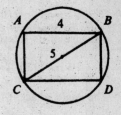

$\dfrac{.8}{1.0} = \dfrac{d}{.027}$

$.8(.027) = d = .0216 \doteq .022$

$d = .0216 \doteq .022$

$\tan 36.8^\circ = .727 + .022 = .749$ (23-19)

[24] Ⓓ The equation will have one and only one real root when the discriminant, $b^2 - 4ac$, equals 0.

$b^2 - 4ac = 9 - 4(2)(c) = 9 - 8c$

If $9 - 8c = 0$, then $c = 9/8$.   (19-9)

[25] Ⓔ $g(x) = x^2 - 1$

$g(f(x)) = [f(x)]^2 - 1$

$= [x + 1]^2 - 1$

$= x^2 + 2x + 1 - 1$

$= x^2 + 2x$

If $x^2 + 2x = 0$, then $x(x + 2) = 0$ and $x = 0$ or -2.   (20-9)

[26] Ⓒ $(a^x)^{2/3} = a^{2x/3}$ and $\dfrac{1}{a^2} = a^{-2}$

So $\dfrac{2}{3}x = -2$ and $x = -2(\dfrac{3}{2})$ giving $x = -3$.

(23-7)

[27] Ⓔ Volume of box equals the height, 5, times the area of the base, which is the rectangle shown. Since $AB = 4$ and $BC = 5$, then $AC = 3$ by the Pythagorean Theorem so the area is 12 and the volume is $5(12) = 60$.   (30-2)

[28] Ⓔ If $x^2 - 2x - 3 > 0$, then $(x - 3)(x + 1) > 0$, which is true when both factors are positive or when both are negative. Thus:

$(x - 3 > 0$ and $x + 1 > 0)$

or $(x - 3 < 0$ and $x + 1 < 0)$

$(x > 3$ and $x > -1)$ or $(x < 3$ and $x < -1)$

$x > 3$ or $x < -1$ (8-5)

[29] Ⓒ $f(2b) = \dfrac{3(2b) + 1}{2b} = \dfrac{6b + 1}{2b}$

$2f(b) = 2\left(\dfrac{3b + 1}{b}\right) = \dfrac{6b + 2}{b}$

$\dfrac{6b + 1}{2b} = \dfrac{6b + 2}{b}$

$$6b + 1 = 12b + 4 \ (b \neq 0)$$
$$-3 = 6b$$
$$-\frac{1}{2} = b \qquad (20\text{-}7)$$

[30] Ⓑ Replace y by $3x$ in $y^2 - x^2 = 2$ to get:

$$(3x)^2 - x^2 = 2$$
$$9x^2 - x^2 = 2$$
$$8x^2 = 2$$
$$x^2 = \frac{1}{4}$$
$$x = \pm\frac{1}{2}$$
$$y = 3x \text{ so } y = \pm\frac{3}{2} \qquad (22\text{-}9)$$

[31] Ⓑ The diagonals of a pentagon form three triangles with the sides of the pentagon so the sum of the measures of its angles is $3(180) = 540$. If the cosine of an angle of a polygon is $-\frac{1}{2}$, then its measure is 120 and the four angles, $\angle A$, $\angle B$, $\angle C$ and $\angle D$, total 480 so the remaining angle is 60 with a cosine of $1/2$. $\qquad (24\text{-}9)$

[32] Ⓔ If $\log_{\sqrt{2}}(x - 1) = 4$, then $(\sqrt{2})^4 = x - 1$ and $x - 1 = 4$ so $x = 5$. $\qquad (18\text{-}13)$

[33] Ⓓ By the "Law of Cosines"

$$(BC)^2 = (AC)^2 + (AB)^2 - 2(AC)(AB)\cos \angle A$$
$$(16)^2 = (14)^2 + (12)^2 - 2(14)(12)\cos \angle A$$
$$256 = 196 + 144 - 336 \cos \angle A$$
$$\frac{256 - 340}{-336} = \cos \angle A$$
$$\frac{-84}{-336} = \cos \angle A$$
$$\frac{1}{4} = \cos \angle A \qquad (24\text{-}16)$$

[34] Ⓓ If $a = b$ and $f(a) \neq f(b)$, then $(a, f(a))$ and $(b, f(b))$ are coordinates of two different points on the same vertical line. $\qquad (20\text{-}2)$

[35] Ⓒ In the diagram at right the dotted line indicates the water level. Note that the volume remaining must be half of that of the aquarium. Thus if $V =$ the volume of the aquarium, then

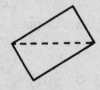

$$\frac{2}{3}V - \frac{1}{2}V = 6$$

$$\frac{4}{6}V - \frac{3}{6}V = 6$$
$$\frac{1}{6}V = 6$$
$$V = 36 \qquad (30\text{-}1)$$

[36] Ⓑ $\log_{10}(x + 4) + \log_{10}(x - 4) = 1$
$$\log_{10}(x + 4)(x - 4) = 1$$
$$\log_{10}(x^2 - 16) = 1$$
$$10^1 = x^2 - 16$$
$$26 = x^2$$
$$\sqrt{26} = x \qquad (23\text{-}13)$$

[37] Ⓐ In the slope-intercept form (found by solving the equation for y) the equation $4x - 2y = 3$ is $y = 2x - \frac{3}{2}$ so the slope is 2. The slope of any line $\parallel$ to it must also be 2. Thus the equation requested is:

$$y - 1 = 2(x + 2)$$
$$= 2x + 4$$
$$y = 2x + 5 \qquad (18\text{-}9)$$

[38] Ⓑ $(\angle AOB)° = (\angle DOC)°$ since they are vertical angles so $(\text{arc } AB)° = (\text{arc } DC)°$ because they are cut off by central angles having the same measure. Thus $\angle AXB$ and $\angle DYC$ are inscribed in arcs of equal measure in the same circle so they in turn must be equal in measure. $\qquad (16\text{-}5)$

[39] Ⓒ By definition $\log_b x = y$ means $b^y = x$. Thus $f(a) = 2^a$ means $\log_2 f(a) = a$. $\qquad (23\text{-}12)$

[40] Ⓓ The set of all points in space equidistant from the points X and Y is the perpendicular bisecting plane of segment XY. $\qquad (14\text{-}2)$

[41] Ⓔ Each term in the expansion of $(x^{-1} + x^2)^9$ is the product of some coefficient, C, and a factor that is $(x^2)^{r-1}$, where r is the number of the term, and a factor that is $(x^{-1})^{9-(r-1)}$. In this question we are not concerned with the coefficient but must find the value of r for which the sum of the exponents is 0, which will yield the required $x^0 = 1$.

$$(x^2)^{r-1} = x^{2r-2}$$
$$(x^{-1})^{9-(r-1)} = x^{-9+r-1} = x^{r-10}$$
$$2r - 2 + r - 10 = 0$$
$$3r = 12$$
$$r = 4 \qquad (29\text{-}4)$$

[42] Ⓑ $\triangle XAB \sim \triangle XYZ$ by AA with the corresponding vertices indicated by the order of listing. Since

the triangles are similar, the ratio of the areas is the square of the ratio of a pair of corresponding sides or

$\left(\dfrac{XA}{XY}\right)^2$. By Pyth. Th. $XA = 2\sqrt{5}$. $XY = 8$.

$\left(\dfrac{2\sqrt{5}}{8}\right)^2 = 4 \times \dfrac{5}{64} = \dfrac{5}{16}$

(15-11 and 17-12)

[43] Ⓑ The range of a function of the form $y = A \sin Bx$ is determined by A, the amplitude. Since $y = \sin Bx$ varies between -1 and 1, then $y = -\dfrac{1}{4} \sin Bx$ varies between $-\dfrac{1}{4}$ and $\dfrac{1}{4}$. *(24-15)*

[44] Ⓐ Segment AB will be the diagonal of a box with the given projection lengths equal to the lengths of the edges of the box. By repeated use of the Pyth. Th. we get:

$$AB = \sqrt{1^2 + 2^2 + 3^2} = \sqrt{14}.\textit{(17-12)}$$

[45] Ⓒ The total number of ways three marbles can be drawn from a bag of seven is the number of combinations of seven marbles taken three at a time:

$$\frac{7!}{4!3!} = 35.$$

Only one of these is the desired combination. *(28-6)*

[46] Ⓑ The complex fraction will be undefined whenever the denominator, $(m^2 - m - 2)/(m^2 - 4)$, is either undefined or zero. This occurs when

$m^2 - m - 2 = 0$ or $m^2 - 4 = 0$.
$m^2 - m - 2 = 0$ $m^2 - 4 = 0$
$(m-2)(m+1) = 0$ $(m-2)(m+2) = 0$
$\{2, -1\}$ $\{2, -2\}$

(20-6)

[47] Ⓑ $\text{Log}_{10} A > 0$ for all $A > 1$. Thus $x - 5 > 1$ and $x > 6$. *(23-12)*

[48] Ⓒ Since the coefficients are real, any imaginary roots must come in conjugate pairs so $-i$ is also a root and $(x + i)$, $(x - i)$ are factors.

$$(x + i)(x - i) = x^2 + 1$$

$$
\begin{array}{r}
x + 2 \\
x^2 + 1 \overline{)\, x^3 + 2x^2 + x + 2} \\
\underline{x^3 + x } \\
2x^2 + 2 \\
\underline{2x^2 + 2} \\
0
\end{array}
$$

Thus $x + 2$ is the remaining factor and -2 the remaining root. *(25-10)*

[49] Ⓔ If f and g are inverses, the domain of g is the range of f that is the set of all $y \le 0$.

(20-10)

[50] Ⓔ $4 \sin^2 x + 4 \cos x - 1 = 0$ Since $\sin^2 x + \cos^2 x = 1$ we replace $\sin^2 x$ with $1 - \cos^2 x$ to get:

$$4(1 - \cos^2 x) + 4 \cos x - 1 = 0$$
$$-4 \cos^2 x + 4 \cos x + 3 = 0$$
$$4 \cos^2 x - 4 \cos x - 3 = 0$$
$$(2 \cos x - 3)(2 \cos x + 1) = 0$$
$$\cos x = \frac{3}{2} \text{ or } \cos x = -\frac{1}{2}$$

But $\cos x = \dfrac{3}{2}$ has no root since $\cos x$ cannot be greater than 1. $\text{Cos } x = \dfrac{1}{2}$ is true for 120° and 240°, which convert to $\dfrac{2\pi}{3}$ and $\dfrac{4\pi}{3}$ radians. Although $\{\dfrac{2\pi}{3}, -\dfrac{2\pi}{3}\}$ are solutions, Ⓒ is not correct because $-\dfrac{2\pi}{3}$ is not between 0 and 2π. *(24-14)*

SELF-EVALUATION CHART FOR TEST 2

SUBJECT AREA	QUESTIONS ANSWERED CORRECTLY	NUMBER OF CORRECT ANSWERS
Algebra (15 questions)	1 3 4 7 10 11 12 14 20 21 24 26 28 32 46	_____
Plane geometry (8 questions)	2 5 8 9 19 22 38 42	_____
Solid geometry (4 questions)	27 35 40 44	_____
Coordinate geometry (5 questions)	6 13 18 30 37	_____
Trigonometry (6 questions)	15 23 31 33 43 50	_____
Functions (7 questions)	16 25 29 34 36 39 49	_____
Miscellaneous (5 questions)	17 41 45 47 48	_____

Total number of correct answers _____

Total score = total number of correct answers $\times$ 4   _____

minus number of incorrect answers   − _____

_____

ANSWER SHEET FOR TEST 3

Determine the correct answer for each question. Then, using a No. 2 pencil, blacken completely the oval containing the letter of your choice.

1. (A) (B) (C) (D) (E)
2. (A) (B) (C) (D) (E)
3. (A) (B) (C) (D) (E)
4. (A) (B) (C) (D) (E)
5. (A) (B) (C) (D) (E)
6. (A) (B) (C) (D) (E)
7. (A) (B) (C) (D) (E)
8. (A) (B) (C) (D) (E)
9. (A) (B) (C) (D) (E)
10. (A) (B) (C) (D) (E)
11. (A) (B) (C) (D) (E)
12. (A) (B) (C) (D) (E)
13. (A) (B) (C) (D) (E)
14. (A) (B) (C) (D) (E)
15. (A) (B) (C) (D) (E)
16. (A) (B) (C) (D) (E)
17. (A) (B) (C) (D) (E)

18. (A) (B) (C) (D) (E)
19. (A) (B) (C) (D) (E)
20. (A) (B) (C) (D) (E)
21. (A) (B) (C) (D) (E)
22. (A) (B) (C) (D) (E)
23. (A) (B) (C) (D) (E)
24. (A) (B) (C) (D) (E)
25. (A) (B) (C) (D) (E)
26. (A) (B) (C) (D) (E)
27. (A) (B) (C) (D) (E)
28. (A) (B) (C) (D) (E)
29. (A) (B) (C) (D) (E)
30. (A) (B) (C) (D) (E)
31. (A) (B) (C) (D) (E)
32. (A) (B) (C) (D) (E)
33. (A) (B) (C) (D) (E)
34. (A) (B) (C) (D) (E)

35. (A) (B) (C) (D) (E)
36. (A) (B) (C) (D) (E)
37. (A) (B) (C) (D) (E)
38. (A) (B) (C) (D) (E)
39. (A) (B) (C) (D) (E)
40. (A) (B) (C) (D) (E)
41. (A) (B) (C) (D) (E)
42. (A) (B) (C) (D) (E)
43. (A) (B) (C) (D) (E)
44. (A) (B) (C) (D) (E)
45. (A) (B) (C) (D) (E)
46. (A) (B) (C) (D) (E)
47. (A) (B) (C) (D) (E)
48. (A) (B) (C) (D) (E)
49. (A) (B) (C) (D) (E)
50. (A) (B) (C) (D) (E)

34. Model Test 3

For each of the following, select the best choice—A, B, C, D or E—to answer the question or complete the statement. Then locate the number of the question on the answer sheet, and indicate your choice by filling in completely the corresponding oval.

[1] Which of the following is the simplified form of $x - [2x - (3 - x)]$?

  Ⓐ x Ⓑ 3   Ⓒ $3 - 2x$ Ⓓ $2x - 3$
  Ⓔ $4x + 3$

[2] If $a - b > 0$, which of the following is NOT equal to $|a - b|$?

  Ⓐ $|a - b|$ Ⓑ $-(a - b)$ Ⓒ $|b - a|$
  Ⓓ $-(b - a)$ Ⓔ $\dfrac{2a - 2b}{2}$

[3] $\sqrt{\dfrac{2}{3}}\sqrt{\dfrac{15}{4}} =$

  Ⓐ $\dfrac{\sqrt{30}}{6}$ Ⓑ $\dfrac{\sqrt{10}}{2}$ Ⓒ $\sqrt{30}$ Ⓓ $\sqrt{5}$
  Ⓔ $\dfrac{\sqrt{10}}{3}$

[4] If $x - y = 0$, then which of the following is NOT equal to xy?

  Ⓐ $(-y)^2$ Ⓑ $-y^2$ Ⓒ y^2 Ⓓ $(-x)^2$
  Ⓔ x^2

[5] If $x < -x$, then

  Ⓐ $x > 0$ Ⓑ $x < 0$ Ⓒ $x = 0$ Ⓓ $\dfrac{1}{x} > 0$
  Ⓔ $x^2 < 0$

[6] The first and last terms of a perfect square trinomial are $36x^2$ and $4y^2z^2$. Which of the following could be the middle term?

  Ⓐ $24xyz$ Ⓑ $2xyz$ Ⓒ $12x^2y^2z^2$ Ⓓ $12xyz$
  Ⓔ $24x^2y^2z^2$

[7] What number of pennies is equivalent to $4x$ nickels plus $2x$ dimes?

  Ⓐ $6x$ Ⓑ $8x^2$ Ⓒ $15x$ Ⓓ $40x$ Ⓔ $30x$

[8] If $x - 2y - z = 2$, $x - y + 2z = 9$ and $2x + y + z = 3$, then $z =$

  Ⓐ -1 Ⓑ 0   Ⓒ 1   Ⓓ 2   Ⓔ 3

[9] Which of the following is the reciprocal of

$$\frac{a}{b} + \frac{b}{a}?$$

  Ⓐ $\dfrac{ab}{a + b}$ Ⓑ $\dfrac{b}{a} + \dfrac{a}{b}$ Ⓒ $ab^{-1} + ba^{-1}$
  Ⓓ $\dfrac{1}{a^2 + b^2}$ Ⓔ $\dfrac{ab}{a^2 + b^2}$

[10] Which of the following can never be zero, if x is a real number?

  Ⓐ $x^2 - 1$ Ⓑ $|x|$ Ⓒ $\dfrac{x}{4}$ Ⓓ $x^3 + 1$
  Ⓔ $2x^2 + 2$

[11] If the diagonal of a square is 20, the length of a side is

  Ⓐ $15\sqrt{2}$ Ⓑ $\sqrt{2}$ Ⓒ $5\sqrt{2}$ Ⓓ $10\sqrt{2}$
  Ⓔ $20\sqrt{2}$

[12] If $f(x) = 3x^2 + kx - 2$ and $f(-2) = 2$, then $k =$

  Ⓐ 1   Ⓑ 2   Ⓒ 3   Ⓓ 4   Ⓔ 5

[13] Which of the following is the completely factored form of $5x^4 - 20$ in the real number system?

  Ⓐ $5(x^4 - 4)$ Ⓑ $5(x^2 - 2)(x^2 + 2)$
  Ⓒ $(x^2 - 2)(5x + 10)$
  Ⓓ $5(x - \sqrt{2})(x + \sqrt{2})(x^2 + 2)$
  Ⓔ $(x - \sqrt{2})(x + \sqrt{2})(5x + 10)$

[14] If the sides of a right triangle have lengths of $x - 7$, x and $x + 1$, then $x =$

  Ⓐ $\{1, 7\}$ Ⓑ $\{7, -1\}$ Ⓒ $\{7, 4\}$ Ⓓ $\{7, 12\}$
  Ⓔ $\{7, 12\}$

[15] Which of the following is NOT true for all real numbers x, y and z?

  Ⓐ $x(y + z) = xy + xz$ Ⓑ $x(y + z) = x(z + y)$ Ⓒ $x(y + z) = (y + z)x$
  Ⓓ $x(y - z) = x(z - y)$ Ⓔ $x(y - z) = xy - xz$

[16] If $\dfrac{3a}{a - 1} = 1 + \dfrac{2a}{a + 1}$, then $a =$

  Ⓐ $\{1, -1\}$ Ⓑ $\{-\dfrac{1}{5}, 1, -1\}$ Ⓒ $\{-\dfrac{1}{5}\}$
  Ⓓ $\{-5\}$ Ⓔ $\{-\dfrac{1}{5}, 0\}$

[17] What is the greatest integer x for which $-6x - 1 > 12$?

   Ⓐ -2 Ⓑ -3 Ⓒ 3 Ⓓ 2 Ⓔ -1

[18] The sum of two numbers is 21, and the difference of their squares is 63. The numbers are

   Ⓐ $\{10, 11\}$ Ⓑ $\{8, 13\}$ Ⓒ $\{9, 12\}$
   Ⓓ $\{14, 7\}$ Ⓔ $\{6, 15\}$

[19] If $(a + 1)(2 - a) < 0$, then

   Ⓐ $-2 < a < 1$ Ⓑ $a < -2$ or $a > 1$
   Ⓒ $a < -2$ or $a < 1$ Ⓓ $-1 < a < 2$
   Ⓔ $a > 2$ or $a < -1$

[20] If a student's first two test grades are 100 and 91, what grade must she make on her third test for the average of the three to be 90?

   Ⓐ 79 Ⓑ 78 Ⓒ 77 Ⓓ 76 Ⓔ 75

[21] The volume of Cube A is three times the volume of Cube B. If the sum of the areas of all of the faces of Cube B is 18, then the volume of Cube A is

   Ⓐ $\sqrt{3}$ Ⓑ 3 Ⓒ $3\sqrt{3}$ Ⓓ 9 Ⓔ $9\sqrt{3}$

[22] If $f(x) = x^2 + 3x - 4$, then $f(x + 1) =$

   Ⓐ $x^2 + 3x - 3$ Ⓑ $x(x + 5)$
   Ⓒ $x^2 + 5x - 3$ Ⓓ $x^2 + 3x - 1$
   Ⓔ $3x + 1$

[23] The ratio of the length of a rectangle to its width is 5 to 4. If the perimeter of the rectangle is 36, the length is

   Ⓐ 10 Ⓑ 3 Ⓒ 4 Ⓓ 5 Ⓔ 6

[24] If $P = (4, 1)$, $O = (0, 0)$ and $Q = (0, -2)$, then $\sin \angle POQ =$

   Ⓐ $\dfrac{3}{4}$ Ⓑ $-\dfrac{4}{5}$ Ⓒ $-\dfrac{3}{4}$ Ⓓ $\dfrac{4}{5}$ Ⓔ $\dfrac{4}{\sqrt{17}}$

[25] Given $\angle A$ is a right angle and $AB = AC$. Which of the following constructions will NOT yield the bisector of $\angle A$?

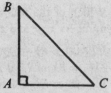

   Ⓐ Construct a line through A and any point in the exterior of the triangle and equidistant from B and C. Ⓑ Construct a perpendicular from A to segment BC. Ⓒ Construct the perpendicular bisector of segment BC. Ⓓ Construct a line containing any two points equidistant from B and C. Ⓔ Construct a line containing the midpoint of BC and any point equidistant from all three vertices.

[26] Which of the following is equal to $\tan \theta + \cot \theta$?

   Ⓐ $\dfrac{1}{\cot \theta + \tan \theta}$ Ⓑ $\dfrac{\sin \theta + \cos \theta}{(\sin \theta)(\cos \theta)}$
   Ⓒ $\tan^2 \theta + 1$ Ⓓ $(\sec \theta)(\csc \theta)$ Ⓔ $\sec^2 \theta$

[27] $BC \parallel AD$, $CE \perp AD$, $CF = FE$, $AF = 8$, $FD = 2$, $BC = 6$. The area of pentagon $ABCDE$ is

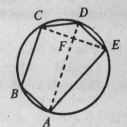

   Ⓐ 24 Ⓑ 30
   Ⓒ 36 Ⓓ 52 Ⓔ 64

[28] Which of the following is a quadratic equation with roots of $-\dfrac{3}{4}$ and $\dfrac{1}{2}$?

   Ⓐ $8x^2 + 5x - 3 = 0$ Ⓑ $8x^2 - 5x - 3 = 0$
   Ⓒ $8x^2 + 5x + 3 = 0$ Ⓓ $8x^2 - 2x - 3 = 0$
   Ⓔ $8x^2 + 2x - 3 = 0$

[29] What is the increase in volume V of a rectangular box if its width is doubled, its length is tripled and its height quadrupled?

   Ⓐ $23V$ Ⓑ $8V$ Ⓒ $9V$ Ⓓ $16V$ Ⓔ $12V$

[30] If $f(x) = 4^{-x}$, then $f\left(\dfrac{a}{2}\right) =$

   Ⓐ 2 Ⓑ 1 Ⓒ $2^{1/a}$ Ⓓ $\dfrac{1}{2^a}$ Ⓔ 2^a

[31] $\triangle BCD$ is equilateral with $BC = 4$. AE is perpendicular to plane F. $AE = 4$. The volume of the pyramid is

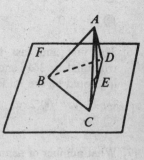

   Ⓐ 48 Ⓑ $\dfrac{16}{3}$
   Ⓒ $16\sqrt{3}$ Ⓓ 16
   Ⓔ $\dfrac{16\sqrt{3}}{3}$

[32] If $6a - 2$, $3a$ and $a + 2$ are in arithmetic progression, then $a =$

   Ⓐ 0 Ⓑ 1 Ⓒ 2 Ⓓ 3 Ⓔ 4

[33] Which of the following sets of lines will NOT determine a plane?

Ⓐ A pair of parallel lines   Ⓑ A pair of perpendicular lines   Ⓒ Two lines perpendicular to the same plane   Ⓓ Any two nonintersecting lines   Ⓔ Any two intersecting lines

[34] What is the range of the function defined by

$$y = \frac{|x|}{x}?$$

Ⓐ $y > 0$ Ⓑ $\{1, -1\}$ Ⓒ $y < 0$ Ⓓ All real numbers except zero   Ⓔ No real numbers

[35] If the sum of the measures of the angles of a polygon is 1440, how many sides does the polygon have?

Ⓐ 14   Ⓑ 8   Ⓒ 12   Ⓓ 10   Ⓔ 16

[36] Which of the following has the greatest y- intercept?

Ⓐ $x + 2y = 3$ Ⓑ $2x + 3y = 4$
Ⓒ $3x + 4y = 5$ Ⓓ $4x + 5y = 6$
Ⓔ $5x + 6y = 7$

[37] $DF \parallel AB$, $BC \perp AB$,
$BC = 5$, $BG = 4$,
$BA = 12$, $DA = 3$.
$CE =$

Ⓐ $\frac{50\sqrt{2}}{13}$ Ⓑ $\frac{5\sqrt{2}}{13}$
Ⓒ $\frac{10\sqrt{2}}{13}$ Ⓓ $\frac{3\sqrt{2}}{10}$
Ⓔ $\frac{10\sqrt{41}}{13}$

[38] The axis of symmetry of $y = -3x^2 + 12x - 9$ is

Ⓐ $x = 3$ Ⓑ $x = -3$ Ⓒ $x = 6$
Ⓓ $x = -2$ Ⓔ $x = 2$

[39] If $z = 7 - 24i$, then $|z| =$

Ⓐ 5   Ⓑ 17   Ⓒ 31   Ⓓ 168   Ⓔ 25

[40] The expression $\frac{a^{-1} - b^{-1}}{a^{-2} - b^{-2}} =$

Ⓐ $\frac{b - a}{ab}$ Ⓑ $\frac{b + a}{ab}$ Ⓒ $\frac{ab}{b + a}$
Ⓓ $\frac{a^2 - b^2}{a - b}$ Ⓔ $a - b$

[41] The radian measure of an angle of 16° is

Ⓐ $\frac{4}{45}$ Ⓑ 16π Ⓒ $\frac{4\pi}{45}$ Ⓓ $\frac{45\pi}{4}$ Ⓔ 11.25

[42] For what real values of x and y is the following true?

$$x - y + 2i = 6 + (x + y)i$$

Ⓐ $(4, -2)$ Ⓑ $(1, 2)$ Ⓒ $(2, 4)$ Ⓓ $(3, 1)$
Ⓔ $(3, 2)$

[43] If $x > 0$ and $\log_{3x} 27 = 1$, then $x =$

Ⓐ 9   Ⓑ $-\frac{1}{3}$ Ⓒ -3 Ⓓ $\frac{1}{3}$ Ⓔ 3

[44] Which of the following is a point in the intersection of $x^2 + y^2 < 4$ and $x - 3y < -3$?

Ⓐ $(0, 1)$ Ⓑ $(1, -1)$ Ⓒ $(1, 0)$ Ⓓ $(-1, 1)$
Ⓔ $(0, 0)$

[45] If n is the number of any term, then the nth term of the geometric sequence $2\sqrt{2}, 8, 16\sqrt{2}, \ldots$ is

Ⓐ $n\sqrt{2}$ Ⓑ $(n\sqrt{2})^2$ Ⓒ $(2\sqrt{2})^n$
Ⓓ $(2\sqrt{2})^{n+1}$ Ⓔ $(2\sqrt{2})^{n-1}$

[46] In how many different ways can the letters of the word "WINDOW" be arranged?

Ⓐ 720   Ⓑ 360   Ⓒ 180   Ⓓ 90   Ⓔ 45

[47] Which of the following is a point of intersection of the graphs of $y = \frac{1}{2} \sin 2x$ and $y = \frac{1}{2}$?

Ⓐ $\left(\frac{\pi}{4}, \frac{1}{2}\right)$ Ⓑ $\left(\frac{\pi}{3}, \frac{1}{2}\right)$ Ⓒ $\left(\frac{\pi}{2}, \frac{1}{2}\right)$
Ⓓ $\left(\pi, \frac{1}{2}\right)$ Ⓔ $\left(2\pi, \frac{1}{2}\right)$

[48] The graph of $xy = 0$ is
Ⓐ A point   Ⓑ A line   Ⓒ A pair of intersecting lines   Ⓓ A pair of parallel lines   Ⓔ A hyperbola

[49] If 40 percent of a 20 gallon solution is alcohol, how many QUARTS of water must be added to make a new solution which is 25 percent alcohol?

Ⓐ 60   Ⓑ 48   Ⓒ 36   Ⓓ 24   Ⓔ 12

[50] If $y^2 - 9x^2 = 25$, then the maximum negative value of y is

Ⓐ -25 Ⓑ -1 Ⓒ -5 Ⓓ $-\frac{5}{3}$
Ⓔ The maximum negative value cannot be determined

ANSWER KEY

1. C	11. D	21. E	31. E	41. C
2. B	12. D	22. B	32. A	42. A
3. B	13. D	23. A	33. D	43. A
4. B	14. E	24. E	34. B	44. D
5. B	15. D	25. E	35. D	45. C
6. A	16. C	26. D	36. A	46. B
7. D	17. B	27. D	37. E	47. A
8. E	18. C	28. E	38. E	48. C
9. E	19. E	29. A	39. E	49. B
10. E	20. A	30. D	40. C	50. C

ANSWER EXPLANATIONS

[1] Ⓒ $x - [2x - (3 - x)]$
$= x - [2x - 3 + x]$
$= x - 2x + 3 - x$
$= -2x + 3 = 3 - 2x$ (7–1)

[2] Ⓑ If $a - b > 0$ then $-(a - b) < 0$, which cannot be the absolute value since the absolute value of every real number is nonnegative.   (8–1)

[3] Ⓑ $\sqrt{\dfrac{2}{3}}\sqrt{\dfrac{15}{4}} = \sqrt{\dfrac{2 \cdot 15}{3 \cdot 4}} = \sqrt{\dfrac{2 \cdot 5}{4}}$
$= \dfrac{\sqrt{10}}{\sqrt{4}} = \dfrac{\sqrt{10}}{2}$ (6–12)

[4] Ⓑ If $x - y = 0$ then $x = y$. Thus $xy = y^2$ when x is replaced by y, and $xy = x^2$ when y is replaced by x. Each answer except $-y^2$ simplifies to either x^2 or y^2.

[5] Ⓑ If $x < -x$, then $0 < -2x$.
$-\dfrac{1}{2} \cdot 0 > -\dfrac{1}{2}(-2x)$
$0 > x$ (6–7 and 8–1)

[6] Ⓐ A perfect square trinomial is the square of a binomial. The first term of the trinomial is thus the square of the first term of the binomial and the last term of the trinomial is the square of the last term of the binomial. Thus the trinomial in question is either

$(6x + 2yz)^2 = 36x^2 + 24xyz + 4y^2z^2$

or

$(6x - 2yz)^2 = 36x^2 - 24xyz + 4y^2z^2$ (19–3)

[7] Ⓓ Each nickel is equivalent to 5 pennies so $4x$ nickels equals $4x(5) = 20x$ pennies. Each dime is equivalent to 10 pennies so $2x$ dimes equals $2x(10) = 20x$ pennies; $20x + 20x = 40x$.

[8] Ⓔ In the following system:

(1) $x - 2y - z = 2$
(2) $x - y + 2z = 9$
(3) $2x + y + z = 3$

if we subtract equation (2) from equation (1) to get a new equation (2)′ and then subtract twice equation (1) from equation (3) to get a new equation (3)′, we get the following equivalent system:

(1) $x - 2y - z = 2$
(2)′ $\quad - y - 3z = -7$
(3)′ $\quad 5y + 3z = -1$

In this new system we will add five times equation (2)′ to equation (3)′ to get a new equation (3)″:

(3)″ $-12z = -36.$
Thus $\quad z = 3.$ (22–8)

[9] Ⓔ $\dfrac{1}{\dfrac{a}{b} + \dfrac{b}{a}} = \dfrac{1}{\dfrac{a^2}{ab} + \dfrac{b^2}{ab}} = \dfrac{1}{\dfrac{a^2 + b^2}{ab}} = \dfrac{ab}{a^2 + b^2}$

[10] Ⓔ If $2x^2 + 2 = 0$, then $2x^2 = -2$ and $x^2 = -1$. No root for this equation exists in the real number system.   (21–1)

[11] Ⓓ Let $s =$ one side; then the diagonal forms a right triangle with two adjacent sides so that:
$s^2 + s^2 = (20)^2$
$2s^2 = 400$
$s^2 = 200$
$s = \sqrt{200} = \sqrt{100 \times 2} = 10\sqrt{2}$ (17–14)

[12] Ⓓ $f(-2) = 3(-2)^2 + k(-2) - 2$
$= 12 - 2k - 2 = 10 - 2k$
If $f(-2) = 2$, then
$2 = 10 - 2k$
$2k = 8$
$k = 4$ (20–7)

[13] Ⓓ $5x^4 - 20$
$= 5(x^4 - 4) = 5(x^2 - 2)(x^2 + 2)$
$= 5(x - \sqrt{2})(x + \sqrt{2})(x^2 + 2)$ (7–5)

[14] Ⓔ x must be positive for these to be sides of a triangle so $x + 1$ is the longest side and:
$(x + 1)^2 = (x - 7)^2 + x^2$
$x^2 + 2x + 1 = x^2 - 14x + 49 + x^2$
$0 = x^2 - 16x + 48$
$= (x - 4)(x - 12)$

The values of x are $\{4, 12\}$, but 4 makes $x - 7 = -3$.   (17–12)

[15] ⒟ Note that for ⒟ to be true, $y - z$ must equal $z - y$ for all real numbers. But $4 - 3 \neq 3 - 4$.

(6–6)

[16] ⒞ $\dfrac{3a}{a-1} = 1 + \dfrac{2a}{a+1}$; $LCD = (a-1)(a+1)$

Therefore:

$$\frac{3a(a+1)}{(a-1)(a+1)} = \frac{(a-1)(a+1)}{(a-1)(a+1)} + \frac{(a-1)(2a)}{(a-1)(a+1)}$$

Multiply both sides by the *LCD* to get:

$$3a(a + 1) = (a - 1)(a + 1) + (a - 1)(2a)$$
$$3a^2 + 3a = a^2 - 1 + 2a^2 - 2a$$
$$3a = -1 - 2a$$
$$5a = -1$$
$$a = -\frac{1}{5}$$

(9–14)

[17] ⒝ If $-6x - 1 > 12$, then:

$$-6x > 13$$
$$x < -\frac{13}{6}$$
$$x < -2\frac{1}{6}$$

The greatest integer less than $-2\dfrac{1}{6}$ is -3.

(8–2)

[18] ⒞ Let x = the smaller; then $21 - x$ is the larger and

$$(21 - x)^2 - x^2 = 63$$
$$441 - 42x + x^2 - x^2 = 63$$
$$-42x = 63 - 441$$
$$-42x = -378$$
$$x = 9$$
$$21 - x = 12$$

(22–6)

[19] ⒠ If $(a + 1)(2 - a) < 0$, then one factor is negative while the other is positive so:

$(a + 1 < 0$ and $2 - a > 0)$
  or $(a + 1 > 0$ and $2 - a < 0)$
$(a < -1$ and $2 > a)$ or $(a > -1$ and $2 < a)$
  $(a < -1)$ or $(a > 2)$

(8–5)

[20] ⒜ Let x be the third grade; then:

$$\frac{100 + 91 + x}{3} = 90$$
$$191 + x = 270$$
$$x = 79$$

[21] ⒠ Each face of Cube B is a square of side b with an area of b^2. The total surface is composed of six such faces.

$$6b^2 = 18$$
$$b^2 = 3$$
$$b = \sqrt{3}$$

The volume of Cube B is $(\sqrt{3})^3 = 3\sqrt{3}$, so the volume of Cube A is $3(3\sqrt{3}) = 9\sqrt{3}$. *(30–1)*

[22] ⒝ $f(x + 1) = (x + 1)^2 + 3(x + 1) - 4$
$\qquad\qquad = x^2 + 2x + 1 + 3x + 3 - 4$
$\qquad\qquad = x^2 + 5x$
$\qquad\qquad = x(x + 5)$

(20–7)

[23] ⒜ If the ratio is 5 to 4, then the length is $5x$ and the width $4x$, where x is the common factor (if any) removed in the reduction to $\dfrac{5}{4}$. The perimeter contains two lengths and two widths, so:

$$2(5x) + 2(4x) = 36$$
$$18x = 36$$
$$x = 2$$

Thus the length is $5(2) = 10$ and the width is $4(2) = 8$.

[24] ⒠ The graph of the points is shown at right. To find the sine of the angle, put the angle in standard position by choosing segment OQ to lie on the positive ray of the x-axis and adjusting the coordinates (you can visualize this by turning the page so that OQ of the upper diagram is to your right).

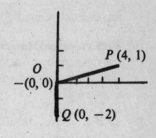

The sine of $\angle POQ$ is the y-coordinate of P, 4, over the distance of P to the origin, $\sqrt{17}$.

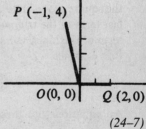

$$\sin \angle POQ = \frac{4}{\sqrt{17}}$$

(24–7)

[25] ⒠ The midpoint of BC is the only point equidistant from the vertices of the right triangle. Thus only one point is specified by ⒠, and this point will not determine a line. *(11–6)*

[26] (D) $\tan\theta + \cot\theta = \dfrac{\sin\theta}{\cos\theta} + \dfrac{\cos\theta}{\sin\theta}$

$$= \frac{\sin^2\theta}{\cos\theta\,\sin\theta} + \frac{\cos^2\theta}{\cos\theta\,\sin\theta}$$

$$= \frac{\sin^2\theta + \cos^2\theta}{\cos\theta\,\sin\theta}$$

$$= \frac{1}{\cos\theta\,\sin\theta}$$

$$= \frac{1}{\cos\theta} \cdot \frac{1}{\sin\theta}$$

$$= \sec\theta\,\csc\theta \qquad (24\text{--}13)$$

[27] (D) $CF = FE$ and $(CF)(FE) = (AF)(FD)$ so:

$$(CF)^2 = 8 \cdot 2 = 16$$
$$CF = 4 = FE$$

Area $\triangle CFD = \dfrac{1}{2}(CF)(FD) = \dfrac{1}{2}(4)(2) = 4$

Area $\triangle DFE = \dfrac{1}{2}(FE)(FD) = \dfrac{1}{2}(4)(2) = 4$

Area $\triangle AFE = \dfrac{1}{2}(FE)(AF) = \dfrac{1}{2}(4)(8) = 16$

Area trapezoid $AFCB = \dfrac{1}{2}(FC)(BC + AF)$

$$= \frac{1}{2}(4)(6 + 8) = 28$$

Total area $= 52$

or, alternative method:

Area trapezoid $ABCD = \dfrac{1}{2}(FC)(BC + AD)$

$$= \frac{1}{2}(4)(6 + 10) = 32$$

Area $\triangle AED = \dfrac{1}{2}(AD)(FE) = \dfrac{1}{2}(10)(4) = 20$

$\therefore$ Total area $= 32 + 20 = 52$

$$(16\text{--}11 \text{ and } 17\text{--}8)$$

[28] (E) If the roots are $-\dfrac{3}{4}$ and $\dfrac{1}{2}$, then the factors are

$\left(x + \dfrac{3}{4}\right)$ and $\left(x - \dfrac{1}{2}\right)$.

$\left(x + \dfrac{3}{4}\right)\left(x - \dfrac{1}{2}\right) = x^2 + \dfrac{3}{4}x - \dfrac{1}{2}x - \dfrac{3}{8}$

$$= x^2 + \frac{1}{4}x - \frac{3}{8}$$

An equation with these roots then is:

$$x^2 + \frac{1}{4}x - \frac{3}{8} = 0$$

Multiply both sides by 8 and you will get:

$$8x^2 + 2x - 3 = 0 \qquad (19\text{--}10)$$

[29] (A) Let $V = lwh$ be the original volume. Then the new volume is $V' = (2w)(3l)(4h) = 24lwh$. $V' - V = 24lwh - lwh = 23lwh$. $\qquad(30\text{--}1)$

[30] (D) $f\left(\dfrac{a}{2}\right) = 4^{-a/2} = (2^2)^{-a/2} = 2^{-a} = \dfrac{1}{2^a}$

$$(20\text{--}7 \text{ and } 23\text{--}9)$$

[31] (E) Pyramid volume $= \dfrac{1}{3}(\text{area } \triangle BCD) \times$ (height of pyramid). Using the 30-60-90 triangle relations on $\triangle BDC$, we get the figure opposite. So area $\triangle BCD = \dfrac{1}{2}(2\sqrt{3})(4) = 4\sqrt{3}$. Height of pyramid is $AE = 4$.

$$V = \frac{1}{3}(4\sqrt{3})(4) = \frac{16\sqrt{3}}{3} \qquad (30\text{--}3)$$

[32] (A) If the progression is arithmetic then:

$$3a - (6a - 2) = (a + 2) - 3a$$
$$-3a + 2 = -2a + 2$$
$$0 = a \qquad (26\text{--}2)$$

[33] (D) No plane will contain both L_1 and L_2 below:

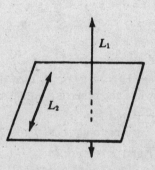

[34] (B) If $x > 0$, then $|x| = x$ and $y = \dfrac{|x|}{x} = \dfrac{x}{x} = 1$.

If $x < 0$, then $|x| = -x$ and $y = \dfrac{|x|}{x} = \dfrac{-x}{x} = -1$.

If $x = 0$, then $\dfrac{|x|}{x}$ is undefined. $\qquad(20\text{--}1)$

[35] ⓓ If n is the number of sides of a polygon, then $(n - 2)180$ is the sum of the measures of its angles.

$$(n - 2)180 = 1440$$
$$n - 2 = 8$$
$$n = 10 \qquad (17\text{--}18)$$

[36]· ⓐ To find the y-intercept, let $x = 0$ and solve for y. $\qquad (18\text{--}21)$

[37] ⓔ By the Pythagorean Theorem:

$$(GC)^2 = (BC)^2 + (GB)^2$$
$$= 25 + 16 = 41$$
$$GC = \sqrt{41}$$
$$(AC)^2 = (BC)^2 + (AB)^2$$
$$= 25 + 144 = 169$$
$$AC = \sqrt{169} = 13$$

$$DC = AC - AD = 13 - 3 = 10$$
$$\triangle DEC \sim \triangle AGC \text{ so:}$$
$$\frac{DC}{AC} = \frac{CE}{GC}$$
$$\frac{10}{13} = \frac{CE}{\sqrt{41}}$$
$$\frac{10\sqrt{41}}{13} = CE \quad (17\text{--}12 \text{ and } 15\text{--}9)$$

[38] ⓔ $y = -3x^2 + 12x - 9$
$$= -3(x^2 - 4x) - 9$$
$$= -3(x^2 - 4x + 4) - 9 + 12$$
$$= -3(x - 2)^2 + 3$$

Thus the axis of symmetry is $x = 2$. $\quad (18\text{--}24)$

[39] ⓔ By definition, $|a + bi| = \sqrt{a^2 + b^2}$
$$|7 + (-24)i| = \sqrt{49 + 576} = \sqrt{625} = 25$$
$$(21\text{--}11)$$

[40] ⓒ
$$\frac{a^{-1} - b^{-1}}{a^{-2} - b^{-2}} = \frac{\dfrac{1}{a} - \dfrac{1}{b}}{\dfrac{1}{a^2} - \dfrac{1}{b^2}} = \frac{\dfrac{b}{ab} - \dfrac{a}{ab}}{\dfrac{b^2}{a^2b^2} - \dfrac{a^2}{a^2b^2}}$$

$$= \frac{\dfrac{b - a}{ab}}{\dfrac{b^2 - a^2}{a^2b^2}} = \frac{b - a}{ab} \times \frac{a^2b^2}{b^2 - a^2}$$

$$= \frac{(b - a)}{ab} \times \frac{(ab)(ab)}{(b - a)(b + a)} = \frac{ab}{b + a}$$
$$(18\text{--}4)$$

[41] ⓒ $\quad 1° = \left(\dfrac{\pi}{180}\right)$ radians, so

$$(16)1° = 16\left(\frac{\pi}{180}\right) \text{ radians} = \frac{4\pi}{45} \text{ radians}$$
$$(24\text{--}2)$$

[42] ⓐ When two complex numbers in standard form are equal, their real parts are equal and their imaginary parts are equal. Thus:

$$\begin{vmatrix} x - y = 6 \\ x + y = 2 \end{vmatrix}$$

Adding the two equations gives:

$$2x = 8$$
$$x = 4$$

By substitution of 4 for x in one of the equations above we find $y = -2$. $\qquad (21\text{--}2)$

[43] ⓐ $\log_{3x} 27 = 1$ means $3x^1 = 27$ so $x = 9$.
$$(23\text{--}13)$$

[44] ⓓ The point $(-1, 1)$ is in the intersection since it satisfies both inequalities. $\qquad (22\text{--}9)$

[45] ⓒ Each term of a geometric sequence is of the form ar^{n-1}, where a is the first term, r the common ratio and n the number of the term.
$$a = 2\sqrt{2}$$
$$r = \frac{8}{2\sqrt{2}} = \frac{4}{\sqrt{2}} = \frac{4\sqrt{2}}{\sqrt{2}\sqrt{2}} = \frac{4\sqrt{2}}{2} = 2\sqrt{2}$$

Thus:
$$ar^{n-1} = (2\sqrt{2})(2\sqrt{2})^{n-1} = (2\sqrt{2})^n$$
$$(26\text{--}6)$$

[46] ⓑ The question asks for the number of permutations of six letters taken all at a time, two of which are identical. By formula:

$$\frac{6!}{2!} = 360 \qquad (27\text{--}5)$$

[47] ⓐ $y = \sin \theta$ varies between -1 and 1 so $y = \dfrac{1}{2} \sin \theta$ varies between $-\dfrac{1}{2}$ and $\dfrac{1}{2}$. Thus $y = \dfrac{1}{2}$ when $\sin \theta = 1$. Since $\sin \theta = 1$ when $\theta = \dfrac{\pi}{2}$,

$$2x = \frac{\pi}{2} \quad \text{and} \quad x = \frac{\pi}{4} \quad (24\text{--}15)$$

[48] ⓒ $xy = 0$ if and only if $x = 0$ or $y = 0$. All points for which $x = 0$ lie on the y-axis and for which $y = 0$ lie on the x-axis. The graph is thus the union of the coordinate axes. $\qquad (6\text{--}5)$

[49] Ⓑ 20 gallons = 4(20) = 80 quarts. 40 percent of 80 = .40(80) = 32 quarts of alcohol. Let x = amount of water added. Then $80 + x$ is the total amount of the new, 25 percent solution, and $.25(80 + x)$ is the amount of alcohol in this solution. But the number of quarts of alcohol is unchanged so $.25(80 + x) = 32$.

$$.25(80) + .25(x) = 32$$
$$20 + .25(x) = 32$$
$$.25(x) = 12$$
$$25(x) = 1200$$
$$x = 48. \qquad (22–5)$$

[50] Ⓒ $y^2 - 9x^2 = 25$ is the equation of a hyperbola with intercepts on the y-axis. The maximum negative value occurs at V in the diagram right. Let $x = 0$, then $y^2 = 25$; $y = \pm 5$.

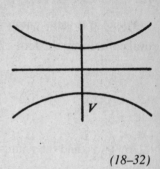

$(18–32)$

SELF-EVALUATION CHART FOR TEST 3

SUBJECT AREA	QUESTIONS ANSWERED CORRECTLY																	NUMBER OF CORRECT ANSWERS
Algebra (17 questions)	1	2	3	4	5	6	7	8	9	10	13	15	16	18	19	20	28	_____
Plane geometry (8 questions)	11	14	23	25	27	33	35	37										_____
Solid geometry (3 questions)	21	29	31															_____
Coordinate geometry (6 questions)	36	38	44	47	48	50												_____
Trigonometry (3 questions)	24	26	41															_____
Functions (6 questions)	10	12	22	30	34	43												_____
Miscellaneous (8 questions)	17	32	39	40	42	45	46	49										_____

Total number of correct answers _____

Total score = total number of correct answers × 4 _____

minus number of incorrect answers − _____

_____

ANSWER SHEET FOR TEST 4

Determine the correct answer for each question. Then, using a No. 2 pencil, blacken completely the oval containing the letter of your choice.

1. (A) (B) (C) (D) (E)
2. (A) (B) (C) (D) (E)
3. (A) (B) (C) (D) (E)
4. (A) (B) (C) (D) (E)
5. (A) (B) (C) (D) (E)
6. (A) (B) (C) (D) (E)
7. (A) (B) (C) (D) (E)
8. (A) (B) (C) (D) (E)
9. (A) (B) (C) (D) (E)
10. (A) (B) (C) (D) (E)
11. (A) (B) (C) (D) (E)
12. (A) (B) (C) (D) (E)
13. (A) (B) (C) (D) (E)
14. (A) (B) (C) (D) (E)
15. (A) (B) (C) (D) (E)
16. (A) (B) (C) (D) (E)
17. (A) (B) (C) (D) (E)

18. (A) (B) (C) (D) (E)
19. (A) (B) (C) (D) (E)
20. (A) (B) (C) (D) (E)
21. (A) (B) (C) (D) (E)
22. (A) (B) (C) (D) (E)
23. (A) (B) (C) (D) (E)
24. (A) (B) (C) (D) (E)
25. (A) (B) (C) (D) (E)
26. (A) (B) (C) (D) (E)
27. (A) (B) (C) (D) (E)
28. (A) (B) (C) (D) (E)
29. (A) (B) (C) (D) (E)
30. (A) (B) (C) (D) (E)
31. (A) (B) (C) (D) (E)
32. (A) (B) (C) (D) (E)
33. (A) (B) (C) (D) (E)
34. (A) (B) (C) (D) (E)

35. (A) (B) (C) (D) (E)
36. (A) (B) (C) (D) (E)
37. (A) (B) (C) (D) (E)
38. (A) (B) (C) (D) (E)
39. (A) (B) (C) (D) (E)
40. (A) (B) (C) (D) (E)
41. (A) (B) (C) (D) (E)
42. (A) (B) (C) (D) (E)
43. (A) (B) (C) (D) (E)
44. (A) (B) (C) (D) (E)
45. (A) (B) (C) (D) (E)
46. (A) (B) (C) (D) (E)
47. (A) (B) (C) (D) (E)
48. (A) (B) (C) (D) (E)
49. (A) (B) (C) (D) (E)
50. (A) (B) (C) (D) (E)

35. Model Test 4

TEST

For each of the following, select the best choice—A, B, C, D or E—to answer the question or complete the statement. Then locate the number of the question on the answer sheet, and indicate your choice by filling in completely the corresponding oval.

[1] If a is positive and b negative, which of the following is negative?

(A) $|ab|$ (B) $a|b|$ (C) $|a|b$ (D) $a + |b|$
(E) $|a| - b$

[2] If the sum of $x - 6y + 2z$ and $3x - 4y + 2z$ is subtracted from $3y - 4z + x$, the result is

(A) $13y - 8z - 3x$ (B) $7y + 5x$
(C) $4x - 10y + 4z$ (D) $x - 6y + 2z$
(E) $3x + 8z - 13y$

[3] If the equation of a circle is $x^2 + y^2 = 3$, which of the following is an x-intercept?

(A) 0   (B) $-\sqrt{3}$ (C) 3   (D) -3 (E) Cannot be determined

[4] If $\dfrac{8a+1}{2} = \dfrac{8a+6}{4} + 5$ then $a =$

(A) 0   (B) 1   (C) 2   (D) 3   (E) 4

[5] Together Mr. Haddick and Mr. Beebe have $20.25. Mr. Haddick has only dimes, and Mr. Beebe only quarters. If Mr. Haddick has twice as many coins as Mr. Beebe, how many does Mr. Beebe have?

(A) 45   (B) 40   (C) 35   (D) 30   (E) 25

[6] If $a = 3b - 5$ and $b = 4a - 2$, then $a =$
(A) 1   (B) 2   (C) 3   (D) -1 (E) 0

[7] $\dfrac{\sqrt{x-y}}{\sqrt{x+y}} =$

(A) $\dfrac{x-y}{x+y}$ (B) $\dfrac{\sqrt{x^2-y^2}}{x+y}$ (C) $\sqrt{x-y}$
(D) $x - y$ (E) $x + y$

[8] X and Y are the sets of all points contained in the circular regions. Which of the following is true?

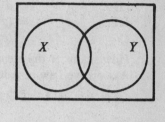

(A) $(X \cup Y)$ is a subset of Y.   (B) $X \cap Y = \emptyset$.   (C) If a point is not in X, then it is not in $X \cup Y$.   (D) If a point is not in $X \cup Y$, then it is not in X.   (E) If a point is not in $X \cap Y$, then it is not in X.

[9] If two angles of a quadrilateral are equal in measure, then the other two must be

(A) Equal in measure   (B) Obtuse   (C) Acute
(D) Supplementary   (E) No conclusion possible

[10] Which of the following is true?

(A) $(13^2)^4 = 13^6$ (B) $3^2 + 3^3 = 3^5$ (C) $4^{-4} \times 4^3 = \dfrac{1}{4}$ (D) $(36)^{1/2} = 18$ (E) $7\sqrt{11} = 11\sqrt{7}$

[11] If $x = -\dfrac{1}{4}$, then $4[(x + 4)(4x - 1)] =$

(A) -120 (B) 0   (C) 30   (D) -15 (E) -30

[12] If $2a^3 - ab^2 + b^3$ is divided by $a + b$, the result is

(A) $a^2 - b^2$ (B) $2a^2 - b^2$ (C) $2a^2 + b^2$
(D) $2a^2 - 2ab + b^2$ (E) $2a^2 + ab$

[13] In $\triangle ABC$, $AC = AB$, ray BD bisects $\angle ABC$, $(\angle ACB)° = 50$. What is the degree measure of $\angle ABD$?

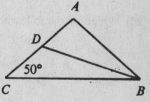

(A) 50   (B) 75
(C) 25   (D) 60   (E) 30

[14] Which of the following is NOT a term in the product of $x^2 - x + 2$ and $x^2 + x + 1$?

(A) x^4 (B) x^3 (C) $2x^2$ (D) x (E) 2

[15] The following is part of the proof of the theorem "If a, b and c are real numbers, then $(a + b) + c = (c + a) + b$."

I $(a + b) + c = a + (b + c)$
II $= a + (c + b)$
III $= (a + c) + b$
IV $= (c + a) + b$

How many of the steps can be justified by the Associative Law of Addition?

Ⓐ None   Ⓑ 1   Ⓒ 2   Ⓓ 3   Ⓔ All

[16] If $2 \le 8x - 1 \le -6$, then

Ⓐ $-\dfrac{5}{8} \le x \le \dfrac{3}{8}$ Ⓑ $x \ge 0$ Ⓒ $x \le 0$

Ⓓ $-\dfrac{7}{8} \le x \le \dfrac{1}{8}$ Ⓔ There are no values for x

[17] $\angle COE$ and $\angle BOD$ are right angles. If the measure of $\angle BOC$ is four times the measure of $\angle COD$, what is the measure of $\angle AOB$?

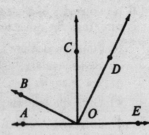

Ⓐ 16   Ⓑ 17
Ⓒ 18   Ⓓ 19   Ⓔ 20

[18] The measure of the positive angle formed by the nonnegative ray of the x-axis and the line defined by $y = -\sqrt{3}x$ is

Ⓐ 30   Ⓑ 120   Ⓒ 90   Ⓓ 45   Ⓔ 150

[19] The simplified form of

$$\dfrac{\dfrac{1}{a} + 1}{a + 1}$$

is

Ⓐ 1   Ⓑ $\dfrac{1}{a}$ Ⓒ a Ⓓ $a + 1$ Ⓔ $(a + 1)^2$

[20] Which of the following is a factor of

$$x^2 - (y + 1)^2?$$

Ⓐ $x - y - 1$ Ⓑ $y + 1$ Ⓒ $x - 1$
Ⓓ $x - y$ Ⓔ $x - y + 1$

[21] If O is the center of the circle, then the degree measure of minor arc CD is

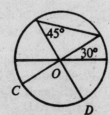

Ⓐ 180   Ⓑ 45
Ⓒ 90   Ⓓ 135   Ⓔ 75

[22] The intersection of a line and a circle may contain how many points?

Ⓐ 0   Ⓑ 0 or 1   Ⓒ 0, 1 or 2   Ⓓ 1, 2 or 3
Ⓔ 1 or 2

[23] If p and q are the coordinates of points on the number line, the distance between the points will always be

Ⓐ $p - q$ Ⓑ $q - p$ Ⓒ $-(p - q)$
Ⓓ $|p - q|$ Ⓔ $\sqrt{p^2 + q^2}$

[24] If $f(x) = |x - 1|$ and $g(x) = 1 - x^2$, then $3f(-2) + 4g(-3) =$

Ⓐ -23 Ⓑ -5 Ⓒ 13   Ⓓ 32   Ⓔ -13

[25] Which of the following is NOT the degree measure of an angle in standard position and coterminal with an angle of $-8°$?

Ⓐ 352   Ⓑ 8   Ⓒ -368 Ⓓ 712   Ⓔ -728

[26] Assuming that a and b are both NEGATIVE numbers, in which quadrant does the point $(a, -b)$ lie?

Ⓐ I   Ⓑ II   Ⓒ III   Ⓓ IV   Ⓔ Cannot be determined

[27] The product of $(-x^{m+1})$ and $(-x^{m-1})$ is

Ⓐ x^{2m} Ⓑ $-x^{2m}$ Ⓒ x^{m-1} Ⓓ $-x^{m^2-1}$
Ⓔ $\dfrac{1}{x^{2m}}$

[28] What is the radian measure of a central angle that cuts off an arc π inches long on a circle of radius 2 inches?

Ⓐ $\dfrac{1}{2}$ Ⓑ $\dfrac{\pi}{2}$ Ⓒ $\dfrac{\pi}{4}$ Ⓓ π Ⓔ 2

[29] Which of the following is equal to $y^{1/2}(y^{1/2} + y^{-1/2})$?

Ⓐ $y + 1$ Ⓑ y Ⓒ 1   Ⓓ 0   Ⓔ $\dfrac{1}{y}$

[30] If $\log_3 (1 + y)^2 = 2$, then $y =$

Ⓐ 1   Ⓑ 2   Ⓒ 3   Ⓓ 4   Ⓔ 5

[31] Which of the following is equal to

$$(\tan \theta)(\csc \theta)?$$

Ⓐ $\sin \theta$ Ⓑ $\cos \theta$ Ⓒ $\sec \theta$ Ⓓ $\csc \theta$
Ⓔ $\cot \theta$

[32] If a solid metal sphere of radius 1 foot is melted and recast to form spheres of radius 1 inch, how many of these smaller spheres can be made?

Ⓐ 12   Ⓑ 36   Ⓒ 144   Ⓓ 432   Ⓔ 1728

[33] What value of Y will be printed when the program below is completed?

(1) LET $Y = 1$.
(2) REPLACE Y BY Y^2.
(3) REPLACE Y BY $Y + 1$.
(4) IF $Y < 25$, GO BACK TO STEP 2, IF NOT, GO TO STEP 5.
(5) PRINT THE VALUE OF Y.

Ⓐ 1   Ⓑ 2   Ⓒ 25   Ⓓ 26   Ⓔ 36

[34] In $\triangle ABC$, if $AB = 6$, $AC = 4$, and the degree measure of $\angle A$ is 30, the area of the triangle is

Ⓐ 2   Ⓑ 3   Ⓒ 6   Ⓓ 12   Ⓔ The area cannot be determined

[35] If $\log_{10}3 = .4771$ and $\log_{10}2 = .3010$, then $\log_{10}5 =$

Ⓐ .7781   Ⓑ .1761   Ⓒ .6532   Ⓓ .6990
Ⓔ .5229

[36] What is the number of square inches in the area of the base of a right circular cone with a volume of 40π cubic inches and a height of 6 inches?

Ⓐ 40π Ⓑ 20π Ⓒ 10π Ⓓ 5π Ⓔ π

[37] Line AB is tangent to the circle at T. Radius ED has length 6. $TE \perp CD$ and ray ET bisects $\angle AEB$. $AB =$

Ⓐ 6   Ⓑ 5   Ⓒ 12
Ⓓ 9   Ⓔ Cannot be determined

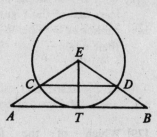

[38] If a polygon is inscribed in a circle, then

Ⓐ It is equilateral   Ⓑ It is equiangular   Ⓒ It is BOTH equiangular and equilateral   Ⓓ It has a finite number of sides   Ⓔ It has at least one right angle

[39] Which of the following is the equation of a line that is neither parallel nor perpendicular to the line defined by $y + x = 0$?

Ⓐ $y = x$ Ⓑ $y = x + 2$ Ⓒ $y - x + 2 = 0$
Ⓓ $2y - 2x = 1$ Ⓔ $2y = 4x + 1$

[40] If t can represent any positive integer, then

Ⓐ $\sqrt{t}$ is always irrational   Ⓑ $\sqrt{t}$ is not always real   Ⓒ t^2 is always an even integer   Ⓓ $2t + 1$ is always an odd integer   Ⓔ $\dfrac{t}{3}$ is never an even integer

[41] If a point X lies in the interior of $\triangle ABC$ at right, then which of the following must be true?

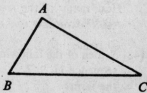

Ⓐ $BX < BA$ Ⓑ $BX > BA$ Ⓒ $BX = BA$
Ⓓ $BX \leq BA$ Ⓔ $BX < BC$

[42] In a geometric proof the reason "corresponding parts of congruent triangles are congruent" refers to

Ⓐ The definition of "triangle"   Ⓑ The definition of "correspondence"   Ⓒ The definition of "congruent triangles"   Ⓓ A congruence postulate such as SAS Ⓔ A theorem already proved

[43] If the measures of the exterior angles of a certain polygon are added and this sum is divided by the number of sides of the polygon, the result is 18. How many sides does the polygon have?

Ⓐ 36   Ⓑ 24   Ⓒ 20   Ⓓ 12   Ⓔ 10

[44] What is the middle term in the expansion of
$$(2x - \tfrac{1}{2}y)^6?$$

Ⓐ $-20x^3y^3$ Ⓑ $-80x^2y^4$ Ⓒ $-20x^2y^4$
Ⓓ $-80x^3y^3$ Ⓔ $-20x^4y^4$

[45] Which of the following completely describes the symmetry of $\{(x, y): |x| = 2\}$?

Ⓐ x-axis only   Ⓑ y-axis only   Ⓒ x-axis and y-axis only   Ⓓ Origin, x-axis and y-axis   Ⓔ Origin only

[46] The domain of the function defined by
$$f(x) = \frac{x}{\sqrt{x}}$$
is

Ⓐ All reals   Ⓑ All positive reals   Ⓒ All non-negative reals   Ⓓ All reals except zero   Ⓔ All negative reals

[47] The graph of one cycle of $y = 3 \sin \frac{1}{2}x$ is given at right. What is the x-coordinate of P?

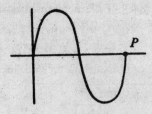

ⓐ $\frac{\pi}{2}$ ⓑ π ⓒ 2π

ⓓ 4π ⓔ 6π

[48] Which of the following is the general term of the sequence 11, 9, 7, . . . , where n is the number of the term?

ⓐ n ⓑ $11 + n$ ⓒ $11 - 2n$
ⓓ $11 - 2(n - 1)$ ⓔ $n - 2$

[49] The minimum value of $f(x) = x^2 + x + 4$ is

ⓐ 2   ⓑ − 2   ⓒ 4   ⓓ $\frac{15}{4}$ ⓔ $\frac{17}{4}$

[50] If cos 3.52 = − .9287, then cos 6.66 =

ⓐ − .9287   ⓑ .9287   ⓒ .0713   ⓓ − .0713
ⓔ − 1.8574

ANSWER KEY

1. C	11. E	21. C	31. C	41. E
2. A	12. D	22. C	32. E	42. C
3. B	13. C	23. D	33. D	43. C
4. D	14. B	24. A	34. C	44. A
5. A	15. C	25. B	35. D	45. D
6. A	16. E	26. B	36. B	46. B
7. B	17. C	27. A	37. E	47. D
8. D	18. B	28. B	38. D	48. D
9. E	19. B	29. A	39. E	49. D
10. C	20. A	30. B	40. D	50. B

ANSWER EXPLANATIONS

[1] ⓒ $|a|$ is positive and b negative so their product is negative.   (6–8)

[2] ⓐ $(3y - 4z + x) - [(x - 6y + 2z)$
$+ (3x - 4y + 2z)]$
$= (3y - 4z + x) - [4x - 10y + 4z]$
$= 3y - 4z + x - 4x + 10y - 4z$
$= 13y - 8z - 3x$ (7–1)

[3] ⓑ Let $y = 0$, then $x^2 = 3$ and $x = \pm\sqrt{3}$. Thus $+\sqrt{3}$ and $-\sqrt{3}$ both qualify as x-intercepts.   (18–21)

[4] ⓓ Multiply both sides of the equation by 4 to get:
$$2(8a + 1) = 8a + 6 + 4(5)$$
$$16a + 2 = 8a + 6 + 20$$
$$8a = 24$$
$$a = 3 \qquad (9\text{–}14)$$

[5] ⓐ Let x = the number of quarters; then $.25x$ = the total value of the quarters, $2x$ = the number of dimes, and $.10(2x)$ = the total value of the dimes.
$$.25x + .10(2x) = 20.25$$
$$.25x + .20x = 20.25$$
$$.45x = 20.25$$
$$x = \frac{20.25}{.45} = 45 \qquad (22\text{–}6)$$

[6] ⓐ Substitute $4a - 2$ for b in the first equation:
$$a = 3(4a - 2) - 5$$
$$= 12a - 6 - 5$$
$$-11a = -11$$
$$a = 1 \qquad (22\text{–}3)$$

[7] ⓑ $\dfrac{\sqrt{x - y}}{\sqrt{x + y}} = \dfrac{\sqrt{x - y}}{\sqrt{x + y}} \cdot \dfrac{\sqrt{x + y}}{\sqrt{x + y}}$
$$= \frac{\sqrt{(x - y)(x + y)}}{x + y}$$
$$= \frac{\sqrt{x^2 - y^2}}{x + y} \qquad (6\text{–}14)$$

[8] ⓓ $X \cup Y$ is the set of all points that belong to at least one of the regions X and Y. Thus a point cannot be in either X or Y if it doesn't belong to their union.   (10–1)

[9] ⓔ No restriction exists on the measures of the angles of a quadrilateral except that their sum be 360.   (14–8)

[10] ⓒ $4^{-4} \times 4^3 = 4^{-4+3} = 4^{-1} = \dfrac{1}{4}$ (23–3)

[11] ⓔ Replace x with $-\dfrac{1}{4}$ to get:
$$4[(-\tfrac{1}{4} + 4)(4(-\tfrac{1}{4}) - 1)]$$
$$= 4[(-\tfrac{1}{4} + \tfrac{16}{4})(-1 - 1)]$$
$$= 4[(\tfrac{15}{4})(-2)] = 15(-2)$$
$$= -30$$

[12] ⓓ

$$a + b \overline{)2a^3 - ab^2 + b^3}$$

$$\frac{2a^2 - 2ab + b^2}{}$$

$$\underline{2a^3 + 2a^2b}$$
$$-2a^2b - ab^2$$
$$\underline{-2a^2b - 2ab^2}$$
$$ab^2 + b^3$$
$$\underline{ab^2 + b^3}$$
$$0$$

(7–3)

[13] ⓒ Since $AC = AB$, then $(\angle ABC)° = 50$ by the Isosceles Triangle Theorem. $(\angle ABD)° = \frac{1}{2}(50) = 25$ by definition of angle bisector.   *(12–4)*

[14] ⓑ $x^2 + x + 1$

$$x^2 - x + 2 \overline{)x^4 + x^3 + x^2}$$

$$\underline{- x^3 - x^2 - x}$$
$$+ 2x^2 + 2x + 2$$
$$\overline{x^4 + 2x^2 + x + 2}$$

(7–2)

[15] ⓒ Steps I and III are by the Associative Law, but steps II and IV show the Commutative Law.   *(6–3)*

[16] ⓔ If $2 \le 8x - 1 \le -6$, add 1 to each member to get $3 \le 8x \le -5$. Divide each member by 8 to get $\frac{3}{8} \le x \le -\frac{5}{8}$. Since no real number is both less than a negative number and greater than a positive number, there is no solution.   *(7–3)*

[17] ⓒ Let $(\angle COD)° = x$; then $(\angle COB)° = 4x$ and $(\angle BOD)° = 4x + x = 5x = 90$. Thus $x = \frac{90}{5} = 18$. $\angle COD$ and $\angle AOB$ are complements of the same angle, $\angle BOC$, and thus have the same measure.   *(11–3)*

[18] ⓑ In the diagram let P be the point on the line $y = -\sqrt{3}\, x$ for which $x = -1$.

(24–7)

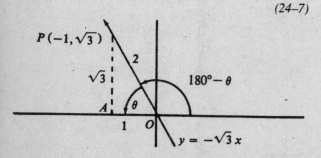

Thus $y = -\sqrt{3}(-1) = \sqrt{3}$ and

$$OP = \sqrt{(\sqrt{3})^2 + (-1)^2} = \sqrt{3 + 1} = 2$$

$\triangle OPA$ is therefore a 30-60-90 triangle with $\theta = 60°$ so the angle in question is 120°.

[19] ⓑ $\dfrac{\dfrac{1}{a} + 1}{a + 1} = \dfrac{\dfrac{1}{a} + \dfrac{a}{a}}{a + 1}$

$$= \frac{\dfrac{1 + a}{a}}{a + 1} = \frac{1 + a}{a} \cdot \frac{1}{a + 1} = \frac{1}{a}$$

(19–13)

[20] ⓐ The given expression is the difference of two squares:

$$x^2 - (y + 1)^2 = [x - (y + 1)][x + (y + 1)]$$
$$= [x - y - 1][x + y + 1]$$

(7–5)

[21] ⓒ Since $(\angle ABD)° = 45$, (arc AD)° $= 90 = (\angle AOD)°$. AC is a diameter so $\angle AOD$ is supplementary to $\angle COD$, which must also be 90. Hence (arc CD)° $= 90$.   *(16–3)*

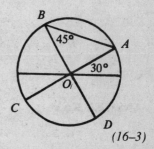

[22] ⓒ The possibilities are shown by L_1, L_2 and L_3. If you chose ⓓ, you probably made the mistake of assuming that the center of a circle is a point of the circle.

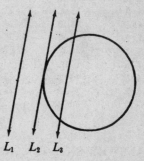

[23] ⓓ ⓓ satisfies the definition of "distance" on the number line.   *(19–1)*

[24] ⓐ $3f(x) + 4g(x) = 3|x - 1| + 4(1 - x^2)$
$3f(-2) + 4g(-3) = 3|-2 - 1| + 4[1 - (-3)^2]$
$= 3|-3| + 4(-8)$
$= 9 + (-32) = -23$.

(20–7)

[25] ⓑ $-8°$ terminates in quadrant IV, 8° terminates in quadrant I.   *(24–4)*

[26] Ⓑ Since a and b are negative, $-b$ is positive and the point has a negative first coordinate with a positive second coordinate.   (18–3)

[27] Ⓐ $(-x^{m+1})(-x^{m-1}) = (-1)(x^{m+1})(-1)(x^{m-1})$
$$= (-1)(-1)(x^{m+1+m-1})$$
$$= x^{2m}$$ (23–1)

[28] Ⓑ θ in radians $= \dfrac{\text{arc length}}{\text{radius}} = \dfrac{\pi}{2}$ (24–3)

[29] Ⓐ By the Distributive Law, the given expression equals:

$y^{1/2} \cdot y^{1/2} + y^{1/2}\, y^{-1/2} = y^{1/2+1/2} + y^{1/2-1/2}$
$$= y^1 + y^0 = y + 1$$
    (23–6)

[30] Ⓑ $\log_3(1+y)^2 = 2$ means $3^2 = (1+y)^2$
$$9 = 1+2y+y^2$$
$$0 = y^2+2y-8$$
$$= (y+4)(y-2)$$
$$y = -4 \text{ or } y = 2$$
    (23–13)

[31] Ⓒ $\tan \theta = \dfrac{\sin \theta}{\cos \theta}$ and $\csc \theta = \dfrac{1}{\sin \theta}$

Thus:

$(\tan \theta)(\csc \theta) = \dfrac{\sin \theta}{\cos \theta} \cdot \dfrac{1}{\sin \theta} = \dfrac{1}{\cos \theta}$
$$= \sec \theta$$ (24–14)

[32] Ⓔ $V = \dfrac{4}{3}\pi r^3$ Let $r = 1$ foot $= 12$ inches, then:

$$V = \frac{4}{3}\pi(12)^3 = \frac{4}{3}\pi(1728).$$

Let $r = 1$ inch, then:

$$V' = \frac{4}{3}\pi(1).$$

Thus $V = (1728)V'$.   (30–5)

[33] Ⓓ Y starts with the value 1, is replaced by 1, then by 2. This value is looped back to be squared, giving 4, and then raised by 1 to give 5. The 5 is looped back to be squared, yielding 25, and raised by 1 to give 26. Since 26 is not less than 25, the computer will print it in step 5.   (11–1, 2, 3)

[34] Ⓒ By the 30-60-90 triangle relations, $h = 2$ so

Area $\triangle ABC = \dfrac{1}{2}(2)(6)$
$$= 6.$$
    (24–17)

[35] Ⓓ $\log_{10} 5 = \log_{10} \dfrac{10}{2} = \log_{10} 10 - \log_{10} 2$
$$= 1 - .3010$$
$$= .6990$$ (23–14)

[36] Ⓑ $V = \dfrac{1}{3}hA$, where $A =$ area of base and $h =$ height of cone.

$$40\pi = \frac{1}{3}(6)A$$
$$40\pi = 2A$$
$$20\pi = A$$ (30–4)

[37] Ⓔ The given figure and information are not contradicted regardless of the length of AB.

[38] Ⓓ No restriction on angle measure or length of side is implied by inscribing the polygon; by definition of "polygon," the number of sides is finite.   (17–18)

[39] Ⓔ In slope-intercept form the line $y + x = 0$ is $y = -x$ giving a slope of -1. Any parallel line has a slope of -1 and any perpendicular a slope of 1. The equation in Ⓔ is $y = 2x + \dfrac{1}{2}$ when in slope-intercept form and thus has a slope of 2.   (18–9, 10)

[40] Ⓓ For any integer t, $2t$ will always be even (since it has a factor of 2) so $2t + 1$ will always be odd.

[41] Ⓔ Trial and error will demonstrate this.   (13–2)

[42] Ⓒ Definition of congruent triangles.   (12–3)

[43] Ⓒ The sum of the measures of the exterior angles of a polygon is always 360. Let $n =$ the number of sides (hence the number of exterior angles—counting one to a vertex). Then $\dfrac{360}{n} =$ the measure of each angle and:

$$\frac{360}{n} = 18$$
$$360 = 18n$$
$$20 = n$$

[44] Ⓐ There are seven terms so the middle term is the fourth. By formula:

$_6C_3(2x)^3\left(-\dfrac{1}{2}y\right)^3 = \dfrac{6!}{3!3!}(8x^3)\left(-\dfrac{1}{8}y^3\right)$
$$= 20(-1)(x^3)(y^3) = -20x^3y^3$$
    (29–3)

[45] ⓓ Note the graph. The *x*- and *y*-axis symmetry are obvious. For origin symmetry note that each nonvertical line through the origin intercepts the graph in two points, *A* and *A'*, such that *OA* = *OA'*.

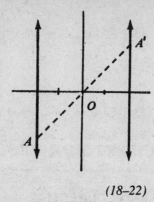

(18–22)

[46] ⓑ *x* = 0 leads to division by zero. *x* < 0 leads to the square root of a negative number.

(20–6)

[47] ⓓ Since the *y*-coordinate of *P* is 0,

$$0 = 3 \sin \frac{1}{2}x$$

Divide both sides by 3:

$$0 = \sin \frac{1}{2}x$$

The smallest positive angle whose sine is zero has radian measure 2π so:

$$\frac{1}{2}x = 2\pi$$

$$x = 4\pi$$

(24–15)

[48] ⓓ The sequence is arithmetic with *a* = 11 and *d* = −2, so, by formula, the general term, a_n, is given by:

$$a_n = 11 + (n - 1)(-2)$$
$$= 11 - 2(n - 1)$$

(26–2)

[49] ⓑ The graph of $y = x^2 + x + 4$ is a parabola opening upward so the minimum value of $f(x)$ is the *y*-coordinate of the vertex, which can be found by transforming the equation as follows:

$$y = x^2 + x + 4$$
$$= (x^2 + x) + 4$$
$$= (x^2 + x + \frac{1}{4}) + 4 - \frac{1}{4}$$
$$= (x + \frac{1}{2})^2 + \frac{15}{4}$$

Thus the vertex is $(-\frac{1}{2}, \frac{15}{4})$.

(20–17)

[50] ⓑ The two diagrams show unit circles that have arcs of length 3.52 and 6.66, respectively, marked off:

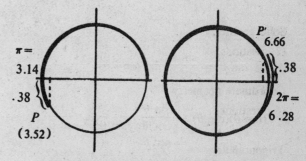

As you can see from the symmetry, points *P* and *P'* have *x*-coordinates that differ only in sign. The cosine of each arc (which is the *x*-coordinate in each case) then must differ only in sign.

(24–11)

SELF-EVALUATION CHART FOR TEST 4

SUBJECT AREA	QUESTIONS ANSWERED CORRECTLY																NUMBER OF CORRECT ANSWERS
Algebra (16 questions)	1	2	4	5	6	7	10	12	14	15	16	19	20	27	29	30	_____
Plane geometry (10 questions)							9	13	17	21	22	37	38	41	42	43	_____
Solid geometry (2 questions)															22	36	_____
Coordinate geometry (6 questions)											3	18	23	26	39	45	_____
Trigonometry (6 questions)											25	28	31	34	47	50	_____
Functions (5 questions)												11	24	35	46	49	_____
Miscellaneous (5 questions)												8	33	40	44	48	_____

Total number of correct answers _____

Total score = total number of correct answers × 4 _____

minus number of incorrect answers − _____

_____

ANSWER SHEET FOR TEST 5

Determine the correct answer for each question. Then, using a No. 2 pencil, blacken completely the oval containing the letter of your choice.

1. (A) (B) (C) (D) (E)	18. (A) (B) (C) (D) (E)	35. (A) (B) (C) (D) (E)
2. (A) (B) (C) (D) (E)	19. (A) (B) (C) (D) (E)	36. (A) (B) (C) (D) (E)
3. (A) (B) (C) (D) (E)	20. (A) (B) (C) (D) (E)	37. (A) (B) (C) (D) (E)
4. (A) (B) (C) (D) (E)	21. (A) (B) (C) (D) (E)	38. (A) (B) (C) (D) (E)
5. (A) (B) (C) (D) (E)	22. (A) (B) (C) (D) (E)	39. (A) (B) (C) (D) (E)
6. (A) (B) (C) (D) (E)	23. (A) (B) (C) (D) (E)	40. (A) (B) (C) (D) (E)
7. (A) (B) (C) (D) (E)	24. (A) (B) (C) (D) (E)	41. (A) (B) (C) (D) (E)
8. (A) (B) (C) (D) (E)	25. (A) (B) (C) (D) (E)	42. (A) (B) (C) (D) (E)
9. (A) (B) (C) (D) (E)	26. (A) (B) (C) (D) (E)	43. (A) (B) (C) (D) (E)
10. (A) (B) (C) (D) (E)	27. (A) (B) (C) (D) (E)	44. (A) (B) (C) (D) (E)
11. (A) (B) (C) (D) (E)	28. (A) (B) (C) (D) (E)	45. (A) (B) (C) (D) (E)
12. (A) (B) (C) (D) (E)	29. (A) (B) (C) (D) (E)	46. (A) (B) (C) (D) (E)
13. (A) (B) (C) (D) (E)	30. (A) (B) (C) (D) (E)	47. (A) (B) (C) (D) (E)
14. (A) (B) (C) (D) (E)	31. (A) (B) (C) (D) (E)	48. (A) (B) (C) (D) (E)
15. (A) (B) (C) (D) (E)	32. (A) (B) (C) (D) (E)	49. (A) (B) (C) (D) (E)
16. (A) (B) (C) (D) (E)	33. (A) (B) (C) (D) (E)	50. (A) (B) (C) (D) (E)
17. (A) (B) (C) (D) (E)	34. (A) (B) (C) (D) (E)	

36.   Model Test 5

For each of the following, select the best choice—A, B, C, D or E—to answer the question or complete the statement. Then locate the number of the question on the answer sheet, and indicate your choice by filling in completely the corresponding oval.

[1] The number of oranges in 8 crates of 24 each is the same as the number of oranges in

 (A) 4 crates of 48 each (B) 2 crates of 36 each
 (C) 6 crates of 12 each (D) 3 crates of 75 each
 (E) 7 crates of 10 each

[2] $\dfrac{4}{7} \times \dfrac{8}{7} =$

 (A) $\dfrac{1}{2}$ (B) $\dfrac{56}{28}$ (C) $\dfrac{32}{7}$ (D) $\dfrac{16}{7}$ (E) $\dfrac{32}{49}$

[3] Which of the following sets of numbers could be the degree measures of the three angles of an isosceles triangle?

 (A) 50, 50, 60 (B) 30, 60, 90 (C) 45, 45, 90
 (D) 100, 100, 80 (E) 50, 60, 70

[4] $(3b)^2 =$

 (A) $6b$ (B) $6b^2$ (C) $3b^2$ (D) $9b^2$ (E) $9b$

[5] If $\dfrac{x}{5} = 2$, then $x =$

 (A) $\dfrac{5}{2}$ (B) $\dfrac{2}{5}$ (C) 10 (D) 5^2 (E) 7

[6] If $D = RT$, then, when $D = 6$ and $T = \dfrac{1}{2}$, $R =$

 (A) 12 (B) 3 (C) 6 (D) $6\dfrac{1}{2}$ (E) 15

[7] Which of the following statements about the diagonals of a rectangle is (are) true?

 I. The diagonals always have the same length.
 II. The diagonals always are perpendicular.
 III. The diagonals always bisect each other.

 (A) I only (B) I and II only (C) I and III only
 (D) II and III only (E) I, II and III

[8] $\dfrac{9a^2 + 3a}{3a} =$

 (A) $4a$ (B) $6a$ (C) $9a^2$ (D) $3a + 1$
 (E) $9a^2 + 1$

[9] If A is an angle in standard position, sin A is positive and cos A is negative, in what quadrant is the terminal side of angle A?

 (A) I (B) II or III (C) II (D) IV (E) III or IV

[10] If $\dfrac{x + 5}{x - 1} = \dfrac{x}{x - 5}$, then $x =$

 (A) -5 (B) 25 (C) 0 (D) 1 (E) 10

[11] sin 30° =

 (A) cos 30° (B) sin 60° (C) 1 + cos 30°
 (D) sin 90° − sin 60° (E) cos 60°

[12] If $5x - 4 = 2x + 8$, what does $3x = ?$

 (A) 12 (B) 4 (C) 8 (D) -4 (E) 2

[13] If you are given that each of two angles of a triangle is acute, what conclusion can you draw about the third?

 (A) It is obtuse. (B) It is a right angle. (C) It is acute. (D) It cannot exist since the triangle is impossible. (E) It can have any measure between 0 and 180.

[14] In quadrilateral $ABCD$, if angles A and D are right angles, what is the value of y in terms of x?

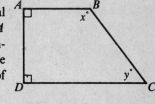

 (A) $\dfrac{x}{2}$ (B) $180 - x$ (C) $\dfrac{x}{3}$ (D) $x - 90$
 (E) $\dfrac{180 - x}{2}$

[15] If the area of the square is 9, then the area of the circle is

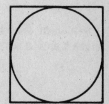

 (A) 9π (B) 3π
 (C) $\dfrac{9}{4}\pi$ (D) $\dfrac{3}{2}\pi$ (E) 6π

[16] In decimal form, 15% of $\dfrac{1}{2}$ is

 (A) .025 (B) .075 (C) 7.5 (D) .30 (E) .75

[17] If *DE* is parallel to *AB,* and the length of the sides are as shown in the diagram, what is the length of *DE?*

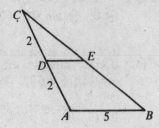

    Ⓐ 3 Ⓑ $\frac{4}{5}$ Ⓒ $1\frac{1}{4}$

    Ⓓ $2\frac{1}{2}$ Ⓔ 2

[18] $\frac{x}{yz} \div y =$

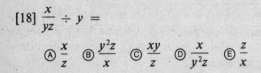

    Ⓐ $\frac{x}{z}$ Ⓑ $\frac{y^2z}{x}$ Ⓒ $\frac{xy}{z}$ Ⓓ $\frac{x}{y^2z}$ Ⓔ $\frac{z}{x}$

[19] If $f(x) = x^3 - 5x^2 + 7$, then $f(-2) - f(2) =$

    Ⓐ -26 Ⓑ -16 Ⓒ 8 Ⓓ -6 Ⓔ -7

[20] If $\log 25 - \log 2 = \log x$, then $x =$

    Ⓐ 23 Ⓑ 50 Ⓒ 5 Ⓓ 27 Ⓔ $12\frac{1}{2}$

[21] $\frac{\text{Cot } \theta}{\text{Cos } \theta} =$

    Ⓐ Sin θ Ⓑ Sec θ Ⓒ Tan θ Ⓓ Csc θ
    Ⓔ 1

[22] Which of the following is a value of x for which $1 + \cos x + \sin^2 x = 0$ is true?

    Ⓐ $\frac{\pi}{2}$ Ⓑ π Ⓒ $\frac{2\pi}{3}$ Ⓓ 2π Ⓔ 0

[23] If x is a positive number, which of the following has the greatest value?

    Ⓐ $\frac{x}{x}$ Ⓑ $\frac{x + 1}{x}$ Ⓒ $\frac{x}{x + 1}$ Ⓓ $\frac{x + 1}{x - 1}$

    Ⓔ $\frac{x + 2}{x + 3}$

[24] Which of the following points is in the graph of the solution set of the system

$$x + y < 7$$
$$x - y < 3$$

    Ⓐ (7,0) Ⓑ (3, −3) Ⓒ (7, 7) Ⓓ (7, 3)
    Ⓔ (0, 0)

[25] If $3(x + 4) = 9$, then $x =$

    Ⓐ $\frac{5}{3}$ Ⓑ -1 Ⓒ 3 Ⓓ 7 Ⓔ 2

[26] A rectangle has a width of 9 and a diagonal of 15. What is its length?

    Ⓐ 12 Ⓑ 10 Ⓒ 11 Ⓓ 13 Ⓔ 14

[27] If the point $(b, -2)$ is on the graph of the equation $2x + y = 7$, then $b =$

    Ⓐ -3 Ⓑ 3 Ⓒ $2\frac{1}{2}$ Ⓓ -5 Ⓔ $4\frac{1}{2}$

[28] $3\sqrt{3} =$

    Ⓐ $\sqrt{12}$ Ⓑ $\sqrt{9}$ Ⓒ $\sqrt{27}$ Ⓓ $\sqrt{6}$
    Ⓔ $\sqrt{15}$

[29] For the triangles shown below, which set of given information would NOT NECESSARILY lead to the conclusion that $\triangle ABC \cong \triangle XYZ$?

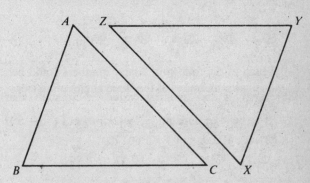

    Ⓐ $AB = XY$, $AC = YZ$, and $\angle C = \angle Z$ Ⓑ $AB = XY$, $\angle B = \angle Y$, and $\angle C = \angle Z$ Ⓒ $AB = XY$, $AC = XZ$, and $\angle A = \angle X$ Ⓓ $AB = XY$, $\angle B = \angle Y$, and $\angle A = \angle X$ Ⓔ $AB = XY$, $BC = YZ$, and $AC = XZ$

[30] The area of a certain triangle is one-quarter the area of a certain rectangle. If the two figures have equal heights, the ratio $\frac{\text{base of rectangle}}{\text{base of triangle}}$ is

    Ⓐ 4 Ⓑ 1 Ⓒ 8 Ⓓ 2 Ⓔ $\frac{1}{4}$

[31] If $\frac{4^x}{4^2} = 4^8$ then $x =$

    Ⓐ 6 Ⓑ 16 Ⓒ 4 Ⓓ 10 Ⓔ 64

[32] A cup is in the shape of a cone with a circular lip. The radius of the lip is 2 inches, and the height of the cone is 4 inches. When the cup is filled to half its volume, the height of the liquid, h, is

    Ⓐ $2h^2 = 5$ Ⓑ $3h = 4$ Ⓒ $\frac{h}{3} = 12$

    Ⓓ $h^2 = 16$ Ⓔ $h^3 = 32$

[33] In the figure, if $\dfrac{AB}{AC}$

$= \dfrac{1}{2}$, then $\sin \angle A =$

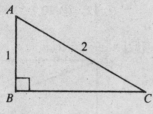

(A) $\dfrac{1}{3}$ (B) $\dfrac{1}{2}$

(C) $\dfrac{\sqrt{3}}{2}$ (D) $\sqrt{3}$

(E) 2

[34] Which of the following is an expression for $\sqrt{-81} - \sqrt{-36}$ in the form $x + yi$, where x and y are real?

(A) $0 + (\sqrt{117})i$ (B) $0 + 3i$ (C) $3 + 0i$
(D) $0 + 45i$ (E) $0 + (\sqrt{45})i$

[35] If $y = x + 3$, then $|x-y| + |y-x| =$

(A) 0 (B) 6 (C) -6 (D) 3 (E) Cannot be determined

[36] What is the smallest value of x such that $0 < x < \dfrac{\pi}{2}$ and $\tan\left(\dfrac{\pi}{4} + 2x\right) = \cot\left(\dfrac{\pi}{6} - x\right)$?

(A) $\dfrac{\pi}{12}$ (B) $\dfrac{\pi}{9}$ (C) $\dfrac{\pi}{3}$ (D) $\dfrac{\pi}{10}$ (E) $\dfrac{\pi}{15}$

[37] If a, b, c and d are positive numbers, $b > c$, and $d > a$, which of the following is (are) true?

I $a + b > c + d$
II $b + c > a + d$
III $b + d > a + c$

(A) I only   (B) II only   (C) III only   (D) I, II, III
(E) None

[38] The base of an isosceles triangle lies on the x-axis. What is the sum of the slopes of the three sides?

(A) 0 (B) 1 (C) -1 (D) $2\sqrt{3}$ (E) Cannot be determined

[39] Which of the following is the set of all real numbers x such that $|x| - 6 \le |x - 6|$?

(A) $\{6\}$ (B) $\{-6\}$ (C) $\{x : x \ge 0\}$
(D) $\{x : x \le 0\}$ (E) All real numbers

[40] If $\dfrac{x}{x+1} \ge 1$, then

(A) $-1 < x < 0$ (B) $x > -1$ (C) $x \ge -1$
(D) $x < -1$ (E) $-1 \le x < 0$

[41] $\dfrac{\csc 25°}{\sec 65°} =$

(A) 0 (B) $\tan 40°$ (C) $\cot 40°$ (D) 1 (E) -1

[42] If three numbers are added in pairs, the sums equal 5, 16 and 27. The greatest of the three numbers is

(A) 15   (B) 17   (C) 19   (D) 21   (E) 23

[43] Two planes, P and Q, are perpendicular to each other. If S is the set of all points that are 5 inches from P and 3 inches from Q, which of the following describes S?

(A) Two parallel lines   (B) Two intersecting lines
(C) Two points   (D) Four points   (E) Four parallel lines

[44] The area of a square is 81, and the coordinates of one corner are $(5, -4)$. The coordinates of an adjacent corner are

(A) $(5 - 6\sqrt{2}, 1)$ (B) $(-8, 6\sqrt{2} - 4)$
(C) $(2, 6\sqrt{2} - 4)$ (D) $(6\sqrt{2} - 5, -1)$
(E) $(8, 4 - 6\sqrt{2})$

[45] If f and g are inverse functions and if $(2, -3)$ is a point on the graph on $y = g(x)$, then f is

(A) $f(x) = 2x + 8$ (B) $f(x) = 4x - 11$
(C) $f(x) = x^2 - 1$ (D) $f(x) = 5x - 7$
(E) $f(x) = x - 5$

[46] A rectangular solid has length 4, width 3, and height 5. If AB is a diagonal of the base and AC is a diagonal of the solid, then $\tan \angle BAC =$

(A) $\dfrac{3}{4}$ (B) 1 (C) $\dfrac{4}{5}$ (D) $\dfrac{3}{5}$ (E) $\dfrac{4}{3}$

[47] In rectangle $XYZW$, at right, $YZ = 2$ and $YW = 2\sqrt{5}$. How long is the side of a square whose area is the same as the area of $XYZW$?

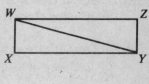

(A) $\sqrt{10}$ (B) $2\sqrt{10}$
(C) 12 (D) $2\sqrt{2}$
(E) $2\sqrt{3}$

[48] In the graph at right, an equation of the given line is

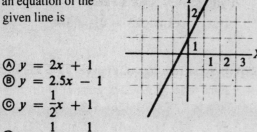

   Ⓐ $y = 2x + 1$
   Ⓑ $y = 2.5x - 1$
   Ⓒ $y = \frac{1}{2}x + 1$
   Ⓓ $y = \frac{1}{2}x - \frac{1}{2}$
   Ⓔ $y = -2x + 1$

[49] If $\log_2 k^3 = 6$, then $k =$

   Ⓐ $3\frac{1}{3}$ Ⓑ $6\frac{1}{3}$ Ⓒ 1 Ⓓ 4 Ⓔ 8

[50] When simplified, $\dfrac{2 - \dfrac{1 - 2x}{x - 2}}{\dfrac{x^2 + 4x + 4}{x^2 - 4}} =$

   Ⓐ $\dfrac{2x + 1}{x + 2}$ Ⓑ $\dfrac{4x - 3}{x + 2}$ Ⓒ $-\dfrac{5}{x + 2}$
   Ⓓ $\dfrac{(x - 2)(4x - 5)}{x + 2}$ Ⓔ $\dfrac{4x - 5}{x + 2}$

ANSWER KEY

1. A	11. E	21. D	31. D	41. D
2. E	12. A	22. B	32. E	42. C
3. C	13. E	23. D	33. C	43. E
4. D	14. B	24. E	34. B	44. C
5. C	15. C	25. B	35. B	45. A
6. A	16. B	26. A	36. A	46. B
7. C	17. D	27. E	37. C	47. D
8. D	18. D	28. C	38. A	48. A
9. C	19. B	29. A	39. E	49. D
10. B	20. E	30. D	40. D	50. E

ANSWER EXPLANATIONS

[1] Ⓐ $8 \times 24 = 4 \times 48$ (5)

[2] Ⓔ $\dfrac{4}{7} \times \dfrac{8}{7} = \dfrac{4 \times 8}{7 \times 7} = \dfrac{32}{49}$ (5-9)

[3] Ⓒ Two angles must have the same measure (since the triangle is isosceles), and their sum must be 180.   (14-7)

[4] Ⓓ $(3b)^2 = (3b)(3b) = 9b^2$ (23-4)

[5] Ⓒ $\dfrac{x}{5} = 2$ so $x = 5(\dfrac{x}{5}) = 5 \cdot 2 = 10$ (9-5)

[6] Ⓐ $6 = R \times \dfrac{1}{2}$. Multiply each side by 2 to get $12 = R$.

[7] Ⓒ

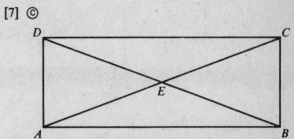

For a rectangle such as $ABCD$, $\triangle DBA \cong \triangle CAB$ by SAS so $DB = AC$ by CP. Also, $\triangle DEA \cong \triangle CEB$ by ASA so $DE = EB$ and $CE = EA$ by CP. DB and CA are clearly not perpendicular.
                          (20-9,10,11)

[8] Ⓓ $\dfrac{9a^2 + 3a}{3a} = \dfrac{9a^2}{3a} + \dfrac{3a}{3a} = 3a + 1$ (9-4)

[9] Ⓒ A device for remembering the quadrants for which the basic trig functions (sin, cos, tan) are positive is

ALL	Seniors	Turn	Crazy
I	II	III	IV

[10] Ⓑ Cross-multiply:
$$(x + 5)(x - 5) = x(x - 1)$$
$$x^2 - 25 = x^2 - x$$
$$-25 = -x$$
$$25 = x \qquad (9-14)$$

[11] Ⓔ Sine and cosine are cofunctions, meaning $\sin A = \cos (90 - A)$.   (24-9)

[12] Ⓐ $(5x - 4) - 2x = (2x + 8) - 2x$
$$3x - 4 = 8$$
$$3x = 12$$

[13] Ⓔ Every triangle must have at least two acute angles.   (14-7)

[14] Ⓑ Since AB is parallel to CD, $\angle B$ and $\angle C$ are supplementary, so $x + y = 180$.   (14-6)

[15] Ⓒ Area of square is 3^2 so side is 3. Radius of circle must be $\dfrac{3}{2}$. Area is $\pi r^2 = \pi \left(\dfrac{3}{2}\right)^2$. (17-1, 9)

[16] Ⓑ $15\% = .15$
$$\dfrac{1}{2} = .5$$
$(.5)(.15) = .075$ (5-18, 15)

[17] Ⓓ $\triangle CDE \cong \triangle CAB$

$$\frac{CD}{CA} = \frac{DE}{AB}$$

$$\frac{2}{4} = \frac{DE}{5}$$

$$\frac{5}{2} = DE \qquad (15-9)$$

[18] Ⓓ $\dfrac{x}{yz} \div y = \dfrac{x}{yz} \cdot \dfrac{1}{y} = \dfrac{x}{y^2z}$ $(9-3)$

[19] Ⓑ $f(-2) = (-2)^3 - 5(-2)^2 + 7 = -21$
$f(2) = (2)^3 - 5(2)^2 + 7 = -5$
$(-21) - (-5) = -16$ $(10-7)$

[20] Ⓔ $\log 25 - \log 2 = \log \dfrac{25}{2}$

$$\frac{25}{2} = x = 12\frac{1}{2} \qquad (23-14)$$

[21] Ⓓ $\dfrac{\cot \theta}{\cos \theta} = \dfrac{\cos \theta}{\sin \theta} \cdot \dfrac{1}{\cos \theta}$

$$= \frac{1}{\sin \theta}$$

$$= \csc \theta \qquad (24-13)$$

[22] Ⓑ $1 + \cos x + \sin^2 x = 0$
$1 + \cos x + (1 - \cos^2 x) = 0$
$2 + \cos x - \cos^2 x = 0$
$\cos x = 2$ or $\cos x = -1$
$\cos x = 2$ is impossible
$\cos x = -1$ at $180°$ or π radians $(24-13)$

[23] Ⓓ Greatest value occurs when the ratio of numerator to denominator is greatest. Denominators are greater than numerators in Ⓐ, Ⓒ, and Ⓔ, so they are eliminated. In Ⓑ the numerator is only one unit more than its denominator as compared with two units in Ⓓ. $(9-6)$

[24] Ⓔ The cross-hatched region of the graph below contains all solutions. $(22-7)$

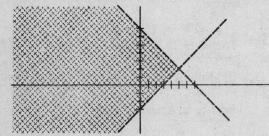

[25] Ⓑ $\dfrac{3(x+4)}{3} = \dfrac{9}{3}$

$$x + 4 = 3$$

$$x = -1$$

[26] Ⓐ If length $= x$ then $x^2 + 9^2 = 15^2$ by the Pythagorean Theorem and

$$x^2 = 225 - 81 = 144$$

$$x = 12$$

[27] Ⓔ Substitute $(b, -2)$ for (x, y) in the equation.

$$2b - 2 = 7$$

$$2b = 9$$

$$b = \frac{9}{2}$$

[28] Ⓒ
$$3\sqrt{3} = \sqrt{9}\sqrt{3} = \sqrt{9 \cdot 3} = \sqrt{27} \quad (6-12)$$

[29] Ⓐ Correspondence in Ⓐ is SSA, which is not a congruence. $(12-2)$

[30] Ⓓ $\dfrac{A_t}{A_r} = \dfrac{1}{4} = \dfrac{½b_t \cdot h}{b_r \cdot h} = \dfrac{b_t}{2b_r}$

Therefore $4b_t = 2b_r$, so $\dfrac{b_r}{b_t} = 2$. $(17-1)$

[31] Ⓓ $x - 2 = 8$
$x = 10$ $(31-16)$

[32] Ⓔ The volume of the cone is

$$\frac{1}{3}\pi r^2 h = \frac{16}{3}\pi$$

Therefore half the volume is $\dfrac{8}{3}\pi$. The liquid contents form a second cone in the same proportion as the first; in other words, the height of the cone is twice its radius. Since $r = \dfrac{1}{2}h$ and $V = \dfrac{8}{3}\pi$,

$$\frac{8}{3}\pi = \frac{1}{3}\pi \left(\frac{1}{2}h\right)^2 h$$

$$32 = h^3 \qquad (30-4)$$

[33] Ⓒ $BC = \sqrt{3}$ by the Pythagorean Theorem

$$\sin \angle A = \frac{\text{opposite side}}{\text{hypotenuse}} = \frac{\sqrt{3}}{2} \qquad (24-8)$$

[34] Ⓑ $\sqrt{-81} = 9i$, $\sqrt{-36} = 6i$
$9i - 6i = 3i.$ $(21-4)$

[35] Ⓑ Substitute $x + 3$ for y
$|x - x - 3| + |x + 3 - x| = 3 + 3 = 6.$
$(6-8 \text{ and } 31-14)$

[36] Ⓐ Since cofunctions of complementary angles are equal,

$$\left(\frac{\pi}{4} + 2x\right) + \left(\frac{\pi}{6} - x\right) = \frac{\pi}{2}$$

$$x = \frac{\pi}{2} - \frac{\pi}{6} - \frac{\pi}{4} = \frac{\pi}{12} \qquad (31-6)$$

[37] Ⓒ By addition of the given inequalities $b + d > a + c$, so III is correct. If a, b, c and $d = 1, 2, 3$ and 4, respectively, it can be seen that I and II are false. *(31)*

[38] Ⓐ Situate the triangle on a coordinate system as shown. Slope of base = 0. Therefore

sum of slopes =

$$0 + \frac{a}{b} - \frac{a}{b} = 0 \qquad \textit{(18–6 and 24–12)}$$

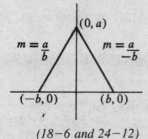

$(0, a)$

$m = \dfrac{a}{b}$ $m = \dfrac{a}{-b}$

$(-b, 0)$ $(b, 0)$

[39] Ⓔ If $x \geq 6$, both sides of inequality are equal. If $-6 < x < 6$, the left side is negative and the right side is positive, so inequality is true.
If $x \leq -6$, both sides are positive but left side is always less than the right side. Therefore inequality is always true. *(8–7)*

[40] Ⓓ If $x + 1 > 0$, $x > x + 1$, which is never true. If $x + 1 < 0$, inequality is reversed when multiplying through, so $x \leq x + 1$. Therefore, when $x < -1$, $0 \leq 1$, so inequality is true for all $x < -1$.

[41] Ⓓ Since cofunctions of complementary angles are equal, $\sec 65° = \csc 25°$

$$\frac{\csc 25°}{\sec 65°} = \frac{\csc 25°}{\csc 25°} = 1 \qquad \textit{(31–6)}$$

[42] Ⓒ $x + y = 5$
      $y + z = 16$
      $x + z = 27$

z is largest.
Subtract first from second, and add result to third to get

$$2z = 38$$
$$z = 19 \qquad \textit{(22–8)}$$

[43] Ⓔ The set of all points 5 inches from P is a pair of parallel planes (call them M and N), one on each side of P. Likewise, the set of all points 3 inches from Q is a pair of parallel planes (call them R and S). Planes M and N are both perpendicular to planes R and S. The four planes intersect in pairs to form four parallel lines.

[44] Ⓒ The other corner must lie on a circle with center $(5, -4)$ and radius 9. The equation is $(x - 5)^2 + (y + 4)^2 = 81$.
Ⓓ and Ⓔ can be ruled out because the radical does not drop out when substituted and squared.
Trying the others:
Ⓐ $72 + 25 \neq 81$
Ⓑ $169 + 72 \neq 81$
Ⓒ $9 + 72 = 81$. *(18–26)*

[45] Ⓐ $f(-3) = -6 + 8 = 2$. *(20–10)*

[46] Ⓑ Refer to the diagram:

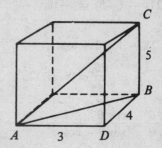

C

5

B

4

A 3 D

If the dimensions of the base are 3 by 4, diagonal $AB = 5$ by the Pythagorean Theorem. $\triangle ABC$ is a right triangle. Therefore

$$\tan \angle CAB = \frac{BC}{AB} = \frac{5}{5} = 1$$

(17–12, 24–8, and 30–1)

[47] Ⓓ $WZ = 4$ by Pythagorean Theorem.
Area = 8
Therefore, the side of the square with area of 8 is $\sqrt{8} = 2\sqrt{2}$. *(17–1, 12)*

[48] Ⓐ $m = \dfrac{\text{change in } y\text{-coordinates}}{\text{change in } x\text{-coordinates}} = \dfrac{2}{1}$
y-intercept = 1
$y = 2x + 1$. *(18–18)*

[49] Ⓓ By definition of logs,
$2^6 = k^3$
$2^6 = (2^2)^3 = k^3$
Therefore $2^2 = k = 4$. *(23–16)*

[50] Ⓔ Multiply top and bottom of original fraction by $x^2 - 4$:

$$\frac{2(x^2 - 4) - (1 - 2x)(x + 2)}{x^2 + 4x + 4} =$$

$$\frac{2x^2 - 8 - x - 2 + 2x^2 + 4x}{x^2 + 4x + 4} =$$

$$\frac{4x^2 + 3x - 10}{x^2 + 4x + 4} = \frac{(x + 2)(4x - 5)}{(x + 2)(x + 2)} \quad \textit{(9–12)}$$

SELF-EVALUATION CHART FOR TEST 5

SUBJECT AREA	QUESTIONS ANSWERED CORRECTLY	NUMBER OF CORRECT ANSWERS
Algebra (15 questions)	4 5 6 8 10 12 18 25 28 31 35 37 39 42 50	_____
Plane geometry (10 questions)	3 7 13 14 15 17 26 29 30 32	_____
Solid geometry (3 questions)	32 43 46	_____
Coordinate geometry (5 questions)	24 27 38 44 48	_____
Trigonometry (7 questions)	9 11 21 22 33 36 41	_____
Functions (5 questions)	19 20 23 40 45	_____
Miscellaneous (5 questions)	1 2 16 34 49	_____
Total number of correct answers		_____

Total score = total number of correct answers × 4 _____

minus number of incorrect answers − _____

_____

ANSWER SHEET FOR TEST 6

Determine the correct answer for each question. Then, using a No. 2 pencil, blacken completely the oval containing the letter of your choice.

1. Ⓐ Ⓑ Ⓒ Ⓓ Ⓔ
2. Ⓐ Ⓑ Ⓒ Ⓓ Ⓔ
3. Ⓐ Ⓑ Ⓒ Ⓓ Ⓔ
4. Ⓐ Ⓑ Ⓒ Ⓓ Ⓔ
5. Ⓐ Ⓑ Ⓒ Ⓓ Ⓔ
6. Ⓐ Ⓑ Ⓒ Ⓓ Ⓔ
7. Ⓐ Ⓑ Ⓒ Ⓓ Ⓔ
8. Ⓐ Ⓑ Ⓒ Ⓓ Ⓔ
9. Ⓐ Ⓑ Ⓒ Ⓓ Ⓔ
10. Ⓐ Ⓑ Ⓒ Ⓓ Ⓔ
11. Ⓐ Ⓑ Ⓒ Ⓓ Ⓔ
12. Ⓐ Ⓑ Ⓒ Ⓓ Ⓔ
13. Ⓐ Ⓑ Ⓒ Ⓓ Ⓔ
14. Ⓐ Ⓑ Ⓒ Ⓓ Ⓔ
15. Ⓐ Ⓑ Ⓒ Ⓓ Ⓔ
16. Ⓐ Ⓑ Ⓒ Ⓓ Ⓔ
17. Ⓐ Ⓑ Ⓒ Ⓓ Ⓔ

18. Ⓐ Ⓑ Ⓒ Ⓓ Ⓔ
19. Ⓐ Ⓑ Ⓒ Ⓓ Ⓔ
20. Ⓐ Ⓑ Ⓒ Ⓓ Ⓔ
21. Ⓐ Ⓑ Ⓒ Ⓓ Ⓔ
22. Ⓐ Ⓑ Ⓒ Ⓓ Ⓔ
23. Ⓐ Ⓑ Ⓒ Ⓓ Ⓔ
24. Ⓐ Ⓑ Ⓒ Ⓓ Ⓔ
25. Ⓐ Ⓑ Ⓒ Ⓓ Ⓔ
26. Ⓐ Ⓑ Ⓒ Ⓓ Ⓔ
27. Ⓐ Ⓑ Ⓒ Ⓓ Ⓔ
28. Ⓐ Ⓑ Ⓒ Ⓓ Ⓔ
29. Ⓐ Ⓑ Ⓒ Ⓓ Ⓔ
30. Ⓐ Ⓑ Ⓒ Ⓓ Ⓔ
31. Ⓐ Ⓑ Ⓒ Ⓓ Ⓔ
32. Ⓐ Ⓑ Ⓒ Ⓓ Ⓔ
33. Ⓐ Ⓑ Ⓒ Ⓓ Ⓔ
34. Ⓐ Ⓑ Ⓒ Ⓓ Ⓔ

35. Ⓐ Ⓑ Ⓒ Ⓓ Ⓔ
36. Ⓐ Ⓑ Ⓒ Ⓓ Ⓔ
37. Ⓐ Ⓑ Ⓒ Ⓓ Ⓔ
38. Ⓐ Ⓑ Ⓒ Ⓓ Ⓔ
39. Ⓐ Ⓑ Ⓒ Ⓓ Ⓔ
40. Ⓐ Ⓑ Ⓒ Ⓓ Ⓔ
41. Ⓐ Ⓑ Ⓒ Ⓓ Ⓔ
42. Ⓐ Ⓑ Ⓒ Ⓓ Ⓔ
43. Ⓐ Ⓑ Ⓒ Ⓓ Ⓔ
44. Ⓐ Ⓑ Ⓒ Ⓓ Ⓔ
45. Ⓐ Ⓑ Ⓒ Ⓓ Ⓔ
46. Ⓐ Ⓑ Ⓒ Ⓓ Ⓔ
47. Ⓐ Ⓑ Ⓒ Ⓓ Ⓔ
48. Ⓐ Ⓑ Ⓒ Ⓓ Ⓔ
49. Ⓐ Ⓑ Ⓒ Ⓓ Ⓔ
50. Ⓐ Ⓑ Ⓒ Ⓓ Ⓔ

37. Model Test 6

For each of the following, select the best choice—A, B, C, D or E—to answer the question or complete the statement. Then locate the number of the question on the answer sheet, and indicate your choice by filling in completely the corresponding oval.

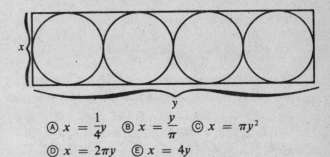

[1] If $\frac{1}{5}$ of a cup of liquid weighs 3 ounces, how many ounces will $\frac{3}{5}$ of a cup of the same liquid weigh?

(A) 10   (B) 6   (C) 1   (D) 15   (E) 9

[2] If ray R_1 and ray R_2 are parallel in the figure below, then $a + b + c =$

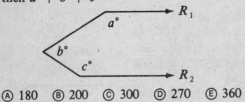

(A) 180   (B) 200   (C) 300   (D) 270   (E) 360

[3] If a point (x, y) is in the third quadrant, which of the following must be true?

(A) $x + y < 0$ (B) $x = -y$ (C) $x > y$
(D) $x + y = 3$ (E) $xy < 0$

[4] The coordinates of A are

(A) $(-8, 2)$
(B) $(-4, 2)$
(C) $(-4, 4)$
(D) $(-2, -2)$
(E) $(-4, -4)$

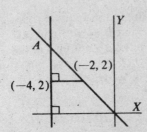

[5] What is the area of the triangle formed by the x-axis and the lines $x - y = 4$ and $x + y = 12$?

(A) 48   (B) 8   (C) 16   (D) 3   (E) 20

[6] If a is a positive number, then $\frac{a^{1/3}}{a^{-2/3}} =$

(A) $-a$ (B) $-\frac{1}{2}$ (C) $a^{-1/3}$ (D) a (E) -2

[7] Which of the following is the relationship between x and y if the circles shown are tangent to each other and to the sides of the rectangle?

(A) $x = \frac{1}{4}y$ (B) $x = \frac{y}{\pi}$ (C) $x = \pi y^2$
(D) $x = 2\pi y$ (E) $x = 4y$

[8] If $m = 2b$ for the linear function $f(x) = mx + b$, and $f(1) = 12$, then $b =$

(A) 6   (B) 3   (C) -6 (D) 8   (E) 4

[9] If $x^{-1} = 2^{-1} + 3^{-1}$, then $x =$

(A) 5   (B) $\frac{6}{5}$ (C) -5 (D) $\frac{2}{3}$ (E) $\frac{1}{5}$

[10] If $p + q = a$ and $p \cdot q = b$, then the average of p and q is

(A) $a + \frac{b}{2}$ (B) $\frac{a}{2}$ (C) $\frac{a+b}{2}$ (D) $\frac{a-b}{2}$ (E) $\frac{ab}{2}$

[11] If $a^2 - b^2 = a - b$, then $a + b =$

(A) 0   (B) 3   (C) 1   (D) -2 (E) Cannot be determined

[12] If $XYZW$ is a square inscribed in a circle for which C is the circumference, XY is the length of one side and XZ is the length of the diagonal, then

(A) $4XY < C < 4XZ$
(B) $C < 4XY < 4XZ$
(C) $4XY < 4XZ < C$
(D) $C < 4XZ < 4XY$
(E) $4XZ < 4XY < C$

[13] If θ is the angle formed by the x-axis and a ray of the line $y = 2x$, then $\sin \theta =$

(A) $\frac{1}{2}$ (B) 2   (C) $\frac{1}{3}$
(D) $\frac{2\sqrt{5}}{5}$ (E) $\frac{\sqrt{5}}{2}$

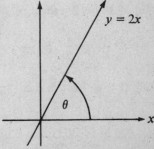

[14] Which of the following is an arrangement of a, b and c in order from least to greatest if $a = \cos p$, $b = \cos \frac{p}{2}$ and $c = \cos 2p$ where p is a number between 0 and $\frac{\pi}{6}$?

   Ⓐ cab Ⓑ bac Ⓒ abc Ⓓ cba Ⓔ bca

[15] If x is an integer greater than -10 but less than 10, and $|x - 2| < 3$, then the values of x are

   Ⓐ $-10, -9, -8, -7, -6, -5, -4, -3, -2, -1, 0, 1, 2, 3, 4$ Ⓑ $0, 1, 2, 3, 4, 5, 6, 7, 8, 9, 10$ Ⓒ $0, 1, 2, 3, 4$ Ⓓ $-4, -3, -2, -1, 0, 1, 2, 3, 4$ Ⓔ $-1, 0, 1$

[16] If a and b are both positive integers divisible by 5 without remainder, then which of the following will *not* be divisible by 5 without remainder?

   Ⓐ ab Ⓑ $a + b$ Ⓒ $a - b$ Ⓓ $a^2 + b^2$ Ⓔ $\dfrac{a}{b}$

[17] If MN is parallel to AC, $BC = 21$, $NC = 9$, and $AB = 14$, then $BM =$

   Ⓐ 9   Ⓑ 7   Ⓒ 8   Ⓓ 10   Ⓔ 6

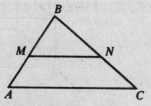

[18] The formula $S = at^2 + b$ provides values according to the following table:

t	S
0	3
2	11

The values of a and b are

   Ⓐ $a = -1, b = 3$ Ⓑ $a = 0, b = 11$ Ⓒ $a = 3, b = 8$ Ⓓ $a = 2, b = 14$ Ⓔ $a = 2, b = 3$

[19] If $8x = 25$, then $\frac{2}{5}x =$

   Ⓐ $\dfrac{5}{4}$ Ⓑ $\dfrac{4}{5}$ Ⓒ $\dfrac{125}{4}$ Ⓓ $\dfrac{125}{16}$ Ⓔ $\dfrac{16}{25}$

[20] If $y = \log_{10} 5$, then

   Ⓐ $y = \dfrac{1}{2}$ Ⓑ $y = 2$ Ⓒ $10^y = 5$ Ⓓ $5^y = 10$ Ⓔ $y^5 = 10$

[21] $\dfrac{4}{2 - 2i} =$

   Ⓐ $1 - i$ Ⓑ $1 + i$ Ⓒ i Ⓓ $2i$ Ⓔ $-2i$

[22] $\sqrt{\cos^2 4\theta + \sin^2 4\theta} =$

   Ⓐ $\cos 4\theta + \sin 4\theta$ Ⓑ $\cos 2\theta + \sin 2\theta$ Ⓒ 1   Ⓓ $\sec^2 4\theta$ Ⓔ $\sec 2\theta$

[23] If $(a, \sin a)$ and $(b, \sin b)$ are any two points on the graph of $y = \sin x$, then the greatest value of $\sin a - \sin b$ is

   Ⓐ 1   Ⓑ 2   Ⓒ 0   Ⓓ π Ⓔ 2π

[24] If $\log (x + 2) - \log (x - 1) = \log 4$, what is x?

   Ⓐ -2 Ⓑ 2   Ⓒ 1   Ⓓ -1 Ⓔ 4

[25] In triangle ABC, M and N are the midpoints of sides AB and BC, respectively. If $MN = 3x - 2$ and $AC = 5x + 7$, then $x =$

   Ⓐ 11   Ⓑ 10   Ⓒ 6   Ⓓ 31   Ⓔ 24

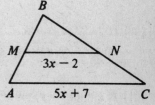

[26] In the figure at right, $AB = BC$ and $AD = CD$. Which of the following is NOT true?

   Ⓐ BD bisects $\angle ABC$.
   Ⓑ BD bisects AC.
   Ⓒ BD is perpendicular to AC.
   Ⓓ AC bisects BD.
   Ⓔ $\angle BAC$ and $\angle BCA$ are equal in measure.

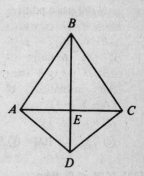

[27] Figure $ABCD$ is a parallelogram. If the measures of the angles are represented in terms of x as shown, then $x =$

   Ⓐ 45   Ⓑ 30   Ⓒ 60   Ⓓ 50   Ⓔ 55

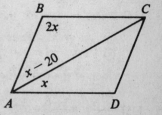

[28] If $f(x) = \sin x + \dfrac{1}{\sin x}$, then

Ⓐ $f(x) = \dfrac{1}{f(x)}$ Ⓑ $-f(x) = f(-x)$ Ⓒ $f(x)$

$= -f(x)$ Ⓓ $f(-x) = f(\dfrac{1}{x})$ Ⓔ $f(\dfrac{1}{x}) = -f(x)$

[29] In the figure at right, $CD \parallel XY$ and $AB \parallel XY$. W and Z are equidistant from XY. If $AB = a$ and $CD = 3a$, then the ratio $\dfrac{\text{area of } \triangle AWB}{\text{area of } \triangle CZD} =$

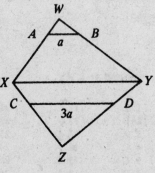

Ⓐ a^2 Ⓑ $\dfrac{1}{9}a^2$

Ⓒ $\dfrac{1}{9}$ Ⓓ $\dfrac{1}{3}$ Ⓔ $\dfrac{1}{3}a$

[30] If $2 \sin^2 x = \sin x$, then a value of x is

Ⓐ 30° Ⓑ 45° Ⓒ 60° Ⓓ 120° Ⓔ 360°

[31] If $x * (x - y) = x^2 + y^2$, then $5 * 3 =$

Ⓐ 34 Ⓑ 8 Ⓒ 64 Ⓓ 16 Ⓔ 29

[32] In the figure at right, $\triangle ABD$ has a point C of side AD for which $AB = BC = CD$. If the measure of $\angle BCD$ is 110, then the measure of $\angle ABD =$

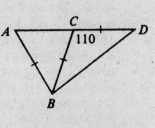

Ⓐ 90 Ⓑ 80
Ⓒ 75 Ⓓ 100 Ⓔ 95

(The figure is not drawn to scale.)

[33] If $3^x < 0$, then

Ⓐ All $x < 1$ Ⓑ All $x < 0$ Ⓒ All $x > 0$
Ⓓ All $x < 3$ Ⓔ No x

[34] If $f(x) = x^2 - ax$, then $f(-1) =$

Ⓐ $-1 - a$ Ⓑ a Ⓒ $1 - a$ Ⓓ $a + 1$
Ⓔ 1

[35] $\dfrac{\sin\dfrac{\pi}{6} + \cos\dfrac{\pi}{6}}{\sqrt{3}\,\tan\dfrac{\pi}{6}} =$

Ⓐ $\dfrac{1}{\sqrt{3}}$ Ⓑ 2 Ⓒ $\sqrt{3} + 1$ Ⓓ $\dfrac{1}{2} + \sqrt{3}$

Ⓔ $\dfrac{1 + \sqrt{3}}{2}$

[36] If in the figure at right $PQ = PR$, then

Ⓐ $a = 120$
Ⓑ $b = 40$
Ⓒ $a + b = 180$
Ⓓ $a - b = 90$
Ⓔ $b - a = -10$

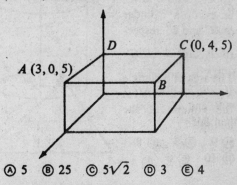

[37] In a three-dimensional coordinate system, the coordinates of A are $(3, 0, 5)$ and of C are $(0, 4, 5)$. How far is B from D?

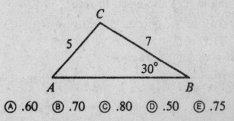

Ⓐ 5 Ⓑ 25 Ⓒ $5\sqrt{2}$ Ⓓ 3 Ⓔ 4

[38] For the parabola that is the graph of $y = x(a - x)$, the vertex is

Ⓐ $\left(\dfrac{a}{2}, \dfrac{a^2}{4}\right)$ Ⓑ $\left(\dfrac{a}{2}, \dfrac{a}{2}\right)$ Ⓒ $(a, 0)$ Ⓓ (a, a)

Ⓔ $\left(a, \dfrac{a}{2}\right)$

[39] If $AB = DB$, $\angle A = 70°$, $\angle DBC = 20°$ and $\angle C = x°$, then $x =$

Ⓐ 70 Ⓑ 60
Ⓒ 45 Ⓓ 50
Ⓔ 65

[40] In $\triangle ABC$, if the parts have the measures shown, then $\sin A =$

Ⓐ .60 Ⓑ .70 Ⓒ .80 Ⓓ .50 Ⓔ .75

[41] Which of the following is not equal to
$(x + 2)(3x - 3)$?

Ⓐ $3(x + 2)(x - 1)$ Ⓑ $(2 + x)(3x - 3)$
Ⓒ $-(2 + x)(3 - 3x)$ Ⓓ $(2 + x)(3 - 3x)$
Ⓔ $3x^2 + 3x - 6$

[42] Which of the following is the solution set of
$7x^2 - 7x - 14 = 0$?

Ⓐ $\{1, 2\}$ Ⓑ $\{7, -2\}$ Ⓒ $\{2, -7\}$
Ⓓ $\{-14, 1\}$ Ⓔ $\{-1, 2\}$

[43] If $\dfrac{\sqrt{5} + x}{\sqrt{5} - x} = 1$, then $x =$

Ⓐ $\sqrt{5}$ Ⓑ $-\sqrt{5}$ Ⓒ 5 Ⓓ $\dfrac{1}{\sqrt{5}}$ Ⓔ 0

[44] The centers of the upper and lower bases of a cylinder are C and C', respectively. $AC = \dfrac{1}{2}C\,C'$.

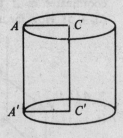

The area of rectangle $ACC'A'$ is 2. What is the volume of the cylinder?

Ⓐ 2π Ⓑ 4π
Ⓒ π Ⓓ 2 Ⓔ 4

[45] If $x^2 - 3x + 2 = (x - k)^2 + p$, then $p =$

Ⓐ $-\dfrac{1}{4}$ Ⓑ 2 Ⓒ 3 Ⓓ -2 Ⓔ -1

[46] If S is a set of six distinct points of a circle, how many chords can be drawn if any pair of elements of S can be endpoints?

Ⓐ 6 Ⓑ 20 Ⓒ 10 Ⓓ 15 Ⓔ 36

[47] $\sqrt{16 + 16x^2} - \sqrt{9 + 9x^2} =$

Ⓐ $1 + x^2$ Ⓑ $7 + x^2$ Ⓒ $\sqrt{7 + 7x^2}$
Ⓓ $1 + x$ Ⓔ $\sqrt{1 + x^2}$

[48] If $f(x)$ is a function for which $f(2 + k) = f(2 - k)$ and $f(-3) = 0$, for which of the following is $f(x)$ also equal to zero?

Ⓐ $x = 3$ Ⓑ $x = 5$ Ⓒ $x = -1$ Ⓓ $x = 6$
Ⓔ $x = 7$

[49] If $\dfrac{1}{x + 1} + \dfrac{1}{x - 1} = \dfrac{a}{x^2 - 1}$, then $a =$

Ⓐ $2x$ Ⓑ x Ⓒ 2 Ⓓ x^2 Ⓔ $2x + 2$

[50] If $f(x) = x + 3$, then the equation of the graph at right is

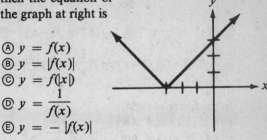

Ⓐ $y = f(x)$
Ⓑ $y = |f(x)|$
Ⓒ $y = f(|x|)$
Ⓓ $y = \dfrac{1}{f(x)}$
Ⓔ $y = -|f(x)|$

ANSWER KEY

1. E	11. C	21. B	31. E	41. D
2. E	12. A	22. C	32. C	42. E
3. A	13. D	23. B	33. E	43. E
4. C	14. A	24. B	34. D	44. A
5. C	15. C	25. A	35. E	45. A
6. D	16. E	26. D	36. C	46. D
7. A	17. C	27. D	37. A	47. E
8. E	18. E	28. B	38. A	48. E
9. B	19. A	29. C	39. D	49. A
10. B	20. C	30. A	40. B	50. B

ANSWER EXPLANATIONS

[1] Ⓔ Since $\dfrac{3}{5}$ is three times $\dfrac{1}{5}$, the number of ounces is three times 3 ounces.   *(15–1)*

[2] Ⓔ Draw line XY as shown. The sum of angles 1, 2 and 3 is 180. Angles 4 and 5 are supplementary since R_1 and R_2 are parallel. The sum of the measures of all five angles is 360.   *(14–6, 7)*

[3] Ⓐ In the third quadrant, both x and y are negative so $x + y$ is negative.   *(18–3)*

[4] Ⓒ First coordinate must be -4 because all points on the same vertical line must have the same first coordinate. Second coordinate must be 4 since the line through the points A, $(-2, 2)$ and the origin must be $y = -x$.   *(13–2, 18)*

[5] Ⓒ Lines $x - y = 4$ and $x + y = 12$ intersect at $(8, 4)$. The equations can be solved simultaneously by adding the left sides and the right sides:

$$(x - y) + (x + y) = 4 + 12$$
$$2x = 16$$
$$x = 8$$

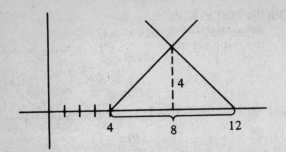

Since $x - y = 4$, $y = 4$. From the diagram, the triangle has altitude 4 and base 8. Therefore the area is $\frac{1}{2}(4)(8) = 16$.   *(17–1 and 22–1)*

[6] Ⓓ $\dfrac{a^{1/3}}{a^{-2/3}} = a^{(1/3) - (-2/3)} = a^{3/3} = a$ *(23–17)*

[7] Ⓐ x is the diameter of one circle; y is the diameter of four circles, all having the same size.   .

[8] Ⓔ Since $m = 2b$, $f(x) = 2bx + b$. Since $f(1) = 12$,
$$12 = 2b + b$$
$$4 = b$$
    (18–19 and 20–7, 14, 15)

[9] Ⓑ $x^{-1} = 2^{-1} + 3^{-1}$
$$\frac{1}{x} = \frac{1}{2} + \frac{1}{3}$$
$$\frac{1}{x} = \frac{5}{6}$$
$$x = \frac{6}{5}$$ *(23–1, 6)*

[10] Ⓑ The average is found by adding p and q, then dividing by 2. Since $p + q = a$, the result is $\frac{a}{2}$. Note that the fact $p \cdot q = b$ is not needed.

[11] Ⓒ $a^2 - b^2 = (a - b)(a + b)$
Since $a^2 - b^2 = a - b$, $a + b = 1$.   *(7–5)*

[12] Ⓐ $4XY$ is the perimeter of the square, which can be easily seen to be less than the circumference, C. Since $C = \pi D$, C is approximately 3.14 (XZ). Therefore $4 XZ > C$.   *(17–18, 19)*

[13] Ⓓ Pick any point on line $y = 2x$, say, $(1, 2)$. Its distance r from the origin is $\sqrt{5}$. Therefore
$$\sin \theta = \frac{2}{\sqrt{5}} = \frac{2\sqrt{5}}{5}$$ *(24–6, 11)*

[14] Ⓐ Cosine is a decreasing function from 0 to $\frac{\pi}{2}$ meaning that the function decreases as the angle increases. To put cosine θ in increasing order, put θ in the decreasing order $2p$, p, $\frac{p}{2}$.   *(24–15)*

[15] Ⓒ If $|x - 2| < 3$, then
$$-3 < x - 2 < 3$$
$$-1 < x \quad\quad < 5$$ *(8–6)*

[16] Ⓔ If 5 is a factor of a and b, it will also be a factor of ab, $a + b$, $a - b$ and $a^2 + b^2$, but not of $\frac{a}{b}$. To test the latter, try $a = 10$ and $b = 5$, for example. In this case, $\frac{a}{b} = 2$.   *(31–9)*

[17] Ⓒ Since $\triangle BMN \cong \triangle BAC$,
$$\frac{BM}{AB} = \frac{BN}{BC} \quad \frac{BM}{14} = \frac{12}{21} = \frac{4}{7}$$
$$BM = 14\left(\frac{4}{7}\right) = 8$$ *(15–9)*

[18] Ⓔ Substituting $t = 0$ and $s = 3$ gives
$$3 = a(0)^2 + b$$
$$3 = b$$
Substituting $t = 2$, $s = 11$ and $b = 3$ gives
$$11 = a(4) + 3$$
$$8 = 4a$$
$$2 = a$$

[19] Ⓐ To find $\frac{2}{5}x$, divide each side of $8x = 25$ by 20 (since 20 is 4 times 5):
$$\frac{8x}{20} = \frac{25}{20}$$
$$\frac{2}{5}x = \frac{5}{4}$$

[20] Ⓒ $y = \log_{10} 5$ means $10^y = 5$ by definition.   *(23–12)*

[21] Ⓑ $\dfrac{4}{2 - 2i} = \dfrac{2(2)}{2(1 - i)} = \dfrac{2}{1 - i}$
$$= \frac{2(1 + i)}{(1 - i)(1 + i)} = \frac{2(1 + i)}{1 - i^2}$$
$$= \frac{2(1 + i)}{2} = 1 + i$$ *(21–7)*

[22] Ⓒ $\sqrt{\cos^2 4\theta + \sin^2 4\theta} = \sqrt{1} = 1$ *(24–13)*

[23] Ⓑ The greatest value of sin x is 1, and the least value is -1. Therefore the greatest difference between two values is $1 - (-1) = 2$.   *(24–15)*

[24] Ⓑ $\log (x + 2) - \log (x - 1) = \log \dfrac{x + 2}{x - 1}$. Since

$\log \dfrac{x + 2}{x - 1} = \log 4$, $\dfrac{x + 2}{x - 1} = 4$.

Therefore $x + 2 = 4x - 4$ by cross multiplying, and $x = 2$.   *(23–13, 14)*

[25] Ⓐ Because M and N are midpoints,

$$MN = \frac{1}{2}AC$$

$$3x - 2 = \frac{1}{2}(5x + 7)$$

$$6x - 4 = 5x + 7$$

$$x = 11 \quad \textit{(15–9 and 17–1, 4)}$$

[26] Ⓓ $\triangle ABD \cong \triangle CBD$ by SSS

∴ $\angle ABD \cong \angle CBD$ by CPCTC

$\triangle ABE \cong \triangle CBE$ by SAS

$AE = CE$ by CPCTC

$\angle BEA \cong \angle BEC$ by CPCTC

$\angle BEA$ and $\angle BEC$ are right angles because they are congruent and supplementary.

$\angle BAC \cong \angle BCA$ by CPCTC   *(12–3, 4)*

[27] Ⓓ Because $BC \parallel AD$, $\angle ABC$ and $\angle BAD$ are supplementary.

$$2x + x - 20 + x = 180$$

$$4x - 20 = 180$$

$$4x = 200$$

$$x = 50 \quad \textit{(14–6)}$$

[28] Ⓑ Since $\sin (-x) = -\sin x$, $-f(x) = f(-x)$.

[29] Ⓒ $\triangle XWY$ and $\triangle XYZ$ have equal altitudes and equal bases, so they have equal areas. Since $AB \parallel XY$,

$$\frac{\text{area of } \triangle AWB}{\text{area of } \triangle XWY} = \left(\frac{AB}{XY}\right)^2 = \frac{a^2}{XY^2}$$

Since $CD \parallel XY$,

$$\frac{\text{area of } \triangle ZCD}{\text{area of } \triangle XYZ} = \left(\frac{CD}{XY}\right)^2 = \frac{9a^2}{XY^2}$$

$$\frac{\text{area of } \triangle AWB}{\text{area of } \triangle XWY} \cdot \frac{\text{area of } \triangle XYZ}{\text{area of } \triangle ZCD}$$

$$= \frac{a^2}{XY^2} \cdot \frac{XY^2}{9a^2} = \frac{1}{9}$$

(15–9 and 17–1, 4, 11)

[30] Ⓐ $2\sin^2 x = \sin x$.

When $\sin x \neq 0$, $2\sin x = 1$.

$$\sin x = \frac{1}{2}$$

$$x = 30° \quad \textit{(24–14)}$$

[31] Ⓔ $5 * 3 = 5(5 - 2) = 5^2 + 2^2 = 29$

[32] Ⓒ $x + x + 110 = 180$

$2x = 70$

$x = 35$

$2y + z = 180$

$y = 70$

$140 + z = 180$

$z = 40$

$x + z = 75$ *(12–4 and 14–7)*

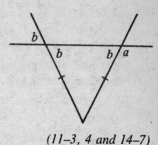

[33] Ⓔ Regardless of the value of x, 3^x is positive.

(23–10)

[34] Ⓓ $f(-1) = (-1)^2 - a(-1) = 1 + a$ *(20–7)*

[35] Ⓔ $\sin \dfrac{\pi}{6} = \dfrac{1}{2}$, $\cos \dfrac{\pi}{6} = \dfrac{3}{\sqrt{2}}$, $\tan \dfrac{\pi}{6} = \dfrac{1}{\sqrt{3}}$

Substitute the values into the given expression and simplify.   *(24–15 and 6–12, 13, 14)*

[36] Ⓒ From the figure at right,

$$b + a = 180$$

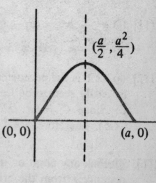

(11–3, 4 and 14–7)

[37] Ⓐ $AD = 3$

$AB = 4$

$DB^2 = AD^2 + AB^2$

$= 3^2 + 4^2$

$DB = \sqrt{25}$

$= 5$ *(31–15)*

[38] Ⓐ The diagram at right shows the parabola, its intercepts and its axis of symmetry. The first coordinate of the vertex of the parabola can be easily seen from the sketch. The second coordinate is found by substituting into the equation.   *(20–16)*

[39] ⒟ Since $AB = DB$, $\angle BDA \cong \angle A$, so $\angle BDA$ is 70°. Since $\angle BDA$ is an exterior angle of $\triangle BDC$, its measure is the sum of the measures of $\angle B$ and $\angle C$.

$$70 = 20 + x$$
$$50 = x \qquad (14\text{--}7)$$

[40] ⒝ By the Law of Sines,
$$\frac{BC}{\sin A} = \frac{AC}{\sin B}$$
$$\frac{7}{\sin A} = \frac{5}{1/2}$$
$$5 \sin A = \frac{1}{2}(7)$$
$$\sin A = \frac{1}{2}(7)(\frac{1}{5}) = \frac{7}{10} \qquad (24\text{--}18)$$

[41] ⒟ $3x - 3 = -1(3 - 3x)$. The factor -1 is missing in ⒟, but it appears in ⒞ as the opposite of the quantity. $(7\text{--}7)$

[42] ⒠ $7x^2 - 7x - 14 = 0$
$$7(x^2 - x - 2) = 0$$
$$7(x - 2)(x + 1) = 0,$$
so $x - 2 = 0$ or $x + 1 = 0$.
Therefore $x = 2$ or $x = -1$.
$(7\text{--}7 \text{ and } 19\text{--}1, 2)$

[43] ⒠ Cross-multiply to get $\sqrt{5} + x = \sqrt{5} - x$
$x = -x$, so $2x = 0$ and $x = 0$. $(9\text{--}7)$

[44] ⒜ Area of $ACC'A' = (AC)(CC')$
$$2 = (AC)(2AC)$$
$$1 = AC^2$$
$$1 = AC$$
The volume of the cylinder is
$$h(\pi r^2)$$
$$2(\pi \cdot 1^2)$$
$$2\pi \qquad (30\text{--}2)$$

[45] ⒜ $x^2 - 3x + 2 = (x^2 - 3x + \frac{9}{4}) + 2 - \frac{9}{4}$
$$= (x - \frac{3}{2})^2 - \frac{1}{4} \qquad (19\text{--}4)$$

[46] ⒟ From any point A, there are five chords that have the other five points as endpoints. From B, there are four chords since AB has already been drawn. From C, there are three chords since AC and BC have already been drawn. From D, two (not drawn) remain. From E, one (not drawn) remains. From F, none remains.

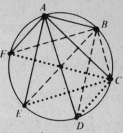

[47] ⒠ $\sqrt{16 + 16x^2} - \sqrt{9 + 9x^2} =$
$4\sqrt{1 + x^2} - 3\sqrt{1 + x^2} = \sqrt{1 + x^2}$
$(6\text{--}12)$

[48] ⒠ Since $f(2 + k) = f(2 - k)$, $x = 2$ is an axis of symmetry for $f(x)$. Since $x = -3$ is 5 units to the left of $x = 2$, its reflection is $x = 7$, which is 5 units to the right of $x = 2$. $(18\text{--}23)$

[49] ⒜ The lowest common denominator is $(x + 1)(x - 1) = x^2 - 1$, so
$$\frac{1}{x + 1} + \frac{1}{x - 1} = \frac{x - 1 + x + 1}{x^2 - 1}$$
$$= \frac{2x}{x^2 - 1} \qquad (9\text{--}11)$$

[50] ⒝ The graph of $f(x) = x + 3$ is as follows:

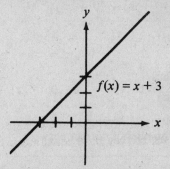

The graph of $|f(x)|$ is the same for $x \geq -3$, but when $x < -3$, $|f(x)|$ is $-f(x) = -(x + 3)$, which is graphed below:

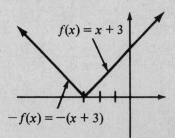

SELF-EVALUATION CHART FOR TEST 6

SUBJECT AREA	QUESTIONS ANSWERED CORRECTLY	NUMBER OF CORRECT ANSWERS
Algebra (14 questions)	1 6 11 15 19 20 24 31 33 41 42 43 47 49	_____
Plane geometry (10 questions)	2 7 12 17 25 26 27 32 36 39	_____
Solid geometry (3 questions)	29 31 44	_____
Coordinate geometry (6 questions)	3 4 5 23 38 45	_____
Trigonometry (5 questions)	13 22 30 35 40	_____
Functions (6 questions)	8 18 28 34 48 50	_____
Miscellaneous (6 questions)	9 10 14 16 21 46	_____
Total number of correct answers		_____

Total score = total number of correct answers $\times$ 4   _____

minus number of incorrect answers − _____

_____

Index

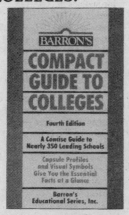